Postzionism

Postzionism

A Reader

EDITED BY LAURENCE J. SILBERSTEIN

RUTGERS UNIVERSITY PRESS
NEW BRUNSWICK, NEW JERSEY, AND LONDON

LIBRARY OF CONGRESS CATALOGING-IN-PUBLICATION DATA

Postzionism : a reader / edited by Laurence J. Silberstein.
 p. cm.
 Includes bibliographical references and index.
 ISBN 978-0-8135-4346-8 (hardcover : alk. paper)—ISBN 978-0-8135-4347-5 (pbk. : alk. paper)
 1. Post-Zionism. I. Silberstein, Laurence J. (Laurence Jay), 1936–
 DS113.4P68 2008
 320.54095694—dc22   2007039077

A British Cataloging-in-Publication record for this book is available from the British Library.

This collection copyright © 2008 by Rutgers, The State University

For copyrights to individual pieces please see first page of each essay.

All rights reserved

No part of this book may be reproduced or utilized in any form or by any means, electronic or mechanical, or by any information storage and retrieval system, without written permission from the publisher. Please contact Rutgers University Press, 100 Joyce Kilmer Avenue, Piscataway, NJ 08854–8099. The only exception to this prohibition is "fair use" as defined by U.S. copyright law.

Visit our Web site: http://rutgerspress.rutgers.edu

Manufactured in the United States of America

To the memory of Baruch Kimmerling:
Creative Scholar, Courageous Critic, Caring Colleague

CONTENTS

Acknowledgments   xi

Reading Postzionism: An Introduction   1
LAURENCE J. SILBERSTEIN

PART I
New Historians and Critical Sociologists: Critical Reflections on Israeli/Zionist Narratives

1   The New Historiography: Israel Confronts Its Past   31
BENNY MORRIS

2   Land, Labor, and the Origins of the Israeli-Palestinian Conflict, 1882–1914   46
GERSHON SHAFIR

3   Introduction to *The Palestinian People: A History*   56
BARUCH KIMMERLING AND JOEL S. MIGDAL

4   Postzionist Studies of Israel: The First Decade   61
URI RAM

PART II
Expanding the Range of Critique: Engaging the Discourse

5   The Identity of the Victims and the Victims of Identity: A Critique of Zionist Ideology for a Postzionist Age   81
ADI OPHIR

6   Academic History Caught in the Cross-Fire: The Case of Israeli-Jewish Historiography   102
BARUCH KIMMERLING

7	Ethnocracy: The Politics of Judaizing Israel/Palestine OREN YIFTACHEL	121
8	A First Step in a Difficult and Sensitive Road: Preliminary Observations on *Qaadan v. Katzir* ALEXANDRE (SANDY) KEDAR	148
9	Save as Jerusalems ARIELLA AZOULAY	165

PART III
Minority Discourse:
Voices from the Margins

Minority Discourse in Israeli Culture

10	Hebrew in an Israeli Arab Hand: Six Miniatures on Anton Shammas's *Arabesques* HANNAN HEVER	193

Palestinian Citizens

11	At Half Mast—Myths, Symbols, and Rituals of an Emerging State: A Personal Testimony of an "Israeli Arab" ANTON SHAMMAS	219
12	Arab Citizens of Palestine: Little to Celebrate AZMI BISHARA	226

Arab Jews/Mizrahim

13	Rupture and Return: Zionist Discourse and the Study of Arab Jews ELLA SHOHAT	233
14	History Begins at Home YEHOUDA SHENHAV	257
15	A Mizrahi Call for a More Democratic Israel PNINA MOTZAFI-HALLER	275

Gender and Sexuality:
Women, Gays, and Lesbians

16	Body and Territory: Women in Israeli Cinema ORLY LUBIN	283

17	Introduction to *Beyond Flesh: Queer Masculinities and Nationalism in Israeli Cinema* RAZ YOSEF	294
18	The Construction of Lesbianism as Nonissue in Israel ERELLA SHADMI	308

PART IV
American Jews

19	Diaspora: Generation and the Ground of Jewish Identity DANIEL BOYARIN AND JONATHAN BOYARIN	329
20	From Diaspora Jews to New Jews CARYN AVIV AND DAVID SHNEER	345
21	The Charge of Anti-Semitism: Jews, Israel, and the Risks of Public Critique JUDITH BUTLER	369

About the Contributors   387
Index   393

ACKNOWLEDGMENTS

Over the years, many individuals have helped me to deepen my understanding of postzionism's growth and development. Adi Ophir has been a constant source of information and encouragement and has offered many useful suggestions for the current book. While not necessarily agreeing with my views, Gerald Cromer and Jim Diamond have been willing conversation partners, gently prodding me to clarify my thoughts. I thank Laura Levitt, Ruth Knafo Setton, and Ken Daley for reading and commenting on my introductory chapter. Their skills as readers have helped me to sharpen my arguments, clarify my thoughts, and avoid numerous missteps. I also thank Laura Levitt for her suggestions on several of the readings. I thank Esther Fuchs, who served as a reader for the original proposal, for her helpful comments and suggestions. Hannan Hever has been a reliable guide through the labyrinth of Israeli culture. Among the others with whom I have had useful exchanges about this project or about postzionism in general, I thank Gershon Shafir, Laura Levitt, Yehouda Shenhav, Ella Shohat, Oren Yiftachel, and the late Baruch Kimmerling.

My fellow participants in the Berman Center's ongoing colloquium on Judaism and postmodern culture have, over the years, patiently read and commented on my continuing efforts to clarify my thoughts on issues relating to postzionism. These include Zak Braiterman, Daniel Boyarin, Jonathan Boyarin, Michelle Friedman, Shai Ginsburg, Anita Norich, Peter Ochs, Miriam Peskowitz, Moshe Reem, Susan Shapiro, Oren Stier, and David Watt.

I thank my colleagues in Lehigh's Department of Religion Studies for giving me an opportunity to conduct a departmental faculty seminar on Foucault and Religion. Their repeated challenges helped me to refine my own understanding and test my application of Foucault's ideas. Chava Weissler and Michael Raposa have given generously of their time to read and comment on earlier efforts to view postzionism through the lens of contemporary theory. The invitation from Ian Buchanan and Adrian Parr to contribute to their edited volume, *Deleuze and the Contemporary World* (Edinburgh 2006) provided me with a wonderful opportunity to enhance my understanding of the usefulness of Deleuze and Guattari for the interpretation of Zionism and postzionism. Their rigorous editorial judgment encouraged me to take risks that I might otherwise not have taken.

At Rutgers University Press, Kristi Long was the first to recognize the value of a reader on postzionism. Her successor, Adi Hovav, has been both supportive and patient as I struggled to bring *Postzionism: A Reader* to fruition.

I am again indebted to my colleagues at the Berman Center, Shirley Ratushny and Carolyn Hudacek, for their unwavering support. Shirley's carefully honed editorial skills were, as in the past, a great help to me in the writing of my introductory chapter. Without Carolyn's technical skills, her ability to navigate the Web, and her unstinting commitment to this project, it would never have materialized.

My wife, Mimi, has spent more hours without my company than I could possibly count. Were it not for her faith in me and her unceasing encouragement, none of this would have been possible.

Postzionism

Reading Postzionism

An Introduction

LAURENCE J. SILBERSTEIN

In 1998, as Israel prepared to celebrate the state's fiftieth birthday, a public controversy erupted. Israeli television presented a twenty-two-part series, *Tekumah* (renewal or rebirth), which, drawing on original footage and contemporary interviews, sought to provide viewers with an overview of Israel's history. Yet the outbursts that the series provoked showed it to be much more than a simple historical overview. Israel's minister of communications Limor Livnat announced that she had forbidden her fourteen-year-old son to view the series. Livnat claimed that the series "depicts the Palestinian side sympathetically, systematically distorts the great Zionist deeds and causes severe and probably irreparable damage to our image." "According to my understanding," she continued, "the Israeli public broadcasting channel is not supposed to show the propagandistic position of the Palestinians while pushing aside our myths."[1]

Ariel Sharon, at the time a cabinet minister known for his hawkish views, sent a letter to the education minister arguing that the film "distorts the history of the rebirth and undermines any moral basis for the establishment of the state of Israel and its continued existence."[2] Sharon urged him "to ban the series from schools." Livnat, calling the series "postzionist," demanded that it be taken off the air.

The controversy over *Tekumah* was, to one observer, an indication that Israelis "are still in the process of forming our identity."[3] To one viewer, the outcry was an indication that Israelis were experiencing "the end of a loss of innocence," while another saw the anger as a reflection of a widespread sense of guilt and denial: "we don't want to know and we can't bear the sense of guilt. The establishment of the State of Israel was justice for the Jews, but it was accompanied by a terrible injustice for the Palestinians."[4]

The public controversy over *Tekumah* was part of a broader cultural conflict in Israel over collective memory, collective identity, and collective meaning. To Israelis, like all national groups, the narratives of their nation's past provide a framework through which to view and interpret the events of the past and the present. As the author of a study of American collective memory observed, controversies over national narratives are actually less about the past than "how the past affects the present."[5] Accordingly, to challenge such is to unsettle the foundations on which the national identity is constructed.

As Livnat's comments suggest, the conflict over *Tekumah* was an extension of an earlier cultural conflict that had erupted in the mid-1990s. This conflict emerged in response to a series of books and articles by a group of Israeli scholars who came to be known as new historians and critical sociologists.

A useful summary of the issues raised by the new historians and critical sociologists has been provided by historian and journalist Tom Segev. In *1949: The First Israelis,* first published in Hebrew in 1986, Segev provided one of the first historical accounts to make use of recently declassified documents.[6] To Segev, the new scholarship had "shattered a firmly established self-image and exposed as mere myths a large number of long excepted truisms" (viii).[7]

The "myths" Segev called into question were deeply held beliefs that served as the foundation for most Israelis' national identity. These included the following ideas: (1) that although Israel had done everything possible to bring about peace in 1948 (and after), the Arabs continually refused all initiatives; (2) that the Palestinian Arab refugees, deceived by leaders who promised them that they would soon return, along with the conquering Arab armies, had willingly left their homes; (3) that the primary purpose of the state of Israel was to serve as a refuge for the persecuted Jews throughout the world and provide a secure place for the ingathering of the "exiles"; (4) that, in addition to providing Jews with a safe haven, Israel also provided them with the opportunity to live freely as Jews, unhampered either by political persecution or economic and social discrimination, which had characterized life in "exile";[8] and (5) that only in Israel could Judaism flourish, functioning as a unifying force for world Jewry.

To Segev and the other scholars, however, the dominant accounts of Israeli history were simply not supported by the documentation: "it became apparent that the Arabs had not always refused to discuss peace with Israel and that Israel had not done all it could possibly do to reach peace with its neighbors at all costs. A large number of Palestinian Arabs were expelled from their homes, not only during the war of 1948–1949 but afterwards as well."

Nor did the evidence support the dominant Zionist vision of Israel as a welcoming refuge for all Jews: "It was not the 'gathering of exiles' in accordance with the Zionist ideal that was the primary purpose for Israel to encourage Jewish immigration, but rather its needs for manpower in agriculture, industry and the army. Jewish immigrants from Arab countries have been discriminated against, partly as a result of explicit decisions, and many of them were deliberately stripped of their cultural and religious identity."[9]

Far from being a cohesive society in which Jews of varying backgrounds lived in harmony, the Israel reflected in the newly declassified documents was, from the beginning, beset with conflict.[10] Nor were these conflicts only a matter of the past. "Thirty-eight years after the Declaration of Independence, Israel still faces the very same problems and conflicts that troubled the first Israelis. It is a country still searching for its principles and its identity."[11]

The scholars whose writings were designated as postzionist were, for the most part, members of a generation that had either been born or had grown to maturity in the decades following the 1948 war. The perspective of the previous generation, the so-called '48 generation, had been shaped by the ideology and practices of pre–state labor Zionism, the trauma of the Holocaust, and the challenges of the 1948 war. In contrast, the dominant factors shaping the perspective of the younger generation were very different. In contrast to their elders, the experiences of the younger generation were shaped by the post-1967 Israeli occupation of the West Bank and Gaza; the near defeat of Israel in the Yom Kippur War of 1973; the controversial 1982 invasion of Lebanon and its aftermath; the growing intensification of Palestinian national identity; and the growing impact of globalization.

During this same period, the character of Israeli society and culture was undergoing major changes and transformations. While the Israeli victory in the 1967 war was perceived by most observers in the immediate aftermath to have a unifying effect on the nation, the internal conflicts over the occupation were to have a disruptive impact. In addition, factors such as the emergence of a militant religious right, the increasing number and influence of Israeli settlers in the West Bank and Gaza, and the emergence of a powerful Palestinian national identity both within the occupied territories and among Israel's Arab citizens produced challenges unknown to the previous generation. At the same time, the growth and awakening identity of Jews from Middle Eastern countries, who eventually came to be known as Mizrahim, and the intensifying conflict between religious and secular Israeli Jews brought to light fault lines within Israeli society and culture that belied the dominant Zionist narrative of Israel as a welcoming refuge for all Jews. As minority voices within Israeli society grew stronger and more assertive, the more simplistic view of Israeli society and culture became, for many, increasingly untenable. Accordingly, criticisms of the dominant narratives that had previously been voiced primarily by those on the margins or by those opposed to the existence of the state, were now being voiced by a cross-section of Israeli citizens as well as Jews in other countries. As described by political scientist Michael Shalev, a member of the post-'48 generation:

> In the 1970's, in the face of painful evidence of social inequality, political turmoil, and military and economic vulnerability several strands of

intellectual insurgency arose to challenge accepted thinking. Much of this work produced revisionist histories which cast the labour movement elite in a quite unflattering light. Critical scholarship was also driven by the search for theoretical alternatives to a sociological orthodoxy which had plainly failed to reckon with the conflicts and inequalities accompanying nation- and state- building and capitalist economic development. Israel's invasion of Lebanon, its continuing occupation of the West Bank and Gaza, and the intense political polarization surrounding these issues lent a further impetus to the critical social science in the 1980's.[12]

Strongly affected by the force of the growing Palestinian nationalism and its growing resistance to Israeli rule, many Israeli intellectuals and academicians reached the conclusion that rather than a passing phenomenon, the Israeli-Palestinian conflict stands at the center of Israeli history and exercises a powerful impact on Israeli society and culture. Many of them recount moments of awakening that shook their previously held beliefs and identifications.

In early 1994, Zionist critics publicly expressed their growing concern over the new body of scholarship. In the words of one of these critics, "What has previously been known in limited academic circles should now be revealed to the community at large: There has arisen a scholarly school among Israeli social scientists that challenges the Zionist world view, the Zionist settlement of the land of Israel, and the right of the state of Israel to exist."[13]

To Zionist critics, the new scholarship threatened not only the moral fiber but also the very survival of Israeli society. In the opinion of one critic, if allowed to continue unchallenged, the effects of this scholarship would soon be widely felt: "owing to their abilities as scholars and debaters, their views are receiving a wider hearing. They are directing generations of students in research, and their subversion of the Zionist narrative will contribute, intentionally or unintentionally, to a delegitimation of the Jewish state at home and abroad."[14]

In the eyes of the Zionist critics, these scholars were guilty of berating such basic Zionist principles as "redemption of the land," "conquest through labor," "ingathering of the exiles," and "defense." In addition, they represent Zionism as "a kind of evil, colonialistic conspiracy to exploit the people ('am) living in Palestine, to subjugate them, to dispossess them."[15] Finally, by insisting that "Israel should be a normal democratic society without a specifically Jewish mission," these scholars had transgressed the boundaries of legitimate Israeli national discourse. Consequently, they could not be considered to be Zionists, but postzionists.[16]

As used by Zionist critics, the term "postzionism" was one of reproach. In their eyes, those whom they labeled postzionist were guilty of three basic transgressions: they cast aspersions on the motives and intentions of the Zionist settlers and the founders of the state; they abandoned the Zionist vision of Israel as a Jewish State; and they sought to transform Israel into a democratic state of all of its citizens.[17]

As was the case with *Tekumah*, the angry attacks on postzionism indicated the extent of the identity crisis of Israeli society. To one scholar sympathetic to postzionism, Ilan Pappe, it was the crisis "of a society that stands on the threshold of a period of peace, in which the national consensus, previously built upon threats to survival and security problems, clears a space for a debate across the society and its culture."[18]

Many Zionists equate postzionism with antizionism, that is, opposition to the state of Israel itself.[19] Such a criticism is roundly rejected by the accused scholars, including those who openly identify with the term "postzionism." As loyal, concerned Israeli citizens, they view their criticism of the Zionist underpinnings of the state as a necessary step in the effort to produce a more complex and realistic interpretation of Israel's past and present. Courageously facing the problematic aspect of its Zionist past does not weaken the state, they argue, but strengthens it. By creating possibilities for a more open, honest conversation in the present, they are working toward the emergence of a more diverse, fully democratic state in the future.

Postzionism: A Reader seeks to introduce the reader to postzionism and the issues raised in these controversies. As the range of selections shows, the issues relating to postzionism are by no means limited to Israel. Already in the early stages of the postzionist critique, American Jewish voices, some of which are included in this book, could be heard. As they help to make clear, the issues raised by postzionism concern not only Zionism but also broader issues of Jewish identity and Jewish life.

Among Israelis, the growing usage of the term "postzionism" reflects an increasing sense that the maps of meaning provided by Zionism are simply no longer adequate. To critics and detractors, postzionism presents a challenge to the basic principles and values of Zionism. To its detractors, postzionism is a prelude to national fragmentation and moral decline. To its advocates, however, the postzionist critique is a necessary prerequisite to Israel's emergence as a fully democratic society.

As with any term ending in "ism," including Zionism, postzionism lacks an essential meaning. Instead, its meaning shifts according to who uses it and how. In many ways, the ambiguity and multiple, often conflicting, meanings ascribed to the term "postzionism" mirror the ambiguity and multiple, often conflicted, meanings ascribed to the term "Zionism."[20] Accordingly, rather than engage in the futile task of seeking out any essential meaning of the term, I find it far more useful to ask how the term operates, and inquire into what it does.

As a majoritarian discourse, Zionism may be seen as an effort to regulate what can and cannot be said about topics such as the Israeli nation, identity, society, culture, and history. Zionism thus imposes limits on the ways in which Jewish history, Jewish homeland, Jewish culture, and Jewish identity are represented and discussed.[21] Like all nationalist discourses, Zionism also functions to produce a certain kind of subject. It positions those subjects, loyal Israelis, to conform to the dominant model of good citizens. These, in turn, accept, embrace, and identify with the knowledge that Zionist discourse takes to be true, natural, and commonsensical. Likewise, they take the practices that derive from and render plausible Zionist discourse to be "normal." Conversely, they categorize as abnormal those whose discourse and practices deviate from these norms.[22]

If we view Zionism as a majoritarian discourse that provides the dominant models within Israeli culture, then postzionism may be seen as a minoritarian discourse.[23] Using the language of the majority, postzionism seeks to bring to light and challenge the neglected, unseen, or concealed power effects of Zionist discourse on present-day Israeli society and culture.[24] Thus, rather than designating the passing of an era or period of time, postzionism functions to open cultural spaces in the present wherein alternative or counter discourses can be produced.[25] Far from suggesting that the Zionist era has passed into a new, postzionist era, it seeks to render visible the multiple effects of Zionist discourse and its accompanying practices on the diverse areas of Israeli life. Rather than announce Zionism's passing, postzionism functions as an ongoing critique of zionisms continuing effects.

Approaching Zionism or any other nationalist movement as discourse helps to make us aware of the multiple and diverse forms of power relations it entails. It thus enables us to see the many ways in which Zionism functions to produce, distribute, and perpetuate the knowledge that renders its existence possible. In viewing Zionism and postzionism as discourse, the important question is not whether or not a particular scholar or writer "is" or identifies as "a postzionist." Instead, one is led to ask how and in what ways do particular writings contribute to the production of a postzionist discourse.

Toward that end, this book presents a variety of writings that render such a contribution. These include writings by historians who came to be known as "new historians"; sociologists identified as "critical sociologists"; interdisciplinary, theoretically informed scholars engaging in a wide-ranging critique of Israeli society and culture; and members of marginalized and excluded minority groups, including Palestinian Arabs, Mizrahi or Arab Jews, women, gays, and lesbians. A concluding section contains readings by American Jews that contribute to a growing American Jewish critique of Zionism.

It should be noted that the current postzionist critique did not emerge in a vacuum. Earlier critics, both within and outside of the Zionist camp, formulated thoughtful and insightful critiques of Zionism. These include such Zionist writers as Martin Buber, Uri Avneri, Amos Elon, and Meron Benvenisti. Outside of the Zionist body, groups such as the Marxist organization Matzpen, the Canaanites, and writers like Boaz Evron also formulated important criticisms.[26]

Space limitations make it impossible to include any of their writings in this book. Similarly, space limitations have prevented me from including important contributions to the postzionist critique by, among others, Amiel Alcalay, Sara Chinski, Yitzkah Laor, Ian Pappe, Dan Rabinowitz, Amnon Raz-Krakotzkin, Tom Segev, and Idith Zertal.

While Israel has been the setting for the debates described above, the place of Zionism and Israel in Jewish culture and history has also been the subject of an ongoing debate in the United States.[27] As the contributions by several American Jewish scholars to this reader make clear, the issues raised by postzionism extend beyond the borders of Israel.[28]

Zionism, although primarily identified with the State of Israel, plays a major role in shaping the ways that American Jews, and many non-Jews, understand Jewish history, identity, and culture. Owing to Israel's prominent role within American Jewish life, one scholar has designated identification with that state as a basic component of the civil religion of American Jews.[29] Thus, debates over the Jewishness of the State of Israel directly relate to the identity construction of American Jews.

New Historians and Critical Sociologists: Telling the Story Differently

According to cultural studies pioneer Stuart Hall, narratives of the past play a decisive role in shaping present-day identities: "Far from being grounded in a mere 'recovery' of the past, which is waiting to be found and which, when found, will secure our sense of ourselves into eternity, identities are the names we give to the different ways we are positioned by, and position ourselves within, the narratives of the past."[30]

It is not surprising, therefore, that the first charges of postzionism were leveled at a group of historians who challenged the dominant Zionist narratives. At the same time, a group of sociologists began to challenge the dominant Zionist representations of Israeli society. The writings of these scholars, who came to be known as the new historians and critical sociologists, are represented in part 1.

In the first reading in the book, historian Benny Morris provides an overview of the factors contributing to the emergence of these groups. Morris's own book, *The Origins of the Palestinian Refugee Problem* (1987), was considered to be an outstanding example of the new historiography. Notwithstanding Morris's repeated assertions that he was a Zionist, his book rendered a major contribution to the emergence of postzionist discourse.

Morris was one of a group of younger scholars who, in the early 1980s, had gained access to newly declassified documents relating to the beginnings and early history of the state. Working his way through these documents, he quickly recognized that they contradicted the dominant versions of Israeli history. Trying to explain the flight of approximately 600,000 Arabs from Israel during the 1948 war, Morris was led to a shocking conclusion: "From the new documents of that period it became clear that much of what had been told to the people—to children at school and adults in newspapers—in the memoirs and historical writings—was in the best instances distortion, and in many other instances, simply the ignoring of facts and plain lies."[31]

As Morris explained, applying a set of questions characteristic of a new generation of scholars, he and other historians produced works that challenged many of the dominant narratives of Zionist scholarship. Whereas the dominant narratives had assigned primary responsibility for the flight to the Arabs and basically exonerated the Israelis of any blame, Morris explained the flight, village by village, in terms of multiple factors. Yet Zionist critics were outraged at his conclusion that deliberate expulsions by Israeli military forces and acts of mass violence by unofficial Israeli military units played an important role.[32]

While Morris's research focused on retelling the story of the period of 1947–48, political scientist Gershon Shafir focused his attention on the prestate period of Zionist settlement. As he explains in the second reading in part 1, his research led him to take issue with the deeply embedded Israeli interpretation of Zionist settlement in terms of the humane motives and idealistic goals of the settlers. Applying a form of Marxist historical analysis, Shafir emphasized the economic and social effects of Zionist settlement practices on the indigenous Arab population rather than the settlers' motives. Previously, the application of the term colonialist had been limited to scholars and political leaders hostile to Zionism. However, after carefully examining the various scholarly usages and in the face of the virtually universal Israeli rejection of the term, Shafir also argued that Zionist settlement was best described as a form of colonialism.[33]

The third reading in part 1 by sociologist Baruch Kimmerling and political scientist Joel Migdal directly challenges the dominant Israeli scholarly practice of excluding the Palestinian perspective from accounts of Israeli history. Whereas Israeli Jews regard the emergence of a Jewish state in 1948 as the historical fulfillment of a two-thousand-year dream, and, in the case of religious Zionists, the beginning of a redemptive process, Israel's Palestinian citizens experienced the 1948 war as *al Naqba*, a catastrophe of enormous proportions. Arguing against the dominant ethnocentric approach, Kimmerling and Migdal seek to provide a corrective. In their pioneering book, *Palestinians: The Making of a People*, from which the reading is taken, Kimmerling and Migdal undertake to produce a balanced account of the history of the Palestinian nation, one that gives credence to Palestinian national aspirations.[34]

Alongside the work of the new historians, Israeli sociologists were also engaged in questioning the prevailing representations of Israeli society. The dominant Israeli sociology had represented Israeli society through the Zionist concept of "ingathering of the exiles" and depicted Israel as a national refuge.

Challenging this representation, sociologist Uri Ram argues the need for a new, more complex view.

Ram, one of the few Israeli scholars to openly embrace the term "postzionist,"[35] produced an anthology of writings by a group of Israeli sociologists who challenge the dominant social scientific views of Israeli society. In his Hebrew anthology *Israeli Society: Critical Perspectives,* he seeks to provide an alternative view. Incorporating the perspectives of women, Jews from Middle Eastern countries, and Palestinian Arabs, groups commonly neglected in Israeli sociological writings, Ram argues the need of a postzionist sociology that moves out from under the umbrella of Zionist discourse.[36] As he summarized it in his 1995 book, "the time is now ripe for the formulation of a postzionist sociological agenda that would be congruous with the consolidation of a democratic Israeli civil society, a society of free and equal citizens and of diverse identities. Rather than national integration, the focus of such an agenda should be the issue of citizenship in a modern democratic society."[37] Whereas Zionist sociology "promoted the idea of an identity among unequals and the exclusion of the others," postzionist sociology envisions an Israel that is "characterized by equality among non-identicals and the inclusion of the others."[38]

In a more recent article, reproduced below, Ram seeks to summarize the career of postzionism through 2005. In contrast to those who view postzionism as solely an Israeli phenomenon, Ram seeks to show its connections to such global processes as postnationalism, globalization, postcolonialism, and post-Fordist economics.[39] Ram also describes the ways that different groups within Israeli society have reacted to postzionism. Rejecting recurring claims that postzionism, a phenomenon of the "Oslo" era, had basically run its course by the end of the 1990s, Ram seeks to show its continuing, expanding effects on Israeli society and culture.

Beyond History and Sociology: Postzionism as Critique

As the general public was becoming aware of the work of the new historians and critical sociologists, another group of Israeli scholars and intellectuals was pursuing a different form of postzionist critique. Applying insights drawn from feminist, postcolonial, poststructuralist, and postmodern theory, they directed their attention to Zionist discourse. Of particular concern were the multiple and diverse ways that Zionist discourse and its related practices marginalized, excluded, and disempowered various groups within and outside of Israeli society. Their task, as they understood it, was not simply to revise historical accounts but also to develop a new critical discourse. Within the Israeli academy, there was little interest in such a critique, as well as strong resistance. Consequently, they sought to create new cultural spaces wherein they could critically engage and rethink the dominant Zionist representations of Israeli life, history, and politics.

The new critical discourse they developed was an effort to reveal the multiple power relations that were instantiated in the capillaries of everyday Israeli life.[40] This required, on the one hand, rendering visible the commonly "unseen" power effects of diverse and recurring practices inscribed into the fabric of Israeli society and culture. Through intellectual critique, they sought to render visible power relations that the dominant discourses and regimes of truth obscure, conceal, or neglect.[41] They also seek to show how, within the dominant Zionist discourse, these power relations are taken to be normal.[42]

If we view postzionism as a form of what Michel Foucault considers to be intellectual critique, the writings in this section directly contribute to a critique of the discourses, practices, and institutions produced by Zionism. On one level, this form of postzionist critique challenges Zionism's position as the dominant discourse for defining and imbuing with meaning the daily realities of Israeli life, society, and culture. In the process, it reveals the contingency of the prevailing Zionist definitions of Israeli national identity, territory, history, and law. It thus helps us to see that things can be otherwise, that there are alternative possibilities of Israeli national identity, and that what keeps the dominant forms of knowledge in place are regimes of truth and relations of power rather than national destiny or national mission. At the same time, as a transformative force, what Gilles Deleuze calls a "line of flight," the postzionist critique is by no means merely negative. The purpose of undoing the unjust effects brought about by Zionist discourse and practices is to transform Israeli society into one that is more open to and accepting of difference.

Drawing upon such critical discourses as feminism, poststructuralism, postcolonialism, and postmodernism, the writings in parts 2 and 3 extend the postzionist critique to such fields as literature, art, gender relations, sexuality, law, and space. Scholars like Baruch Kimmerling, Oren Yiftachel, Alexandre (Sandy) Kedar, Ariella Azoulay, and Hannan Hever engage in a rethinking of Zionism's basic assumptions, the models embraced by the majority. The same is true of the writings by members of minoritarian groups in part 4. These critics shed light on the marginalizing, exclusionary, and oppressive effects of Zionist discourse that most Israelis have come to see as normal. They thus help bring to light the normalizing effects of the dominant Zionist discourse on the diverse realms of Israeli life. In so doing, as philosopher Adi Ophir observes, they confront their fellow Israelis and Jews worldwide with the numerous ways in which victims can become victimizers.

The two articles at the beginning of part 3 provide a useful bridge from the historical and sociological writings to this theoretically informed postzionist critique.[43] In the first article, Adi Ophir, analyzing the multiple and problematic meanings of the concept of postzionism, seeks to explain its distinctive function in Israeli society. Ophir likens postzionist critics to therapists who seek to bring to light the emotional investments that generate denial. Embracing the identity of victims, Israelis resist seeing their own role in creating victims. Were they to do so, Ophir argues, they would have to acknowledge the senselessness of their own losses, which their victim narrative could no longer explain.

Ophir, the founding editor and moving force behind the journal *Theory and Criticism*, played a seminal role in the development of a theoretically informed postzionist critique. Through a series of "inversions," Ophir describes the many contradictions of Zionism, contradictions that are painful for Israelis to recognize. Through postzionist critique, many of Zionism's successes are revealed as failures that Israelis must confront and address. These contradictions, he argues, necessitate a move beyond Zionism into a postzionist era. A member of the post-'48 generation, Ophir recounts his own dramatic story of rudely awakening to the truths of Israeli history.

Baruch Kimmerling, a sociologist in the tradition of Simmel and Weber, argues for the need to look beyond the knowledge produced by Israeli scholars and focus on the discourse by means of which they produce this knowledge. Conscripted to the Zionist cause, Israeli academicians, he argues, work within "a Jewish bubble." Writing from a Jewish perspective and using Zionist concepts, most Israeli scholarship marginalizes and excludes both Palestinian Arabs and Mizrahi Jews from Arab lands, the victims to whom Ophir referred.[44]

By uncritically accepting the Zionist representation of the land of Israel as the homeland of the Jewish people and the state of Israel as a Jewish state belonging to the entire Jewish people, Israeli scholars, according to Kimmerling, reinforce the disenfranchised position of Israel's Arab citizens. Moreover, the recurring usage of Zionist concepts like "ingathering of the exiles" to describe Zionist settlement conceals and silences the history and claims of the Palestinian "others" who were already living in the land.[45]

Kimmerling sees Israeli scholars as functioning in the role of a "an ultimate supreme court," deciding what in the collective memories of Jews and Arabs is true and constructing a canonical national historical narrative. Like Ophir, he confronts his fellow scholars with the ways in which the knowledge they produce actually contributes to shaping and reinforcing Zionism's hegemonic power. In so doing, he moves beyond the boundaries of history and sociology and engages in a critique of the discourse through which scholars frame the issues, pose the problems, and select and interpret the data.[46] The solution, he argues, is for scholars to move out from under the bubble of Zionist discourse and embrace a more objective, non-Zionist scholarly discourse. Only in this way can Israeli scholars avoid contributing to what Ophir referred to as Israel's victimizing practices.[47]

The selections by Oren Yiftachel, Alexandre (Sandy) Kedar, and Ariella Azoulay all address the problem of space. In different ways, each reveals the ways in which space, rather than a given physical reality, is a product of powerful mechanisms and discourses. The imagining, labeling, and striating of space are power-laden processes. Yiftachel, a political geographer, attempts to unravel the prevailing Israeli discourse that defines and divides space through a set of Judaizing discourses and practices. To Yiftachel, these practices belie Israel's claim to be a democracy. Instead, he considers Israel to be an ethnocracy, a society in which power is concentrated in the hands of a particular ethnic group (Jews). In an ethnocracy such as Israel, all other ethnic groups (Arabs, Thai workers, Mizrahi Jews) are marginalized and disempowered. By labeling the land as Jewish and creating an apparatus of institutions and practices that enact and perpetuate this concept, Israel essentially excludes its others, particularly its Palestinian population. In Zionist and Israeli discourse, the land that they live on, and that their ancestors in most cases had lived on, belongs not to them, and not to their state, but to the Jewish people.[48]

Moreover, while Jewish settlers who live in the occupied territories beyond the conventional "green line" borders have citizenship, Palestinians in these territories do not. The result is that while the Israeli settlers enjoy full participation in the Israeli political system, Palestinians in the territories do not. One result of this inequity is to effectively erase any clear state borders, which is commonly considered to be a prerequisite for a democratic society. This results in a state that, while incorporating a number of democratic characteristics, falls short of satisfying the criteria for a fully democratic nation.[49]

Alexander (Sandy) Kedar's analysis of the widely publicized case of *Qaadan v. Katzir* extends the critique of Judaizing practices into the legal sphere. In this case, a Palestinian citizen of Israel was denied the right to purchase land in a Jewish cooperative community. The denial was based largely on the argument that the land, owned by the Jewish people, cannot be sold to a non-Jew. Although the Israeli Supreme Court, after five years, decided in favor of the Qaadans, it did not provide the mechanisms whereby its decision could be put into effect. Kedar describes the tension within Israeli jurisprudence between an ethnocentric, Judaizing discourse and one that is liberal and democratic.[50]

Kedar sees the Supreme Court's decision as marking "not a categorical transformation, but a big leap, from the 'Jewish/Zionist,' toward the 'Democratic/equality' pole within the 'Jewish-Democratic state' legal tenet. Through its "interference with the allocation component of the Israeli land regime," and its limiting of the Jewish-Zionist aspects of the state, the court took a firm stand against discrimination on the basis of religion or nationality. Yet, as Kedar acknowledges, the court's unwillingness to engage with the nation's past, a step taken by many other settler states, and its refusal to directly address the nationalization (Judaization) of the land stopped far short of enacting its transformative potential.[51] Also, insofar as the courts "liberal-individualistic prism" isolates the case from the Qaadans' "collective identity and needs as Palestinian citizens of Israel," it avoids the wider problem of the Palestinian Arab minority in Israel. Kedar nonetheless remains hopeful about the possibilities of finding solutions to these problems within the legal system.

Taking up many of the same issues raised by Yiftachel and Kedar, Ariella Azoulay, a cultural critic, provides a complex, interdisciplinary spatial analysis to elucidate what she calls the "Jewification of Jerusalem." Problematizing the conventional understandings of space as given, homogeneous and fixed, Azoulay describes the multiple, complex processes that constitute the spaces known as Jerusalem. According to Azoulay, the multiplicity of forces, subjects and objects, times, and narratives that constitute Jerusalem cannot be reduced to one unified meaning. Criticizing Israeli efforts to project essentialistic, hierarchical nationalistic meanings on to Jerusalem, Azoulay puts forth an alternative view of multiple, diverse, multileveled interconnecting Jerusalems. Applying concepts drawn from Foucault and Deleuze, she argues that all efforts to impose a homogeneous meaning and institute a system of control are both problematic and futile.

Like all cities, Jerusalem encompasses multiple spaces—material, intellectual, cultural, ethnic, religious, national, virtual. Mechanisms of control such as cartography, law, and the planning process by means of which Israel seeks to "Jewify" Jerusalem actually produce opposite effects. Consequently, they further complicate the city. Azoulay's primary concern is the effort to Jewify Jerusalem. However, her analysis renders problematic all efforts, including Jewish, to essentialize and project transcendent meanings on the endlessly interconnecting, heterogeneous, multiplicitous, economic, political, religious, ethnic relations and events that make up the spaces of Jerusalem.

Viewing discourse and power relations as central to the critique of Zionism and Israeli life, the scholars represented in this section aspire to a new critical discourse.[52] However, their primary concerns are by no means theoretical. They regard theory to be significant only insofar as it can help to reveal social and cultural inequities and injustices. Accordingly, their turn to theory is primarily a function of their desire to transform the prevailing power relations in Israeli life. Toward that end, they critically engage the dominant discourse and practices of Israeli life and scholarship. As intellectuals, they use theory as a tool in the struggle that, in Foucault's words, is "aimed at revealing and undermining power where it is most visible and invidious."[53] The ultimate goal, however, is to open the way to a different Israel, one that accepts, honors, and empowers all of its citizens.

Minoritarian Writings: Voices from the Margins

In his analysis of Anton Shammas's Hebrew novel, *Arabesques*, postcolonial critic Hannan Hever provides an important tool for framing the minority writings in the following section. In Hever's view, Shammas's Hebrew novel is a powerful exemplar of what Gilles Deleuze and Félix Guattari call a minority literature.[54] According to Deleuze, what defines majority is not a numerical advantage, but rather "a model you have to conform to," a face according to which everyone is measured and judged. Minority, in this usage, refers to a process that "has no model, it's a becoming, a process."[55] Whereas the majority seeks to position minorities as deviant, abnormal, or marginal, Deleuze represents them as transformative forces. Whereas conventional Western thought privileges continuity, identity, and unity, Deleuze emphasizes transformation, difference, and multiplicity.

To Hever, Shammas's use of the dominant Hebrew language problematizes and transforms the dominant Zionist conception of Hebrew literature as Jewish literature, and Israeli culture as Jewish culture. Shammas's book, written from the perspective of the oppressed minority, reveals numerous paradoxes in Israeli culture. Although Israel claims to be a democracy, by proclaiming itself as the state of the Jewish people, it essentially disenfranchises its non-Jewish minority. While Palestinian citizens comprise almost 20 percent of its citizenry, the dominant Israeli discourse represents the cultural identity of the state as Jewish. Shammas also confronts the dominant Israeli linear historical discourse with a cyclical discourse that finds its paradigm in the interweaving lines of the arabesque. As read by Hever, Shammas's novel is a powerful contribution to a postzionist critique.

Hever's use of Deleuze suggests a powerful tool for framing the role of Palestinian citizens, Mizrahi Jews, women, gays, and lesbians in Israeli society. In Deleuze's terms, rather than simply constituting numerical minorities, such groups represent powerful transformative forces that challenge the dominant majoritarian models. Accordingly, as suggested by one commentator, they exemplify "a new way of posing the problem of the political," one in which political regimes are judged "in terms of the space they allow for 'multiplicities' and their 'individuations.'"[56]

Although the Israeli scholars discussed above help to make visible the marginalizing and exclusionary forces in Israeli society, they belong, for the most part, to the male, Jewish, Ashkenazi majority. Consequently, to regard them as spokespeople for oppressed minorities is to reinforce the minority's disempowered condition. At the same time, by making visible power relations and their enabling conditions, they help make it possible for oppressed peoples to engage in their own struggle, "a struggle that concerns their own interests, whose objectives they clearly understand and whose methods only they can determine.[57]

With one exception, part 4 presents writings by members of minorities who have been marginalized and excluded. In the memoir included here, Anton Shammas effectively brings to light the often unseen power effects of the dominant culture. Through what many would see as a benign system of language, symbols, and education, the state, perpetuating a Jewish discourse, effectively excludes the almost 20 percent of the population comprised of Palestinian citizens.[58] For Palestinians living in Israel, these cultural practices and narratives are mechanisms for exclusion and alienation. Consequently, the issues go far beyond the individual's civil rights and entail more deeply seated issues of power.

As Shammas's description of the cultural impact of the new state on his father's generation makes clear, culture is by no means benign. To the majority and minority alike, culture is intertwined with power. Shammas thus poses a most difficult challenge to those Israeli liberals who see the problem in terms of individual civil rights. With the source of exclusion inscribed into the fabric of the culture, legal efforts to protect civil rights do not suffice.[59]

While Shammas's diary represents the cultural marginalization of Israel's Palestinian citizens, Azmi Bishara's article extends the conversation to encompass legal and political issues. Bishara, a former member of the Israeli parliament, emphasizes the ways that the Jewishness of the Israeli state, inscribed in its legal and political systems, disenfranchises its Palestinian Arab population. So long as Israel is defined as a state that is Jewish, he argues, its Palestinian citizens, identifying with the Palestinian people, the Arab nation, and Arab culture, will be part of the state's form, but not its essence. Bishara represents the position of Israel's Palestinian citizens as a group torn between their desire for equality and their desire for an independent Palestinian national identity.

Bishara has been very vocal in arguing the right of Israel's Arab citizens to be recognized as both a political and cultural minority in a state that would also recognize their Palestinian national identity. In "Arab Citizens of Palestine: Little to Celebrate," written as the state was celebrating its fiftieth year, Bishara argues that only by becoming a state of all of its citizens can Israel justifiably claim to be a true democracy.[60] To achieve this, it must grant cultural and political rights to its Palestinian citizens not only as individuals, but as a collective. According to both Shammas and Bishara, the majoritarian model of Israel as a Jewish state necessarily results in the exclusion and disempowerment of its Palestinian citizens.[61]

While Palestinian Arabs are the most obvious victims of Zionism, a critique of Zionism is increasingly also being voiced by Jewish minoritarian groups. From the outset, the dominant Zionist narratives and representations of Israeli society have been produced by male Jews of European ancestry. These narratives, taken as normal by Ashkenazi Jews, have marginalized and excluded not only Palestinian citizens of Israel but also Mizrahi Jews. Moreover, as the readings reproduced in part 3 show, several Jewish minoritarian groups have come forward to criticize the marginalizing and exclusionary practices that characterize Israeli society and culture. Each of these groups experiences the discourse, practices, and identity norms with which the majority of Israelis identify as exclusionary, alienating, and oppressive.

As the articles by Ella Shohat, Yehouda Shenhav, and Pnina Motzafi-Haller make clear, Jews from Middle Eastern countries or Arab Jews, once referred to mistakenly as Sephardim, also constitute minoritarian voices within the state. Building upon previous writings which were among the first to address the issue of Arab Jews in Israel, Shohat describes the reductive and exclusionary effects of Zionism, with its concepts of *aliya*, redemption, and ingathering of the exiles.[62] This Orientalist discourse, she argues, produced primarily by European Ashkenazi Jews, fails to do justice to the complex and diverse experiences of Jews from Arab lands. Taking issue with what she sees as a monolithic Zionist historical discourse, she interrogates it in light of the experiences of Arab Jews. Whereas Zionist discourse is marked by a sense of continuity, the experiences of Arab Jews are marked by spatial disruption and cultural displacement.

Criticizing Zionism's teleological model in which Israel is represented as the natural culmination of the long path of Jewish history, Shohat argues that efforts to absorb all Jews into a new Israeli identity occlude or erase the distinct cultural and ethnic qualities of Arab Jews. Shohat thus calls for a new Mizrahi epistemology, a suggestion reiterated by Yehouda Shenhav. Shohat also criticizes Israelis' aversion to the concept of Arab Jews, which brings together cultural and social elements that Israeli culture struggles to keep separate.

Shenhav, in his postcolonialist, historical study *Arab Jews*, analyzes the history of Iraqi Jews as a case study that reveals Zionism's exclusions, distortions, and power effects. Expanding on the earlier work of Shohat, Shenhav seeks to unravel "methodological Zionism's" reduction of all social processes to nationalist Zionist categories. Rather than following the conventional Zionist path of beginning the narrative with the arrival of Iraqi Jews in the new state, Shenhav begins with the colonial encounter in Abadan, an Iranian city on the Persian Gulf. In addition, refusing to separate the external political Arab-Israeli conflict from the "internal" ethnic Mizrahi-Ashkenazi one, Shenhav, like Shohat, resists all efforts to depoliticize the subject of the Arab Jews.

Rejecting Zionism's attempt to fuse the categories of nationalism, religion, or ethnicity, Shenhav unravels the national-religious-ethnic package in order to bring to light the mechanisms "by which they acquire a unifying logic." In contrast to Zionist efforts to unify discourse, identity, and narrative, Shenhav, through his case studies, seeks to open the way to alternative, non-, or postzionist possibilities. He also highlights Zionism's contradictory effort to sever the Arab Jews' ties to their Arabness while enlisting them in the service of the state.

The issues of Israeli identity are further problematized by Pnina Motzafi-Haller, who connects the discussion of Mizrahi identity to that of women and Palestinians. An anthropologist, a feminist, and an activist in the cause of Mizrahi women of all classes, Motzafi-Haller uses the example of her son's Israeli textbooks to highlight the persistence of exclusionary practices against Mizrahi Jews. In her view, these textbooks are but another example of the numerous ways that Zionist historiography distorts, disfigures, and destroys "the historical agency of Mizrahim." Challenging the state's claim to effectively represent all Israelis, Motzafi-Haller asserts the need to challenge such claims as well as the Orientalist mentality that dominates Israeli society.

Specifically calling for a postzionist Israeli society, Motzafi-Haller encourages the deconstruction of the Ashkenazi-Zionist apparatus while advocating deeper and expanding democratic processes. As she envisions a transformed postzionist Israel, difference would replace otherness, while the state would be held accountable to the demands of all of Israel's multiple ethnic, social, cultural, and gender groups.[63]

In addition to Palestinian Arabs and Arab Jews, the emerging voices of feminists, gays, and lesbians within Israel further complicate the majoritarian model of a cohesive, unified, national identity. As these readings show, the experiences of women, gays, and lesbians help to further clarify, albeit in different ways, the marginalizing and exclusionary effects of Zionism within Israeli society.

In her discussion of the Israeli film *Jacky*, film scholar Orly Lubin seeks to bring to light the ways that Israeli women are represented in Israeli culture. According to Lubin, the common representation of women depicts them as subordinate, dependent, and lacking in agency. Owing largely to the ways that they are viewed in the Zionist imagination, women are rarely shown as agents with the power to construct their own subjectivity. In *Jacky*, however, Lubin finds a different, more empowering representation of women. Transgressing accepted cultural norms and striking out on her own, the female protagonist uses drug dealing as a way to establish an independent power base.

By situating the action in a development town, the film shifts the locus away from the privileged spaces of the national homeland to the marginalized spaces of the ethnic—that is, the Mizrahi home. In the drug culture of the development town, the actors structure their lives on the basis of their own needs rather than those of the nation. Thus, the protagonists live their daily lives out from under the prevailing national Ashkenazi narratives. Reading *Jacky* as a critique of the majority Israeli society, Lubin renders an important contribution to a feminist postzionist critique. Her analysis suggests possibilities for a critical feminist alternative to the dominant Israeli ethos in the interstices of gender, ethnicity, and territory.

Raz Yosef, depicting the victimized position of gay men within Israeli society, seeks to undermine the masculine heterosexual character of Zionist/Israeli discourse. Following such scholars as Daniel Boyarin, Yosef argues that Zionism's masculine discourse represents the ideal Israeli as manly.[64] Exploring, like Lubin, the exclusionary effects of Israeli popular culture, Yosef focuses on the representation of the queer, the (homo) eroticized Mizrahi Jew, and the Palestinian male, the abject others.

Acknowledging his debt to scholars like Boyarin, Sander Gilman, and Ella Shohat, Yosef represents Zionism as a sexual, as well as a political and ideological, project. One of Zionism's goals was to transform European, diasporic male masculinity into the new Hebrew man, a strong, athletic, military model. This, in turn, became the image of the Sabra, the militarized and masculine model of Israeliness. To Yosef, the queer, beyond serving as the other of the Zionist self, actually functions as a structural component of that self, one that must be disavowed. Applying postcolonial theory, Yosef explores the ways that ethnic, national, and racial factors intertwine with sexuality to construct the Zionist national subject. He further argues that racial and racist discourse, rather than being an effect or a byproduct of Zionist sexual politics, is actually one of its constitutive elements.

Erella Shadmi's analysis of the situation of lesbians in Israel further complicates the issues of national identity. Revealing the effects of the dominant Zionist discourse on yet another minority group, Shadmi shows how the Zionist privileging of heterosexuality, marriage, and children excludes and silences lesbians. Subordinating gender and sexuality to the needs of the nation, Zionism thus fosters a lesbophobic patriarchal society.

Shadmi further argues that insofar as they view their problems in terms of individual rights, lesbians lack the forum for questioning the "naturalness" of heterosexuality. As a result, they are left without an alternative lesbian form of life. Insofar as they cannot formulate an effective lesbian political critique, they remain politically powerless. Even queer theory, which raises issues such as pleasure, desire, and fantasy, does not address the specific needs of lesbians. Although acknowledging that in recent years lesbians have come into public view in Israel, she argues that the radical transformative force of lesbianism has yet to emerge.

Postzionist Critique among American Jews

As the writings of the American Jewish scholars included in this reader clearly indicate, the debates over postzionism extend beyond the borders of Israel. Although primarily identified with the state of Israel, Zionism has played a powerful role in shaping the ways that American Jews and many non-Jews understand Jewish history, identity, and culture. To highlight the prominent role of Israel in the life of the American Jewish community, one scholar describes it as a basic component of American Jews' civil religion.[65]

Somewhat ironically, most Americans, Jewish and non-Jewish alike, lack an in-depth knowledge of the basic axioms and concepts of Zionist discourse. For example, although Zionism defines Jews as a nation, most American Jews, identifying with the American nation, do not consider themselves to be part of a Jewish nation in any real sense. In addition, Zionism, from its beginnings, rejected the possibilities of a viable Jewish life in the Diaspora, which it more commonly designates as Exile. Yet many American Jews actively participate in creating a vital, dynamic Jewish culture in the United States.

To co-authors Caryn Aviv and David Shneer, significant numbers of Jews in the United States and elsewhere are rethinking their relation to Israel, and to the Zionist binary of Diaspora/homeland. In the process, they have begun to dismantle the Zionist concept of Diaspora. Mirroring concerns that have been labeled postzionist, some Jews, both religious and secular, have come to question the viability of the Zionist idea of a Jewish state in a multicultural, transnational world. Eschewing the use of terms like "Diaspora" and "homeland" to define the geography of world Jewry, Aviv and Shneer prefer to speak of new Jews as "global." In so doing, they call into question the conventional Zionist spatial divisions. In addition, new Jews question the very notion of a unified Jewish people, a basic Zionist axiom. Such concepts, Aviv and Shneer argue, fail to capture the complex realities of Jewish identity and Jewish communal life. In their view, power in the Jewish world is multidirectional. This, in turn, leads them to speak of Jewish peoples rather than a single Jewish people.

Although presenting Zionist representations of Jewish life as highly problematic, Aviv and Shneer refrain from the kind of critique exemplified in the writings of many postzionists. This leads the reader to conclude that perhaps changing realities obviate the need for such a critique. However, such a claim would clearly be rejected by Daniel and Jonathan Boyarin and Judith Butler, the authors of the last two readings.

To the Boyarins, Zionism's effectiveness in representing itself as the authentic culmination of Jewish history demands a nuanced, critical counterreading of Jewish texts and Jewish history. Moving deftly but selectively among a series of classical Jewish texts and historical experiences, they seek to establish their claim that Diaspora has been a powerful and persistent creative force within Judaism. Taking issue with the Zionist claim, the Boyarins argue that there is no essential link between Jews and territory or between Jewishness and political sovereignty. Moreover, their reading reveals that the Zionist rendering of Diaspora and homeland constitutes but one possibility within Judaism. Criticizing the many victimizing practices and injustices carried out in the name of the Israeli state, they provide their readers with textual and historical grounds for an alternative Jewish model, a Diasporic model.

The Boyarins also point to the presence of racist and fascist tendencies within contemporary Judaism, particularly in Israel. Attributing these to the Zionist generated political and cultural system, they argue that Zionism fosters the subversion of Jewish ethics and culture rather than their culmination. Numerous Jewish sources reject political domination and autochthony, thereby providing the basis for a viable alternative concept of Diaspora. This, in turn, enables a Jewish identity that integrates respect for cultural difference, proclivity for cultural mixing, and passionate concern for all human beings. In the final analysis, they argue, Diaspora, rather than monotheism may be Judaism's most important contribution to the world.

As Israeli speakers in the United States often discover, American Jews are far more cautious than their Israel counterparts when it comes to criticizing Zionism and Israel. As Judith Butler argues, this caution often takes the form of censorship. To demonstrate this, Butler sets forth a critique of a widely circulated statement by Harvard president Lawrence Summers concerning the growing criticism of Israel on university campuses. According to Butler, Summers's statement reflects a perspective commonly found within the Jewish community, one that seeks to impose sharp limits on public discourse concerning Israel. Butler, a prominent philosopher, feminist scholar, and queer theorist, views Summers's statement as raising important questions concerning the construction of Jewish identity. Of particular concern is Summers's assumption of the "full and seamless identification" of Jews with the state of Israel. It is precisely this unexamined linking of Jewish identity to an uncritical acceptance of Israeli policies and practices that Butler regards as problematic: At the same time, she rejects Summers's assumption that to criticize Israel is anti-Israel, and is the equivalent of questioning Israel's right to exist.

While acknowledging her emotional investment in the state of Israel, Butler nonetheless calls for the creation of spaces of critique within Jewish pubic discourse. Such spaces will, in turn, help to reveal the dynamic, multiplicitous, and contested character of Jewish identity. In such spaces, Jews could freely express criticisms of Israel without being subjected to charges of being anti-Israel. In her critique and in her call for a radical restructuring of Israeli life, Butler positions herself in close relation to many of the Israeli postzionist critics represented in this reader.[66]

As the previous discussion makes clear, the issues raised by *Postzionism: A Reader* are of deep concern to Jews outside of as well as within Israel. In an age commonly identified as global, the basic underpinnings of the nation-state has been subjected to extensive reexamination. Israel, one of the younger nation-states, has, since its inception, experienced continual conflict and warfare. This has, in turn, significantly intensified the responses to critiques such as postzionism. Yet, like many nation-states, Israelis are increasingly being asked to confront the expansion of transformative forces such as postzionism. Significantly challenging the prevailing forms of Israeli national identity, such forces open the way to alternative national and postnational forms. To Zionist critics, such challenges are threatening and ultimately destructive. Conversely, to those sympathetic to postzionism, they are signs of hope and the possibility of a more viable, diverse, and open national life.

To readers deeply concerned about the Middle East in general and Israel in particular, these articles provide a broader, more complex understanding of the issues at stake. They also provide access to diverse, critical, transformative forces in Israeli national life. They thus suggest possibilities for a scope of vision and range of understanding all too often occluded within American political life in general, and Jewish communal life specifically.

Outside of Israel, particularly in the United States, Zionism has played a major role in shaping Jewish identity construction. Consequently, to challenge Zionist axioms is to put into question the ways that many American Jews understand what it means to be Jewish. For American Jews, the postzionist critique challenges them to critically reflect on the premises of their own Jewish identity.[67] Those who resist such reflection regard postzionism as a distinct danger. On the other hand, to that minority who welcome and encourage such reflection, postzionism offers possibilities for a more dynamic, ethically consistent, and intellectually satisfying Jewish life.

NOTES

1. *New York Times*, April 10, 1998.
2. Ibid.
3. Ibid.
4. Ibid. On the wider significance of *Tekumah* see Laurence J. Silberstein, *The Postzionism Debates: Knowledge and Power in Israeli Culture* (New York and London: Routledge, 1999), 1–14, and Ilan Pappe, "Israeli Television's Fiftieth Anniversary 'Tekumma' Series: A Post-Zionist View," *Journal of Palestine Studies* 27 (Summer 1998): 99–105.
5. Marita Sturken, *Tangled Memories: The Vietnam War, the AIDS Epidemic, and the Politics of Remembering* (Berkeley and Los Angeles: University of California Press, 1997), 2.
6. Tom Segev, *1949: The First Israelis* (New York: Free Press, 1986).
7. For other critiques of the "myths" of Israeli society see Simcha Flapan, *The Birth of Israel: Myths and Realities* (New York: Pantheon, 1987) and the scholarly analysis of Nachman ben Yehuda, *The Masada Myth* (Madison: University of Wisconsin, 1995).
8. Shalev succinctly summarizes the critique leveled at this premise by critical sociologists from Haifa University. See Michael Shalev, "Time for Theory: Critical Notes on Lissak and Sternhell," *Israel Studies* 1 (Fall 1996): 185 n. 11. See also Uri Ram, *The Changing Agenda of Israeli Sociology* (Albany: SUNY Press, 1995), chaps. 5–6.
9. Segev, *The First Israelis*, vii.
10. These conflicts are clearly set forth by A. B. Yehoshua in "Israeli Identity in a Time of Peace: Prospects and Perils," *Tikkun* 10 (November/December 1996): 33–40, 94. Yehoshua, an ardent although often critical defender of Zionist ideology, reflects on the possibilities for resolving these conflicts in the context of a Zionist state. In *In the Land of Israel* (New York: Vintage Books/Random House, 1984), Amos Oz, another widely recognized Israeli writer, depicts, at greater lengths, many of these same conflicts.
11. Segev, *The First Israelis*, viii.
12. Michael Shalev, *Labour and the Political Economy in Israel*, Library of Political Economy (New York: Oxford University Press, 1992), 14.
13. Yisrael Landers, "The Sin That We Committed in Establishing the State" [in Hebrew], *Davar HaShavua*, March 18, 1994, 8–9.
14. Ibid.
15. Aharon Megged, "The Israeli Instinct for Self-Destruction," *Musaf Haaretz* (June 10, 1994): 28. Megged took specific aim at sociologist Baruch Kimmerling and his American colleague Joel Migdal, particularly their effort, the first by Israeli/Jewish scholars, to produce an unbiased history of the Palestinian people; see Baruch Kimmerling

and Joel Migdal, *Palestinians: The Making of a People* (New York: Free Press, 1993) See notes 56–60 below. In Megged's view, Kimmerling and Migdal simply reiterated that form of anti-Zionist attack that had roots in Soviet propaganda. Reiterating the standard Labor Zionist position, Megged argued that the early Zionist settlers never intended "to exploit the cheap labor of the natives, to steal their lands by force, to subjugate them through denying them rights, individually or collectively. Just the opposite: [their goal was] to create an independent economic and cultural system alongside the Arab system, independent and non-exploitative." Far from doing harm to the Arab economic system, the labor Zionist movement sought only "to develop and advance it."

16. Landers, "The Sin That We Committed," 8. Although the term "postzionist" had been previously used in Israeli society, it was primarily used to refer to the idea that insofar as Zionism had succeeded in its endeavor to establish a Jewish state, Israelis now live in a postzionist era. See on this Silberstein, *Postzionism Debates*, 222 n. 4. The current usage significantly differs.

17. At no point in these articles is there any suggestion that the scholarship was faulty. Instead, the criticisms were based on ideological grounds, speaking more to the present than to the past.

18. Ilan Pappe, "New History of Zionism: The Academic and Public Confrontation" [in Hebrew], *Kivvunim: A Journal of Zionism and Judaism* 8 (June 1995): 45. For Pappe's overview of the academic debates over postzionism, see "Post-Zionist Critique on Israel and the Palestinians. Part I: The Academic Debate," *Journal of Palestine Studies* 26 (Winter 1997): 29–41. Parts 2–3 appear in vol. 26 (3): 37–43 and 26 (4): 60. See also Ephraim Nimni, ed., *The Challenge of Post-Zionism: Alternatives to Fundamentalist Politics in Israel* (London: Zed Books, 2003) and Uri Ram, "Post-Zionism: The First Decade," a section of which is reprinted below. The full article appears in *Israel Studies Forum* 20 (2): 22–45.

19. Evidence that this charge is still being leveled is the article "The Lie of Postzionism: Whoever Calls Him/Herself a Postzionist Is Simply an Old Time Anti-Zionist," written by well-known political theorist Shlomo Avineri and published in *Haaretz*, July 3, 2007. I thank Anton Shammas for calling my attention to this article.

20. For critiques of terms ending in "ism" see Arthur O. Lovejoy, *The Great Chain of Being: The History of an Idea* (New York: Harper and Row, 1965), and Paul Veyne, "Foucault Revolutionizes History," in *Foucault and His Interlocutors*, edited and introduced by Arnold I. Davidson (Chicago: University of Chicago Press, 1997), 146–182. In *The Challenge of Postzionism: Alternatives to Fundamentalist Politics in Israel* (London: Zed Books, 2003), Nimni refers to the concept postzionism as an empty signifier, a term he borrows from Ernesto Laclau and Chantal Mouffe (11).

21. This is clearly reflected in the controversies surrounding the television series *Tekumah* and new secondary school textbooks that the Likud government eventually removed from Israeli schools. In each case, the term "postzionism" was widely applied. For a brief discussion of these controversies, see the introduction to Silberstein, *Postzionism Debates*, 1–14.

22. For a more extensive analysis of Zionist discourse, see Silberstein, *Postzionism Debates*. For the various practices through which Zionist discourse has been enacted, see Meron Benvenisti, *Conflicts and Contradictions* (New York: Dillard Books, 1986), and idem, *Sacred Landscapes: The Buried History of the Holy Land Since 1948* (Berkeley: University of California Press, 2000). See also Oz Almog, *The Sabra: The Generation of the New Jew* (Berkeley: University of California Press, 2000), and Anton Shammas, "At

Half Mast—Myths, Symbols, and Rituals of An Emerging State: A Personal Testimony of an 'Israeli Arab,'" in *New Perspectives on Israeli History: The Early Years of the State*, ed. Laurence J. Silberstein (New York: New York University Press, 1991), 216–224, reprinted in this volume.

23. Following Gilles Deleuze and Félix Guattari, I use the term minority not as a numerical designation, but to designate groups who do not identify with the dominant (majority) models or representations of Israeli society. For a discussion of the concept as employed in this book, see Gilles Deleuze and Felix Guattari, *Kafka: Toward a Minor Literature*, trans. Dana Polan (Minneapolis: University of Minnesota Press, 1986), *The Deleuze Dictionary*, ed. Adrian Parr (New York: Columbia University Press, 2005), pp. 164–170. See also, Abdul R. Jan Mohammed and David Lloyd, eds., *The Nature and Context of Minority Discourse* (New York: Oxford University Press, 1990). I discuss the concept more fully in relation to Israeli society in Laurence J. Silberstein, "Becoming Israeli/Israeli Becoming," in *Deleuze and the Contemporary World*, ed. Ian Buchanan and Adrian Parr (Edinburgh: University of Edinburgh Press, 2000), 146–160.

24. For a discussion of postzionism as critique, see Laurence J. Silberstein, "Postzionism: A Critique of Israel's Zionist Discourse," *Palestine Israel Journal* 9 (2002), 84–91, 97–106, and Postzionism and Postmodernism Theory: The Challenge to Jewish Studies in *Modern Judaism and Historical Consciousness: Identities-Encounters-Perspectives*, ed. Andreas Gotzmann and Christian Wiese (Boston: Brill, 2007), 445–471.

25. As Shenhav and Hever emphasize, the term "postcolonial" "does not refer to a period 'after colonialism,' but rather refers to an effort to become liberated from the modes of colonialist discourse and speech" regardless of when they were manifested. Yehouda Shenhav and Hannan Hever, "Currents in Postcolonial Studies" [in Hebrew], in *Colonialism and the Postcolonial Situation*, ed. Yehouda Shenhav (Jerusalem: Van Lear Jerusalem Institute and Hakibbutz Hameuchad, 2004), 189–200. See also Homi K. Bhabha's concept of "third space" in idem, *The Location of Culture* (London and New York: Routledge, 1994).

26. See Silberstein, *Postzionism Debates*, chaps. 2 and 3.

27. See, for example, Michael Staub, *Torn at the Roots* (New York: Columbia University Press, 2002); Leonard Fein, *Where Are We?* (New York: Harper and Row, 1988); Jacob Neusner, *Stranger at Home: "The Holocaust," Zionism, and American Judaism* (Chicago: University of Chicago Press, 1981); Bernard Avishai, *The Tragedy of Zionism: How Its Revolutionary Past Haunts Israeli Democracy* (New York: Helios Press, 2002) and Tony Kushner and Alisa Solomon, eds., *Wrestling with Zion: Progressive Jewish-American Responses to the Israeli-Palestinian Conflict* (New York: Grove Press, 2003).

28. The critiques by Ella Shohat, who was born in Iraq and for whom Israel was home for many years, were formulated within the academic and cultural climate of the United States.

29. See Jonathan Woocher, *Sacred Survival: The Civil Religion of American Jews* (Bloomington: Indiana University Press, 1986).

30. Stuart Hall, "Cultural Identity and Diaspora," in *Identity: Community, Culture, Difference*, ed. Jonathan Rutherford (London: Lawrence and Wishart, 1990), 225.

31. Morris, *1948 and After: Israel and the Palestinians* (Oxford: Oxford University Press, 1994), 40. The shock and disappointment experienced by many in the current generation upon learning that they had been lied to is a common theme among younger, critical scholars. This is clearly revealed in the title of an article by Morris, "The Lied to Us, They Concealed, They Covered Up: Interview with Rami Tal" [in Hebrew], *Yediot Aharonot*, December 16, 1994, 29–30. See also Adi Ophir, this volume, 84-101;

Shafir, *Israel Studies* 1, no. 2 (fall 1996): 189–213; Michael Shalev, preface to *Labor and The Political Economy of Israel* (Oxford: Oxford University Press, 1992); and idem, "Time for Theory: Critical Notes on Lissak and Sternhell," *Israel Studies* 1 (Fall 1996): 14; and Nahman Ben-Yehuda, *The Masada Myth: Collective Memory and Mythmaking in Israel* (Madison: University of Wisconsin Press, 1995), 3–7. For a more recent expression of disillusionment with Zionism by a longtime devotee, see Avraham Burg, "The Zionist Revolution Is Dead," originally published in Hebrew in *Yediot Aharonot* and reprinted in *The Forward,* August 29, 2003.

32. In a widely discussed interview in *Haaretz,* January 9, 2004, Morris created a furor when he endorsed Israel's policy of "ethnic cleansing" in the 1948 war and suggested the desirability of "transferring" the current Palestinian citizens of Israel out of the state. See Morris, "Peace? No Chance," in *Guardian Unlimited,* February 20, 2002. For a critique of Morris's position, see Adi Ophir, "Genocide Hides Behind Expulsion," at www.dissidentvoice.org, January 17, 2006.

33. Baruch Kimmerling was one of the first Israeli scholars to raise the issue of colonialism in *Zionism and Territory: The Socio-Territorial Dimension of Zionist Politics* (Berkeley: University of California Press, 1983), but he developed it in a different direction than did Shafir. See also Gershon Shafir, *Land, Labor and the Origins of the Israeli-Palestinian Conflict: 1882–1914* (Cambridge: Cambridge University Press, 1996).

34. Prior to the late Prime Minister Yitzhak Rabin's 1993 speech in the White House Rose Garden, no Israeli prime minister publicly acknowledged the legitimacy of Palestinian national aspirations.

35. For a discussion of previous uses of the term "postzionism," see Silberstein, *Postzionism Debates,* 222 n. 4. See also the article by Uri Ram, "Post-Zionism: The First Decade," in *Israel Studies Forum* 20, no. 2 (2005): 22–45.

36. In *The Changing Agenda of Israeli Sociology* (Albany: SUNY Press, 1995), Ram explores the changing theoretical perspectives that have informed the writings of Israeli sociologists since the beginnings of the state.

37. Ram, *Changing Agenda,* 206.

38. Ibid. For an excellent example of the kind of postzionist sociology Ram had in mind, see Baruch Kimmerling, *The Invention and Decline of Israeliness: State, Society, and the Military* (Berkeley: University of California Press, 2001).

39. For a brief discussion, see Silberstein, *Postzionism Debates,* 94–96.

40. For a more extensive discussion of this group of scholars and the context of its emergence, see Silberstein, *Postzionism Debates,* chap. 6. See also Silberstein, "Postzionism: A Critique of Israel's Zionist Discourse," in *Palestine Israel Journal* 9 (Summer 2002): 2–3, 84–91, 97–106, and "Theory as Practice: Postzionism and the Critique of Power" in *Israel Studies Bulletin* (Fall 2000): 30–35.

41. Judith Butler provides a lucid analysis of the practice of critique in "What Is Critique," in *The Judith Butler Reader,* ed. Sara Salih, with Judith Butler (Malden, MA: Oxford, Victoria, 2004): 202–222. See also Wendy Brown, *Edgework: Critical Essays on Knowledge and Politics* (Princeton: Princeton University Press, 2005), esp. 1–16, and see Michel Foucault, "What Is Critique?" in *The Politics of Truth,* ed. Sylvère Lotringer and Lysa Hochroth (New York: Semiotexte, 1997), 23–82. In addition to the articles referred to in note 40, I discuss the concept of critique and its application to the field of Jewish Studies in "Postzionism and Postmodernism: The Challenge to Jewish Studies," in *Modern Judaism and Historical Consciousness: Identities—Encounters—Perspectives,* ed. Andreas Gotzmann and Christian Wiese (Boston: Brill Publishers, 2007).

42. It's not so much that most Israelis did/do not see the power relations operating between Jews and Israelis, but that they do not see the inherent injustice of such power relations and the extent to which they are instantiated in virtually all dimensions of Israeli society and culture. The problem, therefore, is not just that of obtaining civil liberties and equality, but rather, as the writings by Shammas, Bishara, and Hever demonstrate, seeing and addressing the inequitable workings of power in the capillaries of everyday Israeli life.

43. For the purpose of distinguishing this theory oriented group of critical Israeli intellectuals from the "new historians" and "critical sociologists," I have previously, notwithstanding the problems it entails, chosen to refer to them as postmodern postzionists. In so doing, I call attention to the affinity of their work with various perspectives and practices commonly identified as postmodern. These include a focus on the critique of discourse and practices and the ways that meaning is constituted and knowledge produced and disseminated. See Silberstein, *Postzionism Debates*, chap. 5.

44. Ilan Pappe, a scholar whose works are commonly regarded as postzionist, had also commented on the narrow, exclusionary orientation of Israel scholarly discourse. Insisting that any legitimate history of Israel must take into consideration Palestinian perspectives, he edited several Hebrew books in which he presented both Jewish and Palestinian perspectives. See Ilan Pappe, *The Israel/Palestine Question* (New York and London: Routledge, 1999). The Hebrew reader is referred to *Jewish-Arab Relations in Mandatory Palestine: A New Approach to the Historical Research* [in Hebrew] (Givat Havivah: Institute for Peace Studies, 1995); and Ilan Pappe and Shlomo Swirski, eds., *The Intafada: An Inside View* [in Hebrew] (Tel Aviv: Mefaresh, 1992).

45. Kimmerling focuses on the ideologically embedded character of historiography more clearly and incisively than most other Israeli social scientists. However, although acknowledging the importance of discourse, he refrains from analyzing the processes by means of which the discourse is produced and inscribed as a part of Israeli hegemonic culture. In contrast, as indicated above, a postmodernist critique would focus on the processes by means of which the scholarly discourse is constructed and disseminated.

46. Kimmerling's analysis provides an example of Foucault's claim that the discourse employed in the production of knowledge is imbricated in complex relations of power. To effectively reveal and confront the power effects of Zionist scholarly discourse requires a critique of that discourse and the knowledge it produces. What is needed, he argued, is a new, non-Zionist mode of scholarly discourse. While providing an excellent example that supports Foucault's claims regarding the relationship of power and knowledge, there is no indication that Kimmerling's critique owed anything to Foucault. Nor is this kind of critique representative of his scholarly work as a whole. While Kimmerling has gained a reputation as one of Israel's most prolific intellectual critics, he continued to position himself primarily as a devotee of and practitioner of objective social science; see Kimmerling, *The Invention and Decline of Israeliness*, introduction.

47. For useful discussions of the relationship of postmodernism to social theory, see Steven Seidman and David Wagner, eds., *Postmodernism and Social Theory* (Cambridge, Mass.: Blackwell, 1992); and Steven Best and Douglas Kellner, *Postmodern Theory: Critical Interrogations* (New York: Guildford Press, 1991).

48. In addition to the articles in this volume by Oren Yiftachel and Alexandre (Sandy) Kedar, see Oren Yiftachel, *Ethnocracy: Land and Identity Politics in Israel/Palestine* (Philadelphia: University of Pennsylvania Press, 2006).

49. Applying postnational conceptions of space and Diaspora, Dan Rabinowitz has criticized the dominant Israeli discourse that represents territory, culture, and national identity as essentially interconnected. Highlighting processes of globalization and transnationalism, he questions the continued privileging of state and nation by Israeli scholars. See Dan Rabinowitz, "Postnational Palestine/Israel? Globalization, Diaspora, Transnationalism, and the Israeli-Palestinian Conflict," *Critical Inquiry* (Summer 2000): 757–781; idem, "Borders and Their Discontents: Israel's Green Line, Arabness and Unilateral Separation," *European Studies: A Journal of European Culture, History, and Politics* 19 (2003): 217–231. In "The Palestinian Citizens of Israel, the Concept of Trapped Minority and the Discourse of Transnationalism in Anthropology," *Ethnic and Racial Studies* 24, no. 1 (2001): 64–85, Rabinowitz represents the Palestinian citizens of Israel as a "trapped minority" torn between two national narratives and two national spaces.

50. As of August 2007, the Qaadans have still not been permitted to purchase land.

51. For an analysis of a situation mentioned by Kedar in which the courts adopted a far more transformative position, see the discussion of *Mabo v. Queensland* in Paul Patton, *Deleuze and the Political* (London and New York: Routledge, 2000), chap. 6.

52. In discussions at Van Leer during late 1988 and 1989, a small group of young scholars sought to formulate an appropriate discourse for the critique of Israeli social and cultural life. These concerns are summarized in unpublished documents in my possession, and in a document written by Ophir and Hannan Hever, a professor of Hebrew literature at Tel Aviv University. I am grateful to Adi Ophir for providing me with copies of these documents. I discuss this document and the emergence and early activities of this group, in Silberstein, *Postzionism Debates*, 167–169.

53. Michel Foucault, *Foucault Live: Interviews, 1961–84*, ed. S. Lotringer (New York: Semiotexte, 1996), 75–76.

54. Hever is one of the only Israeli scholars to make use of Deleuze and Guattari's ideas. I am grateful to Hever for first showing me the significance of Deleuze for the analysis of Zionism and Israel. For Deleuze and Guattari's significance for postcolonial studies, see Paul Patton, *Deleuze and the Political*, and Robert Young, *Colonial Desire: Hybridity in Theory, Culture, Race* (New York and London: Routledge, 1995), 166–174.

55. Gilles Deleuze, *Negotiations:1972–1990* (New York: Columbia University Press, 1995), 173.

56. John Rajchman, *The Deleuze Connection* (Cambridge: MIT Press, 2000), 82.

57. The phrasing is Foucault's. See Foucault, *Foucault Live*, 81.

58. For recent population figures, see Yiftachel, *Ethnocracy: Land and Identity Politics in Israel/Palestine*, chap. 3. See also Kimmerling, *The Invention and Decline of Israeliness: State Society and the Military* (Berkeley: University of California Press, 2001).

59. In other writings, Shammas has argued that laws such as Israel's law of return, along with the entire apparatus around which Israeli national identity has been constructed, privilege Jewish Israelis while disenfranchising and disempowering Palestinian Israelis. The law of return, a uniquely Zionist institution that is a source of pride to Jews throughout the world, is, in his view, incompatible with a fully democratic society. According to this law, a manifestation of the discourse that defined Israel as a state of the Jewish people, any Jew from any place in the world who immigrated to Israel would be welcome and, with rare exceptions, granted citizenship. In contrast, Palestinians who fled the state in 1948 and whose families had lived on

the land for generations, even centuries, are denied permission to return. How is it, argued Shammas, that a non-Hebrew-speaking Jew from Brooklyn who had never set foot in Israel could be pretty much guaranteed citizenship, while Palestinians fluent in Hebrew with a map of the landscape inscribed in their consciousness could never hope for citizenship. For a thorough discussion of these issues in which Shammas confronts and challenges A. B. Yehoshua, one of Israel's leading writers and liberal intellectuals, see David Grossman, *Sleeping on a Wire: Conversations with Palestinians in Israel* (New York: Farrar, Straus, and Giroux, 1993), chap. 15.

60. For other examples of Bishara's thoughts on these matters, see his lecture "Palestine, and the Question of Citizenship," revised Web version, February 6, 2004, http://www.sant.ox.ac.uk/areastudies/lecturesarchive/Bishara.pdf.

61. While most Arab citizens of Israel identify with the Palestinian people, the basic terms the Israeli majority uses to label them conceal and erase this identification. The majority's nomenclature for Arabs of Israel has, over the years, included Arviei Yisrael (Arabs of Israel or Israeli Arabs), Aravim Yisraelim (Israeli Arabs), and simply Aravim (Arabs). However, according to Dan Rabinowitz, this language conceals "the contestatory nature of the land" (Dan Rabinowitz, "Oriental Nostalgia: The Transformation of Palestinians to Israeli Arabs" [in Hebrew], *Theory and Criticism* 4 [Fall 1993]: 145). According to Rabinowitz, the use of the generic concept "Arabs" to refer to Palestinian citizens of Israel shifts attention from the internal political conflict to internal cultural differences, thereby feeding into the liberal discourse of cultural pluralism. Yet Israeli Jews, when speaking of Arabs outside of Israel, have no difficulty referring to their national identity (Jordanians, Egyptians, etc.) rather than their (Arabic) cultural identity. See also Silberstein, *Postzionism Debates*, 183–185.

62. See Ella Shohat, "Sephardim in Israel: Zionism from the Standpoint of Its Jewish Victims," *Social Text* 19/20 (Fall 1988): 1–35, and "The Invention of the Mizrahim," *Journal of Palestine Studies* 29 (Autumn 1991): 5–20.

63. For an extensive analysis of and proposal for the study of Mizrahi women, see Pnina Motzafi-Haller, "Scholarship, Identity and Power: Mizrahi Women in Israel," *Signs* 26 (Spring 2001): 697–734.

64. See Daniel Boyarin, *Unheroic Conduct: The Rise of Secularity and the Invention of the Jewish Man* (Berkeley: University of California Press, 1997). Miki Gluzman, whose writings on the topic have not yet appeared in English, focuses on issues of sexuality and homosexuality in Hebrew and Israeli literature. See "Longing for Heterosexuality: Zionism and Sexuality in Herzl's Altneuland" [in Hebrew], *Theory and Criticism* 11 (Winter 1997): 145–162.

65. See Jonathan Woocher, *Sacred Survival: The Civil Religion of American Jews* (Indianapolis: Indiana University Press, 1986). The term "Israelism" has also had wide circulation as a concept that reflects the central role of Israel in American Jewish life. See Gerald Sorin, *Tradition Transformed: The Jewish Experience in America* (Baltimore: Johns Hopkins University Press, 1997), 214–217, 243–244.

66. For Butler's views on the Palestinian-Israeli conflict, see Judith Butler, "Jews and the Bi-National State," in *Logos* 3 (Winter 2004), http://www.logosjournal.com/. For another widely discussed critique of Zionism by a prominent American Jewish intellectual, see Tony Judt, "Israel: The Alternative," *New York Review of Books* 50 (October 23, 2003). For reactions to Judt's position, see "An Alternative Future: An Exchange by Abraham H. Foxman, Amos Elon, Michael Walzer, Omer Bartov, Reply by Tony Judt," *New York Review of Books* 50 (December 4, 2003).

67. I apply Butler's ideas regarding the relation of ethics and identity to the problem of American Jewish identity in "Becoming Jewish: Jewish Becomings: Critical and Ethical Reflections," *Transversal: Zeitschrift für Jüdische Studien*, Special Issue on Jewish Identity (Fall 2006). I expand this discussion in "Minority Voices and the Ethics of Jewish Identity: Critical Reflections," in *Kulturelle Grenzraüme im Judischen Kontext*, ed. Klaus Hödl (Innsbruck: Studien Verlag, 2008).

PART I

New Historians and Critical Sociologists

Critical Reflections on Israeli/Zionist Narratives

1

The New Historiography

Israel Confronts Its Past

BENNY MORRIS

On July 11, 1948, the Yiftah Brigade's Third Battalion, as part of what was called Operation Dani, occupied the center of the Arab town of Lydda. There was no formal surrender, but the night passed quietly. Just before noon the following day, two or three armored cars belonging to the Arab Legion, the British-led and -trained Transjordanian army, drove into town. A firefight ensued, and the scout cars withdrew. But a number of armed townspeople, perhaps believing that the shooting heralded a major Arab counterattack, began sniping from windows and rooftops at their Israeli occupiers. The Third Battalion—about four hundred nervous Israeli soldiers in the middle of an Arab town of tens of thousands—fiercely put down what various chroniclers subsequently called a "rebellion" by firing in the streets, into houses, and at the concentrations of POWs in the mosque courtyards. Israeli military records refer to more than 250 Arabs killed in the town that afternoon. By contrast, Israeli casualties in both the firefight with the Arab Legion scout cars and the suppression of the sniping were between two and four dead (the records vary) and twelve wounded. Israeli historians called the affair a rebellion in order to justify the subsequent slaughter; Arab chroniclers, such as Aref al-Aref, did likewise in order to highlight Palestinian resolve and resistance in the face of Zionist encroachment.

Operation Dani took place roughly midway through the first Israeli-Arab war—the War of Independence, in official Israeli parlance. The Arab states' invasion on May 15 of the fledgling state had been halted weeks before; the newly organized and freshly equipped Israel Defense Forces (IDF) were on the offensive on all fronts—as was to remain true for the remainder of the war.

On July 12, before the shooting in Lydda had completely died down, Lt. Col. Yitzhak Rabin, officer in command of operations for Operation Dani, issued

Reprinted, by permission, from *Tikkun: A Bimonthly Interfaith Critique of Politics, Culture and Society* 3, no. 6 (1988): 19–23, 99–102.

the following order: "1. The inhabitants of Lydda must be expelled quickly without attention to age. They should be directed towards Beit Nabala. Yiftah [Brigade HQ] must determine the method and inform [Operation] Dani HQ and Eighth Brigade HQ. 2. Implement immediately." A similar order was issued at the same time to the Kiryati Brigade concerning the inhabitants of the neighboring Arab town of Ramle.

On July 12 and July 13, the Yiftah and Kiryati brigades carried out their orders, expelling the fifty to sixty thousand inhabitants of the two towns, which lie about ten miles southeast of Tel Aviv. Throughout the war, the two towns had interdicted Jewish traffic on the main Tel Aviv–Jerusalem road, and the Yishuv's leaders regarded Lydda and Ramle as a perpetual threat to Tel Aviv itself. About noon on July 13, Operation Dani HQ informed IDF General Staff/Operations: "Lydda police fort has been captured. [The troops] are busy expelling the inhabitants [*oskim be'geirush ha'toshavim*]." Lydda's inhabitants were forced to walk eastward to the Arab Legion lines, and many of Ramle's inhabitants were ferried in trucks or buses. Clogging the roads (and the legion's possible routes of advance westward), the tens of thousands of refugees marched, gradually shedding possessions along the way. Arab chroniclers, such as Sheikh Muhammad Nimr al-Khatib, claimed that hundreds of children died in the march from dehydration and disease. One Israeli witness at the time described the spoor: The refugee column "to begin with [jettisoned] utensils and furniture and, in the end, bodies of men, women and children." Many of the refugees came to rest near Ramallah and set up tent encampments (which later became the refugee camps supported by the United Nations Relief and Works Agency [UNRWA], and the hotbeds of today's Palestinian rebellion which current Defense Minister Rabin is trying to suppress).

Israeli historians in the 1950s, 1960s, and 1970s were less than honest in their treatment of the Lydda-Ramle episode. The IDF's official *Toldot Milhemet Ha'kornemiut* (History of the War of Independence), written by the General Staff/History Branch and published in 1959, stated, "The Arabs [of Lydda], who had violated the terms of the surrender and feared [Israeli] retribution, were happy at the possibility given them of evacuating the town and proceeding eastwards, to Legion territory: Lydda emptied of its Arab inhabitants."

A decade later, the former head of the IDF History Branch, Lt. Col. Netanel Lorch, wrote in 1968 in *The Edge of the Sword*, the second revised edition of his history of the war, that "the residents, who had violated surrender terms and feared retribution, declared they would leave and asked [for] safe conduct to Arab Legion lines, which was granted."

A somewhat less deceitful, but also misleading, description of the events in Lydda and Ramle is provided by Lt. Col. Elhannan Orren, another former director of the IDF History Branch, in his *Ba'derekh el ha'ir* (On the road to the city), a highly detailed description of Operation Dani published by the IDF in 1976. Orren, like his predecessors, fails to state anywhere that what occurred was an expulsion, and one explicitly ordered from on high (originating, according to Ben-Gurion's first major biographer, Michael Bar-Zohar, from the prime minister himself). Orren also repeats a variant of the "inhabitants asked, the IDF graciously complied" story.

Yitzhak Rabin, ironically more frank than his chroniclers, inserted a passage into his autobiography, *Pinkas sherut* (Service notebook), which more or less admitted that what had occurred in Lydda and Ramle had been an expulsion. But the passage was excised by order of the Israeli government. (Subsequently, to everyone's embarrassment, Peretz Kidron, the English translator of *Pinkas sherut*, sent the offending passage to the *New York Times*, where it was published on October 23, 1979.)

The treatment of the Lydda-Ramle affair by past Israeli historians is illustrative of what can be called, for want of a better term, the "old" or "official" history. That history has shaped the way Israelis and Diaspora Jews—or, at least, Diaspora Zionists—have seen and, in large measure, still see Israel's past; and it has also held sway over the way gentile Europeans and Americans (and their governments) see that past. This understanding of the past, in turn, has significantly influenced the attitudes of Diaspora Jews, as well as the attitude of European and American non-Jews, toward present-day Israel—which affects government policies concerning the Israeli-Arab conflict.

The essence of the old history is that Zionism was a beneficent and well-meaning progressive national movement; that Israel was born pure into an uncharitable, predatory world; that Zionist efforts at compromise and conciliation were rejected by the Arabs; and that Palestine's Arabs, and in their wake the surrounding Arab states, for reasons of innate selfishness, xenophobia, and downright cussedness, refused to accede to the burgeoning Zionist presence and in 1947 to 1949 launched a war to extirpate the foreign plant. The Arabs, so goes the old history, were politically and militarily assisted in their efforts by the British, but they nonetheless lost the war. Poorly armed and outnumbered, the Jewish community in Palestine, called the Yishuv, fought valiantly, suppressed the Palestinian gangs (*knufyot* in Israeli parlance), and repelled the five invading Arab armies. In the course of that war, says the old history—which at this point becomes indistinguishable from Israeli propaganda—Arab states and leaders, in order to blacken Israel's image and facilitate the invasion of Palestine, called upon/ordered Palestine's Arabs to quit their homes and the "Zionist areas"—to which they were expected to return once the Arab armies had proved victorious. Thus was triggered the Palestinian Arab exodus which led to the now forty-year-old Palestinian refugee problem.

The old history makes the further claim that in the latter stages of the 1948 war and in the years immediately thereafter Israel desperately sought to make peace with all or any of its neighbors, but the Arabs, obdurate and ungenerous, refused all overtures, remaining hell-bent on destroying Israel.

The old historians offered a simplistic and consciously pro-Israeli interpretation of the past, and they deliberately avoided mentioning anything that would reflect badly on Israel. People argued that since the conflict with the Arabs was still raging, and since it was a political as well as a military struggle, it necessarily involved propaganda, the goodwill (or ill will) of governments in the West, and the hearts and minds of Christians and Diaspora Jews. Blackening Israel's image, it was argued, would ultimately weaken Israel in its ongoing war for survival. In short, raisons d'état often took precedence over telling the truth.

The past few years have witnessed the emergence of a new generation of Israeli scholars and a "new" history. These historians, some of them living abroad, have looked and are looking afresh at the Israeli historical experience, and their conclusions, by and large, are at odds with those of the old historians.

Two factors are involved in the emergence of this new history—one relating to materials, the other to personae. Thanks to Israel's Archives Law (passed in 1955, amended in 1964 and 1981), and particularly to the law's key "thirty-year rule," starting in the early 1980s a large number (hundreds of thousands, perhaps millions) of state papers were opened to researchers. Almost all the Foreign Ministry's papers from 1947 to 1956, as well as a large number of documents—correspondence, memoranda, minutes—from other ministries, including the prime minister's office (though excluding the Defense Ministry and the IDF), have been released. Similarly, large collections of private papers and political party papers from this period have been opened. Therefore, for the first time, historians have been able to write studies of the period on the basis of a large collection of contemporary source material. (The old history was written largely on the basis of interviews and memoirs, and, at best, it made use of select batches of documents, many of them censored, such as those from the IDF archive.)

The second factor is the nature of the new historians. Most of them were born around 1948 and have matured in a more open, doubting, and self-critical Israel than the pre–Lebanon War Israel in which the old historians grew up. The old historians had lived through 1948 as highly committed adult participants in the epic, glorious rebirth of the Jewish commonwealth. They were unable to separate their lives from this historical event, unable to regard impartially and objectively the facts and processes that they later wrote about. Indeed, they admit as much. The new historians, by contrast, are able to be more impartial.

Inevitably, the new historians focused their attention, at least initially, on 1948, because the documents were available and because that was the central, natal, revolutionary event in Israeli history. How one perceives 1948 bears heavily on how one perceives the whole Zionist/ Israeli experience. If Israel, the haven of a much-persecuted people, was born pure and innocent, then it was worthy of the grace, material assistance, and political support showered upon it by the West over the past forty years—and worthy of more of the same in years to come. If, on the other hand, Israel was born tarnished, besmirched by original sin, then it was no more deserving of that grace and assistance than were its neighbors.

The past few months have seen the publication in the West of a handful of "new" histories, including Avi Shlaim's *Collusion across the Jordan* (Columbia University Press, 1988); Ilan Pappe's *Britain and the Arab-Israeli Conflict, 1948–51* (Macmillan/St. Anthony's, 1988); Simha Flapan's *The Birth of Israel* (Pantheon, 1987); and my own *The Birth of the Palestinian Refugee Problem, 1947–1949* (Cambridge University Press, 1988). Taken together, these works—along with a large number of articles that have appeared recently in academic journals such as *Studies in Zionism, Middle Eastern Studies,* and the *Middle East Journal*—significantly undermine, if not thoroughly demolish, a variety of assumptions that helped form the core of the old history.

Flapan's work is the least historical of these books. Indeed, it is not, strictly speaking, a "history" at all but rather a polemical work written from a Marxist perspective. In his introduction, Flapan—who passed away in 1987 and who was the former director of the left-wing Mapam Party's Arab department and editor of the monthly *New Outlook*—writes that his purpose is not to produce "a detailed historical study interesting only to historians and researchers," but rather to write "a book that will undermine the propaganda structures that have so long obstructed the growth of the peace forces in my country." Politics rather than historiography is the book's manifest objective.

Despite its explicitly polemical purpose, Flapan's book has the virtue of more or less accurately formulating some of the central fallacies—which he calls "myths"—that informed the old history. These were (1) that the Yishuv in 1947 joyously accepted partition and the truncated Jewish state prescribed by the UN General Assembly, and that the Palestinians and the surrounding Arab states unanimously rejected the partition and attacked the Yishuv with the aim of throwing the Jews into the sea; (2) that the war was waged between a relatively defenseless and weak (Jewish) David and a relatively strong (Arab) Goliath; (3) that the Palestinians fled their homes and villages either voluntarily or at the behest/order of the Arab leaders; and (4) that, at the war's end, Israel was interested in making peace, but the recalcitrant Arabs displayed no such interest, opting for a perpetual—if sporadic—war to the finish.

Because of poor research and analysis—including selective and erroneous use of documents—Flapan's demolition of these myths is far from convincing. But Shlaim, in *Collusion*, tackles some of the same myths—and far more persuasively. According to Shlaim, the original Zionist goal was the establishment of a Jewish state in the whole of Palestine. The acceptance of partition, in the mid-1930s as in 1947, was tactical, not a change in the Zionist dream. Ben-Gurion, says Shlaim, considered the partition lines of "secondary importance . . . because he intended to change them in any case; they were not the end but only the beginning." In acquiescing to partition schemes in the mid-1930s, Ben-Gurion wrote: "I am certain that we will be able to settle in all the other parts of the country, whether through agreement and mutual understanding with our Arab neighbors or in another way." To his wife, Ben-Gurion wrote: "Establish a Jewish state at once, even if it is not in the whole land. The rest will come in the course of time. It must come."

Come November 1947, the Yishuv entered the first stage of the war with a tacit understanding with Transjordan's king, Abdullah—"a falcon trapped in a canary's cage"—that his Arab Legion would take over the eastern part of Palestine (now called the West Bank), earmarked by the UN for Palestinian statehood, and that it would leave the Yishuv alone to set up the Jewish state in the other areas of the country. The Yishuv and the Hashemite kingdom of Transjordan, Shlaim persuasively argues, had conspired from 1946 to early 1947 to nip the UN Partition Resolution in the bud and to stymie the emergence of a Palestinian Arab state. From the start, while publicly enunciating support for the partition of the land between its Jewish and Arab communities, both Ben-Gurion and Abdullah aimed at frustrating the UN resolution and sharing among themselves the areas earmarked for Palestinian Arab statehood. It was to be partition—but between Israel and Transjordan. This "collusion" and "unholy alliance"—in Shlaim's loaded phrases—was sealed at the now-famous clandestine meeting between Golda Myerson (heir) and Abdullah at Naharayim on the Jordan River on November 17, 1947.

This Zionist-Hashemite nonaggression pact was sanctioned by Britain, adds Shlaim. Contrary to the old Zionist historiography—which was based largely on the (mistaken) feelings of Israel's leaders at that time—Britain's Foreign Secretary Ernest Bevin, "by February 1948," had clearly become "resigned to the inevitable emergence of a Jewish state" (while opposing the emergence of a Palestinian Arab state). Indeed, he warned Transjordan "to refrain from invading the areas allotted to the Jews."

Both Shlaim and Flapan make the point that the Palestinian Arabs, though led by Haj Amin al-Husayni, the conniving, extremist former mufti of Jerusalem, were far from unanimous in supporting the Husayni-led crusade against the Jews. Indeed, in the first months of the hostilities, according to Yishuv intelligence sources, the bulk of Palestine's Arabs merely wanted quiet, if only out of respect for the Jews' martial prowess. But gradually, in part due to Haganah overreactions, the conflict widened and eventually engulfed the two communities throughout the land. In April and May 1948, the Haganah gained the upper hand and the Palestinians lost the war, most of them going into exile.

What ensued, once Israel declared its independence on May 14, 1948, and the Arab states invaded on May 15, was "a general land grab," with everyone—Israel, Transjordan, Syria, Iraq, Lebanon, and Egypt—bent on preventing the birth of a Palestinian Arab state and carving out chunks of Palestine for themselves.

Contrary to the old history, Abdullah's invasion of eastern Palestine was clearly designed to conquer territory for his kingdom—at the expense of the Palestinian Arabs—rather than to destroy the Jewish state. Indeed, the Arab Legion—apart from one abortive incursion around Notre Dame in Jerusalem and the assault on the Etzion Bloc (a Jewish settlement zone inside the Arab state area)—stuck meticulously, throughout the war, to its nonaggressive stance vis-à-vis the Yishuv and the Jewish state's territory. Rather, it was the Haganah/IDF that repeatedly attacked the legion on territory earmarked for Arab sovereignty (Latrun, Lydda, Ramie).

Nevertheless, Shlaim, like Pappe in *Britain and the Arab-Israeli Conflict, 1948–51*, is never completely clear about Egypt, Syria, Iraq, and Lebanon's main purpose in invading Palestine: Was their primary aim to overrun the Yishuv and destroy the Jewish state, or was it merely to frustrate or curtail Abdullah's territorial ambitions and to acquire some territory for themselves?

Flapan argues firmly, but without evidence, that "the invasion . . . *was* not aimed at destroying the Jewish state." Shlaim and Pappe are more cautious. Shlaim writes that the Arab armies intended to bisect the Jewish state and, if possible, "occupy Haifa and Tel Aviv" or "crippl[e] the Jewish state." But, at the same time, he argues that they were driven into the invasion more by a desire to stymie Abdullah than by the wish to kill the Jews; and, partly for this reason, they did not properly plan the invasion, either militarily or politically, and their leaders were generally pessimistic about its outcome. Pappe points out that Egypt initially did not seem determined to participate in the invasion, and all the Arab states failed to commit the full weight of their military power to the enterprise—which indicates perhaps that they took the declared aim of driving the Jews into the sea less than seriously. In any event, Transjordan frustrated the other Arabs intentions throughout and rendered their military preparations and planning ineffective.

One of the most tenacious myths relating to 1948 is the myth of "David and Goliath"—that the Arabs were overwhelmingly stronger militarily than the Yishuv. The simple truth—as conveyed by Flapan, Shlaim, Pappe, and myself—is that the stronger side won. The map showing a minuscule Israel and a giant surrounding sea of Arab states did not and, indeed, for the time being still does not accurately reflect the military balance of power. The pre-1948 Yishuv had organized itself for statehood and war; the Palestinian Arabs, who outnumbered the Jews two to one, had not. And in war, command and control are everything, or almost everything. During the first half of the war (December 1947–May 14, 1948), the Yishuv was better armed and had more trained manpower than the Palestinians, whose forces were beefed up by several thousand "volunteers" from the surrounding Arab states. This superior organization, command, and control meant that at almost every decisive point in the battle the Haganah managed to field more and better-equipped formations than did the Palestinians. When the Yishuv put matters to the test, in the Haganah offensives of April and early May 1948, the decision was never in doubt; the Arab redoubts fell, in domino fashion, like ripe plums—the Jerusalem corridor, Tiberias, Haifa, Eastern Galilee, Safad. When one adds to this the Yishuv's superiority in morale and motivation—it was a bare three years after the Holocaust, and the Haganah troopers knew that it was do-or-die—the Palestinians never had a chance.

The old history is no more illuminating when it comes to the second stage of the war—the conventional battles of May 15, 1948, to January 1949. Jewish organization, command, and control remained superior to those of the uncoordinated armies of Egypt, Syria, Iraq, and Lebanon; and throughout the Yishuv also, the IDF had an edge in numbers. In mid-May 1948, for example, the Haganah fielded 35,000 armed troops, while the Arab invaders fielded 25,000 to 30,000 troops. By the time of Operation Dani in July, the IDF had 65,000 men under arms, and by December it had 80,000 to 90,000—outnumbering its combined Arab foes at every stage of the battle. The Haganah/IDF also enjoyed the immensely important advantage, throughout the conventional war, of short lines of communication, while the Iraqis and Egyptians had to send supplies and reinforcements over hundreds of kilometers of desert before they reached the front lines.

Two caveats must be entered. First, Transjordan's Arab Legion was probably the best army in the war. But it never numbered much more than five thousand troops, and it had no tanks or aircraft. Second, in terms of equipment, during the crucial three weeks between the pan-Arab invasion of Palestine on May 15 and the start of the first truce on June 11, the Arab armies had an edge in weaponry over the Hagana/IDF. The Haganah was much weaker in terms of aircraft, and had no artillery (only heavy mortars) and very few tanks or tracked vehicles. For those three weeks, as the Haganah's officer in command of operations, Yigael Yadin, told the politicians, it was "fifty-fifty." But before May15 and from the first truce onward, the Yishuv's military formations were superior both in terms of manpower and in terms of weaponry.

Apart from the birth of the State of Israel, the major political outcome of the 1948 war was the creation of the Palestinian refugee problem. How the problem came about has been the subject of heated controversy between Israeli and Arab propagandists for the past four decades. The controversy is as much about the nature of Zionism as it is about what exactly happened in 1948. If the Arab contention is true—that the Yishuv had always intended "transfer" and that in 1948 it systematically and forcibly expelled the Arab population from the areas that became the Jewish state—then Israel is a robber state that, like young Jacob, has won the sympathy and support of its elders in the West by trickery and connivance, and the Palestinians are more or less innocent victims. If, on the other hand, the Israeli propaganda line is accepted—that the Palestinians fled "voluntarily" or at the behest of their own and other Arab leaders—then Israel is free of original sin.

As I have set out in great detail in *The Birth of the Palestinian Refugee Problem, 1947–1949,* the truth lies somewhere in between. While from the mid-1930s most of the Yishuv's leaders, including Ben-Gurion, wanted to establish a Jewish state without an Arab minority, or with as small an Arab minority as possible, and supported a "transfer solution" to this minority problem, the Yishuv did not enter the 1948 war with a master plan for expelling the Arabs, nor did its political and military leaders ever adopt such a master plan. There were Haganah/IDF expulsions of Arab communities, some of them with Haganah/IDF General Staff and/or cabinet-level sanction—such as at Miska and Ad-Dumeira in April 1948; at Zarnuqa, Al-Qubeiba, and Huj in May; in Lydda and Ramle in July; and along the Lebanese border (Bir'im, Iqrit, Tarbikha, Suruh, Al-Mansura, and Nabi Rubin) in early November. But there was no grand or blanket policy of expulsions.

On the other hand, at no point during the war did Arab leaders issue a blanket call for Palestine's Arabs to leave their homes and villages and wander into exile. Nor was there an Arab radio or press campaign urging or ordering the Palestinians to flee. Indeed, I have found no trace of any such broadcasts—and throughout the war the Arab radio stations and other press were monitored by the Israeli intelligence services and Foreign Ministry, and by Western diplomatic stations and agencies (such as the BBC). No contemporary reference to or citation from such a broadcast, let alone from a series of such broadcasts, has ever surfaced.

Indeed, in early May 1948 when, according to Israeli propaganda and some of the old histories, such a campaign of broadcasts should have been at its height, in preparation for the pan-Arab invasion, Arab radio stations and leaders (Radio Ramallah, King Abdullah, and Arab Liberation Army commander Qawuqji) all issued broadcasts calling upon the Palestinians to stay put and, if already in exile, to return to their homes in Palestine. References to these broadcasts exist in Haganah, Mapam, and British records.

Occasionally, local Arab commanders and/or politicians ordered the evacuation of women and children from war zones. Less frequently, as in Haifa on April 22, 1948, local Arab leaders advised or instructed their communities to leave rather than stay in a potential or actual war zone or "treacherously" remain under Jewish rule. But there were no Arab blanket orders or campaigns to leave.

Rather, in order to understand the exodus of the 600,000 to 760,000 Arabs from the areas that became the post-1948 Jewish state, one must look to a variety of related processes and causes. What happened in Haifa is illustrative of the complexity of the exodus (though it, too, does not convey the full complexity of what transpired in the various regions of Palestine at the time).

The exodus from Haifa (which initially had an Arab population of 70,000), as from the other main Arab Palestinian centers, Jaffa and Jerusalem, began in December 1947 with the start of sporadic hostilities between the various Jewish and Arab neighborhoods. The exodus slowly gained momentum during the following months as the British Mandate administration moved toward dissolution and final withdrawal. The first to go were the rich and the educated—the middle classes with second homes on the Beirut beachfront, in Nablus or Amman, or those who had either relatives abroad with large homes or enough money to stay in hotels for long periods. The Palestinians' political and economic leadership disappeared. By mid-May 1948, only one member of the Arab Higher Committee, the Palestinians' shadow government, was still in the country.

The flight of the professionals, the civil servants, the traders, and the businessmen had a harsh impact on the Haifa Arab masses, who already were demoralized by the continual sniping and bomb attacks, by the feeling that the Jews were stronger, and by the sense that their own ragtag militia would fail when the test came (as, indeed, it did). The Arabs felt terribly isolated and insecure—Arab Haifa was far from other major Arab population centers and was easily cut off by Jewish settlements along the approach roads. Businesses and workshops closed, policemen shed their uniforms and left their posts, Arab workers could no longer commute to jobs in Jewish areas, and agricultural produce was interdicted in ambushes on the approach roads to the city. Unemployment and prices soared. Thousands of people left.

Then came the Haganah attack of April 21 to April 22 on the Arab districts. Several companies of Carmeli Brigade troops, under cover of constant mortar fire, drove down the Carmel mountain slopes into the Arab downtown areas. Arab militia resistance collapsed. Thousands of Arabs fled from the outlying Arab neighborhoods (such as Wadi Rushmiya and Hailssa) into the British-controlled port area, piled into boats, and fled northward to Acre. The leaders who remained sued for a cease-fire. Under British mediation, the Haganah agreed, offering what the British regarded as generous terms. But then, when faced with Moslem pressure, the Arab leaders, most of them Christian Arabs, got cold feet; a cease-fire meant surrender and implied agreement to live under Jewish rule. They would be open to charges of collaboration and treachery. So, to the astonishment of the British officers and the Jewish military and political leaders gathered on the afternoon of April 22 at the Haifa town hall, the Arab delegation announced that its community would evacuate the city.

The Jewish mayor, Shabtai Levy, and the British commander, Maj. Gen. Hugh Stockwell, pleaded with the Arabs to reconsider. The Haganah representative, Mordechai Makleff, declined to voice an opinion. But the Arabs were unmoved, and the mass exodus, which had begun under the impact of the Haganah mortars and ground assault, moved into top gear, with the British supplying boats and armored car escorts to the departing Arab convoys. From April 22 to May

1, almost all the Arab population departed. The rough treatment—temporary evictions, house-to-house searches, detentions, the occasional beating—meted out to the remaining population during those days by the Haganah and the IZL (Irgun Zvai Leumi) troops who occupied the downtown areas led many of the undecided also to opt for evacuation. By early May, the city's Arab population had dwindled to three or four thousand.

The bulk of the Palestinian refugees—some 250,000 to 300,000—went into exile during those weeks between April and mid-June 1948, with the major precipitant being Jewish (Haganah/IZL) military attack or fears of such attack. In most cases, the Jewish commanders, who wanted to occupy empty villages (occupying populated villages meant leaving behind a garrison, which the units could not afford to do), were hardly ever confronted with deciding whether or not to expel an overrun community: Most villages and towns simply emptied at the first whiff of grapeshot.

In conformity with Tokhnit Dalet (Plan D), the Haganah's master plan, formulated in March 1948, for securing the Jewish state areas in preparation for the expected declaration of statehood and the prospective Arab invasion, the Haganah cleared various areas completely of Arab villages—in the Jerusalem corridor, around Kibbutz Mishmar Ha'emek, and along the coast road. But in most cases, expulsion orders were not necessary; the inhabitants had already fled, out of fear or as a result of Jewish attack. In several areas, Israeli commanders successfully used psychological warfare ploys ("Here's some friendly advice. You better get out now, before the Jews come and rape your daughters.") to obtain Arab evacuation.

The prewar basic structural weaknesses of Palestinian society led to the dissolution of that society when the test of battle came. Lack of administrative structures, as well as weak leaders, poor or nonexistent military organization beyond the single-village level, and faulty or nonexistent taxation mechanisms, all caused the main towns to fall apart in April and May 1948. The fall of the towns and the exodus from them, in turn, brought a sense of fear and despondency to the rural hinterlands. Traditionally, the villages, though economically autarchic, had looked to the towns for political leadership and guidance. The evacuation by the middle classes and the leaders, as well as the fall of the towns, provided the Palestinians in the hinterlands with an example to emulate. Safad's fall and evacuation on May 10 and May 11, for example, triggered an immediate evacuation of the surrounding Arab villages; so, earlier, did the fall of Haifa and the IZL assault on Jaffa.

Seen from the Jewish side, the spectacle of mass Arab evacuation certainly triggered appetites for more of the same: Everyone, at every level of military and political decision making, understood that a Jewish state without a large Arab minority would be stronger and more viable both militarily and politically. Therefore, the tendency of local military commanders to "nudge" Palestinians into flight increased as the war went on. Jewish atrocities—far more widespread than the old historians have indicated (there were massacres of Arabs at Ad-Dawavima, Eilaboun, Jish, Safsaf, Hule, Saliha, and Sasa besides Deir Yassin and Lydda)—and the drive to avenge past Arab wrongs also contributed significantly to the exodus.

The last major fallacy tackled incidentally or directly by the new historians concerns an Israel that in 1948 to 1949 was bent on making peace with its neighbors, and an Arab world that monolithically rejected all such peace efforts. The evidence that Israel's leaders were not desperate to make peace and were unwilling to make the large concessions necessary to give peace a chance is overwhelming. In Tel Aviv, there was a sense of triumph and drunkenness that accompanied victory—a feeling that the Arabs would "soon" or "eventually" sue for peace, that there was no need to rush things or make concessions, that ultimately military victory and dominance would translate into diplomatic-political success.

As Ben-Gurion told an American journalist in mid-July 1949: "I am prepared to get up in the middle of the night in order to sign a peace agreement—but I am not in a hurry and I can wait ten years. We are under no pressure whatsoever." Or, as Ben-Gurion records Abba Eban's telling him: "[Eban] sees no need to run after peace. The armistice is sufficient for us; if we run after peace, the Arabs will demand a price of us—borders [i.e., in terms of territory] or refugees [i.e., repatriation] or both. Let us wait a few years."

As Pappe puts it in *Britain:* "Abdullah's eagerness [to make peace] was not reciprocated by the Israelis. The priorities of the state of Israel had changed during 1949. The armistice agreements brought relative calm to the borders, and peace was no longer the first priority. The government was preoccupied with absorbing new immigrants and overcoming economic difficulties."

Israel's lack of emphasis on achieving peace was manifested most clearly in the protracted (1949–1951) secret negotiations with Abdullah. Israeli Foreign Minister Moshe Sharett described his meeting with Transjordan's king at the palace in Shuneh on May 5, 1949, in the following way: "Transjordan said—we are ready for peace immediately. We said—certainly, we too want peace but one shouldn't rush, one should walk." Israel and Jordan signed an armistice agreement, after much arm-twisting by Israel, which British and American diplomats compared to Hitler's treatment of the Czechs in 1938 to 1939. (As Abdullah put it, quoting an old Turkish saying: "If you meet a bear when crossing a rotten bridge, call her 'dear Auntie.'") But the two sides never signed a peace treaty or a nonbelligerence agreement—something that was proposed at one point by Abdullah.

Shlaim—who in *Collusion* expands the description of the secret Israeli-Jordanian negotiations first provided in Dan Schueftan's *Ha'Optziya Ha'Yardenit* (The Jordanian option), published in Hebrew in Israel in 1986—more or less lays the blame for the failed negotiations squarely on Israel's shoulders. A more generous, less anti-Israeli interpretation of the evidence would blame the Israelis and the Jordanians equally.

Israel refused to offer major concessions in terms of refugee repatriation or territory (Abdullah was particularly keen on getting back Lydda and Ramie) and was for too long unwilling to offer Jordan a sovereign corridor through its territory to the sea at Gaza. Throughout, Israel was prodded if not guided by the "blatant expansionism" of some of Ben-Gurion's aides, such as Moshe Dayan. As Yehoshafat Harkabi, one of Dayan's military colleagues, put it (according to Shlaim): "The existential mission of the State of Israel led us to be demanding and acquisitive, and mindful of the value of every square metre of land." In any case, Ben-Gurion refused to meet Abdullah, and the Israeli leaders often spoke of Abdullah with undeserved contempt.

Shlaim writes that "two principal factors were responsible for the failure of the postwar negotiations: Israel's strength and Abdullah's weakness." Nevertheless, Shlaim seems to attribute too much weight to the first and too little to the second. Shlaim does not sufficiently acknowledge the importance of the "Palestinization" of Jordan following the Hashemite annexation of the West Bank, which quickly resulted in a curtailment of Abdullah's autonomy and his freedom of political movement both within Jordan and in the Arab world in general. The twin pressures exercised by the Arab world outside and by his successive cabinets inside the kingdom successfully impeded Abdullah's ability to make a separate peace with Israel. He almost did so a number of times, but he always held back at the last moment and refused to take the plunge. It is possible, Shlaim argues, that more generous concessions by Tel Aviv at certain critical points in the negotiations would have given Abdullah greater motivation to pursue peace as well as the ammunition he needed to silence his antipeace critics, but the truth of such a claim is uncertain. What is clear is that Abdullah, though showing remarkable courage throughout, simply felt unable in those last years to go against the unanimous or near-unanimous wishes of his ministers and against the unanimous antipeace stand of the surrounding Arab world.

What happened with Abdullah occurred in miniature and more briefly with Egypt and with Syria. In September to October 1948, Egypt's King Farouk, knowing that the war was lost, secretly sent a senior court official to Paris to sound out Israel on the possibility of a peace based on Israeli cession of parts of the Negev and the Gaza Strip to Egypt. Sharett and the senior staff at the Foreign Ministry favored continued negotiations, but Ben-Gurion—bent on a further round of hostilities to drive the Egyptian army out of the Negev—flatly rejected the overture. Shlaim summarizes: "[Ben-Gurion] may have been right in thinking that nothing of substance would come out of these talks. But he surely owed his cabinet colleagues at least a report on what had taken place so that they could review their decision to go [again] to war against Egypt on the basis of all the relevant information." New Egyptian peace overtures in November, after Israel's Operation Yoav, again came to naught.

As for Syria, in May 1949, its new ruler, Husni Za'im, made major peace proposals which included recognition of Israel as well as Syrian readiness to absorb hundreds of thousands of Palestinian refugees. Za'im wanted Israel to concede a sliver of territory along the Jordan River. He asked to meet with Ben-Gurion or Sharett. Again, Ben-Gurion rejected the proposal, writing on May 12: "I am quite prepared to meet Colonel Za'im in order to promote peace ... but I see no purpose in any such meeting as long as the representatives of Syria in the armistice negotiations do not declare in an unequivocal manner that their forces are prepared to withdraw to their prewar territory [i.e., withdraw from the small Syrian-occupied Mishmar Ha'yarden salient, west of the Jordan]."

Continued feelers by Za'im resulted again in Israeli refusal. As Sharett put it on May 25: "It is clear that we ... won't agree that any bit of the Land of Israel be transferred to Syria, because this is a question of control over the water sources [i.e., of the Jordan River]." Shabtai Rosenne, the legal adviser at the Foreign Ministry, put it simply: "I feel that the need for an agreement between Israel and Syria pressed more heavily on the Syrians." Therefore, why rush toward peace? A few weeks later Za'im was overthrown and executed, and the Syrian peace initiative died with him. Whether the overture was serious or merely tactical—to obtain Western sympathy and funds, for example—is unclear. What is certain is that Israel failed to pursue it.

What was true of Israel's one-to-one contacts with each of the Arab states was true also of its negotiations with the Arabs under UN auspices at Lausanne in the spring and summer of 1949. There, too, Israel was ungenerous (though, needless to say, the Arabs were equally obdurate). For months, UN officials and the United States pressed Israel to make what they felt might be the redemptive gesture: to proclaim its willingness to take back several hundred thousand refugees. As the months dragged on and Israel remained inflexible, the Arabs became just as obstinate. When, at last, Israel offered to take back 100,000, which, in reality, as Sharett explained to his colleagues, was only 65,000 (Sharett told his colleagues in Mapai that some 35,000 refugees had already returned to Israel illegally or were about to return as part of the family reunification scheme, and these refugees would be deducted from the 100,000), it was a case of too little too late. And Israel's more realistic offer—to take the Gaza Strip with its resident and refugee populations—was never seriously entertained by Egypt. Lausanne was probably the last chance for a comprehensive Israeli-Arab peace.

In Pirkei Avot it is written: "Rabbi Shimon Ben Gamliel was wont to say: On three things the world rests: On justice, on truth and on peace" (1:18). And he would quote Zechariah: "execute the judgment of truth and peace in your gates" (8:16). Telling the truth thus seems to be an injunction anchored in

Jewish tradition, and the scriptures apparently link truth to peace in some indeterminate manner.

The new history is one of the signs of a maturing Israel (though, no doubt, there are those who say it is a symptom of decay and degeneration). What is now being written about Israel's past seems to offer us a more balanced and a more "truthful" view of that country's history than what has been offered hitherto. It may also in some obscure way serve the purposes of peace and reconciliation between the warring tribes of that land.

2

Land, Labor, and the Origins of the Israeli-Palestinian Conflict, 1882–1914

GERSHON SHAFIR

This book was originally written between 1983 and 1988 in order to revisit what I consider to be the most critical period of Israeli history: the generation of the founders. Though I focused on the founders, it was their interaction with the Arabs of Palestine that I wished to highlight. In undertaking this project I was following in the footsteps of Baruch Kimmerling, a trailblazer among critical sociologists who studied the effects of the Israeli-Palestinian conflict on Israeli society.[1] Such reassessment was called for because the bifurcation of Israeli society into Jewish and Arab sectors has been reproduced in Israeli social sciences and extrapolated into Israeli history. Consequently, the formative impact of the conflict on the character of the Israeli state and society was rendered invisible, and so were the reasons for the intransigence associated with the conflict.

Jewish-Arab relations in the period of the founders, I concluded, were already in the process of assuming a distinctly colonial cast. But I also pointed out that colonialism is not made of one cloth. The book, in fact, analyzes the confrontation between the First and Second Aliyot over their separate approaches to the Arab population as a conflict between alternative versions of colonialism. The Second Aliya's strategy made Israeli state-building viable but, in the process, intensified the Jewish-Arab conflict in Palestine.

Since this book first appeared in 1989 two major developments, one intellectual, the other political, have abated the resistance to this thesis and its implications and hastened its integration with Israeli historiography and sociology. A sustained debate over the "new historiography"—which, as the writer Aharon Megged correctly observed, is focused on the colonial character of Zionism—has begun to undermine historiographic orthodoxies.[2] Anita Shapira,

---

Reprinted, by permission, from Gershon Shafir, *Land, Labor, and the Origins of the Israeli-Palestinian Conflict* (Berkeley: University of California Press, 1996), ix–xix.

in a special 1995 issue of *History and Memory* devoted to Israeli historiography, acknowledges that the use of the colonial model in studying Israel "is both legitimate and desirable," since "defining a movement as settlement-colonialism may well help to clarify the relations between the settling nation and the native one." As she points out, such an admission would not have been forthcoming in the past.[3]

The Israeli-Palestinian accords form steps in a process of peacemaking between enemies who have long delegitimized each other and their respective historiographies. The recognition of the Palestinian people's existence and a willingness to come to a historical accommodation with it, in Shapira's words, increased "the readiness to accept the notion that the establishment of Israel brought a disaster upon the Palestinians."[4] Political reconciliation also amplified the moral and intellectual fortitude needed to come face to face with the colonial dynamic of the conflict that was uncovered by the new historiography and sociology and to countenance its resolution through decolonization. In this preface I will examine the thesis of this work in relation to the historiographic debate and the peace process.

The publication in 1989 of *Land, Labor, and the Origins of the Israeli-Palestinian Conflict, 1882–1914* coincided with the appearance of works by historians Benny Morris, Avi Shlaim, and Ilan Pappe.[5] The four books, and others published in the past decade, share many concerns. Noting the similarity, Morris, in a manifesto-style article, labeled these works the "new historiography" and saw them as an indication that Israeli history had come into its own, the result of a maturing of a new, more self-critical generation of the post–Six Day War and post–Lebanon War era in Israel, and the release of documents from the 1948 period by Israel's liberal Archives Law.[6]

In spite of our similarities there are some crucial differences between my sociological study and the work of the new historians, but also some yet unexplored connections. An obvious variation is that the archival sources I used were not newly opened but had already been available to scholars in the past. Although the sources were available, I discovered in many instances that a fresh reading of them was necessary in order to reinstate in them what was overlooked by previous readers' blind spots. A more crucial divergence between the work of the new historians and my own was their different chronological locus. The new historians focused on the War of Independence and its immediate antecedents and consequences while I studied the founders' era. Further, the historians concerned themselves with what they self-consciously labeled the "myths" of Israeli society,[7] whereas I examined its ideological substructure.

Myths lend themselves easily to interpretations in which shades of gray are missing. They are symbolic systems in which significance is derived not from the content, but from the arrangement of the constituent elements as pairs of polar opposites—for example, the archetypes of man and woman, good and evil. The relationship of the pairs is usually fixed and is played out repeatedly without the influence of historical context. The main myth contested by Pappe, Shlaim, and Morris is that the War of Independence and the subsequent peace talks pitted the forces of peace and compromise against the forces of unreason and belligerence. Israel, consequently, stood unequivocally vindicated.

But how did it happen that mythical accounts of Israeli state formation developed only in later stages of the Israeli-Palestinian conflict—that is, after it had swelled into the Israeli-Arab conflict and led to a cycle of war that would repeat itself once a decade? How were Jewish-Arab relations understood previously?

During the first thirty years of Zionist immigration and settlement, which is the focus of this work, neither the First nor the Second Aliya had evolved a consistent myth of the Arab. Instead, after the First World War an ideologization of Zionism—especially Labor Zionism—and its effects was born and left the legacy of an ideological mind-set.

Whereas myths magnify conflict and transpose it to a cosmic level where it takes on the characteristics of an unsolvable contest, a major component of ideological thinking is that it hides social contradictions behind a facade of harmonious social relations. Ideologies, generally, attempt to negate or conceal contradictions that remain unsolved. This is done by presenting the interests of a class, party, or nation as forward-looking and even revolutionary and, therefore, as representative of the broader society as a whole. Ideological thinking is also the teleological narrative typical to modern nationalism. The labor movement and its founders from the Second Aliya were viewed in retrospect as having been determined to shape history in their image all along.

The labor movement sought to minimize and mask conflicts with the Palestinian population by invoking two ideologies in tandem, which ironically contradicted each other: the first ideology asserted that Labor Zionism had a beneficial influence on Palestinian society, whereas the second held that it had no impact.

According to the first view, "for the Labor Zionists the economic benefits of Jewish settlement appeared to be the decisive response to Arab nationalism."[8] It was expected that the Arab masses would be beneficiaries of the modernization brought on by Jewish immigration and settlement. Therefore, it was argued that only the narrow circles of the elite—be they land-owning effendis, the Christian middle class, or later the reactionary leaders of the surrounding Arab states—were the opponents of Zionism.

Modernization undertaken by the Zionist movement, however, was embedded in a colonial relationship, and the goals of Jewish colonization—conquest of labor and conquest of land—and the colonizing institutions that supported them, such as the Histadrut and the Jewish National Fund (JNF), were exclusivist.[9] "Conquest of labor" aimed at the displacement of Arab workers by Jewish workers in all branches and skill levels. Arab land, once purchased by the JNF, could not be resold to Arabs,[10] and JNF land was not available for employment of Arab workers. The *kibbutzim,* which customarily were built on JNF land and had only Jewish members, were the most exclusivist of all the creations of the Second Aliya, and in that fashion also thoroughly nationalist. In fact, the labor movement's institutions were the ones that were least able to benefit the Arabs of Palestine.

Jewish immigrants, and subsequently historians and social scientists, also expounded another ideology stating that Jewish immigrants could not have exploited the Palestinians because the two societies remained separate. In Gorny's presentation, it was expected that the balance between the Jewish and Arab societies, and consequently peaceful and good neighborly relations between them, may be accomplished not through mutual integration, but only through separation.[11]

Horowitz and Lissak used the term "dual society" and "dual economy" to postulate the existence of "two distinct economic systems . . . with only limited market relations."[12] Undoubtedly, the two societies and economies were at different levels of development, otherwise the Jewish colonial settlement could not have succeeded. But Lissak and Horowitz failed to see that as long as Jewish society was bent on expansion, it could never remain self-contained. The Yishuv directly interacted with its Palestinian counterpart and, through the purchase of some of its land, limited its traditional subsistence and later, through conquest, uprooted a large share of its population. The colonialism of the First Aliya was based on sparse settlement and exploitation and the employment of low-paid Palestinian workers on Jewish-owned farms. The Second Aliya replaced it with the colonialism of dense settlement in exclusive Jewish colonies and displacement of Arab residents. Separation was the result, not the cause, of the Israeli-Palestinian conflict.

Recently, some Israeli historians and historical geographers have sought to give a new lease on life to the separation perspective. Aaronsohn and Tsahor, for example, argue that Zionist settlement in Palestine was colonization without colonialism.[13] But this could only be true as long as colonial intrusion did not take place in an unpopulated territory. The inherent hostility between the indigenous population and the immigrants was principally because the immigrants insisted the territory chosen by them was "empty" of other nationalities. In practical terms this meant that the newcomers viewed the native population as part and parcel of the environment that was to be subdued, tamed, and made hospitable for themselves. The native inhabitants, in the process of losing part of their traditional holdings and fearful that with the passage of time their territory would indeed become emptied of them, were intent on forcefully protecting what remained.[14] In short, colonization presumed the justification and practices of a colonial endeavor.

Whereas differences with other colonial undertakings—such as absence of a metropolis and evident nationalist aims, and the secondary role played by capitalist calculations—gave Zionist colonization its own particular cast, they did not eliminate the fundamental similarity of the Second Aliya's goals with those of other "pure settlement" colonies (i.e., colonies aimed at creating a homogeneous settler-immigrant population). Many of the unique characteristics of Zionist colonization were not a result of its purportedly noncolonial character, but were merely policies intended to compensate the settler-immigrants for the adverse conditions prevailing in the land and labor markets of Palestine. The goal of Zionism, however, was to successfully colonize Palestine while at the same time justifying the creation of a homogeneous Jewish settlement through an intensifying denial of Palestinian national aspirations. This was the main reason for the intractable nature of the conflict, and, significantly, until the Oslo Accord, none of the Zionist approaches were able to dissolve Palestinian resistance.

Though myths are usually related to origins, here ideological thinking preceded the construction of myths but is also closely linked with it. The ideological *denial* of a conflict between Jewish settler-immigrants and the Arabs of Palestine at the very least hindered the conflict's resolution and more likely contributed to its escalation and transformation into a full-scale military confrontation, which then became fertile ground for the birth of the Israeli-Arab mythologies. The work of the new historians and critical sociologists, including myself, therefore present two related parts of the same story.

The rethinking of the conflict still touches a raw nerve, as evidenced in Aharon Megged's vitriolic article in *Haaretz*. Significantly, Megged never disputes the new historians and critical sociologists' works or theses. Instead, he decries the loss of certainty, the sense of security in knowing that the Israeli cause is just, which he believes they undermine.[15] Megged is terrified of the price that has to be paid for giving up certainties, but he seems unaware of the price being paid to hold on to spurious certainties. Both ideological and mythical certainties, however, bequeathed problematic legacies. Ideologies spared history makers some of the anguish of being unable to reconcile their behavior with their convictions, but ultimately left unfulfilled interests invisible and rendered their expression illegitimate. Consequently, ideological convictions prolonged the conflict, even as they left the door open for its eventual resolution. Myths provided moral satisfaction by presenting the world as a place full of unsolvable situations and predetermined fates even as they justified behavior that brought on repeated conflict and offered no way out of it. Though ideological convictions embodied a more optimistic approach, the blinders they required led to far more sinister mythical views.

I recognize that contemporary theories have long ago abandoned the view that myth and ideology are primitive or faulty ways of thinking that should be superseded by scientific research, and in fact I accept that they fulfill important cultural roles. But especially in a culture long dominated by myth and ideology, I think that the advent of autonomous historiography is a welcome event. By presenting historical processes in their many-sided complexity, giving them back their rich, if frequently tragic, texture as well as their contradictory and dialectical features, new historiography and critical sociology facilitate, at the least, the unlearning of mythical and ideological certainties. This might be a weak claim on their behalf, but, in my mind, even if this is all that they could accomplish, it would go a long way toward revisiting and revising our knowledge of the Israeli-Palestinian conflict and our attitude toward it during a trying period. A more ambitious role for the revision of historical consciousness, however, is also possible. At its best, critical historiography can take us beyond the negative task of unlearning and give new meaning to research as a tool for discovering what was and is possible. By having contributed to the unlearning of myths and ideologies, and possibly even to relearning the past, these new perspectives on Israeli history and society contributed to an atmosphere that facilitated and possibly promoted the present efforts at peacemaking.

The Oslo agreement of September 1993 and the subsequent agreements between the Rabin-Peres government and the PLO have begun to de-escalate over a century of conflict by reversing its confrontational dynamic. The PLO's moderation, which reluctantly evolved by leaps and bounds, led to an official recognition of Israel in November 1988. Though the shift of the Rabin-Peres government was as radical as it was sudden, and therefore confounded almost all observers, its causes were in the making for some years. Before pondering these causes, however, we need to explore what peacemaking between Israel and the PLO encompasses.

In my view, by agreeing to withdraw from the Gaza Strip, Jericho, and the urban centers of the West Bank (with the exception of Hebron), Israel has undertaken a partial process of decolonization. The new relationship between Israel—under the Labor government—and the PLO (as well as its parallels in South Africa and possibly Northern Ireland) amounts to decolonization of a partially successful "pure settlement colony." Peacemaking between Israel and the PLO signals a new, late wave in the decolonization of overseas European societies. It also lays to rest the radical opinion, prevalent after the Second World War, that colonial conflict is total, and therefore irreconcilable.

Colonization, or the founding of "new societies," as Fieldhouse and Fredrickson pointed out, had many strands.[16] Correspondingly, processes of decolonization vary. Whereas settler-immigrants and their descendants on Europe's other "frontiers of settlement" mixed (in different measures) with the native populations, marginalized and destroyed them, or expelled them, Palestinians still continue to pose a basic challenge to the resolve and identity of Jewish Israelis. At the same time, although Jewish immigration to Palestine was small in comparison to the masses of Jews that migrated to the United States and other destinations, the settler-immigrants in Israel had no colonial metropolis to return to and over time evolved into their own native population. (Likewise, the ANC and the South African Communist Party recognized white settlement in South Africa as "colonialism of a special type.") The partial realization of the goals of the settler-immigrants, who sank deep roots and established societies with distinct cultural, ethnic, and religious markers, means that the decolonization required for peacemaking in Israel will also be partial and will be played out in Gaza, the West Bank, and East Jerusalem.

Presently, Israeli willingness to undertake partial decolonization is the combined result of two sets of factors. The first is a cumulative realization by the security elites that Israeli security apparatuses could not subdue the Palestinian *intifada* or obliterate the nationalist aspirations that animated it. However, the massive Palestinian resistance did not defeat the Israeli military or cripple its economy, but merely spurred Israeli leaders in new directions already made attractive by ongoing changes that affected politically and economically potent groups in the society.

The second set of factors concerns domestic transformations, those catalyzed by global processes. Over the years, Israel's economic development, funded to a large extent by externally generated resources, has weakened the state's and Histadrut's control of the economy in favor of private business interests. This sectoral shift has manifested itself in policy changes that began as early as the late 1960s and have gradually intensified over the last two decades. Among these changes were the greater role played by market forces in the labor market and the opening up of the financial markets, as well as substantial privatization, the institution of a stable exchange rate, reduced capital subsidies and increasing governmental resistance to "bailouts," and cuts in the defense budget and budget deficit.[17] Correspondingly, the export-oriented high-tech sectors have grown considerably and led to the expansion of the Israeli professional and middle classes. These strata feel confident enough to compete in the open market, both domestically and internationally, and their concern—the converse in many ways of that of the Jewish labor movement—is no longer to be protected within this market, but rather to expand it as much as possible. The new economic elites have been the principal champions of economic liberalization and also of the integration of Israel's economy with the world and, if possible, regional markets. As long as the Israeli-Palestinian and Israeli-Arab conflicts destabilized the region, Israel was boycotted by multinational companies and remained outside the international investment circuit. Peacemaking was the Israeli way of gaining security as well as access to a more global economy.[18]

The rise of the new strata has been further precipitated by the crumbling and faltering of the massive, costly, and frequently inefficient extra-market institutions built up by Labor Zionism and associated with the Histadrut, institutions that in the past provided Jewish settler-immigrants and their descendants with conditions favorable for settlement and prosperity. In the Israeli context the historical association of state, colonization, and social rights gives an added dimension to the weakening of the sphere of state and semipublic institutions. The call for reduced state intervention in the economy—which by the early 1990s was heard as frequently in Israel as it had been in the United Kingdom and the United States in the early 1980s also entailed dismantling the framework and legacy of state-subsidized colonization drives, seen as a continuation of pre-1948 settlement, in the West Bank and Gaza Strip.

Just as the institutional edifice created by the labor movement around the Histadrut—and by extension the welfare state in general—was viewed by the new economic and professional strata as a hindrance to their own well-being, so the settlement ethos and its corresponding social institutions, which were crucial for Israel's state- and nation-building and provided the labor movement with much of its identity, privilege, and hegemony, became anachronistic and viewed as an obstacle to these strata's economic and political interests. It was the settlement ideologies, however, that had in the past justified the delegitimation of the Palestinians' national rights. The gradual decline of these ideologies, the anxiety in the face of the mythologies replacing them, and the slow but steady expansion of a civil, more liberal, discourse, out of which the new historiography itself emerged, had the effect of moving the Israeli state to moderate its opposition to Palestinian nationalism and question the wisdom of territorial expansion. Under the influence of these elites, the stage of state-building has ended for most Israelis, and Israel has effectively entered into the era of post-Zionism.

The process of decolonization at the present moment is still at its beginning stage, though it seems to have passed the point of no return. The recognition of the PLO and the very process of negotiations have tarnished the appeal of the myth of irreconcilable differences between Israelis and Palestinians. Doing away with mythologies, however, made possible, and even likely, the rebirth of the two types of ideological thinking associated with the labor movement: the illusion that disengagement can and should bring about complete separation, on the one hand, and the delusion that what is good for Israel is beneficial for Palestinians, thus leading to the reestablishment of previous relations of superiority through neocolonial practices, on the other.

The process of decolonization is justified by the rationale that territorial separation of Israelis and Palestinians will provide security to the former and sovereignty to the latter. While these two goals would certainly be enhanced by Israeli withdrawal, Israeli and Palestinian negotiators have already discovered just how difficult it would be to separate two groups who live on such a small strip of land and share many of its resources, most importantly water and the environment. Some of the circumstances that argue against separation are East Jerusalem, where the two populations are roughly of equal size; the Gaza Strip and West Bank, which are physically split by Israel itself and are in need of a land bridge; and, of course, the desire of about one-sixth of Israel's own Arab citizens for a measure of integration. The separatist legacy of the labor movement that first evolved in the Jewish sector of the economy before the

First World War has clear limits. Separation in these areas may only be partial, and attempts to drive it further will achieve inimical results. These situations require that Israelis and Palestinians learn to live together in addition to living side by side.

The ideology of the inherently beneficial character of Zionist economic development for the Arab residents of Palestine that masked the transfer of resources into Jewish hands and established Jewish superiority has also appeared in a new guise. Attempts to continue yoking cheap Palestinian labor to benefit Israeli capital clearly have the potential to re-create neo-colonial relations in the economic arena. Such development can only lead to the replacement of the labor movement's exclusionary practices with that of exploitation by Israeli businesses. Conversely, abandoning the Palestinian workers whose labor benefited the Israel economy for a quarter century would only maintain the enormous gap between the two societies' standards of living. The possibility of mutually beneficial economic relations requires that the one-sided advantages acquired during the twenty-five years of Israeli domination not structure future links. After all, past experience shows that ideologically motivated disregard of legitimate interests may bring on mythical beliefs and sharpen conflict.

When the old is dead and the new is not yet born, in the interregnum many morbid symptoms appear, Antonio Gramsci warned us. The noxious intentions and destructive actions of religious zealots—Palestinian and Jewish—who wish to scuttle the peace process prove the accuracy of his observation. By upholding its perspective, the historiographic revolution will likely help avert the backlash and panic that spread so easily after acts of terrorism and political assassinations. The coincidence of the Palestinian-Israeli peace process and the maturation of a new historiographical and sociological perspective on Israeli society allows a measure of interlocking political and intellectual openness—a recognition of separate and complementary legitimate interests that will prevent the morbid phenomena and its symptoms from prevailing. As long as the categories in which Palestinians and Israelis view each other are not frozen into ahistorical classifications, their relations have a better chance of remaining flexible and accommodating instead of reverting to ideological or mythical excesses.

NOTES

1. Baruch Kimmerling, *Zionism and Territory* (Berkeley: Institute of International Studies, 1983); and Baruch Kimmerling in collaboration with Irit Backer, *The Interrupted System: Israeli Civilians in War and Routine Times* (New Brunswick: Transaction Books, 1985).
2. Aharon Megged, "The Israeli Suicide Instinct" [in Hebrew], *Haaretz*, 10 June 1994.
3. Anita Shapira, "Politics and Collective Memory: The Debate over the 'New Historians' in Israel," *History and Memory* 7, no. 1 (Spring/Summer 1995): 30.

4. Ibid., 32.
5. Benny Morris, *The Birth of the Palestinian Refugee Problem, 1947–1949* (Cambridge: Cambridge University Press, 1987); Avi Shlaim, *Collusion across the Jordan: King Abdullah, the Zionist Movement, and the Partition of Palestine* (Oxford: Oxford University Press, 1988); and Ilan Pappe, *Britain and the Israeli-Arab Conflict, 1948–1951* (New York: Macmillan, 1988).
6. Benny Morris, "The New Historiography: Israel Confronts Its Past," *Tikkun* (November/December 1988): 19–23, 99–102.
7. One of the first historians to use the term "myth" as its nemesis was Simha Flapan, who subtitled his 1987 work *The Birth of Israel* (New York: Pantheon) as a contrast of "Myths and Realities," but this is an agenda and term used by other new historians as well. See, for example, Ilan Pappe, "Critique and Agenda: The Post-Zionist Scholars in Israel," *History and Memory* 7, no. 1 (Spring/Summer 1995): 77–78; and Avi Shlaim, "The Debate About 1948" (paper presented at the Association for Israel Studies Conference, Gratz College, Melrose Park, June 12–13, 1994).
8. Howard Morley Sachar, *A History of Israel: From the Rise of Zionism to Our Time* (New York: Knopf, 1979), 172.
9. A recent study of Palestinian agriculture during the Mandate, by Charles Kamen, *Little Common Ground: Arab Agriculture and Jewish Settlement in Palestine, 1920–1948* (Pittsburgh: University of Pittsburgh Press, 1991), concluded that "Jewish settlement, and in particular the Zionist policy of economic exclusiveness, hindered Arab economic development" (271).
10. When the Mandatory authorities tried to suggest alternative land to displaced Palestinian fellahin, Zionist land purchasing organizations were opposed on the grounds that eventually they hoped to acquire that land as well.
11. Yosef Gorny, "The Ideology of the Conquest of Labor" [in Hebrew], *Keseth*, no. 38 (Winter 1968): 77–78.
12. Dan Horowitz and Moshe Lissak, *The Origins of the Israeli Polity: Palestine under the Mandate* (Chicago: University of Chicago Press, 1978), 16–17.
13. See, for example, Ran Aaronsohn, "Baron Rothschild and the Initial Stage of Jewish Settlement in Palestine (1882–1890)," *Journal of Historical Geography* 19, no. 2 (1993); Zeev Tsahor, "Colonialist or Colonizer" [in Hebrew], in *Haaretz*, December 22, 1994; and see also my reply, "The Colonial Question" [in Hebrew], *Haaretz*, January 5, 1995.
14. See my "Changing Nationalism and Israel's 'Open Frontier' on the West Bank," *Theory and Society* 13 (November 1984): 803.
15. Megged, "The Israeli Suicide Instinct."
16. For their typology, see Gershon Shafir, *Land, Labor, and the Origins of the Israeli-Palestinian Conflict, 1882–1914* (Berkeley: University of California Press, 1996), 8–9.
17. Michael Shalev, *Labor and the Political Economy in Israel* (Oxford: Oxford University Press, 1992); and Michael Shalev, "The Death of the 'Bureaucratic' Labor Market? Structural Change in the Israeli Political Economy," unpublished paper, Department of Sociology, Hebrew University, Jerusalem.
18. See Yoav Peled and Gershon Shafir, "The Roots of Peacemaking: The Dynamics of Citizenship in Israel, 1948–1993," *International Journal of Middle Eastern Studies* 28 (August 1996): 391–413.

3

Introduction to
The Palestinian People: A History

BARUCH KIMMERLING AND JOEL S. MIGDAL

Toward the end of the eighteenth century, powerful economic and political forces at work in Europe began to affect everyday life in the Middle East, eventually impelling its peoples to redefine both their communities and their vision. Such change did not come without great struggle, continuing in one form or another until the present. Social boundaries—those factors defining insiders and outsiders and what binds the insiders together—have been as much a source of the struggle as the political boundaries of the new Middle Eastern states. In the case of the Palestinians, the process of redefinition has been obscured, and even transformed, by the ongoing conflict with the Jews.

The creation of a nation involves a melding of values and myths, of people's imaginations and their identities. It demands leadership, but also a social foundation empowering the leaders and establishing the limits of what they can achieve. In *The Palestinian People: A History*, we are less interested in protocols and diplomacy than in the dynamics and beliefs of peasants, urban workers, merchants, and landowners, and their relationships to the leaders. For particularly with *al-Nakba*—the catastrophic shattering of the Palestinian community in the 1948 war with the Jews—we find the content of what it means to be Palestinian shaped as much by this foundation as by the old, established leadership.[1] The Palestinian people were not mere victims, as so many accounts have presented them (although, to be sure, fate has not treated them kindly), but were active participants in the creation of their people's collective character.

We hope to write against the grain of the sort of history that has been written as part and parcel of mythmaking national projects. In different ways,

---

Reprinted from Baruch Kimmerling and Joel S. Migdal, *The Palestinian People: A History*, xv–xxix, by permission of Carol Mann Agency. Originally published as *The Palestinians: The Making of a People* in 1994. Copyright © 1994, 2003 Baruch Kimmerling and Joel S. Migdal published by Harvard University Press.

Palestinians have suffered a great deal from such mythmaking. The historiographical debate has been an integral part of the conflict between Palestinians and Jews. Note the account of one national historian:

> The Palestinians' claim is predicated on the right of ownership evidenced by uninterrupted possession and occupation since the dawn of recorded history. They lived in the country when the Hebrews (of whom the Jews claim descent) came and lived there for a comparatively short period. They continued to live there during the Hebrew (and Jewish) occupation. They remained there after the last Hebrew or Jew left the country nearly two thousand years ago.... The people today called Palestinians or Palestinian Arabs, who have been fighting the Zionists and State of Israel which Zionism created in 1948, are largely the descendants of the Canaanites, the Edomites, and the Philistines who lived in Palestine when it was invaded by the Hebrews in ancient times. But the Hebrews finally left or were driven out two thousand years ago.[2]

The search for connection with the past has sometimes transformed history into a handmaiden of those seeking to give the nation a proper pedigree—an effort that involves denigrating the adversary's experience of the past. This exercise has been as evident on the part of Jews as Palestinian advocates. Historians sympathetic with Israel have frequently shared Golda Meir's perspective: "There was no such thing as Palestinians. When was there an independent Palestinian people with a Palestinian state? . . . It was not as though there was a Palestinian people in Palestine considering itself as a Palestinian people and we came and threw them out and took their country from them. They did not exist."[3]

One of the best-known expressions of such a viewpoint has been Joan Peters's *From Time Immemorial: The Origins of the Arab-Jewish Conflict over Palestine*, heavily documented and, apparently, a serious work of scholarship. Its basic argument is that most of Palestine's Arab population was not indigenous. Rather it consisted of migrants, attracted by opportunities offered by Jewish settlement, who came from disparate streams and certainly did not (do not) constitute a people. "The 'Palestinians' claim," Peters explains, "is avowedly based upon 'history' and their goal is the dissolution of another state. Their alleged right of 'self-determination' is based upon the erroneous alleged '90% majority of Arabs' in 1917 on the Jewish-settled areas that became Israel in 1948."[4] But as numerous sober historians have shown,[5] Peters's tendentiousness is not, in fact, supported by the historical record, being based on materials out of context and on distorted evidence.

Almost nothing was shared willingly between Jews and Arabs in the historiographical battle, which began in the reincarnated Palestine of the interwar years. Even the appropriation of the term "Palestinian" became a source for controversy, as seen in Golda Meir's and Joan Peters's protests. The term eventually became attached to the Arabs living in Palestine prior to British withdrawal, as well as to their descendants, while the Jews discarded it in 1948 in favor of "Israelis." For the Arabs, the term indicated not only a land of origin, but also an increasing sense of a shared past and future. Here I refer to Palestinian Arabs as Palestinians, and to the country as Palestine, even when applied to periods in which such usage is anachronistic—when the Arabs' sense of participating in a common history had not yet evolved, and when the territory was administratively fragmented. But the use of the term for the nineteenth or early twentieth centuries should not obscure the main point, the one that has so often been missed on both sides of the historiographical divide: a Palestinian national identity, like those of other modern nations, has been created—invented and elaborated—over the course of the last two centuries.

In some ways, the Jewish national movement has shaped the Palestinian people almost as much as it did the Jews themselves. Had it not been for the pressures exerted on the Arabs of Palestine by the Zionist movement, the very concept of a Palestinian people would not have developed; and Palestinians quite accurately understand their society's essential, existential status as the direct result of Jewish political rejuvenation and settlement. They see their own lives as reflections of a catastrophe, with Zionism—as Palestinian writer Fawaz Turki has put it—"having its day and the Palestinian [movement] its eclipse," individual Palestinians ending up in "the world of the exile. The world of the occupied. The world of the refugee. The world of the ghetto. The world of the stateless."[6] Nevertheless, focusing attention exclusively on the Palestinian Arab conflict with the Jews would obscure other important factors, particularly the extension of the world market into Palestine and the imposition of politically and administratively capable states, both beginning in the nineteenth century. Until quite recently, Palestinian writers paid scant attention to the contours of their own society, preoccupied as they were with the other, the Jews—the key to unlocking the secrets of those forces that turned their world upside down. For their part, the Zionists have been absorbed in a nationalist project rendering the Palestinians almost incidental. In the process, they have failed to grasp the extent to which their own society has been shaped by its ongoing encounter with the Palestinians. Perhaps doing so would involve too painful an encounter with Zionism's political counterpart—what we might call "Palestinism": the belief that the Arab population originating in the area of the Palestine mandate is distinct from other Arab groups, with a right to its own nation-state in that territory.[7]

As young academics, the authors of this book joined a handful of Jewish social scientists beginning, in the wake of the 1967 war, to view the Palestinians not as anthropological curiosities, but as a social group deeply affecting the future of the Jews. In addition to its 2.4 million Jews, Israel then governed almost 1.5 million Arabs, including around 400,000 citizens of Israel, 665,000 in the West Bank and East Jerusalem, and 356,000 in the Gaza Strip. We both came to know many Palestinians, mostly in West Bank villages and on the campus of the Hebrew University. Kimmerling wrote about Jewish and Palestinian interdependence in the half century since World War I, while Migdal focused on the longstanding impact of different rulers, including the Israelis, on Palestinian society. Hovering behind all this work has been an awareness that mutual Jewish-Palestinian denial will disappear slowly, if ever. Still, recent events have made one thing quite clear: The Palestinian dream of self-determination will likely be realized only with the assent of a secure, cohesive Israel, and the Israeli dream of acceptance throughout the Middle East will likely need Palestinian approval.

As much as any people in the world, the Palestinians have suffered from media stereotypes: "terrorists" and "freedom fighters," "murderers" and "victims." At times, the Palestinian leadership has reinforced such images by insisting on a national consensus denying the rifts in their society. In the following pages, we intend to satisfy neither the demonic nor idyllic vision of the Palestinian Arab. Rather, we will describe the contours of a people at the center of one of the most volatile conflicts of our time.

NOTES

1. The term "al-Nakba" (catastrophe, disaster) was coined by Syrian scholar Constantine Zurayk in the event's immediate aftermath: "The defeat of the Arabs in Palestine is no simple setback or light, passing evil. It is a disaster in every sense of the word and one of the harshest trials and tribulations with which the Arabs have been afflicted throughout their long history—a history marked by numerous trials and tribulations." See *The Meaning of Disaster* (Beirut: Khayat's College Book Cooperative, 1956), 2. The Arabic title of the book is *Ma'na al-Nakbah*.

2. Frank C. Sakran, *Palestine, Still a Dilemma* (Washington, D.C.: American Council on the Middle East, 1976), 104–105. There are numerous other works making similar points. See, for example, Samir S. Saleeby, *The Palestine Problem* (London: Institute of International Studies, 1970), chap. 2.

3. Cited in *Sunday Times* (London), June 15, 1969.

4. *From Time Immemorial: The Origins of the Arab-Jewish Conflict over Palestine* (New York: Harper & Row, 1984), 402–403.

5. Her numbers were characterized by Norman Finkelstein (*In These Times*, September 1984) as "the most spectacular fraud ever published on the Arab-Israeli conflict ... a field littered with crass propaganda, forgeries and fakes." Similar evaluations were expressed by notable historians: Albert Hourani, *The Observer*, March 5, 1985; Yehoshua Porath, "Mrs. Peters' Palestine," *New York Review of Books*, January 16, 1986. In *Trends in the Demographic Development of Palestinians, 1870–1987* (Tel-Aviv: Shiloach Institute, Tel-Aviv University, 1989), Gad Gilbar shows that, contrary to what Peters contends, the migration factor was far less significant than natural increase. See also Justin McCarthy, *The Population of Palestine: Population History and Statistics of the Late Ottoman Period and the Mandate* (New York: Columbia University Press, 1990), who writes, "These and myriad other methodological and factual errors make Peters' work demographically worthless" (41). Besides the manipulative use of facts, the book suffers from a failure to take account of Palestinian social structure and

its inner dynamics and development. (More interesting, perhaps, is the acceptance the book gained in intellectual circles.) In any case, our position is in line with this statement from Porath's review: "But even if we put together all the cases [Peters] cites, one cannot escape the conclusion that most of the growth of the Palestinian Arab community resulted from a process of natural increase" (37).

6. Turki, a refugee who grew up in Lebanon, has written some of the most poignant and biting material about the condition of exile, most notably in his book, *The Disinherited: Journal of a Palestinian Exile* (New York: Monthly Review Press, 1972).

7. See Muhammad Y. Muslih, *The Origins of Palestinian Nationalism* (New York: Columbia University Press, 1988). For the best overall account of the history of Palestinian nationalism, see the three-volume history by Y. Porath, *The Emergence of the Palestinian-Arab National Movement: 1918–1929* (London: Frank Cass, 1974); *The Palestinian Arab National Movement: 1929–1939* (London: Frank Cass, 1977); and *In Search of Arab Unity* (London: Frank Cass, 1986).

4

Postzionist Studies of Israel

The First Decade

URI RAM

The postzionist critique on what may be called "nationalist epistemology" (or nationalist point of view) is felt today in all disciplines of knowledge and creative arts in Israel (even if not always explicitly under the postzionist heading). This is the situation in the field of history, where the "new historians" or "revisionist historians" had a lasting impact on history writing and on historical memory (Ne'eman-Arad 1995; Pappe 1995; Ram 2003; Weitz 1997), in sociology (Shenhav 2003, 2003a), in anthropology (Rabinowitz 1997, 2004), in archeology (Finkelstein and Silberman 2002; Herzog 1999; Levine and Mazar 2001), in geography (Bar Gal 1999, 2002; Newman 2004; Yiftachel 1999), in planning and architecture (Yacobi 2004; Segal, Tartakover, and Weizman 2003), in literature (Hever and Silberstein 2002), in women's studies (Feldman 1999; Lubin 2003), in film studies (Gertz, Lubin, and Neeman 1998; Shohat 1989), in studies of the body and of sexuality (Kedar 2003; Weiss 2005), in studies of law (Barak-Erez 2003; Barzilai 2004; Shamir 1999), and more.

The presence of postzionism in Israeli culture in general and of postzionist studies of Israeli society in particular is pervasive and unequivocal. But how to explain this phenomenon? Let us turn now to a sketching of several theoretical approaches to postzionism.

Since the 1990s a number of explanations have been provided to the phenomena of postzionism. It is convenient to classify the theoretical approaches to postzionism into four sections, which are discussed below: a postideological

---

An initial version of this paper was presented at the conference "Changing European Societies—The Role for Social Policy," Copenhagen, 13–15 November 2003. My sincere thanks to Noah Lewin-Epstein, Michal Shamir, and Stefan Svallfors for supplying me with data and being patient with my many questions over the long period in which this study has been gestating. I am also indebted to Gal Levy and Zeev Rosenhek for stimulating cooperative work in related areas. Reprinted by permission of Uri Ram. Originally published as "Postzionist Studies of Israel: The First Decade," *Israel Studies Bulletin* 20, no. 2 (2005): 22–45.

approach, a postmodernist approach, a postcolonial approach, and a post-Marxist approach.

The Postideological Perspective

In the postideological perspective, postzionism is considered as a process of cultural "normalization" that comes naturally after the successful accomplishment of the basic ends of Zionism—i.e., Jewish "ascendance" (Aliya) to Israel and the establishment and consolidation of a Jewish state. Zionism is considered here as a scaffold, which turns redundant after the building is accomplished, or as author A. B. Yehoshua put it in his famous essay *In Praise of Normalcy*, a "climber" is no more a "climber" once he reaches the peak of the mountain (Yehoshua 1984). Such a notion of postzionism was proposed, among else, by philosopher Menachem Brinker (1986).

This may be described as the most Zionist approach to postzionism, or even as a Ben-Gurionian approach to it, as it resembles the attitude of the state's first prime minister to the Jewish Agency, when he argued that with the establishment of the state the latter's role had expired. The prefix "post" represents, then, in this case, the distinction between "becoming" (the Zionist stage) and "being" (the postzionist stage).

Sociologist Erik Cohen has presented the Durkheimean-Weberian, or shall we say Eisenstadtian, version of the postideological approach to postzionism. According to it, Zionism was a charismatic movement of radical transformation; in the course of time it passed routinization and left behind it a vacuum of "anomie." Postzionism is thus an anxiety, arising out of the absence of a generally accepted system of legitimization (Cohen 1995). This perspective is in congruence with recent views of S. N. Eisenstadt on the breakdown of the "original mold," which was designed by the dominant elite, and the subsequent proliferation of alternative discourses, including the postzionist one, but without the emergence of a substitute that will unify society (Eisenstadt 1996). Eisenstadt may be thus termed a "cognitive postzionist," as distinct from normative ones—that is, someone who recognizes the postzionist situation, without being happy about it. Not few of Israel's veteran Zionist intellectuals share this position with him. In somewhat parallel terms, coined within the framework of an earlier discussion by political scientists Charles Liebman and Eliezer Don Yehiya, postzionism may be considered as a situation of a "state without vision" (or a "service state"), in distinction from a "visionary state" (which they deem the Zionist state to have been) (Liebman and Don Yehiya 1976). The works of Baruch Kimmerling also contribute to the postzionist analysis, even though he avoids the concept (Kimmerling 2001, 2004).

This postideological approach is in fact a late Israeli version of the "end of ideology" thesis (Bell 1960). It is an evolutionary "historical stages" approach, according to which Israeli society is experiencing a normal transition from a nation-building phase to an institutionalized phase; or from a "stormy nationalism" to "banal nationalism," as befits a mature liberal state (Billing 1995). It is from this perspective that some commentators draw a distinction between "positive" and "negative" postzionism—positive or negative in terms of acquiescence with Zionism (see Gorni 2003; Wheeler 2003).

The Postmodernist Perspective

As against the postideological approach, the postmodernist approach does not consider postzionism as the maturation of Zionism, but, on the contrary, as signifying its demise. Nationalism is not considered simply as the conventional expression of peoplehood, but rather as a rack, forced upon fluctuating identities. Nationalism is thus a form of oppression, postnationalism a form of liberation. The incredulity toward nationalism is a private case of the incredulity toward the other great emancipatory narratives of modernity (Lyotard 1984). The ambition of nationalism to melt various identities into a cohesive universal identity, and its simultaneous strive to exclude differing identities, is substituted in postmodern times by a discourse of otherness, difference, and multiculturalism—and the umbrella term for this trend in Israel is "postzionism" (Azoulay and Ophir 1998).

The proponents of this perspective view postzionism not as a new historical phase, but rather as a new point of view, a new epistemology, which subverts and undermines the linear and essentialist point of view of nationalism. Postzionism is the exposition of the multifarious identities that have been repressed under the national banner and an expression of the heterogeneity that Zionism attempted to homogenize. Laurence Silberstein, author of the most comprehensive text on postzionism to date, defined the relations between postmodernism and postzionism as a complex web, which has its nodes of joint as well as nodes of disjoint (Silberstein 1999). The most significant node of joint is the deconstruction of the "regime of truth," or the power/knowledge network, and the attention given to different voices and new narratives. To sum up, as against the postideological approach, which considers postzionism as a "Zionism with a normal face," so to speak, the postmodern approach considers postzionism as a subversion of Zionism and as a deconstruction of it into components and narratives it used to deny or marginalize. Thus Eliezer Schweid from the Hebrew University, committed opponent of postzionism, considers it as the "Israeli version of post-modernism" (Schweid 1996a, 1996b). (On the relationships between postzionism and postmodernism see also Levine 1996.)

While the above is a Foucauldian, identity-oriented version of the postmodern approach, there is also a Habermasian, citizenship-oriented, approach to postzionism. This approach refers to the distinction between ethnic-nationalism and territorial-nationalism (Brubaker 1994). In this view, postzionism represents a postnational concept of Israeli citizenship, or even of Israeli constitutional nationalism, de-linked from the Jewish (or any other) communal belonging. This type of nationalism, based on a present common framework of life, rather than on past myth, may overcome the unresolved tension between the Jewish component in Israeli identity, which may turn into a matter of private or subcommunal affiliation, and the democratic component of Israeli identity, which must turn into the state's constitutional basis. As long as Israel is a state of the Jewish ethnos, rather than of its citizens, it cannot be considered as a proper democracy (Ram 1999, 2001; Yiftachel 1999).

The most thorough analysis from this perspective is offered by Shafir and Peled (2002). In their view, three distinct citizenship regimes (or incorporation regimes) obtain in Israel: an ethnonationalist regime, which ensures the primacy of Jews; a liberal regime, which ensures equal rights to individual citizens; and a republican regime, which allocates ranks and privileges on the basis of "civic virtue," which practically means contribution to the common Zionist cause. Up to recent times the contradictory ethnic and liberal regimes could dwell together under the legitimization provided by the republican regime. As of recently, republicanism is receding and the conflict between the ethnic and the liberal regimes comes to the fore. In terms of the current discussion, it is the conflict between neozionism and postzionism.

A specific question within the postmodern approach to postzionism is the question of the relationship between Israeli and Jewish identities. In both the Foucauldian and the Habermasian versions mentioned above, postzionism is understood to draw a sharp distinction between Israeli and Jewish identities. Yet the constitutional-oriented version is keen on emphasizing the autonomy of Israeliness as a basis for democratic legitimization, while the identity-oriented version is keen on emphasizing the autonomy of Jewishness, as a basis for new diasporic Jewish identities (Raz-Krakotzkin 1993 and 1994; Levy and Weingrod 2004). In the latter spirit, critic Dan Miron presents postzionism as "a position that does not see the state of Israel as a necessary response to the home quest of the protagonists . . . (but rather one that deconstructs) the binary pairs from which the Israeli ethos was constructed, such as Holocaust versus heroism, death versus new life, Diaspora versus homeland, weakness versus power and passivism versus activism" (Lev Ari 2004).

The Postcolonialist Perspective

The postcolonialist approach to postzionism is a particular case of the postmodern perspective. It shares the latter's challenge to modernity but superimposes on the self-other dichotomy the West-East dichotomy. Zionism is thus rendered as Western, and postzionism receives an Eastern tilt—ideally conjoining both Arab-Palestinian and Jewish-Oriental identities, as in Yehuda Shenhav's "Jewish-Arabs" conceptualization (Shenhav 2003a, 2003b). This approach draws heavily of course on the Orientalism perspective of critics like Said (1978), as well as on the hybrid version of it, by critics like Bhabha (1990; Shenhav 2004).

The postcolonial discourse invents new-old identities and composes new narratives, which give voice to subaltern sectors of the population, and which (re)create old-new hyphenated identities, which defy the simplicity of the nationalist boundaries. When this perspective is applied to Israel, postzionism receives the sense of the empowerment of the "internal other" of Zionism—that is, Oriental Jews—and concomitantly of the transgression of the internal-external national boundaries, which are substituted (conceptually) with the Occidental-Oriental distinction. In other words, Zionism is conceived as a European-Ashkenazi-White-Colonial movement, which has victimized both the internal Orientals and the external Arabs (Shohat 1989, 2001).

The goal of postcolonial postzionism is, in any event, to undo the "conspiracy of silencing" that clouded the Mizrahi identity in Israel. By exposing exclusionary practices it also undoes the national narrative, which assumes a common essence and denies inherent otherness (Motzafi-Haller 1998, 2002). According to the new postcolonial postzionism, the denial of Mizarahim was performed, first, by mainstream sociology, which imputed to them cultural backwardness and thus denied the Israeli context of their underrated situation, but second, also, by critical sociology, which considered Mizrahim in class terms, thus denying their cultural history and identity (Shenhav 2003a, 2003b). Postcolonial postzionism thus deconstructs the tissue of the national "us" to its distinct hierarchical layers, subverts the concept of a pregiven "nation," and proposes alternative notions, or at the least complementary ones, of collective identity.

Whereas the postcolonial approach to postzionism aims to speak in the name of the Orient, Jewish and Arab combined, it remains in fact mostly an in-Jewish affair. The Palestinian Arabs, being excluded from Israeli society and identity and being the ultimate "others" in the country, find it more difficult to perform the delicate postcolonial conceptual dance on the inside-outside boundary; they are mostly "outsiders," even when they are full citizens. Thus while for postzionism the question of the status and conditions of the Palestinian citizens in Israel is absolutely central (Ozacky-Lazar, Ghanim, and Pappe 1999; Shafir and Peled 2002; Yiftachel 1999), Palestinians in Israel usually speak from a national point of view, rather than from a postnational one. Postnationalism seems to be the privilege of well-established nations.

The Post-Marxist Perspective

The post-Marxist approach differs from the three approaches mentioned above in considering economic and social changes as major factors in the shaping of the political and cultural transformations associated with postzionism. In other words, this approach is post-Marxist in the sense that it relates postmodernism itself to the recent transformation of the capitalist mode of regulation, namely the emergence of post-Fordism, and to the subsequent transformations in the balance of power between the classes. It is the only approach cognizant of the affinities between the economic and social changes and the political-cultural changes. It is a post-Marxist perspective nevertheless, in the sense that it shares some aspects of postmodern thought, such as nondeterministic and nonlinear analysis, and also in the sense that it recognizes the postmodern dimensions of contemporary culture.

Post-Fordist capitalism differs from Fordist capitalism in the following aspects: a transition from hierarchical bureaucratic firm to a flexible entrepreneurial network; a transition from Keynesian interventionism in the economy and production-side developmentalism to neoliberal and consumption-side economics; a transition from labor market collective regulation to non-organized labor market and "new forms" of employment; a transition from a universal welfare state (the European model) to a safety network welfarism (the American model); and a transition from a national economy to a global economy (Aglietta 2001; Jessop 2003). Overall, this transition disrupts the balance of power between capital, labor, and state, which prevailed in the corporatist (Fordist) state, and it ushers in an unbalanced power structure under capital's tutelage. Two "noneconomic" results of this major shift of the social regime are the rise of inequality in the distribution of income and a trend of fragmentation of the population into identity groups. How does all this relate to postzionism?

To make a long answer short, the argument is as follows: the Israeli "traditional" social regime was collectivist because this was conditional to the success of the early settlement and conquest phase of Zionism in Palestine, a region that was unattractive to capital and labor alike. The national project could take off only on the basis of labor enclaves and the exclusion of Arab laborers, based on injunction of Jewish capital. The combination of "public" finance and privileged labor made the Labor strategy triumphant (Shafir 1996; Shalev 1992). In the early state era, during the 1950s and 1960s, the national project was bequeathed to the state administration, which was manifested in the *mamlachtiyut* etatist ideology of the era. In the 1970s, especially since the rise of the Likud in 1977, a liberal change started, but until the mid-1980s, the new economy floundered because of failed management (which caused three-digit inflation). Since the new economic program of the mid-1980s, and in conjunction with the hi-tech revolution of the 1990s, the transition from Fordism to post-Fordism in Israel has finally materialized.

By this time, the veteran elites have already turned their preference from military mobility to entrepreneurial accumulation, and from national adherence to postnationalist aspirations (Levy 2003). The state and the Histadrut privatized their large corporations (a process completed for the Histadrut, not yet so for the state) and together with the new influx of international investment (in the early 1990s encouraged by the peace process), the ideology of the business sector has become dominant in Israel. The interclass pact was disbanded and inequality bounced. As a reaction to it, the lower classes, a category which in large part overlaps with Oriental descent, low education, and traditionalist culture, turned en masse to look for consolation for the loss of identity and compensation for the loss of status, which it found in populist propaganda and chauvinist politics. Thus emerged inside Israel a local postzionist/neozionist version of the global dialectics of "McWorld versus Jihad" (Jewish Jihad in this case) (Barber 1996; Ram 2005; Shafir and Peled 2000).

Hence the change from Fordism to post-Fordism is associated with the change from a nation and class coalition into a clash between localist neozionist ethno-fundamentalism and globalist postzionist civic-liberalism.

Postzionism: Ideological Controversies

During the 1990s postzionism was the pivot around which the past, present, and future of Israel have been evaluated and disputed. One may venture here only a sketch of the intellectual and ideological controversies surrounding postzionism.

A hostile attack on postzionism germinates obviously from neozionist quarters. Postzionism is naturally the nemesis of neozionism. This is obvious since these are the two diametrical opposites in contemporary Israeli political culture (instances of this clash from the neozionist side include the writings of Eliezer Schweid (e.g., Schweid 1996a, 1996b, as well as the daily diatribes of Yisrael Harel in *Haaretz*). This is a clear case of "clash of civilizations"—the universalistic, cosmopolitan, libertarian civilization on the "post" side, and particularistic, chauvinist, communal civilization on the "neo" side. It will not be far-fetched to argue that this clash is a late incarnation of the Enlightenment-Romantic clash in turn-of-the-century European culture and of an even earlier clash between Enlightenment Judaism (*Haskala*) and Orthodox Judaism (Feiner 2003). Multifarious controversies in contemporary Israel receive a coherent structure when looked at from this perspective.

Another source of antagonism toward postzionism is mainstream liberal Zionism. The thinkers of this stream share with the neozionists the nationalistic assumptions, yet they pledge allegiance to liberal democracy. The debate between national-liberals and postzionists is centered on the idiom of "a Jewish and democratic state." The idea behind this formula is that the "and" which combines the sides of the equation is possible—that is, that there is no contradiction here. Some argue in this vein that Israel is not an exception among other liberal democracies (Yacobson and Rubinstein 2003), while others argue that Israel is an epitome of a new version of democracy, namely "ethnic democracy" (Smooha 2002). Postzionists argue that "Jewish and democratic" are an oxymoronic, and that Israel's regime is better described as an "ethnocracy" (Yiftachel 1999). Shafir and Peled frame the question, as was mentioned, in terms of three regimes of incorporation that have prevailed in Israel: the liberal, the ethnic, and the republican. The latter mitigated between the former two. In the recent era, they maintain, the republican ethos is tarnished; hence the emerging clash between liberalism and communalism (Shafir and Peled 2002). Therefore postzionists think that Israel faces a stark choice: Jewish or democratic.

A third source of objection to postzionism is the circle of intellectuals affiliated with the "social" agenda of the Labor Party's left wing (this wing had in fact evaporated from actual Labor politics long ago). The defense of old nationalism is performed in this case in the name of socialism or—in its glaring absence—of "social solidarity." The argument is that postzionism supports inadvertently the neoliberal attack on the Israeli welfare state. Like in classical Zionism, these thinkers collapse under the banner of "collectivism" both social meaning (socialism) and cultural meaning (nationalism), and they reject the unpacking of this parcel. Postzionists rebuff this argument on three grounds: first, because of its entanglement with the Zionist project, the Israeli welfare state was segmental and exclusive toward categories of people who did not form the "hard core" of the nation (women, Mizrahim, Arabs). Second, social solidarity may turn into a civic and constitutional, rather than a "national" provenience. Third, postzionism is not exclusively liberal (thus expressing the middle classes) but also multicultural (thus expressing the excluded and marginalized populations) (for a theoretical discussion on the relations between the interests and identities, see Fraser 1997).

A final source of disapproval of postzionism is a trend that aims to bypass it from the left, so to speak—postcolonialism. Some of the speakers of this trend tend to deride postzionism as representing the rebellious intellectuals of the Ashkenazi elite (exuberant exemplars are scattered in Livneh 2000). Yet in the general public discourse these speakers themselves are usually conceived as postzionist. For instance, Livneh asserts, rightly, that the Democratic Mizrahi Rainbow "was founded upon a Postzionist position" (2001, 20). Postcolonialism is indeed a private case of postzionism, and, in fact, in recent years some of the best of postzionist research comes from writers who affiliate with postcolonialist critique (e.g., Hever, Shenhav, and Motzafi-Haller 2002).

Finally, some advance the argument that postzionism is inherently Jewish. Since Arabs have not been Zionists from the first place (obviously!) why should they become postzionist anyway? Postzionists regard this as an ad absurdum rhetoric. Postzionism is a vision of a civic and multicultural Israeli society, which will be a democratic version of the state of Israel. Some other thinkers prefer the vision of "binational state" to the vision of "a state of citizens." From a postzionist perspective, this vision complies with the fundamental assumptions of nationalism, which are inherently not democratic (even if in some circumstances binationalism may be more democratic, relative to a one nation rule). Yet on a principled level (to be distinguished from practical politics), postzionists prefer, as said, the liberal "state of its citizens," which leaves to the level of voluntary civil society the options of communions around cultural preferences (religious, national, sexual, or any others).

Postzionism: Concluding Comments on Its Presumed Decline and Fall

Before closing this interim account of postzionism in its first decade, one last issue should be tackled: the announcement of the early death of postzionism, even before passing its tenth birthday. Let us consider the life span and future prospects of postzionism.

The first thing to note is that postzionism is indeed very young; as said above it entered the public domain at the end of 1993. It should be no surprise, then, to find out that despite the burgeoning of postzionist elements in Israeli culture, the status of postzionism is still merely of an emerging counter-hegemonic culture

A number of reasons may account for this. First is the usual conservative inertia of existing national institutions. Second is the depth in which Zionist culture is ingrained in the population by a huge educational and ideological enterprise. Third is the robust development of the countertrend of neozionism, which has succeeded in consolidating ethnonationalism as a common denominator of Israeli political culture. A fourth cause for the currently low status of postzionism is the change of global atmosphere since September 11, 2001, which has caused a setback to multiculturalism and libertarianism all over the Western world. And, last but not least, the second Intifada (started in 2000), with its undifferentiating attacks on Israeli civilians, has certainly contributed to a "closing of the ranks" effect among Israeli Jews.

The backward rolling of postzionism in the early 2000s generated a widespread sense that it was a passing incident that may be considered, posthumously, as an episode belonging to the Oslo period. Some noted that postzionism "lost much of its 'trendy' glitter" (Yuval Davis 2003, 182) and announced its "decline and fall" (Livneh 2000) or its "expiration" (Pappe in Livneh 2002, 18; for a realistic consideration see Kelman 1998). In 2003 it was announced on national television news that "Postzionism is out; Zionism is in" (*Mabat Lachadashot*, Channel 1, 2003). It is only logical to conclude that during some period before that breaking news postzionism was "in." Despite the news about the "outing" of postzionism, the Likud ruling party remained worried and the first clause in its 2003 program proclaimed that "the continuation in the thrive of Israel will be guaranteed despite Postzionism and the condition of the global village" (Likud 2003). But the great savior of Zionism in its struggle with postzionism happens not to have been the Likud, but rather the Palestinians, as was explained in *Yediot Ah'Ronot*:

> Recent Palestinian violence had one positive consequence: the arousal of Jewish nationalism, namely Zionism. Whereas until the recent Israel was bloomed with Postzionist ideas and sophisticated concepts of a global village, which conveyed the message that Zionism is lost for posterity, the recent events in the territories and among Israeli Arabs revived Zionism anew and showed its relevancy to our times. Zionism went out of citizenship courses and returned to be a relevant political position" (Guy Bechor, cited in Goldberger 2002, 101).

It is evident, as mentioned above, that the events of September 11, 2001, their military fallout from Afghanistan to Iraq, and their cultural fallout within the Western world, as evinced by the reception of Huntington's concept of "Clash of Civilizations" (Huntington 1998), and on top of it the refueling of hostilities in Israel-Palestine since 2000, all these indeed encourage the ethnonationalist agenda of neozionism.

Yet, while in political terms postzionism is not in its peak in the first half of the first decade of the 2000s, this is not necessarily the case with regard to the impact of postzionism on Israeli culture, especially the elite culture. In this regard the talk of "decline and fall" is in all probability shortsighted. Postzionism seems to have been diffused rather deep into the public consciousness. Hence, the circumstantial political state of postzionism should not be confused with its structural position.

It may be argued by postzionists that the proclamation of its expiration are founded upon the categorical mistakes of weighting postzionism prematurely in the positivistic terms of popular spread or of political effect. It should be remembered that what is discussed here is an emergent counterhegemonic trend, and that its discursive achievements are what matters. In other words, in critical theory terms, postzionism is a concept of both "immanence"—taping actual undercurrents—and "transcendence"—pointing toward an exogenous normative horizon (Fraser and Honneth 2003; Horkheimer 1975). The category of postzionism may thus be better thought about as a "actual potentiality," rather than as "potential actuality." In addition, it must also be added that postzionism is just one flip of the coin, the other being neozionism, and that the struggle between the two has not been decided yet.

To sum up, in its first decade postzionism has become the prism through which the augmenting tensions between the democratic and the Jewish dimensions of the state of Israel are exposed.

We have presented four approaches to postzionism. The postnational approach considers postzionism as a process of "normalization"; the postmodern approach considers it a shaking-off of the oppressive nationalist grand-narrative; the postcolonial approach considers it a Mizrahi counter-hegemonic politics of identity; and the post-Marxist approach considers it the political-cultural counterpart of post-Fordist restructuring of the inter-class balance of power. Taken together, these four approaches highlight the various dimensions of postzionism: the decline of nationalism; the rise of individualism; the spread of pluralism; and the overarching hegemony of neoliberalism. The interrelationships between these dimensions, the combined weight of these developments, and their relationship with the continued colonial domination of Israel over the Palestinians are yet to be seen. The progression of postzionism in Israel is certainly not linear; the backlash of ethnonationalist collectivism and fundamentalist neozionism lurks around the corner, awaiting a chance to be inflamed by an eventual new cycle of Israeli-Palestinian hostilities, or in fact awaiting a chance to inflame such hostilities.

This interim report of the first decade of postzionist studies of Israel may thus conclude with the note that the death of postzionism was proclaimed too early and too hastily. The deceased has not yet exhausted its full potential. It is also true, however, that there is no guarantee that it ever will.

REFERENCES

Agassi, Joseph. 1999. *Liberal Nationalism for Israel: Towards an Israeli National Identity*. New York: Gefen Books.
Aglietta, Michael. 2001. *A Theory of Capitalist Regulation: the US Experience*. London: Verso
Aharonson, Shlomo. 1997. "Zionism and Post-Zionism: The Historical-Ideological Context" [in Hebrew]. In Y. Weitz 1997, 291–309.
Alboim-Dror, Rachel. 1997. "'Liberated from Nationalistic Shuvinism': On Herzl in a Post-Zionist Mirror" [in Hebrew]. *Iton 77* (208): 17–19.
Almog, Oz. 1997. "The Democratic Faith" [in Hebrew]. *Panim* 2:10–20.
Aloni, Shulamit. 1997. "Back to Independence" [in Hebrew] *Haaretz*, November 21.
Avneri, Uri. 1968. *Israel without Zionists: A Plea for Peace in the Middle East*. New York: McMillan.
Azoulay, Ariella, and Adi Ophir. 1998. "100 Years of Zionism: 50 Years of a Jewish State." *Tikkun*, 13 (2): 68–71.
Balaban, Avraham. 1995. *A Different Wave in the Israeli Fiction: Postmodernist Israeli Fiction* [in Hebrew]. Jerusalem: Keter.
Barak-Erez, Dafna. 2003. *Milestone Judgments of the Israeli Supreme Court* [in Hebrew]. Tel Aviv: Broadcast University, Misrad Habitachon.
Barber, Benjamin. 1996. *Jihad vs. McWorld: How Globalism and Tribalism Are Reshaping the World*. New York: Ballantine Books.
Bar Gal, Yoram. 1999. "On the Tribe's Elders: Continuation and Renewal in Israeli Geography" [in Hebrew]. *Ofakim be-Geographya* 51:7–39.
———. 2002. "Maps and Nationalism: New Reading in Israel Atlas" [in Hebrew]. *Ofakim be-Geographya* 55:8–29.
Barzilai, Gad. 2004. *Communities and Law: Politics and Cultures of Legal Identities*. Ann Arbor: University of Michigan Press.
Beit-Hallahmi, Benjamin. 1992. *Despair and Deliverance: Private Salvation in Contemporary Israel*. New York: Suny Press.
Bell, Daniel. 1960. *The End of Ideology*. Glencoe, Ill.: Free Press.

Ben Amos, Avner ed. 2002. *History, Identity and Memory: Images of the Past in Israeli Education* [in Hebrew]. Tel Aviv: Ramot.
Ben Eliezer, Uri. 2004. "Civil Society and Military Society in Israel: Neo-Militarism and Anti-Militarism in the Post-Hegemonic Era." In *In the Name of Security: The Sociology of Peace and War in Israel in Changing Times*, ed. Majid Al-Haj and Uri Ben Eliezer, 29–76. Haifa: University of Haifa and Pardes, 2003.
Bhabha, Homi. 1990. *Nation and Narration*. New York: Routledge.
Billing, Michael. 1995. *Banal Nationalism*. New York: Sage.
Boger, Hagit. 1996. "Post-Zionist Discourse and the Israeli National Consensus: What Has Changed?" *Response* 66: 28–44.
Boyarin, Daniel, and Boyarin Jonathan. 1994. "Israel Has No Motherland" [in Hebrew]. *Theory and Criticism* 5:79–104.
Brinker, Menachem. 1986. "After Zionism" [in Hebrew]. *Siman Kria* 19: 21–29.
Brubaker, Roger. 1994. *Citizenship and Nationhood in France and Germany*. Cambridge, Mass.: Harvard University Press.
Chinski, Sarah. 1993. "Silence of the Fish: The Local Versus the Universal in Israeli Discourse of Art." [in Hebrew]. *Theory and Criticism* 4:105–122.
Cohen, Erik. 1995. "Israel as a Post-Zionist Society." In Wistrich and Ochana 1995.
Director, Ruti. 2004. "Current Israeli Art—An Outline." http://www.saltarbutartzi.org.il/_Articles/Article.asp?CategoryID=134andArticleID=101
Duvdevani, Shmulik. 2000. "Not Walking in the Fields: The New Immigrant in Dover Kisashvili Movie 'Late Marriage'" [in Hebrew]. http://www.ynet.co.il/articles/0,7340,L-1272608,00.html.
Ehrlich, Avishai. "Zionism, Anti-Zionism, Post-Zionism." In Nimni 2003a, 63–97.
Eisenstadt, Shmuel N. 1996. "The Struggle over Symbols of Collective Identity and Its Boundaries in Post-Revolutionary Israeli Society" [in Hebrew]. In Ginossar and Bareli 1996.
———. 2004. *Changes in Israeli Society* [in Hebrew]. Tel Aviv: Broadcast University.
Evron, Boas. 1995. *Jewish State or Israeli Nation?* Bloomington: Indiana University Press.
Feige, Michael. 2002. *One Space, Two Places: Gush Emunim and Peace Now and the Construction of Israeli Space* [in Hebrew]. Jerusalem: Hebrew University Magnes Press.
Feiner, Shmuel. 2003. *The Jewish Enlightenment*. Philadelphia: University of Pennsylvania Press.
Feldman, Yael. 1999. *No Room of Their Own*. New York: Columbia University Press.
Feldt, Jakob. 2004. *The Israeli Memory Struggle: History and Identity in the Age of Globalization*. Ph.D. diss., Institute for Cross-Cultural and Regional Studies, University of Copenhagen.
Fisher, Eran. 2000. "Post-Historicism and Post-Nationalism: Tekuma Television Series and the Crisis of Identity in Israel" [in Hebrew]. Master's thesis, Ben Gurion University.
Fraser, Nancy. 1997. "From Redistribution to Recognition? Dilemmas of Justice in a 'Postsocialist' Age." In *Justice Interruptus: Critical Reflections on the 'Postsocialist' Condition*. New York: Routledge.
Fraser, Nancy, and Axel Honneth. 2003. *Redistribution or Recognition? A Political-Philosophical Exchange*. London: Verso.
Friedman, Marsha. 1998. "Thoughts over Post-Zionism" [in Hebrew]. *Noga* 33:19.
Friling, Tuvia, ed. 2003. *An Answer to a Post-Zionist Colleague* [in Hebrew]. Tel Aviv: Yediot Achronot.
Fuhrer, Ronald. 1998. *Israeli Painting: From Post-Impressionism to Post-Zionism*. New York: Overlook Press.
Gavison, Ruth. 2003. "The Jews' Right to Statehood: A Defense." *Azure* 15:70–108.

Gertz, Nurith, Orly Lubin, and Jad Neeman, eds. 1998. *Fictive Looks on Israeli Cinema* [in Hebrew]. Tel Aviv: Open University.

Ghanem, As'ad. 2003. "Zionism, Post-Zionism and Anti-Zionism in Israel: Jews and Arabs in Conflict over the Nature of the State." In Ephraim Nimni, 98–116.

Gilerman, Danna. 2003. "In Berlin We Declared Post-Zionism" [in Hebrew]. *Haaretz*, April 29.

Ginossar, Pinhas, and Avi Bareli, eds. 1996. *Zionism: A Contemporary Controversy (Special Issue of Iyunim BeTkumat Israel Series)* [in Hebrew]. Sede Boqer: Ben Gurion Research Center.

Goldberger, Dorit. 2002. "The Post-Zionist Debate in Israeli Press, 1994–1998" [in Hebrew]. Master's thesis, Bar Ilan University.

Gorni, Yossef. 2003. "Zionism as a Renewing Idea" [in Hebrew]. In Friling 2000, 457–480.

Gottwein, Daniel. 2003. "Left and Right Post-Zionism and the Privatization of Israeli Collective Memory" [in Hebrew]. In Shapira and Penslar 2001, 9–42.

Gross, Eyal. 2003. "Queer Globalization and Human Rights: Dana International/Emnesti International" [in Hebrew]. *Theory and Criticism* 23:227–236.

Gurevitch, David. 1997. *Postmodernity: Culture and Literature in the End of the Twentieth Century* [in Hebrew]. Tel Aviv: Dvir.

Gur-Zeev, Ilan. 2004. *Toward A Diasporic Education: Multi-Culturalism, Post-Colonialism and Counter-Education in a Post-Modern Era* [in Hebrew]. Tel Aviv: Resling.

Hazony, Yoram. 2000. *The Jewish State: The Struggle for Israel's Soul*. New York: Basic Books.

Herzog, Hanna. 2003. "Post-Zionist Discourse in Alternative Voices." In Nimni 2003, 153–167.

Herzog, Zeev. 1999. "Truth from the Holy Land" [in Hebrew]. *Haaretz Supplement*, October 29.

Hever, Hannan, and Laurence J. Silberstein. 2002. *Producing the Modern Hebrew Canon: Nation Building and Minority Discourse*. New York: New York University Press.

Hever, Hannan, Yehuda Shenhav, and Pnina Motzafi-Haller, eds. 2002. *Mizrahim in Israel: A Critical Observation into Israel's Ethnicity* [in Hebrew]. Tel Aviv: Hakibbutz Hameuchad.

Horkheimer, Max. 1975. "Traditional and Critical Theory." In *Critical Theory*, ed. Max Horkheimer, 188–244. New York: Continuum.

Huntington, Samuel. 1998. *Clash of Civilizations: And the Remaking of the World Order*. New York: Simon and Schuster.

Inbari, Assaf. 1999. "End of the Seculars Season" [in Hebrew]. *Haaretz Supplement*, three-part series, September 10, 17, and 24

Israel Studies Forum. 2003. vol. 19 (1).

Jessop, Bob. 2003. *The Future of the Capitalist State*. New York: Polity Press.

Judt, Tony, 2003. "Israel: The Alternative." *New York Review of Books* 50:16.

Karpel, Motti. 2003. *The Revolution of the Faithful: The Decline of Zionism and the Rise of the Faithful Alternative* [in Hebrew]. Alon Shvut: Lechatchila.

Kedar, Yair, Amalya Ziv, and Oren Kner. 2003. *Beyond Sexuality: Selected Homo-Lesbian Articles and Queer Theory* [in Hebrew]. Tel Aviv: Hakibbutz Hameuchad.

Kelman, Herbert C. 1998. "Israel in Transition from Zionism to Post-Zionism." *Annals of the American Academy* 555:46–61.

Kemp, Adriana, David Newman, Uri Ram, and Oren Yiftachel, eds. 2004. *Israelis in Conflict: Hegemonies, Identities and Challenges*. Sussex: Sussex Academic Press.

Kimmerling, Baruch. 2001. *The Invention and Decline of Israeliness: State, Society and the Military*. Berkeley, Calif.: Berkeley University Press.

Koren, Dani. 1998. *The End of Political Parties: Israeli Democracy in Stress* [in Hebrew]. Tel Aviv: Hakibbutz Hameuchad.

Lerner, Michael. 1998. "Post-Zionism: Restoring Compassion, Overcoming Chauvinism." *Tikkun* 13 (2):33–38.

Lev Ari, Shiri. 2004. "Alexander Sand, 1921–2004" [in Hebrew]. *Haaretz*, September 12.

Levine, Mark. 1996. "Is Post-Zionism Postmodern?" *Response* 66:14–27.

Levine, Yisrael, and Amichai Mazar, eds. 2001. *The Controversy over Historical Truth in the Bible* [in Hebrew]. Jerusalem: Yad Yizhak Ben Zvi.

Levy, Andre, and Alex Weingrod, eds. 2004. *Homelands and Diasporas: Holy Lands and Other Places*. Stanford: Stanford University Press.

Levy, Yagil. 2003. "Social Convertibility and Militarism: Evaluation of the Development of Military-Society Relations in Israel in the Early 2000s." *Journal of Political and Military Sociology* 31 (1): 71–96.

Liebman, Charles S., and Eliezer Don-yehiya. 1983. *Civil Religion in Israel: Traditional Judaism and Political Culture in the Jewish State*. Berkeley: University of California Press.

Likud, The. 2003. Party Program towards the 16th Knesset. http://www.knesset.gov.il/elections16/heb/lists/plat_16.htm.

Livneh, Neri. 2001. "The Rise and Fall of Post-Zionism" [in Hebrew]. *Haaretz Supplement*, September 21, 18–21.

Lomsky-Feder, Edna, and Tamar Rapport. 2001. "Homecoming, Immigration, and the National Ethos: Russian-Jewish Homecomers Reading Zionism." *Anthropological Quarterly* 74 (1): 1–14.

Lubin, Orly. 2003. *A Woman Reads a Woman* [in Hebrew]. Haifa: Haifa University and Zemora Bitan.

Lustick, Ian. 2003. "Zionist Ideology and Its Discontents." *Israel Studies Forum* 19 (1): 98–103.

Lyotard, Jean-Francois. 1984. *The Post-Modern Condition: A Report on Knowledge*. Minneapolis: University of Minnesota Press.

Matiash, Yehoshua, and Naama Zabar Ben-Yehosha. 2004. "Reforms in the State Education Curriculum and the Struggle over Identity" [in Hebrew]. *Megamot* 44 (1): 84–104.

Mechman, Dan, ed. 1997. *Post-Zionism and the Holocaust: The Public Controversy on Post-Zionism in the Years 1993–1996* [in Hebrew]. Ramat Gan: Bar-Ilan University.

Motzafi-Haller, Penina. 2002. "Mizrahi Intellectuals, 1946–1951: Ethnic Identity and Its Boundaries" [in Hebrew]. In Hever, Shenhav, and Motzafi-Haller 2002, 152–190.

———. 1998. "A Mizrahi Call: For a More Democratic Israel." *Tikkun* 13 (2): 50–52.

Nativ. 2004. *Index 1988–2004* [in Hebrew]. Jerusalem: Merkaz Ariel.

Naveh, Eyal, and Esther Yogev. 2002. *Histories: Towards a Dialogue with the Israeli Past* [in Hebrew]. Tel Aviv: Bavel.

Ne'eman-Arad, Gulie, ed. 1995. *Israeli Historiography Revisited*. Special issue of *History and Memory* 7 (1).

Newman, David. 2004 "Territorial Identities in a Deterritorialized World: From National to Post-national Territorial Identities in Israel/Palestine." In *Living on the Margins: Citizenship and Identity in Contemporary Israel*, ed. A. Kemp, D. Newman, O. Yiftachel, and U. Ram. Sussex, UK: Sussex Academic Press.

Nimni, Ephraim. 2003a. *The Challenge of Post-Zionism: Alternatives to Fundamentalist Politics in Israel*. London: Zed Books.

———. 2003b. "From *Galut* to *T'futsoth*: Post-Zionism and the Dislocation of Jewish Diasporas." In Nimni 2003a, 117–152.

Noam, Vered. 1996. "Religious Zionism in the Age of the Post" [in Hebrew]. *Nekuda* 198: 66–71.

Ozacky-Lazar, Sara, Asad Ghanim, and Ilan Pappe, eds. 1999. *Seven Ways: Options for the Status of Arabs in Israel*. Givat Havivah: Institute for Peace Studies.
Ophir, Adi. 1999. *Fifty to Forty-Eight: Critical Moments* [in Hebrew]. Tel Aviv: Van Leer and Hakibbutz Hameuchad.
Orr, Akiva. 1994. *Israel: Politics, Myths and Identity Crises*. London: Pluto Press.
Oz, Yuval, and Amiram Barkat. 2005. "INF: The State Attorney became Post-Zionist." *Haaretz*, January 27.
Pappe, Ilan. 1995. "Critique and Agenda: The Post-Zionist Scholars in Israel." In Ne'eman-Arad 1995, 66–90.
Pappe, Ilan. 1997. "Post Zionist Critique of Israel and the Palestinians." Parts 1–3 in *Journal of Palestine Studies* 26 (2): 29–41; 26 (3): 37–43; 26 (4): 60–69.
Peled, Yoav, and Adi Ophir, eds. 2001. *Israel: From Mobilization to Civil Society?* [in Hebrew]. Tel Aviv: Hakibbutz Hameuchad and Van Leer.
Peled, Yoav. 1994. "Luxurious Diaspora: On the Rehabilitation of the Concept of Diaspora in Boyarin and Raz-Karkotzkin" [in Hebrew]. *Theory and Criticism* 5:133–140.
Peled, Yoav. 1998. "Toward a Definition of Nationalism in Israel? The Enigma of Shas." *Ethnic and Racial Studies* 21:703–727.
Rabinowitz, Dan. 1997. *Overlooking Nazareth: the Ethnography of Exclusion in Galilee*. Cambridge: Cambridge University Press.
———. 2004. "Writing Against the State: Transnationalism and the Epistemology of Minority Studies, with Special Reference to Israel." In *Israelis in Conflict: Hegemonies, Identities and Challenges*, ed. A. Kemp, D. Newman, U. Ram, and O. Yiftachel, 81–100. Brighton: Sussex Academic Press.
Ram, Uri, ed. 1993. *Israeli Society: Critical Perspectives* [in Hebrew]. Tel Aviv: Breirot.
———. 1995. *The Changing Agenda of Israeli Sociology: Theory, Ideology and Identity*. New York: SUNY Press.
———. 1999. "The State of the Nation: Contemporary Challenges to Zionism in Israel." *Constellations* 6 (3): 325–338.
———. 2001. "Historiographical Foundations of the Historical Strife in Israel." *Journal of Israeli History* 20 (2/3): 43–61.
———. 2003. "Postnationalist Pasts: The Case of Israel." In *States of Memory*, ed. J. K. Olick, 227–258. Durham: Duke University Press.
———2005. *The Globalization of Israel: McWorld in Tel Aviv, Jihad in Jerusalem* [in Hebrew]. Tel Aviv: Resling.
Ravizki, Aviezer. 1997. "Religious and Seculars in Israel—Post-Zionist Cultural War?" [in Hebrew]. *Alpayim* 14:970–980.
Raz-Krakotzkin, Amnon. 1993/1994. " Exile in the Midst of Sovereignty; A Critique of 'Shlilat HaGalut' in Israeli Culture" [in Hebrew]. *Theory and Criticism* 4:23–55; 5:113–132.
———. 1997. "Bi-Nationalism Is the Solution." *News from Within* 8 (9): 19–21.
Roniger, Luis, and Michael Feige. 1992. "From Pioneer to Freier: The Changing Models of Generalized Exchange in Israel" [in Hebrew]. *European Journal of Sociology* 33 (2): 280–307.
Rouhana, Nadim N., and Nimer Sultany. 2003. "Redrawing the Boundaries of Citizenship: Israel's New Hegemony." *Journal of Palestine Studies* 38 (1): 5–22.
Said, Edward. 1978. *Orientalism*. New York: Vintage.
Scholte, Jan Aart. 2000. *Globalization: A Critical Introduction*. London: McMillan.
Schweid, Eliezer. 1996a. *Zionism after Zionism* [in Hebrew]. Jerusalem: Mosad Bialik.
———. 1996b. *Zionism in a Postmodernistic Era* [in Hebrew]. Jerusalem Hasifriya Haziyonit: Mosad Bialik.

Segal, Rafi, David Tartakover, Eyal Weizman, eds. 2003. *A Civilian Occupation: The Politics of Israeli Architecture.* London: Verso.
Segev, Tom. 1996. "Herzl—The First Post-Zionist" [in Hebrew]. *Haaretz*, March 3.
Segev, Tom. 2003. *Elvis in Jerusalem: Post-Zionism and the Americanization of Israel.* New York: Owl Books.
Shafir, Gershon, and Yoav Peled. 2000. *The New Israel: Peacemaking and Liberalism.* Boulder, Colo.: Westview.
Shafir, Gershon, and Yoav Peled. 2002. *Being Israeli: The Dynamics of Multiple Citizenship.* Cambridge: Cambridge University Press.
Shafir, Gershon. 1996. *Land, Labor and the Origins of the Israeli-Palestinian Conflict, 1882–1914.* Berkeley: University of California Press.
Shaked, Gershon. 1993. *Hebrew Narrative Fiction, 1880–1980, Vol IV* [in Hebrew]. Tel Aviv: Hakibbutz Hameuchad.
Shalev, Michael. 1992. *Labour and the Political Economy in Israel.* London: Oxford University Press.
Shalev, Michael. 2003. "Placing Class Politics in Context: Why Is Israel Welfare State So Consensual?" http://www.geocities.com/michaelshalev/Papers/Shalev_WelfareConsensus.pdf.
Shamir, Ronen. 1999. *The Colonies of Law : Colonialism, Zionism and Law in Early Mandate Palestine.* Cambridge: Cambridge University Press.
Shapira, Anita. 1997. "Ben Gurion and the Bible: The Creation of Historical Narrative" [in Hebrew]. *Alpayim* 14: 207–231.
Shapira, Anita, and Derek Jonathan Penslar. 2001. *Israeli Historical Revisionism: From Left to Right.* London: Frank Cass.
Sharan Shlomo, ed. 2003. *Israel and the Post-Zionists: A Nation at Risk.* Sussex: Sussex Academic Press.
Shechter, Nathan. 2004. "Truth from Yishmael's Land: Post-Zionism in 'MiKan U-Mikan'" [in Hebrew]. *Keshet HaHadasha* 9:160–178.
Sheleg, Yair. 2004. "There Are Fewer Jews, But They Live Better" [in Hebrew]. *Haaretz*, June 24.
Shenhav, Yehuda, ed. 2004. *Coloniality and the Postcolonial Condition: Implications for Israeli Society* [in Hebrew]. Tel Aviv: Hakibbutz Hameuchad–Van Leer.
Shenhav, Yehuda. 2003a. *The Arab-Jews: Nationalism, Religion and Ethnicity* [in Hebrew]. Tel Aviv: Am Oved.
———. 2003b. "The Cloak, the Cage and the Fog of Sanctity: The Zionist Mission and the Role of Religion among Jews in the Middle East." *Nations and Nationalism* 9 (4): 497–515.
Shohat, Ella. 1989. *Israeli Cinema: East/West and the Politics of Representation.* Austin: University of Texas Press.
———. 2001. *Forbidden Reminiscences: A Collection of Essays* [in Hebrew]. Tel Aviv: Kedem and the Author.
Silberman, Neil Asher, and Israel Finkelstein. 2002. *The Bible Unearthed: Archaeology's New Vision of Ancient Israel and the Origin of Its Sacred Texts.* New York: Free Press.
Silberstein, Laurence, J. 1999. *The Post-Zionism Debates: Knowledge and Power in Israeli Society.* New York: Routledge.
Smooha, Sammy. 2002. "The Model of Ethnic Democracy: Israel as a Jewish and Democratic State." *Nations and Nationalism* 8 (4): 475–504.
Sternal, Zeev. 2003. "Settlers Post-Zionism" [in Hebrew]. *Haaretz*, June 20.
"A Survey of Israel: After Zionism." 1998. *Economist*, April 25, 4–18.
Weiss, Meira. 2005. *The Chosen Body: The Politics of the Body in Israeli Society.* New York: Sup.

Weitz, Yechiam. 1997. *From Vision to Revision: A Hundred Years of Historiography of Zionism* [in Hebrew]. Jerusalem: Zalman Shazar Center.

Wheeler, Deborah L. 2003. "Does Post-Zionism Have a Future?" In *Traditions and Transitions in Israel Studies—Books on Israel*, ed. Laura Zittrain Eisenberg, 6:159–180. New York: SUNY Press.

Williams, Raymond. 1985. *Marxism and Literature*. Oxford: Oxford University Press.

Wistrich, Robert S., and David Ohana, eds. 1995. *The Shaping of Israeli Identity: Myth, Memory and Trauma*. London: Frank Cass.

Wolk, Dvir. 2004. "On Dag Nachash." http://www.mixer.co.il/Article/?ArticleID=124605and sid=49.

Yacobi, Haim, ed. 2004. *Constructing a Sense of Place: Architecture and the Zionist Discourse*. Hampshire: Ashgate.

Yacobson, Alexander, and Amnon Rubinstein. 2003. *Israel and the Family of Nations: Jewish Nation-State and Human Rights* [in Hebrew]. Jerusalem: Schocken.

Yadgar, Yaakov. 2002. "From the Particularistic to the Universalistic: National Narratives in Israel's Mainstream Press." *Nations and Nationalism* 8 (1): 55–72.

Yehoshua, A. B. 1984. *In Praise of Modernity: Five Essays on Zionism* [in Hebrew]. Jerusalem: Schoken.

Yiftachel, Oren. 1999. "Ethnocracy: The Politics of Judaizing Israel/Palestine." *Constellations* 6 (3): 364–390.

Yishai, Yael. 2003. *Between Mobilization and Pacification: Civil Society in Israel* [in Hebrew]. Jerusalem: Carmel.

Yuval, Davis, Nira. 2003. "Conclusion: Some Thoughts on Post-Zionism and the Construction of the Zionist Project." In Nimni 2003a, 182–196.

Zanberg, Wester. 2003. "From Vanunu to Topaz" [in Hebrew]. *Haaretz*, April 13.

Zimmermann, Moshe. 2001. "Hannah Arendt, the Early Post-Zionist." In *Hannah Arendt in Jerusalem*, ed. Steven Aschheim, 165–180. Berkeley: University of California Press.

PART II

Expanding the Range of Critique

Engaging the Discourse

5

The Identity of the Victims and the Victims of Identity

A Critique of Zionist Ideology for a Postzionist Age

ADI OPHIR

The Position of the Victim

In his revealing discussion of the concept of *differend* J.-F. Lyotard observed that "it is in the nature of a victim not to be able to prove that one has been done a wrong."[1] In other words, one *becomes* a victim when one undergoes a damage or an injury one is unable to prove. When one is unable to prove a damage, no compensation—no replacement for one's loss—is possible; one's loss is irretrievable. When there is a victim, there is an irretrievable loss; as long as one's loss is irretrievable, one *is* a victim.

Being a victim means being the "owner" of an irretrievable loss. When a damage can be demonstrated and compensation can be claimed and accepted, one's loss is retrievable. When compensation takes place and the loss is retrieved, one ceases being a victim. Through some act of exchange, an object that seemed to be irreplaceable is retrieved or replaced. Such an exchange may be prevented due to certain social, economic, and discursive conditions. It is the victim alone, however, who determines when such conditions take place. It is in the nature of a victim to be unable not only to obtain a replacement for a lost object for which she cares but also to conceive of an obtainable replacement as appropriate. The status of an object or a person as irreplaceable depends on an interested subject that would recognize it, him, or her as such, in its singularity and uniqueness. An object becomes replaceable and one ceases being a victim when one is capable of giving up this sense of singularity and is ready to do so and be content with a certain equivalence of value. A loss becomes absolute and one becomes its "owner" and victim when the lost object is conceived of and experienced as singular and hence irreplaceable.

Reprinted by permission from Adi Ophir, *Mapping Jewish Identities* (New York and London: New York University Press, 1997), 174–200.

The subjective economy of loss cannot be reduced to the objective economy of things. The two are obviously inextricably linked, but at the moment of absolute loss, this link seems to be severed. The absolute loss of an object means that the object is now entirely at the mercy of those who remember it. The object is completely subjectivized; it seems entirely flexible; its contours blur; its resistance diminishes; it has been lost and evaporated into the airy stuff of which memory consists. It is at this moment that the subject assumes full mastery over the object; the object is finally fully possessed. But what seems at first a moment of complete subjectivization *of* the object may turn out to be a moment of complete subjectivization *by* the object. The subject who does not forget and refuses to accept substitutes for an absolute loss is preoccupied with the disappearance of the singular object; he or she is possessed by the very cessation of being of the lost object. The victim of absolute loss is subjugated by the presence of an absence, dominated by a void.

To forget and to remember are two seemingly opposite ways of coping with the presence of an irretrievable loss. The forgetting of a lost object can console because—and as long as—the loss is forgotten together with the object. Remembering a lost object (through its representation in tales, paintings, songs, and, recently, in video clips) is capable of consoling because—and as long as—the representing image or text serves as a replacement, and the loss of the irreplaceable is forgotten. In both cases, the singularity of the lost object is negated. When the object is truly singular and irreplaceable and the loss is absolute indeed, even representation must fail, and memory can only betray this failure. It is in the nature of the victim to insist on this failure and never be content with substitutes and consoling representations.

In most cases, the work of memory, both collective and private, conceals the failure of representation through its very use of ordinary language, common tropes, and images. Hence it is the duty of the artist or the poet who faces an absolute loss to force into presence, in and through the very activity of representation, the failure of representation.[2] Faced with this failure, readers and spectators, who are not necessarily "owners" and victims of this loss, would be reminded of the immemorial; they would not be allowed to forget a debt that can never be paid.[3] Through this work of representation and mourning, they would acquire a sense of absolute loss and would share the position of the victim of a loss of something that has never been in their possession.

Contemporary Jewish culture, in Israel and elsewhere, is inflated with agents that do just that: urge us not to forget the immemorial and remind us of the failure of representation. Several cultural institutions and products come easily to mind here in the context of the commemoration of the Holocaust: Yad va-Shem, the Holocaust Memorial Museum in Washington, the nonmonument for the victims of the Holocaust that is planned for the city of Berlin, the death-camps pilgrimage, Claude Lanzmann's *Shoah*, Steven Spielberg's *Schindler's List*. The learned public often criticizes these institutions and products for their failure to remain within the boundaries of failure, and some of this criticism is justified. The point, however, is not how faithful these cultural agents are to the new standard of representation but that the display of the failure to represent through the work of representation itself has, indeed, become such a standard and is now framing the discourse about memory, remembrance, and loss. At the same time, a sense of an irretrievable loss has become something to be produced, acquired, or purchased; even the experience of absolute loss has become a cultural commodity.

The aura of absolute loss is a cultural construct; cultural agents and institutions of all kinds are involved in its construction. But while much of contemporary Jewish culture is devoted to the production of the aura of absolute loss, other segments of culture are busy, as always, with its effacement—that is, with the systematic effacement of losses as they occur. Both types of cultural practices—both the production and the effacement of the aura of absolute loss—are involved in the making and unmaking of victims, and they do so in opposite directions.

Both types produce victims. In the first case, the position of the victim is acquired through (more or less) willful participation in those practices that produce the aura of singularity by bringing representation to fail. Individuals and groups addressed by an act of failing representation are capable of purchasing a sense of loss with regard to objects that have never been in their possession. They thus learn to share the victim position and are made into subjects of absolute losses. At the same time, in the name of this loss, these individuals are capable of entering social struggles in which some of that loss would be transformed and become retrievable again and thereby would be put back into a circulation in a certain exchange system.

In the second case, when culture effaces absolute losses and negates the aura of singularity of lost objects, the position of the victim may be enforced. The failure of representation is a result of an obstacle imposed by a hegemonic discourse. Such a discourse is inevitably mute to some kinds of phrases; anyone who needs these phrases to articulate a damage would therefore be deprived of the means to prove that damage.[4] This happens because the damage cannot be represented within the constraints of the hegemonic discourse, because one is deprived of access to that discourse, or because there is nobody to take note of one's complaint. The deprived plaintiff becomes a victim.[5]

And yet, as much as *both* types of cultural practices are involved in victimization, *both* may help to unmake victims. When a victim is deprived of the means to prove a damage and the loss she suffers is effaced by a dominant discourse, one should help her re-create an aura of irretrievable loss and let her express her experience in a way that can be shared with others. Against the cultural mechanism and the social system that efface both the loss and the *différend* that accompanies it, one's duty is to identify traces of the loss by recovering a disguised failure of representation. But the reverse may also be true. When consoling practices provide a victim objects and representations to substitute for the lost object, when a consoling discourse distracts attention from the lost object and makes space for forgetfulness and forgiveness, the loss is gradually, even if never completely, effaced. When memory mediates between a subject and the presence of an absence by which he or she has been possessed, the victim may gradually recover.

The Identity of the Victim

People become victims in many, more or less cruel ways. Too often they lose and suffer what they do not deserve, deprived of compensation and relief, in unfair, let alone violent, ways. Yet they do not necessarily get stuck in the victim position. They do not identify with this position; they do not conceive of or imagine themselves through the figure of the victim; and they do not commerce and communicate with others through the mediation of this position and that figure. More accurately, they do it quite often, but without consolidating the figure, without insisting on being hooked to that position, and without melting different victim positions they happen to occupy in different social spheres and in different times into one quasi-transcendental position of an eternal victim. They let others occupy the victim position when it so happens and recognize them as such, and they are ready to leave that position vacant whenever it is possible.

Some modern (especially, but not only, Israeli) Jews are not like other people in this respect. They seem fascinated by the victim position, in love with their losses.[6] It is from there that they start constructing their identity. It may seem that it is because they have suffered a great loss—the loss of a coherent Jewish identity—that they are busy reconstructing their Jewish identity to begin with. But in truth, it is the other way around: it is because they have been in need of a discourse of identity, for various, unrelated reasons, that they have reconstructed this Jewish identity as a loss that could never be fully retrieved. Since they already think about this loss from within the victim position—they are always already there—they cannot imagine that loss of identity apart from the many ways in which they or their ancestors have always been victims. In fact, because changes in Jewish life have been so immense and rapid in this century, sharing the victim position with their ancestors has become for many of them the safest and easiest way to relate to their genealogical roots and construct their identity as the victims' heirs. The many, variegated, and quite different cases in which Jews fell victim to non-Jewish aggression throughout history boil down to one long, repetitive story of victimization.

The apogee of this story is the Holocaust, no doubt. Hence the Holocaust is conceived of, thought, learned, and taught through the prism of the question of Jewish identity. The Holocaust is used and abused as a means in the construction of Jewish identity, and identity questions frame and shape the domain of Holocaust discourse. Therefore many Jews tend to think that they have inherited that unimaginable loss as one receives any other inheritance, by virtue of name and genealogy alone. Hence these Jews are mesmerized by an identity constructed around a victim position, which is mesmerized in its turn by an unimaginable loss, into which all other losses lead or are assembled. It is from an understanding of this mechanism of mesmerism by an absolute loss, by a loss invested with an aura of the irretrievable, that a discussion of "the question of Jewish identity" should commence.[7]

Indeed, the destruction of European Jewry is not the only traumatic event around which the identity of the victim is constructed in Zionist discourse. There is a structural similarity between the fascination of the nationalist Zionist discourse with the loss of the Land and the commemoration of the Holocaust in Israeli culture. Both cases involve a similar structure of identification, constructed in an analogous way around two very different losses: Exile (i.e., the loss of the Land and of sovereignty) and the Holocaust. The whole project of colonization initiated by the right-wing Zionist–religious movement Gush Emunim after the 1967 war may be interpreted in this light as an attempt to endow the Land of Israel with an aura of absolute loss.

In 1961 the trial of Adolf Eichmann transformed the way in which Israeli Jews cope with the memories of the Holocaust. It generated a new culture of memory and commemoration in which the extermination of European Jewry became the paradigm of absolute loss around which the new Jewish identity should be constructed. Six years later, during the weeks before the outbreak of the war, the traumatic preoccupation with the Holocaust shaped how Israeli Jews experienced both the threat posed by the Arab enemies before the war and their victory over their enemies after the war. Fear of an imminent Holocaust was replaced by a euphoric celebration of a miraculous triumph, and in both cases the reading of the political, military, and diplomatic reality was utterly distorted. It is from within this distortion that Gush Emunim was born.

Gush Emunim took it upon itself to accomplish a double displacement of the object of absolute loss. The object of the traumatic loss was displaced from the destruction of European Jewry to the destruction of the temple and the dispossession of the Land. The subject of loss was displaced from the position of eternal witness to the unfinished business of extermination, to the position of an eternal agent working in the unfinished business of redemption. What drove the Jewish colonizers was not simply a claim to regain their hold on a lost and now-reconquered piece of Land; something else was manifested in their discourse and activities. It was the insistence on expressing their claims in the most complicated political circumstances, in ways that have always made it impossible to cater fully to their demands. An immanent complaint about an unfinished business was there from the very beginning. In fact, this is a mark of messianism in general—the present is always conceived as an unfinished business of redemption. Gush Emunim did not introduce the messianic moment into Zionist discourse—that moment had been there from the beginning—but the religious nationalists brought it to perfection with a certain twist. In the case of the Jewish colonizers, what is unfinished is not simply the lack in redemption, imagined from the utopian perspective of a world to come, but precisely the opposite: the excess of loss imagined from the nostomanic perspective of a world that passed away long ago.

The work of colonization, that is, the work of return, of regaining the losses, has not been completed not because "the movement" (i.e., the "Gush") was too weak, or the stubborn people of Israel did not respond to the call, or the time was not ripe. The success of the colonizing project has never been complete because an immanent failure has been inscribed in its logic from the very beginning—an incarnation of the remainder of the loss. This has been the colonizers' greatest success so far. A whole nation is now possessed by the loss of an imaginary object that has never been hers—the Land of Israel. A whole nation is now prepared for the losses of a new war soon to come, which it is willing to justify in advance on the basis of the call emanating from the remainders—reminiscences and reminders—of the old loss.

The displacement of absolute loss by the religious nationalists did not, however, mean a replacement of one project (the commemoration of the Holocaust) by the other (the redemption of the Land). In fact, the two projects were quickly interwoven, feeding each other, each thriving on the myths and practices of the other. In both cases, an identification is constructed through the cultural work that makes present an irrecoverable loss. The visit of Benjamin Netanyahu to Auschwitz in the spring of 1998, marching with the Israeli flag in the death fields and preaching his "lesson" covered with a tallith, was a symbol of both the culmination and the merger of these two projects of identification cum victimization. It was, as Saul Friedlander would have said, a perfect performance of Kitsch and Death performed by Israel's greatest performance artist, its present prime minister.[8]

Being a Victim of Identity: The Postzionist Critique

Various cultural practices cope with the presence of absolute loss. The most paradigmatic is probably psychotherapy, but there are many others: bedtime stories; religious myths of redemption; the national oration that renders the stupid, senseless death of war into a beautiful death worth dying.[9] No doubt, it is not only compassion that motivates these discourses. The very presence in society of individuals possessed by a loss is a disruption of social order, a source of annoying embarrassment and a burden on any economy, since that which is beyond substitution immediately becomes a magnet for an unending stream of pacifying substitutes poured in vain into the abyss. The victim position gained by absolute loss creates debts whose interest one may enjoy for a long time; hence, holding a victim position can always be a strategy in social relations. Moreover, an object may always be endowed with the aura of singularity after it has been lost. Indeed, one of the main targets of psychoanalysis is to expose the economy of investments and gains associated with the subject's insistence on hanging onto the position of a victim of absolute loss. When a whole culture clings to such a position, the only therapy possible is critique, cultural and social criticism. This is, I believe (but will not be able to develop here), part of the role of critical theory in Israel today. Here is a case where a hegemonic culture and a hegemonic ideological discourse have not stopped exploiting the position of the victim as a strategy in both internal and external power struggles. And they have made consistent efforts to maintain this position, even in the many, recurrent situations in which they have represented practices of cruel victimization of others.

Yet, even when the consoling discourse is not simply pacifying but critical, exposing the strategic aspect of the victim position, the experience of loss it has to cope with should not be considered a mere fake. Misrecognition of losses does not reduce pain. The dilemma of the critic is even more acute when critique exposes a loss as senseless and its substitutes as bogus, thus forcing the subject to cope with absolute loss. Truth may be as unbearably painful in this case as misrecognition and fantasy were in the former case. What the so-called postzionists, new historians, and critical sociologists have been doing in Israel in the last decade is precisely to cause this pain. And they have caused it both ways: by depriving Israeli Jews of their victim position, and by forcing them to confront the fact that they have been victimizing others.

This new wave of cultural criticism deprives many Israelis of their ability both to profit from their victim position and to give meaning to their losses when they truly deserve the victim position. The new historians thus exemplify a basic truth about *being* a victim. Unlike *becoming* a victim, which may be a result of contingent, ephemeral forces, *being* a victim means taking, holding to, or being stuck in a victim position, which is always also an effect of a certain structured cultural field. The position of the victim is a cultural construct. It is produced, distributed, acquired, purchased, and sometimes even offered for free. In the case of the new historians, it is taken away, to a lesser or greater extent, from those who feel entitled to it by name, right of inheritance, and personal losses. No wonder those critics have been met with so much anger, condemnation, and contempt, and with so few sober counterarguments.

The victim position has been a major asset of the Zionist movement and, later, of the State of Israel. The point is not to ask how Israeli Jews have become victims and heirs to victims whose injuries cannot be healed and whose losses cannot be retrieved. The point is to understand how the victim position functions in Israeli culture; in the state's ideology, the apparatuses in which it is embodied; and in the construction of the constituting narrative of the Jewish state. The critique of Zionism demonstrates that the victim position functions as a key structural element in the discursive fields in which Jewish and Israeli identities are shaped, negotiated, and fought for.

On the explicit thematic level of the basic Zionist narrative, Israeli Jews are represented as victims and heirs to victims (European Jews) who sought refuge and homeland in their fatherland, where they became victims of Arab violence. Their ongoing struggle against the various forms of violence that permeate every sphere of social life has been carried out in justice with great courage and talent.

In recent years, however, the so-called new historians, using new methodological and ideological perspectives and gathering new historical data, have questioned this narrative. They have taught us that Arab violence was all too often a response to Jewish aggressive colonization. Their writings reveal that Jews had options other than to fight; that their fight was not always courageous and was often unjust and cruel; and that once victorious, Israeli Jews have never shown the generosity necessary to turn an enemy into a friendly neighbor.

On a more implicit level, the new historians question the pragmatics of the Zionist narrative. They expose crucial gaps between this narrative's narrator (the hegemonic subject of Zionist ideology, usually the Ashkenazic Jew), its addressee (every Israeli Jew), and its protagonists (the Chalutz and its contemporary heirs—the settler or the agent of the secret services, etc.). The new historians call into question the all-too-easy collapse of these three narrative figures into the seemingly solid, universal figure of the Israeli Jew. This collapse makes it possible to identify uncritically the narrative's addressee with the figure of the Israeli Jew as a victim-hero.

The problematization of identity enacted by the new historians and critical sociologists, however, does not cease with questioning the identity of victim, whether as a theme of Zionist discourse or as one of its effects. Being a victim is not a ready-made identity but a position with which one identifies, a strategic position to be attained and maintained in various cultural fields. Understanding this enables us to expand and radicalize the critique of the new historians and critical sociologists, for it exposes the ideological work through which the victim position is constructed and maintained. This position is not merely a crucial component of the identity of the Israeli Jew but a key element in the mechanisms that construct it. In other words, what is at stake in the problematization of identity by the critics of Zionism is not merely identity but the forms and practices of identification. It is also the positions that one holds, maintains, loses, or gives up in order to be entitled to an identity and to become authorized to represent it or bestow it on others. The problematization of identification by a critique that radicalizes the work of the new historians subverts the basic structure of Zionist discourse and its ability to continue fabricating the identity of Israeli Jews.

Postzionism: Epoch or Cultural Critique?

As in the debates surrounding postmodernism, so, too, in the debates surrounding postzionism it is useful to distinguish, if only heuristically, between, on the one hand, (post)modernity as a set of historical conditions and, on the other hand, (post)modernism as a style or cultural position or a set of discursive strategies in the realms of art, literature, aesthetics, critical theory, and historiography. Modernism and postmodernism coexist in the contemporary world alongside and against a third major rival—the traditional antimodernist, who longs for a return to a premodern age. One of the main questions at stake in the dispute among these three ideal-types is whether there has been a real epoch-making difference between a modern and a postmodern age. An important difference among the three positions can be articulated through the responses to this question.

Similarly, one may distinguish between two senses of Zionism. On the one hand, Zionism may be conceived as a national movement, a vision, and a discursive regime (all three being interrelated in one project). In this case, anti- or postzionism may be conceived as certain critical stances vis-à-vis Zionist ideology. On the other hand, one may think of Zionism in terms of a set of historical conditions created and dominated by the Zionist project. "Antizionist" may express longings for a prezionist age, while "postzionist" may herald—or mark—the closure of the Zionist epoch. Once Zionism is understood as an epoch that may come to an end, the Zionist narrative of both ancient and modern Jewish history is called into question. At the same time, a Jewish history told from a non-Zionist perspective emerges as a proper context for a critical examination of the Zionist project, declaring the closure of the Zionist epoch, announcing it as a fait accompli, an imminent event, or a desired goal.

Was there indeed a Zionist epoch in the history of the Jews? What was this epoch? Has it really come to an end? If it has, what are the distinguishing features of this postzionist age? The answers to these questions are exactly what is at stake in the debate between Zionists and their anti- and postzionist critics. If there are clear-cut distinctions among these three positions, such distinctions must be articulated in relation to the question of the desired, accomplished, or threatening closure of a Zionist epoch in the history of the Jews. At the same time, the question of this Zionist epoch and its closure cannot be approached without taking a stance in the imaginary triangle defined by these three ideal-type positions.

In response to the question "Has the Zionist epoch come to an end?" Zionists, even critical Zionists, answer with a more or less reserved "no." Zionism is an ongoing project; therefore, one should still work hard to accomplish its unachieved goals. The present history of the Jews, it is argued, should still be thought of from the perspective of Zionist discourse, and its future should still be determined by a Zionist agenda. Antizionists are those who, having opposed

Zionism from its inception, wish to recover a world that was still devoid of its nationalist ideas and political and cultural practices. Antizionists base their identity on the negation of Zionism. They acknowledge that the Zionist epoch is not over yet, that the Zionist project is still alive and kicking, perhaps more violently than ever. For this reason, Zionism should be opposed whenever possible. Thus, Zionist discourse still determines, by way of negation, the antizionists' cultural and political agenda. Understanding Israeli society through the prism of the Zionist project, they conceive of it as a force that still structures this society and determines many of its ruptures and transformations.

Postzionists are presumably those who, while not necessarily accepting old antizionist positions, deny the ongoing viability of Zionism. Thus, for postzionists, the Zionist epoch, an epoch in which the Zionist project held center stage, has come to an end. The major political, social, and cultural problems faced by Israeli and Diaspora Jews today should no longer be formulated within the framework of a Zionist discourse; nor can they be solved according to the principles of a Zionist agenda. Israeli Jews, argue the postzionists, should develop a new democratic, civic discourse, or a new non-Zionist political discourse, rooted in the present conditions of Israeli society. Diaspora Jews should develop their own response to the new conditions of Jewish life; this response is not necessarily related to the Israeli conditions and to the problems facing Israeli Jews.

The Postzionist Label

Before elaborating on the question of the (post)Zionist epoch, I would like to ponder for a moment a simple, somewhat surprising matter of fact. In Israel today, there are very few real, living and kicking, *self-professed* postzionists who adhere to the position I have just defined for them. Moreover, very few people identify themselves as postzionists. I personally know only three or four self-proclaimed postzionists. One is Uri Ram, a sociologist from Ben-Gurion University. For Ram, postzionism is a position that critically accepts certain aspects of postmodern culture and uses them to foster a strong Israeli civil society that would counter recent chauvinistic, nationalist, and fascist trends. Ram's postzionism accepts the existence of a Palestinian state alongside Israel as a fait accompli. Instead of conceiving Israel as a Jewish state, he views it as "a state of all its citizens," Palestinians and Jews alike. In other words, for the postzionist, nationality should not determine citizenship but vice versa: citizenship should determine the boundaries of the Israeli nation. Judaism would then be regarded as a religion, a community affair, or a matter of a particular ethnicity, one among many.[10]

Important as this ideological position is—and I think it is both important and just—it fails to do justice to the term it tries to define. Some liberal Zionists, as well as many antizionists, accept the inversion of the relation between nationhood and citizenship. Many Zionists share with Ram the idea of a strong Israeli civil society that would oppose Jewish nationalism and racism. And, indeed, some of Ram's closest associates in the debate, scholars and intellectuals like Tom Segev, Benny Morris, Yoav Peled, Moshe Zuckermann, and Amnon Raz-Krakotzkin, do not conceive themselves as postzionist or at least have never declared themselves as such. Thus, for example, Moshe Zuckermann, a social theorist who wrote an important study about the ways the imagery of the Holocaust was used during the Gulf War, is a communist and a straightforward antizionist. Benny Morris, who coined the term *new historians* and whose contribution to the historians' debate is perhaps the most important, is a self-proclaimed Zionist. The historian Amnon Raz-Krakotzkin, whose treatise on Zionist "negation of exile" (*shlilalt hagola*) is one of the most influential contributions to the formation of what Zionists understand as a postzionist consciousness,[11] refuses the title consistently. Postzionism, he argues, is an ideology for Jews only. A Palestinian Israeli cannot identify with it even if he or she accepts it to the letter. Thus, postzionism reproduces Zionism's main fault—the radical separation between Israeli Jews and Israeli Arabs.[12] Yet, notwithstanding their disavowal of the label, all these people have been called postzionists, and their works have often been presented as paradigms of postzionist discourse. For their opponents, at least, they occupy a position that precedes them and determines in advance the way they should be read.

The fact that the postzionist position is often associated with postmodernism, as the analogy presented above suggests, only intensifies the impression that the postzionist position has been ready and fixed in advance, regardless of the particular features of the works of those who occupy it. Among the growing group of new historians and critical sociologists, only one historian, Ilan Pappe, has tried to develop a postmodern historiography.[13] But even for him, those explicit postmodern historiographical reflections have never become part of his historical studies. Instead, they mainly serve him as a kind of apology for the ideological non-Zionist position he takes as a historian.

Only recently, however, a new generation of scholars, educated in the United States, England, and France, have introduced concepts, sensibilities, theoretical attitudes, and discursive practices that may be associated with postmodern forms of discourse, especially with postcolonial and feminist theories and with gay studies.[14] While they, too, hardly ever claim to be postzionist, they have been called postzionists by others.

Most of these so-called postzionists have been pushed into that position because of their more or less systematic critique of Zionist ideology and the apparatuses of the Israeli state in which this ideology is embodied and which it serves to legitimate. They are often accused of doing what any decent scholar of culture and society is supposed to do—questioning the conceptual grids and discursive practices of those whom they study, Zionists among others. Thus, for example, the so-called postzionists do not speak about *ohm* but about immigrants; they do not mistake colonization for "redemption of the Land" or occupation for liberation. They examine economic interests behind the "conquest" of the labor market by Jewish hands.[15] Refusing to fully embrace the common image of Israel as "the only democracy in the Middle East," they critically analyze the apartheid aspects of Israeli citizenship.[16] Others explore/reveal the power relations involved in the formation of cultural entities such as Hebrew literature and Israeli art.[17] And they question the binary and teleological structure of the Zionist narrative and its self-evident divisions between "us" and "them," "our enemies." If this is enough to warrant the label "postzionist," then they are postzionists in the same way that critical students of capitalism are postcapitalists and critical students of liberal democracy are postliberals. The "post" affixed to the Zionist stance of those critics of Zionism designates merely a critical examination of an object of discourse and is not very useful.

The "post" may be more informative if, instead of looking for the meaning of the label, one seeks out its pragmatics. For "postzionism" is a label, and labeling is a speech act that serves Zionists as a mechanism of distinction and differentiation, a means of taking and allocating positions in a discursive field. The label functions mainly within Zionist discourse, in academic circles more than elsewhere, and it is certainly used by Zionists much more often than by their critics. Zionist scholars, the old hegemony in the fields of Jewish and Israeli studies (in Jewish history and thought, Israeli sociology, political science, Middle East studies, Hebrew literature), use this label to designate and address certain forms of critique that undermine their claim for legitimacy and authority. By doing this, they achieve two things at once: they determine who is an authorized speaker in the debate and which claims are to be taken seriously.

First, as Raz-Krakotzkin and Silberstein have noted,[18] the label frames the critique of Zionism as an internal Jewish controversy. Israeli Palestinians cannot be postzionists; they have been antizionist all along. The critical discourse developed in the radical left in Israel is thus split in two. The all-too-important voices of Azmi Bishara and a few other Palestinian intellectuals, both in Israel and in the territories, are dissociated from those of their Jewish colleagues and relegated to the old niche of irreconcilable antizionism. As for the Jews, they are often divided between an old form of antizionism, mostly presented as outdated and irrelevant, and postzionism, which is considered worthy of some attention and presented as a deviation "within the family" caused mainly by the corrupting influences and bad intellectual manners of our time, namely, postmodernist theories and jargon. This association means that one should not take the arguments of the postzionists too seriously; it is more important to address the bad, corrupting effects of their discourse. As everyone knows, what postmodernists are best at is the deconstruction of narratives; hence, one should try to retell the narratives they are trying to dismantle.[19]

Indeed, this is the second effect of labeling: it is a convenient way to avoid coming to terms with the opponent's critique. The opponent's position is labeled in a way that undermines his or her authority, sincerity, and objectivity. Postzionist critique, we too often hear, is mean, heartless, cynical, full of self-hatred, and ignores the point of view of those it claims to study; it is relativist, ideologically biased, and imposes its interpretation on the facts or ignores them altogether.[20] These denunciations are well recognized and are repeated again and again, like tropes associated with a certain villain type in an old drama. As such, they are part of the preset position of the postzionist scholar. Their enunciation is supposed to screen out some of the more disturbing claims and effects of Zionism's contemporary critics. These denunciations protect the Zionist scholar from hearing the claims of its critic and seeing what the latter tries to show. Thus, the label "postzionist" functions as an obstacle for a critical dialogue between Zionists and their critics; in other words, it encloses Zionist ideology in a dogmatic position. Or better, it is a symptom of how dogmatic and ossified the latter has already become.

But it is misleading to say that Zionists neither hear what their critics try to tell them nor see what they are trying to show. They hear and see all too well. It is from what they hear and see that the negative reception and vehement rejection of some key postzionist works stem. (I think, for example, of the hostile reception accorded Tom Segev's *The Seventh Million,* Idith Zertal's *The Gold of the Jews,* and, of course, Benny Morris's *The Birth of the Palestinian Refugee Problem.*)[21] What they hear and see is the slow but irreversible process of untying that web of beliefs that used to be Zionist ideology.

One of the key factors in the conditions leading, to the postzionist critique has been a growing sense on the part of Israelis of the post-1948 generation that they have been lied to and deceived. While there are many examples of this sense to be found in the writings of Morris, Gershon Shafir, and Michael Shalev, among others, I offer here a personal testimony. It was not until the autumn of 1982 that I learned the truth about the April 1948 massacre in the village of DirYassin, where two right-wing Jewish militias, the Irgun and the Stern groups, killed more than two hundred villagers after the village had surrendered. Before then, I consistently denied the claim of both Arabs and left-wing Israelis that a massacre had occurred. I refused to believe these claims because my father, who was a member of the Irgun and had actually played a minor part in the atrocities, told me otherwise; and I believed him wholeheartedly. After the massacre in Sabra and Shatila in September 1982, under the impact of the terrible news, he told me that the massacre reminded him too much of another massacre to which he had been a witness many years ago. These are the same kind of inhuman people, he said. It was then that I learned for the first time that he had been lying to me all along. I also learned that he had distorted the truth in a history book, in which he documented the Irgun's activities in Jerusalem during the 1948 war.[22] And I also learned that he did not tell me the whole truth about either the writing of this book or the conflicting versions of the massacre, which the book tries to refute.

I emphasize this experience of disillusionment because it helps convey a sense of how the rather simple feeling of having been duped has led many people, including many of the so-called postzionists, to embrace a critical stance toward Zionist ideology. We have all too often been duped by our parents and teachers, by our army commanders, by our public officials, and by so many representatives who spoke in the name of the state. We have been deceived about the myth of "a few against the many"—there were more Jewish than Arab soldiers in 1948;[23] about the flight of the Palestinian refugees—too many Palestinians were expelled or forced to leave, or shot dead when they tried to return to their homes and fields;[24] about the reasons for the Sinai war; and about the reasons and planning for the Lebanon war.[25] And even as I write these lines, we are being lied to about the so-called peace process and Israel's responsibilities for the stalemate after Rabin's assassination.

The postzionist critique of Zionist ideology, however, goes much further and much deeper than the refutation of some lies or of dubious propaganda. The refutation of these lies and the replacement of euphemisms with proper names clears the space for the acknowledgment that in the Zionist story there are victims other than Jews. Revealing the deception in the dominant Zionist narratives makes possible the representation of the "other" as a victim, not only a victimizer, and consequently allows Israelis the opportunity to accept responsibility for the victimization of others. In other words, the critic of Zionist ideology challenges the dominant image of the Israeli Jew as someone who always already occupies the victim position. This, I think, has been one of the main cultural effects of the research and writing of the so-called new historians and critical sociologists in the last fifteen years.

The Critique of Zionist Ideology

Thus, the new critique of Zionism deprives Israelis of the possibility of continuing to wallow in the identity of eternal, passive, and innocent victims. At the same time, it prevents them from imbuing their losses with a false heroic meaning or significance. "You have not been only victims and heirs to victims," the postzionists are telling their fellows, "you have been constantly victimizing others—Palestinians, Arab-Jews, and even the Holocaust survivors themselves."[26] And they argue this as well: "More than a portion of the sacrifices you have made and of the losses you have suffered have not been necessary. These losses cannot be justified by the usual edifying discourse of the 'beautiful death' for the sake of one's homeland—they have simply been superfluous. And they have been caused to a large extent by your insistence on the role of the victim that has made you blind both to your responsibility for the suffering of others and to the real options you have had to prevent at least some of those unnecessary losses."[27]

However, the "lessons" and some of the arguments that the new historians and critical sociologists make are not entirely new. Without going into details, I mention only some earlier critics of Zionism, such as Hannah Arendt, Martin Buber, and other members of Brith Shalom, and later the Ichud movement, the Palestinian Communist Party, the Matzpen movement, Uri Davis, Uri Avneri, and Simcha Flapan.[28] What distinguishes the new historians and critical sociologists from antizionists, however, and makes them "postzionists" (as Avi Shlaim and Amnon Raz-Krakotzkin have noted)[29] is the fact that, for the first time, the critique of Zionism is being carried out in the discourse of and with the authorial stamp of the academic world, both within Israel and outside it. And yet, this reflects more than a change in the academic world alone. The critique of Zionism became a legitimate academic enterprise and was undertaken by mainstream intellectuals only because, for many Israelis, some of the major themes of that critique have long been self-evident. What has changed is not so much the content of the critique of Zionism but the place it holds within Zionist discourse and within Israeli culture at large. This very change is one of the clear marks of a postzionist epoch.

We may now return to the question posed above: Has the Zionist epoch come to an end? It is through the figure of the victims of the Zionist project, which various kinds of postzionist discourse help to delineate, that the closure of the Zionist epoch appears both inevitable and desirable. By this I do not mean a simple judgment of an end according to the means necessary for achieving it or according to the price that has to be paid. What I mean is that the figure of Zionism's victims is a mirror that reflects—for those capable of seeing—the end of Zionism.

The early Zionists conceived of Jews as victims of anti-Semitic persecutions and of their own degenerate way of life in the Diaspora, yet they did not assume the victim position. They engaged not in mourning irretrievable losses but in creating new forms of Jewish life in (what for them was) a new country. Only later, in Palestine, when conditions changed radically and others became the unexpected victims of their enterprise did they gradually assume the position of the victim. Even the Holocaust did not place them in that position before the Eichmann trial, in which David Ben-Gurion, his attorney general, Eichmann's prosecutor, and a group of court journalists made the easy association between the Nazis of yesterday and the Arab enemies of today.[30] Zionists embraced the victim position after June 1967, when their victimization of others grew both in number and in scope. In the summer of 1982 in south Lebanon, many Israeli Jews realized for the first time that they, too, had become victims of the expanding Zionist enterprise and the Israeli state that speaks in its name. And there were tens of thousands of Arab victims as well. Then came the Intifada, in which Palestinian victims claimed their rights in a way that many Israelis could no longer ignore. It was at that moment, perhaps, that the other was perceived not simply as an accidental victim of some "deviations" (*charigim*) in the functioning of an otherwise decent system of governance but as a victim of the Zionist enterprise itself. The figure of the other as victim subverted the self-image of the Zionist occupying the victim position and has come to reflect the end of Zionism.

The reflection of this end may be formulated by a series of inversions of Zionism's initial claims, goals, and tenets. In each of these inversions, the Zionist project is contrasted with its contemporary realization, which always involves victimization of others.

> The idea of a national liberation movement and the right of national self-determination, upon which the main political claim of Zionism was based, have been systematically undermined, negated, and denied by the success of the Zionist movement. This success has produced the ongoing oppression of another national movement and repeated attempts to destroy it.

> Zionism was a revolt against European anti-Semitism and, later, against racism, and many of those who took part in this struggle were later victims of racism and anti-Semitism. But the struggle has yielded a society that tolerates, and sometimes actively supports, the emergence and consolidation of a Jewish racism that constantly victimizes its others.

> The enlightened struggle to guarantee full civil rights to Jews by means of a sovereign Jewish political entity gave birth to an apartheid system of citizenship. The Jewish state administers populations, territories, and lives according to a strict distinction among six classes of subjects: Jewish citizens; Palestinian citizens ("Israeli Arabs"); Palestinians devoid of citizenship under Israeli martial law; Palestinian semi-citizens of the Palestinian authority in the Gaza Strip, under permanent military curfew; Palestinian semi-citizens of the Palestinian authority in the West Bank, under partial military curfew; and, finally, guest workers denied any legal rights, who too often resemble slaves more than guests.

> The Jewish state achieved some but by no means all of the objectives of Zionism. Even before it was established, the Zionist vision had been embodied in the ideological apparatuses of the emerging state. Today, the state is not an instrument of the Jewish national movement but vice versa. Jewish nationalism in general and Zionist ideology in particular are the state's instruments, used for political purposes. Old and new forms of Zionist discourse serve to legitimate the apartheid system of the Jewish state, Jewish control of the land, continuous

involvement in warfare activities, the ongoing occupation, and the intentional undermining of the processes of negotiation and reconciliation with the Palestinians that were built in Oslo.

Zionism was supposed to transform Jewish economy and turn Jews into productive workers. In the Jewish state, Jews have abandoned most kinds of manual and traditional industrial labor to others. A system of labor relations has formed in which Jews control capital and the means of production while non-Jews work in their fields and factories, sometimes in inhuman conditions, underpaid and exploited.

It is clear that much more than the position of the victim is at stake here. Many of the contemporary conditions of Jewish life in Israel are an inverted realization of the basic tenets of Zionist ideology. The series of inversions presented above may be further extended to include other inversions in which the figure of the other as a victim (or of the victim as other) blurs into the background but does not entirely disappear. At the same time, more Israeli Jews recognize themselves as victims (or potential victims) of the Zionist project and its consequences.

Jews have gained political sovereignty and a mighty army, but Israel, whose population is constantly threatened by conventional, chemical, and nuclear weapons, has become the most dangerous place on the globe for Jews.

Messianic themes have always been present in Zionist discourse, animating its vision. In today's Israeli politics, political themes sometimes animate the messianic form that Zionist discourse has taken. Not that all Zionists have become messianic; but it is in and through discourse dominated by messianic political theology that they articulate their claims.

The melting pot of Jewish ethnic communities has become an overboiling pot of ethnic and religious conflicts. "National Unity" is an empty slogan that witnesses the shattering of unity to pieces. The only thing that keeps all these communities together is the state with its apparatuses, and a war that never ends.

Zionist ideology contained a vision about building a Jewish community in Palestine that would be a spiritual center. To the extent that this Jewish community still maintains spiritual aspirations, they are the most eccentric that Jews have known since the collective suicide on Masada. To the extent that this community maintains a central position in the Jewish world, this position is due first and foremost to the most nonspiritual element in Jewish tradition, the contemporary forms of the sword—conventional, chemical, nuclear. If some spiritual merit is preserved nevertheless, it is either not particularly Jewish or not particularly central.

The Zionist epoch has come to a close precisely because the Zionist vision has been realized. We live in a postzionist age as a direct result of the success of the Zionist enterprise; the realization of the basic tenets of Zionist ideology has inverted these tenets. This is not the place to try to explain why it has all happened this way, nor even to demonstrate that the inversion described above really took place. I assume that it did take place, and that to show this, it suffices to juxtapose a series of commonplaces about Zionism with a series of commonplaces about Israel today. The commonsense nature of this juxtaposition is telling. It makes the systematic failure of Zionist discourse to comprehend the present historical conditions of Jewish life, especially in Israel, both understandable and unavoidable. Zionist discourse reflects the reality it seeks to explain, but this reflection is inverted. Zionist discourse denies this inversion and projects that denial on an imaginary enemy, the postzionist. Zionism was once a vision, a national movement with a political and cultural agenda. The concrete realization of the vision has turned Zionist discourse into an ideology in the strict and most simplistic Marxist sense of the term, except for one thing: the inversion takes place in the open, outside the *camera obscura* and without its help.

Everything that this ideology touches melts into air, into the void created by the straightforward contradictions between what anyone can see for oneself and what a Zionist can say. The contradictions can be observed by everyone; anyone can be the critic of that ideology. The contradictions I have described above are not something I have exposed with the clear mind and analytic tools of an unbiased observer (which I am not) or of a Marxist dialectician (which I also am not). The interesting point about Zionist ideology, since the mid-1980s at least and certainly in the late 1990s, is that the two contradictory descriptions of social reality coexist, side by side, in the public sphere and in the media. They are pronounced by the agents themselves, by the subjects of ideology. They are sometimes even uttered by the same people in the same context of enunciation. Politicians and generals keep telling us how strong and militarily potent and yet entirely vulnerable Israel is. Those who speak about "national unity" exemplify discord and irreconcilable differences in their very preaching to unity. Those who speak for human rights quite often support the major element of the apartheid system—the so-called separation *(hafrada)* between Israelis and Palestinians. Those who condemn racism in one context are willing to tolerate or even support it in other contexts.

There exists an unbridgeable gap between the Zionist representation of historical-political reality and many of its commonsense representations. Many Israelis, so it seems, are not really bothered by this contradictory situation, perhaps because they hardly care for the Zionist discourse anymore.

There is also a frightening minority of dogmatic Zionists who do not care for the real and therefore do not sense any contradiction. But there are many who do sense the contradiction but, being deeply invested in Zionist discourse, are too reluctant to admit it outright and too quick to dismiss or overlook it, hoping that the embarrassment will somehow disappear.

Postzionism plays an important role in how ordinary, commonsense Zionists cope with the contradictory situation created by Zionist ideology. Postzionism serves as a displacement of the contradiction as well as a screen on which it can be projected and become bearable. The contradiction no longer takes place between Zionist representation of historical-political reality and its ordinary, commonsense representation but rather between Zionism and postzionism, conceived as two ideologies with rival truth claims. The figure of the other as a victim also becomes bearable, for it emerges from within a rival ideology that lacks any authority. This displacement may explain why Zionists so often invoke a simplistic association of postzionism with vulgar postmodernism and relativism; they need this caricature of postmodernism in order to salvage themselves from their own embarrassing contradiction. The contradiction is related to the existence of a rival ideological position, and the debate is stuck in a methodological muddle, pushing aside issues of substance. The real, historical conditions that Zionist ideology represents in an inverted way can once again be recognized and ignored, thought and unthought at the same time.

This situation, I believe, is short-lived. In a few years, Zionism will become a relic, an object for museums and history departments only. Postzionism will be remembered as the name for the moment in which Israeli Jews became fully aware of the passing of the Zionist epoch in the history of the Jews. This is the moment in which Israeli Jews will allow people other than Jews to assume the position of victim and assume responsibility for all those "other" victims of the Zionist enterprise.

NOTES

1. Jean-François Lyotard, *The Differend: Phrases in Dispute* (Minneapolis: University of Minnesota Press, 1988), 9.
2. Lyotard develops this theme in his reading of Kant's analytic of the sublime and in many of his essays on paintings. See, e.g., Jean-François Lyotard, *Lessons on the Analytic of the Sublime* (Stanford, Calif.: Stanford University Press, 1994) and "Representation, Presentation, Unpresentable," in *The Inhuman* (Stanford, Calif.: Stanford University Press, 1988): 119–128.
3. The debt stems from the irreplaceability of the singular. If replacement had been possible, the debt would have been canceled, and the loss would have been lost without a trace.
4. This is Lyotard's definition of "wrong" *(tort)* in *The Differend*, 7.
5. This is Lyotard's paradigmatic case, for which many examples can be easily given: for instance, the Bedouin, the Aborigine, and the American Indian cannot prove their

entitlement to a piece of land because their cultures never inscribed the relation between men and their lands in terms of property and ownership.

6. The history of the Jews, in this century at least, may explain this tendency, but it certainly does not justify it. The problem is, however, that this history is already told, for the most part, from within a victim position.

7. I have elaborated on this theme elsewhere. See Adi Ophir, "The Infinity of the Lost and the Finitude of the Solution," in *The Holocaust in Jewish History* [in Hebrew], ed. Dan Michman (Jerusalem: Yad Vashem, 2005), 637–681.

8. Saul Friedlander, *Reflections on Nazism: An Essay on Kitsch and Death* (New York: Harper & Row, 1984).

9. Cf. Lyotard, "Beautiful Death," in Lyotard, *The Differend*, 156.

10. Uri Ram, "Post-Nationalist Pasts: The Case of Israel," *Social Science History* 24, no. 4 (1998): 513–545; idem, "Zionist and Post-Zionist Historical Consciousness in Israel: A Sociological Analysis of the Historians' Debate," in *Zionist Historiography between Vision and Revision* [in Hebrew], 275–289, ed. Yechiam Weitz (Jerusalem: Zalman Shazar Center for Jewish History, 1997); idem, "Between Neozionism and Post-Zionism: A Sociological Clarification" [in Hebrew], *Gesher* 132 (Winter 1996): 93–97. See also Laurence Silberstein, *The Postzionism Debates: Knowledge and Power in Israeli Culture* (New York: Routledge, 1999), introduction and 89–113.

11. Amnon Raz-Krakotzkin, "Exile within Sovereignty: Toward a Critique of the 'Negation of Exile' in Israeli Culture," *Theoria ve-Bikoret* 4 (1994): 23–55 and 5:113–132; Silberstein, *Postzionism Debates*, 175-83.

12. Amnon Raz-Krakotzkin, "Historical Consciousness and Historical Responsibility," in *Between Vision and Revision*, ed. Y. Weitz, 97–134 (Jerusalem: Merkaz Zalman Shazar, 1997).

13. Ilan Pappe, "The New History of the 1948 War," *Theoria ve-Bikoret* 3 (1993): 99–114; and "Critique and Agenda: The Post-Zionist Scholars in Israel," *History and Memory* 7, no. 1 (1995): 66–90.

14. See Silberstein, *Postzionism Debates*, chap. 6.

15. Gershon Shafir, *Land, Labor, and Origins of the Israeli-Palestinian Conflict, 1882–1914* (Cambridge: Cambridge University Press, 1989).

16. See, e.g., Yoav Peled, "Ethnic Democracy and the Legal Construction of Citizenship: Arab Citizens of the Jewish State," *American Political Science Review* 86, no. 2 (1992): 432–443; idem, "Strangers in Utopia: The Israeli Palestinian Citizens" [in Hebrew], *Theoria ve-Bikoret* 3 (1993): 21–35; Danni Rabinowitz, *Overlooking Nazareth* (Cambridge: Cambridge University Press, 1996).

17. For literature, see, e.g., Hannan Hever, "The Struggle over the Canon," *Theoria ve-Bikoret* 5 (1994): 55–77. For art, see, e.g., Ariella Azoulay, "The Possibility for Critical Art in Israel," *Theoria ve-Bikoret* 2 (1992): 89–117; and Sara Chinski, "The Silence of the Fish," *Theoria ve-Bikoret* 4 (1994): 105–122.

18. Raz-Krakotzkin, "Historical Consciousness and Historical Responsibility"; and Silberstein, *Postzionism Debates*, 113–126.

19. See, e.g., Anita Shapira, "Politics and Collective Memory: The Debate over the 'New Historians' in Israel," *History and Memory* 7, no. 1 (1995): 9–40; Aharon Megged, "Israeli Suicidal Desire," *Haaretz*, June 10, 1994, 27–28.

20. See, e.g., Megged, "Israeli Suicidal Desire"; Gideon Kersel, "Mentality: Intelligence, Morality, and Jewish-Arab Conflict," *Theoria ve-Bikoret* 8 (1996): 47–72.

21. Tom Segev, *The Seventh Million: The Israelis and the Holocaust* (New York: Hill and Wang, 1993); Idith Zertal, *The Gold of the Jews* (Berkeley: University of California Press, 1998); Benny Morris, *The Birth of the Palestinian Refugee Problem* (Cambridge: Cambridge University Press, 1987).
22. Yehushua Ophir, *Al Hachomot* [On the walls] (Ramat-Gan: Massada, 1960).
23. There were more Jewish than Arab soldiers in 1948, at least until the invasion of the Arab states in May 1948. Cf. Uri Milstein, *History of the War of Independence* (Lanham, Md.: University Press of America, 1996), 1:184.
24. Morris, *Birth of the Palestinian Refugee Problem*; and idem, *Israel's Border Wars, 1949–1956: Arab Infiltration, Israeli Retaliation, and the Countdown to the Suez War* (Oxford: Clarendon, 1997).
25. About the Sinai war, see Motti Golani, *Israel in Search of a War: The Sinai Campaign, 1955–1956* (Brighton: Sussex Academic Press, 1994). About the Lebanon war, see Zeev Schiff and Ehud Yaari, *The War of Deceit* (Jerusalem: Schocken, 1984).
26. See, e.g., Segev, *Seventh Million*, part 3; Ella Shohat, "Sephardim in Israel: Zionism from the Standpoint of Its Jewish Victims," *Social Text* 19–20 (1988): 1–35.
27. Avi Shlaim, *Collusion across the Jordan* (Oxford: Clarendon, 1988); Gershon Shafir, The Yaring Affair," *Theoria ve-Bikoret* 12–13 (1999): 205–213.
28. Nira Yuval Davis, "Matzpen, the Socialist Organization in Israel" (Master's thesis, Hebrew University of Jerusalem, 1977); Simcha Flapan, *The Birth of Israel: Myths and Realities* (New York: Pantheon, 1987); Uri Avneri, *Israel without Zionists: A Plea for Peace in the Middle East* (New York: Macmillan, 1968); Silberstein, *Postzionism Debates*, chaps. 2 and 3.
29. Avi Shlaim, "The Debate about 1948," *Journal of Middle Eastern Studies* 27 (1995): 287–304; Raz-Krakotzkin, "Exile within Sovereignty."
30. See Idith Zertal, "From the People Hall to the Wailing Wall: A Study in Memory, Fear, and War," *Representations* (March 2000): 96–126.

6

Academic History Caught in the Cross-Fire

The Case of Israeli-Jewish Historiography

BARUCH KIMMERLING

The main purpose of this essay is to analyze the interplay of the creation of an Israeli academic historiography with the process of building a settler society, which has continually experienced violent resistance to its basic precepts and corresponding problems of internal and external legitimacy. This historiography was an integral part of the process of nation and collective-identity building, which placed the discipline under cross-pressures of Zionist commitment, on the one hand, and an effort to meet the standards of professional ethics, on the other, including a positivistic philosophy that assumed the negation of ideological influences, as formulated by Leopold von Ranke in the late nineteenth century.

Building an Immigrant-Settler Society

Political Zionism crystallized and emerged on the eve of the European colonial period, which perceived as self-evident the right of Europeans to settle any available non-European land. However, "Zion," contrary to the other lands targeted for colonization by Europeans, was not selected because of the abundance and quality of its land, its natural wealth, or its political accessibility. Zion was chosen because it was the only land that could awaken the sentiments needed among world Jewry in order to develop a movement devoted to immigration and the building of a new society, as opposed to the personal and familial salvation-emigration to North America.[1] In order to mobilize the Jews,

---

Reprinted, by permission of Indiana University Press, from Baruch Kimmerling, "Academic History Caught in the Cross-Fire: The Case of Israeli-Jewish Historiography," *History and Memory* 7, no. 1 (Spring/Summer 1995): 41–65. I would like to acknowledge the valuable comments I received on a previous version of this paper from Don Handelman, Eric Cohen, and Ilan Troen. I am grateful to Ezra Kopelowitz for his assistance in editing this article.

a selected arsenal of primordial symbols and myths taken from Jewish religion was partially secularized and nationalized to suit Zionist purposes.[2] This secularization of selected ingredients of the religion contributed to creating a new nationalism, in which the partially reconstructed and partially invented past, or history, was employed to fuse the past with the present and the future. The overt purpose of these activities was to make a direct linkage between the "Jewish past" of the land and the contemporary situation of Zionist colonization. The "Jewish past" and history were perceived as a major source of legitimacy for the Zionists' claim for title over the land in opposition to the local Arab population's counterclaim to be the exclusive legitimate owner of the land.[3]

Some immigrant-settler societies, such as those in North America, Australia, or New Zealand, succeeded in annihilating the native populations; others managed to absorb the native population within new stratification systems and established newly assimilated nations. In other cases—as in Algeria, Rhodesia, and South Africa—the local native population succeeded, following long and bloody struggles, in overthrowing the immigrant-settler ruling system. However, in the Jewish-Arab (later relabeled the Jewish-Palestinian) conflict over the land of Palestine, which has lasted about one hundred years through the present, none of the parties is strong enough to achieve a decisive victory. The conflict has changed from time to time in its patterns of conduct, rules, and means, but has basically remained a total conflict, perceived by both parties as being of a zero-sum character.[4] In such a conflict, material and human resources are mobilized most of the time, including intellectual capacities; history, historians and historiography also play a crucial role.

For this reason a nationalist historiography is not only created as part of nation-building efforts. Such "nationalist historiography," asserts Elie Kedourie, "operates a subtle but unmistakable change in traditional conceptions. In Zionism, Judaism ceases to be the raison d'être of the Jews, and becomes, instead, a product of Jewish national consciousness. In the doctrine of Pakistan [ism] Islam is transformed into a political ideology and used in order to mobilize Muslims against Hindi."[5] Moreover, in such cases historiography became both a part of, and a weapon in, the process of conflict management. One of the consequences in Zionist (as well as Arab) historiography is what E. H. Carr has called the "inability to achieve even the most elementary measure of imaginative understanding of what goes on in the mind of the other party, so that the words and actions of the other are always made to appear mauling, senseless or hypocritical."[6] As will be demonstrated later, Israeli historiography used several sophisticated strategies to recruit history as a powerful tool in its struggle on two fronts: in the struggle of Zionism against other streams in Judaism, and in the struggle against the Arabs and Palestinians.[7] Both "fronts" have double targets: the external enemy and the need to legitimize Zionist ideology and realities amongst the domestic "constituency," in order to avoid an internal legitimation crisis.[8]

Making a Zionist Historiography

Germany before the rise of Nazism was considered the largest academic center of Judaic studies. When the Nazi regime came to power most of the scholars of Jewish origin left Germany, with a group of them emigrating to Palestine. While the most influential professors in the field such as Eugen Taeubler (1879–1953) or Ismar Elbogen (1874–1943) emigrated to the United States, many of their students came to Palestine.[9] The tiny Hebrew University of Jerusalem and its Institute for Jewish Studies were able to hire only a small minority of these and other German-speaking scholars. Both inside and outside the university, including the original founders of the Hebrew University's Jewish Studies Department, most historians were German speakers or heavily influenced by German historiography. Of those considered as key figures and included amongst the most influential and powerful figures at the Hebrew University were Yitzhak Fritz Baer and Ben Zion Dinur in Jewish national historiography.[10]

From the very beginning, the Hebrew University benefited from the presence of other outstanding and charismatic scholars in history and other closely related disciplines within Jewish studies, most of whom had developed within the German tradition. Martin Buber, an established German philosopher and sociologist, did important work on the Hasidic movement and ideology. Gershom Gerhard Scholem, a founder of the Hebrew University and a scholar of Jewish mysticism and its history, was educated at the University of Berlin. Arthur Ruppin was born in Prussia and was a graduate of the University of Berlin in economics, sociology, demography, and law. Ruppin, who held the chair of the "sociology of the Jewish people" at the Hebrew University from 1926 until his death in 1943, was an important Zionist political leader who initiated the major settlement drives in Palestine of his time. Yehezkel Kaufmann, who was born in the Ukraine and studied at the University of Bern, was appointed Professor of Bible at the Hebrew University in 1939; he had spent much time in Berlin contributing to the German Jewish Encyclopedia. Samuel Hugo Bergman, who was of Czech origin and a philosophy graduate of the universities of Prague and Berlin, was appointed lecturer at the Hebrew University in 1928. Although he was not clearly considered a "Judaist," he was influenced by Buber and contributed to modern Jewish thought. Joseph Klausner, born in Vilna and educated in Germany, specialized in the history of Hebrew literature and of the Second Jewish Kingdom; he held a double chair at the Hebrew University. To this group can be added the likes of Raphael Mahler, Ernst Simon, the economist Alfred Bonné, the Talmudist E. E. Urbach, and others.[11] Most of them had received a traditional-religious yeshivah education.

Despite many of the thematic, educational, temperamental, and generational differences, this group of scholars shared not only a common fate, as relatively marginal immigrants who formed part of an elite that was in many ways alienated from mainstream Zionist political life in Palestine, but also a common cultural and intellectual tradition. In a sense their approach was the inverse of that of Heinrich Graetz and Simon Dubnow, who were the founding fathers of modern Jewish historiography. Graetz and Dubnow emphasized the national character of Judaism, although they presented the Jewish nation in the modern era as a nonterritorial entity. Thus, Eretz Israel (the Land of Israel) was considered as a part of Jewish history, but not as a necessary condition for survival. This non-territorial form of nationalism was unacceptable in Zionist historiosophy and the reconstruction of Jewish history in terms of territorial ethnonationalism.

In constructing a new Zionist historiography, they relied on important ingredients of German neo-Romanticism and historicism. Researchers such as Robert Jutte and Shmuel Almog have not hesitated to call this group a school; while others like David Myers have doubts about the existence of a homogeneous "Jerusalem School."[12] At the very least Scholem, Dinur, and Baer shared a common perception of Jewish history as an internally coherent unity extending beyond the particularities of place and time, and despite the dispersal of the Jews. The Jewish people was presented as a national organism that had survived several millennia thanks to its vitality and acute historical consciousness. They stressed the centrality and inevitability of the "Land of Israel" (Eretz Israel) in this consciousness and situated the exile (*galut*) in a dialectical relationship with the "Land of Israel." They viewed the political organization of the Jewish communities in exile (the *kehillah*) and its relative autonomy as an alternative structural framework that had preserved the Jewish Volk. This issue was probably the only departure from the Zionist ideology of the time, which tended to refer to the Jews in exile as powerless and sought to negate the galut. In 1936 the group founded a Hebrew scholarly periodical, entitled Zion, which set the boundaries of "legitimate," "good," or "acceptable" Jewish-Zionist historiographical writings.[13]

This was the historical ideological background and starting point of the academic and canonical new Jewish historiography which crystallized in Jerusalem and radiated its impact on the future establishment of Israeli social science.[14] Since those early days, Israeli historiography has both expanded enormously and diversified. New, and in some senses competing, departments, schools, and research institutions were created, new generations of scholars made their appearance, and almost every part of the Jewish past and contemporary Israeli history was analyzed and reanalyzed. New scholarly journals in Hebrew and English were established, with an enormous quantity of books and papers published in all genres. The very nature of history as a vocation changed as new paradigms appeared and disappeared along with their associated methodologies, especially given the involvement of almost all the subfields of the social sciences in Israel in the creation of Israeli historiography.[15]

From another angle, some of the basic characteristics of Zionist society, as shaped in the 1920s and 1930s, changed their scope and composition, while the concepts used to describe it remained the same. At the university level one of the first chairs established at the new Hebrew University was dedicated to Palestine Studies and was held (from 1924 to 1940) by Samuel Klein, a Hungarian rabbi, educated at the Orthodox Rabbinseminan of Budapest and Berlin (where he developed his interest in the historical geography of Palestine) as well as at the universities of Berlin and Heidelberg. Klein was an Orthodox Jew who had converted to Zionism and had published before his immigration political essays, which asserted the exclusive right of the Jewish people to settle Palestine. His courses at the Hebrew University were in great demand by the students and provided in Klein's words "a testimony to ourselves, and in face of the nations of the world, that we never gave up the right of existence in our land, and also evidence of the justice of our demand to build an eternal home in it, like any other people inhabiting their own country."[16]

At the present time, Israeli historiography is still forced to confront these concepts when discussing issues such as the basic legitimacy of a Jewish collectivity in the context of the struggle with the Palestinian national movement (as formulated by Klein), the continuously perceived threat to the very existence of the collectivity, as well as the relations of the Zionist enterprise and ideology vis-à-vis other Jewish alternatives and diasporas. The issue of the nature of the collective identity here and now, as a result of its changing form over the ninety years of Zionist colonization of the territory, has never been resolved, and historians and scholars in other related "sciences" have been charged with supplying instant answers, which are always regarded as socially and politically pressing. In other words, the persons who dealt with historiography were required not only to maintain a high professional (and, for some, academic) standard as historians, but also to write as devoted Zionists (which is indeed how they perceived themselves).

Historiography in the Cross-Fire

As Eric Hobsbawm has asserted,

> no serious historian of nations and nationalism can be a committed political nationalist, except in the sense in which believers in the literal truth of the Scriptures while unable to make contributions to evolutionary theory, are not precluded from making contributions to archaeology and Semitic philology. Nationalism requires too much belief in what is patently not so.... Historians are professionally obliged not to get it wrong, or at least to make an effort not to. To be Irish and proudly attached to Ireland is not itself incompatible with a serious study of Irish history. To be a Fenian or an Orangeman is not so compatible, any more

than being a Zionist is compatible with writing a genuine serious history of the Jews; unless the historian leaves his or her convictions behind when entering the library or the study.[17]

The Israeli case seems different from Hobsbawm's assertion, as the vast majority of contemporary academic historians and social scientists in Israel are not only Zionists, but also "proudly attached" to their Zionist convictions when producing their historiographical output, no less than the founding fathers of their vocation. At the same time they try to maintain high standards of scholarship, including the publication of their works in respectable referee journals and university presses abroad. However the major body of Israeli-Zionist historiography is still only available in Hebrew (in contrast with the works published by social scientists). There is an awareness of the danger of producing a parochial or sectarian "science of history," due to the small size of the academic community and the distance of the country from the leading scientific centers. However, when ideological commitments collide with standards of objectivity and impartiality, usually the "Zionist orientations" receive primacy. This general argument must be broken into smaller parts, in order to demonstrate the specific techniques, methods and practices that are employed to produce a heterogeneous Zionist historiography. As Zionist ideology is far from a monolithic world view, Zionist history also has many variations. However, two presumptions are common to all the variations: (1) the unequivocal right of the Jewish people to the Land of Israel (referring to the fact that the geopolitical boundaries of this right are under permanent dispute, or the subject of bargaining); and (2) the ultimate and only correct Zionist "solution" to the so-called "Jewish problem" is the creation of an independent Jewish state (sometimes called a "commonwealth," "polity," or "national home") in what is perceived as the ancient fatherland, here and now (and not in a messianic or utopian future).

This historiography, over and above its internal variations, has an ideological bias that appears in the implicit and explicit use of seven main methods.

1. Key Concepts

It is well known that words and concepts shape our cognition and patterns of thinking. Israeli historiographers use two key concepts—mainly in Hebrew—that in many cases precondition the results and the conclusions of their research, without even being aware of the far-reaching consequences of their use. The first basic concept is the name of the territory that became the target land of the Zionist aspiration, *Eretz Israel*. The literal translation of the term is of course the Land of Israel (or the Land of the Jews), which is used indiscriminately for all historical periods, including periods when there were no Jews living in the land or when the territory was ruled by other powers, as in the expressions "Eretz Israel in the Byzantine Era," "Eretz Israel under the

Crusaders" or "Eretz Israel in the Ottoman Period." By using the concept in such a way, the historian grants the Jews an eternal title over the territory, regardless of who populated or governed it, even in a situation when the "legitimate ownership" of the land was under dispute.[18]

The second key concept is the Hebrew term *aliyah* (literally "ascent"). It has two major meanings in modern Hebrew that overlap its meaning in historiography. The first meaning is the act of Jewish immigration to Palestine/Eretz Israel/Israel. Some would add that this implies that aliyah is not just immigration, but an ideologically or religiously motivated activity. However, it is accepted today that regardless of motivation any immigration to Israel is aliyah. The Hebrew word for immigration/emigration, *hagirah*, is applied to other kinds of Jewish or non-Jewish voluntary population movements. The second use of the term "aliyah" is in reference to one of the five officially recognized waves of pioneer Zionist immigration to the country between 1882 and approximately 1939.

However, the origin of the term "aliyah" is purely sacred, or religious. It initially referred to the pilgrimage made three times a year during the Second Jewish Commonwealth period, when, on the three major holidays, Jews were obliged to ascend to the Jerusalem Temple and to bring tributes and sacrifices to God and his holy servants, the priests of the Temple. After the dispersal, the term was used in two contexts: in the synagogue, calling a person to read from the holy scriptures was an "aliyah to the Torah," the supreme act of affinity to the holiness; and the pilgrimage of those who succeeded in immigrating to Eretz Israel, mainly for burial purposes, was called aliyah. Zionist terminology, incorporated the term for any kind of immigration to Eretz Israel or Israel, in order to present the act as ideological-Zionist immigration, even though the majority of Jewish immigrants were not motivated by Zionist convictions (which is not to say that they did not subsequently absorb Zionist tenets into their self-identity in varying degrees).

With very few exceptions Israeli-Zionist historiography adopted this term, and it is often routinely used even in foreign-language publications. Other biased or loaded terminology is also systematically used, particularly in reference to the Arabs and the Jewish-Arab conflict. Any Arab or Palestinian resistance to Jewish colonization is described as "riots," "disturbances," or even "pogroms." The use of the term "pogrom" has the effect of reducing the Jewish-Arab/Palestinian national conflict over the land to the traditional relations between persecuted Jews and antisemitic gentiles, thus relocating the conflict through the use of terminology within a different, and seemingly more convenient, historical, conceptual, and political context.[19]

2. Periodization

Any kind of periodization, or division of the past into distinct categories, shapes to a large measure the patterns and the content of the past (and maybe the present as well).[20] Zionist historiography employed three kinds of periodization. The first is based on a division into two periods—before and after the rise of the independent and sovereign State of Israel. Several consequences of this periodization will be discussed later. The second periodization is based on the five main waves of immigration: the "First Aliyah" (1882–1903), the second (1904–1914), the third (1919–1923), the fourth (1924–1931), and the fifth (from approximately 1932–1945 or 1948). The third basis for periodization is the Arab-Israeli wars (e.g., 1948–1956, 1956–1967, and so forth).

In itself, periodization according to the *aliyot* (plural of aliyah) makes sense as each wave of immigration changed the composition, the scope and the major agendas of the collectivity. However, the actual use of this specific form of periodization has several implicit results:

(a) The definition of the wave of immigration from 1882 to the turn of the century as the "First Aliyah" within a successive continuity creates the impression that this was a Zionist ideological settlement enterprise which predated the Zionist movement proper. In fact, the first wave was the result of a Jewish religious impulse, not very different from the German Templer immigration to Palestine a decade earlier. The Zionization of this immigration deepens the roots of the Zionist movement; after all, these early settlers did become *post factum* part and parcel of the Zionist collectivity, although the inclusion process of this group is usually missing from Zionist historiography.

(b) The immigrants of the second and third waves were highly ideological and politically motivated, coming from the hard core of the newly established Zionist movement. The fourth and fifth waves of immigrants were refugees who arrived in Palestine from Poland and Germany, mostly as a result of the extremely restrictive immigration laws that had been adopted in the United States. The use of the same term "aliyah" regardless of the differences between the waves of immigration—ideological or not—constructed a "reality" common to all the immigrants, who were all considered as ideologically motivated, and this in turn limited the scope and questions of historical research.

(c) The aliyot were connected to the heroic Zionist ethos of sacrifice, asceticism, and pioneering, demanded by the grand struggle against nature, human nature, and external political powers in order to build a new nation and a new Jewish man (the women were marginal in this "story"). Since 1945 or 1948 there have been at least five great waves of immigration to Israel, each of which has considerably changed the social fabric and culture of Israeli society. Ending the periodization of history, according to aliyot in 1948, had at least two implications: First, the latecomers were not considered on a par with the heroic earlier immigrants, which meant that they were not entitled to the cultural rewards reaped by the founding fathers of the nation.[21] Second, the shift to another basis of periodization—the binary, periodization of before and after the establishment of the sovereign state—implied that the process of state and society building had been concluded by the first five aliyot and that the changes that had since occurred were only extensions or improvements (or even a worsening) of the basic sociopolitical patterns that had been established between 1882 and 1948. Needless to say, such social construction of history served to bolster the "stability" of the basic sociopolitical order and the existing ruling elites, as well as the attempt to reproduce this order in subsequent generations, despite the fundamental social changes that had taken place.

(d) The switch to periodization of history according to wars meant stressing the "statist" nature of the society since 1948. As Tilly put it, "wars make states and states make wars," and the Israeli state was without doubt consolidated over the course of several wars, mainly those of 1948, 1956, and 1967.[22] War became the central common and private experience of the "Israeli man."[23]

3. Teleological Explanations

Teleological explanations give meaning to historical events in terms of the implications they might have for other events and grant them significance in terms of some "destiny" toward which history is supposedly moving. By and large, most of the secular historiography produced by Jews in Israel, or in the presovereign Jewish community in Palestine, leads to the statist "Zionist solution" of the "Jewish question." A commodified version of the entire span of Jewish history, including the Holocaust, is recruited in order to lead the consumer of historiography to this one inevitable conclusion to the exclusion of any alternatives. Some "canonic" historiographical enterprises exemplify this and the other techniques mentioned here, such as most of the entries in the Encyclopaedia Hebraica, especially the entry on Eretz Israel, and the planned four-volume History of the Jewish Community in Eretz Israel since the First Aliyah.[24]

4. Exceptionalism

Many historical schools of thought consider every historical event, and even more so every single "case study," as a unique and incomparable instance, while other historians, and especially social scientists, tend to view historical events from within a comparative theoretical framework. In this light, Israeli historians and sociologists see Zionism as the only utopia ever implemented, even though it still suffers from a number of troubles.[25] Most Israeli historians and social scientists argue explicitly or implicitly for the historical exceptionality and uniqueness of the Jewish and Israeli case. The survival of the Jews as a nation (sic!) over a period of at least 3,000 years is presented as a unique historical case (what about the Gypsies, the Greeks, the Chinese, and the Japanese?). Antisemitism is presented and analyzed as a unique phenomenon of Jew-hatred, which included the Holocaust.[26] The creation of Israel, through the "ingathering of the exiles" and its victory in the 1948 "War of Independence" over the Palestinian community and "seven Arab states" are presented not only as unique, but often in metaphysical or mythological terms. This approach of uniqueness by historians and social scientists is borrowed directly from the Zionist ideological handbook, which was written under the strong influence of the exclusionary tendencies that exist in many streams of Judaism.

Resistance to comparing Israeli society with any other existing society plays a specific role in Israeli historiography. By defining their material a priori as a unique case, historians and social scientists are freed from the need to characterize Israeli society as a specific societal type.[27] A historical-comparative approach would define Israel as an immigrant-settler society, comparable on the one hand to the North and South American nations, Australia or New Zealand, and, on the other hand, to Algeria (of the *pieds noirs*), Rhodesia or the Boers' society of South Africa. It would thus oblige the historian to deal with Israel's colonial legacy, the very allusion to which is taboo, in both Israeli society and Israeli historiography.[28]

5. Boundaries of the Examined Collectivity

The Judeocentric trends among Israeli historians are not only a psychological or cultural trait, but also part of the shaping of diverse sociopolitical control systems in different historical periods. For example, during the British colonial period (1918–1948) the major sociopolitical efforts of the Jewish community, the so-called Yishuv, were toward building a separate, segregated polity as independent as possible from the British colonial state's services (excluding security and law enforcement) and the Arab majority's supply of merchandise and labor. The policy was formulated as a strategy for creating a quasi-state, or an apparatus for the state-in-the-making, that would fill the power vacuum after the predicted British withdrawal and take control over a substantial part of the land, despite the Jewish population's minority status within the colonial state.[29] Jewish and Israeli historiography followed this logic, drawing the boundaries of the collectivity (i.e., the subject of research and analysis) as an almost exclusive "Jewish bubble." Conceptually the British state and the Arab population were not included within the collective boundaries. When the Arabs and the British do appear, they are treated as external forces and residual categories, entering and exiting from the analysis like the *deus ex machina* of Greek tragedies.[30]

After the 1948 war about 150,000 Arabs remained within the cease-fire frontiers of Israel and were granted formal citizenship and citizen rights. Between 1949 and 1966 these Arabs were excluded from "Israeli society" and its labor market by a harshly imposed military government which implemented extremely restrictive control and surveillance methods. Correspondingly, within Israeli history and the social sciences the Arab population of Israel has been almost unanimously neglected.[31] When historians and social scientists analyze "Israeli society," they include only Jews in their research samples. When social research on pluralism and social mobility in Israel is done, the subjects are self-evidently Jewish.[32] Even public opinion polls have until recently included exclusively Jewish samples. This seems to work congruently with the political and legal perception of Israel as the state of the Jewish people residing both within and outside its boundaries, rather than as the state of its citizens (which would also include Arabs). Thus, Israel's boundaries have been drawn in a way that potentially includes a greater population than those who are actually citizens of the state, but partially excludes the non-Jewish citizens. Israeli historiography and sociography both reflect and reinforce the sociopolitical reality.

The use and abuse of boundary-drawing became even more salient after the 1967 war. Approximately two million Palestinian residents of the West Bank of Jordan and the Gaza Strip were incorporated within the Israeli control system, all without citizen rights (and the different agreements with the Palestinians have not changed this situation). Most of the occupied territories were not annexed (in order to avoid Palestinian claims for citizen rights or even their partial inclusion within any "boundary" that could qualify them to make a right-associated claim); yet, the land became a frontier space for Israeli-Jewish settlements and for many years a reservoir of cheap labor and a market for Israeli products. For exclusionary purposes an ethnonational boundary of the collectivity was drawn (the State of Israel), while for purposes of inclusion a boundary of coercive military control was fixed for the Palestinians, which coincided with the primordial Jewish boundaries (Eretz Israel).[33] Keeping control of and settling the occupied territories, while excluding the Palestinian population from the boundaries of the collectivity, made it possible to continue pretending that the rules-of-the-game within the State of Israel were democratic and in accord with accepted Western political standards. Hence the possible avoidance of references to the entire control system as a single unified sociopolitical entity, which would make Israel more like a model of Herrenvolk-democracy than that of a Western-style democracy. Israeli historiography and sociography almost completely adopted the exclusionary model of the polity, which not incidentally was more convenient ideologically.[34]

6. Antiquity

Zionist historiography—the historiography of an immigrant-settler nation— heavily stressed the ancient roots of the Jewish people in Eretz Israel, not simply on the general historical level, but also by the restructuring and invention of specific myths, such as the Masada myth or what Harkabi has labeled the Bar Kokhba syndrome.[35] On their side, the Palestinian "natives" were challenged to invent and create a countermythology. This land became known as Palestine following the Philistines and other Canaanite peoples who settled the coastal plain of the country in 1190 B.C., but were routed by King David in a series of bitter battles over the land. These semihistorical and semimythological occurrences of 3,000–3,500 years ago are still used and abused as "historiography" in the present struggle over the land of Palestine. Now, the Palestinians insist that they are the direct successors of the Canaanites in general and the Philistines in particular.[36]

The strange "historical race" between the Jews and Palestinians over the question of who succeeded whom has other less anecdotal consequences. Yehoshua Porath's pioneering and well-researched history of the Palestinian national movement was unable to establish—due to the lack of a conceptual or comparative framework—whether such a national movement existed at all and, if it existed, what its nature was. Arbitrarily, Porath's Palestinian history more or less began with the inception of the British colonial regime, and the whole enterprise placed the Palestinian collectivity within an ahistorical context.[37] However, when a social history of the Palestinians was published that predated the beginning of Palestinian collective activity to the Jewish colonization of the country, it provoked a kind of moral panic in Israel and an unprecedented public intellectual debate about the essence of history, the nature of Zionism, and relations with the Arabs and Palestinians.[38]

7. Intentions versus Consequences

Israeli-Zionist historiography tends to stress the inward and outward intentions of the settlers. Internally, their intentions were to build a just and harmonious society, which would not cause harm to another collectivity. Even though the land was not "empty," as some Zionist ideologues put it at the beginning of the colonization process, Jewish settlement was expected to be a benevolent enterprise that would bring progress and prosperity to all the inhabitants of the land. The complete rejection of Zionist colonization by the local population was perceived by mainstream Zionism as a lack of understanding of the benefits that would accrue to both Arabs and Jews. For the Jews this was a strategy of conflict reduction, necessary in a situation in which they constituted a small fragment of the population.[39] From the Arab perspective, Zionist colonization from its incipient stages was perceived in terms of its consequences; namely, the creation of a polity at the expense of the local population. The zero-sum quality of the land as well as the changing composition of the population (as the result of Jewish immigration) was stressed, and the "Zionist invasion," especially since the British colonial era, was equated with the "Crusader conquest" of the Holy Land by European colonialists.

Several Conclusions

Historiography in general, and academic discourse in particular, are embedded in an active form of knowledge that shapes collective identity by bridging between different pasts (recovered, imagined, invented, and intentionally constructed) and creating meanings and boundaries for the collectivity. Within a highly ideological and mobilized society, which within a relatively short span of time created a culturally heterogeneous immigrant-settler society and shortly thereafter a state, the agents who create the "past" occupy a central position. The scope of historiographical "output" is intensified by the internal struggles of different elite groups—political, military, cultural and economic— each with diverse personalities and "celebrities," all of whom are anxious to assure their place in the nation-building epic or to whitewash various "misdeeds," preferring to place responsibility upon the shoulders of their rivals. The armed forces have their own "history branch," whose aim is not only to document "everything that happened" in the army, but also to "determine the truth" about events under dispute. Dozens of nonacademic institutions, affiliated with different political streams or parties, maintain private and public archives and are involved in "historiographical production." There are also many nonacademic professional historians and biographers who produce a vast "knowledge of the past." An additional genre is the widely developed writing of personal memoirs, which are generally connected with "grand" national narratives such as pioneering, the Holocaust, the rescue of Jews, wars or espionage. Under such circumstances a vast depository of knowledge about the past is accumulated, based on a complex mixture of myths, subjectivized events, and fabricated stories.

Professionalized academic historiography and sociography have a crucial role to play in such a situation. Apart from their routine activities, they function as an ultimate "supreme historical court," which deciphers from all the accumulated "pieces of the past" the "true" collective memories that are appropriate for inclusion in the canonical national historical narrative.

However, academic historiography is not a body of knowledge that is autonomous from its cultural, ideological, and political milieu. Historiography, any historiography, is part of a sociopolitical hegemony and is committed to serving it. This article has demonstrated that Israeli historiography is not only an active and central actor in the process of shaping Jewish-Zionist hegemony, but also a subject of this shaping process. Only an awareness of these limitations can enable the historian to partially overcome their effect.

On the individual as well as professional-community levels, Israeli academic historians are caught in the cross-fire. On the one hand, they are committed to certain professional requirements derived from the presumed autonomy of the profession; on the other hand, they are committed, not much less than their predecessors in the "Jerusalem School," to the supreme goals of the collectivity. It seems important to clarify that the historian's commitment is not to a kind of mobilized science such as Zhdanovism in the Stalinist Soviet Union, but is rather part of the historian's conviction of the correctness of his or her self-mobilization for a larger and just cause. Yet this phenomenon is even more dangerous as it is part of a sociopolitical hegemony. In a Zhdanovist system of direct control of the cultural elites, it is possible to build countercultures which spread through a "samizdat" (underground publishing) system. In a hegemonic situation the self-recruitment of the elites is latent and considered self-evident and "correct." To challenge a hegemonic body of knowledge is far more complicated than the struggle against a politically directed elite.[40] Who other than the historian dealing with Jewish and Israeli history should be more aware of and concerned with his or her own people's "fate" and feel personal responsibility toward their own collective identity? Any dissonant ("revisionist"?) voice is perceived as an assault threatening the cosmological and ontological worldview of the nationalist players and their rules of the game. The recent changes, actual and presumed, in the world order, in the Middle East and in Arab-Jewish relations, makes this the perfect time for the Israeli historian to follow Bernard Lewis's advice and "take a broader look at the nature of his vocation and discipline."[41]

NOTES

1. Baruch Kimmerling, "Religion, Nationalism and Democracy in Israel" [in Hebrew], *Zmanim* (Tel Aviv), no. 50 (December 1994): 116–131.

2. Baruch Kimmerling, "Between the Primordial and the Civil Definitions of the Collective Identity: The State of Israel or Eretz Israel," in *Comparative Social Dynamics: Essays in Honor of Shmuel Eisenstadt*, ed. Erik Cohen, Moshe Lissak, and Uri Almagor (Boulder, Colo., 1984), 262–283.

3. Baruch Kimmerling and Joel S. Migdal, *Palestinians: The Making of a People* (Cambridge, Mass., 1994).

4. See Baruch Kimmerling, *Zionism and Territory: The Socio-Territorial Dimensions of Zionist Politics* (Berkeley, 1983); and idem, *Zionism and Economy* (Cambridge, Mass., 1983). ("ZS character" is a situation in which there is a fixed amount of a given resource, so that the gain of one side in a conflict over that resource entails the other side's losing the same amount.)

5. Elie Kedourie, *Nationalism* (London, 1961), 76. The abuse in different measures of what I call "applied history," or history as it is presented in textbooks and taught, is a universal phenomenon. See Roy Preiswerk and Dominique Perot, *Ethno-centrisme et histoire* (Paris, 1975); and Marc Ferro, *The Use and Abuse of History, Or How the Past Is Taught* (London, 1984). Ferro examined fourteen case studies of national histories as constructed by their school systems. For an examination of contents of Hebrew history textbooks used between 1900 and 1984, see Ruth Firer, *The Agents of Zionist Education* [in Hebrew] (Tel Aviv, 1985).

6. E. H. Carr, *What Is History?* (New York, 1961), 27.

7. Benny Morris puts it in a simplistic way: he divides the historians into the "old" and the "new." The former, being completely committed to the Zionist cause, lied in order

to conceal most of the atrocities and injustices committed by Jews against Arabs and Palestinians. The few "new historians," committed to objectivity and to the professional duty of divulging the truth, write a genuine historiography. They deal mainly with the context of the 1948 war, the partial ethnic cleansing that occurred during this war, and Israeli military reprisal activities during the 1950s and early 1960s. See Benny Morris, "The New Historiography: Israel Confronts Its Past," *Tikkun* (November December 1988): 19–23, 99–102, where he includes Avi Shlaim, Ilan Pappe, Uri Milstein, Simha Flapan, Uri Bar-Joseph, Yitzhak Levy, and of course himself among the "new historians." To this list he added Yehoshua Porath's books on the emergence of the Palestinian national movement. On the controversy following this initial presentation, see idem, *1948 and After: Israel and the Palestinians* (Oxford, 1994), 1–48.

8. See Kimmerling, *Zionism and Territory*, chap. 7.

9. According to Jutte, from 1933 to 1945 about one hundred Jewish historians, with different academic degrees and achievements, emigrated from Germany to Palestine. Most of them were absorbed by the Jewish secondary (but also elementary) school system. Others found work in different fields, managing to continue independent historiographical research, such as the social historian Raphael Straus. See Robert Jutte, *Die Emigration der deutschsprächenden "Wissenschaft des Judentums": Die Auswanderung jüdischer Historiker nach Palästina, 1939–1945* (Stuttgart, 1991); cf. Daniel Schwarz, "The Wandering of Jewish Historians to Palestine" [in Hebrew] *Cathedra*, no. 69 (September 1994): 14–57.

10. Dinur (Dinaburg) was born in the Ukraine and in addition to his religious studies graduated from the universities of Bern and Petrograd. Despite this he was a part and parcel of German historiography. Although he emigrated to Palestine in 1921, it was only in 1948 that he was appointed professor at the Hebrew University. Thus Dinur and Baer were relative latecomers to this group.

11. For an acute and sarcastic description of the 1920s and 1930s Jerusalem professors, see Nobel Laureate Shmuel Yosef Agnon's novel *Shira*, trans. Zeva Shapiro (Jerusalem, 1989). In the early 1990s the Hebrew University itself began to write its own history; however, none of this multivolume project has yet been published. The idea of a Jewish national university was first proposed in the early 1880s by a rabbi, Hermann Schapira, who was a professor of mathematics at Heidelberg, and was raised again at the first Zionist Congress in 1897. The cornerstone of the university was laid on Mt. Scopus in 1918, and the institution—initiated by Judah L. Magnes (an American Zionist Rabbi), Dr. Chaim Weizmann and Professor Albert Einstein—was officially opened in 1925. At that point the Institutes of Chemistry, Microbiology, and Jewish Studies had already been established.

12. David N. Myers prefers to call them "an aggregate of 'Jerusalem scholars'": "Was there a 'Jerusalem School': An Inquiry into the First Generation of Historical Research at the Hebrew University," in *Studies in Contemporary Jewry*, ed. Jonathan Frankel (New York and Oxford, 1994), 10:66–93. See also Myers, "History as Ideology: The Case of Ben Zion Dinur: Zionist Historian par excellence," *Modern Judaism* 8 (1988): 167–193. For a more decided view, see Shmuel Almog's eulogy of Shmuel Ettinger in his *Nationalism, Zionism and Antisemitism: Essays and Research* [in Hebrew] (Jerusalem, 1992), 13–21. According to Almog, Ettinger, a second-generation Jerusalemite historian, was fully aware of the limitations of his teachers Dinur and Baer, as were Israel Kolatt, Yehoshua Arieli, and Jacob Talmon.

13. A very important academic publishing house for this group was the Jewish Publication Society of America, which published their works in other languages. This also

signaled the local academic community's turn from Europe to America as a reference culture.

14. Of course, within this limited framework this presentation of the beginnings of Israeli historiography is necessarily superficial. A comprehensive study of this subject has yet to be done.

15. The "intrusion" of the social sciences into the field was perceived by some historians as very threatening and led them to engage in "territorial behavior," to attempt to define more clearly not only what history is, but also who is entitled to be considered a "historian." For an ambivalent discussion of the relations between history and various branches of social science, see Israel Kolatt's programmatic essay on the occasion of the inauguration of the historical periodical *Cathedra*, "On Research and the Researcher of the History of the Yishuv and Zionism" [in Hebrew], *Cathedra: For the History of Eretz Israel and Its Yishuv*, no. 1 (1976): 3–35. The term "Yishuv" refers to the polity, or the politically organized Jewish community, in colonial Palestine from approximately 1918 to 1948. The term "Eretz Israel" (Land of Israel) and its problematic status will be discussed later. For a more favorable view of the relation between history and sociology, see Jacob Katz, "The Concept of Social History and Its Possible Use in Jewish Historical Research," *Scripta Hierosalymitana* 3 (1956): 201–231; see also idem, *With My Own Eyes: An Autobiography of a Historian* [in Hebrew] (Jerusalem, 1989).

16. Shmuel Klein, *The Land of Judea since the Return from Babylon through the Conclusion of the Talmud* [in Hebrew] (Tel Aviv, 1939), unpaginated introduction.

17. Eric J. Hobsbawm, *Nations and Nationalism since 1780: Programme, Myth, Reality* (Cambridge, 1990), 12–13.

18. It is true that when historians' works are translated into, or written in, a language other than Hebrew, in many cases this term "Eretz Israel" is changed to "Palestine," "Israel" (to designate the State of Israel) or "The Holy Land." However, many times the original term is retained. Generally, foreign-language Zionist historiography is less loaded with biased terms, as their original meaning is lost in translation or because the writer is aware that a foreign readership cannot accept as self-evident such heavily ideologized concepts.

19. Since 1967 another term has entered Israeli political culture as well as the social sciences. The occupied territories are referred to simply as "territories" in order to avoid defining them as either conquered or liberated.

20. See William A. Green, *History, Historians and the Dynamics of Change* (Westport, Conn., 1993), 18–20, 204–210.

21. This was also reflected in the paternalistic and manipulative relations toward the post-1948 immigrants, especially toward those who immigrated from Asian and African countries. See Shlomo Swirski, *Israel: The Oriental Majority* (London, 1989).

22. See Charles Tilly, "War Making and State Making as Organized Crime," in *Bridging the State Back In*, ed. Peter Evans, Dietrich Rueschmeyer, and Theda Skocpol (Cambridge, 1985), 161–191; Michael N. Barnett, *Confronting the Costs of War: Military Power, State and Society in Egypt and Israel* (Princeton, 1992); Baruch Kimmerling, "Patterns of Militarism in Israel," *European Journal of Sociology* 2 (1993): 1–28.

23. See Baruch Kimmerling, *The Interrupted System: Israeli Civilians in War and Routine Times* (New Brunswick, N.J., 1985).

24. Published by the prestigious Israeli Academy for Science and Humanities and edited by three leading Israeli historians, Israel Kolatt, Moshe Lissak (also a sociologist),

and Gavriel Cohen. Interestingly enough the English translation of the series title replaces the term "First Aliyah" with the date "1882." The foreign reader has to guess the meaning of this date. The joint publisher of this ambitious definitive summary of the history of contemporary Jewish settlement on the territory through the establishment of the State of Israel is the Bialik Institute. The first volume was published in Jerusalem in 1989, with only half of the project currently published. The project was supported financially by the Ministry of Education and Culture. Similar trends can also be observed in most of the entries in *Encyclopaedia Judaica,* 25 vols. (Jerusalem, 1971–1992), as well as in the semipopular periodical *Cathedra,* founded in 1976 by the Ben Zvi Institute.

25. See for example Dan Horowitz and Moshe Lissak, *Origins of the Israeli Polity: Palestine under the Mandate* (Chicago and London, 1989); idem, *Troubles in Utopia* (Albany, N.Y., 1989).

26. Most mainstream Israeli historians and social scientists agree upon the incomparability of the Holocaust with other organized genocides and invest much energy in "proving" this argument. Any counterargument is defined as "revisionism" and virtually seen as equivalent to the denial of the Holocaust itself. When in 1995 the Ministry of Education tried to introduce an optional curricular program for high schools about the Armenian and Gypsy genocides, the plan was vetoed by several respectable history professors, who argued that the subject was better presented as part of the more general program dealing with World War II.

27. Here is a logical and methodological trap. How can something be considered "unique" without systematic comparative study, which is the only way to prove "uniqueness"? S. N. Eisenstadt has compared from time to time Israeli society with the United States, although his comparison is always with the post–Civil War United States, which had lost its character as a frontier society.

28. Among the very few who have referred to the Israeli case in terms of an immigrant-settler or colonial type of society are Gershon Shafir, *Land, Labor and the Origins of the Israeli-Palestinian Conflict, 1882–1914* (Cambridge, 1989); and Kimmerling, *Zionism and Territory;* see also idem, "State Building, State Autonomy, and the Identity of Society: The Case of the Israeli State," *Journal of Historical Sociology* 6, no. 4 (1993): 397–429.

29. The Jews constituted about 35 percent of the population of Palestine at the end of the colonial period and owned about 7 percent of the land. From the Jewish point of view the major danger was the accepted decolonization pattern of transferring the colonial state's authority and major institutions—such as the state bureaucracy, police, courts, educational and health systems—to the representatives of the (Palestinian-Arab) majority population. See, Kimmerling, "State Building."

30. Some major exceptions are the economic historians who included in their paradigm the three-way construction of colonial Palestine, devoting attention to the fiscal, monetary, agrarian, and welfare policies in "Mandatory" Palestine. See Jacob Metzer, "Fiscal Incidence and Resource Transfer between Jews and Arabs in Mandatory Palestine," *Research in Economic History* 7 (1982): 87–132; Nachum T. Gross, "The Economic Policy of the Mandatory Government in Palestine" [in Hebrew], Falk Institute for Economic Research, Discussion Paper no. 81.06 (Jerusalem, 1981); Ylana N. Miller, Government and Society in Rural Palestine—1920–1948 (Austin, 1985); and Barbara Jean Smith, *The Roots of Separatism in Palestine: British Economic Policy, 1920–1929* (Syracuse, N.Y., 1992).

31. Baruch Kimmerling, "Ideology, Sociology and Nation Building: The Palestinians and Their Meaning in Israeli Sociology," *American Sociological Review* 57 (August 1992):

446–460. Ilan Troen, "Calculating the 'Economic Absorptive Capacity' of Palestine: A Study of the Political Use of Scientific Research," *Contemporary Jewry* 10, no. 2 (1989): 19–38. See Ian Lustick's review of S. N. Eisenstadt's book *The Transformation of Israeli Society: An Essay in Interpretation* (London, 1985), "The Voice of a Sociologist, The Task of an Historian: The Limits of a Paradigm," in *Books on Israel*, ed. Lustick (Albany, N.Y., 1988), 1:9–16.

32. Moshe Lissak, *Social Mobility in Israel Society* (Jerusalem, 1969).
33. See Baruch Kimmerling, "Boundaries and Frontiers of the Israeli Control System," in *The Israeli State and Society: Boundaries and Frontiers*, ed. Kimmerling (Albany, NY, 1989), 265–284; idem, "Between the Primordial and the Civil Definitions of the Collective Identity."
34. This description is much more relevant to Israeli social science proper than to history, which is supposed to deal with the "past." The problem for the historian begins with the very difficult and professionally challenging attempt to define "when the past begins to be the past."
35. See Yael Zerubavel, *Recovered Roots: Collective Memory and the Making of Israeli National Tradition* (Chicago, 1994); Yehoshafat Harkabi, *The Bar Kokhba Syndrome: Risk and Realism in International Politics* (Chappaqua, N.Y., 1983). (The Bar Kokhba syndrome refers to a national rebellion that from its beginning was destined to fail and led to a collective disaster.)
36. Ifrah Zilberman, *The Palestinian Myth of Canaanite Origin* [in Hebrew] (Jerusalem, 1993); see also Kimmerling and Migdal, Palestinians, vi.
37. See Yehoshua Porath, *The Emergence of the Palestinian National Movement, 1917–1929* (London, 1974); and idem, *The Palestinian National Movement: From Riots to Rebellion* (London, 1977).
38. The book under dispute was Kimmerling and Migdal, *Palestinians*. Some Israelis accused the authors of "delegitimizing the Zionist enterprise" by predating Palestinian history to 1831 (the Egyptian conquest of the territory), which was before the Zionist settlement of Palestine (1882). See Moshe Lissak's interview to Israel Landress, *Davar Magazine*, March 18, 1994 [in Hebrew]; and the same assertion made by the writer Aharon Megged against a group he calls the "new historians" (Benny Morris, Ilan Pappe, Zeev Sternhell, Yehoshafat Harkabi, Baruch Kimmerling, and Joel Migdal), *Haaretz Magazine*, June 10, 1994 [in Hebrew], and *Jerusalem Post*, June 17, 1994. See Kimmerling, "La grande misère des idéologues: La paix possible, on peut enfin étudier la réalité du passé, sans fard," *Courier International*, November 10–16, 1994. The issue of "who preceded whom" on the territory became one of the most heated intellectual and political issues in Israel in many years. Most leading intellectuals and historians participated in the debate, and the Israeli Historical Society dedicated a three-day conference to the issue of "revisionism" and "post-Zionism" (November 29–December 1, 1994). "Zionist history is being rewritten in the spirit of our enemies," accused Megged. The debate itself is deserving of further sociological research.
39. For example, Anita Shapira, analyzing Jewish defense policy during the colonial period, argues that at the beginning this policy was "defensive," in reaction to the Arab challenge. Only when the Jews realized that a reconciliation could not be achieved did they take the "offensive," a policy that led to the expulsion of most of the Arab population from the conquered lands. Shapira, *Land and Power: The Zionist Resort to Force, 1881–1948* (New York, 1992). What she ignores is the fact that the settlement process itself was perceived by the Arabs as an act of aggression and that

the Zionists' resort to force happened whenever the force was available. See also Yosef Gorni, *Zionism and the Arabs, 1882–1948: A Study of Ideology* (Oxford, 1987).

40. For a case study of the complex relations between Israeli intellectuals and the political establishment, see Michael Keren, *Ben Gurion and the Intellectuals: Power, Knowledge and Charisma* (DeKalb, Ill., 1983).

41. Bernard Lewis, *History: Remembered, Recovered, Invented* (Princeton, 1975), preface.

7

Ethnocracy

The Politics of Judaizing Israel/Palestine

OREN YIFTACHEL

During Israel's fiftieth year of independence (1997–1998), the country's high court of justice was grappling with an appeal known as the *Katzir* case.[1] It was lodged by an Arab citizen who was prevented from leasing state land in the village of Katzir on grounds of not being a Jew.[2] The court has so far deferred decision on the case. Its president, Judge Aharon Barak, known widely as a champion of civil rights, noted that this case has been among the most strenuous in his legal career.

The fact that in Israel's fiftieth year the state's highest legal authority still finds it difficult to protect a basic civil right such as equal access to state land provides a telling starting point for pursuing the goals of this essay. In the pages following I wish to offer a new conceptual prism through which the formation of Israel's regime and its ethnic relations can be explained. A theoretical and empirical examination of the Israeli regime leads me to argue that it should be classified as an "ethnocracy."

The chapter begins with a theoretical account of ethnocratic regimes, which are neither authoritarian nor democratic. Such regimes are states that maintain a relatively open government, yet facilitate a nondemocratic seizure of the country and polity by one ethnic group. A key conceptual distinction is elaborated between ethnocratic and democratic regimes. Ethnocracies, despite exhibiting several democratic features, lack a democratic structure. As such, they tend to breach key democratic tenets, such as equal citizenship, the existence of a territorial political community (the *demos*), universal suffrage, and protection against the tyranny of the majority.

Following the theoretical discussion, the chapter traces the making of the Israeli ethnocracy, focusing on the major Zionist project of Judaizing Israel/

Reprinted, by permission of Blackwell Publishing, from Oren Yiftachel, "'Ethnocracy': The Politics of Judaizing Israel/Palestine," *Constellations* 6, no. 3 (1999): 364–390.

Palestine. The predominance of the Judaization project has spawned an institutional and political structure that undermines the common perception that Israel is both Jewish and democratic.[3] The Judaization process is also a major axis along which relations between various Jewish and Arab ethnoclasses can be explained. The empirical sections elaborate on the consequences of the ethnocratic Judaization project on three major Israeli societal cleavages: Arab-Jewish, Ashkenazi-Mizrahi, and secular-orthodox.[4]

The analysis places particular emphasis on Israel's political geography. This perspective draws attention to the material context of geographical change, holding that discourse and space constitute one another in a ceaseless process of social construction.[5] The critical political-geographical perspective problematizes issues often taken for granted among analysts of Israel, such as settlement, segregation, borders, and sovereignty. As such it aims to complement other critical analyses of Israeli society.

Theorizing Ethnocracy

The theorization of ethnocracy draws on the main political and historical forces that have shaped the politics and territory of this regime. It focuses on three major political-historical processes: the formation of a (colonial) settler society, the mobilizing power of ethnonationalism, and the "ethnic logic" of capital. The fusion of the three key forces in Israel/Palestine has resulted in the establishment of the Israeli ethnocracy and determined its specific features. But the formation of ethnocracy is not unique to Israel. It is found in other settings where one ethnonation attempts to extend or preserve its disproportional control over contested territories and rival nation(s). This political system also typically results in the creation of stratified ethnoclasses within each nation. Other notable cases include Malaysia, Sri Lanka, Estonia, Latvia, Northern Ireland (pre-1972), and Serbia. Let us turn now in brief to the three structural forces identified above.

A Settler Society

Settler societies, such as the Jewish community in Israel/Palestine, pursue a deliberate strategy of ethnic migration and settlement that aims to alter the country's ethnic structure. Colonial settler societies have traditionally facilitated European migration into other continents, and legitimized the exploitation of indigenous land, labor, and natural resources. Other settler societies, mainly non-European, create internal migration and resettlement in order to change the demographic balance of specific regions. In all types of settler societies a "frontier culture" develops, glorifying and augmenting the settlement and expanding the control of the dominant group into neighboring regions.[6]

One common type of colonial-settler society has been described as the "pure settlement colony," which has been shown to be most appropriate to the Israeli-Zionist case.[7] Further studies have shown that "pure" settler societies are generally marked by a broad stratification into three main ethnoclasses: a founding charter group, such as Protestant-Anglos in North America and Australia; a group of later migrants, such as southern Europeans in North America; and dispossessed indigenous groups, such as the Aborigines in Australia, Maoris in New Zealand, Amerindians in North America, and Palestinians in Israel/Palestine.[8] The charter group establishes the state in its "own vision," institutionalizes its dominance, and creates a system that segregates it from the other ethnoclasses. But the pattern of control and segregation is not even, as immigrants are gradually assimilated into the charter group in a process described by Y. N. Soysal as "uneven incorporation."[9] Such a system generally reproduces the dominance of the charter group for generations to come.

The establishment of "pure" settler societies highlights the political and economic importance of extraterritorial ethnic links that are crucial for the success of most colonial projects. The links typically connect the settler society to a co-ethnic metropolitan state or to supportive ethnic diasporas. As elaborated later, extraterritorial ethnic links are a defining characteristic of ethnocracies. These regimes rely heavily on support and immigration from external ethnic sources as a key mechanism in maintaining their dominance over minority groups.

Ethnonationalism

Ethnonationalism, as a set of ideas and practices, constitutes one of the most powerful forces to have shaped the world's political geography in general, and that of Israel/Palestine in particular. Ethnonationalism is a political movement that struggles to achieve or preserve ethnic statehood. It fuses two principles of political order: the post-Westphalian division of the world into sovereign states and the principle of ethnic self-determination.[10] The combined application of these two political principles created the nation-state as the main pillar of today's world political order. Although the nation-state concept is rarely matched by political reality (as nations and states rarely overlap), it has become a dominant global model due to its dual moral basis: popular sovereignty (after centuries of despotic and/or religious regimes) and ethnic self-determination.

The principle of self-determination is central for our purposes here. In its simplest form, as enshrined in the 1945 United Nations Charter, it states that "every people has the right for self-determination." This principle has formed the political and moral foundation for the establishment of popular sovereignty and democratic government. Yet most international declarations, including the United Nations Charter, leave vague the definition of a "people" and the meaning of "self-determination," although in contemporary political culture it is commonly accepted as independence in the group's "own" homeland state. Once such a state is created, the principle is reified, and issues such as territory and national survival become inseparable from ethnonational history and culture. This possesses powerful implications to other facets of social life, most notably male dominance, militarism, and the strategic role of ethnic-religions, although a full discussion of these important topics must await another essay.

The dominance of the ethnonational concept generates forms of ethnic territoriality that view control over state territory and its defense as central to the survival of the group in question, often based on selective and highly strategic historical, cultural, or religious interpretations. The application of this principle has been a major bone of contention in the struggle between Jews and Palestinians and in the formation of the Israeli ethnocracy, which attempted to Judaize the land in the name of Jewish self-determination.

The global dominance of ethnonationalism and the nation-state order has prompted Billig to consider national identities as "banal."[11] But despite its dominance, the political geography of nation-states is far from stable, as a pervasive nation-building discourse and material reality continuously remolds the collective identity of homeland ethnic minorities. Such minorities often develop a national consciousness of their own that destabilizes political structures with campaigns for autonomy, regionalism, or sovereignty.[12]

The Ethnic Logic of Capital

A third structural force to shape the political geography of Israel/Palestine and the nature of its regime has been associated with the onset of capitalism and its ethnic and social consequences. Here the settings of a settler society and ethnonationalism combine to create a specific logic of capital flow, development, and class formation on two main levels. First, labor markets and development are ethnically segmented, thereby creating an ethnoclass structure that tends to accord with the charter-immigrant-indigenous hierarchy noted earlier. Typically, the founding charter group occupies privileged niches within the labor market, while migrants are marginalized, at least initially, from the centers of economic power and thus occupy the working and petit bourgeois classes. Indigenous people are typically excluded from access to capital or mobility within the labor market and are thus virtually trapped as an underclass.[13]

Second, the accelerating globalization of markets and capital have weakened the state's economic power. This has been accompanied by the adoption of neoliberal policies and the subsequent deregulation of economic activities and privatization of many state functions. Generally, these forces have widened the socioeconomic gaps between the charter, immigrant, and indigenous ethnoclasses. Yet in the setting of militant ethnonationalism, as prevalent in Israel/Palestine, the globalization of capital, and the associated establishment of supranational trade organizations, may also subdue ethnonationalism and expansionism, previously fueled by territorial ethnic rivalries. Particularly significant in this process is the globalization of the leading classes among the dominant ethnonation, which increasingly search for opportunities and mobility within a more open and accessible regional and global economy. A conspicuous tension between the global and the local thus surfaces, with a potential to intensify intranational tensions, but at the same time also to ease international conflicts, as has recently been illustrated in South Africa, Spain, and Northern Ireland.[14]

Ethnocracy

The fusion of the three forces—settler society, ethnonationalism, and the ethnic logic of capital—creates a regime-type I have called "ethnocracy."[15] An ethnocracy is a nondemocratic regime that attempts to extend or preserve disproportional ethnic control over a contested multiethnic territory. Ethnocracy develops chiefly when control over territory is challenged and when a dominant group is powerful enough to determine unilaterally the nature of the state. Ethnocracy is thus an unstable regime, with opposite forces of expansionism and resistance in constant conflict.[16] An ethnocratic regime is characterized by several key principles:

1. Despite several democratic features, mainly ethnicity (and not territorial citizenship) determines the allocation of rights and privileges; a constant democratic-ethnocratic tension characterizes politics.
2. State borders and political boundaries are fuzzy: there is no identifiable demos, mainly due to the role of ethnic diasporas inside the polity and the inferior position of ethnic minorities.
3. A dominant "charter" ethnic group appropriates the state apparatus, determines most public policies, and segregates itself from other groups.
4. Political, residential, and economic segregation and stratification occur on two main levels: ethnonations and ethnoclasses.
5. The constitutive logic of ethnonational segregation is diffused, enhancing a process of political ethnicization among subgroups within each ethnonation.
6. Significant (though partial) civil and political rights are extended to members of the minority ethnonation, distinguishing ethnocracies from *Herrenvolk* democracies or authoritarian regimes.

Ethnocratic regimes are usually supported by a cultural and ideological apparatus that legitimizes and reinforces the uneven reality. This is achieved by constructing a historical narrative that proclaims the dominant ethnonation as the rightful owner of the territory in question. Such narrative degrades all other contenders as historically not entitled, or culturally unworthy, to control the land or achieve political equality.

A further legitimizing apparatus is the maintenance of *selective openness*. Internally, the introduction of democratic institutions is common, especially in settling societies, as it adds legitimacy to the entire settling project, to the leadership of the charter ethnoclass, and to the incorporation of groups of later immigrants. But these democratic institutions commonly exclude indigenous or rival minorities. This is achieved either formally, as was the case in Australia until 1967, or more subtly, by leaving such groups outside decision-making circles, as is the case in Sri Lanka.[17] Externally, selective openness is established as a principle of foreign relations and membership in international organizations. This has become particularly important with the increasing opening of the world economy and the establishment of supranational organizations, such as the EU and NAFTA. Membership in such organizations often requires at least the appearance of open regimes, and most ethnocracies comply with this requirement.

Given these powerful legitimizing forces, ethnocratic projects usually enjoy a hegemonic status that originates among the charter group and is successfully diffused among the populace. The hegemonic moment, as convincingly formulated by Antonio Gramsci, is marked by a distorted but widely accepted fusion of a given set of principles and practices. It is an order in which a certain social structure is dominant, with its own concept of reality determining most tastes, morality, customs, and political principles. Given the economic, political, and cultural power of the elites, a hegemonic order is likely to be reproduced unless severe contradictions with "stubborn realities" generate counterhegemonic mobilizations.[18]

Ethnocracy in the Making: The Judaization of Israel/Palestine

The analysis of the Israeli regime in this chapter covers the entire territory and population under Israeli rule. Prior to 1967, then, it is limited to the area within the Green Line (the 1949 armistice lines), but after that date it covers all of Israel/Palestine, or what Baruch Kimmerling has called the "Israeli control system."[19] While the occupied territories are often treated in studies of Israel as an external and temporary aberration, they are considered here as an integral part of the Israeli regime, simply because Israel governs these areas. This appears to be the situation even following the 1993 Oslo agreement, because the areas under limited Palestinian self-rule are still under overall Jewish control.[20] The appropriate political-geographical framework for the analysis of Israel/Palestine since 1967 is thus: *one ethnocracy, two ethnonations*, and *several Jewish and Palestinian ethnoclasses*.

Jews account for about 80 percent of Israel's 5.9 million citizens and Palestinian-Arabs about 17 percent (the rest being non-Jewish and non-Arab). An additional 2.7 million Palestinians reside in the occupied territories of the West Bank and Gaza Strip. Hence, the population of the entire contested

"Land of Israel" (Palestine) is roughly 55 percent Jewish and 43 percent Palestinian-Arab.[21]

Ethnic and religious division is also marked within each national community. About 41 percent of Jews are Ashkenazi and about 43 percent Mizrahi. The rest are mainly recent Russian-speaking immigrants, mostly of European origin, who form a distinct ethnocultural group, at least in the short term. Of the Palestinian-Arabs in Israel, 77 percent are Muslims (a fifth of whom are Bedouin), 13 percent are Christian, and 10 percent Druze. In the occupied territories, 95 percent are Muslim and 4 percent Christian. In both the Jewish and Muslim communities, a major cultural division has also developed between orthodox and secular groups. About 20 percent of Jews are orthodox, as are about 30 percent of Muslims on both sides of the Green Line.[22]

Zionism has been a settler movement, and Israel a settler state, whose territory was previously inhabited by Palestinian-Arabs. Despite notable differences with other colonial movements, the actual process of European settlement classifies Zionism (both before and after 1948) as a "pure" colonial settler movement.[23] After independence and following the mass entry of Jewish refugees and migrants, conspicuous social stratification emerged. In broad terms, the Ashkenazim have constituted the charter group and have occupied the upper echelons of society in most spheres, including politics, the military, the labor market, and culture. The Mizrahim have been the main group of later immigrants, recently accompanied by a group of Russian-speakers and a small group of Ethiopian Jews. These groups are placed in a middle position, lagging behind the Ashkenazim, but above the indigenous Palestinian-Arabs. Strikingly, and despite an official ideology of integration and equality toward the Mizrahim, a persistent socioeconomic gap has remained between them and the Ashkenazi group.[24]

As is typical in settler societies, Israel's indigenous Arab minority has occupied from the outset the lowest strata in most spheres of Israeli life, and has been virtually excluded from the political, cultural, and economic centers of society. Following the conquest of the occupied territories in 1967, their Palestinian residents became partially incorporated into Israeli economy, mainly as day laborers, but were denied political and civil rights.[25]

A Jewish State

Israel was pronounced a "Jewish state" upon declaring its independence in 1948. In some ways, the declaration of independence was quite liberal, promising non-Jews "full and equal citizenship" and banning discrimination on grounds of religion, ethnic origin, gender, or creed. The central political institutions of the new state were established as democratic, including a representative parliament (the Knesset), periodic elections, an independent judiciary, and relatively free media.

During the following years, however, a series of incremental laws enshrined the ethnic and partially religious Jewish character of the state (rather than its *Israeli* character, as accepted international standards of self-determination would require). Chief among these have been the state's immigration statutes (Laws of Return and Citizenship), which made every Jew in the world a potential citizen, while denying this possibility to many Palestinians born in the country. Other laws further anchored the Jewish character of the state not only in the symbolic realm, but also as a concrete and *deepening reality* covering areas such as citizenship, education, communication, and land ownership. As the Israeli High Court declared in 1964, in what became known as the *Yerdor* case, "the Jewishness of Israel is a constitutional given."[26] In 1985, revisions made to the Basic Law on the Knesset added that no party would be allowed to run if it rejected Israel's definition as a state of the Jewish people.[27] The combination of these laws created a structure nearly immune to democratic attempts to change its Zionist character.

During the early 1990s two Knesset basic laws defined the state as "Jewish and democratic," thereby further enshrining the state's Jewish character, but also coupling it with a democratic commitment. As argued below, this coupling is problematic not as an abstract principle, but against the ongoing reality of Judaization, which has unilaterally restructured the nature of the state through immigration and land policies. This transformation was supported by the uniethnic arms of the state, including army, police, courts, economic institutions, development agencies, and most decision-making forums.

Hence, a main obstacle to Israeli democracy does not necessarily lie in the declaration of Israel as "Jewish," which may be akin to the legal status of Finland as a "Lutheran state" or England as "Anglican." The main problem lies in the mirror processes of *Judaization and de-Arabization* (that is, the dispossession of Palestinian-Arabs) facilitated and legitimized by the declaration of Israel as "Jewish," and by the ethnocratic legal and political structures resulting from this declaration.[28] Let us turn now to some detail and explore the dynamic political geography behind the establishment of the Israeli ethnocracy.

Judaizing the Homeland

Following independence, Israel entered a radical stage of territorial restructuring. Some policies and initiatives were an extension of earlier Jewish approaches, but the tactics, strategies, and ethnocentric cultural construction of the pre-1948 Jewish *Yeshuv* (community) were significantly intensified. This was enabled with the aid of the newly acquired state apparatus, armed forces, and the international legitimacy attached to national sovereignty.

The territorial restructuring of the land has centered around a combined and expansionist Judaization and de-Arabization program adopted by the nascent Israeli state. This began with the flight and expulsion of approximately 750,000 Palestinians during the 1948 war. Israel prevented the return of the refugees to their villages, which were rapidly demolished.[29] The authorities were quick to fill the "gaps" created by this involuntary exodus with Jewish settlements inhabited by migrants and refugees who entered the country en masse during the late 1940s and early 1950s.

The Judaization program was premised on a hegemonic myth cultivated since the rise of Zionism, namely that "the land" (*Haaretz*) belongs to the Jewish people, and only to the Jewish people. An exclusive form of settling ethnonationalism developed in order quickly to "indigenize" immigrant Jews and to conceal, trivialize, or marginalize the Palestinian past.

The "frontier" became a central icon, and its settlement was considered one of the highest achievements of any Zionist. The frontier *kibbutzim* (collective rural villages) provided a model, and the reviving Hebrew language was filled with positive images such as *aliva lakaraka* (literally "ascent to the land," i.e., settlement), *ge'ulat karka* (land redemption), *hityashvut, hitnahalut* (positive biblical terms for Jewish settlement), *kibbush hashmama* (conquest of the desert), and *hagshama* (literally "fulfillment" but denoting the settling of the frontier). The glorification of the frontier thus assisted both in the construction of national-Jewish identity, and in capturing physical space on which this identity could be territorially constructed.

Such sentiments were translated into a pervasive program of Jewish-Zionist territorial socialization, expressed in school curricula, literature, political speech, popular music, and other spheres of public discourse. Settlement thus continued to be a cornerstone of Zionist nation-building, even after the establishment of a sovereign Jewish state. To be sure, the arrival of Jews to their ancestors' mythical land, and the perception of this land as a safe haven after generations of persecution, had a powerful liberating meaning. Yet the darker sides of this project were nearly totally absent from the construction of an unproblematic "return" of Jews to their biblical promised land. Very few dissenting voices were heard against these Judaizing discourses, policies, or practices. If such dissent did emerge, the national-Jewish elites found effective ways to marginalize, co-opt, or gag most challengers.[30]

Therefore, 1948 should be regarded as a major political turning point, not only due to the establishment of a state pronouncing a democratic regime, but also as the beginning of a state-orchestrated and essentially nondemocratic Judaization project. Two parallel processes have thus developed on the same land: the visible establishment of democratic institutions and procedures, and a more concealed, yet systematic and coercive, seizure of the territory by the dominant ethnic group. The contradiction between the two processes casts doubt on the pervasive classification of Israel in the academic literature as a democracy, a point to which we return later.

The perception of the land as only Jewish was premised on a distorted national discourse of a "forced exile" and subsequent "return."[31] A parallel discourse developed in reaction to the Arab-Jewish conflict (and Arab rejectionism), elevating the exigencies of national security onto a level of unquestioned gospel. These discourses blinded most Jews to a range of discriminatory policies imposed against the state's Palestinian citizens, including the imposition of military rule, lack of economic or social development, political surveillance and underrepresentation, and—most important for this essay—large-scale confiscation of Palestinian land.[32]

Prior to 1948, only about 5–6 percent of the country was in Jewish hands, and about 10 percent was vested with the representative of the British Mandate. The Israeli state, however, quickly expanded its landholdings, and it currently owns and controls 93 percent of the area within the Green Line. The lion's share of this land transfer was based on expropriation of Palestinian refugee property, but about two-thirds of the land belonging to Palestinians who remained as Israeli citizens was also expropriated. At present, Palestinian-Arabs, who constitute around 17 percent of Israel's population, own only around 4 percent of its land, while their local government areas cover 2.5 percent of the country.

A central aspect of land transfer was its legal unidirectionality. Israel created an institutional and legal land system under which confiscated land could not be sold. Further, such land did not merely become state land, but a joint possession of the state and the entire Jewish people. This was achieved by granting extraterritorial organizations, such as the Jewish National Fund, the Jewish Agency, and the Zionist Federation, a share of the state's sovereign powers and significant authority in the areas of land, development, and settlement. The transfer of land to the hands of unaccountable bodies representing the "Jewish people" can be likened to a "black hole," into which Arab land enters but cannot be retrieved. This structure ensures the unidirectional character of all land transfers: from Palestinians to Jewish hands, and never vice versa. A stark expression of this legal and institutional setting is that Israel's Arab citizens are currently prevented from purchasing, leasing, or using land in around 80 percent of the country.[33] It can be reasonably assumed that the constitutions of most democratic countries would make such a blatant breach of equal civil rights illegal. But Israel's character as a Judaizing state has so far prevented the enactment of a constitution which would guarantee such rights.

During the 1950s and 1960s, and following the transfer of land to the state, over six hundred Jewish settlements were constructed in all parts of the land. This created the infrastructure for the housing of Jewish refugees and immigrants who continue to pour into the country. The upshot was the penetration of Jews into most Arab areas, the encirclement of most Arab villages by exclusively Jewish settlements (where non-Jews are not permitted to purchase housing), and the virtual ghettoization of the Arab minority.

Settlement and Intra-Jewish Segregation

Let us turn now to the issue of ethnoclasses. Beyond the obvious consequences of the Jewish settlement project on the ethnonational level, it also caused processes of segregation and stratification between Jewish ethnoclasses. This aspect is central for the understanding of relations between the various Jewish ethnoclasses, and especially Ashkenazim and Mizrahim. Notably, it is not argued that relations between Jewish ethnic groups are nondemocratic, but rather that the ethnocratic-settling nature of Jewish-Palestinian relations has adversely affected intra-Jewish relations. To illustrate the geography of these processes, let us outline in more detail the social and ethnic nature of the Jewish settlement project, which advanced in three main waves.

During the first wave, between 1949 and 1952, some 240 communal villages (*kibbutzim* and *moshavim*) were built, mainly along the Green Line. During the second wave, from the early 1950s to the mid-1960s, twenty-seven "development towns" and a further fifty-six villages were built. These were mainly populated, at times using coercion, by North African Jewish refugees and immigrants. During the same period large groups of Mizrahim were also housed in "frontier" urban neighborhoods, which were either previously Palestinian or adjacent to Palestinian areas. Given the low socioeconomic resources of most Mizrahim, their mainly enemy-affiliated Arab culture, and lack of ties to Israeli elites, the development towns and "the neighborhoods" quickly became, and have remained to date, distinct concentrations of segregated, poor, and deprived Mizrahi populations.[34] This geography of dependence, achieved in the name of Judaizing the country, has underlain the evolution of Ashkenazi-Mizrahi relations to the present day, despite a countervailing assimilation process.

The third wave, during the last two decades, saw the establishment of over 150 small nonurban settlements known as "community" or "private" settlements (*yeshuvim kehilatiyim*) on both sides of the Green Line. These are small suburbanlike neighborhoods, located in the heart of areas on both sides of the Green Line. Their establishment was presented to the public as a renewed effort to Judaize Israel's hostile frontiers, using the typical rhetoric of national security, the Arab threat to state lands, or the possible emergence of Arab secessionism. In the occupied territories, additional rationales for Jewish settlement referred to the return of Jews to ancient biblical sites, and to the creation of "strategic depth." But, despite the continuation of a similar Zionist discourse, a major difference characterized these settlements. They ruptured, for the first time, Israel's internationally recognized borders, a point to which I return later.

From a social perspective, the people migrating into most of these high-quality residential localities were mainly middle-class Ashkenazi suburbanites seeking to improve their housing and social status. In recent years, urban Jewish settlement in the West Bank accompanied the ongoing construction and expansion of small *kehilatti* settlements. These towns have increasingly accommodated religious-national and ultra-orthodox Jews.[35]

Notably, the different waves of settlement were marked by social and institutional *segregation* sanctioned and augmented by state policies. A whole range of mechanisms was devised and implemented not only to maintain nearly impregnable patterns of segregation between Arabs and Jews, but also to erect fairly rigid lines of separation between various Jewish ethnoclasses. Segregation mechanisms included the demarcation of local government and education district boundaries, the provision of separate and unequal government services (especially education and housing), the development of largely separate economies, the organization of different types of localities in different statewide "settlement movements," and the uneven allocation of land on a sectoral basis.[36]

As a result, layered and differentiated Jewish spaces were created, with low levels of contact between the various ethnoclasses. This has worked to reproduce inequalities and competing collective identities. Movement across boundaries has been restricted by allowing most new Jewish settlements (built on state land!) to screen their residents by applying tests of "resident suitability." This practice has predictably produced communities dominated by middle-class Ashkenazim. At least part of the ethnoclass fragmentation and hostility currently evident in Israeli society can thus be traced to the Judaizing settlement system and its institutionalized segregation. In this process we can also note the working of the ethnic logic of capital, mentioned earlier as a major force shaping social relations in ethnocracies. Development closely followed the ethnoclass pattern prevalent in Israeli society. This created spatial circumstances for the *reproduction* of the "ethnic gap" between Ashkenazim and Mizrahim, through location-based mechanisms such as education, land control, housing, social networks, local stigmas, and accessibility to facilities and opportunities.

Democracy or Ethnocracy?

As we have seen, the politico-geographic analysis of Jewish land and settlement policies highlights three key factors, often neglected in other interpretations of Israeli society: (1)The Israeli regime has facilitated a constant process of expanding Jewish control over the territory of Israel/Palestine; (2) Israel is a state and polity without clear borders; and (3) the country's organization of social space is based on pervasive and uneven ethnic segregation. An elaboration of these assertions leads me to question the taken-for-granted notion that Israel is a democracy.[37] Instead, I would argue that the polity is governed by an ethnocratic regime, as defined earlier. It is a rule for and by an expanding ethnic group, within the state and beyond its boundaries, which is neither democratic nor authoritarian.[38]

Democracy, on the other hand, is a regime that follows several main principles, including equal and substantial civil rights, inclusive citizenship, periodic and free elections, universal suffrage, separation between arms of government, protection of individuals and minorities against the majority, and an appropriate level of government openness and public ethics.[39] A factor often taken for granted by regime analysts (but far from obvious in the Israeli case) is the existence of clear boundaries to state territory and its political community. The establishment of a state as a territorial-legal entity is premised on the existence of such boundaries, without which the law *of the land* and the activity of democratic institutions cannot be imposed universally, thus undermining the operation of inclusive and equal democratic procedures.

This brings us back to the question of Israeli boundaries and borders. As shown above, the Jewish system of land ownership and development, as well as the geography of frontier settlement, have undermined the territorial-legal nature of the state. Organizations based in the Jewish Diaspora possess statutory powers within Israel/Palestine. World Jewry is also involved in Israeli politics in other significant ways, including major donations to Jewish parties and politicians, open and public influence over policy-making and agenda-setting, as well as lobbying on behalf of Israeli politicians in international fora, especially in the United States.[40] Hence, extraterritorial (noncitizen) Jewish groups have amassed political power in Israel to an extent unmatched by any democratic state. This is an undemocratic structural factor consistent with the properties of ethnocratic regimes.

As mentioned, Jewish settlement in the occupied territories has also ruptured the Green Line (Israel's pre-1967 internationally recognized borders) as a meaningful border. At the time of writing, some 340,000 Israeli Jews resided in the territories (including al-Quds, or East Jerusalem), and Israeli law has been unilaterally extended to each of these settlements.[41] The Green Line has been transformed into a geographical mechanism of separating between (citizen from noncitizen) Palestinians, but not between Jews.[42]

The combination of the two factors means that "Israel," as a definable democratic-political entity, simply *does not exist*. The legal and political power of extraterritorial (Jewish) bodies and the breaching of state borders empty the notion of Israel from the broadly accepted meaning of a state as a territorial-legal institution. Hence, the unproblematic acceptance of "Israel proper" in most social science writings (including some of my own previous work) and in the public media has been based on a misnomer.[43]

Given this reality, Israel simply does not comply with a basic requirement of democracy—the existence of a demos. The demos, as defined in ancient Greece, denotes an inclusive body of citizens within given borders. It is a competing organizing principle to the *ethnos*, which denotes common origin. The term "democracy" therefore means the rule of the demos, and its modern application points to an overlap between permanent residency in the polity and equal political rights as a *necessary democratic condition.*

As we have seen, Israel's political structure and settlement activity have diminished the relevance of such boundaries, and in effect undermined the existence of universal suffrage (as settlers can vote to the parliament that governs them, but not their Palestinian neighbors). The significance of this observation is clear from Israel's 1996 elections: counting only the results within "Israel proper," Shimon Peres would have beaten Benjamin Netanyahu by a margin of over 5 percent. Netanyahu's victory was thus based on the votes of Jews in the Occupied Territories (that is, outside Israel), as were the previous successes of the Likud camp in 1981, 1984, and 1988. The involvement of the settlers in Israeli politics is of course far deeper than simply electoral. In the 1996–1999 parliament, they were represented by 18 Knesset members (out of 120), 4 government ministers, and held a host of key positions in politics, the armed forces, and academia.

Hence, a basic requirement for the democratization of the Israeli polity is not only to turn it into a state of all its citizens (as most nonzionist groups demand), but to *a state of all its resident-citizens, and only them.* This is the only way to ensure that extraterritorial and politically unaccountable bodies, such as the Jewish Agency, the Jewish National Fund, and Jewish settlers in occupied territories, do not unduly affect the state's sovereign territory. This principle would thus lay appropriate geographical foundations for a democratic rule, for and by the state's political demos.

Beyond the critical issue of borders, several other major impediments to the establishment of sound democratic regime have existed throughout Israel's political history. These have included a very high level of regime centrality, relative lack of political accountability, weakness of judiciary, pervasive militarism, male dominance and associated discrimination against women in most walks of life and the inseparability of religion and state. Lack of space prevents discussion on all but the last of these issues, to which we now turn.

Ethnocracy or Theocracy?

Some scholars claim that a growing influence of orthodox Jewish groups on Israeli politics is leading Israel toward theocratic, and not ethnocratic, rule.[44] Yet the orthodox agenda appears compatible with the Jewish ethnocratic project, as orthodox groups take the rule of the Jewish ethnos as a given point of departure, and chiefly aim to deepen its religiosity. As such, their campaign is geared to change the nature of the Israeli ethnocracy without challenging its very existence or the ethnic boundaries of its membership.

Yet, the orthodox agenda in Israeli politics is indeed significant, as it, too, challenges the prevalent perception of Israel as "Jewish and democratic." Despite significant differences, all orthodox parties support the increasing imposition of religious rule in Israel (*Halacha*), as stated by the late leader of the National Religious Party, Z. Hammer, who was considered a moderate: "I genuinely wish that Israel would be shaped according to the spirit of Tora and Halacha . . . the democratic system is not sacred for me."[45] Likewise, one of the leaders of Shas, often considered a relatively moderate orthodox party, declared recently: "We work for creating a *Halacha state* . . . such as state would guarantee religious freedom, but the courts will enforce Jewish law . . . we have the sacred Tora which has a moral set of laws, why should anyone be worried?"[46] Although the initiatives taken in recent times by these bodies attempt to mainly influence the character of public (and not private) spheres, there exists a fundamental contradiction between the orthodox agenda and several basic features of democracy, such as the rule of law, individual liberty and autonomy, civil equality, and popular sovereignty.[47]

This challenge is somewhat obscured by the duality in the interpretation of Judaism as ethnic and/or religious. The secular interpretation of Judaism treats it as mainly ethnic or cultural, while orthodox and ultra-orthodox groups interpret it as an inseparable whole (that is, both ethnicity and religion). This unresolved duality is at the heart of the tension between the secular and orthodox Jewish camps: if the meaning of "Jewish" is unresolved, how can the nature of the "Jewish state" be determined?

The challenge to democracy from the orthodox agenda has become more acute, because the orthodox political camp has grown stronger in Israeli politics over the last decade. In the 1996–1999 period it held 28 of the Knesset's 120 seats (with orthodox parties holding 23 and the rest being orthodox members of other parties). The orthodox camp has held the parliamentary balance of power for most of Israel's history.

Notably for this essay, the rising power of orthodox sectors in Israel is closely linked to the state's political geography and to the Zionist project of Judaizing the country. There are four main grounds for this. First, all religious movements, and most conspicuously Gush Emunim ("Loyalty Bloc," the main Jewish religious organization to settle the West Bank), fully support the settling of Jews in occupied Palestinian territories and the violent military occupation of these areas. This is often asserted as part of a divine imperative, based on the eternal Jewish right and duty to settle all parts of the "promised land." Such settlement is to be achieved while ignoring the aspirations of Palestinians in these territories for self-determination or equal civil rights. Needless to say, this agenda undermines even the possibility of democratic rule in Israel, and has already caused several waves of intra-Jewish religious-secular violence, including the assassination of Prime Minister Rabin in 1995.

Second, repeated surveys show that the religious public in Israel is the most intransigent in its opposition to granting civil equality to Israel's Arab citizens. This does not mean that the entire orthodox public opposes democratic rule, or that it is homogenous in its political views. But nearly all opinion studies, as well as the platforms of main religious political organizations, rank democratic values lower than the Jewishness of the state or Jewish control over the entire Israel/Palestine territory.[48]

Third, there is a discernible link between the rising power of orthodox bodies and the rupturing of Israel's borders. Political analyses and surveys show that as the Judaization of the occupied territories deepened, so have the Jewish elements in the collective identity of Israeli-Jews at the expense of Israeli components.[49] This trend stems from the confusion in the meaning of "Israeli," when both state borders and boundaries of the Israeli polity are blurred. In other words, the breaching of Israeli borders with settlement activity and the involvement of world Jewry in internal politics have eroded the territorial and civil meaning of the term "Israeli" and simultaneously strengthened the (nonterritorial and ethnoreligious) Jewish collective identity. This process has grave implications for democracy, principally because it bypasses the institution of territorial citizenship, on which a democratic state must be founded. In the Israeli context it legitimizes the stratification between Jews (with full rights) and Arabs (second-class citizens), thus denying Arabs much of the status attached to their "Israeli" affiliation. Only the demarcation of clear Israeli borders, and the subsequent creation of a territorial political community, can halt the undemocratic ascendancy of Judaism over Israeliness.

Finally, the Judaization project is perceived by many in the orthodox camp not only as ethnic-territorial, but also as deepening the religiosity of Israeli Jews. This is based on interpretation of a central percept: "all Jews are guarantors for one another." Here "guarantee" entails "bringing back" all "straying" nonbelievers to God's way. This mission legitimizes the repeated (if often unsuccessful) attempts to strengthen the religious character of laws and public spaces. The state's religious character is already anchored in a variety of areas: the Jewish Sabbath is the official Israeli day of rest; public institutions only serve Kosher food; no import of pork is allowed; all personal laws are governed with the national rabbinate (which prohibits civil marriage); and most archaeological digs need approval from religious authorities.

Orthodox parties justify the imposition of these regulations on the secular public by asserting that they ensure the state's ethnic-cultural character for future generations. As such, this would prevent the incorporation of non-Jews and create a state which "deserves to be called Israeli ... and Jewish."[50] Accordingly, the theocracy sought by religious parties already presupposes a Jewish ethnic state (ethnocracy). Their agenda is simply to transform it into a *religious ethnocracy*.[51] In this light, we should note not only the conflict between orthodox and secular Jews, but also their long-standing *cooperation* in the project of establishing a Jewish ethnocracy.

Hence, the religious challenge to the democratization of Israel and the relations between orthodox and secular elements in Israeli society cannot be separated from the political geography of a *Jewish and Judaizing state*. The leading Israeli discourse in politics, academia, and the general public tends to treat separately Arab-Jewish and religious-secular issues. But, as shown above, the conflicts and agreements between secular and orthodox Jews cannot be isolated from the concerns, struggles, and rights of Palestinian-Arabs. This is mainly because at the very heart of the tension between orthodox and secular Jews lies the drive of Israel's Arab citizens to transform the state from ethnocracy to democracy, and to halt and even reverse the ethnocratic Judaization project.

A Segregative Settling Ethnocracy

As we have seen, the project of Judaizing the state, spearheaded by Jewish immigration and settlement, and buttressed by a set of constitutional laws and a broad consensus among the Jewish public, has been a major (indeed constitutive) feature of the Israeli regime. Israel thus fits well the model of an ethnocratic regime presented earlier in the chapter. More specifically, and given the importance of settlement, it should be called a settling *ethnocracy*.

But beyond regime definitions, and beyond the fundamental chasm between Palestinians and Jews, the fusion of ethnocentric principles and the dynamics of immigration, settlement, and class formation created uneven and segregated patterns among Jews. This was exacerbated by the geographic nature of the Jewish settlement project, which was based on the principal unit of the locality (*Yeshuv*). The Jewish settlement project advanced by building localities that were usually ethnically homogeneous, and thus created from the outset a segregated pattern of development. As noted, this geography still stands behind much of the remaining tension between Mizrahim and Ashkenazim in Israel.[52] The political, legal, and cultural mechanisms introduced for the purpose of segregating Jews from Arabs were thus also used to segregate Jewish elites from other ethnoclasses, thereby reinforcing the process of "ethnicization" typical of ethnocratic regimes.

To be sure, these mechanisms were used differently, and more subtly, among Jews, but the persistent gap between Ashkenazim and Mizrahim cannot be understood without accounting for the geography of intra-Jewish relations. In the main, Mizrahim were spatially marginalized by the Israeli settlement project, whether in the isolated periphery or in poor and stigmatized neighborhoods of Israel's major cities. This has limited their potential economic, social, and cultural participation.

There is a clear nexus connecting the de-Arabization of the country with the marginalization of the Mizrahim, who have been positioned—culturally and geographically—between Arab and Jew, between Israel and its hostile neighbors, between a "backward" Eastern past and a "progressive" Western future. But, we should remember: the depth and extent of discrimination against Palestinians and Mizrahim has been quite different, with the latter included in Jewish-Israeli nation-building as active participants in the oppression of the former.

A similar segregationist logic was also used to legitimize the creation of separate neighborhoods and localities for ultra-orthodox and orthodox Jews, recent Russian immigrants, and Palestinian-Arabs. In other words, the uneven segregationist logic of the ethnocratic regime has been infused into spatial and cultural practices, which have worked to further ethnicize Israeli society.

Of course, not all ethnic separation is negative, and voluntary separation between groups can at times function to reduce ethnic conflict. But in a society that has declared the "gathering and integration of the exiles" (*mizug gahtyot*) a major national goal, levels of segregation and stratification between Jewish ethno-classes have remained remarkably high. Referring back to our theoretical framework, we can note the fusion of settler-society mechanisms (conquest, immigration, and settlement) with the power of ethnonationalism (segregating Jews from Arabs) and the ethnic logic of capital (distancing upper and lower ethnoclasses) in the creation of Israel's conflict-riddled contemporary human geography.

This process, however, is not unidimensional and must be weighed against countertrends, such as growing levels of assimilation between Mizrahim and Ashkenazim, and increasing formal equality in social rights among all groups. In addition, solidarity among Jews in the face of a common enemy has often eased internal tensions and segregation, especially between Mizrahim and Ashkenazim, as both have merged into a broadening Israel middle class. Here we can also note that the original Ashkenazi charter group has broadened to incorporate the Mizrahim, especially among the assimilated middle and upper classes.[53] Yet, the ethnicization trend has also been powerful, as illustrated by the growing tendency of political entrepreneurs to exploit "ethnic capital" and draw on ethnoclass-religious affiliations as a source of political support. In the 1996 elections such sectoral parties increased their power by 40 percent, and for the first time in Israel's history overshadowed the largest two parties, Labor and Likud, which have traditionally been the most ethnically heterogeneous.

Moreover, the situation has not been static. The strategy of Judaization and population dispersal has recently slowed, responding to the new neoliberal agendas of many Israeli elites.[54] It has also encountered growing Palestinian-Arab resistance and Mizrahi grievances, which in turn have reshaped some of the strategies, mechanisms, and manifestations of Israel's territorial, planning, and development policies. Both Arabs and Mizrahim have progressed in their absolute (if not relative) socioeconomic standards, partially due to Israel's development policies. Likewise, Palestinian resistance in the occupied territories, culminating in the *Intifada*, has slowed Jewish expansion in several regions, brought about the Oslo agreement, and achieved a measure of limited Palestinian self-rule.[55] But these changes, important as they are, have still occurred within the firm boundaries of the dominant, ethnocratic

Zionist discourse, where Jewish settlement and control and the territorial containment of the Arab population are undisputed Jewish national goals both within the Green Line and in large parts of the occupied territories.[56]

Conclusion: The Enigma of Distorted Structures

In the foregoing I have attempted to probe the nature of the Israeli regime from a political-geographic perspective. I have shown that three main forces have shaped the Israeli polity: the establishment of a settler society, the mobilizing force of ethnonationalism, and the ethnic logic of capital. The fusion of these forces has created a regime I have termed "ethnocracy," which privileges ethnos over demos in a contested territory seized by a dominant group. Ethnic relations in Israel are thus more comparable to other ethnocracies, such as Malaysia, Sri Lanka, Serbia, or Estonia, than to Western liberal democracies, as commonly suggested in scholarly literature or popular discourse.[57]

More specifically to Israel, I have shown that the Israeli regime has been significantly shaped by the ethnocratic project of Judaizing the land of Israel/Palestine. This has been legitimized by the need to "indigenize" "de-territorialized" Jews in order to fulfill a claim for territorial self-determination. The momentum of the Judaization project has subsequently led to the rupture of the state's borders, the continuing incorporation of extraterritorial Jewish organizations into the Israeli government, the persistent and violent military rule over the occupied Palestinian territories, and the subsequent undermining of equal citizenship. As shown above, the Judaization project provides a "genetic core" for understanding the Israeli polity because it shaped not only the Jewish-Palestinian conflict but also the relations between Ashkenazim and Mizrahim, as well as between secular and orthodox Jews.[58]

A key factor in understanding the Israeli regime thus lies in uncovering the sophisticated institutional setting that presents itself as democratic, but at the same time facilitates the continuing immigration of Jews (and only Jews) to Israel, and the unidirectional transfer of land from Arab to Jewish hands. Here we can observe that the legal and political foundations of the Jewish state have created a distorted structure that ensured a continuing uniethnic seizure of a biethnic state. Once in place, this structure became self-referential, reifying and reinforcing its own logic.

But the dominant view unequivocally treats Israel as a democracy.[59] This view is augmented by the durable operation of many important democratic features (as distinct from structures), especially competitive politics, generous civil rights, a relatively autonomous judiciary, and free media. In particular, Israel's democratic image has also been promoted in the academy by nearly all scholars in the social sciences and humanities.

Israeli scholars use a range of definitions for the Israeli regime, including liberal democracy,[60] constitutional democracy,[61] consociational democracy,[62] and ethnic democracy.[63] The enactment of two new basic laws during the 1990s has prompted a wave of writing hailing the "constitutional revolution" as a major move toward legal liberalism.[64] Even critical writers such as Azmi Bishara, Yoav Peled, Yonattan Shapiro, Uri Ben-Eliezer, Shlomo Swirsky, and Uri Ram still treat "Israel Proper" (the imaginary unit within the Green Line) as a democratic, though seriously flawed, regime.[65] Most Palestinian writers have refrained from analyzing the specific nature of the Israeli regime, although here a number of significant challenges to the common democratic definition of Israel began to appear, most notably by Elia Zureik,[66] Asad Ghanem, and Nadim Rouhana, with the latter two defining Israel as a nondemocratic "ethnic state."[67]

Yet, none of these works has incorporated seriously the two principal political-geographical processes shaping the Israeli polity: the ongoing Judaization of the country and the vagueness of its political borders. Even critical writers tend to ignore the incongruity between the definition of Israel within the Green Line, and the residence of people considered as full Israelis in occupied territories beyond the state's boundaries. This is not a minor aberration, but rather a structural condition that undermines the claim to a democratic regime. "Israel Proper" is a political and territorial entity that has long ceased to exist, and hence cannot provide an appropriate spatial unit for analyzing the nature of the polity.

In many ways, the situation resembles the hegemonic moment observed by Gramsci, when a dominant truth is diffused by powerful elites to all corners of society, preventing the raising of alternative voices and reproducing prevailing social and power relations. It appears that this hegemony has reached even the most enlightened and putatively democratic realms of Israeli-Jewish society.

How can this enigma be explained? How can enlightened circles who declare themselves to be democratic square the "Jewish and democratic" account with the continuing process of Judaization? I suggest here a metaphor in which Israeli-Jewish discourse is analogous to a tilted tower, such as the Tower of Pisa. Once one enters the tower, it appears straight, since its internal structural grid is perfectly perpendicular and parallel. This is akin to the introverted discourse about the Jewish and democratic state: once inside this discourse, most Jews accept the Jewish character of the state as an unproblematic point of departure, much like the floor of the tilted tower. From that perspective, Judaization appears natural and justified—or perhaps does not appear at all.[68]

On the basis of this tilted foundation, Israel has added laws and policies over the years that can be likened to the tower's walls. Given the tilted foundation, these walls could only be built on an angle, yet they appear straight to those observing from the inside. One needs to step outside and away from the tilted building and measure its coordinates against truly vertical buildings in order to discern the distortion. In the Israeli case, then, scholars are urged to step outside the internal Jewish-Israeli discourse and analyze the Israeli regime systematically against the "straight" principles of a democratic state.[69]

In this vein, let us explore briefly the principle of self-determination, which forms the basis of popular sovereignty and thus of democracy itself. Because the modern state is a legal-territorial entity, and because the fullest expression of self-determination is the governance of a state, it must be exercised on a territorial basis. But Israel maintains a placeless entity (the Jewish people) as the source of its self-determination, and thus defines the state as "the state of the Jewish people." This nonterritorial definition presents two serious problems for democratic rule: it prevents the full political inclusion of non-Jews by degrading the status of (territorial) state citizenship and it reinforces Judaization through the role of world Jewry in immigration and land transfer.[70]

The case of Finland may again help illustrate the problem: while that state is declared to be Lutheran, it is also defined as a (territorial) Finnish political community. As such, it allows non-Lutheran minorities to fully identify as Finnish. But because the state of Israel is defined (nonterritorially) as Jewish, and Arabs can never become Jewish, their right to equal citizenship is structurally denied. Hence, a democratic state requires a territorial form of self-determination that enables the equal inclusion of minorities into the state's civil society.[71] This recognition casts doubt over the validity of one of the most significant statements made by the Israeli High Court, which declared in 1988 that "Israel's definition as the state of the Jewish people does not negate its democratic character, in the same way that the Frenchness of France does not negate its democratic character."[72] This statement harbors a conceptual distortion: if France is French, Israel should be *Israeli* (and not Jewish). Hence, stepping outside the internal Israeli-Jewish discourse reveals that the maintenance of a nonterritorial (Jewish) form of self-determination structurally breaches central tenets of democracy. It constitutes, instead, the foundation of the Israeli-Jewish ethnocracy.

Epilogue: Ethnocracy and Negev Lands

To conclude, let us return once again to the "coal face" of land control issues in Israel. Since September 1997, the Israeli government has announced on several occasions the introduction of new strategies to block the "Arab invasion" into state lands within the Green Line, and to curtail "illegal" Bedouin dwellings, construction, and grazing. In most cases, "illegal dwellings" and "Arab invasion" are code terms for Bedouin residence on traditional tribal land and resistance to involuntary concentration in a small number of towns designated by the state in the Negev and Galilee.[73] The recently announced strategy would combine the development of small Jewish settlements (mainly in the Negev's northeastern hills), the establishment of single-family Jewish farms, the sale of Negev land to the Jewish Agency and Diaspora Jews, and the application of greater pressure on Bedouins to migrate to the state-planned towns. The initiator of the policy was the (then) director of the prime minister's office, Avigdor Lieberman, an immigrant from the former Soviet Union and a resident of a West Bank Jewish settlement.

A closer look at the latest land control strategy raises several hard questions: if the Bedouin-Arabs were Israeli citizens, as they are, why would their use of state land be considered an "invasion"? How do other sectors of Israeli society, such as *moshavim* and *kibbutzim*, which regularly build without planning permission, escape treatment as "invaders"? Given that the initiator of the policy is a West Bank settler (illegal according to international law), who is actually the invader here? How can a recent immigrant to the country campaign to evacuate residents who have been on the land for several generations, since well before the state was established? How can the state lease large tracts of land to noncitizen (Jewish) organizations and continue to block its own (Arab) citizens from using it for residential purposes?[74]

At the end of its first Jubilee, then, Israel's ethnocratic features keep surfacing: the ongoing Judaization project, the stratification of ethnic rights, the fuzziness of geographical and political boundaries, and the legal and material involvement of extraterritorial Jewish organizations. Against this reality, scholars, students, and activists are called upon to destabilize the hegemonic Jewish discourse of a "Jewish and democratic state" and to participate in the task of transforming Israel from ethnocracy to democracy.

NOTES

1. I am grateful for the encouragement and comments received from Uri Ram, and for the useful remarks on earlier drafts received from Adriana Kemp, Yossi Yonah, Michael Shalev, Asa'd Ghanem, Ian Lustick, Amnon Raz, and Nira Yuval-Davis. Parts of this chapter appeared in my "Ethnocracy or Democracy? Settler Politics in Israel," *Bulletin of Middle East Report and Information Project* (MERIP) 217 (1998): 8–14.

2. *Ka'adan v. Israel Land Authority et al.*, Bagatz 6698/95.

3. Here my work joins previous critiques of the Israeli regime. See, for example: U. Ben-Eliezer, *The Emergence of Israeli Militarism* [in Hebrew] (Tel Aviv: Kibbutz Me'uhad, 1995); B. Kimmerling, "Religion, Nationalism and Democracy in Israel" [in Hebrew], *Zemanim* 56 (1995): 116–131; A. Ghanem, "State and Minority in Israel: The Case of Ethnic State and the Predicament of Its Minority," *Ethnic and Racial Studies* 21, no. 3 (1998): 428–447; J. Shapiro, *Democracy in Israel* (Ramat Gan: Messada, 1977).

4. Ashkenazi Jews ("Ashkenazim" in plural) are of European origins, while Mizrahi Jews ("Mizrahim" in plural, also termed "Sephardim" or "Oriental Jews") hail from the Muslim world.

5. Following H. Lefebvre, *The Production of Space* (Oxford: Blackwell, 1991).

6. See Yiftachel and T. Fenster, "Introduction: Frontiers, Planning and Indigenous Peoples," *Progress in Planning* 47, no. 4 (1997): 251–260.

7. G. Fredrickson, "Colonialism and Racism: United States and South Africa in Comparative Perspective," in *The Arrogance of Racism*, ed. G. Fredrickson, 112–131 (Middletown: Wesleyan University Press, 1988); G. Shafir, *Land, Labor and the Origins of the Israeli-Palestinian Conflict 1882–1914* (Cambridge: Cambridge University Press, 1989).
8. D. Stasiulis and N. Yuval-Davis, "Introduction: Beyond Dichotomies: Gender, Race, Ethnicity and Class in Settler Societies," in *Unsettling Settler Societies*, ed. D. Stasiulis and N. Yuval-Davis, 1–38 (London: Sage, 1995). This broad classification fluctuates according to the specific circumstances of each settler society.
9. Y. N. Soysal, *Limits of Citizenship: Migrants and Postnational Membership in Europe* (Chicago: University of Chicago Press, 1994).
10. A. Murphy, "The Sovereign State System as a Political-Territorial Ideal: Historical and Contemporary Considerations" in *State Sovereignty as Social Construct*, ed. T. Biersteker and S. Weber, 81–120 (Cambridge: Cambridge University Press, 1996).
11. M. Billig, *Banal Nationalism* (London: Sage, 1995).
12. B. Anderson, "Introduction," in *Mapping the Nation*, 1–16, ed. G. Balakrishnan (New York: Verso, 1996); W. Connor, *Ethnonationalism: The Quest for Understanding* (Princeton: Princeton University Press, 1994): A. D. Smith, *Nations and Nationalism in a Global Era* (Cambridge: Polity, 1995).
13. Stasiulis and Yuval-Davis, "Beyond Dichotomies."
14. For the global process, see D. Held, "The Decline of the Nation State," in *New Times: The Changing Face of Politics in the 1990s*, 191–204, ed. S. Hall and M. Jacques (London: Lawrence and Wishart, 1990); D. Harvey, *The Condition of Postmodernity* (Oxford: Blackwell, 1989). For its Israeli manifestations, see U. Ram, "Citizens, Consumers and Believers: The Israeli Public Sphere between Capitalism and Fundamentalism," *Israel Studies* 3. no. 1 (1998): 24–44; G. Shafir and Y. Poled, "Citizenship and Stratification in an Ethnic Democracy," *Ethnic and Racial Studies* 21, no. 3 (1998): 408–427.
15. The term "ethnocracy" has appeared in previous literature. See J. Linz and A. Stepan, *Problems of Democratic Transition and Consolidation* (Baltimore: Johns Hopkins University Press, 1996), 69; Linz, "Totalitarian vs. Authoritarian Regimes," in *Handbook of Political Science (1975)*, ed. F. Greenstein and N. Polsby, 175–411 (Reading, Mass.: Addison-Wesley),; A. Mazrui, *The Making of Military Ethnocracy* (London: Sage, 1975); D. Little, *Sri Lanka: The Invention of Enmity* (Washington: US Institute of Peace, 1994), 72. However, as far as I am aware, it was generally used as a derogatory term, and not developed into a model or concept, as formulated here. For an earlier formulation, see my "Israeli Society and Jewish-Palestinian Reconciliation: 'Ethnocracy' and Its Territorial Contradictions," *Middle East Journal* 51, no. 4 (1997): 505–519.
16. As noted, ethnocracies have existed for long periods in countries such as Sri Lanka, Malaysia, and Northern Ireland (until 1968), and more recently in Estonia, Latvia, Slovakia, and Serbia.
17. Here the advent of "illiberal democracy" (F. Zakaria, "The Rise of Illiberal Democracy," *Foreign Affairs* 76, no. 6 (1997): 22–43) is instrumental, by establishing a regime with formal democratic appearance but with centralizing, coercive, and authoritarian characteristics. See also Y. Yonah, "A State of all Citizens, a Nation-State or a Multicultural State? Israel and the Boundaries of Liberal Democracy," *Alpayim* 16 (1998): 238–263.
18. A. Gramsci, *Selections from Prison Notebooks* (New York: International Publishers, 1971); see also Lustick's illuminating discussion of the notion of hegemony in his *Unsettled States, Disputed Lands* (Ithaca: Cornell University Press, 1993).

19. B. Kimmerling, "Boundaries and Frontiers in the Israeli Control System: Analytical Conclusions," in *The Israeli State and Society: Boundaries and Frontiers*, ed. B. Kimmerling, 267–288 (Albany: SUNY Press, 1989).
20. This is supported by repeated statements of Israeli leaders. For example, Prime Minister Netanyahu claimed that "only one government has and will have sovereign power west of the Jordan" (*Maariv*, February 18, 1998); similarly, Minster of Justice Y. Hanegbi claimed on September 14, 1998 (Channel One, Israeli TV) that "sovereignty in Eretz Yisrael will never be divided and will remain Israeli, and Israeli only."
21. BS, Israel's Bureau of Statistics, *Israel Yearbook* (Jerusalem: Government Printers, 1998); figures relate to December 31, 1997.
22. E. Rekhes, "The Moslem Movement in Israel," in *The Arab Minority in Israel: Dilemmas of Political Orientation and Social Change*, ed. E. Rekhes (Tel Aviv: Dayan Centre, University of Tel Aviv, 1991).
23. The differences from "typical" European settler movements include Zionism's nature as an ethnonational and not an economic project, the status of most Jews as refugees, the loose organization of Diasporic Jewish communities as opposed to the well-organized metropolitan countries, and the notion of "return" to Zion enshrined in Jewish traditions.
24. See, for example, Y. Cohen and Y. Haberfeld, "Second Generation Jewish Immigrants in Israel: Have the Ethnic Gap in Schooling and Earnings Declined?" *Ethnic and Racial Studies* 21, no. 3 (1998): 507–528; S. M. Lewi-Epstein and N. Semyonov, "Ethnic Mobility in the Israeli Labor Market," *American Sociological Review* 51 (1986): 342–351.
25. For the historical evolution of Israel's ethnic political economy and labor relations in Israel, see L. Grinberg, *Split Corporatism in Israel* (Albany: SUNY Press, 1991); M. Shalev, *Labour and the Political Economy in Israel* (Oxford: Oxford University Press, 1992).
26. P. Lahav, *Judgment in Jerusalem: Chief Justice Simon Agranat and the Zionist Century* (Berkeley: University of California Press, 1997).
27. The 1985 law also disqualifies parties using a racist platform.
28. See D. Kretzmer, *The Legal Status of the Arabs in Israel* (Boulder: Westview, 1990); Adalah, *Legal Violations of Arab Rights in Israel* (Sehfa'amre: Adala, 1998).
29. See B. Morris, *Israel's Border Wars, 1949–1956* (Oxford: Oxford University Press, 1993).
30. According to Peled and Shafir ("The Roots of Pacemaking: The Dynamics of Citizenship in Israel, 1948–93," *International Journal of Middle East Studies* 28 [1996]: 391–413), the intensity of the Judaization project has slowed down recently, in part because of the global orientations of Israeli elites. But despite the decline, the logic of Judaization is still fundamental to Israeli-Jewish politics and should be treated as the historical "genetic core" of the Israeli regime.
31. See U. Ram, "Zionist Historiography and the Invention of Modern Jewish Nationhood: The Case of Ben Zion Dinur," *History and Memory* 7, no. 1 (1995): 91–124. Records show that Jews remained in the land of Israel for centuries after the destruction of the Second Temple and in most cases emigrated voluntarily.
32. On policies affecting Palestinian-Arabs in Israel, see also G. Falah, "Israeli Judaisation Policy in Galilee and Its Impact on Local Arab Urbanisation," *Political Geography Quarterly* 8 (1989): 229–253; I. Lustick, *Arabs in the Jewish State: Israel's Control over a National Minority* (Austin: University of Texas Press, 1980): S. Smooha, "Existing and Alternative Policy Towards the Arabs in Israel," *Ethnic and Racial Studies* 5 (1982): 71–98; O. Yiftachel, *Planning a Mixed Region in Israel: The Political Geography of Arab-Jewish Relations in the Galilee* (Aldershot, U.K.: Avebury, 1992); E. T. Zureik, *Palestinians in Israel: a Study of Internal Colonialism* (London: Routledge and Kegan Paul, 1979).

33. That is, the area of Israeli regional councils, where world Jewry organizations are part of most land leasing and ownership arrangements.
34. See Hasson, "Social and Spatial Conflicts: The Settlement Process in Israel during the 1950s," *L'Espace Geographique* 3 (1981): 169–179; Y. Gradus, "The Emergence of Regionalism n a Centralised System: The Case of Israel," *Environment and Planning D: Society and Space* 2 (1984): 87–100; S. Swirski and B. Shoshani, *Development Towns: Toward a Different Tomorrow* (Tel Aviv: Breirot, 1985).
35. See Falah, "Israeli Judaisation Policy in Galilee"; Lustick, *Unsettled Stares, Disputed Lands*; D. Newman, "The Territorial Politics of Exurbanisation: Reflections on 25 Years of Jewish Settlement in the West Bank," *Israel Affairs* 3, no. 1 (1996): 61–85; Yiftachel, "Israeli Society and Jewish-Palestinian Reconciliation."
36. See Yiftachel, "Israeli Society and Jewish-Palestinian Reconciliation."
37. There exists a wide body of literature that debates the characteristics of Israeli democracy, all assuming a priori that Israel is governed by such a regime. See A. Arian, *The Second Republic: Politics in Israel* (Tel Aviv: Zmora-Bitan, 1997); B. Neuberger, *Democracy in Israel: Origins and Development* (Tel Aviv: Open University, 1998); S. Smooha, "Ethnic Democracy: Israel as an Archetype," *Israel Studies* 2, no. 2 (1997): 198–241.
38. For elaboration of the historical evolution of the Israeli-Jewish "ethnocracy," see my "Israeli Society and Jewish-Palestinian Reconciliation." A similar formulation of Israel as an "ethnic state" can be found in N. Rouhana, *Palestinian Citizens in an Ethnic Jewish State: Identities and Conflict* (New Haven: Yale University Press, 1997); Ghanem, "State and Minority in Israel."
39. See D. Held, *Models of Democracy* (Stanford: Stanford University Press, 1988); Linz and Stepan, *Problems of Democratic Transition and Consolidation*. Needless to say, pure democracy is never implemented fully, although Linz and Stepan list forty-two countries that fall over a democratic threshold. We use the democratic model here as an analytical tool with which the Israeli regime can he examined.
40. A striking example of the involvement of world Jewry was the declaration by ultra-orthodox Australian millionaire, and major donor to religious parties, David Guttnick, that he would work to "topple the Netanyahu government" in case it decides to withdraw from occupied territories (*Haaretz*, August 14, 1998).
41. Jewish settlements in the occupied territories were established under military rule; the settlements are closed to Palestinian-Arabs.
42. For a thorough, groundbreaking analysis of the role of borders in Jewish politics, see A. Kemp, "Talking Boundaries: The Making of Political Territory in Israel 1949–1957" [in Hebrew] (Ph.D. diss., Tel Aviv University, 1997).
43. Most accounts of the Israeli regime, including critical analyses, have continued to treat Israel concurrently as the land bounded by the Green Line and the body of Israeli citizens (including Jewish settlers of the occupied territories). This contradiction was rarely problematized in the literature. For examples of critical accounts that take this approach, see Y. Peled, "Ethnic Democracy and the Legal Construction of Citizenship; Arab Citizens of the Jewish State," *American Political Science Review* 86, no. 2 (1992): 432–443; U. Ram, "Citizens, Consumers and Believers"; Rouhana, *Palestinian Citizens in an Ethnic Jewish State*; Smooha, "Ethnic Democracy." For earlier debates with this approach, see Kimmerling, "Boundaries and Frontiers in the Israeli Control System"; Migdal, "Society-Formation and the Case of Israel," in *Israel in Comparative Perspective*, ed. M. Barnett, 173–198 (Albany: SUNY Press, 1996).
44. Sec Kimmerling, "Religion, Nationalism and Democracy in Israel"; Y. Nevo, "Israel: From Ethnocracy to Theocracy" (paper delivered at "The Conflictual Identities

45. Quoted in Neuberger, *Democracy in Israel*, 41.
46. Interview of Rabbi Azran, *Globes*, September 28, 1998.
47. Kimmerling, "Religion, Nationalism and Democracy in Israel"; C. Liebman, "Attitudes Towards Democracy among Israeli Religious Leaders," in *Democracy, Peace and the Israeli-Palestinian Conflict*, ed. E. Kofman, A. Shukri, and R. Rothstein, 135–161 (Boulder: Lynne Reiner Publishers, 1993).
48. See Y. Peres and E. Yuchtman-Yaar, *Between Consent and Dissent: Democracy and Peace in the Israeli Mind* (Jerusalem: Israel Democracy Institute, 1998); S. Smooha, *Arabs and Jews in Israel: Change and Continuity in Mutual Intolerance* (Oxford: Westview, 1992).
49. See Migdal, "Society-Formation and the Case of Israel" ; Peres and Yuchtman-Yaar, *Between Consent and Dissent*.
50. See Stukhammer, "Israel's Jubilee and Haredi-Secular Relations from a Haredi Perspective," *Alpayim* 16 (1998): 219; see also a recent interview with the new leader of the Religious National Party, Rabbi Y. Levi, who claimed that the main goal of his party is to ensure the Jewishness of the state for future generations (*Haaretz*, August 12, 1998).
51. As observed by E. Don-Yehiya, the most striking feature of orthodox-secular relations is their cooperation, and not conflict, as the two groups differ sharply on most values, goals, and aspirations (*The Politics of Accommodation: Settling Conflicts of State and Religion in Israel* [Jerusalem: Floresheimer Institute for Policy Studies, 1997]). I suggest here that the central project of Judaizing the country has formed the foundation for this cooperation.
52. See E. Shohat, "The Narrative of the Nation and the Discourse of Modernisation: the Case of the Mizrahim," *Critique* (Spring 1997): 3–18; S. Swirski, *Israel: The Oriental Majority* (London: Zed, 1989).
53. T. Bensky, "Testing Melting Pot Theories in the Jewish Israeli Context," Sociological Papers, Sociological Institute for Community Studies, Bar Ilan University, vol. 2, no. 2, 1993, 34–62.
54. Peled and Shafir, "The Roots of Peacemaking."
55. On protest and resistance in the Israeli peripheries, see my "Israeli Society and Jewish-Palestinian Reconciliation."
56. It can even be argued that the Oslo process has accelerated the process of Judaizing large parts of the occupied territories, by legitimizing the construction of further Jewish housing and pervasive land confiscation for "by-pass roads." In this vein, the long closures of the territories, and the subsequent importation of hundreds of thousands of foreign workers to replace Palestinian labor, are also part of the post-Oslo process of Judaization.
57. For recent attempts to compare Israel to Western democracies, see A. Dowty, *The Jewish State: One Hundred Years Later* (Berkeley: University of California Press, 1998); G. Shefer, "Has Israel Really Been a Garrison Democracy? Sources of Change in Israel's Democracy," *Israel Affairs* 3, no. 1 (1996): 13–38.
58. I do not claim, of course, that the Judaization process can explain every facet of ethnic relations in Israel/Palestine; rather, it is a factor that helped shape these relations while remaining largely overlooked in scholarly literature. But the Judaization process has also affected greatly power relations between groups not covered in this essay, including military-civil society, gender relations, and local-central tensions.

See K. Ferguson, *Kibbutz Journal: Reflections on Gender, Race and Nation in Israel* (Pasadena, Calif.: Trilogy Book, 1993).

59. This includes some own previous writings, such as *Planning a Mixed Region in Israel*(1992), where I classified Israel as a bi-ethnic democracy.

60. Neuberger, *Democracy in Israel*; Shefer, "Has Israel Really Been a Garrison Democracy?"

61. S. N. Eisenstadt, *The Transformation of Israeli Society* (London: Weidenfeld and Nicholson, 1985).

62. Don-Yehiya, *The Politics of Accommodation*; Liebman, "Attitudes Towards Democracy among Israeli Religious Leaders"; D. Horowitz and M. Lissak, *Trouble in Utopia: The Overburdened Polity of Israel* (Albany: SUNY Press, 1990).

63. Smooha, "Ethnic Democracy: Israel as an Archetype"; Shafir and Peled, "The Roots of Peacemaking."

64. See Arian, *The Second Republic*; A. Barak, "Fifty Years of Israeli Law" [in Hebrew], *Alpayim* 16 (1998): 36–45.

65. See A. Bishara, "On the Question of the Palestinian Minority in Israel" [in Hebrew], *Teorya Uvikkoret (Theory and Critique)* 3 (1993): 7–20; U. Ben-Eliezer, "Is Military Coup Possible in Israel?" *Theory and Society* 27 (1998): 314–349; Peled, "Ethnic Democracy and the Legal Construction of Citizenship"; Shapiro, *Democracy in Israel*; Swirsky, *Israel: The Oriental Majority*; Ram, "Citizens, Consumers and Believers."

66. E. Zureik, "Prospects of Palestinians in Israel (I)," *Journal of Palestine Studies* 12, no. 2 (1993): 90–109.

67. See Ghanem, "State and Minority in Israel"; Rouhana, *Palestinian Citizens in an Ethnic Jewish State*.

68. Here we can note that the political disagreement between the Jewish left and right in Israel, which is often portrayed as a bitter rivalry, is not on the broadly accepted "need" to Judaize Israel, but only on the desired extent of this project.

69. A step in this direction has already been taken, see Ghanem, "State and Minority in Israel"; Rouhana, *Palestinian Citizens in an Ethnic Jewish State*; Yiftachel, "Questioning 'Ethnic Democracy,'" *Israeli Studies* 3, no. 2 (1998): 253–267.

70. This affects adversely the political rights of Israeli Jews, too, as it undermines the extent of their own sovereignty.

71. Political theorists discuss in recent debates the possibility of cultural or linguistic forms of self-determination, which may be nonterritorial (see W. Kymlicka, *Multicultural Citizenship: A Liberal Theory of Minority Rights* [Oxford: Clarendon Press, 1995]). However, these forms also allow the possibility of civil entrance into the collectivity. This is different in Judaism, which is neither territorial, cultural, or linguistic, and thus prevents the possibility of civil inclusion.

72. *Neiman v. Central Elections Committee*, Judgment of High Court President Judge M. Shamgar.

73. On this issue, see detailed analysis by T. Fenster, "Settlement Planning and Participation under Principles of Pluralism," *Progress in Planning* 39, no. 3 (1993): 169–242.

74. The government's new strong-arm approach became evidently clear in early April 1998, when three homes built by Bedouins on private Arab land in the Galilee were demolished. The event was followed by demonstrations and strikes and community efforts to rebuild the homes.

8

A First Step in a Difficult and Sensitive Road

Preliminary Observations on *Qaadan v. Katzir*

ALEXANDRE (SANDY) KEDAR

The state of Israel allocated land to the Jewish Agency in order to establish Katzir.[1] This so-called community settlement was founded in 1982 in the Wadi Ara (Nahal Eirun) region. In 1995, the Qaadans, a Palestinian-Israeli family, attempted to acquire land in Katzir but failed to do so. Until the supreme court *Qaadan v. Katzir* decision, Arabs could not acquire land in any of the hundreds of settlements of this kind existing in Israel.[2] A sophisticated discriminatory procedure, involving the state, the Jewish National Fund (JNF), the Israel Land Administration (ILA), the Jewish Agency, and Community Cooperatives guaranteed the ethnonational purity of these settlements. In October 1995, the Association of Civil Rights in Israel (ACRI), which represented the Qaadans, petitioned the supreme court. Chief Justice Aharon Barak confessed this to be one of the most difficult cases he ever encountered.[3] The court made many attempts to convince the parties to find an out-of-court solution. Finally, after five years of failed attempts, a four-to-one majority ruled in favor of the Qaadans.[4] Chief Justice Barak, with Justices Zamir, Or, and Heshin, ruled that the state could not "allocate State land to the Jewish Agency for the establishment of the Katzir community settlement on the basis of discrimination between Jews and non Jews" (par. 40).[5] Notwithstanding this seemingly clear decree, its operative part was lacking. It merely instructed the state to consider whether "on the basis of the equality principle," and taking into consideration factors "concerning the Jewish Agency and the settlers in the place . . . it could allow the petitioners . . . to establish a home in the confines of the Katzir community settlement" (par. 40). The duality of this decree, proclaiming simultaneously the illegality of the discriminatory procedure, while apparently leaving

---

Reprinted by permission of Alexandre Kedar. Originally published as "A First Step in a Difficult and Sensitive Road: Preliminary Observations on *Qaadan v. Katzir*," *Israel Studies Bulletin* 16 (2000): 2–11.

the respondents with discretion whether to continue this illegal practice, symbolizes the essence of the case as being, in the words of the court, "a first step in a difficult and sensitive road."

What is the significance of this road and where would it lead? I believe that there are at least three major perspectives to look at this question. While these perspectives are closely interrelated and often blurred, it is helpful to differentiate them. The first is the difficult attempt to assess the impact of the decision upon Israeli society at large. How will it affect the Jewish, Zionist, and Democratic fabric of Israel? How will it influence its ethnic and political geography? The second is the normative perspective that asks whether this decision is "justified" according to particular ethical criteria. The third is an attempt to understand the "inner" meaning of Qaadan—that is, its significance on the position, direction, and role of the court itself.

I have doubts as to current predictions on Qaadan's impact. Nevertheless I will address this question in the conclusion. As to the normative perspective, I entertain strong views and beliefs on the case, and undoubtedly they influence my understanding of Qaadan. However, as a legal historian and a land regime scholar, I decided to focus primarily on the "inner" aspects of the case.

What then is the inner significance of Qaadan? I believe the case represents an essential shift in the court's position. It signals a transition from a collective and "settling" into more individualist and "liberal" jurisprudence. Nevertheless, it is not a categorical transformation, but a big leap, from the "Jewish/Zionist" toward the "Democratic/equality" pole within the "Jewish-Democratic State" legal tenet. Moreover, Qaadan is a forward-looking precedent, which endeavors to draw a line: accepting past practices while initiating "a first step in a difficult and sensitive road." This road simultaneously embodies considerable promises and significant drawbacks. I will first look at the promises and then at the drawbacks.

Interference with Discriminatory Land Allocation

A major contribution of Qaadan is its interference with the allocation component of the Israeli land regime. To evaluate this contribution, it is important to understand the making of the Israeli land regime. Beginning with the creation of Israel, the court contributed to the constitution of the Israeli land regime as a system geared to promote the Zionist project of Judaizing Israeli space and society.[6] As Oren Yiftachel has argued, similarly to other settler states, Israel initiated a comprehensive land and settlement policy.[7] This policy rested on new, powerful legislation that transferred land use, control, and ownership into Jewish-Israeli hands. It is important to highlight here two major aspects: (1) nationalization of public and Arab land, and (2) selective allocation of possessory land rights within the Jewish population. This distinction is important, since Qaadan addressed only the latter component.

At the end of the Israeli War of Independence, land officially owned by the state and Jewish individuals and organizations amounted to about 13.5 percent of the state's territory.[8] To fulfill the Zionist project of Judaizing the land, Israel fashioned a national-collectivist land regime, rapidly and systematically expanding the land in its control.[9] By the 1960s approximately 93 percent of the Israeli territory came to the ownership and control of public and Jewish institutions aggregated together into Israel Lands [Mekarkei Israel].[10] The land nationalization took place through two major channels. One channel was the nationalization of Palestinian land through the military, administrative, and legal sovereign powers of Israel. The property of the Palestinian refugees was fully transferred to public/Jewish ownership. In addition, Palestinians that remained and became Israeli citizens lost approximately 40–60 percent of the land they had possessed.[11] Another channel was the normal registration of all British Mandate's land in the state of Israel's name. Much of the million of dunums transferred to state ownership during this process had hitherto been unregistered, but indeed legally belonged to the state. However, additional land was transferred from its Arab and Bedouin landholders as a result of crafty changes in land possession rules, mainly those concerning "Mewat" (dead land) and adverse possession.[12] Thus, Palestinian land served as a major source in the making of the Israeli land regime.

The creation of the Israeli land regime involved also the allocation of possession (but not ownership) of much of the land now belonging to Israel Lands. The possession of this public land, including Arab land transferred to it, was allocated to Jewish residents and settlements.[13] While rural land was allocated principally to Kibbutzim and Moshavim, Arab citizens of Israel remained excluded from this covert and complex allocation system.[14] A different classification of possessory rights in land into distinctive spatial/legal categories permitted the implementation of discriminatory rules while simultaneously maintaining a neutral facade.

On the basis of this system, Israel developed during the late 1970s a new settlement type, the Mitzpim (Lookouts). A major motivating force for the establishment of the Mitzpim has been the desire to Judaize the Galilee. This region was perceived as representing a "demographic threat," because of the high proportion of Arabs residing in the area and its proximity to the northern border. The Mitzpim were established in strategic locations in order to promote Jewish presence in the area and prevent Arab encroachment over public land. Such settlements offered high quality suburban residence at subsidized prices geared to induce Jews to move to the Galilee.[15] The Mitzpim then expanded into additional Israeli regions and this new type of settlement became known as "community settlements." Katzir was established in the same way, in an area densely populated by Arabs and bordering the 1967 Green Line.

As part of the process of establishing community settlements, a sophisticated system designed to exclude Arabs crystallized. Jews receive public land in these areas by a complex land allocation system. Initially, the whole settlement land is assigned through a system known as a "three-party lease." According to this arrangement, three parties sign the initial land allocation contract: ILA as the public landowners' agent,[16] the Jewish Agency, and the Jewish settlement as a collective (its legal entity is a cooperative). In order to lease (normally at a subsidized price and sometimes free of charge) an individual plot of land in such a settlement, a person must be accepted as a member of a cooperative that incorporates all residents of the community. The cooperative (often with participation of the Jewish Agency) has the power of selection and practical veto power over acceptance. This delegation of state power, the major rationale of which is to preclude Arabs from access to land, serves simultaneously to preserve the mainly middle-class character of these settlements. This has been the system at the core of the Qaadan decision.

While the Qaadan decision left untouched the issue of nationalization (which was not addressed in the petition), it dramatically interfered with the allocation part. The court ruled that "every person, whatever its nationality, is qualified to participate in the contest over the right to build his house in the Katzir community settlement" (par. 33, 38). It is likely that from Qaadan on, the power of the state and Jewish national organs such as the Jewish Agency and the JNF to allocate land to Jews only will be greatly curtailed.[17]

A Limited Interpretation of the Jewish-Zionist State Tenet

Land issues stand at the core of Jewish-Zionist and Palestinian national identities as well as of Liberal and Zionist ideologies. While the supreme court contributed to the formation of the Israeli land regime when it adjudicated land issues, it usually succeeded to avoid ideological language.[18] This can be explained in the legitimating function of the court. It preferred to use a technical and professional style, which strengthened the impression that it just implemented the law.[19]

The Qaadan petition shoved straight into an unenthusiastic court these ideological tensions.[20] While the court disregarded the Palestinian narrative and recounted only the Jewish-Zionist version,[21] its self-identity and public perception as a liberal court prevented the court from avoiding the clash of Liberal and Zionist visions.

Relying on traditional settling Zionist tenets, the Jewish Agency, one of the respondents, justified its position by arguing that its very purpose is to "settle Jews in the expanses of Israel generally, and especially in frontier areas as well as regions where the presence of Jews is sparse" (par.10). Barak reiterated such rhetoric, referring to collective ownership of land, the desire to prevent such land from "unwanted elements" (a euphemism for Arabs), and to the importance of Aliya, agricultural settlements, and security.[22]

Yet, notwithstanding the persistence of this rhetoric, it is important to highlight the emergence of a different voice, which promotes a softer version of Zionism and attempts to adjust it with a liberal individualist order. According to Qaadan, the Jewish-Zionist state is limited to two major areas. Aliya—the immigration of Jews to Israel[23]—and the national attributes of the nation.

> Indeed, the return of the Jewish People to its homeland stems concurrently from the values of Israel as a Jewish and a Democratic State. . . . From these values . . . several conclusions are drawn: [. . .] that Hebrew will be a principal language . . . and . . . that Jewish tradition [Moreshet Israel] will constitute a central component of [Israel's] religious and cultural tradition, and there are additional inferences that we do not need to address here. But from the values of Israel as a Jewish and Democratic State does not stem at all that the state will discriminate between its citizens. Jews and non-Jews in Israel are equal in rights and duties. (Par. 31; see also par. 19, 35, 36)

Equality

The explicit and unambiguous pronouncement that the Jewish attributes of Israel cannot justify the discrimination of non-Jews, elevates equality into an overriding legal principle that trumps in most cases even the state's Jewishness. This pronouncement is undoubtedly a major innovation. In the past, similarly to other settlers' courts, the Israeli supreme court constructed legal categories that concealed the existence of discriminatory rules and practices promoting Jewish appropriation of land. Furthermore, while there is no question that the Israeli supreme court shaped a civil rights jurisprudence in many areas, the court did not apply this jurisprudence with the same force across the board.[24] For a while, the court practiced this jurisprudence mainly in issues closer to the Jewish "enlightened public" consensus.[25] Particularly in the sensitive areas closest to the core of settling Zionism, such as security, land, and settlements, the court evaded the full equal implementation of its civil rights jurisprudence upon non-Jews.[26] Recently, the court made several steps into dangerous waters. Thus, after almost a decade of dragging its feet, the court finally outlawed torture. Likewise, it decided, again after more than a decade, to outlaw the utilization of Lebanese abducted by Israel as "trading cards" for the return of Israeli soldiers.[27]

Qaadan is part of this pattern. Especially after the so-called constitutional revolution of 1992, the court began to develop the doctrine of equality. However it did not apply in the same force to Palestinians. In Qaadan, the court faced an agonizing dilemma. Under the carefully crafted petition of ACRI, it had to decide either to reject the petition and pay the heavy price of being perceived as insincere, or extend its jurisprudence to the taboo area of Arab land rights.[28] After attempting to evade the decision for almost five years, the court resolved to build upon its previous equality jurisprudence and extend it to Palestinians as well. The court rejected the argument that the Jewish values of Israel justify the discrimination of non-Jews: "Equality is a fundamental value of the State of Israel. Each [public] agency in Israel—and above all the State of Israel, its agencies and employees—must act equally between the different individuals in the State. . . . The State's duty to act equally extends to all its actions. It applies therefore also to the allocation of State land" (par. 21, 23).

In extending its equality jurisprudence, the Israeli court, as courts often do, attempted to provide its novel decision with the legitimacy of past precedents. To do so, the court relied on precedents addressing equality of women, of business actors in their relation with the state, and similar issues (par. 21–24). The mere resolution to use these precedents in the sensitive issue of land allocation to Arabs announces that the court's equality jurisprudence is not for Jews only. Thus, as Ilan Saban argued, the "peripheral radiation" of the court's progressive jurisprudence seems to emanate.[29]

Interference with Discriminatory Mechanisms

The fourth contribution of Qaadan is its unmasking and rejection of certain potent devices used in the past to facilitate and legitimate the discriminatory Israeli land regime. Since I have analyzed elsewhere at length the history of Israeli supreme court in these issues,[30] and since the Israeli court resembled other settlers' courts; it will suffice to offer a condensed and general characterization of high courts during the construction of settlers land regimes.[31]

Legal systems in general, and high courts in particular, play a special role in creating and legitimating settlers' land regimes.[32] Typically, settlers' courts attribute to the new land system an aura of necessity and naturalness that protects the new status quo and prevents future redistribution.[33] Formalistic legal tools play a meaningful role in such legitimization. Rules of procedure and evidence, embedded with a heavy dose of technical and seemingly scientific language and methods, conceal the violent restructuring with an image of inevitability and neutrality. The discrimination of nonsettler groups and individuals is often masked by the construction of seemingly neutral legal categories that denote in truth particular social and ethnic groups. The legal system often imposes insurmountable procedural obstacles that prevent natives and other outsiders from effectively affirming and protecting their land rights. Courts also adopt a selective deferential position, leaving the administrative authorities with ample powers to apply rules differentiating settler and nonsettler populations in relation to land. Furthermore, the channeling of the issues into the technical realms of procedure, evidence, and legal presumptions makes it possible to keep most of the issues out of public debate and facilitates the legitimization of land dispossession, transfer, and discriminating allocation. These devices allow the application of differential criteria without admitting doing so. They also have the advantage of altering legal rules while maintaining the semblance of continuity.[34] The combined application of these legal tropes silences the fundamental questions at the foundation of these methods and contributes to the creation and endurance of discriminatory land regimes. As I will argue below, a major contribution of Qaadan has been its rejection of some (though not all) of these mechanisms. In this short article I would like to point to three major areas where the supreme court interfered with these discriminatory devices: the use of procedural barriers, the noninterference with administrative discretion, and the question of burden of proof.

The Israeli legal system, like other settler states, constructed procedural obstacles hampering Arab landholders.[35] For example, the Israeli law erected sophisticated and sometime even contradictory "legal time barriers"[36] that hampered attempts of Arab long-term possessors to secure their land.[37] In Qaadan, the respondents attempted to use similar procedural barriers to dismiss the petition. They argued simultaneously that petitioners were too late and too early (par. 8). Chief Justice Barak dismissed these procedural attempts. Thus, it rejected the argument that since the petitioners never filled a formal request to become members of the community cooperative the petition was too early. He decided that since it was clear that such a request would have been dismissed, this requirement was futile and therefore unnecessary (par. 12).

The supreme court has for a long time deferred to administrative discretion pertaining to the Israeli land regime.[38] During the nationalization of Arab land, it construed administrative discretion in ways that left the authorities with ample powers to expropriate Arab land without judicial interference.[39] In Qaadan, Barak interfered with this discretion and decided that the state could not discriminate in its allocation of land. Furthermore, the state had no discretion to release itself from this duty, by using a third body, even if it was the Jewish Agency (par. 34–38).

In the past, the Israeli supreme court often imposed the burden of proof in ways that hampered Arab attempts to hold land.[40] A substantial contribution of Qaadan is that it discarded respondents' attempts to use this legal device. This novel approach is suggested already in the statement of the case by Chief Justice Barak.[41] The authoritative language of Barak in his opening paragraph released the petitioners from the burden of proving that they could not reside in Katzir merely because they were Arabs. Furthermore, Barak framed the legal question in a way that accepted as evident not only that the Qaadans could not acquire land in Katzir, but that all state land allocated to the Jewish Agency is closed to Arabs. While this unambiguous depiction assisted the petitioners, it simultaneously put a strong spotlight on Israel's discriminatory land allocation system.

Furthermore, the court ruled that any differential treatment on the basis of religion or nationality is suspect and prima facie discriminatory. It seems that from now on it suffices to prove a differential attitude on ethnic-national basis, and the onus shifts to the state to prove that this difference is justified (par. 24).[42]

This onus is not easy to lift. In Qaadan, respondents conceded that Katzir itself consisted also of a noncooperative area where Arabs and Jews could live together. Chief Justice Barak lay the onus on the respondents to prove that there was a relevant difference between the two sections of Katzir. The state argued that the disputed sector differed because it was a cooperative. Other respondents, including the Katzir Community Cooperative and the Jewish Agency, argued that the Community Cooperative differed since it constituted part of the "chain of lookouts designed to preserve Israeli expanses for the Jewish people" and because Arabs would not be able to participate in the guard duties (par. 27). Barak refused to accept these answers. He "could not understand—and no factual evidence has been presented before us, why the dwelling of the petitioners in the Community Cooperative, situated about two kilometers" from the noncooperative sector of Katzir, "justifies the violation of the equality principle" (par. 26, 29). He stressed that "in fact, the Katzir Cooperative is open to any Jew. The result is that there is no relevant peculiarity of the residents of the settlement except their national ethnicity which serves . . . in these circumstances as a discriminatory criterion" (par. 30).

The court also casts off an attempt to introduce the "separate but equal" doctrine. It is important to stress that the court rejected this argument not only relying upon *Brown v. Board of Education*—but also on factual grounds.[43] Dismantling the veil of legitimization, Barak proclaimed that "in actuality the State of Israel allocates land exclusively to Jewish Cooperative settlements. The effect of the separation policy practiced today is discriminatory" (par. 30).

Isolating the Case

While Qaadan undoubtedly constitutes a tremendous change in the court's rhetoric, the court raised several stumbling blocks, which limit, or potentially limit, the decision's import and could lead also to conservative directions. The major obstacles are the court's refusal to look at the past, its liberal-individualist outlook, and the maintenance of escape mechanisms.

Qaadan draws a line. The past is to be left unchallenged, untouched and unspoken. Moreover, the story of the Qaadans is isolated from their collective identity and needs as Palestinian citizens of Israel.

It is worthwhile to contrast the court's escape from the past with the radical changes that are taking place in some older settlers' states. Certain courts in settler societies start to look afresh at their past land policies. Thus the Australian supreme court, which until the last decade refused to recognize land rights of aborigines, began recently to reframe the legal and political discourse by laying down its famous *Mabo v. Queensland* (1992)[44] and *Wik v. Queensland* (1996)[45] decisions. In Mabo, the court rejected the legal doctrine of terra nullius, which categorized Australia as an empty continent, and instead recognized Aboriginal title. "The nation as a whole would remain diminished until there is an acknowledgment of, and retreat from, those past injustices," explained the court.[46] Similar moves can be observed in high courts of other settler societies such as New Zealand and Canada.[47] Notwithstanding the limitations of these legal decisions,[48] there are those who perceive them as "catalytic events in Aboriginal decolonization"[49] or as manifestations of a "jurisprudence of regret."[50] This judicial trend is an engaging attempt to simultaneously acknowledge an excruciating past while taking into account contemporary needs and constraints. It gives hope to the prospect of constructing a common and equitable future in these divided societies.

This tone is missing from Qaadan. Chief Justice Barak commended the petitioners for not "ignoring the Jewish element in the identity of the State of Israel, nor the settlement history of Israel. Their petition is forward looking" (par. 7). Indeed, the only history present in the case is the Zionist narrative. Katzir itself is built at least partly on land previously owned by Palestinians.[51] But the nationalization side of the Israeli land regime is left not only untouched but also untold. Furthermore, the court decision could be understood as leaving past allocation intact. That is, a narrow reading of the case leaves immune all settlements established until Qaadan. Indeed, the refusal to touch upon the past goes as far as returning the question whether the Qaadans will be allowed to acquire land in Katzir to the respondents' discretion.[52]

This attitude goes hand in hand with the liberal-individualist prism of the decision. Due to some extent to the framing of the petition, the Qaadans' case is isolated from their collective identity and needs as Palestinian citizens of Israel. Their story is solely of a family that desired "to live in a place where there is a different quality of life and level of life than where they live today."[53]

I believe that these two omissions could be related to wider changes taking place in Israeli society. Israeli collectivist ideology and structure has been gradually weakening recently. This goes hand with hand with pressures for the alignment of Israeli society with Western globalization and the principles of free-market economics in general and doctrines of privatization in particular.[54]

This general movement manifest itself in the Israeli land regime as well. From the early 1990s the Israeli land regime has been undergoing profound (but selective) privatization.[55] This move is likely to grant monopoly over most valuable land in Israel to a limited segment of Jewish society. Simultaneously, it is important to note the concurrent constitutional and legal changes that have taken place in the last years, notably an expanding definition and an increasing protection of property rights. When Palestinian land was nationalized during the state's formative period, no constitutional guarantee of property existed. Today, after the comprehensive process of land nationalization, property rights have become constitutional due to new basic laws and trends in supreme court interpretation. Thus, Qaadan could be interpreted as setting the premises for a new, seemingly liberal and individualist property system. Yet, this new system, which does not touch upon past nationalization, nor upon the collective needs of Israeli-Palestinians, could be perceived as a move that legitimates and safeguards the present baseline and the power structure of Israeli society.[56] Thus, Qaadan could be understood as contributing to the adjustment to globalization and privatization while maintaining the power structure of Israeli society and keeping most Israeli Palestinians in their relatively powerless position. A small number of affluent Palestinians will be able to buy land. In many cases they will acquire from Kibbutzim and Moshavim land previously held or owned by Palestinians. Most Israeli Palestinians will remain, however, in their powerless position in Israeli space and society.[57]

Maintaining Escape Legal Devices

While the court dismantled some of the major legal tools that permitted the systematic discrimination of Palestinians in relation to land, and concomitant with its refusal to touch the past, the court maintained at least three additional legal devices. First, Barak left open the use of security arguments to prevent Arabs from residing in Jewish settlements (par. 37). Second, the court carefully framed its decision, as affecting only state land, leaving uncertain the bearing of the decision upon land formally owned by the JNF.[58] Considering that much of Israeli agricultural land as well as many of the rural settlements are on land owned by the JNF, this can further weaken the scope of the decision. Furthermore, true to its forward-looking approach, the court ignores that most land currently in formal ownership of the JNF was nationalized from Palestinian refugees and transferred to the JNF after 1948.[59] Finally, Barak stresses, on the basis of the petitioners' argument, that the case does not address Kibbutzim, Moshavim, and Mitzpim (par. 37). The combined effect of the refusal to address the past, the individualist outlook, and the persistence of these escape legal devices could hamper the practical effects of the Qaadan decision.

Conclusion

To conclude, I believe that Qaadan is a first step in a long, difficult, and twisting road. It represents an essential transformation in the court's jurisprudence. It signals a transition from a collective and settling into a more individualist and liberal court. Nevertheless, it is not a categorical transformation, but a big leap, from the Jewish/Zionist toward the Democratic/equality pole within the Jewish-Democratic state legal tenet. I believe that the most significant aspects of the case are that it interferes with the discriminatory land allocation component of the Israeli land regime; it offers a narrow reading of the Jewish part in the Jewish-Democratic legal paradigm; it expands its Democratic side and especially elevates equality into a fundamental legal principle that in most issues confronts successfully the ethnocentric dimensions of Israel's Jewishness; and it unmasks and dismantles many, though not all, of the potent legal devices used in the past to discriminate against Arabs in land issues.

The case retains, however, several powerful impediments. First and foremost, it attempts to avoid the past history of the Israeli land regime. It aspires to establish a forward-looking precedent. As a result, the court does not touch upon the nationalization component. It also leaves open the question of past discriminatory allocation. The case also retains several escape mechanisms that could be used to continue the discriminating land practices.

These powerful tensions are exposed in the concluding paragraphs of Barak's decision. Situated in the present, Barak seems to be torn between past and future, Zionism and democracy, the desire to settle Jews and the recognition that all should have equal access to land.

In the future, it would be illegal to discriminate against non-Jews in land allocation. But past allocations seem to be immune. Thus, at least for existing Jewish settlements and residents, the case seems to imply that the desire to live in an Arab-free community is a legitimate expectation that might give rise to a legal right to do so.[60] This last point is crucial, since it seems to tilt the final outcome against ordering the respondents to permit the Qaadans to live in Katzir. While the court ruled that the discrimination of the Qaadans is illegal, it nevertheless left the decision of whether the Qaadans will acquire a house in Katzir to the respondent's discretion.[61] At the time that this article was written, in September 2000, more than five years after they began their attempts, the Qaadans still do not live in Katzir.[62]

I also believe that Qaadan could lead to various directions. The Knesset could attempt to override the decision, and discriminatory practices could be invented. Furthermore, notwithstanding its individualist outlook, and while it could lead to the establishment of shared Jewish and Arab settlements, it is likely that the case would actually lead to a more equal distribution of land to Arab communities. To prevent Arabs from migrating to Jewish settlements, it is likely that the state and ILA would allocate land to existing Arab localities, as well as for the establishment of new ones.[63] It could also serve as precedent in petitions demanding allocation of land for Arab settlements. Indeed, I believe that given the choice of living in equal conditions in Jewish or Arab localities, many Israeli-Palestinians would prefer to retain their collective identity and live where schools, culture, and community are Arab.[64] Furthermore, I believe that Qaadan would have a strong impact on the discriminatory practices within the Jewish population. The practices of preventing single-parent families or lower income groups from residing in community settlements would receive a serious blow.[65] Finally, I believe that Qaadan has the potential to become an important precedent toward a more equal allocation of land and resources in Israel.[66]

Recently Ibrahim and Hilda Dwiri, an Arab couple from Nazareth who failed to acquire land in the "enlargement" (*Harhava*) of Kibbutz Hassollelim petitioned the court.[67] While this neighborhood adjoins Hassollelim, its future dwellers will not become members of the Kibbutz. Yet, the Kibbutz retains the power of selection, not only as to its members, but also as to the identity of the residents of this locality. Unlike the Qaadan case, this is a new neighborhood, and thought it is located near the Kibbutz, it is not part of it. I believe that this is a test case for assessing the future trends of the court. A narrow reading that upholds the Kibbutz's refusal will practically nullify the significance of Qaadan.

In explaining his Qaadan decision, Chief Justice Barak writes that we should "know and remember that we are doing today a first step in a difficult and sensitive road. We should advance in this road ploddingly, in order not to fall or fail, but we should progress in this road carefully, from case to case, according to the particulars of each case. However, even if the road will be long, it is important that we should always know, not only from where we come, but also where we are going" (par. 37).

This road would probably wind and twist with setbacks and turns. Yet, I believe the Israeli supreme court began in Qaadan an indispensable journey. The Dwiri case is the next step. Let us hope that it will signal that Qaadan was not an isolated one but an important step on the road leading to a more equitable Israel.

Postscript

This essay was written before the latest events and the violence that erupted between Jews and Arabs in Israel proper. While the tone by which I ended the article might seem out of place, I remain convinced that only full equality to the Arab citizens of Israel will ensure the stability and strength of Israeli society. Interestingly, this position seemed to be shared by the Shabak, Israeli internal security forces. In an interview held on October 14, 2000, on Israeli television—that is, after the internal violence erupted—Ami Ayalon, former head of the Shabak, revealed that his organization had recommended to grant full equality to Israeli Arabs, and that he believes that this should be done immediately. I am convinced that both moral and pragmatic reasons require the strengthening of the democratic aspects of Israeli society in line with the above analysis of Qaadan.

NOTES

1. The land is owned by the state and is allocated to the Jewish Agency in a renewable lease (par. 1–2).

2. BGZ 6698/95 *Qaadan v. ILA, Katzir and others* (not yet published) at par. 37 of President Barak's decision. I will refer to the paragraphs of Barak's decision without further mentioning the full citation.
3. See Moshe Reinfeld, "Bagaz Recommends to Find an 'Appropriate Solution' to the Arab Couple's Desire to Acquire Land in Kazir," *Haaretz*, February 18, 1998; Michael Goldberg, "Today the Window of Equality Has Opened," *Yediot Aharonot*, March 9, 2000.
4. Justice Kedmy was in the minority. This article addresses only the majority opinion.
5. Justice Chishin wrote a short separate opinion but agreed to the ruling of Barak.
6. See Oren Yiftachel and Alexandre (Sandy) Kedar, "Landed Power: The Making of the Israeli Land Regime" [in Hebrew], *Theory and Criticism* 16 (2000): 67–100.
7. Oren Yiftachel has extensively researched and developed the concept of "Ethnocracy" and applied it to Israel. According to Yiftachel, a major character of Israel as a settling ethnocracy is its project of Judaization. See Oren Yiftachel, "'Ethnocracy,' Geography and Democracy: Comments on the Politics of the Judaization of the Land" [in Hebrew], *Alpayim* 19 (2000): 78–105; Oren Yiftachel, "'Ethnocracy': The Politics of Judaizing Israel/Palestine," *Constellations* 6 (3): 364–390.
8. For details, see Yiftachel and Kedar, "Landed Power." R. Kark, "Planning, Housing and Land Policy, 1948–1952: The Formation of Concepts and Governmental Frameworks" in *Israel—The First Decade of Independence*, ed. I. Troen and N. Lucas (Albany: State University of New York Press, 1995), 461, 478.
9. Alexandre (Sandy) Kedar, "Minority Time, Majority Time: Land, Nation, and the Law of Adverse Possession in Israel" [in Hebrew], *Tel Aviv University Law Review* 21 (3) (1998): 665, 681–682; Yiftachel and Kedar "Landed Power," 78.
10. That is the state, the Development Authority, and the Jewish National Fund, which form together "Israel Land." See section 1 of *Basic Law: Lands of Israel* (1960).
11. Hillel Cohen, *Present Absentees: The Palestinian Refugees in Israel Since 1948* [in Hebrew] (Jerusalem: Vann Leer Institute, 2000), 100. Yiftachel and Kedar, "Landed Power."
12. See Alexandre (Sandy) Kedar, "Israeli Law and the Redemption of Arab Land, 1948–1969" (SJD, Harvard Law School, 1996); Kedar, "Minority Time, Majority Time," 686; Alexandre (Sandy) Kedar, "The Jewish State and the Arab Possessor," in *The History of Law in a Multi-Cultural Society: Israel 1917–1967*, ed. Ron Harris, Alexandre (Sandy) Kedar, Asaf Likhovsky, and Pnina Lahav (Aldershot, U.K.: Ashgate, 2002); Ronen Shamir, "Suspended in Space: Bedouins under the Law of Israel," *Law and Society Review* 30 (1996): 23.
13. The ethnic logic of the system functioned mainly to remove Arabs from the land. Yet, typical to an ethnocratic regime, it had an impact on stratification and fragmentation within the Jewish sector as well. See Oren Yiftachel, "Nation-Building and National Land: Social and Legal Dimensions" [in Hebrew], *Iyunei Mishpat* 21 (1998): 637–664.
14. As late as 1995, Arab citizens of Israel were allocated approximately 0.25 percent of all public land. Yiftachel and Kedar, "Landed Power."
15. See Oren Yiftachel, "Power Disparities in the Planning of a Mixed Region: Arabs and Jews in the Galilee, Israel," *Urban Studies* 30, no. 1 (1993): 157–182.
16. That is, the agent for Mekarkei Israel (the state, the Development Authority, or the JNF.)
17. But see paragraph 12 on escape mechanisms.
18. See Kedar, "The Jewish State and the Arab Possessor"; Menachem Hofnung, *Israel—Security Needs vs. The Rule of Law* [in Hebrew] (Jerusalem: Nevo, 1991); David Kretzmer,

The Legal Status of the Arabs in Israel (Boulder: Westview Press, 1990), Shamir, "Suspended in Space."

19. In other areas, the court used more overtly Zionist rhetoric. See, for example, E.A., 1/65, *Yeredor v. Chairman of the Central Election Committee*, P.D. 19 (3): 365, and Pnina Lahav, *Judgment in Jerusalem: Chief Justice Agranat and the Zionist Century* (Berkeley: University of California Press, 1997). See also Alexandre (Sandy) Kedar, "The Right to Elect and to Be Elected" [in Hebrew], in *The Courts of Law: Fifty Years of Adjudication in Israel*, ed. David Cheshin et al. (Tel Aviv: Misrad ha-Bitakhon, 1999), 84.

20. Only a few years earlier, Barak wrote that the Jewish-Zionist values embodied in the new Basic Laws included the settling of Jews in the expanses of Israel. See Aharon Barak, "The Objective Purpose of a Contract," *Interpretation in Law* 3 (1994): 330.

21. This is partly due to the framing of the petition. For an Israeli Palestinian criticism of the framing of this petition, see Maruan Dallal (Adalah) to ACRI, on file with the author.

22. "The special purposes that lie at the foundation of ILA, are the preservation of Israel Land [Mekarkei Israel] in State ownership and the concentration of the administration and development of land in Israel within one statutory agency. This, in order to prevent the transfer of the ownership of the land to unwanted elements, to execute a security policy, and allow the execution of national projects such as the absorption of Aliah, the dispersal of population, and agricultural settlement" (par. 19). In addition the court stressed the importance of "preventing speculative commerce in state lands" (par. 19).

23. "Indeed, a special key for the entrance to the house is given to members of the Jewish People (See the Law of Return, 1950), but when a person is present in the house as a legal citizen, he enjoys equal rights as all the other members of the house" (par. 31).

24. In Justice Zamir and Moshe Sobel, "Equality before the Law," *Mishpat U Mimshal* 5, no. 1 (1999): 165, one could find almost no references to supreme court cases positively applying the equality principle on Palestinians. For an argument that unlike its jurisprudence concerning discrimination on the basis of gender, the court did not apply an activist approach when the discrimination is based on ethnic/national grounds. See David Kretzmer, "Fifty Years of Jurisprudence on Human Rights," *Mishpat U Mimshal* 5, no. 1 (1999): 297, 317.

25. See Ronen Shamir, "The Politics of Reasonableness—Discretion as Judicial Power" [in Hebrew], *Theory and Criticism* 5 (1994): 7; Andrei Marmor, "Judicial Review in Israel" [in Hebrew], *Mishpat U Mimshal* 4 (1997–1998): 133; Eli Salzberger and Alexandre (Sandy) Kedar, "The Quiet Revolution—More on Judicial Review According to the New Basic Laws" [in Hebrew], *Mishpat U Mimshal* (1998): 489.

26. Often the court did so by using an ethnic neutral language and leaving large areas of discretion to administrative bodies. See Ilan Saban, "The Legal Status of Minorities in Democratic Deeply Divided Countries: The Arab Minority in Israel and the Francophone Minority in Canada Thesis" [in Hebrew] (Ph.D. diss., Hebrew University of Jerusalem, 2000).

27. See Moshe Gureli, "Did the Day of the Arabs in Court Arrive?" *Globes*, April 17, 2000, 77.

28. For the crafting of the petition, see Neta Ziv and Ronen Shamir, "Build Your House: Small and Big Politics in the Struggle against Discrimination in Land" [in Hebrew], *Theory and Criticism* 16 (2000): 45. For a criticism of Adalah of the crafting of the petition, see Maruan Dallal to ACRI, December 16, 1997, on file with the author.

29. See Ilan Saban, "The Impact of the Supreme Court on the Status of the Arabs in Israel" [in Hebrew], *Mishpat U Mimshal* 3, no. 2 (1996): 541. The outcome of previous cases implicating questions of Arab equal access to land usually tolerated their discrimination. Nevertheless, the Qaadan court managed to use this problematic repertoire as support for the application of the equality principle to Arabs. See for example the court's use of BGZ 114/78 *Burkan v. the Treasor Minister*, P.D. 32(2) 800.

30. See Kedar, "Israeli Law"; idem, "Minority Time, Majority Time"; idem, "The Jewish State and the Arab Possessor." See also Saban, "The Impact of the Supreme Court on the Status of the Arabs in Israel."

31. This is a preliminary part of a work in progress.

32. See for example J. W. Singer, "Sovereignty and Property," *Northwestern University Law Review* 86, no. 1 (1992): 1, 3, 44–45; J. W. Singer, "Well Settled? The Increasing Weight of History in America Indian Land Claims," *Georgia Law Review* 28 (1994): 481, 482; P. Russell, "High Courts and the Rights of Aboriginal Peoples: The Limits of Judicial Independence," *Saskatchewan Law Review* 61 (1998): 247–276; E. A. Daes, "Special Rapporteur, Human Right of Indigenous Peoples: Indigenous People and their Relationship to Land (Second Progress Report)," June 3, 1999, available o at http://www.un.org. On the attitude of U.S law to Chicanos in the southwestern United States, see Guadelupe T. Luna, "Chicana/Chicano Land Tenure in the Agrarian Domain: On the Edge of 'Naked Knife,'" *Michigan Journal of Race and Law* 4 (1998): 39; idem, "Beyond/Between Colors: On the Complexities of Race: The Treaty of Guadalupe Hidalgo and *Dred Scott v. Sanford*," *University of Miami Law Review* 53 (1999): 691; W. W. Fisher III, "Property and Power in American Legal History," in *The History of Law in a Multi-Cultural Society: Israel 1917–1967*, ed. Ron Harris, Alexandre (Sandy) Kedar, Asaf Likhovsky, and Pnina Lahav (Aldershot, U.K.: Ashgate, 2001).

33. Compare D. Kennedy, "Form and Substance in Private Law Adjudication," *Harvard Law Review* 89 (1976): 1685; idem, "Freedom and Constraints in Adjudication: A Critical Phenomenology," *Journal of Legal Education* 36 (1986): 518–562; idem, *A Critique of Adjudication: Fin de Siècle* (Cambridge: Harvard University Press, 1997); M. Horwitz, *The Transformation of American Law, 1780–1960* (Cambridge: Harvard University Press, 1977); idem, *The Transformation of American Law, 1870–1960* (Oxford: Oxford University Press, 1992).

34. As a result, settlers' courts can maintain that they were only applying existing law, while they were in fact altering the rules in the detriment of nonsettler possessors. See, for example, D. Geier, "Power and Presumptions: Rules and Rhetoric, Institutions and Indian Law," *Brigham Young University Law Review* (1994): 451, 454.

35. Thus, for example, the legislation of the 1958 Statute of Limitations and the initiation of settlement process in the Galilee and the Negev led to such procedural barriers. See Kedar, "Minority Time, Majority Time"; idem, "The Jewish State and the Arab Possessor"; Shamir, "Suspended in Space."

36. The phrase is from Shamir, "Suspended in Space," 245.

37. Thus, in the case of changes in adverse possession litigation, Israeli law simultaneously pushed the limitation period forward, extending the period needed to secure the right of possessors, and backward, applying the extension period retroactively, thereby preventing possessors who already fulfilled the previous limitation period from acquiring their land. See Kedar, "Minority Time, Majority Time."

38. See Kretzmer, "Fifty Years of Jurisprudence on Human Rights," 319; Oren Bracha, "Unfortunate or Perilous: The Infiltrators, the Law and the Supreme Court, 1948–1954" [in Hebrew], *Tel Aviv University Law Review* 21 (1998): 333–385; Yifat Holzman-Gazit,

"Immigration Policies, Housing Supply and Supreme Court Jurisprudence of Land Expropriation in Early Statehood," in *The History of Law in a Multi-Cultural Society: Israel 1917–1967*, ed. Ron Harris, Alexandre (Sandy) Kedar, Asaf Likhovsky, and Pnina Lahav (Aldershot, U.K.: Ashgate, 2001); Saban, "The Legal Status of Minorities in Democratic Deeply Divided Countries."

39. See, for example, BGZ 5/54 *Younes v. The Finance Minister*, P.D. 8, 314; AC 58/54 *Habbab v. The CAP*, P.D. 10 912. See also a contrary example in BGZ 64/51 *Daoud v. The Defense Minister and Others*, P.D. 5 1117. For a general review, see Kedar, "Israeli Law."

40. See Kedar, "Israeli Law"; idem, "Minority Time, Majority Time; idem, "The Jewish State and the Arab Possessor."

41. "The State of Israel has allocated land to the Jewish Agency for Eretz Israel. The Agency has established a rural community settlement on the land. This was done by way of a Community Cooperative [Aguda Shitufit].... In practice, the Community Cooperative accepts as members Jews only. The result in this situation is that an Arab can not build his house on state land allocated to the Agency. Under these circumstances—and taking into account the particulars of the case—is the decision of the state to allocate land to the Agency illegal because of a wrongful discrimination of an Arab? This is the question we are facing in this petition." Qaadan, opening paragraph of Barak's opinion.

42. See for example the difficulties encountered by petitioner in BGZ 6532/94 *Abu Kaf v. The Agriculture Minister*, P.D. 50(4) 391.

43. Barak quoted Brown's decision that "separate but equal" is "inherently unequal." Barak, however, left open the possibility to apply differential treatment, but it seems that he thought mainly on affirmative action for minorities (par. 30).

44. *Mabo v. Queensland* [No. 2]. 175 CLR 1.

45. *The Wik Peoples v. Queensland* 141 ALR 129.

46. *Mabo v. Queensland*, 82.

47. See Russell, "High Courts and the Rights of Aboriginal Peoples," 247–276.

48. See, for example, Daes, "Special Rapporteur," 1999.

49. Russel, "High Courts and the Rights of Aboriginal Peoples," 258.

50. J. Webber, "The Jurisprudence of Regret: The Search for Standard of Justice in Mabo," *Sydney Law Review* 17, no. 1 (1995): 5–28.

51. Letter from attorney Tawfik Jabareen, August 18, 2000, on file with the author. Attorney Jabareen bases his response on a British Mandate land registration of block 12176, parcel 26, registered in 1947 in the name of Latifa Yunes, who in 1948 became an absentee. The land was then registered in the name of the Israeli Development Authority. This parcel is included in the leasing agreement between ILA and the Jewish Agency in relation to the establishment of Katzir.

52. See par. 40. This is the way that paragraph is understood by Adi Niv from the JNF. See Adi Niv, "JNF and ILA—The End of the Joint Way?" in *Karka* 49 (2000): 5, 6, and by Elyakim Rubinstein, Israel's attorney general. See Elyakim Rubinstein, "Not the End of the Fulfillment of Zionism," *Karka* 49 (2000): 15, 18–19. For a similar interpretation see Meir Alfia, "In the Essence of the JNF There Are 'Special Circumstances' Allowing It to Operate without Applying the Equality Principle on the Management of Its Land," *Karka* 49 (2000): 21.

53. Par. 4. It should be noted, however, that the court recognizes the possibility of affirmative action in favor of religious or national minorities such as Bedouins (par. 24, 30, 31). Thus, simultaneously with its refusal to look at the past and its

liberal-individualist outlook, the mere recognition that minorities are entitled to affirmative action contains a potential promise for future decisions.

54. Uri Ram, "Between Weapons and Markets: Liberal Postzionism in the Age of Globalism," working paper no. 12, "Ethnocracy and Globalism: New Approaches to the Study of Society and Space in Israel," ed. Uri Ram and Oren Yiftachel, 1999; Menachem Mautner, "The Decline of Formalism and the Rise of Values in Israeli Law" [in Hebrew], *Tel Aviv University Law Review* (1993): 503–596; Eyal Gross, "Property as a Constitutional Right and Basic Law: Human Dignity and Liberty" [in Hebrew], *Tel Aviv University Law Review* 21, no. 3 (1998): 405–447.

55. This process includes steps to transfer the full ownership of urban and suburban houses held in long-term leases, the attempts to permit public housing residents to buy their apartments, and, foremost, the process of gradual transfer of property rights in agricultural land to Kibbutzim, Moshavim, and agricultural companies. See Yiftachel and Kedar, "Landed Power."

56. See Gross, "Property as a Constitutional Right and Basic Law."

57. See ibid.; Salzberger and Kedar, "The Quiet Revolution"; Yiftachel and Kedar, "Landed Power."

58. Par. 14. This was indeed the way it was understood by JNF officials. See, for example, Alfia, "In the Essence of the JNF," 21, 24, the analysis of the JNF's legal counselor.

59. See, for example, Cohen, *Present Absentees*; Yiftachel and Kedar, "Landed Power."

60. Barak stresses that Katzir was established in 1986 as a Jewish settlement. The settlers in Katzir acquired houses relying on the situation as it was then. These expectations, as well as those of the Jewish Agency, bear some difficulties (par. 39).

61. "On the basis of the equality principle, and taking into account relevant considerations—including considerations pertaining to the Jewish Agency and the local settlers.... On the basis of these considerations, the state should decide in the appropriate speed if it could permit the petitioners, in the confines of the law, to establish a home for themselves in the confines of the Katzir community settlement" (par. 40).

62. Nor have they received any formal response to their request to acquire land in this community settlement. Interview with Dan Yakir, ACRI, September 1, 2000.

63. See, for example, *Globes*, April 11, 2000, 30, reporting that Israeli authorities are considering the allocation of land for Arab villages, and even the establishment of a new Arab city, as a reaction to Qaadan. See also Prof. Amiram Gonen, "From Bitter Will Maybe Emerge Sweet," *Globes*, March 30, 2000.

64. See G'amil Dakuar (Attorney for Adalah), "How Much of an Achievement?" [in Hebrew], *Haaretz*, March 15, 2000. Dakuar argues that unlike African Americans, Arabs in Israel do not demand integration, but a solution to their land problems, such as the return of "internal refugees" to their villages, recognition of "unrecognized villages," and the allocation of land to Arab localities.

65. See, for example, Raviv Druker, "They Don't Accept Everybody," *Maariv*, April 6, 1997.

66. Indeed, recently the Democratic Mizrachi Rainbow and a group of academics, including myself, petitioned the supreme court against the selective privatization of public land and the transfer of much of it to Kibbutzim, Moshavim, and Agricultural Companies. I believe that Qaadan could serve as an important precedent for this decision.

67. See petition of *Ibrahim and Hilda Dwiri v. ILA, Hassollelim, and Others*, unpublished, on file with the author.

9

Save as Jerusalems

ARIELLA AZOULAY

Jerusalem, as everyone knows, is a name of a city. But what is this city whose name is Jerusalem? That is a more difficult question. There is an earthly city whose name is Jerusalem, and there is also a heavenly one. There is a Jerusalem of stone and a Jerusalem of paper, a Jerusalem of iron, and a Jerusalem of gold. There is a Christian, a Muslim, and a Jewish Jerusalem. Evidently there is also Jerusalem as the capital of a Palestinian state, which is but a dream and a symbol of a national struggle, as well as Jerusalem as the capital of the State of Israel, which claims today to encompass all the other cities in one city "united forever."

"Jerusalem" is the hero of this chapter—Jerusalem in quotation marks, as a name for a heterogeneous ensemble of spaces, events, and meanings. This ensemble includes the struggle over the city's geographical and historical borders, its transformations along these two axes of time and space, the mapping of the city, the nature and structure of its urban networks (both physical and virtual, those that are contained within it and those that cross it and spread far beyond its geographical borders), and, finally, the politics of naturalization and citizenship in and of the city, the city as a subject, and the subjects of the city. I try to argue that any discussion of "Jerusalem" must encompass all these aspects at once and account for their interrelations. To understand the (human) reality of the city, one must understand the (discursive) reality of its name and through it ponder relations between maps and warfare, between history and strategies of producing truth and subjectivity, between the inscription in concrete space and transcendent temporality. I try to touch on this complexity by way of theoretical interpretation of Foucault's

Reprinted by permission of The MIT Press, from Ariella Azoulay, *Death's Showcase: The Power of Image in Contemporary Democracy* (Cambridge, Mass.: Massachusetts Institute of Technology), 182–188, 192–204. Copyright © 2001 Massachusetts Institute of Technology.

conception of space and spatialization, focusing on the notion of heterotopia (a space composed of different and contradictory layers). I relate this interpretation to an analysis of the administration of Jerusalem's urban space and to two artistic projects of Israeli artists—an itinerary traced by Sigalit Landau from the Israeli Museum to the Palestinian neighborhood El Azariya and an interactive map of one of its neighborhoods prepared by Aya and Gal.

During the three decades and a half of the Israeli occupation of East Jerusalem the organization of space and the distribution of representations in the public space of Jerusalem have been in the hands of one authority, one body determining the rules of the place—the rules according to which Jerusalem is governed and preserved as an archive of past and present. The occupation is also—always—an occupation of representations. Palestinians were deprived of most resources and positions that enable the representations of (their) past and the production and distribution of images of (their) city. A recent demonstration of this fact was the yearlong celebration of the supposed three thousandth anniversary of Jerusalem organized by the municipal authorities with support from the state and Jewish organizations abroad. The entire event, the history it unfolded, and the future it promised was wholly biased, representing mainly the Jewish point of view of the city and eliminating the present national conflict. The opening ceremony took place in the Palestinian village of Silwan, located in the valley between the Old City and the Mount of Olives. The moment was one of elation and joy for Israelis and one of intrusion and threat for Palestinians, who protested at the end of the ceremony by flying balloons colored in black, green, and red, the colors of the Palestinian flag. For a few, ephemeral moments the Palestinians occupied a nonlocated space in the city's heaven in which they could inscribe their own images and representations. But neither then nor now could they actualize their representations in a public space. The Palestinian residents of Jerusalem have no archive in which documents and images from the history of their city can be compiled, stored, classified, and displayed at will, and there is no Palestinian agency that claims the authority for stating and enacting the rules for a Palestinian representation of the history of Jerusalem.[1]

This is a not uncommon description of the Palestinian situation in Jerusalem, and its importance for the political struggle against the many evils of the Israeli occupation of the eastern part of the city cannot be denied. And yet, politically useful as it may be, the description is questionable. One may ask, for example, What exactly is this space administered by the Israeli government, how homogeneous is it, and to what extent is it indeed governed and controlled by the Israeli authorities alone?[2] One may ask whether this description, just like those it seeks to replace, does not deny the heterogeneity of the different spaces gathered under the name "Jerusalem" and reduce it to a homogeneous, single space—the national one. For if one considers Jerusalem only as a site of a national struggle, then its space must follow the rules of a single master narrative that contains two adverse versions and two possible ends, or "solutions"—either a domination by one nation and the subjugation of another (whose traces in the city are wiped out much like the remnants of an old tenant) or a partition of the city that actually doubles the national space. I try to show that in both cases the national space is made sacred and is privileged over all the other spaces of the city, in which there actually exist, and could have existed, complex interrelations that cannot be reduced to a model consisting of two parties that are external to one another.[3]

I start with a very short version of such a unidimensional history of an ethnic and religious space, which I then try to somewhat reformulate. When the Muslims conquered Jerusalem in the seventh century, they had to remove vast quantities of accumulated garbage that covered the Temple Mount compound. They then built the El-Aqsa Mosque on the site. The Crusaders conquered the city in 1099, slaughtered Jews and Muslims, removed all signs of Islam from the Temple Mount site, and transformed the mosque into a Christian basilica. One hundred years later, Jerusalem was again purified when the Muslims returned and removed all crosses and symbols of Christian ritual. Descriptions of Jerusalem from the eighteenth century tell of a neglected city in ruins, overflowing with garbage. Extended Ottoman rule had neglected the acts of purification. Afterward there was an Egyptian occupation, then Ottoman rule again, followed by British, Israeli, and Jordanian rule, each occupation accompanied by removal activities. The Israeli army conquered East Jerusalem, including the Old City, in the 1967 war. Immediately after the conquest of the Temple Mount, the Israeli army set about "cleansing" the buildings and the minarets of Arab Legion soldiers and then vacated and razed an adjacent Muslim neighborhood. The David Tower Museum, founded in 1988, was the climax of a conservation practice that effectively aimed at cleansing and purifying. The story of the city of Jerusalem, as written inside this museum, is a result of the cleansing of the story from any disturbing details that might trouble the causal order that enables the occupation to continue.[4]

But does the city exist only in one ethnic, religious, or national space? Does it really respond only to one (hi)story? The common description aimed at banishing simultaneity and heterogeneity and imposing—each time anew—an image of one hegemony, can be told differently, using a less common description that attempts to illuminate the simultaneity and heterogeneity existing—despite the main history—within the city. Jerusalem's first museum—the museum of the Greek Orthodox patriarchy—was established in 1858. In 1902, the Franciscan Museum was established in the Church of the Flagellation. In 1905, Bezalel's museum was established with the goal of collecting Jewish cultural treasures from all over the world.[5] Indeed, this collection was the basis of the Israel Museum, which opened in 1965. In 1923, the Supreme Muslim Council established the Islamic Museum. In 1938, the Rockefeller Museum was established in East Jerusalem, its main goal being to house archaeological treasures. Each of these museums represents its own point of view, a point of view that determines the rules of the place and its exhibits. The establishment of a museum marks a threshold consisting of hoarding treasure and controlling the entrance gates regarding what is let in. But the museum is part of a discourse within and through which its status, position, and authority are determined. The severe procedures of selection that a certain museum exercises reflect only the rules and constraints of the discourse within which it operates; rejected objects may still flourish outside this discursive space and its museum incarnation. When a museum exercises more than one discourse and is more loosely anchored in any of the discourses it exercises, it may allow more objects to pass though its space and employ multiple heterogeneous space-time frameworks—those that it crosses and those that it frames. This was the situation of the museums described above in 1948, at the time of the foundation of the Israeli state. These museums existed side by side in the space of simultaneity and heterogeneity.

The first description follows a "sequential," diachronic pattern and presents the history of the city as a continuum of stories of occupation, defeat, and domination. Each story replaces its predecessor and suppresses its claims to shape the city's present. The second description follows a spatial and rather static pattern and emphasizes certain privileged sites without the specific narratives associated with them. In the diachronic, sequential description, time and space are taken to be empty, homogeneous containers of events that the historian collects. In the spatial description, space and time are taken to be clusters of intersections, links, and transmission points in a way that allows the simultaneous coexistence of heterogeneous frameworks of spatialization and temporization (for example, of the museum as a cultural site, of the objects and artifacts displayed in it, and of the visitors who pass through it).

The spatial description may be read, of course, as but another ring in the diachronic chain of domination stories—in fact, as the culmination and resolution of the ongoing conflict, leading to a kind of urban harmony in which the peaceful coexistence of different points of views and competing positions is made possible. But such a reading would miss the essential difference between the two descriptions. The sequential pattern rests on the logic of detachment and purification: each new ring in the chain seeks to replace its predecessor and either removes or incorporates its traces into its new regime of identity. The spatial pattern, on the other hand, rests on the logic of simultaneity in the *present*, without governing the elements that comprise it.[6] In other words, subordinating the spatial logic to the logic of the sequential pattern eliminates the difference between the two descriptions, establishes the sequential pattern as a metanarrative, and imposes a homogeneous conception of space-time.

For this reason, the spatial description is presented here as neither the culmination of the sequential narrative nor as its replacement. At most, the spatial description provides a sketch for an attempt to deconstruct the logic of the sequential description. Space, under the former description, is fragmentary, multiple, extending beyond the physical and the visible, and never fully subject to the domination of its masters or even of those who claim to map and represent it adequately. Among the many subjects and objects that inhabit it, it has also an agency of its own. The spatial narrative proposes a grid, a network of interrelation, a structure of junctions in which not all possible passages and connections are manageable or can be brought under control according to a preconceived plan.[7]

The diachronic, sequential narrative exists within—but is not controlled by—the spatial description, as a possible link, another junction, a way out to another dimension, a passage to and from (hi)story, being always more and less than the story that unfolds it. Space is organized in many ways, and it is impossible to describe it as a product of the acts and conscious intentions of urban agents—civilian, military, or paramilitary—that claim to administer it. Space is not an object, a container, and these agents can never really become its master, for space is not written in the language of agency and authorship and does not respond to its syntax and semantics. Both space and the agents who use it are part of the networks in which they are enmeshed, in ways that undermine their professed identities and fool their explicit intentions, turning them all into knots of acted-upon actions. I try to exemplify this through the case of "the Green Line," the borderline that tends to reemerge when spatial agents try to wipe it out and disappear when they try to reinscribe it.

In November 1948 Israel and Jordan signed an armistice agreement and drew a dividing line. Both parties considered the line in the nature of a temporary concession and hoped that the political reality, which it created, would soon change. At the talks, their representatives insisted on drawing the line with two different pencils. Abdallah El-Tal, the Jordanian, used a red pencil, while the Israeli, Moshe Dayan, used a green one.[8] The map was of small scale (1:20,000), and the two lines together had a certain width, which meant in reality a long stretch of no-man's-land, 60 to 70 meters wide and many kilometers long.[9] The line crossed streets and even houses, thus enlarging the area of friction and conflict between the two parties. The two leaders tried hard to keep their agreements and disagreements in check, believing, so it seems, that they were capable of bringing everything under control, letting nothing evade their planning. Unfortunately, the result was just the opposite, and all along the dividing line—that narrow and long no-man's-land created by a pencil—emerged an unexpected, unplanned area of conflict. It was as if the pencil took revenge on the hand that wielded it as an innocent, indifferent, and available means of control. A year after the agreement, a fence was erected along the dividing zone. None of the parities liked the idea of such a conspicuous delineation of the borderline, so the fence was officially named "a fence for the prevention of infiltration." Infiltration had to be fought without a formal recognition of the transgressed boundary.

Heterotopia (*heteros topos*, other place/space), says Foucault in his article "Of Other Spaces," is a site that is designed for human activity; well demarcated, both spatially and temporally, and is characterized by the simultaneous coexistence of two or more spatial settings. Foucault mentions a few examples—the museum, the cemetery, and the holiday village. Foucault's examples (closed and demarcated sites created by humans), I argue, prevent one from fully realizing the power of the heterotopic idea. These examples restrict the concept of heterotopia to the point of view of sovereign subjects who define the rules of the game in heterotopic sites.

Heterotopia concerns the users of a site and not only its spatial organization. Spaces may be multiplied, and the simultaneous presence of the individual in these different spaces may be multiplied as well. The individual may be a citizen in civic space, an address in virtual space, an outlet in a network, or a body in a physical environment. Moreover, heterotopia is no longer just a matter of well-demarcated sites. The whole world, or at least large portions of it, has become heterotopic. Heterotopic spaces are not mastered or administered by the subjects that inhabit them; their rules are not determined according to their will. If the world is heterotopic, or if being-in-space means being-in-heterotopic-space, going into and out of "other" spaces is a matter of making and unmaking links and contacts, hooking or unhooking appliances, being in touch with someone, being exposed to the gaze of someone, being in reach of something.

Let me now go back to the passage from [Michel] Foucault's "Of Other Spaces" concerning tension between the paradigm of time (history) and the paradigm of space—and the transition between them.[10] History is a diachronic paradigm characteristic of the nineteenth century; space is a paradigm characteristic of our own age. That transition itself is still described by Foucault (who is usually associated with the spatial paradigm) in terms of the diachronic time-space paradigm and the historicity that it entails. Furthermore, Foucault reduces temporality to historical temporality and actually dissociates spatialization and temporization. His genealogical researches, which undermine the concept of historical time as an ahistorical container indifferent to the stuff it contains, still write the history of space within the framework of the diachronic paradigm. In "Of Other Spaces" he mentions some of the main stages in the history of space without thinking about the spatial dimension of this history itself, once again assuming space to be a homogeneous trunk in which some stuff—a variety of spaces in this case—is being accumulated. But time is a rhizome that springs out everywhere, and the rhizome has no trunk, historical or otherwise.[11] One may domesticate some chunks of time, call them by the names of periods and ages, and divide them into centuries and decades, and yet each one of these chunks may root itself in a different spot on a ground that changes continuously and loses its coherency due to these multiple temporizations that cut through, cut across, and interweave space in so many different ways. Space and time are always in the plural.

But for Foucault the history of time is still written in the singular. For this reason, perhaps, his analyses of social formations stopped at the disciplinary society. Disciplinary society is characterized by sites well demarcated by a single, recognized, and visible borderline in which all the participants in the power relations share a single geographic and architectural space. In the second half of the twentieth century these sites existed and flourished, but new technologies and new economic and geopolitical relations allowed them to be woven into and crossed by a variety of other spaces, to be shared differently by different inhabitants of the site, and to be opened and responded to in different, differentiating ways to their gaze and movement. Mobility in these new other spaces is not measured by the ratio between traveling time and traveled distance but by other means, such as the ratio between time and the number of links crossed and created or the ratio between a site's surface and the intensity of temporizations that cross it. The forms of space-time in the late twentieth century were characterized above all by new and intense means for temporizing space and spatializing time (such as access to air time for reaching more listeners in a wider zone or access to historical time through visiting "historical sites" or digging deeper into the ground of archaeological sites).

Gilles Deleuze touches on these issues in a small essay entitled "Postscript on the Societies of Control." There he describes the new social formation that replaces the disciplinary society in the West, briefly mentioning its new spatiotemporal dimensions: "Control is short-term and has rapid rates of turnover but also is continuous and without limit, while discipline was of long duration, infinite, and discontinuous. Man is no longer man enclosed but man in debt" (Deleuze 1992, 6).

Mastery and domination are not inscribed in space, and physical borders are no longer a main mechanism of control. Man is no longer "man enclosed" because the boundaries of domination have become complex and undetermined: they are disseminated everywhere, and yet they are mostly invisible. The seemingly inevitable link between a physical and a conceptual limit has been loosened, and the positioning of an individual in any particular place in social space is no longer necessary. Man, Deleuze claims, has become "man in debt." Debt may be disseminated over different spatiotemporal frameworks. It is not physically associated with the individual who is in debt (as was the case when the individual was enclosed) but is linked to his or her address in so many virtual and nonvirtual spaces.[12] In such a world, not only are time and space multiplied and fragmented, but individuals are fragmented and multiplied according to the number of spatiotemporal frameworks within which they are linked. Individuals do not act on a world but are part of an action that they never begin and their organs (hand, eye, mouth) are not means for a purpose or expressions of subjectivity but are links in unanimous chains of action and reaction. Together with many other instruments and objects, hand, mouth, and eye enable the functioning of systems (observation, communication, production) that in their turn make these organs effective and useful to the individual to whom they supposedly belong.[13] A short discussion of the hand and its spatial environment serves here as an example of these new spatiotemporal dimensions.

The hand is a link in the network. It belongs neither to a sovereign citizen nor to an instrument that is supposed to serve the citizen. It is the hand of the "neturalized" citizen,[14] the heterotopic citizen, the one who becomes a citizen of liminal zones, of intermediate spaces, a citizen of passages, a citizen in passing, one who is always in the process of becoming a citizen. Such a heterotopic citizen tries to create an intermediate environment "inside" the networks of social interaction, knowing all too well that there is no place "out there." The heterotopic citizen lives in the immanent tension between two elements that structure the field of social action—(1) the position of the subject within a defined field of discourse and action, which allows them to judge and act with a certain authority and claim to knowledge (these are remnants of the disciplinary society) and (2) the unavoidable intertwining of the subject's acts within conflicting networks of interaction that lie beyond their control, undermining their plans and intentions and constantly robbing their actions of meaning.

When this is the nature of our most basic spatial condition, the spatial inscription of sociopolitical demarcations, boundaries, and borders cannot be presented any longer only in terms of territory and territorialization. The individual, too, cannot be "contained" within the space occupied by his or her body. The limited space of the body is multiplied in these "other spaces" and is represented or has correlates in these spaces. But all these spaces are always somehow "out of joint": there is no exact overlapping, no one set of spatial coordinates that contains them all. All these other spaces are populated with persons, bodies, objects, instruments, and appliances. They are interwoven in different, partly intersecting and partly unrelated networks of speech, vision, and interaction. And in the constant shifts and transitions among these spaces the hand provides the ticket, the license, the right of passage. It serves as a gatekeeper and a bridge, it crosses and builds distances. In short, it allows space to become spatialized.

When the concept of heterotopia thus applies to space and also to those who use space, it is indeed possible to overcome the constituting subject, which Foucault targeted as something to get rid of to escape the strictures of historical discourse. By extending heterotopia to include space users and by understanding the hand as an agent that is not subject to the logic of subjectivity, I can question or even deconstruct the claim of the national constituting subject in the city of Jerusalem. I follow different hands in the heterotopic urban space of Jerusalem to escape the hold of that national subject over the city and undermine its attempt to gather the multiple segments of a fragmentary, heterogeneous, urban space and incorporate them into its own, single-voice history.

Before the conquest of East Jerusalem, the Israeli and Jordanian parties to the conflict recognized the armistice line, usually called the Green Line, as an international boundary only de facto, but never de jure; their city was one and was only temporarily and brutally divided. In June 1967 the Israeli army crossed the Green Line between Jordan and Israel and conquered East Jerusalem (along with the rest of the West Bank).[15] The unrecognized borderline was unilaterally erased by Israel, and ever since then the entire city has been in Israeli hands, which alone have handled all its municipal affairs. Shortly after the war, in defiance of international law, Israel annexed East Jerusalem along with other territories surrounding it. After June 1967 the Green Line was systematically erased from all official maps and gradually disappeared on the ground as a result of massive urban development. Erasing the line was the form of its inscription, and massive urban building projects were soon planned and performed to further erase what the initial erasure had inscribed. When Israel tried to erase the borderline unilaterally, the city was actually divided for the first time in consciousness, not only on the ground, and a dividing line that both parties recognized—one party to wipe out its traces and the other to reestablish it—was inscribed.

Following the occupation of East Jerusalem in 1967 and as an expression of its claim to sovereignty over the entire city, Israel annexed the occupied part and granted its 66,000 Palestinian inhabitants the status of permanent residents, giving them the option of becoming its citizens. As permanent residents, they had to swear allegiance to the Jewish state, the political incarnation of the Jewish national subject. Not surprisingly, very few Palestinians (no more than two thousand) accepted this offer of a change of sovereignty and quick naturalization. As a result, unification again divided the city into classes of inhabitants. Most Palestinians are not citizens in their own city. Their status of permanent residency continues to be conditional: Palestinians who leave the city for a long period of time for purposes other than education lose their right to live there (B'tselem report, 1997). Legally, they have become foreigners who immigrated to their own birthplace, and their right to stay there is not automatically granted to their children. Thus the unified city is based on a system of nationalist apartheid in which non-Jewish residents are systematically discriminated against in terms of rights, housing, urban and economic development, and education.[16]

The ambivalence and indeterminacy of the Green Line that divided the city between 1948 and 1967 embodied the heterogeneity of the city and the fact that it inhabits simultaneously heterogeneous spaces and times that cannot be reduced to a single geopolitical space or contained in a single historical span. The conflict was inscribed onto the surface of the city, and its resolution was visibly postponed. Direct confrontation between the hostile parties was deferred, allowing for a certain coexistence between conflicting fantasies and narratives. The different heterogeneous segments of which the city consists—national, religious, and ethnic groups, forms of life, collective memories, and collective dreams—were not forced into a hierarchical system, and no primacy could have been granted to any of them.

Such a hierarchical system was an inevitable consequence of the Israeli occupation and annexation of East Jerusalem and of the official, imposed unification of the city. The hierarchical system has been maintained within a fixed demographic framework. A special governmental committee for the development of Jerusalem found in 1973 that the population ratio was 73.5 percent Israeli Jews and 25 percent Palestinians, and the official policy of all Israeli governments since has been to maintain this ratio by various means. Massive development of Jewish neighborhoods and Israel's legal administration of the city have created a continuous, even if fragmentary, Jewish area in and around the city and have cut deeply into the Palestinian settled areas, shattering the Palestinian presence in and around the city into isolated fragments.

There are three main mechanisms for maintaining this population ratio, as well as the Zionist image of Jerusalem:

- *Cartography.* The Israeli sovereign draws the city maps and uses cartography as a means of maintaining its demographic balance. The annexation of East Jerusalem and its surroundings incorporated as much land as possible for future Jewish development and as few Arab suburbs as possible. Later changes in rather flexible municipal boundaries brought more Jewish neighborhoods into the city. Today 411,000 Jews and 166,000 Palestinians live within the jurisdiction of the city of Jerusalem. But a different map, which would have taken into account the dynamics of Palestinian life in and around the city and the geographical reality in the Palestinian sections of the city, would have yielded a very different demographic ratio.
- *The legal apparatus.* The conditional residency granted to the Palestinians enables the Israeli authorities to control the demographic composition of the city on an almost daily basis.
- *Planning and housing.* The ratio of new housing for Palestinians and Israelis is one to eight. Palestinians are denied permission to build much more often than Israelis. Between 1967 and 1995, 64,000 apartments were built in Jewish neighborhoods (half of them on confiscated land that mostly belonged to the Jordanian government), and only 8,000 were built for Palestinians.[17]

The Israeli occupation and administration of Jerusalem is based on a misleading ambiguity between representations (maps, statistical tables) and the represented objects (urban space, population). On the one hand, the occupation regime uses the clean, objective language of scientific discourse and assumes its distinction between objects and their representations. On the other hand, the same regime takes an active part in the production of both the represented objects and their discursive representation, as if there were nothing to distinguish between them.[18] When the data gathered "in the field" do not yield the desired map of Jerusalem, the map changes. When the reading of the map yields data that smack too much of apartheid, the data change. Jerusalem, too, that most metaphysical of all cities, has witnessed the loss of the clear metaphysical distinction between the original and its simulacra, between territory and map, between the "thing itself" and its representation.

However, this is not a result of the fragmentation of the visual field and the field of action or of the dissemination of the forces acting in Jerusalem. On the contrary, it is the result of Israel's domination and overdetermination of these fields of vision and action. What seems for a moment as a postmodern practice of representation—a free and open market of identities, territories, maps, and narratives, a real fair of simulations—appears on closer scrutiny to be the result of conscious manipulation of the data, the map, and the territory; of rigid control of the different markets; and of massive intervention in the various practices of exchange. Israel administers the city to fit its desired map, and it draws the maps to fit its desired city. As a result 70,000 out of the 170,000 Palestinian permanent residents find themselves living in suburbs outside the official territory of Jerusalem, and they are gradually losing their status of residency.

At the basis of Israel's illegal policies in Jerusalem lies the faith that the Israeli state and its agents are at one and the same time an incarnation of a universal principle of transcendent subjectivity and the most powerful expression of one particular national subject. Israeli governments have acted and spoken as the sole legitimate representative of the Jewish people and their holy city. They have acted as if they believed that the world, history, and their neighbors are but clay in the hands of the potter, the Israeli sovereign, and that they can impose their will on reality and mold it singlehandedly to their own view. "Let there be no Green Line," they have declared: "let the city be united." And the divided city has become one. Jerusalem thus becomes the arena for the manifestation of two aspects of subjectivity: (1) the subject as an origin and an expression of mastery over others and (2) subjectivity as self-mastery and self-determination. Presented from the perspective of this double subjectivity, the Green Line appears as a scar in the heart of the holy city, and the city itself appears as an entity that has existed continuously, with no interruptions, throughout three thousand years of history. The city has sometimes been desolate, of course, in ruins, and fifty years ago it was divided, but there has always been one discrete entity, they claim, which has undergone destruction and division. However, the Israeli attempts to present a unified city never succeeded in erasing completely the real and imaginary line that still exists in some other spaces separating two hostile communities, two peoples, conquerors and conquered.

So many hands have a stake in the city of Jerusalem. So many people and groups are fighting to lay their hands on the city, to manipulate its past and future, digging its ground to find new data to support these conflicting claims, reconstructing the evidence and preparing themselves, and their city, for the day of judgment. Hands intermingle with and interfere in the work of other hands. Hands build energetically and destroy, no less energetically, what others (and they themselves) have built. Hands draw maps, open some paths and close others, inscribe some dividing lines and erase others. Above all, hands try to mold the city's image and superimpose it on all other competing images.[19] These latter hands are an extension of a national subject, acting as if there may never be another chance to do whatever is not done today in this city where time stretches to eternity, and almost all this work is being done in the name of a *past* and for the sake of a certain future in a diachronic time conceived as a homogeneous, empty container in which events are chained uninterruptedly from the depths of the past to the most distant future.

But what about the *present*? When one cares only for the past and only for the sake of a future, the present tends to disappear. When one ignores for a moment both the past and the future, this hectic urban scene I have just described is suddenly emptied of all national and religious narratives and transcendent subjects that animate it. One can see the city as a multiplicity of heterogeneous spaces and irreconcilable points of view. All one can see are busy hands, gentle and violent actions, rapid, seemingly arbitrary changes in the city's surface. People work, travel, stay home, surf the Internet, turn on their televisions, zap from station to station, watch a local network, then watch a global one, go shopping at a shopping center, get stuck in traffic jams, sit in a bar or a coffee house, visit friends, go to the movies or to the theater, play with their children in the streets or in public gardens. These sites of social life change from area to area, from neighborhood to neighborhood, differing among themselves not only according to the great division of the city between East and West Jerusalem. The way the Israeli occupation divides the city is not unambiguous. Today the city seems to function as a single urban unit. For the innocent, or ignorant, eye, the few checkpoints manned by a few policemen and soldiers scattered here and there on the outskirts of Arab neighborhoods, as well as the ruins of some old military posts, are the only visible, often misleading witnesses to the Green Line. The checkpoints are especially ambivalent signs. As a symbol of the passage from the Jewish part of the city to the Arab one, they certainly defy Israel's policy of unification (though Jews and Arabs clearly have different access to and mobility through these checkpoints). For the purpose of security they are quite ridiculous, since the imaginary dividing line may be crossed at numerous other points. The national logic of unification creates the need to control passage from the Arab part to the Jewish part of the city; but too strict a control contradicts the unifying imperative. In fact, the checkpoint is a symbol of paradox for the Israeli domination over Jerusalem, where the unifying efforts only deepen the dividing forces that resist unification. Recently, a possible ethnic solution to the paradox has been tested by Israeli authorities—an ethnic purification of the city ("the silent transfer," as this process was termed by the B'tselem organization). Such a purification would enable a peaceful coexistence of the spatial and (Jewish) sequential narratives of the city. If the city became entirely Jewish, it would be possible to subject the spatial narrative to the sequential (national) one, to transform Jerusalems into "Jerusalem—a city united forever." In the meantime, the checkpoint functions as a filter, but various spaces leak through the holes, link into other spaces, escape all efforts at unification—diachronic or synchronic.

The refugee camps on the city's outskirts bear witness to the most difficult, brutal, and painful aspects of the occupation of Jerusalem. Most Jews who inhabit the western part are hardly aware of the camps. In the seams of the city, however, in neighborhoods like Pat and Beit-Tzaffafa, the differences between east and west are not that visible, especially for one who is not a resident of the area. A visitor may mistake the Arab houses of Beit-Tzaffafa for the villas of the occupiers and mistake the eight-story building project in neighboring Pat for the housing estates of the occupied. As a matter of fact, the difference in height is just one more example of the evils of the occupation. High-rise construction is permitted only in Jewish neighborhoods; the Palestinians must solve their problems of density and overpopulation in other areas, outside Jerusalem.

The professed policy of the Israeli state since 1967 has been to turn Jerusalem into a Jewish city. The unification of the city has not been a political utopia that is meant to serve all parties involved. Its aim has not been to build bridges between hostile nations and religions. It is, rather, a unilaterally metaphysical fantasy projected by Israelis onto thousands of years of the history of Jerusalem. But the city is harsh and stubborn; it does not respond in kind.

The "Jewification" of Jerusalem follows a logic of "catch as catch can." Every area under the city's municipal jurisdiction that has not yet become Jewish is a target for a second conquest that would make it Jewish or at least more Jewish than it is now.[20] The Jewification of the city, which is closely related to its unification, seeks to increase the Jewish areas of the city at the expense of the Palestinian areas and thus gradually to homogenize the entire urban space, imposing on it a national Jewish identity. However, the practice of "catch as catch can" yields opposite results. Instead of expanding the homogeneous Jewish areas, it creates more and more heterogeneous areas, which are complex and fragmented, containing more zones of friction and conflict. The entire city has become riddled with enclaves. Israeli authorities imagine themselves to be the subject and master of the city, responsible for the production and management of its space and its borderlines, capable of administering trends of mobility, routes of passage, movement of populations, patterns of construction and modes of exchange (of instruments, artifacts, smells, news, weapons, health, friendship, and love).[21] But despite all the means and measures of control, surveillance, and repression at their disposal, which keep the Palestinians in a kind of a third-world enclave, circulation and exchange take place constantly in ways that defy the nationalist rules set by the Israelis.[22]

The circulation of goods, messages, images, and people takes place in "other spaces" that are not necessarily subject to the rules of the national space determined by the Israeli authorities. Apart from and besides the authorized routes, communication, circulation, and exchange take advantage of the many loopholes scattered all along the borderlines in Jerusalem. These loopholes are not accidental gaps but the very stuff of which those lines consist. Due to the presence of these loopholes, the border may interpellate all its users with a double message: "Respect me" and "Transgress me." It may declare at one and the same time, "Here is a border" (discriminating between Israelis and Palestinians), but "There is no border" (for the city is united and welcomes all its residents alike). This Janus face of the border appears in the national space but also in economic, educational, and other daily spaces.

Israeli authorities act as if they believe themselves capable of controlling which face of the borderline will appear where and when. But the borderlines have a life of their own and users of different kinds who use and abuse them in many different ways. Thus, for example, Israel has built Jewish neighborhoods as enclaves in the midst of Palestinian areas in a step-by-step attempt to accumulate more and more urban territory; hoping that somehow the new enclaves will form a new border. However, the rapidly growing Jewish enclaves have turned the Palestinian neighborhoods, too, into enclaves that continue to spread (through mostly illegal construction of new houses) and often trespass borderlines, erasing some and inscribing, or threatening to inscribe new ones.[23] Whereas Jewish neighborhoods were supposed to purify the national space, fortify it, and demonstrate Jewish sovereignty in it, they too often serve opposite ends. Instead of purifying space, they emphasize its heterogeneous nature; instead of fortifying it, they create more areas of friction and increase the threats to the safety and well-being of those who dwell in and around them; and instead of demonstrating Jewish sovereignty, they create more opportunities to challenge and question the claim of the sovereign.

Straightforward Jewification seems politically impossible under the present circumstances. Therefore, the urban space is planted with as many Jewish spots as possible, in a way that makes any neat division of the city between Jewish and Arab practically impossible. Israel has set the ends and chosen the means to realize them, without understanding, however, that the means are not solely determined by the ends that they serve or by the ruling subjects who impose them. Israel's policies in Jerusalem have brought the city to the verge of a spatial unification of such a heterogeneous kind that no transcendent temporality could chain it in a consecutive chain, no single narrative could contain it, and no political subject could master it. Unification—if one still wants to use this word—takes place in such a space by way of numerous links and a constant weaving and unweaving of knots in an undefined network that escapes the rule of any sovereignty that claims transcendent, ahistorical authority.

Is it possible to avoid one single narrative that has primacy over others, one single narrative that channels and directs the multiplicity of actions for the purpose of one preconceived or predetermined telos (a telos that seemingly lies outside the field of social action and endows it with meaning and justification)? Does not such a reading of the city (which seeks to interpret the present as an ensemble detached from the past and from the subjects who claim to act in its name and insist on its representation) produce one more single narrative? Aren't these two readings—one that obliterates the past and one that obliterates the present—rather similar? The two strategies—a spatial strategy that ignores the past while focusing on the present and a sequential historical strategy that ignores the present while focusing on the past—do not exist as ready-made artifacts, ready to be picked up and used to shape reality according to one's will. Opting for one of these strategies would not change the heterogeneous nature of reality. When one of the two strategies is enacted successfully, it may strengthen one competing element at the expense of the other, but it is incapable of eliminating the latter. No strategy, however successful it may be, can homogenize the heterogeneity of the city

Yet between the two strategies lies a radical difference. The first, a spatial and "presentist" strategy, reads the city as a heterogeneous multiplicity of relations—economic, political, religious, ethnic—that cannot be reduced to the national narrative. When the national narrative is thus completely ignored, the national subject that animates that narrative is deconstructed, its transcendent status is denied, and its legitimating power is annihilated. The claims of nationalism are so radically denied that national narratives are not allowed even the existence of one type of force, relations, and legitimacy, among the many of which the heterogeneous space consists. This strategy is self-defeating. Instead of *recognizing* the existing heterogeneous multiplicity and conceiving the national narrative to be one element of this multiplicity, it seeks to eliminate unwanted elements and *produce* an abstract, "better" multiplicity. Thus the present is endowed with an abstract heterogeneity that ignores nationalism, its embodiment, and its role in urban life and space. As a result, this abstraction actually works to create a new chain in the sequential narrative in the form of a multiple spatialization that would be the new historical agent that replaces the national subject, the old hero to be driven off the stage. But even if it were to be triumphant, the spatial strategy does not have either the means or the motivation to eliminate the national subject, the many forms of its narrative, and its various agents.

The second, more common strategy is the one enacted by the Israeli government. The heterogeneous multiplicity of the city is made subject to the Jewish national narrative, to the mechanism of its exclusions, and to the constraints of its temporality, which stretches from antiquity to eternity and is constructed in cycles of (Jewish) destruction and redemption. Within this framework, Jerusalem is "a city united forever," temporarily spoiled by elements that introduce divisions and fractions. Unity is understood as "united under Jewish sovereignty," and the threatening elements are interpreted accordingly, in nationalist and ethnic terms. Hence unity implies, to some at least, Jewish purity and requires efforts at purification. Dividing elements are impure elements, and they must be removed. Jerusalem as "a city united forever" can maintain its unity only under the perspective of eternity, and if purity has not been achieved yet or cannot be achieved due to present circumstances, it is certainly aimed at for some point in the city's eternal future.

NOTES

1. This is a general and generalizing claim. It characterizes the condition of the Palestinians as being deprived of their own place, which means, among other things, the archive as a possible Palestinian place. The fact that there may be some archives in which documents about the Palestinian past are stockpiled does not contradict the exclusion of Palestinians from the archive as a possible place of their own. See also my discussion of the structural subjugation of the Palestinian narrative to the Zionist one (Azoulay 1996). On the archive as a place, see Derrida (1995). For the conflict between Israelis and Palestinians over the organization of the public space and collective memory, see Bishara (1992). Bishara relates the exclusion of Palestinian traces from Israeli public space to the Zionist ideology of "rejection of the Jewish Diaspora!" The Diaspora Jew and the Palestinian are two "others" that the Israeli Zionist discourse systematically excludes.

2. This text is an attempt to think about Jerusalem outside and against the binary logic imposed by the occupation, which necessitates a seemingly clear-cut opposition between conquerors and conquered, unification (imposed by the conquerors), and partition (demanded by the conquered and a few among the Israeli left). As two opposed political solutions, unification and partition adhere to a sacred national space in common. Those who enforce a united city are ready, if not willing, to continue the oppression and discrimination against the Palestinian residents in the name of a sacred Jewish national space. Those who struggle for the partition of the city have as their goal a Palestinian nation-state with its own sacred national space. Instead of this binary logic, this text tries to describe the city as a complex mesh of networks, spaces, and times, which are not given to any clear-cut binary division. The political demand to put an end to the occupation is not abandoned, but the conception of the occupation as an entity with clear-cut "ends" is questioned.

3. The distribution of means and opportunities to create other spaces or link into them is not equal among Israelis and Palestinians. For example, a precondition for links to, and mobility within, globalized spaces is the modernization of physical space, which has usually taken place only when and where this space has been nationalized or at least has become an object for the administration of a nation-state. Without a nationalized space of their own, the Palestinian access to the spaces of globalization is restricted and mediated through different Israeli agencies. Miyoshi (1997)

points to the continuity between old forms of colonialism conducted by different nation-states and postmodern forms conducted by transnational corporations. Even if these corporations call into question the very idea of the nation-state, they can emerge only within its framework. See also in this context Sassen's analysis of the way the global economy is anchored in postmodern, highly developed metropolitan centers (Sassen 1997).

4. The history on display in the museum at the moment completely ignores the partition of the city in 1948 and the Jordanian control of the city for nineteen years. The city is presented as a site and an object of conflicts among the three monotheistic religions, while the national struggle over the city recedes into the background and is depoliticized.

5. The aim of the Betzalel Museum, as in other Zionist museums established in the first half of the century (such as the Ein-Harod Shrine), was to gather "the treasures of Jewish culture" of all times and places. The construction of the realm of knowledge and objects does not differ in principle from similar constructions taking place within the framework of the history museum. However, in a way that reminds one of the classification of animals in Borges's Chinese Encyclopaedia, one of the categories, "the Zionist Museum," tries to include the entire table of categories and threatens to undermine its logic of classification.

6. See Benjamin's discussion of space and the present: "History is the subject of a structure whose site is not homogeneous, empty time, but time filled by the present of the now [jetztzeit]" (Benjamin 1978, 261).

7. The distinction drawn here is indebted to the one formulated by Deleuze and Guattari, between smooth and striated space (Deleuze and Guattari 1980).

8. On drawing the borderline, see Benvenisti (1996).

9. Beside this accidental no-man's-land were other no-man's-lands that were created intentionally. The parties agreed not to agree about these territories and to postpone the division. Thus the map of division actually reflects the reluctance of the two sides to come to terms with the division of the city.

10. For a detailed discussion of this topic in Foucault's article, see chapter 5.

11. The notion of the rhizome is borrowed from Deleuze and Guattari (1980).

12. For more on the relation between time and debt, see Derrida (1991), especially the sections on Mauss's analysis of gift and giving.

13. In *Discipline and Punish* Foucault speaks about handwriting as an apparatus for the constitution of subjectivity (Foucault 1975b). For more on the hand, the eye, and the mouth as instruments and their role in the construction of subjectivity, see Azoulay (1997c).

14. The word *neturalize* and its derivatives was coined by Aya and Gal by replacing *nature* by *network* in the verb *naturalize*.

15. "Temple Mount is in my hands," shouted the commander of the conquering unit into his field radio, coining an idiom that has become a symbol of the Israeli conquest.

16. Much effort is invested in maintaining or inventing the Jewish "character" of the city, especially in building new Jewish neighborhoods all around the eastern part of the city. In the last few years there were discussions of several plans for the development of Jerusalem, all of which support the Israeli policy of Jewification of the city. Speaking before architects about the annexation of an undeveloped area on the western outskirts of the city for the purpose of building new Jewish neighborhoods there, Mayor Ehud Ulmart reiterated this policy: "We have to influence the

patterns of growth in the city so that they would fit the desired character of the city" (Zandberg 1997). The "desired character" means maintaining its Jewish majority, of course.

17. The data are taken from B'tselem Reports, an Israeli organization for human rights in the occupied territories (B'tselem Reports 1995, 1997), and from the daily press.

18. The Israeli policy and plans for the development of the city have always given preference to political considerations over urban ones. The construction of new neighborhoods immediately after the Six-Day War was planned to eliminate the traces of the Green Line. The annexation of new areas all around the city was planned to make possible rapid growth of the Jewish population. The ongoing discrimination in the allocation of construction permits to Arabs and Jews has been a clear attempt to force Palestinians to leave the city.

19. The hectic work being done in Jerusalem is only partly overt. Much of it is clandestine, concealed from the public eye. Some hands work gently, others are violent, but everyone seems very busy, and everything seems awfully urgent. Everything must be done before it is too late—before further urban development takes place, before too many Palestinians infiltrate the city, before more land is confiscated by the Israeli authorities, before the peace talks resume, before the next war, or before the Messiah comes.

20. Seventy square kilometers have been annexed to Jerusalem since the Six-Day War (B'tselem report 1995).

21. The description presents a complex picture of the relation between occupiers and occupied without, however, erasing the differences between Arabs and Jews and the ability to multiply spaces created by the Israeli occupation. The entire urban infrastructure in the Palestinian sections is conspicuously less developed than the infrastructure in the Jewish sections, and the gap keeps widening. But the multiplication of spaces is not merely a result of a more or less developed infrastructure.

22. The border that Israel imposes on the Palestinians does not function according to the intentions of its authors. It acquires new meanings and functions through the interpretations given by those who use it. Conceived as a means to limit, it actually functions as an amplifier of production (Foucault 1976). Instead of closing more tightly the gaps in the boundaries separating Jews and Palestinians, it creates ever more and new gaps, and instead of consolidating governmental control, it dilutes it (see also Lyotard 1979, sec. 13).

23. The man responsible for Jerusalem in the Palestinian Authority, Faisal Husseini, prepared plans to strengthen the city's eastern ring. These plans are like a negative of the Israeli plans for the same area. Israel is capable of blocking Husseini, of course, while the reverse is not true, and yet Israel's capacity to implement its plans does depend, among other things, on Palestinian reactions to those plans.

REFERENCES

Abbeele, G. Van Den. 1992. *Travel as Metaphor: From Montaigne to Rousseau*. Minneapolis: University of Minnesota Press.

Agamben, Giorgio. 1997. *Homo sacer: le portvoir souverain et la vie nue*. Paris: Seuil.

Alon, Gideon. 1996. "Libai: No Minister of Justice Will Ever Reduce Amir's Sentence." *Haaretz*, March 28, 3a.

Azoulay, Ariella. 1992. "Photography and the Disintegration of the Public Space?" [in Hebrew]. *Studio* 37: 36–40.

———. 1994. "With Open Doors: Museums and Historical Narratives in Israel's Public Space." In *Museum Culture*, ed. D. J. Sherman and I. Rogoff. Minneapolis: University of Minnesota Press.
———. 1996. "The Archive Keepers" [in Hebrew]. *Studio*, no. 74: 19–21.
———. 1997a. "Can One Make Works Which Are Not Works of Art?" [in Hebrew]. *Plastika* 1:30–33.
———. 1997b. "Clean Hands." *Documenta\Documents*. Ostfildern: Cantz Verlag, 3:44–57.
———. 1997c. "Un lexique." In *Produire, crier, collectionner*, 78–83. Paris: Hazan.
———. 1999a. *TRAining for ART: A Critique of the Museal Economy*. Porter Institute and Ha-Kibbutz Ha-Meuchad, Tel Aviv.
———. 1999b. *Michal Heiman Test (M.H.T.) No. 2—Manual*. Museum Le Quartier, Quimper.
Azoulay, Ariella, and Adi Ophir. 1998. "Hello Peace, How Are You?" [in Hebrew]. *Plastika* 2: 76–92.
Balibar, Etienne. 1997. *La crainte des masses*. Paris: Galilee.
Baque, Dominique. 1993. *Les documents de la modernite*. Chambon: Editions Jacqueline.
Barel, Zvi. 1996. "Amir Concluded His Testimony in Court." *Haaretz*, March 8, p. 9A.
Barthes, Roland. 1980. *La chambre claire*. Paris: Seuil.
Baudrillard, Jean. 1979. *De la seduction*. Paris: Galilée.
———. 1981. *Simulacres et simulations*. Paris: Galilée.
———. 1983. *Les strategies fatales*. Paris: Grasset.
———. 1987. *Forget Foucault*. New York: Semiotext(e).
———. 1988. *The Ecstasy of Communication*. New York: Semiotext(e).
———. 1990. *La transparence du mal*. Paris: Galilée.
———. 1991. *La guerre du golf n'a pas eu lieu*. Paris: Galilée.
———. 1995. *Le crime parfait*. Paris: Galilée.
Bazin, G. 1967. *Le temps des musses*. Desoer: Liege-Bruxelles.
Benjamin, Walter. 1978. *Illuminations*. New York: Schocken Books.
———. 1979. *Reflections*. New York: Harvest/HBS Books.
———. 1980. "A Short History of Photography." In *Classic Essays on Photography*. New Haven, Conn.: Leete's Island Books.
———. 1983. *Essais*. Vols. 1–2. Paris: Denöel-Gonthier.
———. 1989. *Paris Capitale du X Siecle-Le livre des Passages*. Paris: Les Editions du Cerf.
———. 1991. "L'oeuvre d'art a l'epoque de sa reproduction mecanisee" [1936]. In *Ecritsfrancais*. Paris: NRF Editions Gallimard.
———. 1996a. *Petite histoire de la photographie*. Paris: Etudes Photographiques, Societe Francaise de Photographie.
———. 1996b. *Selected Writings*. Cambridge, Mass.: Belknap Press of Harvard University Press.
Benvenisti, Meron. 1996. *Jerusalem: A Place of Fire* [in Hebrew]. Tel Aviv: Dvir.
Bishara, Azmi. 1992. "Between Place and Space: On the Palestinian Public Space" [in Hebrew]. *Studio* no. 37: 6–9.
Blanchot, Maurice. 1997. "Two Versions of the Imaginary." *Documenta X: The Book*, ed. C. David and J. F. Chevrier. Ostfildern: Cantz Verlag.
Bourdieu, Pierre, and Alain Darbel. 1969. *L'amour de l'art*. Paris: Minuit.
Bourdieu, Pierre. 1979. *La distinction: Critique sociale du jugement*. Paris: Minuit.
Breitberg-Semel, Sarah. 1997. "Know Yourself." *Studio* no. 88:20.
Brener, Elly. 1996. "The Judge: 'Heaven Cries and I Wonder Why." *Davar*, p. 9.
B'tselem Reports. 1995. *Policy of Discrimination* [in Hebrew]. Jerusalem: B'tselem.
———. 1997. *Stop the Quiet Deportation* [in Hebrew]. Jerusalem: B'tselem.
Buchloh, Benjamin. 1988. "From Factura to Factography." In *October: The First Decade*. Cambridge, Mass.: MIT Press.

Buck-Morss, Susan. 1990. *The Dialectics of Seeing*. Cambridge, Mass.: MIT Press.
———. 1992. "Aesthetics and Anaesthetics: Walter Benjamin's Artwork Essay Reconsidered." *October* no. 62: 3–42.
Caruth, Cathy. 1994. *Unclaimed Experience*. Baltimore: Johns Hopkins University Press.
Caygill, Howard. 1994. "Benjamin, Heidegger and the Destruction of Tradition." In *Walter Benjamin's Philosophy*, ed. Andrew Benjamin. New York: Routledge.
Chevrier, Francois. 1992. "Double Lecture." In *Graham/Evans*. Rotterdam: Witte de With Museum.
Crary, Jonathan. 1992. *Techniques of the Observer*. Cambridge, Mass.: MIT Press.
Crow, Thomas, E. 1985. *Painters and Public Life in Eighteenth-Century Paris*. New Haven: Yale University Press.
Daney, Serge. 1997. "Before and After the Image." In *Documenta X: The Book*, ed. C. David and J. F. Chevrier, 610–620. Ostfildern: Cantz Verlag.
De Duve, Thierry. 1989. *Au nom de l'art*. Paris: Minuit.
Deleuze, Gilles. 1968. *Différence et repetition*. Paris: Puf.
———. 1990. *Pourpalers*. Paris: Minuit.
———. 1992. "Postscript on the Societies of Control." *October* no. 59:3–9.
Deleuze, Gilles, and Felix Guattari. 1997. "The Included Middle." In *Documenta X: The Book*, 466–471. Ostfildern: Cantz Verlag.
———. 1980. *Mille Plateaux*. Paris: Minuit.
Derrida, Jacques. 1990. "Force of Law: The 'Mystical Foundation of Authority.'" In *Deconstruction and the Possibility of Justice*, ed. Drucilla Cornell, Michel Rosenfeld, and David Gray Carlson. New York: Routledge.
———. 1991. *Donner le temps*. Paris: Seuil.
———. 1995. *Mal d'archive*, Paris: Galilée.
Dower, John W. 1996. "The Bombed: Hiroshima and Nagasaki in Japanese Memory." In *Hiroshima in History and Memory*, ed. Michael J. Hogan. Cambridge: Cambridge University Press.
Duras, Marguerite. 1967. *Hiroshima mon amour*. New York: Grove Press.
Elkana, Yehuda. 1988. "The Right to Forget." *Haaretz*, March 2, 1988, 13.
Foster, Hal, 1996a. "The Archive without Museums." *October*, no. 77: 97–119.
Foster, Hal, 1996b. "L'artiste comme ethnographe, ou la 'fin de l'histoire' signifietelle le retour a l'anthropologie?" In *Face a l'histoire*, ed. Jean Paul Ameline. Paris: Centre G. Pompidou, Flammarion.
Foucault, Michel. 1963. *La naissance de la dinique*. Paris: PUF.
———. 1966. *Les mots et les choses*. Paris: Gallimard.
———. 1969. *L'archeologie du savoir*. Paris: Gallimard.
———. 1971. *L'ordre du di scours*. Paris: Gallimard.
———. 1975a. *The Birth of the Clinic*. New York: Vintage Books.
———. 1975b. *Surveiller et punir*. Paris: Gallimard.
———. 1976. *Histoire de la sexualize*. Vol. 1. Paris: Gallimard.
———. 1977. *Language, Counter-memory, Practice*. New York: Cornell.
———. 1978. "Qu'est-ce que la critique?" *Bulletin de la Société Française de Philosophie*, 35–63.
———. 1986. "Of Other Spaces." *Diacritics* 16, no. 1:7–22.
———. 1989. *Resumé des cours: 1970–1982*. Paris: Julliard.
———. 1994. *Dits et écrits*. Vols. 3–4. Paris: Gallimard.
Friedlander, Saul. 1982. *Kitsch and Death: On the Reflection of Nazism* [in Hebrew]. Jerusalem: Keter Press.
Gaethgens, T. W. 1986. "Les musées historiques de Versailles." In *Les lieux de me-moire*, ed. P. Nora. Paris: Gallimard.

Gladman, Mordechai. 1997. "You Wake Up in the Morning and Immediately Begin to Worry." *Haaretz*, November 21, p. 10.
Green, David B. 1997. "Shock Treatment." *Jerusalem Report*, December 11, p. 16.
Gurevich, David. 1997. "To Distinguish What Isn't Hell in Hell." *Haaretz*, November 28, literary supplement, p. 1.
Habermas, Jürgen. 1989. *The Structural Transformation of the Public Sphere: An Inquiry into a Category of Bourgeois Society*. Cambridge, Mass.: MIT Press.
Harvey, David. 1985. *The Urbanization of Capital*. Baltimore: Johns Hopkins University Press.
Heidegger, Martin. 1971. *Poetry, Language, Thought*. New York: Harper & Row.
Heidegger, Martin. 1977. *The Question Concerning Technology and Other Essays*. New York: Harper & Row.
———. 1996. "The Age of the World Picture." In *Electronic Culture*, ed. T. Druckrey. New York: Aperture.
Hogan, Michael J., ed. 1996. *Hiroshima in History and Memory*. Cambridge: Cambridge University Press.
Huberman, George Didi. 1982. *L'invention de l'hysterie*. Paris: Macula.
Kant, Immanuel. 1985. *Critique of Pure Reason*. Cambridge: Cambridge University Press.
———. 1991. *Critique of Judgment*. Oxford: Clarendon Press.
Karmi, Jadda. 1997. "One State, Two People" [in Hebrew]. *Haaretz*, September 10, p. 32.
Krauss, Rosalind. 1988. "The Im/Pulse to See." In *Vision and Visuality*, ed. Hal Foster. Seattle: New Press.
———. 1990. "The Cultural Logic of the Late Capitalist Museum." *October*, no. 54:3–18.
Latour, Bruno. 1994. *Nous n'avons jamais ite modernes*. Paris: La Decouverte.
Lyotard, Jean-François. 1979. *La condition postmoderne*. Paris: Minuit.
———. 1983. *Le différend*. Paris: Minuit.
———. 1986. *Le postmoderne explique aux enfants*. Paris: Galilée.
———. 1991. *The Inhumain*. Palo Alto, Calif.: Stanford University Press.
Lyotard, Jean-François, and Jean Loup Thebaud. 1985. *Just Gaming*. Minneapolis: University of Minnesota Press.
Mansbach, Abraham. 1998. *Existence and Meaning* [in Hebrew]. Jerusalem: Magnes Press.
Marx, Karl. 1936. *Capital: A Critique of Political Economy*, ed. Bennett A. Cerf and Donald S. Klopper. New York: Modern Library.
Marx, Karl, and Friedrich Engels. 1951. *On Art and Literature* [in Hebrew]. Merhavya, Israel: Sifryat Hapoalim.
Meidan, Anat. 1995. "I Focused on Yigal Amir Because He Seems to Me to Be a Potential Assassin." *Yediot Acharonot*, December 19, p. 7.
Merleau-Ponty, Maurice. 1964. *Le visible et l'invisible*. Paris: Gallimard.
Miyoshi, Masao. 1997. "A Borderless World?" In *Documenta X: The Book*, ed. C. David and J. F. Chevrier. Ostfildern: Cantz Verlag.
Nancy, Jean Luc. 1990. *La communauté desoeuvrée*. Paris: Christian Bourgois Editeur.
———. 1996. *Etre singulier pluriel*. Paris: Galilée.
Ophir, Adi. 1987. "On Sanctifying the Holocaust an Anti-Theological Treatise." *Tikkun* 2 (1):60–67.
———. 1988a. "Michel Foucault and the Semiotics of the Phenomenal." *Dialogue* 27:387–415.
———. 1988b. "The Cartography of Knowledge and Power: Foucault Reconsidered." In *Cultural Semiosis*, ed. Hugh J. Silverman. New York: Routledge.
———. 1989. "The Semiotics of Power." *Manuscrito* 12 (2):9–34.
Pe'er, Edna. 1996. "Interview with Naji Nasser." *Ma'ariv*, August 9 (weekend supplement), 14–15.

Perry-Lehman, Meira. 1997. "Foreword." *Live and Die as Eva Braun* (exhibition catalog), Israel Museum, Jerusalem (pages unnumbered).
Petrova, Ada, and Peter Watson. 1996. *The Death of Hitler: The Full Story with New Evidence from Secret Russian Archives.* New York: Norton.
Portugali, Yuval. 1996. *Implicate Relations: Society and Space in the Israeli Palestinian Conflict* [in Hebrew]. Tel Aviv: Hakibbutz Hameuchad.
Poulot, D. 1985. "Naissance du monument historique." *Revue d'histoire moderne et contemporaine,* no. 32.
———. 1986. "Richard Lenoir et les musées des monuments historique."
Przyblyski, Jeannene. 1998. "History Is Photography: The Afterimage of Walter Benjamin." *Afterimage* 26 (2): 8–11.
Riegler, Nurit, and Tamar Trebelisi-Chadad. 1997. "Hammer to Israel Museum: Remove the Exhibition of Hitler's Mistress." *Yediot Acharonot,* November 7, p. 22.
Rosen, Roee. 1996. "The Visibility and Invisibility of the Trauma" [in Hebrew]. *Studio* 76: 99–118.
Rosen, Roee, and Galya Yahav. 1997. "Decent, Indecent, and What Lies Between." *Studio* 88:21–30.
Rothman, Roger. 1997. "Mourning and Mania." *Live and Die as Eva Braun* (exhibition catalog). Jerusalem: Israel Museum.
Said, Edward W. 1993. *Culture and Imperialism.* New York: Vintage Books.
Samet, Gideon. 1997. "Holocaust and Other Denials." *Haaretz,* December 5, p. 1B.
Sassen, Saskia. 1997. "Global Cities and Global Value Chains." In *Documenta X: The Book,* ed. C. David and J. F. Chevrier, 736–745. Ostfildern: Cantz Verlag.
Segev, Amira. 1996. "Confrontation between the Israeli Army and Palestinians in Hussan Village after Sawsha Funeral." *Haaretz,* October 30, p. 3A.
Sekulla, Allan. 1989. "The Body and the Archive." In *The Contest of Meaning,* ed. Richard Bolton. Cambridge, Mass.: MIT Press.
Shapira, Sarit. 1994. "A Camera in Limbo." In *Black Holes: The White Locus* (exhibition catalog), Twenty-Second International Biennial of São Paolo, Israeli Ministry of Science and the Arts and Ministry of Foreign Affairs.
Sheffy, Smadar. 1997. "Defending the Unstable Self." *Haaretz,* November 13, p. 3C.
Shragay, Naday. 1997. "Jerusalem's Deputy Mayor Demands the Removal of the Exhibition *Live and Die as Eva Braun.*" *Haaretz,* November 15, p. 1B.
Smith, Adam. 1976. *An Inquiry into the Nature and Causes of the Wealth of Nations,* ed. R. H. Campbell and A. S. Skinner. London: Oxford University Press.
Steiner, George. 1981. *The Portage to San Cristobal of Adolf Hitler.* Chicago: University of Chicago Press.
Tacher, Oren. 1992. "Piaza in Ramat Aviv: The Reaction to the Modernist Time-Space Structure." *Studio* 37:40–41.
Taylor, Mark. 1987. *Altarity.* Chicago: University of Chicago Press.
Trevor-Roper, Hugh. 1947. *The Last Days of Hitler.* New York: Macmillan.
Tsippor, Asaf. 1997. "Don't Call Me a Holocaust Denier, Sweetie." *Ma'ariv,* November 28 (supp.), p. 8.
Venn, Couze. 1997. "Beyond Enlightenment?" *Theory, Culture and Society* 14 (3): 1–28.
Virilio, Paul. 1983. *Pure War.* New York: Semiotext(e).
———. 1989. *War and Cinema.* London: Verso.
———. 1994. "Cyberwar, God and Television: Interview with Paul Virilio." *CTHEORY.* Interview by Louise Wilson. http://ctheoryaec.at.
Yarkoni, Yoram. 1996. "Amir's Father: 'My Son Is an Idiot.'" *Yediot Acharonot,* March 8, p. 3.
Yatom, Ehud, 1996. "I Killed the Terrorists of Bus Line 300." *Yediot Acharonot,* July 23, p. 19.

Yosifon, Golan. 1997. "A Storm in the Wake of Exhibition Opening at Israel Museum: *Live and Die as Eva Braun.*" *Ma'ariv*, November 6, p. 12.

Zandberg, Ester. 1997. "Ulmart Won the Battle" [in Hebrew]. *Haaretz*, June 15.

Zeltzer, Mark. 1998. *Serial Killers*. New York: Routledge.

Ziarek, Krzyszt. 1997. "After Aesthetics: Heidegger and Benjamin on Art and Experience." *Philosophy Today*, 41 (1–4): 199–208.

Zigari, Khaled. 1996. "The Dump in El Azariya," *Kol Ha'ir*, July 12, p. 36.

Zizek, Slavoj. 1992. *Looking Awry*. Cambridge, Mass.: MIT Press.

Zuckerman, Moshe. 1993. "Shoah in the Sealed Room: The "Holocaust" in Israeli Press during the Gulf War" (photocopy).

PART III

Minority Discourse

Voices from the Margins

Minority Discourse in Israeli Culture

10

Hebrew in an Israeli Arab Hand

Six Miniatures on Anton Shammas's *Arabesques*

HANNAN HEVER

The Majority as Minority

In a recent interview a question was asked of the Israeli writer Amos Oz: "Anton Shammas's new novel *Arabesques* has been published to great critical acclaim. Do you consider the presence of this novel, written by an Israeli Arab in Hebrew, to be a turning point in Israeli society?" Oz responded: "I think of this as a triumph, not necessarily for Israeli society, but for the Hebrew language. If the Hebrew language is becoming attractive enough for a non-Jewish Israeli to write in it, then we have arrived."[1]

Oz recognizes the great importance of this book. He is less sure, though, in assessing how central a place it occupies in a particularly Israeli context. Yet despite his slightly patronizing tone—as if admission to "Israeli-ness" were his to give or deny—Oz is, at the same time, publicly acknowledging a certain lack of strength in the Hebrew language. His words can be interpreted, if taken literally, as setting Shammas apart as an Arab and not according him his full cultural rights as a member of Israeli society. But at the same time, Oz's answer sounds almost like a direct quotation from decades of Zionist writings expressing the unflagging hope that the persecuted Jewish minority would someday achieve the status of a majority, and with it political sovereignty in Israel. Oz is presenting the Hebrew language in two lights: as the language of the ruling

---

Translated by Orin D. Gensler. Reprinted, by permission of University of Minnesota Press, from Hannan Hever, "Hebrew in an Israeli Arab Hand: Six Miniatures on Anton Shammas's *Arabesques*," in *The Nature and Context of Minority Discourse* (Minneapolis: University of Minnesota Press, 1990), 267–293. Earlier versions of this essay were presented in Berkeley to the Group for the Study of Colonial Discourse at the University of California, and at the Graduate Theological Union. I would like to express my thanks to Abdul JanMohamed, both for his personal support and for his help and advice in the preparation of this piece.

majority and as the language of a minority compelled to fight for cultural and political recognition.

Anton Shammas's *Arabesques* can be read as a protest, aimed principally at the ambiguous multiplicity that is perhaps the paramount characteristic of Israeli public discourse today. A wealth of examples could be mustered to prove that Israel, though behaving like a nation of rulers and conquerors, still relies heavily on the argumentation and rhetoric of a minority struggling for its very existence. Undoubtedly contributing to this phenomenon is the speed with which Israeli Jews made the transition, immediately after the Holocaust, from a persecuted minority to a ruling majority in their own state. But other considerations enter in as well—for example, the way Jewish history, steeped in suffering, figures so intensely in the worldview of present-day Israel or in the Israeli "fortress mentality" vis-à-vis a largely hostile Arab world. What has developed, as a result, is an astonishingly elastic mode of public discourse, able to adapt itself to almost any dialogical situation. Depending on the requirement of the particular confrontation, it can speak in the voice of an impotent minority, in need of reassurance, or in the voice of a confident majority, sure of itself and its power. In one way or another, then, almost any text found in present-day Israel is liable to fall into the same mode: a blindness to the fundamentally asymmetrical power relationships it enunciates. This holds even—and perhaps chiefly—for texts expressing sympathy or solidarity with the Palestinian cause.[2]

Anton Shammas, as an Israeli Christian Arab, has published a Hebrew novel, a text written in the language of the conquerors. The reaction of the Israeli Jewish writer Oz, on the other hand, is based in large measure on the historical fact that Hebrew is the language of Zionism, the national liberation movement of a Jewish minority which founded the State of Israel. The Arab Shammas was born after Israeli independence, an Arab and an Israeli citizen, in the village of Fasuta in the Galilee, and linked his destiny and his literary career to Hebrew literature and culture. *Arabesques* is his first novel, though he has also published a book of poetry and a children's book—as well as translations from Arabic. He is an active contributor to Israeli newspapers and periodicals.

The identity of an Israeli Christian Arab does not line up in any simple way with the main political forces at work in Israel and the Middle East and in fact stands somewhat apart from them. From this special viewpoint, Shammas has constructed a novel that represents a real challenge to his Hebrew-speaking readers. As an "Israeli Arab," Shammas is a member of a minority group—but as a Christian, he falls outside the Islamic mainstream of the minority that, at least according to the prevalent Israeli conception, tends more "naturally" to be identified with the Palestinians. On the other hand, he writes in Hebrew, the language of the dominant Jewish culture, which is itself a minority within the predominantly Arab Middle East. This peculiar position, which Shammas likens to the image of a Russian babushka doll,[3] gives him a unique perspective on Israeli public discourse from the inside and the outside at once. With this spiritual and political flexibility, Shammas can develop an authorial voice that forces his readers to take a fresh look at their cultural assumptions and expectations. The principal alternatives for critical and popular response to Shammas would tend to represent him as either an *Arab* author writing in *Hebrew* or a *Hebrew* author of *Arab* extraction. Shammas, however, sees himself as neither: he defines himself as someone unable to decide whether Israel represents homeland or exile. For an Arab author to be writing in Hebrew at all is highly unusual in the Israeli cultural landscape—a phenomenon undoubtedly connected with a blurring of the traditional boundaries of Israeli national culture. As a writer, Shammas rejects these polarized images that have been bestowed on him. He responds, instead, on another plane entirely and puts forth his own *Israeli* identity as his personal utopian resolution to the dilemma.

As has been frequently remarked, Shammas may well have created the most truly Israeli novel yet written. But that Israeli essence is imagined through an intricate web of negations. From an *Israeli* viewpoint, at once Jewish and Arab, great significance attaches to this analytical and demystifying negationist stance. The member of a minority within a minority within a minority, Shammas has used the figure of the arabesque as a richly articulated vehicle for minority discourse; such richness is indispensable considering the complexity of the Israeli reality with which Shammas is grappling. As we shall see, this figure has two principal aspects: the one negative, a striving for demystification, and the other positive, an attempt to develop a language adequate to the problems of a minority. This duality will reveal how Shammas's decision to write in the Other's language provides a glimmer of hope, a possible way out of the political and cultural dead end in which Israeli society now finds itself.

As an analysis of Anton Shammas's *Arabesques*, this essay will attempt to respond to the challenge presented by the novel's negationist stance. The comparison between the textual flow of the novel itself and our paraphrases of it will illustrate that the opposition between Shammas's *Arabesques* and any attempt to restate it synoptically is fundamental. The extent to which this opposition is politically charged is quite apparent: we need only note the asymmetry of a Jewish-Israeli text passing judgment on a Hebrew text by an Israeli Arab. And, in fact, a dual consciousness underlies this essay. On the one hand, there is an awareness of the power implications of the hermeneutic acts we perform in imposing hierarchies of meaning on the text. On the other hand, paraphrase is inevitable, even if one takes for granted the irreducible heterogeneity and uniqueness of the text.[4] The division of this essay (sometimes quite abrupt) into chapters, the discontinuous shifts of topic, the fragmentary nature of the exposition, and the avoidance of any sort of harmonious, well-rounded interpretation all constitute a partial response to the unique challenge of the arabesque as a vehicle for minority discourse.

Who Are You, Anton Shammas?

The status of the narrator—his identity, values, potentialities, and especially his relation to the narration—is one of the focal points of this semiautobiographical novel. As part of the "communicative contract" that he offers his readers, Shammas deliberately undermines the authority and unity of the narrative voice in his novel. A sharp formal split differentiates those chapters whose titles mark them as belonging to the "narrative" portion of the book from those chapters comprising the "narrator's" portion. The *narrative* sections unfold the history of the multibranched Shammas family, starting from the early nineteenth century (when the patriarch of the family moved to the Galilee from Syria) on through the period prior to the founding of the State of Israel in 1948 and up to the present-day Israeli occupation of the West Bank and the Gaza Strip. The "narrator" portions relate the journey of the author, Anton Shammas, from Israel to America, to take part in the International Writing Program held annually in Iowa City. This formal thematic split signals the possible absence of conventional, causal links between the narrator and his narrative.

In no small measure, Shammas's novel is organized like a detective story. The Israeli Christian Arab Anton Shammas and his Palestinian doppelgänger Michael Abayyad, from the Center for Palestinian Studies in Beirut, are in effect trying to track each other down. Shammas the narrator is named after his cousin Michel Abayyad, who himself had been named Anton Shammas but, soon after birth, was kidnapped from his natural mother, Almaza, to be raised by a childless couple from "the old Arab nobility" in Beirut (232). From a newspaper article, Shammas the narrator learns of a certain Surayya Sa'id, a blond-haired Christian woman who had converted to Islam and married the son of Abdallah Al-Asbah, one of the heroes of the Great Arab Revolt of 1936. Shammas surmises that she is none other than Layla Khouri, the same woman his father had brought in 1936 from the village of Fasuta in the Galilee to Beirut to live with the Baytar family and who had later been a servant in one of the wealthy neighborhoods of that city. In 1948, Layla Khouri had paid a very brief visit to Fasuta, only to be expelled to the West Bank by the Israeli army. Surayya Sa'id, that is, Layla Khouri, had been a servant in Michel Abayyad's house when the adopted boy was growing up and was secretly in love with him. On the very night in 1948 when Layla returned to Fasuta from Beirut, Michel Abayyad's parents were blackmailed into revealing the terrible secret of their adopted son and were forced to send the young Michel to America.

Shammas himself labels all this an "Arab soap opera" (52). But in the "narrator's" portion of the book, the story reappears. During Shammas's emotional meeting with Michael Abayyad in Iowa City, Abayyad tells his own life story, a story very similar to the one Shammas had extracted from Layla Khouri. But Abayyad's version is not precisely the same as the "narrative" version—it is set a year later (in 1949, instead of 1948), and the servant in the Beirut house of his childhood is identified not as Layla Khouri but as Shammas the narrator's own aunt Almaza.

Abbayad's narrative casts the entire book in a new light. Michael Abayyad had returned from America to Beirut in 1978 to join the staff of the Center for Palestinian Studies in Beirut. There he made the acquaintance of Nur, Anton Shammas's cousin, who suggested to Abayyad that he try to locate his natural mother—the same woman who had suddenly appeared at his adoptive parents' house years ago in 1949 to claim her missing child. But the Beirut of 1978, caught up in a civil war, was not the ideal place for such a search. And on the other hand, the fact of having grown up with Almaza, the bereaved mother, influenced Abayyad so strongly that he came to identify completely with her lost son, Anton. On the basis of Nur's stories, Abayyad decides to write the fictitious autobiography of Anton Shammas and to inject himself into the story in the role of Anton, Almaza's dead child. And now the reader is given a hint that the "narrative" portion of the novel referred to above, including the whole Abayyad-Shammas affair as told by Layla Khouri, is the invention of Michael Abayyad the writer. Here, at least, we seem to have reached a secure epistemological ground: the "narrative" portions of the novel are to be taken as a fabrication. But Shammas the author has not yet exhausted his Chinese puzzle of boxes-within-boxes. The chapter summarizing the "narrator's" section of the novel not only reveals that the "narrative" portion is a fiction—it also includes a statement by Shammas the author that the "narrator's" portion is itself a fiction. Shammas strips Abayyad of the authority of the reliable narration and reveals his own authorial presence even in passages spoken directly by Abayyad. Thus any identity between the "narrative" parts of the novel and the fictitious autobiography written by Abayyad is represented as, at best, an uncertain possibility. And so the novel acquires yet another topmost layer of reliability, undermining in turn the reliability of all the layers beneath.

By this point, the notion of a causal link between the two portions of the novel has been so seriously undercut that it is impossible to tell who is the "authentic" Shammas: the Shammas of the "narrative" part or the Shammas of the "narrator's" part. There is, of course, a temporal discrepancy between the two versions, regarding the moment at which Shammas becomes acquainted with Abayyad's story: relatively early in the "narrative" version, quite late in the "narrator's" version. And yet the two are presented as separate events. In fact, any differences between the two versions can be taken equally well as a contradiction or as a simple matter of mutual indifference. Each story line has its own claim to reality, and the reader has no way of determining which reality is "genuine."

There are in fact two Anton Shammases in the novel. Both appear in the book as protagonist-narrators; both are writers by profession; each calls the other's authority into question. It would be hard to overestimate the importance of this literary gesture. Here the very composition of the novel mirrors Shammas's ambivalent position vis-à-vis the question of his own personal and national identity. And here too he takes an important step forward in encountering the fundamental tensions of Israeli public discourse: the dual representation of the Jews as majority and minority calls for the creation in the novel of a new type of literary subject, a subject who, confronting this duality, is capable of taking steps toward determining its real nature. Indeed, given the absence of such a determination, he can turn even this weakness to his advantage, using it as an analytical tool to crack into the duality and attempt to change it.

The Israeli Arab as Palestinian;
The Palestinian as the Israeli Jew's Jew

The self-identity of the Israeli was formed by Jews who were trying to build a state with a Jewish majority that would, at the same time, in the framework of a liberal democracy respect the identity and rights of all Israelis, Jews, and Arabs alike. This formula included both the ideal of a democratic state and the ideal of a Jewish state with a Jewish majority and a Jewish character, a place of refuge for the Jewish people. The seeds of a contradiction are all too evident here, and they sprouted and grew over the years. The Arab inhabitants of Israel, in fact, never were citizens with truly equal rights. Confiscation of lands, constant pressure from the security forces, neglect of education in the Arab sector—these are only a few examples from a long history of discrimination. The temporary and partial compromises that attempted to reconcile the contradictions became more and more unworkable over the years. The problem was exacerbated by reduced Jewish immigration, with demographic projections indicating that the Jews were likely to lose their majority status in the not-too-distant future. The dramatic climax came, of course, in 1967, when Israel conquered Gaza and the West Bank. The desire to strengthen the ideal of a Jewish state was now reinforced by the desire to hold onto the occupied territories (though inhabited by over a million Arabs)—and the inevitable result was to undermine Israeli democracy while suppressing the Palestinians and their national aspirations.

With the Israeli sense of self-identity caught in this dynamic and contradictory situation, the very act of writing an Israeli novel becomes a highly complex cultural process. And given the bewildering array of sides and opinions in the current Israeli scene, all charged with emotion and almost totally politicized, any attempt at genuine criticism becomes extremely difficult. It is not easy to carry on an incisive political dialogue in a charged situation where all the interlocutors are interested parties automatically slotted into this or that political pigeonhole. Nor is it any easier to carry on a struggle against an occupying power whose past history and present consciousness preclude any neatly categorical analysis in terms of simple categories such as strong-weak or ruler-ruled. Indeed, Israeli public discourse disguises the power of the dominant majority precisely by adopting the linguistic and behavioral style of a minority—one way to circumvent temporarily the contradiction alluded to above, where the image of a small democratic Israel fighting for a homeland for the oppressed Jewish people conflicts with the image of a great Israel engaged in deliberate suppression of the Palestinians. An outrageous expression of this ambivalent imagery can be seen in the protests of the Jewish settlers in the occupied territories at their "abandonment" by the Israeli government and in the rhetoric of self-styled persecuted victims that accompanies their anti-Palestinian activities.

The occupation has created a cultural matrix in which these contradictions have become blurred. One measure of how deeply rooted this culture now is can be seen in the overwhelming use in Israel of Arab workers for manual labor, which has in turn led to a large measure of rhetorical overlap in Israeli discourse between the categories of class and nationality. The ideological and cultural aspects of these phenomena, especially their literary manifestations, evince an opposition between minority and majority—which does not always coincide with the opposition between weakness and strength.[5] The dynamic flexibility of the opposition minority/majority—the mutual dependence between minority and majority, their relative degrees of power as well as a special sensitivity to the link between cultural and linguistic identity, on the one hand, and sovereignty and political legitimacy, on the other, all find expression through the discourse of the arabesque. The importance of this dynamic opposition can be seen most of all in the great strength it imparts to a minority confronted with the defense mechanisms of a majority that, however powerful, feels itself perfectly entitled to minority status and consciousness.

A very special way of seeing and reacting must lie developed in order to crack open this smooth and flexible battery of defense mechanisms, to criticize the presuppositions of the dominant discourse from the outside without losing the vantage of a participant involved personally in events from the inside. To do this in a novel, it is crucial to determine first what identity and authority are available to its narrator. Shammas makes these issues the central focus of his novel and tries in it to delineate the true Israeli image through a dialectical juxtaposition of an Arab Image and a Jewish image.

The mutual undermining of the "narrative" and the "narrator's" segments of the novel is largely responsible for the uncommon dual effect Shammas has created: on the one hand, powerful emotional involvement in *each* of the two segments; on the other, the abstract viewpoint from which *both* parts are formulated. It is from this same viewpoint that Shammas formulates his own identity, through a systematic dialectical negation, almost to the point of absurdity, of the national significance of his own ancestral roots. In one of the most entertaining parts of the novel (15–16), Shammas presents his family's ancestry as an utter hodgepodge of periods, religions, and nationalities. The founder of the family, who immigrated from southwestern Syria to the Galilee only at the beginning of the last century, did so chiefly because the rival family in his old village was trying to kill him. The Christian inhabitants of Fasuta in the Galilee had been persecuted and oppressed by the Moslem inhabitants of nearby Dir El-Qasi, which was renamed Moshav Elqosh after the Israeli War of Independence. The village of Fasuta itself was built not only on the ruins of the Crusader fortress Pasova, but also on the still earlier ruins of the ancient Jewish village Mifshata, where a number of priests had settled after the destruction of the Second Temple. Thus any attempt at any positive statement, made on the basis of a present-day political interpretation of the past, contains the seeds of its own negation. Shammas has created a text that parodies the genre of dynastic political genealogy. And so the text, in purporting to do justice to the political interests of all the parties involved, actually satisfies none of them. In this way Shammas sidesteps the traditional terms of the debate, which has conventionally focused on stating and comparing the historical rights claimed by each of the parties.

Shammas thus exposes the distorted conception of time underlying Israeli public discourse. And he criticizes this conception from a perspective for which he must pay a certain political price. Shammas rejects the whole framework of historical privileges and justifications, and structures the debate instead in futuristic and utopian terms. In this he assumes a risk, evincing a certain weakness, given a volatile political situation articulated precisely in terms of historical questions such as "Who was there first?" One could doubtless regard this as a lack of sensitivity, on Shammas's part, to the concrete political realities of the conflict. But, on the other hand, one could also see it as a concrete exercise in political tactics, crediting Shammas for relinquishing one position of strength to gain a better one.

In his political essays Shammas returns again and again to the demand that the Jewish state should finally adopt the political agenda of an *Israeli* state, a democratic homeland for Jews and Arabs alike.[6] Yet at the same time he demonstrates a sensitivity to the legitimate fears and aspirations of Israeli Jews. His call for an Israeli state as opposed to a Jewish one is actually more a call for a reversal of priorities, an inversion of the hierarchy whereby Jewish considerations automatically take precedence over democratic ones. But the challenge announced in Shammas's novel, a challenge aimed in part at the Israeli left, involves something more: a special sensitivity to the dialogue he is conducting with the presuppositions underlying even the leftist point of view. Shammas develops his Israeli identity as an Arab by confronting his own identity with the Israeli-ness of the Jews. In fact, his primary demand of Israeli Jews is that they change the rules of the game—that, as Jews, they reexamine the function that keeping old scores and accounts has in confusing the issues of their political and moral situation today. This is, however, no more than he demands of himself as he develops his own Israeli identity by rejecting much of the contemporary significance of his own historical and genealogical roots.

In the novel the essence of Shammas's confrontation with the Israeliness of the Jews is embodied in the confrontation between Shammas, the protagonist-narrator, and Yoshi (Yehoshua) Bar-On, the Jewish Israeli author who travels with Shammas to Iowa City. Shammas has hardly bothered to hide the fact that the prototype for Bar-On is the Israeli author A. B. Yehoshua. He is presented satirically in the novel and, indeed, is seen in much the same light as Shammas saw Yehoshua during the stormy debate between the two which was carried on in the Israeli press about a year ago [1989]. The Israeli author Bar-On appears in the novel as a somewhat ridiculous figure, with racist beliefs and impulses, engaging in inner monologues strung together out of colloquial or literary clichés. One of the highpoints of the real-world debate between Shammas and Yehoshua came in a newspaper interview when the "liberal" Yehoshua, who is identified with the moderate-liberal wing of Israeli political opinion, made the following suggestion: after the creation of a Palestinian homeland in the occupied territories—of which he approves—Yehoshua proposed that Shammas find full expression for his nationalism by packing up and moving to the newly formed Palestinian state. In a series of replies that drew many others into this ongoing debate, Shammas tried to show Yehoshua that his suggestion is quite akin to Meir Kahane's proposal to ensure the Jewishness of Israel through an organized expulsion of the Arab population. The unwillingness of Yehoshua, and of many other Israeli liberals, to acknowledge the Arab Shammas as a full-fledged Israeli, whose native land is Israel just as theirs is, was proof for Shammas that the majority is not inclined to relinquish the Jewish primacy of the State of Israel, even at the risk of sacrificing its democratic character. In the novel Shammas focuses on the way liberals fall into the trap of racist discourse patterns. It is precisely for this reason that he conducts the satire with considerable sophistication—the better to expose the two-faced nature of Israeli public discourse.

In Paris, en route to Iowa City, Bar-On wonders what Shammas's reaction would be "if he only knew that to myself I think of him—proud Palestinian-Israeli-Arab that he is—as 'my Jew'" (72). In fact both of these epithets, "Palestinian" and "Jew," belong here to the same discursive universe of stereo typing and discrimination. It is crucial that Shammas refuses to label himself a Palestinian. In the novel, he rebuts attempts to define him as a Palestinian by noting, among other things, that as far back as the 1948 war his father did not consider himself a Palestinian refugee. Bar-On does define Shammas as a Palestinian, thus feeding the discriminatory stereotype of the Israeli Arab as having "alien" loyalties. To be sure, Bar-On is presented as wishing to show empathy for the plight of an Israeli Arab writer. However, as the satire brings out clearly, Bar-On's inner monologue reveals both his feeling of genuine empathy with a fellow minority—an empathy based on the similarity between

Shammas's situation and that of the Jews as a national minority—and the racist stance of a superior majority, in the unconsciously derogatory use of the phrase "my Jew."

Arabesques in Time, Arabesques in Space

Does the novel open with Shammas speaking of the death of his grandmother Alya on April 1, 1954, in the village? Or is he instead speaking of the death of his father in Haifa, in April 1978? In fact, Shammas is doing both at once—a fact that has profound implications for his treatment of time in the novel. The simultaneous interweaving of earlier and later events is a structural principle of the novel; Shammas exploits it chiefly as a concrete means of realizing his cyclical conception of time. The numerous digressions, the twists and turns, the sudden predestined meetings all conform, in one way or other, to the Arabian iconography of the arabesque. This phenomenon stands out particularly in the "narrative" parts, which revolve mostly around the village of Fasuta. But a careful reading of the "narrator's" portion, which describes the trip to Iowa City, also reveals the figure of the arabesque. Even in such a straightforward matter as Shammas's travel journal, things are not what they seem: for one, the entries are not always in chronological order! The connections among events within each part are highly complex, as is the relationship between the two parts. The static arabesque frees the chronological flow of time in the plot from any necessary involvement with such notions as redemption or progress. As mentioned above, Shammas questions the validity of relying on his own family genealogy as a basis for present-day political judgments; and, at the same time, he stands opposed to present-day manifestations of Zionism. Instead, he offers his own Israeli-ness as an alternative, embodying a more modest and far less apocalyptic conception of time.

The traditional figure of the arabesque, pervading the structure of the novel at every level, brings Shammas's representational mode close to a pure statement of formal relations. In the arabesque, Shammas has found a way to relate to the past without falling victim to its nondialectical universalism. Thus he describes the hardships of the Arab refugees of 1948—he attempts to shift the moral debate from considerations of precedence, of who or what came first, to confrontations with undeniably concrete instances of human suffering. The two-dimensional nature of the arabesque motivates the description of the oppression of the Palestinian woman without minimizing its urgency or gravity within the overall web of political oppression depicted in the novel. Thus, for example, in describing the hardships endured by Layla Khouri, Shammas has interwoven her mistreatment by Israeli soldiers in 1948 and 1981 with her misfortunes at the hands of Arab society (for example, her betrayal by a member of Shammas's family, and her sexual and apparently financial exploitation by the woman Sa'ada). Layla the Palestinian is portrayed in the novel as a commodity, passed from hand to hand, from government to government. In this respect, her existence parallels another arabesque, the cyclical course taken by Abayyad, the boy who was kidnapped into adoption and was himself treated as a commodity, whose loss first brought misery to his poverty-stricken natural parents just as it would later to his wealthy adoptive parents. Thus the arabesque takes the fetishization of the individual and the dominance of exchange value and weaves them into a fabric of human relationships existing in a context of social and political repression.[7] This unfolds against the background of the Zionist revolution, with the political realignments and the social and economic modernization which accompanied it, all culminating in the abandonment of the village and its uncommercialized way of life based upon use value.

The arabesque does not serve only a negative, critical function; it also bears a positive, utopian message. It acts as an analogue, in the area of the visual arts, to the position of Islamic "contractualism" in the social sphere. The distinction between Islamic contractualism and Western corporativism is a close parallel to the distinction between the collective *Gemeinschaft*, based on personal relationships, and the impersonal and achievement-oriented *Gesellschaft* usually associated with modern technological society. In contrast to Western corporativism, with its preference for hierarchical structures in which a limited number of conclusions are drawn from a limited number of premises (on the model of geometry), the cyclical rhythms of the arabesque could well be said to characterize an "indefinitely expandable" structure. The arabesque provides a framework within which it becomes possible to reduce the apparently "chaotic variety of life's reality" to manageable proportions, yet without "arbitrarily setting bounds to it." The novel's arabesque style displays the general features of Islam's traditional atomism, an atomism representing an "equal and co-ordinated responsibility of all possible individuals for the maintenance of moral standards."[8]

This moral atomism and, in particular, the special kind of reduction that does not stifle the individuality of certain details are the key to understanding Shammas's arabesque discourse. In a striking passage in the novel, Shammas writes the following:

> That was Uncle Yusef. On the one hand a believing Catholic, whose heart, like that of Saint Augustine, was firm and secure, as if the Virgin herself had promised him that his years were but links in a chain leading to salvation and redemption. And on the other hand he believed, as if to keep an escape hatch open, that if dust were to return unto dust, and the jaws of death were gaping, that the twisting, elusive, cyclical periodicity of things would have the power to withstand death. But he was unaware of these two opposing aspects coexisting within himself; he saw them only as a unitary whole. (204)

Shammas's novel forces these two types of discourse, linear and cyclical, into a confrontation involving not synthesis but an attempt to extract the best from each. Shammas presents himself in the novel as someone in a position both to clarify this temporal duality—the coexistence of Christian time and quasi-pagan time in Uncle Yusef—and to enter into the Christian conception of time as a path leading to salvation (204). But this intermediate stance, in fact a continuation of Uncle Yusef's position, represents a source from which Shammas draws strength. From within this static arabesque of time, but with one foot already on the outside, Shammas is in a position to continue striving toward his goal of a utopia, without paying the price of a nondialectical universalization of the past. Undoubtedly, dehistoricization can be made to serve the purposes of those interested in perpetuating the status quo of oppression, through a deliberate confusion of the notions of development, contingency, and the potential for change.[9] But the arabesque, whose cyclicity has the power "to withstand death," enables Shammas to keep a firm grasp on the absolute reality of suffering and of human existence, whose universal validity is not altered or obscured by its relative position in time. The arabesque creates the effect of static motion, motion without progress. This is its way of "withstanding death" and of undermining attempts to develop a rigidly teleological concept of "national time." It must be emphasized that the great flexibility of the arabesque does not disconnect it from the process of generalization and reduction involved in the creation of a "national subject." But it is never committed to a rigid representation of a national subject, fixed in space and time, and is therefore free to become an *autonomous* critical tool, endowed with its own absolute and self-sufficient validity. With its power thus not contingent upon the exclusive authority of some national subject, it becomes an effective weapon for the minority.

Standing both inside and outside the arabesque, Shammas freezes history; he does this to forge a critical dialogue in which both sides are precluded, in their argumentation, from appealing to selective generalizations based on decontextualized bits of history. Shammas denies Israeli Jews the right to justify present wrongdoings by past grievances, and he holds himself to the same standard. Others have not been so careful. Edward W. Said, for example, rightly criticizes the distortion of history implicit in Zionist claims about the Palestinians, but he falls into the same trap himself in his discussion of the enactment of the Law of Return (which imparts automatic Israeli citizenship to any Jewish immigrant) when the State of Israel was established. He views the law as racist, as a reflection of the inherently discriminatory character of the State of Israel, ignoring the fact that the Law of Return, like affirmative action in the United States, was enacted in an attempt to discriminate in favor of a disadvantaged minority, persecuted and uprooted Jews everywhere.[10] Shammas, too, is conscious of the law's racist implications. But he expresses this awareness in a completely different way than Said, and with sensitivity to its dialectical dimensions, by proposing that the law in its present form be repealed in the not-too-distant future and remain in force only for immigrants from distressed Jewish communities.

The nonmimetic geometrical abstractions of the arabesque are intimately linked to the function of *spatial* patterning in the novel. The entire journey to America in fact shows clear elements of a search for roots and spiritual identity. But here, too, the cyclical arabesque is brought into play, the same motion without progress wherein every destination immediately becomes the take-off point for a new quest. The writers participating in the International Writing Program are housed in a dormitory suggestively called the Mayflower, a name which hints at a connection between Shammas's ideal conception of Israeli identity and the model of a society of immigrants embodied in America and its young history. Yet, at the same time, Shammas has come full circle: he comments, while discussing a letter to his Jewish lover Shlomit in Israel, that only now in Iowa City, "over twenty years after I left my childhood house, do I feel, for the first time in many years, that I can conjure up my childhood house in the village, its smells and sights and sensations, for I am able for the first time to describe it to Shlomit, who never set foot there" (133).

Shammas invests his layover in Paris en route to Iowa City with a special function. First of all, during this intermezzo the novel introduces the figure of Amira, the Jewish writer from Egypt. In fact, the images of women in the novel—including Shammas's Lebanese cousin, his Jewish Israeli lover Shlomit, and Layla Khouri, the Christian woman converted to Islam—make up a representative sample of Middle East geography. There is a large degree of overlap here with the range of male figures. All these serve to lay out, in effect, a map of the different local and national images constituting the cardinal terms in the system of oppositions that collectively define Shammas's Israeli identity. A planned reunion in Paris with Shammas's female cousin from Lebanon represents a new possibility for Shammas to express his identity as an Arab. But at first the meeting does not come off. This fact is another example of the dialectical process—where a possibility is presented only to be rejected—by which Shammas develops his own identity. Indeed, as a "replacement" for his cousin, Shammas immediately makes contact with her opposite: the Jew Bar-On, who is also staying over in Paris.

The Gospel According to Uncle Yusef; or, Hebrew as the Language of Redemption

Uncle Yusef's arabesque tales are described by Shammas in these words: "They flowed about him in a stream of illusion which linked interior and exterior, beginning and ending, reality and fiction" (203). The arabesque, which makes no claim to represent any reality outside itself, is by that very token a fine vehicle for conveying a variety of heterogeneous materials. This constant confusion of domains and categories characterizes the lesson Shammas learns from his uncle's legacy. As he puts it, his uncle has given him all the keys to extricate himself from the arabesque and enter another existence—all the keys but the final one. The key to salvation lies in bringing together the two halves of a single whole—a juncture that comes only once. But the incompleteness in Shammas prevents him, as he puts it, from relying with confidence on any possibility of salvation whatsoever. Like the almost inextricable confusion between fiction and reality, epitomized in the contradiction between the two halves of the story, the novel presents a series of illusory solutions in the form of sets of twins, or near twins, who are intended to complement and complete one another. All this illustrates the novel's clear-sighted appreciation of the political potential of the arabesque. The bond between Shammas the Christian Arab and Bar-On the Jew should be sought not in some sort of messianic eschatology but rather in a close analysis of the Israeli experience and the utopian elements already present in it.

The stories told by Shammas's Christian Arab family from Fasuta depict a static existence, a dimension highlighted even more by the orality of these stories telling of family life in the village in the years before (and even after) the founding of the State of Israel. Oral literature acquires its cultural significance in relation to the time frame in which it is told. Here the time frame of the storyteller is also the political and moral time frame in which Shammas the author wrote and published his book. In this way Shammas simultaneously emphasizes the oral sources of his stories and the radical change that he himself introduces in moving from a traditional oral tale to a written story. Only rarely in the novel does he deny his identity as an Israeli writer and pretend to be a naive folk narrator. Over and over again, Shammas stresses the tension between his connection to oral tradition and his commitment to writing. Indeed, sometimes the very act of storytelling, as in Layla Khouri's case, can undermine the stability of reality. Shammas needs both types, both oral and written narrative, in order to come to terms with his own national literary tradition and to open a gateway to the utopian conception of modern Israeli nationhood outlined in his novel. What he does, in fact, is to rework in writing those stories he heard orally from Uncle Yusef in order to formulate through them a present reality. As remarked earlier, the atemporal, arabesque rhythms of the oral tradition serve as a touchstone for evaluating the nondialectical attitude toward time found in Israeli public discourse. With this in mind, it is noteworthy that Israeli critics reacting to the book have largely ignored the revolutionary function which Shammas gives to the blending of oral and written modes—they delight in the folklore and reject those parts having contemporary political relevance.

The duality with which Shammas displays his oral sources, a blend of estrangement and closeness, parallels the duality of his relationship to Hebrew literature and indeed complements it. In distancing himself from his oral sources, Shammas is forcing his way into written Hebrew literature as an outsider demanding equal rights with the insiders. The conceptual framework that best illuminates the relationship between Bar-On and Shammas is the world of literature and books, a world epitomized by the gathering of writers participating in the International Writing Program. Bar-On, at work on a book about an Israeli Arab, asks to make use of the figure of Anton Shammas. He wants to portray the Arab in his story with real empathy and not reduce him to a stereotype. But the motives underlying this—for example, his desire that his Arab character should play a leading role in a study of the image of the Arab in modern Hebrew literature—only accentuates Bar-On's own stereotypical attitudes toward his Arab characters. The stereotype, of course, is in general an extreme expression of domination. And so, as Shammas shows us, Bar-On's desire to change the surface formulation of the stereotype without addressing the presuppositions of his own discourse leads him, at best, into a new variation on the same stereotype. At one point Bar-On announces his intention to write "about the isolation of the Palestinian Israeli Arab, an isolation greater than any other" (84). This would appear to reveal a special sensitivity to the fate of his protagonist—but the larger context of Shammas's novel makes it clear that it is just another indication of Bar-On's unwillingness to give up control over the representational molds available for the depiction of this fate.

Bar-On's highly practical, utilitarian attitude toward the Other is illustrated by his reaction to Shammas's attempts to preserve his own independence in the face of Bar-On's domination. Bar-On proposes to treat Shammas's private life as an object to be exploited in the creation of his novel. Even when Bar-On gives up on Shammas, he still clings to the same Palestinian stereotype. And so, at one point, he seeks a functional replacement for Shammas, finding it in a Palestinian writer also taking part in the Writing Program; and when things fail to work out with this Palestinian substitute, he leaves America and returns to Israel. But just as the fictional autobiography of Shammas written by Abayyad the Palestinian does not count in the novel as *the* definitive text determining Shammas's identity, so too Shammas provides Bar-On the Jew with misleading information about his life. Shammas develops his own Israeli identity by liberating it from the various political interpretations threatening to swallow it up. And thus he keeps both Abayyad the Palestinian and Bar On the Jew at a distance, allowing neither to gain control over the representation of his life story.

A number of Bar-On's comments on his own forthcoming novel are strikingly applicable to the novel *Arabesques* as well. And the deliberate obscurity which beclouds the whole matter of textual interrelationships, in comparing Shammas's own text with other texts developed within it (that of the Palestinian and that of the Jew), emphasizes their predominant status as mere collections of images rather than as representations of some external reality. In this way, through the world of literature and books, the ideological dilemma of

Shammas's identity is translated into a struggle between texts. The arabesque novel, in its rejection of the authority of all representation, focuses our attention on the *internal* dynamics of the political, national, and cultural images involved. Shammas is contrasted with Bar-On in the context of the Writing Program, at a time when both authors are at work on their own new books. At the same time, though, Shammas was also engaged in a confrontation with Bar On's counterpart, the Israeli writer A. B. Yehoshua, author of the well-known Hebrew short story "Facing the Forests."[11] The central episode of this story concerns the burning of a forest, forests being one of the paramount symbols of Zionist reconstruction. This particular forest was planted on the ruins of an Arab village destroyed in 1948, and it is set on fire by an old Arab villager with the silent cooperation of an eccentric Jewish fire warden.

The arabesque binds literature and metaliterature, the literary, text itself and the critical discourse responding to it. And so Yehoshua's story enters into Shammas's novel, along with the important article written in response to it by the critic Mordechai Shalev.[12] Shalev criticizes the fact that the figure of the Arab in the story, with its political and moral overtones, fulfills a much more general oedipal function: the Arab serves as a means for the young man to carry out an oedipal revolt against the generation of his fathers. In essence Shalev claims that the moral issue, the eviction of the Arabs from their land, is only a pretext for raising the real question: Whose life has the greater vitality, the Jew's or the Arab's? Shammas portrays Bar-On (Yehoshua) as trying, in his new novel, to accommodate the critic Shalev. But Bar-On is unable to see that the attack against him was directed largely against the imposition of individual psychology on what is properly a political and collective matter. Yehoshua's story is thus seen as exploiting the figure of an oppressed Arab in order to fulfill the spiritual needs of an Israeli Jew. The same point is further emphasized by the fact that Yehoshua's Jewish protagonist is an antihero, an eccentric existing on the fringes of society. Even in the protests of the younger generation of Israelis against the injustices accompanying the realization of the Zionist dream—even here, Shammas tells us—the image of the Arab is exploited when a dominant majority ignores its responsibility to examine its own past with maturity and integrity.

Which One Is the Other's Ventriloquist?

In principle, what we are dealing with here is a variation on the Hegelian paradigm of the master-slave relationship, whereby the master's consciousness of himself as master is conditioned by the slave's acknowledgment of the master's superior status. Yehoshua's story "Facing the Forests" and Bar-On's clinging to the stereotype of the Palestinian both emphasize the role played by the figure of the Arab as the key to the identity of the Israeli Jew. But a situation whereby the Israeli "master" draws on a dual consciousness—as minority and majority at once—complicates considerably any attempt at interpretation. And it renders equally problematic the strategies open to those condemned to the role of "slave" in this dialectic. For the Israeli "master," in conformity with the Hegelian paradigm, has attained this status only after winning a life-and-death struggle for independence, and continues to derive its self-consciousness and legitimacy from its still-recent past as an oppressed minority.

But the Hegelian "slave" in the novel, that is, the Israeli Arab, is just as dependent on the Israeli "master" for his own consciousness. His confrontation with Bar-On is especially relevant here. After Bar-On's hurried departure from Iowa City and return to Israel, Shammas is beset by guilt and the sense of having missed an opportunity. Despite the struggle he wages against Bar-On, with Bar-On ultimately recast as his satirical victim, Shammas's life is fundamentally dependent upon Bar-On's. Shammas is afraid that his meeting with Abayyad could be taken by Bar-On as an attempt to enlist Shammas in the PLO; he interprets this as an important clue to his own identity, which cannot exist without the presence, at once threatening and soothing, of Bar-On the Jew. Just as he feels betrayed when Bar-On prefers the Palestinian to himself (152), so he reflects: "How could I react without Bar-On breathing down my neck? How could there even *be* a situation, good or bad, where Bar-On was not breathing down my neck?" (232).

The fact that Shammas is set in opposition to a master who is himself a slave—namely, the Israeli Jew—limits the spiritual and revolutionary power that normally accrues automatically to the slave. It is hardly an accident that the blatant materialistic dimension of Arab life in Israel and the occupied territories, with the Arabs visible and prominent as manual laborers, finds as little genuine political expression in the novel as it does in real life. As an Israeli Arab, Shammas too must confront the dual consciousness of the Israeli Jewish master-slave, and in consequence he has difficulty in crystallizing any sort of revolutionary consciousness. As Fredric Jameson has said, there is a certain advantage to having an overall map of a given situation, a map drawn from the realistic materialist viewpoint of someone who fulfills it in his own work. Shammas has such a map but cannot take advantage of it. Neither Yehoshua nor Shammas can allow himself to take advantage of the national allegory that characterizes the materialism of Third World literature, an allegory "where the telling of the individual story and the individual experience cannot but ultimately involve the whole laborious telling of the experience of the collectivity itself."[13]

As mentioned above, Shalev has criticized the story "Facing the Forests" for substituting an external political dimension for its oedipal concerns. Shalev's attack can now be reinterpreted as an attack on Yehoshua's deviation from the national allegory that is permitted him as an Israeli author belonging to the majority culture. For Shammas the arabesque, with its flexibility and "freedom from any myth-based symbolism," is the appropriate vehicle for coping with the problematic status of allegory in this literary and political situation."[14] He is suspicious of the validity of the Israeli national allegory, both for the Israeli Jew, with his uncertain identity as master, and for himself as a half-slave whose role and identity are no less uncertain; and his suspicion finds expression in the novel in a heterogeneous and discontinuous arabesque of allegorical patterns, many of them Christian, interwoven with passages of local documentary narrative. For Shammas, the allegorical image of the New Testament cock—the image of the cock before it crowed at dawn to signal that Peter had denied his Lord Jesus—introduces in the novel a fascinating blend of mutually incompatible interpretations reflecting both Eastern and Western traditions. The reality depicted in the novel rejects over and over again the promise of redemption implicit in this mythic image. The arabesque blends fact and fiction, realism and romance, tragedy and soap opera, with bits of the real-life biography of the author Anton Shammas thrown in. All this alerts the reader over and over not to expect the ideological satisfaction which a traditional, fixed literary genre is able to supply.

In several senses, Anton Shammas's *Arabesques* both falls into and deviates from the patterns of a "minor literature" as defined by Gilles Deleuze and Félix Guattari.[15] In accordance with this pattern, *Arabesques* is not subject to the authority or the conventions of standard literary genres. First, this Hebrew novel written by an Arab "doesn't come from a minor language; it is rather that which a minority constructs within a major language" (*KML*, 16). At the hands of the Israeli Arab Shammas, Hebrew, the mythic language of Zionism, undergoes a process of *deterritorialization*—the first definitional component, according to Deleuze and Guattari, of a minor literature. Yet this characterization, which at first glance appears to fit the case of Shammas rather well, is somewhat deceptive. For, although Shammas does carry out a process of deterritorialization of Hebrew, at the same time he is reterritorializing it as the language of the *Israeli*.

The second component of a minor literature, whereby *everything* (including the individual) is viewed in *political* terms, also marks a divergence between Deleuze and Guattari's definition and Shammas's novel with the special situation from which it springs. For Deleuze and Guattari, the "political" means a liberation from the unified authority of an autonomous subject, a notion which they apply to Kafka. Politicization undoubtedly plays a significant role in Shammas's novel too: it is a major effect of the mutual undercutting performed by the narrators of the two halves of the novel. Shammas, however, does not politicize everything. His intermediate stance here can be seen both in the novel's critical response to Yehoshua's politicization of the oedipal pattern in "Facing the Forests" and in its refusal to see itself as a national allegory.

Nor does Deleuze and Guattari's third definitional component, whereby "everything takes on a collective value" (*KML*, 17), make the case of Shammas any easier to pigeonhole. This notion of collectivity is to be understood in terms of the opposition between a nonreductionist "collective assemblage of enunciation" and the reductionist concept of a (national) subject (*KML*, 18). In fact, "collectivity" in Deleuze and Guattari's sense is at variance with the dual effect of the arabesque, which simultaneously preserves the independence and particularity of atomic bits of experience while carrying out a reduction, albeit open-ended, which organizes and unites them. Deleuze and Guattari's antireductionist stance carries a price: a disconnection from the inherently reductionist, utopian project of nation making. Indeed, in their discussion of the collective component of a minor literature, they suggest that an author on the margins of the community is all the more able "to express another possible community and to forge the means for another consciousness and another sensibility" (*KML*, 17). By contrast, Shammas does not construct his Israeli utopia from some totally Other consciousness or sensibility, but from the existing, contradiction-ridden inventory of present-day Israeli reality.

But all these differences shrink into insignificance as Deleuze and Guattari proceed to expand the scope of their definition enormously, claiming that the term *minor* "no longer designates specific literatures but the revolutionary conditions for every literature within the heart of what is called great (or established) literature" (*KML*, 18). From here it is only a step to their conception of minor literature as a "machine of expression," a tool for producing mere effects, with no center of gravity (*KML*, 18), thus divorcing it from any possible utopian dimension. Like minor literature, the arabesque is characterized by a lack of obligation to any sort of representation or mythic symbolism. Yet the arabesque does not discard the dream of a national utopia—indeed, it requires it: for the utopian dream creates a context and a target against which the arabesque can level its attack on uncritical, restrictive reductions. In fact, the arabesque undermines the dichotomy that (according to Deleuze and Guattari) any minor literature must address—a dichotomy between, on the one hand, an extreme reterritorialization of language through symbols and archetypes (their example for the political results of this process is the Zionist dream) and, on the other, the process they ascribe to Kafka, a radical deterritorialization of language "to the point of sobriety," culminating in "a perfect and unformed expression, a materially intense expression" (*KML*, 19). Shammas's Hebrew arabesque takes up at the sociopolitical level, the question Deleuze and Guattari had formulated at the linguistic level—that of evaluating "the degrees of territoriality, deterritorialization, and reterritorialization" (*KML*, 25) practiced in Hebrew (the mythic language informing the genesis of Zionism) and other languages in a similar position. Faced with these two conflicting demands—an extreme deterritorialization "to the point of sobriety" vs. a concern for relative degrees of re- and deterritorialization—the arabesque can suggest a dynamic middle way. Shammas's paradigm concedes the importance of the concept of a nation-state, but only as articulated through the arabesque: not as an absolute and rigid notion, defined once and for all, but in a much more critical and flexible sense, as something evolving and responsive to the dialectical process.

These differences between Shammas's model and Deleuze and Guattari's construct in fact could serve to outline a theoretical discussion of the principles implicit in the arabesque as a vehicle for minority discourse. A good example of the especially pertinent advantages afforded by the arabesque is the way Shammas turns to real advantage his own weakness as "slave" vis-à-vis an ambiguous "master." The Hebrew culture's battery of defense mechanisms, which thwarts the development of a revolutionary consciousness, is appropriated by Shammas and used for a different purpose: to illumine the quandary of the slave forced to choose between assignment to a niche in the master culture, thereby condemning himself to imitation, assimilation and loss of identity, and adherence to his traditional culture, thus forcing him into the position of a rejected "savage." Indeed, it is precisely within this unique sort of majority culture, which pretends to be a minority culture and thereby absolves itself of its real responsibilities and commitments as the master culture, that Shammas can realize Derrida's ideal, "to speak the other's language without renouncing [his] own."[16] We should not forget that Hebrew Israeli culture, by virtue of being the dominant majority's culture, acts as a magnet to the minorities who must function within it. But when it represents itself as a minority culture, it undermines its own authority to reject whatever is defined as the Other culture. Bar-On, who in his search for a literary subject shifts his attention from Shammas to the Palestinian from Nablus, compares the two. He himself admits to being troubled by Shammas's complex multiple identity, whose existence transcends the stereotype and violates the binary opposition between Bar-On and the Other: "But my previous hero [Shammas] does not define himself as my enemy, at least not in the accepted sense of the word. And this constitutes a difficulty for me. By contrast, I feel closer to the problems of this Palestinian, and I hope I will not be proved wrong, but my heart tells me that he is the one I will succeed in setting down in writing" (152).

Shammas's *Arabesques* places Israeli Jews in an uneasy position. On the one hand, they cannot just dismiss him or ignore him as someone totally Other, especially in light of his virtuoso command of Hebrew as a literary medium and his vigorous participation in the Israeli mass media as journalist, polemicist, and author. On the other hand, Shammas's violation of the accepted boundaries of Hebrew culture makes it difficult for Israeli Jews to identify easily with him or adopt him as one of their own. This background shows how the novel forces a fundamental revision in some of the political assumptions underlying Israeli public discourse. The very fact that a novel like *Arabesques* exists at all undermines seriously the traditional view of Hebrew literature as a *Jewish national* literature. Through the special device of interweaving oral and folk elements into the narrative, the novel contributes to a process of deterritorialization, challenging the long-standing total coincidence of the Hebrew language with its Jewish subject matter. The Hebrew reader, unable to reject Shammas's challenge out of hand, must either undergo a kind of inner split or develop temporary defense mechanisms (for example, by putting folklore and politics in clearly separate boxes or by making the absurd demand that Shammas become a traditional Zionist). This phenomenon, of Arab authors writing in Hebrew, is still in its infancy, but the trend has already been joined by other writers, such as Na'im Araydi and Muhammad Ana'im. And on the Jewish side, it is noteworthy that parallel attempts to overthrow canonical linguistic boundaries have been made by the writers of Yoram Kanyuk and Yisrael Eliraz, who have actually published Hebrew works under Arab pseudonyms.

It is important now to turn our attention to the other side of the coin, shifting from the deterritorialization to the reterritorialization of Hebrew. "It is essential this time to have an Arab, as an answer to silence, Bar-On muses; "An Arab who speaks in the language of grace, as the exiled Florentine once termed Hebrew. Hebrew, as the language of grace, in contrast to the language of confusion which raged around the world with the fall of the Tower of Babel. My Arab will build his tower of confusion on my own lot. In the language of grace. In my opinion this is his one chance for salvation. Within the accepted limits, of course" (83). We have here a paradox, a simultaneous striving to speak in the Other's language without giving up one's own, as Derrida put it. Thus Hebrew, the old-new language which Shammas, following Dante, called the "language of grace," turns out to offer a political salvation for the Israeli Arab. But it can also suggest a political and existential solution to the confusion of "Jew" and "Israeli." The kind of synthetic Hebrew wielded so ably by Shammas, a popular and modern vernacular, is in fact also a new language, a language created by the Other. The very artificiality of Shammas's language, sometimes even verging on parody, undermines the "self-evident" presuppositions of the entire discourse and encourages the cultural and political reconceptualization so essential to the life and discourse of Israeli Jews. Curiously, this process reenacts, in a sense, the creation during the early days of Zionism of a national *Jewish* consciousness within the Hebrew literature of the late nineteenth and early twentieth centuries, as writers strove to re create Hebrew as a new synthetic language and a source of modern national identity.[17] This work of linguistic invention now serves Shammas in his attempt to build a new-old language as a bridge toward the re-creation of an old-new nation. As an Arab writer, breaking into the linguistic and literary citadel of the Israeli Jews, Shammas calls into question their claim to exclusive possession of the language of traditional Zionism. For him Hebrew is simply the language of present-day Israelis. Acknowledging this revision in the canonical definition of Hebrew literature amounts to acknowledging the radical changes that the Zionist national subject must undergo to cope with the sharp contradictions besetting him in his new historical situation. The immediate (though not exclusive) expression of these changes is an admission of the need to force the values of the Jewish state to approximate better the concrete norms of a truly democratic society.

Shammas's affair with Amira, the Jewish woman writer from Egypt, arouses Bar-On's anger. Bar-On sees in this love an intolerable threat to the established boundaries delimiting his national culture. But Amira has no material connection to the reality of Israel—and therefore for her, existing as a member of the Jewish minority in Alexandria, living in an Arabic and French milieu, Hebrew is indeed the language of the dead past. But for Shammas and Bar-On, Hebrew, as the language of Israel and the Israelis, is the "language of grace," a language capable of reconciling and uniting them. A Dutch author visiting the Writing Program wants to speak with Shammas about "this schizophrenia wherein Bar-On and [Shammas] are but a single individual" (130); and a Norwegian writer acknowledges "that they have not yet made up their minds which one is the other's ventriloquist" (130).

The language of grace, which is supposed to effect a fusion of Shammas and Bar-On, also reminds us of the way the arabesque maps out the future of this special confrontation between master and slave. As previously remarked, the possibility of this fusion is latent in the very ambivalence of the confrontation. Shammas's arabesque does not aim to liberate the slave through a reversal of roles whereby master and slave merely trade places. For, let us recall, a truly Hegelian freedom would involve an *Aufhebung* of the entire opposition. This is the promise held out by the arabesque's composition which "figure[s] forth eternity, presenting the infinite complexity and movement of existence and at the same time resolving it in total harmony of detail with detail and of part with whole so that all that movement is seen in overall repose.... The innumerable details are each felt as precious, *yet no one item stands out to dominate the whole.*"[18]

But the dangers involved in a shift from Hebrew as the language of the past to Hebrew as "the language of grace" are not small. To be sure, the Israeli dream presented here is no Canaanite movement,[19] no apocalyptic vision of a liberation from the fetters of Judaism through an aggressive severing of historical roots. To the contrary: Shammas's Hebrew arabesque represents a utopia, emerging from a detailed critical confrontation between the cultural demands of past and present. But the confrontation is fraught with danger. Indeed, when the husband of Shlomit, Shammas's Israeli Jewish lover, discovers Shammas's Hebrew love letters to his wife, their affair explodes, shattering a delicate and dangerous balance across both family and national boundaries (85). From a language of grace and redemption, Hebrew thus risks once again becoming a language of censure sanctioning racist fears of the Other, whose sexual prowess overcomes the "master's" wife.

The arabesque is a remarkable blend of two conceptions of temporality: a critical approach to time, having no necessary commitment to history or to any promise of progress toward redemption, with an adherence to a static and cyclical temporal continuum. Shammas's Israeli identity is constructed from multiple negations and a critical relationship to prevailing interpretations of the past and future. Shammas's arabesque appropriates the Hebrew language as the language of Israelis. This is an approximation of a relatively autonomous entity present and capable of bringing about a better future. In the current Israeli situation, the arabesque serves as a model for minority discourse, whose flexibility stands it in good stead even in a contradiction-ridden labyrinth that sometimes appears to have no exit. Shammas's book points the way to utopian unification of the language of Arabs and Jews—a unification that is only a contingent possibility, subject to human and political constraints. And yet, coming as it does in the dark days of the occupation of the West Bank and Gaza, the deep sensitivity of Shammas's challenge may open a door to hope.

NOTES

1. David Twersky, "An Interview with Amos Oz," *Tikkun* 1, no. 2 (1986): 26. The interviewer gives the title of Shammas's novel in the singular (i.e., *Arabesque*), as it appears (in English) on the copyright page of the Hebrew edition. I will refer to the book in the plural (i.e., *Arabesques*), as in the Hebrew title. All citations from *Arabesques* (Tel Aviv: Am Oved, 1986) will be from this Hebrew edition and will be included in the text. An English translation of *Arabesques* is forthcoming; in the present essay all translations from the Hebrew are those of Orin D. Gensler.

2. Hannan Hever, "An Extra Pair of Eyes: Hebrew Poetry under Occupation," *Tikkun* 2, no. 2 (May 1987): 84–87, 122–126.

3. Anton Shammas, "Al galut ve-sifrut" [On exile and literature], *Igra* 2 (1987): 67–70; Shammas, "Ashmat ha-babushka" [The guilt of the babushka], *Politika* 5–6 (February–March 1986): 44–45.

4. On this fundamental tension and attempt to resolve it through the problematization of paraphrase, especially in the writing of intellectual history, see Manin Jay, "Two Cheers for Paraphrase: The Confessions of a Synoptic Intellectual Historian," *Stanford Literary Review* 3, no. 1 (Spring 1986): 47–61.

5. For an analysis of the categories of weakness and strength throughout Jewish history, see David Biale, *Power and Powerlessness in Jewish History* (New York: Schocken Books, 1986). Bial shows, among other things, how post-1967 Zionism was mistakenly considered an organic continuation of Jewish history rather than a break in it. This, he suggests, is the background for the widespread tendency to identify anti-Zionism with antisemitism; it likewise explains the characterization of Israeli sovereignty as a contradictory mixture of exaggerated fear and grandiose ambition (146).

6. Anton Shammas, "Milhamti be-tahanot anshe-ha-ruah" [My fight against the windmills of the intellectuals], *Moznayim* 60 (September 1986): 26–27; Anton Shammas, "Ashmat ha-babushka," 45.

7. Abdul R. JanMohamed, "The Economy of Manichean Allegory: The Function of Racial Difference in Colonialist. Literature," in *Race, Writing, and Difference*, ed. Henry Louis Gates Jr. (Chicago: University of Chicago Press, 1986), 79.

8. Marshall G. S. Hodgson, *The Venture of Islam: Conscience and History in a World Civilization* (Chicago: University of Chicago Press, 1974), 344–347. This book approaches the

specific arabesque mode of reduction by viewing it in opposition to geometry, drawing an analogy between the arabesque and the nature of a historical report.

9. JanMohamed, "The Economy of Manichean Allegory," 77.
10. Edward W. Said, "An Ideology of Difference," in *Race, Writing, and Difference*, 40. See also Shammas, "Ashmat ha-babushka," 45.
11. A. B. Yehoshua, "Facing the Forests," in *Three Days and a Child*, trans. Miriam Arad (London: Peter Owen, 1971), 131–174.
12. Mordechai Shalev, "Ha-aravim ke-pitaron sifruti" [The Arabs as a literary solution], *Haaretz*, September 30, 1970.
13. Fredric Jameson, "Third-World Literature in the Era of Multinational Capitalism," *Social Text* 15 (Fall 1986): 69, 85–86. Jameson makes use here of the Hegelian paradigm of the master-slave relationship.
14. Hodgson, *The Venture of Islam*, 510.
15. Gilles Deleuze and Félix Guattari, *Kafka: Toward a Minor Literature*, trans. Dana Polan, foreword by Réda Bensmaia (Minneapolis: University of Minnesota Press, 1986); all further references to this work, abbreviated as *KML*, will appear in the text. Bensmaia's introduction was especially helpful in the following discussion.
16. Jacques Derrida, "Racism's Last Word," *Race, Writing, and Difference*, 333. Shammas writes, "I feel like an exile within Arabic, the language of my blood. I feel like an exile within Hebrew, my step-mother language." Unlike Jewish Hebrew writers in Israel who "see Hebrew as a Jewish language being written in Israel," Shammas by contrast "sees Hebrew and Arabic as two Israeli languages" ("Ashmat ha-babushka," 45). His novel *Arabesques* deals with Hebrew culture and the future of Hebrew as an Israeli language. The fate of Arabic as an Israeli language, in light of the prevailing political asymmetry between Hebrew and Arabic, is another matter.
17. On the need for a new vocabulary to come to terms with the contradictions in present-day Israel, see Bial, *Power and Powerlessness in Jewish History*, 168–169.
18. Hodgson, *The Venture of Islam*, 510; my emphasis.
19. The Canaanite Movement was a Jewish literary and political group active in Palestine (later in Israel) since the 1940s. It advocated shedding Jewish identity in favor of a return to pre-Judaic, Hebrew, pagan culture presumably integral to the Semitic Middle East.

Palestinian Citizens

11

At Half Mast—Myths, Symbols, and Rituals of an Emerging State

A Personal Testimony of an "Israeli Arab"

ANTON SHAMMAS

In the watch-fire-lighting ceremony that opened the celebrations of Independence Day in Israel in 1990 (on the eve of April 30), somebody came up with an ingenious idea for a sign to fit the occasion. As you know, 1990 in Israel marked the first centennial of the revival of the Hebrew language. The establishment of the Jewish state as the national home for the Jewish people was considered by Zionism, to a great extent, as the territorialization of the Hebrew language after two thousand years of uprootedness. Yet, for most of the Israeli Jews, or at least for those who maintain the prevalent cultural tone, as for most of world Jewry, Hebrew still is a Jewish language, not an Israeli one, and all indications show that it is going to remain that way in the foreseeable future.

To celebrate the revival of the tongue and the establishment of the state, and with no apparent intentions of tongue-in-cheek, the tomb of Herzl, the site where the central Independence Day ceremony is held annually, was flanked by a two-part sign, each part carrying two words from a famous biblical verse: "And the whole earth was of one language," according to the King James translation. However, insofar as the Hebrew word for "earth" (*haaretz*), being more humble, implies "land," what the sign meant was that Israel speaks Hebrew; this insinuated, without saying overtly, that Arabic is deterritorialized and its connections to "*haaretz*" are severed.

I saw the picture in *Haaretz* afterwards, and as an amateur but devout reader of biblical narratives, I immediately recognized the verse, as most of you would: Genesis 11:1. And, indeed, the caption read: "In the Bible it did not end well." It ended of course in Babel, with the confusion of the tongues and the scattering of the people.

Reprinted, by permission, from Anton Shammas, *New Perspectives on Israeli History: The Early Years of the State*, ed. Laurence J. Silberstein, 216–224 (New York and London: New York University Press, 1991), 216–224.

In his *De Vulgari Eloquentia*, in which he set out to establish his vernacular, Italian, as a literary language, Dante described Hebrew as "the language of grace," as opposed to Babel's "language of confusion." The Jewish Kabbalists argued that God's actual speech, the idiom of immediacy known to Adam and common to men until Babel, can still be decoded, partially at least, in the inner layers of Hebrew and, perhaps, in other languages of the original scattering—the "original scattering" in this case being, of course, the biblical scattering in the Book of Genesis.

The original deterritorialization and scattering of the Palestinians in 1948 was done in the language of grace. Exile for the Palestinian refugees was a language of confusion. There was no grace in being a confused refugee.

A beautiful midrash has it that "the ruins of the Tower can be seen to this day; but he who sets eyes upon them is cursed with the loss of memory. All the people on earth who go around saying: Who am I? Who am I? are those who have seen the ruins of the tower of Babel" (*Midrash Rabbah*). So I will avert my eyes now and fumble in my memory.

I was born in a small village in the Galilee, two years after the original scattering of the Palestinian refugees. The inhabitants of Fasuta were spared the fate of the wanderers, so there is always a feeling of shame lurking in their memories; the shame of having been privileged, of having been left on their lands, while the others had to carry the land in their memories and go. It was not a tangible feeling which a child could have sensed, but it was there all right, hovering silently above the mourning heads.

My father, those days, was continuously and pensively struggling with the new language that had invaded his small world and ours, imposing upon him confusion and a new type of illiteracy. He needed a special permit, like all the fathers of his generation, to move around in the scenes of his homeland which had turned overnight into "the homeland of the Jewish people"; but no such permits were available for moving around in the cultural scenes.

The permits to travel to Haifa from Fasuta, under the military administration of the 1950s, were written in Hebrew. Wanting to decipher his limits, as it were, he was learning Hebrew for beginners, as if he were an "*Oleh Hadash*," a new immigrant to his own country. He was learning Hebrew with the aid of books which were illustrated with water towers and plowed furrows, depicting a lifestyle in which he had no share, depicting a new set of arcane symbols whose signification were beyond his grasp and beyond his horizon.

I remember standing in line with him in the scorching sun in front of the nearby police station, for hours on end, waiting for his travel permit to Haifa to be issued inside. I say hours on end, using apparently a childish sandglass. As a matter of fact, even now as I commit these memories to paper, I miss those lines because the short journey to the police station in nearby Tarsheeha was our only outing in those days.

I hardly remember seeing the desired permit; apparently I couldn't have cared less about it. But I do remember the silent, scolding looks of my father, blaming me for having so much fun out of a dubious, extremely tedious, and humiliating trip. And I do remember that around that time I started to realize the utter importance of paper.

Besides the official papers, there was another kind which seemed to attract the attention of the occasional police patrols in the village. These were the small, tender, transparent bound batches of cigarette paper, which found their way to the village in mysterious ways from faraway Damascus. The policemen would confiscate these papers on the spot and sometimes even invite the criminal to a friendly interrogation in Tarsheeha.

On the inside cover there were two lines of poetry in praise of the brand, "The Damascene Paper." My uncle taught me how to decipher the calligraphy so I could recite the lines. These were the first two lines of poetry I ever memorized. And there was another charming quality attached to these cigarette papers: the vendors were women whose identity was no secret, let alone their occupation. They were the local informers who were recruited by the Shin-Bet (Security Services) to provide the emerging state with little gossipy secrets of the inhabitants of Fasuta, their alleged political convictions and subversive inclinations, including the number of cigarette papers purchased.

One can talk about the "Myths, Symbols, and Rituals of the Emerging State" in this regard only tongue-in-cheek; retrospectively, that is. After all, the life of Fasuta in the fifties was no tongue-in-cheek matter. True, for the villagers the "emerging state" was an unpredictable being, controlling their lives with a few strings and devices, filling the air with benignly threatening, unequivocally coded messages. My father was determined to decode the messages that had filled his world with a strange—at times even tantalizing—buzz. So he set out one day to single-handedly change the school system in the village. Disenchanted with the management vicissitudes of the private elementary school (run by the local priest who was the local representative of the Catholic archbishop in Haifa), and weary of the tuition demands, he convinced a group of parents and a couple of teachers to join him in a subversive PTA, contacted the Ministry of Education, and converted the "School of the *Mutran*/Archbishop" into a public school. This hardly pleased the young students. My father fell from grace and his image was irrevocably tarnished in their eyes, since they had not previously been forced by law to attend school.

At the end of my first year of primary school, which happened to be the second anniversary of the founding of the public school in my village, we children were sent to bring laurel branches from the tree shading the village spring to decorate an enormous star of David which one of the teachers had built from six planks (it was not even Independence Day). Our principal wished to make a good impression on the Jewish Inspector of Schools who had, apparently, invited himself to have a close look at the achievements of the young new school. The huge star of David, covered in laurel branches, was hung carelessly and loosely above the stage front. As it swayed, it frightened the children taking part in the program, and also frightened their proud parents in the first rows, who thought it might topple down on them. (It didn't.)

I sometimes wonder whether we were not seared by that star, whether it wasn't a branding iron after all—a branding iron to all the Arabs who were left, for some reason or another, inside the borders of Israel, in the year of our Lord Balfour 1948, henceforth to be referred to as the Green Liners. And when you brand someone, you are actually telling him two equally painful things: first, that he belongs to you, that he must abide by your laws, wander only in the regions that you have put under his disposal and keep away from the ones that are out-of-bounds; second, you're telling him that this searing of the skin is just a searing of the skin—you are not after his heart. When he, too, realizes that you do not seek his utter loyalty, then you both break even, confining yourselves to a position lacking any mutual anticipation. You both acquiesce in the rules of the game: Don't call us and we won't call you.

Be that as it may, in those days we were referring to Independence Day as Independence Holiday; special songs, written in Arabic and set to music by Arab composers, were practiced for the occasion. And when the special occasion arrived, blue-and-white flags were fluttering in the timid village wind. And when a special guest was expected (usually a Jewish Inspector of Schools from the big city, flanked by his Arab entourage), we were busy all morning cleaning the unpaved street which led to the school. And when he arrived, we stood on both sides of the street, waving our little flags in his honor. However, we didn't even know what "Hatikvah" (Israel's national anthem) was.

Little did we know then that the state whose flags these were was not ours. Come to think of it, nobody knew, not even the young teacher who had taught us the Arabic translation of the Israeli Declaration of Independence, from a brand-new reader, which also had a relatively detailed biography of Herzl. We were told, through some outlandish reasoning, to learn those texts by heart, and to this day some sentences of the declaration will occasionally pop up out of the blue inside my head.

So even according to the Arabic translation of the declaration, the state was defined as a Jewish state, but nobody seemed to pay any attention to that trivial fact. You see, we had the flags in our hands, so declarations did not matter, nor did the fact which we discovered later—that there was an utter rift between the signified and the signifier; those flags did not signify a single thing. They were meant by the state to be utterly void of any symbolic meaning and were cynically used as mere decorative objects, completely detached from their statism. And we were hung there at half-mast, like a mourning flag: too high to touch the receding Palestinian ground, but still not high enough to have a sense of the Israeli skies.

Years later, after my family had moved to Haifa, I came across an astonishing piece of information which had eluded my childish village attention in the 1950s. It turned out that many of the restrictions placed on Arab residents were lifted come Independence Day, so they could travel freely to the "celebration sites." One of these sites was in the city of Haifa, where Abba Hushi, the then mayor of the city, and whose name became *Abu* (father of) Hushi in the mouths of the villagers, was practicing his games of power over some of the Fasutites for whom this annual "free" trip to Haifa to take a semiforced part in the "celebrations" was their only chance to erase the borders and limits of their travel permits. I did not pay much attention to these highly publicized trips at the time because I had thought, apparently, that they were fully covered in the permits.

But now that I had learned that reality was not always bleak, and that there were full Days—uppercase *D*—of freedom, it only made me the more disoriented. This also meant, incidentally, that those Arabs who had cars could travel as far as they wished to see the otherwise prohibited scenes of "their" countryside, so to speak, provided they came home to roost at the end of the Day; provided they were fully aware that movement, in whichever direction, is a privilege granted by the state—the movement of the body in this case being a mere reflection of the movement of the soul. Otherwise, nobody went anywhere. Besides, in Fasuta there was only one car.

We were the static element in the dynamic formula of the state. We were visited, called upon, by really privileged people—those who had a whole year of 365 Independence Days. Fasuta was an occasional night stop in the ritual called "From Sea to Sea" (*miyyam el yam*): the hiking trip of the high school members of the *Gadna'*, which started near the Mediterranean and ended at the Sea of Galilee (Lake of Tiberias), passing through some Arab villages on the way. They would spend the night in our school, a matter-of-fact business, and the principal of the school, a congenial man of manners, would offer them hot tea.

One of my brothers, who used to have a great partiality for tea, was the assistant in the mission. He would be offered some slices of bread in return; and this was no frivolous matter. We were sick and tired of the monotonous pita bread at home and would expect father to come home from his few trips to Haifa with a couple of crispy, swollen, shiny loaves of *franji* bread; *franji* meaning ceremoniously non-Arab. So for my brother, those three slices were worth even three years of slavery in Egypt, and he would come home and tease us for hours on end with the magic smell of the *franji* bread, then brew himself a large pot of tea and savor every single crumb against our drooling mouths.

These were the big attractions of the outside world for us, the world that started in the nearby *moshav* (settlement) whose name, Elkosh, had supplanted the Arab name Deir el-Qasi. The Muslim inhabitants of Deir el-Qasi had left their homes and lands as a part of the great Palestinian Exodus of 1948, and for new neighbors we got a special mixture of newcomers (Jewish) from the Arab world.

Elkosh at the time was a unique melting pot. Some twenty families of newcomers were brought to settle in the *moshav*—Iraqi and Yemenite Jews together.

They were not even able to understand each other's Arabic dialect, let alone address their problems and disagreements in the holy language of the Bible. They would come to my father's cobbler shop, and later on they would come and visit our home as friends and practice their survival Hebrew with my father. So everybody was happy and understanding, and the lurking, unpleasant memories of the past which belonged to our neighbors' faith and religion were gradually covered up by the endeavors of all parties concerned to master the new language of the new state.

The melting pot in Elkosh was brimming over in no time; the social structure of the newly born *moshav* was falling apart. More and more of the newcomers would come to the Fasutites and suggest a partnership in tilling the soil of Zionism. Agriculture for them was harsh, and harsh was their life and their attempt to get started in what was supposed to be their own state. The Fasutites, a practical bunch and masters of pragmatism, would plant the seedlings of tobacco—their national product of sorts—in the newly conquered land of their new neighbors, and eventually get better prices in the deal. If you happened to be an Arab grower of tobacco in those days, cultivating a plot of land adjacent to an Elkoshite's, you would get some 70 percent of the price he would get on his tobacco. He was subsidized by the Jewish Agency, and that was his state.

We did not only plant seedlings of tobacco in the newly conquered land, we also took part in the "national" operation to cover the mountainsides with trees. On the fifteenth of *Shvat* (*Tu bi-Shvat*), our second-grade teacher led the whole school to a nearby mountainside, with little trees provided by the Ministry of Education in every hand, and after lecturing us about the unequivocal benefits of trees in nature, practically and otherwise, we then contributed our little tiny share in making the desert bloom. Tree Day became a much-awaited holiday in the years to follow; but we never thought of going back to the planting site to check the results of our little green thumbs. We were merely expected to plant trees—so we did. But apparently we were not expected to conduct the follow up; just vegetate.

Then mysterious fires erupted in the surrounding mountains. At least once a month there would be heard a cry for help raised in the village after someone had seen the smoke. Policemen would come in a jeep, carrying brand-new fire extinguishers, and take some of the men to lend a hand. Nobody knew what had caused the fire, and nobody knew who had set the fire, and nobody knew how the jeep arrived always on time. Or maybe the whole thing was just a weird coincidence in a villager's smoking head.

Then there were a couple of hand grenades thrown, exploding in unexpected places, near unexpected houses. And there were some time bombs exploding near out-of-the-way houses. Nobody was seriously injured, but outside walls were scorched and sooted, and so were the minds of the new citizens on whose fears, bafflement, and puzzle the military government thrived. And so did Mapai, the precursor of the Labor Party, through its puppet, Arab Knesset members.

My family, though, had a brief, enlightening affair with the Mapam Party. My elder brother, in his corner at Father's cobbler shop where he had been serving as an apprentice, hung a *Time* magazine cover of Fidel Castro, challenging my father's huge poster of Ben Gurion. He was recruited by one of our cousins to go to work in Kibbutz Kefar Massarik, near Haifa, three months before the elections of 1959. They both joined forces in order to run a well-organized election campaign for Mapam among the young, enthusiastic, first-time voters, including parades with flags of many, colors—red, blue, white—and all Mapam, the United Laborers Party, enjoyed a smashing victory in Fasuta that day. Three days later, a group of Fasutites, my elder brother included, were given the sack in Kefar Massarik. And since that day, my elder brother has been a very lapsed socialist. That was also the year in which he got rid of his astonishing stamp collection, and for a couple of weeks even contemplated growing a beard, but then changed his mind. I wonder if the idea of mourning over a defunct civil religion might have crossed his mind.

The second-grade teacher who led us that Tree Day to the mountains used to surprise us every now and then with some of his artifacts: a three-dimensional map of the village, a white rabbit of cotton balls inside a box and, at one point, a gruesome, still beating heart of a bird; except the bird had flown. But the work I admired most was a framed three-portraits-in-one of President Ben Zvi, Prime Minister Ben Gurion, and Benjamin-Ze'ev Herzl, the Big Founder. He set the picture of Herzl, in one piece, as a background on which he mingled the respective glazed-in strips of Ben Gurion and Ben Zvi in such an undulating way that if you looked at the picture from the left you could see Ben Gurion, from the right—Ben Zvi, and Herzl *en face*. This was sheer magic for us, and our class became "a point of interest" on the otherwise dull map of our dull school. Pupils would come from all grades, at every time imaginable, to look at this new Trinity, this new Wonder of Fasuta.

That same year a painter from Haifa was commissioned to paint a huge work for our local church depicting the prophet Elijah, the patron saint of Fasuta. When the painting was unveiled, there was certainly a stir, a commotion of the devout. But that was nothing compared to the new cult which was emerging around our teacher's triple icon. That icon is one of the most recurrent images of my childhood. I think of it often as the most impressive icon of my school days. But I can no longer see the respective portraits as distinctly and clearly as I could then. All I can see now are some broken lines of faces and glass; and a bird's tiny beating heart.

12

Arab Citizens of Palestine

Little to Celebrate

AZMI BISHARA

There's not much for Israeli Arabs to celebrate as they face the fiftieth anniversary of 1948. What happened in 1948 was the establishment of a Jewish State and the disintegration of a Palestinian reality in this land. Palestinian society was dispersed and destroyed, so you cannot really expect us to look back on that moment with nostalgia or fondness or a celebratory mode—regardless of how one feels about the Israel that subsequently developed.

Arabs in Israel are part of the Palestinian people and the Arab nation, sharing Arab culture, religion, and language; they had this Arabic identity long before the State of Israel. Israel was not founded at Israeli Arabs' choice or in coexistence with them, though they remained in Israel and eventually were allowed to become citizens, unlike their brothers, sisters, cousins, and friends on the West Bank, in Gaza, and in the refugee camps of the Palestinian Diaspora. They remained, but what did not remain was any independent Palestinian economy or any Palestinian city. Except for education, no realm of Israeli Arabs' lives remained autonomous. They had a right to speak and write in Arabic, but in every other respect they were marginalized onto the sidelines of dominant Israeli society. In the early years they lived under Israeli military rule and were only allowed to vote in Israeli elections beginning in 1967. In this same year, 1967, the rest of the Palestinian people came under military rule without becoming citizens, living under military rule just as had Israeli Arabs until that year.

But even when these Israeli Arabs were allowed to vote, it was as part of a Jewish communitarian democracy, a democracy unified not by its Israeliness but by its Jewishness. The Israeli supreme court ruled that Israel was a state

Reprinted, by permission, from *Tikkun: A Bimonthly Interfaith Critique of Politics, Culture and Society* 13, no. 4 (1998): 14–15, 65.

that was Jewish in its essence and democratic in its character. Israeli Arabs then, even today, are part of the form but not part of the essence of the state in which they are citizens. It is not citizenship, but Jewishness, which regulates the relationship between individual and state.

Everything changed for Israel in 1967. Suddenly, worldwide Jewish investment in the state dramatically mushroomed. So did military aid: in one year, 1968, Israel received as much aid from the United States as it had in the entire nineteen previous years of its existence. The implications of 1967 became clear in the 1970s: a rise in investments, a rise in living standards which led to an expanded middle class, the privatization of social services, competition between political parties, the rise of the right wing political bloc, and a loosening of the hold of the Labor Party and agricultural militarism in politics (a phenomenon manifested by the decline of the kibbutzim).

In response to these changes, Israeli Arabs went through two phases: from 1967 to the mid-1970s, they rediscovered their Palestinian identity through their encounter with the West Bank and Gaza, an identity that previously had been repressed through military-occupation–generated fear. This phase also marked the development of a new Arab middle class and intelligentsia that would become the repository of Palestinian nationalist consciousness in the face of the defeat of Arab nationalism as represented by Nasser. After Land Day, March 30, 1976 (the first one-day general strike by the Palestinian people protesting the Israeli confiscation of their land—the first time that Arabs in Israel used civil disobedience), Palestinians began to realize that they were torn between demanding equality in Israeli civil society and demanding an independent national identity. So the second phase, a phase of compromise, began: we began to demand equality in Israel and to demand a Palestinian state in the West Bank and Gaza (a state which we will not become part of).

In the 1980s, as Israel's economy really jumped, and there was a corresponding increase in individual rights, so, too, the economic status and individual rights of Israeli Arabs also increased. So a process of Israelization began among Palestinians, and a section of the Palestinian intelligentsia began to realize that the national identity of Palestinians was becoming even more confused; Palestinians now wanted to emphasize their Israeliness, yet they still were not really being let into the dominant Israeli society. In fact, Israel was becoming even more exclusively Jewish, more right-wing politically, more hostile to the Palestinians. The growing Palestinian middle-class intelligentsia started wanting something more than an economic trickle-down; it wanted to share in the shaping of their own lives, not simply to respond to what others had planned for them. They were told, in response, that they had been given economic opportunities in return for political quiet. And they realized: we are not really citizens, we are tolerated guests. That truth became apparent in the mid-1990s when some Israelis started saying that Yitzhak Rabin's decision to make peace was not legitimate since he relied on Arab votes to constitute his electoral majority—the message was that Arabs are not really part of the society, that relying on their votes made Rabin's government illegitimate, and hence that it would be appropriate, from the standpoint of right-wingers, to kill him. The guy who assassinated Rabin said that he killed him because Rabin was giving away parts of Israel and relying on Arab votes to support this policy. So suddenly in the mid-1990s, the marginalization of Palestinian identity became clearer.

Today, as settlements expand, a genuine Palestinian state in the West Bank seems less possible than it did in the mid-1970s. And equality within Israel seems even more unlikely as Israel becomes more self-consciously not just a Jewish state (that is, a state with a majority of Jews and a Jewish character) but a state of the Jews. Israel is not willing to create an Israeli nation, because it already has another nation, a Jewish nation. So where does this leave Israeli Arabs? How can we get a sense of national identity, a sense of belonging that will give meaning to life?

I came back into politics and was elected to the Knesset to address this issue: the cultural marginalization of Israeli Arabs from their own identity and their civil marginalization from full citizenship. I want Israel to become a society that officially recognizes itself as a state which contains two cultures, one a Jewish majority culture, the other, a Palestinian national minority living inside a Jewish majority, sharing citizenship. Israeli society must recognize Palestinian national identity as a legitimate nationality to be respected. This is my project, and the compass for my political activity. The state itself may have the cultural character of the majority, but its relationship to citizens should be regulated by citizenship and not by their religious identity. In short, I want Israel to become a state of its citizens. By the way, I want this for all the states of this region—that all these states become states of their citizens. So we do not say to the state, "Give me this or give me that," but instead we say that it is our right to be part of the decision making about our society. I do not want a generous state to make good decisions about budgets for my community—I want to be part of the decision-making process that determines my budget.

If a Palestinian state emerges, I believe it is very important that it be democratic. That is why I am critical of Arafat's Palestinian Authority—because the rule of law is better than despotism. Israel does not seek a democratic society in Palestine, but rather the despotic rule of someone who will respond to Israel's demands without having to deal with the messiness that democracy would entail. So I do not see the emergence of a democratic Palestinian state on the West Bank or Gaza. Rather, what I see is the expansion of Israeli settlements and the development of Bantustan regions that approximate the development of a system of apartheid for West Bank Palestinians. This will be apartheid in the sense that one land area is occupied by two groups, one of which has sovereignty, political rights, and the freedom of movement, while the other group does not. As this apartheid system develops, the conflict for Israeli Arabs will become even more complex, because it will mean that we will be asking for political equality in Israel while Israel is oppressing our people in the West Bank; in effect, we will be asking for equality with the oppressors of our own people. So Palestinian Arabs will be torn once again, because their demand for equality will require that they distance themselves from their own people in order to keep their eyes on the living standards and political rights that the oppressor can give you.

Meanwhile, Israeli Arabs do not yet have equal rights: the state invests twice as much money in the education of Jewish students than in the education for Arab students; the development of Israel is based on expropriating Arab land to allow for expansion of Jewish settlements, while not one new Arab village has been built since 1948; there are forty Arab villages that are "unrecognized" and hence do not get any services. Yet if our project eventually succeeds, and we do get equal participation in the Israeli system, and if Israel stays with its current direction of trying to keep Palestine as a Bantustan state without enough economic base for independent survival, then there may come a time when the binational state option will reemerge as a real solution, and we Israeli Arabs will be in a unique position to provide leadership for such a reality. If the separate state that Israel is willing to grant is really just a few separate and detached areas, then the binational demand may become the real demand. If the state that Israel allows is one in which people cannot leave to study or to work without Israeli permission, people will feel in their daily experience that this is not really an independent state even if Arafat proclaims that it is. And in that circumstance, the Palestinian state option may be exhausted and people will be looking for something else—instead of sovereignty, citizenship.

One thing that may make this kind of development more plausible: the fact that within Israel there is emerging from below a new kind of identity, an identity based on Hebrew language and culture, an identity emerging from Tzahal (the Israel Defense Forces) and from a thousand other institutions of life in Israel, and this Hebrew identity is the identity of the majority of Israelis. But people still confuse this emerging identity with a Jewish universal identity, with the universal, ahistorical Am Yisrael, the unterritorial people of Israel that claims a right to citizenship in this land despite the fact that most of its people live elsewhere. Zionism does not recognize this emerging Hebrew nation, but only the nation of the Jewish people all around the world, which is why we in the Knesset end up discussing and deciding laws of conversion to the Jewish religion, laws which actually ought not be decided by national parliament. Imagine: Christian and Moslem members of Knesset discuss and vote on a theological dispute about how to become a Jew! This same abnormality is what prevents the emerging Hebrew nation from recognizing itself and normalizing the State of Israel. Yet I believe that this newly emerging Hebrew nation can form the foundation for the kind of transformation of Israel that may emerge in Israel's second fifty years: a truly binational democratic society.

Arab Jews/Mizrahim

13

Rupture and Return

Zionist Discourse and the Study of Arab Jews

ELLA SHOHAT

Eurocentric and Zionist norms of scholarship that have had dire consequences for the representation of the history and identity of Arab Jews/Mizrahim (that is, Jews from Arab/Muslim regions) vis-à-vis the question of Palestine. In previous publications I have suggested some of the historical, political, economic, and discursive links between the question of Palestine and Arab Jews and argued for a scholarship that investigates the erasure of such links. Here I will trace some moments in the hegemonic production of an isolationist approach to the study of "Jewish History" as crucial to a quite anomalous project in which the state created the nation—not simply in the metaphorical sense of fabrication, but also in the literal sense of engineering the transplant of populations from all over the world. New modes of knowledge about Jews were essential in this enterprise, which placed Palestinians and European Zionist Jews at opposite poles of the civilizational clash. Yet, Arab Jews presented some challenges for Zionist scholarship, precisely because their presence "messed up" its Enlightenment paradigm that had already figured the modern Jew as cleansed from its shtetl past. In Palestine, freed of its progenitor the Ostjuden, the New Jew could paradoxically live in the "East" without being of it

Central to Zionist thinking was the concept of *Kibbutz Galuiot*—the "ingathering of the exiles." Following two millennia of homelessness and living presumably "outside of history," Jews could once again "enter history" as subjects,

---

Ella Shohat, "Rupture and Return: Zionist Discourse and the Study of Arab Jews," in *Social Text* 21, no. 2 (2003): 49–74. Copyright © 2003, Duke University Press. All rights reserved. Used by permission of the publisher.

This essay synthesizes and reworks ideas, arguments, and methodologies that I have been formulating in numerous scholarly publications over the past two decades. Some of these publications are referenced here in the notes. This essay appeared in a longer version, entitled "Rupture and Return: The Shaping of a Mizrahi Epistemology," in the Israeli journal *Hagar* 2, no. 1 (2001): 89–91.

as "normal" actors on the world stage by returning to their ancient birthplace, Eretz Israel. In this way, Jews were thought to heal a deformative rupture produced by exilic existence. This transformation of *Migola le'Geula*—from Diaspora to redemption—offered a teleological reading of Jewish History in which Zionism formed a redemptive vehicle for the renewal of Jewish life on a demarcated terrain, no longer simply spiritual and textual but rather national and political. The idea of Jewish return (which after the establishment of Israel was translated into legal language handing every Jew immediate access to Israeli citizenship) had been intertwined with the imaging of the empty land of Palestine. Its indigenous inhabitants could be bracketed or, alternately, portrayed as intruders deemed to "return" to their Arab land of origins (a discourse that was encoded in the various transfer plans).

A corollary of the notion of Jewish "return" and continuity in Israel was the idea of rupture and discontinuity with diasporic existence. In order to be transformed into "New Jews" (later Israelis), the "Diasporic Jews" had to abandon their diasporic culture, which, in the case of Arab Jews, meant abandoning Arabness and acquiescing in assimilationist modernization, for "their own good." Within this Promethean rescue narrative, concepts of "ingathering" and "modernization" naturalized and glossed over the historical, psychic, and epistemological violence generated by the Zionist vision of the New Jew.[1] This rescue narrative also elided Zionism's own role in provoking ruptures, dislocations, and fragmentation for Palestinian lives, and—in a different way—for Middle Eastern and north African Jews. These ruptures were not only physical (the movement across borders) but also cultural (a rift in relation to previous cultural affiliations) as well as conceptual (in the very ways time and space, history, and geography were conceived).

In this essay I will examine some of the foundational premises and substratal axioms of Zionist discourse concerning Arab Jews, arguing that writing a critical historiography in the wake of nationalism—both Arab and Jewish—requires the dismantling of a number of master narratives. I will attempt to disentangle the complexities of the Mizrahi question by unsettling the conceptual borders erected by more than a century of Zionist discourse, with its lethal binarisms of savagery versus civilization, tradition versus modernity, East versus West, and Arab versus Jew. While one might examine the position of Mizrahim within the restrictive parameters of what Zionist scholarship constructed as "Jewish History," I have long argued against creating such a segregated discursive space for history, identity, and culture. Even if Mizrahi identity was "invented" within the process of the Zionist invention of the "Jewish nation," it is important to unsettle the ghettoized nationalist analytical framework.[2] A diasporized analysis would situate Arab Jewish history, since the advent of Zionism and the partition of Palestine, within a constellation of multidirectional and palimpsest cross-border movements. Although I do not focus here on contemporary intersections between Mizrahim and Palestinians, I am trying to offer a partial genealogy for today's Mizrahi ambivalent positioning as occupying the actantial slot of both dominated and dominators; simultaneously disempowered as "Orientals" or "blacks" vis-à-vis "white" Euro-Israelis and empowered as Jews in a Jewish state vis-à-vis Palestinians. In a sense, Mizrahim are both embedded in and in excess of Zionist history.

This essay offers another dimension to the critique of the denial of Palestinian right of return. It examines the Zionist foundational principle of the Jewish right of return in light of the contradictions that have emerged in the wake of the partition of Palestine for the Jewish minority in Arab/Muslim states. Postzionist revisionist history has Eurocentrically ignored this question and in this sense has retained the contours of a Zionist narrative in which Arab Jews are projected as if always already forming part of the Jewish nation.

The critical project proposed here suggests that Mizrahim have been, at least partly, invented within Zionism, but simultaneously refuses to accept the hegemonic Zionist and postzionist naturalizing of the place of Arab Jews within Jewish nationalism. Furthermore, as Mizrahim are also actively reinventing their identity, a critical Mizrahi scholarship must invent a new understanding of the continuities and discontinuities entailed by the movement across national borders to Israel. The high-velocity history of the past century requires the rethinking of identity designations, intellectual grids, and disciplinary boundaries. Critical scholars especially need to dismantle the zoning of knowledge and rearticulate the relationships between the diverse interdisciplinary practices constituting multicultural Mizrahi inquiry.

My purpose has been to rearticulate a different conceptual framework, one formulated within a *multichronotopic* notion of time and space, highlighting a dynamic palimpsest of identity formations. In this essay, my hope is to suggest the contours of an intellectual/institutional space for critical analysis, called here "Mizrahi studies," that operates within a *relational* approach that highlights a nonfinalized and conjunctural definition of identity as a polysemic site of contradictory positionalities. In the following I will critically explore the dialectics of continuity and discontinuity, of rupture and return, as central to Zionist discourse, especially concerning Jews from west Asia and north Africa I will examine these dialectics through the following grids: (1) *dislocation:* spatiality and the question of naming; (2) *displacement:* the narrative of cross-border movement; (3) *dismemberment:* the erasure of the hyphen; (4) *dischronicity:* temporality and the paradoxes of modernization; (5) *dissonance:* methodology as discursive rupture; and (6) *disciplining:* the move toward Mizrahi studies as a relational inquiry.

Dislocation: Spatiality and the Question of Naming

In the paradigmatically Zionist film *Sallah Shabbati* (Israel, 1964), the spectator is first introduced to the Oriental Jew Sallah when he and his family land in

Israel. He comes from the Levant, but within the film's Eurocentric imaginary mapping, he comes from nowhere: first in the literal sense, since his place of origin remains unknown; and second in the metaphorical sense, since Asian and African geographies are suggested to amount to nothing of substance. While the protagonist's Levantine essence forms the dynamic center of the narrative, his Levantine geography is crucially invisible. Sallah's physical presence in Israel only embodies that geography's absence and highlights the process of erasure. Within the Zionist view, Jews from west Asia/north Africa arrive from obscure corners of the globe to Israel, the Promised Land, to which they have always already been destined. In this way, Mizrahim could be claimed as part of a continuous Jewish history/geography whose alpha and omega is in the Land of Israel, a land that the Zionist movement purported to represent. While superimposing a nationalist discourse on the spiritual messianic idea of Jewish renewal, Zionist ideologues sought not only the physical transfer of Palestinians to Arab countries, but also the transfer of Jews from Arab/Muslim countries to Palestine. However, for the latter, physical dislocation was not adequate, since the displaced Jews had to undergo a metamorphosis. The establishment, in a contemporary retelling of the biblical Exodus from Egypt, called for "the death of the desert generation" in order to facilitate their birth as the New Jews/Israelis, as embodied by the Sabra generation.

The question of continuity and discontinuity is central, therefore, to the Zionist vision of the nation-state. Yet, one could argue that by provoking the geographical dispersal of Arab Jews, by placing them in a new situation "on the ground," by attempting to reshape their identity as simply "Israeli," by disdaining and trying to uproot their Arabness, and by racializing them and discriminating against them as a group, the Zionist project of the ingathering of exiles itself provoked a dislocation that resulted in a series of traumatic ruptures and exilic identity formations. The Israeli establishment obliged Arab Jews to redefine themselves in relation to new ideological paradigms and polarities, thus provoking the aporias of an identity constituted out of its own ruins. The Jews within Islam thought of themselves as Jews, but that Jewishness was part of a larger Judeo-Islamic cultural fabric. Under pressure from Zionism on the one hand and Arab nationalism on the other, that set of affiliations gradually changed, resulting in a transformed cultural semantics.

The identity crisis provoked by this physical, political, and cultural rupture is reflected in a terminological crisis in which no single term seems to fully represent a coherent entity. The very proliferation of terms suggests the difficulties of grappling with the complexities of this identity: Sephardim; non-Ashkenazic Jews; Jews of Islam; Arab Jews; Middle Eastern, west Asian, or north African Jews; Asian and African Jews; non-European Jews; Third World Jews; Levantine Jews; Jews of the Mediterranean; *Maghrebian* and *Mashreqian* Jews (from the western and eastern parts of the Arab world); *Bnei Edot Ha Mizrah* (descendants of the Eastern communities); *yotzei artzot arav ve-ha-Islam* (those who left Arab and Muslim countries); Blacks; Israel ha-Shniya (Second Israel); Mizrahiyim, or Mizrahim; or Iraqi Jews, Iranian Jews, Kurdish Jews, Palestinian Jews, Moroccan Jews, and so forth. Each term raises questions about the implicit history, politics, and discourses that generated the terms and that made them catchwords at specific conjunctures. Each term encodes a historical, geographical, and political point of view.

Prior to their arrival in Israel, Jews in Iraq, for example, had a different self-designation. They had thought of themselves as Jews but that Jewish identity was diacritical—it played off and depended on a relation to other communities. Hyphens, in a sense, were used to highlight diverse aspects of a complexly embedded identity articulated in relation to other communities: Baghdadi Jews (in contrast to Jews of other cities), Babylonian Jews (to mark historical roots in the region), Iraqi Jews (to mark national affiliation), or Arab Jews (in contradistinction to Muslim and Christian Arabs, but also marking affiliation with the greater Arab culture or nation). Even the concept of Sephardicness was not part of the self-definition. That term strictly referred to the Jews of Spain who retained their Spanishness even outside of Iberia—for example, in Turkey, Bulgaria, Egypt, and Morocco. Yet a kind of transregional geocultural Jewish space, from the Mediterranean to the Indian Ocean, was shaped, within which Jews, under the aegis of the larger Islamic world, traveled and exchanged ideas. They were culturally and politically interwoven into that world, even if they retained their Jewishness. Shaped by Arab Muslim culture, they also helped shape that culture in a dialogical process that generated their specific Judeo-Arab identity.

The rise of Zionism and Arab nationalism, along with the implementation of partitions as a colonial solution for regional conflicts, impacted the identity designations of Jews in the Arab Muslim world. Arabness came to signify a national identity, requiring a realignment of Ottoman definitions. Their religion (Jewishness) was rapidly turning into a national marker in the international arena, which gradually conflicted with their affiliation with the Arab nation-state. With the rise of Arab nationalism on the one hand and Zionism on the other, they have come to occupy an ambivalent positioning vis-à-vis both movements. The explosive politics after the partition of Palestine and the establishment of the State of Israel rendered their existence virtually impossible within a context of Arab nationalism. Upon arrival in Israel, shorn of any alternative passport, Arab Jews entered a new linguistic/discursive environment, at once geopolitical (the Israel/Arab conflict), legal (Israeli citizenship), and cultural (East versus West). The normative term became *Israeli,* not merely a signifier of a new passport, but also an indicator of a new cultural and ideological paradigm. Whereas Jewishness in Iraq, for example, formed part of a constellation of coexisting and complexly stratified ethnicities and religions, Jewishness in Israel was now the assumed cultural and political "dominant." Arabness became the marginalized category, and the religion of Arab Jews, for the first time in their history, was now affiliated with the dominant power, equated with the very basis of national belonging. Their culture (their Arabness), meanwhile, became a marker of ethnic, even racial, otherness, a kind of embarrassing excess. If in the Arab world, prior to their "Exodus," their Jewishness (associated now with Zionism) was subjected to surveillance, in Israel their affiliation with an Arab cultural geography was similarly disciplined and punished.

The processes of spatial rupture and cultural displacement have impacted and shifted identity designations.[3] Each term implies a different historical moment, geographical space, and ideological perspective. Throughout this essay, I will move back and forth between different namings, precisely because I am interested in situating identities rather than proposing an essential core identity. Since I am arguing for a conjunctural, historically situated definition of identity, I also want to highlight the processes and discourses that enabled such identity transformation. Although I have often used the term "Arab Jews," I do not use it to suggest a reductive and essential either Jewish or Arab identity. The aim in hyphenating Arab Jewish identity is to call into question the Eurocentric nationalist paradigm that erased the hyphen and made it taboo. The term "Arab Jew" obviously assumes an Arab cultural geography and, therefore, is not meant here to cover, in a global sweep, the histories of *all* Jews. In fact, I have used the term in diacritical opposition to the term "Jewish History," arguing for Jewish histor*ies*. The term "Mizrahi history," meanwhile, implies a recent history, one produced within the ideological space of Israel and Zionism. And while one might rightly argue that there is no single Mizrahi history, the term highlights the dislocation and the shaping of a new hybrid identity, neither simply Arab nor simply Jewish.

Each designation calls attention to a different dimension of a complex history and spatial trajectory, and each term foregrounds specific aspects of communal affiliation. Each frame illuminates only partial aspects of overlapping collective identities shaped within the movement across borders. Each designation addresses specific and even contradictory dynamics between and within different world zones. There is a need for more flexible relations among the various conceptual frameworks—a mobile set of grids, a diverse set of disciplinary as well as cultural-geopolitical lenses—adequate to these complexities. Flexible, yet critical, usage of the terms that can address their politics of location is important not only for pointing out historical and geographical contradictions and differences, but also for reaffirming historical/geographical links and structural analogies.

Displacement: Narratives of Cross-Border Movement

The question of naming is also problematic in relation to the unprecedented movement across borders of west Asian/north African Jews from the late 1940s to the 1960s. Nationalist paradigms cannot capture the complexity of this historical moment, particularly for Arab Jews. Perhaps due to the idiosyncrasies of the situation, for a community trapped between two nationalisms—Arab and Jewish—each term used to designate the displacement seems problematic. None of the terms—*aliya* (ascendancy), *yetzia* (exit), exodus, expulsion, immigration, emigration, exile, refugees, expatriates, and population exchange—seems adequate. In the case of the Palestinians, the forced mass exodus easily fits the term "refugee," since they never wanted to leave Palestine and have maintained the desire to return. In the case of Arab Jews the question of will, desire, and agency remains highly ambivalent and ambiguous. The very proliferation of terms suggests that it is not only a matter of legal definition of citizenship that is at stake, but also the issue of mental maps belonging within the context of rival nationalisms. Did Arab Jews want to stay? Did they want to leave? Did they exercise free will? Did they actually make a decision? Once in Israel, did they want to go back? Were they able to do so? And did they regret the impossibility of returning? Different answers to these questions imply distinct assumptions about questions of agency, memory, and space.

The displacement of Iraqi Jews, for example, was not simply the result of a decision made solely by Arab Jews themselves.[4] Even if some Arab Jews expressed a desire to go to Israel, the question is why, suddenly, after millennia of not doing so, would they leave overnight? The displacement for most Arab Jews was the product of complex circumstances in which panic and disorientation, rather than desire for *aliya*, in the nationalist sense of the word, was the key factor. The "ingathering" seems less natural when one takes into account the circumstances forcing their departure: the efforts of the Zionist underground in Iraq to undermine the authority of community leaders such as Haham Sasson Khdhuri;[5] the Zionist policy of placing a "wedge" between the Jewish and Muslim communities, generating anti-Arab panic on the part of Jews;[6] the anti-Jewish propaganda, especially as channeled through the Istiklal or Independence Party; the failure of most Arab intellectuals and leaders to clarify and act on the distinction between Jews and Zionists; their failure to actively secure the place of Jews in the Arab world; the persecution of Communists—among them Jews who opposed Zionism; the secretive agreements between some Arab leaders and Israeli leaders concerning the idea of "population exchange"; and the misconceptions, on the part of many Arab Jews, about the differences between their own religious identity, affiliation, or sentiments and the secular nation-state project of Zionism, a movement that had virtually nothing to do with those sentiments, even if it capitalized on a quasi-religious rhetoric.

The official term *aliya*, therefore, is multiply misleading. It suggests a commitment to Zionism, when in fact the majority of Jews—and certainly Jews within the Levant—were decidedly not Zionists. Zionist discourse normalized the telos of a Jewish nation-state; the move toward its borders was represented as the ultimate Jewish act. When the actual departure of Arab Jews is represented—as in the 1998 documentary series *Tekumah* produced by the state TV channel in conjunction with the fiftieth anniversary of Israel—it is narrated as merely an act of devotion. Images of Yemeni Jews arriving at the camps set up by the Jewish Agency are juxtaposed with a voiceover that reductively speaks of messianic will and persecution. The Yemeni Jews are represented as *willing* to cross the desert and sacrifice their lives in order to get to the Promised Land, the State of Israel. Most Zionist writings highlight a kind of natural inevitability, while erasing diverse Zionist tactics to actively dislodge these communities.

Even in much of Mizrahi literature and film, the historical complexity of the moment of dislocation, as well as its concomitant emotional, disorienting trauma, operates as a structuring absence. Such texts tend to delineate Jewish life in Israel and in the Arab world as separated existences taking place within disconnected cultural geographies. The production of split spaces that inform most narratives still manifest symptoms of a cultural schizophrenia—the difficulty with articulating the actual moment of departure—that crucial moment whereby overnight one's identity marker as an Iraqi or Yemeni ends and that of an Israeli suddenly begins. This difficulty is present even in texts that do refer to the move. Sammy Michael's Hebrew novel *Victoria* (1993), for example, describes the heroine's life in Iraq from the turn of the century until the 1950s, after which she is magically transferred to her apartment in present-day Israel. The event surrounding her dislocation as well as the novelistic description of her move from Iraq to Israel form a textual silence, in which the move to Israel is a taken-for-granted, obvious, and transparent act in the heroine's life. Yet, the writer more clearly articulates the haunting memory of dislocation in interviews.[7] He speaks of a recurrent nightmare in which he is sitting in his favorite Baghdadi café—a place he is nostalgic for—but when he comes to pay he puts his hand in his pocket and takes out Israeli coins—a telltale sign of his enemy Zionist affiliations. The discursive lacuna concerning the dislocation, however, characterizes most representations that assume the inevitable telos of *aliya* to the Jewish homeland without interrogating its semantics within a specifically Arab Jewish history.

The term *aliya* naturalizes both a negative and a positive pole: the will to escape persecution and the desire to go to the Jewish homeland. Yet this master narrative excludes narratives that relay moments of refusal, questioning, or ambivalence toward the immanent dislocations. The term *aliya* (literally, ascendancy) is borrowed from the realm of religion (*aliya la'regel*), which originally referred to the pilgrimage to the Temple, and later to the holy sites of the land of Zion. Yet, within Zionist discourse, the term *aliya* has been transferred to the realm of citizenship and national identity. In this discursive conflation, the *olim*, according to official ideology, benefited from spiritual and even material ascendancy, a view sharply contrasting with the multifaceted devastation, the social descent (*yerida*) experienced by most Jews from Muslim countries.

Zionist discourse about the transition of Arab Jews to Israel deploys conceptual paradigms in which religious ideas such as redemption, ascent, and the ingathering are grafted onto nationalist paradigms. In this sense, even when scholars acknowledge that *aliya* was not simply voluntary, they often deploy a term that subliminally encodes this Zionist vision.

At the same time, the dominant Arab nationalist discourse represented the mass exodus as an index of the Jewish betrayal of the Arab nation. Ironically, the Zionist view that Arabness and Jewishness were mutually exclusive gradually came to be shared by Arab nationalist discourse, placing Arab Jews on the horns of a terrible dilemma. The rigidity of both paradigms has produced the particular Arab Jewish tragedy, since neither paradigm could contain crossed or multiple identities.[8] The displacement of Arab Jews from the Arab world took place, for the most part, without a fully conscious or comprehensive understanding on their part of what was at stake and what was yet to come. Arab Jews left their countries of origin with mingled excitement and terror, but, most importantly, buffeted by manipulated confusion, misunderstandings, and projections provoked by a Zionism that mingled messianic religiosity with secular nationalist purposes. At times, even Arab Jewish Zionists failed to grasp this distinction, and they certainly never imagined the systematic racism that they were about to encounter in the "Jewish state." Therefore, some Arab Jewish Zionist activists came to lament the day that they set foot in Israel.[9] The incorporation of the non-Ashkenazim into a new culture was far more ambiguous than any simple narrative of immigration and assimilation can convey. Although *aliya* to Israel is celebrated by official ideology and sometimes seen by Sephardim/Mizrahim themselves as a return "home," in fact this return, within a longer historical perspective, can also be seen as a new mode of exile.

Arab Jews, in my view, could never fully foresee what the impossibility of return to their countries of origin would mean.[10] The permission to leave—as in the case of Iraqi Jews—did not allow for a possible return either of individuals or of the community. Therefore, even the term *immigration* does not account for that massive crossing of borders. Iraqi Jews, for example, had to give up their citizenship (*al-tasqit*), losing their right to return. Within Israel, for at least four decades, performing even a symbolic return within the public sphere—the expression of nostalgia for an Arab past—became taboo. The propagandistic description of the dislocation of Arab Jews as "population exchange," which supposedly justifies the creation of Palestinian refugees, meanwhile, is also fundamentally problematic. It elides the simple fact that neither Arab Jews nor Palestinians were ever consulted about whether they would like to be exchanged. Although, following the partition of Palestine, both movements across borders in opposite directions may be described as traumatic, the forced departure of Arab Jews does not exactly parallel the circumstances of the Palestinian no-choice exodus during Al-Nakba (the catastrophe). Furthermore, the right of return for Palestinians has remained a central political issue, even an identity-shaping factor, while for Arab Jews, the idea of return became a murky issue even when limited to the discursive and cultural sphere. Yet, despite these significant differences, the discursive naturalization of such terms as "*aliya*" or "immigration" has to be reevaluated, since the questions of will, desire, and agency remain extremely complex, contingent, and ambivalent.

In sum, at the very core of the invention of Mizrahi identity, within the conceptual space of Zionism and within the physical space of Israel, lies an ambiguous relation to movement across the border. While for the Jews from the Muslim world the Land of Israel/Palestine was continuous with their cultural geography, the Eurocentric construct of the State of Israel on that land required discontinuity. The passage into the political space of Israel initiated Jews from Arab and Muslim lands into a new process within which they were transformed, almost overnight, into a new racialized ethnic identity. Therefore, a critical scholarship cannot afford to assume the Zionist master narrative of choice and desire; rather it needs to look into the deep anxious ambivalences generated by partition and the scars it left on the psyche of the displaced. Such scholarship probes the dialectics of continuity and discontinuity with regards to the Arab Muslim world as a palpitatingly vital issue that informs the transformation of Arab Jews into Mizrahim, as they have ended up, even if after the fact, in a largely colonial-settler enterprise.

Dismemberment: The Erasure of the Hyphen

The master narrative of unique Jewish victimization has been crucial for legitimizing an anomalous nationalist project of "ingathering of the exiles from the four corners of the globe." Yet this narrative has also legitimized the engendering of displacements of peoples from such diverse geographies, languages, cultures, and histories—a project in which, in many ways, a state created a nation. It has been argued that *all* nations are invented, yet I would suggest that *some* nations, such as Jewish/Israel, are more invented than others. Zionist writings made great efforts to normalize not simply "the Jew" but also the very discourses that redefined the multitude of Jewish communities as the "Jewish nation." The metanarrative of the nation constructed one official past while simultaneously destroying other perspectives on that narrative. Noncanonical memories have been suppressed while previous affiliations have been severed. In the new conceptual vacuum, the hyphen, which made possible such terms as "Judeo-Muslim" and "Arab Jew," was dropped, while legitimating others—specifically, "Judeo-Christian," now a marker of a Western geopolitical culture.

Memory of a common past (biblical times), common language (Hebrew), and common land (Eretz Israel) was magnified within a myth-making machine.

The nation's memory was marshaled into suppressing any other possible memories from diverse pasts, languages, and lands. A state of perennial adrenal anxiety has marked the Zionist master narrative. Foregrounding an exceptionalist victimization discourse, this narrative manufactured the Muslim Arab as a common perennial "historical enemy" facing the "Jewish nation." Zionist discourse has represented Palestinians, Arabs, or Muslims as merely one more "non-Jewish" obstacle to the Jewish/Israeli national trajectory. Its historiography concerning Jews within Islam consists of a morbidly selective "tracing of the dots" from pogrom to pogrom. The word "pogrom" itself, it must be noted, derives from and is reflective of the Eastern European Jewish experience. I do not mean to idealize the position of Jews within Islam, rather I argue that Zionist discourse has, in a sense, hijacked Jews from their Judeo-Islamic political geography and subordinated them into the European Jewish chronicle of shtetl and pogrom. This picture of an ageless, relentless oppression and humiliation, however, has produced a double-edged amnesia: one with regard to the Zionist settlement of Palestine, which, for the most part, disregarded the perspective and concerns of the inhabitants of Palestine, culminating in their dispossession and yielding almost a century of Palestinian antagonism to Zionism and Israel, now equated with Jews and Judaism; the second with regard to the Judeo-Islamic history, which deserves to be represented more complexly within a more multiperspectival approach.[11]

The Zionist conception of "Jewish History" presumes a unitary and universal notion of history, rather than a multiplicity of experiences, differing from period to period and from context to context. Positing the vision of Jewish nationalism on a demarcated territory as a "natural evolution" is in itself a problematic claim; but positing this vision as a panacea for *all* Jews is especially bewildering. In the same period that the idea of Zionism was being formulated within a Christian European context, Jews in the Muslim world occupied a different position, one that did not necessarily require a nationalist articulation of their identity. (In this sense, one might argue that the concept of Jewish nationalism was politically irrelevant to their existence as Jews within the Islamic world.) The Zionist "proof" of a single Jewish experience, therefore, allows little space for comparative studies of Jews in relation to diverse religious and ethnic minorities, especially within Muslim spaces. The Zionist vision of a single Jewish experience leads to a historiographical narrative that excludes parallels and overlappings with non-Jewish religious and ethnic communities. Thus, this narrative ejects the idea of hyphenated and syncretic Jewish cultures, as well as the notion of linked and analogous oppressions between Jews and various communities. The selective reading of Judeo-Muslim history, in other words, makes two processes apparent: the unproblematized subordination of Jews within Islam to a "universal" Jewish experience and the rejection of an Arab and Muslim context for Jewish institutions, identities, and histories.

Contemporary cultural practices illustrate this process of dismemberment: that is, the attempt to represent the Jews within Islam detached from Muslim Arab culture, philosophy, and institutions. The exhibition of Turkish Jewish costumes in the Jewish Museum in New York (1989) provides such an example. The exhibition offered its viewers a vehicle for imaginary travel into distant geography and history via the colorful costume of the "other" Jews. Displaced from one geography to another, the museological project removed the costumes from their social habitus, displaying them as exotic objects, fetishistically isolated from the Muslim Ottoman context. This isolationist concept elides the embeddedness of Jewish life in the dominant Muslim culture. Jewish dress codes were shared with the ambient Muslim world—albeit at times with some differences, depending on the specific period. As cultural imperialism was marching into the Muslim world, there was still nothing obvious or natural about a discursive act of "separating" Jews from the Muslim world and "unifying" them with the culture of Ashkenazi Jews.

In fact, in the late nineteenth century, cultural dissonance seems to be most afflicting the relationships among the coreligionists (Ashkenazic and Sephardic Jews) than among the coregionists (Arab Muslims and Jews). Nowhere is it clearer than when the Alliance Israelite Universelle (AIU) was attempting to install what was regarded as an alien culture in the "Levant."[12] The AIU—the schooling system founded in Paris in 1860 by Westernized Ashkenazi Jews—was meant to provide a French curriculum for the Jews of the Levant and to carry the banner of enlightenment and the civilizing mission into the "desolated" regions of the world. The AIU began its programs by requiring its students to change their "outmoded" dress code and hairstyle, perceived as signs of backwardness. The Baghdadi Jewish establishment partially collaborated with the AIU mission to provide education for Baghdadi children, since this type of education was seen as useful within a world of rising Western powers. However, the establishment did not understand the learning of French culture and history to mean the abandonment of Judeo-Arab culture.[13] Consequently, it opposed the cultural power exercised by the AIU toward the students.

The Baghdadi Jewish negative reaction to the practices of the AIU was also shared by Arab Muslims. One of the articles in the Judeo-Arabic newspaper *Perah*, published in India, reports on the Muslims' response to the changes they began to perceive among upper-middle-class Jews: "From one day to the next the phenomenon [of shaving] is spreading so that the one who shaves his beard cannot be distinguished from the gentiles [Christians]. It has also become the occasion of ridicule by the Muslims in the marketplace who say: 'Wonder of wonders, the Jews have forsaken their religion.... See how the Jews have abandoned their religion (heaven forbid)—before, not one of them would touch his beard and earlocks, and now they cut them and throw them into the dustbin.'"[14] In contrast to contemporary representations of an inherent Muslim antisemitism, one detects in this example a Muslim investment in maintaining Jewish identity as it had been known within the Muslim world. Both Muslims and Jews perceived Jewish identity as embedded within a larger Judeo-Islamic civilizational complex, while assimilation into Western style is seen as a betrayal of traditions at once culturally shared and religiously differentiated. In this respect, the Jewish French assimilationist practice is regarded as a violation of these norms. The Judeo-Arabic newspaper of the late nineteenth century cites the Muslim response as invoking the same code that the Jewish Baghdadi leaders also believed in. The anxiety that Arab Jews manifest here, ironically, concerns their image not in the eyes of French Jews, but in the eyes of their Muslim neighbors, who were not seeking the assimilation of Arab Jews.

Zionist historiography advanced the idea of a homogeneous national past and precluded any "deviance" into a more historicized and relational narrative that would see Jews not simply through their religious commonalties but also *in relation* to their non-Jewish contextual cultures, institutions, and practices. Thus a historiography that assumes a pan-Jewish culture is often the same historiography that assumes the bifurcated discourse of "Arab versus Jew" without acknowledging a hyphenated Arab Jewish existence. In this sense, the erasure of the hyphen was crucial to Zionist writings. The Arabness and the Orientalness of Jews posed a challenge to any simplistic definition of Jewish national identity, questioning the very axioms and boundaries of the Euro-Israeli national project. The cultural affinity that Arab Jews shared with Arab Muslims—in many respects stronger than that which they shared with European Jews—threatened the Zionist conception of a homogeneous nation modeled on the European nationalist definition of the nation-state. As an integral part of the topography, language, culture, and history of the "East," Eastern Jews have also threatened the Euro-Israeli self-image that has envisioned itself as a prolongation of "Europe," *in* the "East" but not *of* it. Arab Jews, for the first time in their history, faced the imposed dilemma of choosing between Jewishness and Arabness in a geopolitical context that perpetuated the equation between Arabness, Middle Easterners, and Islam on the one hand and Jewishness, Europeanness, and Westernness on the other. Thus, the religious Jewish aspect of what has been a culturally diverse Jewish identity has been given primacy, a reductive categorization tantamount to dismembering the identity of a community. The continuity of Jewish life meant the ceasing of Arab life for Arab Jews in Israel—at least in the public sphere. What was called by officialdom an "ingathering," then, was also a cultural dismembering, both within and between communities. But the Zionist reading of that dismemberment, both before and after the actual rupture, rendered it as a healing and a return.

The past is subjected to contestation within diverse institutional force fields. Its narrators argue for a privileged ownership of the historical pain, collective memory, and of the copyrights on their deployment. Memories that endanger the hegemonic discourse are forbidden, become taboo, and disappear from the public arena. These taboos are often internalized even by the scarred bodies that might potentially articulate history from a different angle and within a different frame. Zionist discourse, which argued for the "right for normalcy," narrated the historical past and envisioned a utopian future as a homogenous unified model. However, this regulation of "normalcy" created in its wake myriad forms of social "abnormalcy"—the syndromes of which have included the silencing and the kidnapping of the language of critical thinking. Rearticulating the terminology, concepts, and methods is crucial for producing transnational knowledge that undoes the Zionist normative apparatus.

Dischronicity: Temporality and Paradoxes of Modernization

Discursively multifaceted, the ruptures provoked by Zionism were conceived at once geographically—dislodging the communities and transferring their bodies into a newly imagined political space of the *alt-neu-land* of Israel[15]—and historiographically, separating Jews from their culturally ossified habitus and integrating them into the dynamic march of universal culture. The Zionist return to the old biblical land, in other words, was never premised on a simple return to the ways of biblical times, even if it at times expressed nostalgia for ancient ways. Both Bedouins and Yemeni Jews were romanticized within an exoticized temporality. As with all civilizing missions, the "inevitable" march of progress simultaneously produced in its wake the devastation of "primitive" worlds and the mourning for their disappearance. Undergirding these paradoxical conceptualizations was a modernizing assumption of what I call here "dischronicity," or the rupture of time, as though communities live in split time zones, some advanced and some lagging behind. The ideology of modernization thrives on a binarist demarcation of opposed concepts—modernity/tradition, underdevelopment/development, science/superstition, and technology/backwardness. In this sense, modernization functions as a bridge between two opposite temporal poles within a stagist narrative that paradoxically assumes the essential "developedness" of one community over another, while also generating programs to transform the "underdeveloped" into modernity.

In the case of Israel, modernization has been a central mechanism of policy making as well as of identity shaping within the formation of the nation-state. The modernization narrative has projected a Western national identity for a state geographically located in the Middle East and populated by Eastern European Jews as well as by a Middle Eastern majority—both Palestinians and non-Ashkenazi Jews. The dominant discourse of Euro-Israeli policy makers and scholars has suggested that Asian and African Jews—not unlike the Palestinian population—originate from "primitive," "backward," "underdeveloped," "premodern" societies and therefore, unlike Ashkenazim, require modernization.[16] But here modernization can also be seen as a euphemism, at best, for breaking away from Arab Levantine culture. Over the years Euro-Israeli political leaders, writers, and scholars have frequently advanced the historiographically suspect idea that "Jews of the Orient," prior to their "ingathering" into Israel, were somehow "outside of" history. This discourse ironically echoes nineteenth-century assessments, such as those of Hegel, that Jews, like blacks, lived outside of the progressively unfolding spirit of Western civilization.

In the early fifties, some of Israel's most celebrated intellectuals from the Hebrew University in Jerusalem wrote essays addressing the "ethnic problem" and in the process recycled a number of the tropes typically projected onto colonized and non-European people. For Karl Frankenstein, for example, "the primitive mentality of many of the immigrants from backward countries" might be profitably compared to "the primitive expression of children, the retarded, or the mentally disturbed."[17] And in 1964, Kalman Katznelson published his openly racist book *The Ashkenazi Revolution*, in which he argued the essential, irreversible genetic inferiority of the Sephardim, warning against mixed marriage as tainting the Ashkenazi race and calling for the Ashkenazim to protect their interests against a burgeoning Sephardi majority.[18]

In sociological and anthropological studies, the dispossession of Middle Eastern Jews of their culture has been justified by the concept of "the inevitable march of Western progress"—that is, those who have been living in a historically condemned temporality would inevitably disappear before the productive advances of modernity. Within traditional anthropology, one detects a desire to project the Mizrahim as living "allochronically,"[19] in another time, often associated with earlier periods of individual life (childhood), or of human history (primitivism). From the perspective of official Zionism, the *aliya* to Israel signifies leaving behind premodernity. Jews from Arab and Muslim countries enter modernity only when they appear on the map of the Hebrew state, just as the modern history of Palestine is seen as beginning with the Zionist renewal of the biblical mandate. In Israeli history textbooks, Middle Eastern Jewish History has been presumed to begin with the arrival of Jews to Israel.

Contemporary museological projects reproduce this teleological vision of history. The Babylon Jewish Museum in Or Yehuda, Israel, despite its name, is largely dedicated to the triumph of Zionism in Iraq.[20] The exhibition creates a disproportionate spatial gap between life in Babylon/Iraq before and after the arrival of Zionism. The walls dramatically expand on the few decades of Zionist activism in Iraq but minimally condense the millennia of Jewish history lived between the Dijla and the Furat Rivers. This linear narrative naturalizes the transition into the modern nation. The converging discourses of enlightenment, progress, and modernization are central to the Zionist master narrative. A series of mutually reinforcing equations between modernity, science, technology, and the West has legitimized Zionism as an extension of the civilizing mission applied first to Palestine and then to Arab Jews.

Discourses of progress were crucial to the colonization of Palestine, while later playing a central role in the process of incorporating Arab Jews into the

Jewish nation. Rescue tropes such as "making the desert bloom" grounded the claim to Palestine in an argument that was not exclusively biblical but also scientific, buttressed by archeological evidence. Similarly, the "ingathering" project entailed not only a biblical messianic vision but also the idea of modernizing the "Land of the Fathers" and the "traditional Jews."[21] Zionist discourse portrayed Levantine Jewish culture prior to Zionism as static and passive and, like the virgin land of Palestine, lying in wait for the impregnating infusion of European dynamism. While presenting Palestine as an empty land to be transformed by Jewish labor, the Zionist "Founding Fathers" presented Arab Jews as passive vessels to be shaped by the revivifying spirit of Zionism.

Dissonance: Methodology as Discursive Rupture

The rupture shaping the lives of Arab Jews, particularly since the partition of Palestine, has resulted in a scholarship that delineates their lives "before and after their arrival" to Israel. While one might argue about the validity of the facts described in sociological, anthropological, or historical accounts, I want here to point to a discursive oscillation, a conceptual, or even methodological, schizophrenia permeating such scholarship. Rather than a mere coincidence, this disjuncture of paradigms is virtually necessitated by the subliminal privileging of a Zionist vantage point.

Studies of the Jews of Yemen, for example, detail their oppression at Muslim hands, relaying the kidnapping of young Jewish women, their forced conversion to Islam, and imposed marriage to Muslim men. When these same Yemeni Jews are studied within the Israeli framework, however, the writers abandon the historical account of victimization and shift into an anthropological account of folklore and tradition. A mixture of history and anthropology, Herbert S. Lewis's *After the Eagles Landed: The Yemenites of Israel* begins by addressing Muslim persecution in Yemen, but then moves into detailing polygamy and *qat* chewing in Israel.[22] The book mentions the Decree of Orphans in the seventeenth century, which forced fatherless Jewish children to be taken away from their family and community and converted into Islam. Yet the text deploys a selective tale of kidnapping. Although *After the Eagles Landed* was written in the mid-1990s, it fails to mention one of the most traumatic kidnappings to afflict the Yemeni Jewish community between the late 1940s and the 1960s, taking place not in a Muslim country, but rather in the Jewish state.

Disoriented by the new reality in Israel, Yemenis, as well as other Jews from Arab and Muslim countries, fell prey to doctors, nurses, and social workers, most of them on the state payroll. These representatives of the state's welfare institutions were involved in providing Yemeni babies for adoption by Ashkenazi parents largely in Israel and the United States, while telling the biological parents that the babies had died. The conspiracy was extensive enough to include the systematic issuance of fraudulent death certificates for the adopted babies and at times even fake burial sites for the babies who presumably had died, although the parents were never presented with the proof—a body. In this way, the government attempted to ensure that over several decades Mizrahi demands for investigation were silenced, while information was hidden and manipulated by government bureaus. The act of kidnapping was not simply a result of financial interests to increase the state's revenues; it was also a result of a deeply ingrained belief in the inferiority of Jews from Arab and Muslim countries, seen as careless breeders possessing little sense of responsibility toward their own children. Doctors, nurses, and social workers, in this sense, saw themselves as missionaries of Western science and progress, faithful to their duty of carrying out the vision of modernity.[23] Transferring babies from the space of premodernity to that of modernity, where they would be raised according to nuclear family values and Western behavioral norms, was perceived to be logical, rational, and scientific. Within this discursive framework, literally tearing babies away from the arms of their mothers seemed only natural, even redemptive. The act of kidnapping babies, therefore, operated on a continuum with the reigning academic discourses of the time. In this intersection of race, gender, and class, the displaced Jews from Muslim countries became victims of the logic of progress, bearing the marks of its pathologies on their bodies.

A severe human rights violation—kidnapping—was subjected to systematic silencing and censorship.[24] The scholarly elision of this central experience is complicitous with the institutional silencing. Instead, anthropological books tend to be typically organized around such concepts as kinship, marriage, rituals, religious values, and social attitudes. Studies such as *After the Eagles Landed* do not necessarily speak about Yemeni Jews within the sociology of modernization. Rather, they participate in the Eurocentric anthropology of romanticization, longing for the exotic authenticity of its subjects. The author, Herbert S. Lewis, for example, praises Yemeni culture for its simplicity and colorfulness—partially, it seems, as a rebuff to the elitist attitude toward Yemeni Jews. In this sense, romanticizing ethnography differs from modernization sociology. Yet, both the romanticization and the modernization narratives share the discursive production of the Mizrahi family as a site of deviance from an implicit cultural normativity. Therefore, the Orientalist emphasis on the Mizrahi extended family structure (the *hamula*) in both disciplines is unable to contain the devastation experienced by these families through the kidnappings performed with the complicity of certain sectors of the establishment. Both narratives have also kidnapped Mizrahi subjectivity by eliding the perspective of Jews from Muslim countries, who in their worst imaginings could have never predicted an act of kidnapping in—and indirectly sanctioned by—the "Jewish state."

Deploying the framework of either modernizing sociology or romanticizing ethnography to write about Jews within Israel while, at the same time, applying political historiography to write about Jews within Islam produces a selective tale of kidnapping contingent on a political geography. This dichotomous narrativization frames the act of kidnapping in one space as paradigmatic and defamatory, while in the other the *same* act is either ignored or seen as an aberration from the norm. Every negative experience in the Arab world is amplified, allegorized, made synecdochic; it becomes the center of the historical narrative. Every negative experience in Israel, meanwhile, is downplayed within an exoticizing ethnographic account. At a time when both activism and academic research on the issue have entered the public sphere,[25] the structuring absence of the kidnapping case produces the scholarly equivalent of kidnapping—that is, the sequestering of Mizrahi intellectual agency in their own self-historicizing.

The ideological rupture characteristic of Zionist discourse, then, is reflected in much of hegemonic scholarship. The rupture is reproduced not only in the themes but also in the analytical modes, resulting in a kind of a methodological schizophrenia. Moshe Gat's book *A Jewish Community in Crisis: The Exodus from Iraq, 1948–1951,* for example, analyzes the Iraqi political and economic interests in at first refusing and then permitting Iraqi Jews to leave (only upon giving up their citizenship).[26] The book also characterizes the active opposition to Zionism on the part of the Iraqi Jewish leadership of Baghdad, depicting Hakham Sasson Khdhuri as simply fearing the loss of his status and position to the Zionists.[27] Yet this dissection of motives, interest, and power is abandoned once the author moves to examine the activities of the Zionist movement in Iraq as well as the position of the Israeli establishment. Here, the author shifts into a benign and idealistic official discourse to characterize Israel's "concern" for the Iraqi Jews, the very community being uprooted largely to the benefit of the Israeli state apparatus in terms of its political, demographic, and economic necessities: settling the country with Jews, securing the borders, obtaining cheap labor, and getting useful military personnel. As with any historiography, it is not simply the issue of "facts" that is at stake, but also the questions of narrative, tropes, characterizations, and points of view. The studies of Arab Jews tend to be organized around the agency of the Zionist movement and the State of Israel; the reader is sutured into a privileged point of view as well as into an implicit "norms of the text."[28] Thus, despite the methodological/discursive rupture, the historical tale remains coherent through the persistence of a hierarchical narrative structure, in which the Zionist idea provides the discursive "glue" that keeps the various elements together.

A rupture of a different nature operates in Amitav Ghosh's *In an Antique Land,* a book that, unlike most texts, offers a complex picture of Arab Jewish existence within Muslim space.[29] A hybrid of anthropology and history, the book interweaves ethnographic narratives concerning present-day Egyptian Muslims with historiographical accounts of the lives of Arab Jews in the twelfth century. Ghosh chronicles a Judeo-Islamic world largely through the travels of Ben-Yiju, a Tunisian Jewish merchant whose existence is conjured up from the shreds of the Geniza archive. The book vividly captures a geocultural Muslim space stretching from the Mediterranean to the Indian Ocean, where Jews lived, traveled, and exchanged goods and ideas. Within this Muslim space the existence of Jewishness was not perceived in exclusionary terms, as a philosophical and cultural contradiction. Ghosh's anthropology, however, focuses on his visits in the 1980s to an Egyptian village, exclusively dealing with the lives of contemporary Muslim Egyptians. The book produces a fascinating silence about the lives of present-day Egyptian, Tunisian, and other Arab Jews. In this fashion, *In an Antique Land* splits the subjects of his ethnography (Muslim Arabs) and his historiography (Jewish Arabs.) On Ghosh's final trip to Egypt he learns that pilgrims from Israel are on their way to visit the tomb of the cabbalist mystic Sidi Abu-Haseira—a site holy for both Muslims and Sephardic Jews. Yet, for one prosaic reason or another, the anthropologist, Ghosh, ends up never meeting them. Ghosh, at the closure of his historiographical and anthropological odyssey, somehow ends his narrative at the very point where the subject of his historiography could have turned into the subject of his anthropology.

Perhaps Ghosh's missed rendezvous, his packing up and leaving Egypt precisely as the (Sephardic/Mizrahi) Arab Jews visit the Abu-Haseira's holy site, is revelatory of deeper contemporary representational crisis or paralysis. In the hegemonic narrative, the continuity of Jewishness means rupture from the Arab Muslim world. At the same time, in the contemporary Arab Muslim world, the millennia of Jewish existence is at best an unconscious memory, leaving only traces in the footnotes of anti-Zionist ideology. In such discourses, Arab Jews continue to "travel" in the pages of historical texts as imbricated within a legendary Islamic civilization. Yet, as the postcolonial story begins to unfold over the past decades, Arab Jews suddenly cease to exist. This split narrative seems to suggest that once in Israel, Arab Jews have reached their final destination—the State of Israel—and nothing more remains to be said about their Arabness. Even the more critical narratives, in their unguarded moments, reproduce the fait accompli of violent displacements. In this sense, alliances and conflicts between communities (such as Muslims and Jews) not only have shifted historically but have also produced narratives linked to contemporary ideologies. And as certain strands in a cultural fabric become taboo (for example, the Arabness of Jews), this narrative rests on blurring connections that once existed.

Disciplining: Mizrahi Studies as a Relational Inquiry

While for the purpose of the nationalist telos Mizrahim are detached from the Arab Muslim geography of their belonging, a reattachment to that geography occurs for the purpose of explaining their marginalized position within Israeli society. Hegemonic paradigms in the humanities and social sciences have relied on developmentalist and modernization theories that have produced myriad forms of essentialized Oriental "deviance." This scholarship entails a paradoxical relation to the Arab cultural geography of the Arab Jews/Mizrahim, manifested within a disciplinary division of labor. On the one hand, Zionist historiography and literary criticism have exiled Judeo-Arab identity from their texts. On the other, sociology and criminology have placed them at the center, positing Mizrahim as a maladjusted group in Israel. This ruptured discourse extracted Mizrahim from their Arab history only to have it return to explain Mizrahi social pathologies. Mizrahim crowd the pages of Euro-Israeli sociological, criminological, and anthropological texts that provide explanation for the "problem of the gap." Here the Arab Muslim past looms as deformed vestiges in the lives of Israelis of Asian and African origins. Sociology and anthropology detect traces of underdevelopment, while hegemonic historiography and literary criticism tell the story of the past as a moral tale full of national purpose. The scholarly bifurcation of cultural geography cannot possibly capture the traumatic rupture, the complex transformation of an Arab Jewish/Mizrahi identity that is at once past and present, here and there—a palimpsestic identity inhabiting the dissonant, interstitial spaces between citizenship, religion, ethnicity, race, nation, and culture.

The hegemonic study of Mizrahim has been neatly parceled out among the disciplines in a narrative whose terminus lies within the territory of Zionism and Israel, as though there were only rupture without continuities within the Arab Muslim world and only wholeness and redemption in Israel. In this sense, geopolitical borders are superimposed on cultural paradigms; once within the borders of the State of Israel, contemporary Mizrahim are discursively dismembered from the complex Arab cultural space. Performed within the paradigms of development and modernization, the study of Mizrahim has reproduced Eurocentric notions of temporality and spatiality. An Oriental "essence" has also enriched anthropology with an opportunity to study Mizrahim's "exotic" rituals and traditions, often fetishistically detached from their history and politics. The scholarship about the Mizrahim has assumed Israeliness as a telos. Thus present-day Mizrahi culture and activism tend to be narrated reductively, within the framework of a political geography—the State of Israel—lacking the wider perspective of a border-crossing analysis.

In this essay, I have critiqued the study of Arab Jews that employs the Eurocentric and nationalist operations typifying Zionist discourse. A critical Mizrahi scholarship must disengage from the Zionized and nationalist modes of generating knowledge about "Jewish History," often performed within ghettoized and geographically defined discursive spaces. I have argued for a relational understanding of the multiple histories of Jews, histories that stretched over thousands of years, spread over diverse geographies, and lived within different ideological regimes. Eurocentric definitions of the history of Jews in the Islamic world cast them into a fixed stereotypical role, playing a millennial role of passive victims lacking any form of agency. Thus, within standard Zionist writing, any ambivalence, or even refusal, of the Zionist gesture of *aliya* (such as on the part of Communist Arab Jews) is marginalized in relation to canonical historiography. Recognizing these invisible histories works against the Eurocentric legacies of Zionized Jewish studies to rearticulate the spaces, moments, and subjects of a critical Mizrahi studies.

Charting a beginning for a Mizrahi epistemology requires, as we have seen, examining the terminological paradigms, the conceptual aporias, and the methodological inconsistencies plaguing diverse fields of hegemonic scholarship. Producing non-Orientalist and de-Zionized maps of the historical links between the question of Palestine and that of Arab Jews involves crossing a number of disciplinary assumptions and going against the grain of multiple normative political discourses. Such critical knowledge challenges the socialist as well as the capitalist Zionist narrative of modernization of Palestine and of the Mizrahim; it intervenes in the founding premises of naturalizing one return (Jewish) while repressing another (Palestinian); it deconstructs the folklorization and exoticization of non-European cultures; it demystifies the rescue narrative of the land of Palestine and of Arab Jews from their Arab Muslim captors; it rearticulates the place of Jews within the Arab Muslim culture as well as within and in relation to Palestine prior to and in the wake of the Zionist movement. Such critical studies interrupt the modernization narrative whereby anthropology renders Mizrahim as living "allochronically" in "another time"; in which sociology "otherizes" Mizrahim as "ethnicity" in contradistinction to an unmarked Ashkenazi-Sabra normativity; in which criminology forges an essentialist understanding of Oriental corruption; in which historiography fails to discern the political, economic, and discursive links between the question of Palestine and the Arab Jewish question both in Palestine and in the rest of Arab world; and in which political science assumes Arab Jewish/Mizrahi and Palestinian struggles as simply an "internal" versus an "external" problem. Critical scholarship, in contrast, deconstructs nationalist paradigms of "inside" and "outside," yet without blurring questions of power and privilege.

Within this transnational mapping, the critique of the Orientalization of Arab Jews would not entail obscuring the role played by Mizrahim—in their capacity as citizens of the State of Israel—in the continuing occupation and dispossession of Palestinians. This kind of complex positioning recalls other historical situations. In this sense, one might reflect on a useful structural analogy in which Palestinians have replayed the historical role of the dispossessed and occupied Native Americans for Zionism, while Arab Jews were cast as its displaced and exploited blacks.[30] Or, to put it differently, Mizrahim, like U.S. racialized minorities, suffer at the hands of discriminatory ideology and policies, but also have been enlisted in the service of the colonizing nation-state. Yet, throughout the modern history of Arab Jews/Mizrahim, the question of Palestine, like the questions of Zionism, is far from being settled, provoking constant dissonance and a maze of contradictions. The transdisciplinary scholarly frame I am proposing here, for its part, hopes to desegregate intellectual spaces and relocates the issues in a much wider and denser geographic imaginary and historical mapping.

NOTES

1. My critique here of the Zionist antidiaspora discourse, the displacement of Ostjuden onto the Mizrahim, and the menacing heteroglossia is largely taken from *Israeli Cinema: East/West and the Politics of Representation* (Austin: University of Texas Press, 1989), esp. 100, 208. For an elaborate critique of the negation of exile, see Amnon Raz-Krakotzkin, "Exile within Sovereignty: Toward a Critique of the 'Negation of Exile' in Israeli Culture," *Theory and Criticism* 4 (1993): 23–56, and *Theory and Criticism* 5 (1994): 113–132. See also George Steiner, "Our Homeland, the Text," *Salmangudi* 66 (Winter–Spring 1985): 4–25; and Yerach Gover, *Zionism: The Limits of Moral Discourse in Israeli Hebrew Fiction* (Minneapolis: University of Minnesota Press, 1994).

2. On the invention of the Mizrahim, see Ella Shohat, "The Invention of the Mizrahim?" *Journal of Palestine Studies* 29 (Autumn 1999): 5–20.

3. For a detailed review of the terms, see the longer version of this essay in *Hagar*.

4. Even subsequent to the foundation of the State of Israel, the Jewish community in Iraq was constructing new schools and founding new enterprises, a fact hardly indicating an institutionalized intention to leave.

5. This effort is clearly expressed in texts written by Iraqi Zionists; see, for example, Shlomo Hillel, *Ruah Kadim* [Operation Babylon] (Jerusalem: Edanim, 1985), 259–263.

6. One of the most debated cases concerns the Zionist placing of bombs in synagogues. See Abbas Shiblak, *The Lure of Zion* (London: Al Saqi, 1986); and G. N. Giladi, *Discord in Zion* (London: Scorpion, 1990).

7. See interviews in the following documentary films: David Benchetrit, *Samir* (Israel, 1997); and Samir, *Forget Baghdad* (Switzerland, 2002).

8. While the position of Arab Jews is often used to justify the expulsion of Palestinians, there have been a few attempts to reflect on the position of Arab Jews vis-à-vis Arab nationalism from a different angle; see Shiblak, *Lure of Zion*; Ella Shohat, "Sephardim in Israel: Zionism from the Standpoint of Its Jewish Victims," *Social Text*, nos. 19/20 (Fall 1988): 1–35; Moshe Behar, "Time to Meet the Mizrahim?" *al-Ahram*, October 15–21, 1998; essays from "Mizrahim and Zionism: History, Political Discourse, Struggle" (special issue), *News from Within* 13 (January 1997); Tikva Honig-Parnass, "Introduction"; Sami Shalom Chetrit, "The Dream and the Nightmare: Some Remarks on the New Discourse in Mizrahi Politics in Israel, 1980–1996"; Zvi Ben-Dor, "A Short History of the Incredible Mizrahi History"; and Moshe Behar, "Is the Mizrahi Question Relevant to the Future of the Entire Middle East?"; Joseph Massad, "The 'Post-Colonial' Colony: Time, Space, and Bodies in Palestine/Israel," in *The Pre-Occupation of Postcolonial Studies,* ed. Fawzia Afzal-Khan and Kalpana Seshadri-Crooks (Durham, N.C.: Duke University Press, 2000), 311–46; Sami Shalom Chetrit, *HaMahapeikha ha Ashkenazit Meta* [The Ashkenazi revolution is dead] (Tel Aviv: Bimat Kedem, 1999).

9. For example, Naeim Giladi, a former Zionist activist in Iraq who was imprisoned and tortured but was able to escape one week before execution, gradually came to change his outlook after living in Israel and has become an anti-Zionist activist. He left Israel

in the mid-1980s and settled in New York, renouncing his Israeli citizenship. (From my diverse conversations with Giladi in New York during the late 1980s, when we both served as the representatives of the World Organization of Jews from Islamic Countries, an organization member of the United Nation's NGO on "The Question of Palestine.")

10. I am basing this argument on numerous conversations I have had with Iraqi Jews in Israel over the past two decades. It also forms part of a project that Sasson Somekh and I are currently collaborating on, focusing on the moment of dislocation from Iraq to Israel.

11. For more complex accounts of the histories of Jews, see Maxine Rodinson, *Cult, Ghetto, and State: The Persistence of the Jewish Question* (London: Al Saqi, 1983); Ilan Halevi, *A History of the Jews: Ancient and Modern* (London: Zed, 1987); Ammiel Alcalay, *After Jews and Arabs: Remaking Levantine Culture* (Minneapolis: University of Minnesota Press, 1993); Mark R. Cohen, *Under Crescent and Cross* (Princeton, N.J.: Princeton University Press, 1995); Amnon Raz-Krakotzkin, "Historical Consciousness and Historical Responsibilities," in *From Vision to Revision: A Hundred Years of Historiography of Zionism*, ed. Yechiam Weitz (Jerusalem: Zalman Shazar Center, 1997); Joel Beinin, *The Dispersion of the Egyptian Jewry: Culture, Politics, and the Formation of a Modern Diaspora* (Berkeley: University of California Press, 1998); and Nissim Rejwan, *Israel in Search of Identity* (Gainesville: University of Florida Press, 1999).

12. On the history of the AIU, see Aron Rodrigue, *Images of Sephardi and Eastern Jewries in Transition: The Teachers of the Alliance Israelite Universelle, 1860–1939* (Seattle: University of Washington Press, 1993).

13. See Zvi Yehuda, "The Jews of Babylon and Cultural Change through the Educational Activities of Alliance Israelite Universelle" (in Hebrew), *Babylonian Jewry: A Journal for the Research of the History and Culture of the Jews of Babylon*, no. 1 (Fall 1995).

14. *Perah* (Calcutta), September 23, 1885. The translation from the Judeo-Arabic language is mine. A selection from Perah is included in the appendix of Yehuda, "The Jews of Babylon."

15. Herzl's visionary Zionist utopia was the subject of his 1902 German-language book: Theodor Herzl, *Altneuland: Old New Land*, trans. Miriam Kraus (Tel Aviv: Babel, 1997).

16. For other critical approaches to the dominant Israeli sociology, see Shlomo Swirski, *Israel: The Oriental Majority* (London: Zed, 1989); and Uri Ram, ed., *Israeli Society: Critical Perspectives* (in Hebrew) (Tel Aviv: Breirot, 1993). Over the years, Mizrahim have argued against the dominant explanation of the "gap" between Mizrahim and Ashkenazim addressed in such magazines as *Afikim, Hapanter ha Shahor, Apirion, Pa'amon ha-Shkhunut, Hapatish, Iton Aher*, and *Hadshot Hila*.

17. Another scholar, Yosef Gross, saw the immigrants as suffering from "mental regression" and a "lack of development of the ego." Quotations from Frankenstein and Gross are taken from Tom Segev, *1949: The First Israelis* (in Hebrew) (Jerusalem: Domino, 1984), 157. The extended symposium concerning the "Sephardi problem" was framed as a debate about the "essence of primitivism." Only a strong infusion of European cultural values, the scholars concluded, would rescue the Arab Jews from their "backwardness."

18. Kalman Katznelson, *Hamahapeikha HaAshkenazit* [The Ashkenazi revolution] (Tel Aviv: Anach, 1964).

19. The term "allochronic" is borrowed from Johannes Fabian, *Time and the Other: How Anthropology Makes Its Object* (New York: Columbia University Press, 1983).

20. Located in Or Yehuda, the museum was founded by Iraqi Jews who were among the leaders of the Zionist movement.
21. For a more detailed critique of Orientalist modernization and discourse, particularly what I call "the Zionist masternarrative" and its concomitant "rescue fantasies," see Ella Shohat, *Israeli Cinema*; "Sephardim in Israel"; and "Masternarrative/Counter Readings," in *Resisting Images: Essays on Cinema and History*, ed. Robert Sklar and Charles Musser (Philadelphia: Temple University Press, 1990), 251–278. See also Sami Shalom Chetrit, "Castrated Mizrahi Identity," in *The Ashkenazi Revolution Is Dead* (Tel Aviv: Kedem, 1999), 57–60; and Amnon Raz-Krakotzkin, "Orientalism, Jewish Studies, and Israeli Society: A Few Comments," *Gma'a* 3 (1999): 49–52.
22. Herbert S. Lewis, *After the Eagles Landed: The Yemenites of Israel* (Prospect Heights, Ill.: Waveland, 1994).
23. One of the nurses, Rouja Kushinski, was interviewed on the subject for a report on the Israeli television program *Oovda* (Channel 2, 1996), directed by Uri Rozenweig with research prepared by Shoshana Madmoni. Not only did the nurse admit to the act of taking children away, she maintained her belief that forcefully removing children from their biological parents was the right thing to do.
24. On June 30, 1986, for example, the Public Committee for the Discovery of the Missing Yemenite Children held a massive protest rally. The rally, like many Mizrahi protests and demonstrations, was completely ignored by the dominant media. A few months later, however, Israeli television produced a documentary on the subject, blaming the bureaucratic chaos of the period for unfortunate "rumors" and perpetuating the myth of Oriental parents as careless breeders with little sense of responsibility toward their own children. The same discourse was replayed in the mid-1990s, when a forceful protest led by Rabbi Uzi Meshulam overwhelmed the country. Meshulam was delegitimized and portrayed in the media as another David Koresh. Meshulam, who published various documents consisting of firsthand and first-person accounts by Yemeni mothers about the kidnapped babies, is still serving prison time for his campaign demanding access to government files of the case. The Mizrahi struggle to shed light on what exactly took place during those years and, most important, to give the families a chance to meet their kidnapped children, is still a major rallying factor for Mizrahim of diverse persuasions.
25. See Dov Levitan, "The Aliya of the "Magic Carpet" as a Historical Continuation of the Earlier Yemenite Aliyas" (in Hebrew) (Master's thesis, Bar-Ilan University, 1983); and investigative articles written by journalist Shosh Madmoni (in the magazine *Shishi* and the daily *Yedioth Ahronot*) and by Yigal Mashiah (in the daily *Haaretz*) in 1996. See also Shoshana Madmoni, "The Missing Yemenite Children: Sometimes Truth Is Stranger than Fiction," *News from Within* (February 1996).
26. Moshe Gat, *A Jewish Community in Crisis: The Exodus from Iraq, 1948–1951* (Jerusalem: Merkaz Zalman Shazar, 1989).
27. *Hakham* is the Sephardi equivalent of Rabbi.
28. The term "norms of the text" is borrowed from Boris Uspensky, *A Poetics of Composition* (Berkeley: University of California Press, 1973).
29. Amitav Ghosh, *In an Antique Land* (New York: Alfred A. Knopf, 1993).
30. I insist on the words "structural analogy," since I certainly am not trying to argue for an equation. For further exploration of this point, see E. Shohat, "Taboo Memories, Diasporic Visions: Columbus, Palestine, and Arab-Jews," in *Performing Hybridity*, ed. May Joseph and Jennifer Fink, 201–232 (Minneapolis: University of Minnesota Press, 1999).

14

History Begins at Home

YEHOUDA SHENHAV

This book is about the complex, conflict-ridden, and ambivalent encounter of Jews from Arab countries with Zionist nationalism and the Jewish state.[1] These conflicts had a tremendous bearing on my own upbringing, as the following personal story will show.

Some time ago, as I sat down to work in a Tel Aviv café in the area where I live, an elderly man suddenly approached me. "You are the son of Eliahu Shaharabani, of blessed memory," he said, half stating a fact, half asking. I looked at the man standing in front of me. I had never seen him before. He was handsome, about seventy years old, and spoke with a heavy Iraqi accent. This is what my father would look like if he were alive, I thought to myself.

"My name is Avner Yaron," the man explained. "I recruited your father into the intelligence community in the 1950s." The tables in the café were close together, and I had the feeling that everyone in the place was listening to our conversation. "I have proof," he said, as though revealing a secret. "If you like, I'll show you." I felt a sense of relief when he left. I watched him as he walked under the big awning of the café, crossed the street, and receded into the distance.

My discomfort had nothing to do with the suddenness of the man's appearance or his reference to my father's work. What he had told me came as no great surprise. I knew a little about my father's history, and somehow I had expected an episode like this sooner or later. I wasn't sure I would ever hear from Yaron again. Nor did I really want to.

Two weeks later, a fax arrived in my office from the secret agent, saying, "There is an envelope for you in the café." I was a bit put out: unmarked brown

---

Reprinted, by permission, from Yehouda Shenhav, *The Arab Jews: A Postcolonial Reading of Nationalism, Religion, and Ethnicity* (Palo Alto, Calif.: Stanford University Press), 1–17. Copyright © by the Board of Trustees of the Leland Stanford Jr. University.

envelopes have unpleasant connotations these days. Nevertheless, I couldn't resist. The envelope contained two group photographs, in black and white, and a note: "These are photos with your late father from 1950." One photograph showed four young men and a young woman, all in their early twenties, some wearing khaki shirts, the others white shirts. All were Arab Jews. The other photograph showed four young men and two young women standing on a beach. One of the women, in a two-piece bathing suit, did not look as though she belonged to the group. "Hemda was the commander's wife," the agent had written, as though anticipating my question. My father was standing at the back, smiling. I identified him at once by his high mane of hair, rather like Kramer's on the *Seinfeld* show. He must have been about twenty-one at the time the photograph was taken.

The pictures, like Yaron's appearance, confronted me with my complex location within what is often represented as an ancient, insurmountable conflict between Arabs (who are not Jews) and Jews (who are not Arabs). In something as simple as the ways in which Iraqiness marked their bodies, color, and language, Yaron, my father, and the others undermined the basic opposition between Arab and Jew. As a result, the treatment of Israel as a place where Jews can be open and comfortable with their Jewishness so often apt for Jews from Europe and North America—does not even begin to frame the details of my family history, or of the history of the Arab Jews in general. For us, the story is instead about how "Arabness" was underscored, erased, and otherwise managed in order to fit us into the Jewish collectivity. It is about how the accent and bearing of an old Jewish man could be so discomfiting in the Jewish state in the late twentieth century.

The shift from being part of the Arab world to part of the non-Arab Jewish collectivity is evident even in the sparsest details of my background. My grandfather Yosef was a Baghdadi merchant who did a lot of traveling through the colonial territory, selling dates, fish, and eggs. At least once every three months, he took the Baghdad-Palestine railway line, and on one of those trips, he purchased a plot of land in the town of Petah Tikva, outside Tel Aviv. In 1936, the family left Iraq with the intention of settling there, but they returned to Baghdad after just nine months. Only Shlomo, my father's older brother, remained in Palestine. My grandfather continued his commercial travels during World War II as well. My father joined him on one of his trips, in 1942, and decided to remain in Palestine with his brother, Shlomo. I was told that my grandfather had objected, but that my father insisted and prevailed; he was thirteen years old and found construction work in Palestine.

When my father was seventeen, he moved with a group of Iraqi-born friends to Kibbutz Be'eri, on the ruins of the Arab village of Nahbir. In that same year, Avshalom Shmueli, a recruitment officer, came to Be'eri and recruited them into Israel's intelligence community. There is nothing surprising about this. They were part of an inexhaustible reservoir of ambitious young people, loyal to the state, spoke perfect Arabic, and looked like Arabs. They had the ideal profile. As an intelligence man, my father worked hard and was sometimes gone for lengthy periods. His absences enhanced my status as a boy in the neighborhood. By working for the state against the Arab enemy, he earned his entry ticket into Israeliness. I was able to benefit from it vicariously. But this does not mean I was comfortable with his Arabness. As a kid, I fought against my parents and their culture, which I perceived as hostile Arab culture. Employing creative tactics, I would shut the radio off or put it out of commission when they wanted to listen to the great Arab singers Om Kolthoum, Farid al-Atrach, or Abd-el-Wahab. The truth is that I was greatly preoccupied with my own and my family's Arab Jewish origins but kept the subject to myself. Those origins did not provide a valid entry ticket to become an equal member in Israeli society, with its basically Orientalist mentality, then as now.

In a bizarre irony, my Iraqi father died of a heart attack when an Iraqi missile struck the neighborhood in Tel Aviv during the Gulf War. He was then sixty-two. Friends of his whom I met after his death spoke to me in Iraqi Arabic and wanted to be sure that I remembered them from the period when we lived on an intelligence base located in the southern city of Be'er Sheva. Not long ago, Avner Yaron remembered me again and sent me another brown envelope. This one contained a color photograph of our home—an old Arab house—on the base.

My father's colleagues were a "nature reserve," as the Israeli expression goes: they spoke Arabic, read the Arabic press, and listened to Arabic radio stations; some of them spent time in other countries and identified themselves as Arabs. They eavesdropped on the famous radio conversation between Egypt's President Abdel Nasser and Jordan's King Hussein a few days prior to the outbreak of the June 1967 conflict—in Arabic, of course. When they returned home from their assignments, they watched Lebanese television and listened to Radio Cairo. They held frequent all-night *haflot*—traditional Arab parties with plenty of food and communal singing. The greatest Arab Jewish singers in Israel were regular guests in my parents' home. How ironic that their very entry into the Israeli collective—through their intelligence work—demanded that they remain part of the Arab world against which they worked. Such is the logic of the Israeli state: top-heavy with contradictions. On the one hand, it wants to strip its Arab Jews—citizens of Israel known also as Mizrahim—of their Arabness, while on the other, it implores some of them (like my father and his friends) to go on living as Arabs by license.

These recollections bring to mind the story of Eli Cohen, a top Israeli spy who infiltrated the senior ranks of the Ba'ath regime in Syria and was caught, tried, and executed in 1965. Eli Cohen was recruited by the Mossad espionage agency because he was an Arab Jew. In 1968 or 1969, not long after the Six Day War, the Committee of the Babylonian Community in Petah Tikva decided to rename the synagogue located next to the city's produce market after him. My maternal grandfather, Salim, who was one of the senior members of the committee and a *gabai*—an official of the synagogue—asked me to write the speech he was to deliver at the renaming ceremony. I was thrilled by the momentousness of the event. In the municipal library, I found a copy of *Our Man in Damascus*, a biography of Eli Cohen (Ben-Hanan 1968), which served me year after year in the annual commemoration ceremony, when I wrote new variations of that same tired old speech.

The draft of the address that I wrote for my grandfather was studded with quotations from the book. For example, that the handler of Agent 880 was "a cordial man with deep blue eyes"; that Sophie, Eli Cohen's daughter, would ask, "Why isn't my father coming home tonight, like all the other fathers?"; that Cohen's trial proceeded like "a cheap matinee film," like a play written according to the rules of the "Middle Eastern imagination." It declared: "The Damascus mob is thirsty for blood, and the government supplies it to the point of intoxication." The book related that Eli Cohen's mother, who watched her son's execution on television, cried out in tears, "Why did the state send my Eli?"; "Why was it my son, of all people, who had to die among Arabs?" I described his wife, Nadia, with her two infant children and quoted her proudly: "The state, which sent Eli Cohen on his mission, did not hesitate to launch an open struggle to save its agent."

I was about sixteen. I was slightly offended when my grandfather would set aside my text and launch into new realms of melodrama. He thought himself a superb and charismatic orator. Nadia Cohen sat in the women's section of the synagogue, and the entire congregation burst into tears with her. They wanted more of my grandfather's speech. These texts brought in handsome donations for the synagogue. We youngsters passed the time playing in the space between the synagogue chamber and the small yard around it. This was shortly after the 1967 war (the so-called Six Day War), the first full-scale war in which Arab Jews participated—having missed the first "heroic" war, that of 1948. Together with the Eli Cohen affair, their full participation in the 1967 ethos and national epic brought the color back to the cheeks of the Arab Jews. Eli Cohen had been an offering, a sacrifice that constituted an act of redemption and a source of pride, an expression of the symbolic—and concrete—price that the Arab Jews had to pay, then as now, in order to be part of the putative Israeli collectivity.

The only problem was that when Eli Cohen from Bat Yam (a suburb of Tel Aviv) became Kamal Amin Thabat in Damascus, like my father's friends, no one bothered to mention that the primary criterion for his recruitment to the Mossad was his Arab origins. The public discourse denied and ignored that connection. For example, the Ministry of Education decided in the late 1990s to make the Eli Cohen affair a mandatory subject in the curriculum and to issue a commemorative booklet. Among those whom the ministry asked to reminisce about Cohen was the writer Amnon Shamosh, his friend, who wrote a story entitled "Kamal Efendi Returns to Bat Yam," emphasizing the role of Cohen's Arab background. After submitting the story, Shamosh received a furious phone call from the head of the association to commemorate Eli Cohen, Ephraim Hiram, who said he was very upset by it: "This is a national hero, and his ethnic identity is not important," he told Shamosh. "The terms 'Mizrahi' and 'Ashkenazi' are obsolete and their use in the story raises old demons." Shamosh refused to delete what the Ministry of Education termed the "problematic passages," explaining: "I could not forgo the ethnic connection, because Arabness is an integral part of Cohen's story, as was his criticism of his Ashkenazi handlers, who did not understand him or the surroundings into which he was sent.... Naturally, the members of the establishment were Ashkenazim and the people in the field in the Arab states were Mizrahim.... I am obliged to illuminate those aspects that the functionaries would like to sweep under the carpet." Hiram responded in an opinion piece in the daily *Yedioth Aharonoth*: "I insisted that Shamosh write ... using a literary rather than a factual approach, and under no circumstances with a Mizrahi or Ashkenazi motif.... A story, that is all we asked for.... Why do intellectuals have to foment hatred within this nation instead of drawing people closer together?"

Shamosh's story did not appear in the Ministry of Education booklet. The link between Mizrahiness and national politics was perceived as dangerous. The booklet commemorating Eli Cohen denied and rejected any such link.

It may seem eminently reasonable for the new Jewish state to use immigrants' Arab backgrounds as "expertise" and the basis for a "career." As such, my use of Israel's spies to argue that the incorporation of the Arab Jews into the Jewish collective was complex and internally contradictory may seem facile. But first, though Arab Jews were routinely used as spies, their cultural skills were never used to forge positive links with Arab countries. This disjuncture suggests that the state was after more than just practical help. Its practices were used to separate Arab Jews from their Arab backgrounds. Second, the Arabization and de-Arabization evident in the story of Kamal Amin Thabat was not limited to the recruitment of spies; it permeated the society and was part and parcel of its ideological structure. The same ethnicity that Hiram insisted does not matter clearly does matter, as both Mizrahim and Ashkenazim routinely mark it and deny it. For example, after the infamous Nazi war criminal Adolph Eichmann was captured in Argentina and brought to Jerusalem to stand trial in 1961, Hannah Arendt wrote in a letter to Karl Jaspers: "Fortunately, Eichmann's three judges were of German origin, indeed the best German Jewry. [Attorney General Gideon] Hausner is a typical Galician Jew, still European, very unsympathetic, ... boring, ... constantly making mistakes. Probably one of those people who don't know any language. Everything is organized by the Israeli police force, which gives me the creeps. It speaks only Hebrew and looks Arabic. Some downright brutal types among them. They obey any order. Outside the courthouse doors the oriental mob, as if one were in Istanbul or some other half-Asiatic country" (Arendt and Jaspers 1992, 434–435).

Arendt does more here than just mark the Arabness of Arab Jews. As a European Jew (of German origin), she expresses a quintessential Orientalist reading of Israeli society, one that could come directly from Edward Said's *Orientalism*.[2] She ranks Jews on a scale based on the distinction between "Occident" and "Orient," with "European" at one end and "Arab" at the other. At the top, she places the German Enlightenment, whose moral status was not compromised by its tragic history in the twentieth century. Below that, she places the Israeli attorney general. Hausner is still European, but a Galician who is "constantly making mistakes." She probably wonders how an eastern European Jew, the "Asian of Europe," became the "European of Asia," as it were. Below this, she ranks the Arab Jews, who speak Hebrew but look like Arabs. At the bottom of the scale is the "oriental mob," right out of the classical Orientalist descriptions of Cairo, Baghdad, and Istanbul. The Arab Jews gave Arendt the creeps because they exposed a concealed feature—and the unusual mixture—of Israeli society. Bound by the Zionist lexicon, Arendt does not, however, have the terminology to define these hybrids.

Not all Arab Jews participated in de-Arabization as I did. Grandmother Farha, my mother's mother, who sadly passed away in 2005, probably at the age of ninety-three, had the audacity to address that dangerous link and used the Arab Jewish category more explicitly. She explained to me that Eli Cohen's father was named Amin, and his mother was Sa'ida, and that he was an Egyptian Jew and I was an Iraqi Jew. She liked to idealize the Jewish past in Iraq, even after 1967, when a shift (for the worse) occurred in the historical representation of Jewish-Arab relations. Grandmother, who had come to Israel from Iraq in 1950, said that the uprooting of more than 100,000 Jews from Iraq in the 1950s, along with the erasure of their past, was a barbaric act. She would surely have agreed with Walter Benjamin that, from the victim's point of view, history is not a progressive development but an ongoing catastrophe. Contrary to the prevailing fashion, grandmother did not consider Jews and Arabs to be two mutually exclusive categories. She continued to live in Israel as a pious Jew but never disavowed her Arab identity and culture.

I did.

Denial is a key concept in psychoanalysis, but it has a sociological context as well. The moment it became clear to me that the denial that I believed was a private experience was in fact a collective phenomenon would be a moment of discovery for me: the discovery that the experience of denial was a formative one for many in my generation.[3]

In the summer of 1998, I found myself talking to a German audience in Munich about the different modes of the "discourse" about Arab Jews in Israel during the country's first fifty years. I spoke about the connection between the Zionist project and Arab Jews, and I enumerated the intergenerational changes that had taken place among Arab Jews in modes of speech, denial, and silence. The speaker immediately after me was Mahmoud Muhareb, an Israeli Palestinian, who was then a member of the faculty of Birzeit University in the West Bank. His lecture was "naturally" about Zionism and the Palestinians. At the end of the day, a senior member of the Israeli diplomatic mission in Germany approached Muhareb and said to him in a tone of incredulity, "I appreciate your talk. It was perfectly clear to me what you were talking about. But what in the hell was Shenhav talking about? There hasn't been an ethnic problem in Israel for a long time." That diplomat is hardly alone in this view; it is commonplace in the Israeli public arena. By then I knew how to respond to the diplomat. In fact, I had published the response a year and a half earlier in the form of an op-ed piece in the weekend magazine of the daily newspaper *Haaretz*.

The article, entitled "Bond of Silence" (*Haaretz Magazine*, December 27, 1996), dealt with the collective denial, especially by the Zionist left, of the intra-Jewish ethnic rift in Israel. Drawing on my personal experience, I tried to explain how the Israeli society had placed a taboo on any discussion of the Mizrahi question as a political issue (as distinct from a folkloristic phenomenon). The left's recognition of the Palestinian question, I argued, did not stem from a love of the Orient but was rooted in a desire to keep the Palestinians on the other side of the tracks, or fence, where they will not be a threat to the perceived Western hegemony in Israel. However, I pointed out, the Arab Jews cannot be moved to the other side of the fence; at most, bypass roads can be built to skirt the development towns and inner-city ghettos they inhabit. Instead, their Arabness is handled by erasing it. Recognition of the Arab Jews as a collectivity (and not only as individuals) would require rearticulation of Israeli society's basic assumptions and its reorganization. In many senses, my article described the ideological context within which my own personal denial had taken place.

The outburst of reactions proved to me how strongly naming these dynamics violated a social taboo, how much Israeli society needs to keep infra-Jewish ethnicity invisible. The article drew a surprising number of responses, letters, and rebuttals over a period of about four months, and it was quoted widely on radio and television current affairs programs, and even in foreign (English and German) media. I received sharply worded letters, accusing me, among other offenses, of disseminating "hatred" and "rage," creating "antagonism between the communities," and asserting that I was personally "crass," "extremist," "postmodernist," and "sick." Some of my academic colleagues scolded me for making "nonsociological" use of certain terms; others explained to me that I was positioning myself at the extreme end of the scale. The true cause of the emotional response by so many people was not only the article's substance but principally the fact that success had not guaranteed silence in my case. All those who had accepted me as a "success story" in Israeli academia were now unable to forgive my treachery in breaking the silence. One of my colleagues, who is Iraqi-born himself, stated that he personally had not experienced discrimination, and that only the hyperactivity of successful Mizrahim such as myself, "who suffer from endless obsession and chronic restlessness," kept the question on the public agenda. Most of the reactions illustrated the depth of the denial, thus effectively affirming the article's thesis. One professor noted that according to public opinion surveys, the majority of Mizrahim in Israel (88 percent) say they have never experienced ethnic discrimination. However, instead of considering the possibility of interpreting this as a form of denial, he concluded that it demonstrated the absence of an ethnic issue in Israel. This attitude is particularly odd in light of the sociological fact that the gaps between Israeli-born second-generation Ashkenazim and Mizrahim have not decreased in the past thirty years and in some cases have increased (see Cohen and Haberfeld 1998; Khazzoom 1998, 2005). Overall, Mizrahim are now some 45 percent of Israel's population, but they account for only a quarter of the students in the country's universities, and their proportion among university professors, judges, leading media figures, writers, and in the arts remains substantially below their ratio in the population.

Why is the location of Arab Jews in Israel so complex, so emotional, and such dangerous territory? In this book, I move from personal to collective history, and from individual analysis to cultural analysis, in order to analyze the mechanisms of representation of the Arab Jews in the Zionist and Israeli context.

It is essential to clarify at this point that the category of "Arab Jews," used throughout this book, is neither natural nor necessarily consistent and coherent. It is a splicing together of two categories whose relations are at best ambivalent, given the long history of rupture between them. As a viable option of practice and discourse in Israeli society, "Arab Jews" was short-lived, and the label was edited out by historical circumstances, particularly the rise of Jewish and Arab nationalisms. Several Jewish intellectuals in the Arab world have, in fact, used it to identify themselves (see, most notably, Memmi 1975; also Cohen and Udovitch 1989; Udovitch and Valensi 1984). As Albert Memmi says: "The term Jewish Arabs or Arab Jews is not a very good one, of course. But I have found it convenient to use. I simply wanted to remind my readers that because we were born in these so-called Arab countries and had been living in those regions long before the arrival of the Arabs, we share their languages, their customs, and their cultures to an extent that is not negligible" (1975, 29). Memmi adds that the Arabs did not respect the Arab Jews (or Jewish Arabs, as he sometimes refers to them), and that "it is far too late to become Jewish Arabs again" (1975, 20). Last, it should be mentioned that the term "Arab Jews" was used descriptively by Zionist emissaries and state functionaries. Even as late as 1972, interviewed by the Italian journalist Oriana Fallaci, the prime minister of Israel, Golda Meir, referred to the Jews from Arab countries as "Arab Jews" (Fallaci 1976, 104).

Today, given the historical circumstances in the Middle East, the concept does not necessarily depict a real identity, but rather functions as a counterfactual category that seeks to challenge the paradigm I label "methodological Zionism," following Ulrich Beck's concept of "methodological nationalism" (2003). Methodological Zionism refers to an epistemology where all social processes are reduced to national Zionist categories. I challenge methodological Zionism and suggest that the "impossible" juxtaposition of Jews and Arabs as a signifier of one's identity posits a critical option that resembles Max Weber's notion of "objective possibility" (Weber 1949). Indeed, some contemporary intellectuals use "Arab Jews" as a political category to challenge the discursive structure of the Zionist lexicon, among them Shimon Ballas, Samir Naqash, and Ella Shohat. Shohat's work, in particular, was pioneering in establishing this category in contemporary colonial and postcolonial studies (1988, 1997a, 2001).[4]

I argue that insisting on the category of Arab Jews reveals the contradictory practices of Zionist ideology, among them, seeking to absorb the Arab Jews into its ranks while remaining European, and to retain its Jewish primordial character while remaining modern and secular. These are a series of steps that were taken during the building of a coherent national identity and then erased in order to cast that national identity is self-evident and uncontested. The five chapters of this book deal with the social history of these steps, both prior to the establishment of the state of Israel and thereafter. They examine the encounter between Arab Jews and Jewish nationalism in four contexts: the encounter between Zionism and Arab Jews in a colonial context, where colonialism, Orientalism, and nationalism shaped its parameters; the "religionization" of the Arab Jews in that encounter as a way of incorporating them into the Zionist collective while erasing their Arab background; the political economy where the incorporation of the Arab Jews was used to erase the Zionist debts to Palestinians; and Zionist memory, into which one group of Arab Jews tried to incorporate themselves.

In describing these contexts, I draw on Michel Foucault, Bruno Latour, and postcolonial writers such as Edward Said and Homi Bhabha. The story I tell challenges not only naive historical analysis that accepts Zionist narrative as history but also approaches to Israeli society shaped and molded by "methodological Zionism." More concretely, Zionist epistemology has shaped prior work on Israel in at least three ways that I avoid in this book. The most fundamental change I make is to begin the analysis several years prior to the formation of the Jewish state, rather than with the physical immigration of the Arab Jews to Israeli soil in the 1950s (see also Khazzoom 2003; Shohat 1988). This runs counter to Zionist epistemology, which promotes a state-centric, Israelocentric perspective in which inequality, discrimination, and cultural clashes are studied within the context of the state of Israel.[5] While admittedly useful, such studies are limiting, because they treat the Arab Jews as immigrants and as citizens of Israel dealing with an established state and formal institutions.

In contrast, I begin the analysis with the colonial encounter in Abadan, an Iranian city at the head of the Persian Gulf, about 420 miles (675 km) south-southwest of Tehran, where Jews from Arab countries were representationally shaped into appropriate subjects for immigration to the Zionist state. This constitutes the "zero point," or terminus a quo, of the story I seek to tell in this book, because Zionism had never before focused on Arab Jews as potential immigrants to Palestine. Here we find what Bhabha calls a "third space," where any number of outcomes were possible (as opposed to the single outcome necessitated by methodological Zionism). This vantage provides an alternative, and broader, epistemological view of practices that are not easily discerned in the Zionist state-centered perspective.

Furthermore, by highlighting the Arabness of the Arab Jews, rather than treating them as an ethnic group unrelated to the Arab world from which they came, I avoid compartmentalization into the "external national" problem, or Arab-Israeli cleavage, and the "internal ethnic" problem, or Mizrahi Ashkenazi cleavage (Khazzoom 2003; Shohat 1988), a dichotomy that has been part of Zionism since its inception. As Gershon Shafir has explained, Zionism was established as a theory of political legitimation, which demands that ethnic boundaries not cross political boundaries ([1989] 1996). Thus, for example, in analyzing the genesis of the Palestinian refugee problem, the "new" historian Benny Morris (1987) does not mention its inexorable connection with the Arab Jews. Anthropologists analyzing the heritage of the Jews from the Islamic countries (e.g., Deshen and Shokeid 1984) and historians writing about the waves of immigration to Palestine and Israel (e.g., Hacohen 1998; Ofer 1996) address these subjects as an ethnic question that is (seemingly) separate from the Palestinian question. Yosef Meir (1983), analyzing the Yemenite immigration of 1910, does not cite its substantial relevance to the Palestinian question, as opposed to Shafir ([1989] 1996), as well as to Ella Shohat (1988, 1989, 1997a, 1999), and others who have used an integrated approach. Canonical Israeli historiography, then, is based on a system of cultural classification that channels the "different" spheres of discourse into separate tracks. This division of labor depoliticizes the question of the Arab Jews, defines it as an "ethnic" issue (i.e., an intra-Jewish ethnic question), and eliminates the possibility of describing the history of the Arab Jews in its overall—historical and political, let alone colonial—context.

The discourse about the identity of the Arab Jews in Israel is similarly caught between an approach that views it as a natural phenomenon rooted in the Arab Jews themselves and in their Arabic culture (known as essentialism); and a class-based neo-Marxist approach that treats "Mizrahiness" as a homegrown Israeli category that is determined by class, place of residence, education, and labor market conditions. Each approach suffers from innate self-blindness. The essentialist-cultural position ignores the political and cultural context within which the identity of the Arab Jews is forged and overlooks the ideological apparatuses of the Jewish state within which it is reproduced, shaped, and articulated. The class-based approach ignores the Arab origin of the Arab Jews and negates their history. Moreover, both approaches adduce "Mizrahiness" in contradistinction to "Ashkenaziness" and thereby miss the fact that the former, like the latter, is a site that has wide margins and is inconsistent and multifaceted. In this book, I offer a different perspective that attempts to avoid some of these obstacles.

Apart from chapter 1, which sets the stage, the book is organized around four units, represented by chapters 2, 3, 4, and 5. Each of the four units can be read as an independent essay focusing on one question in the social history of the Arab Jews and Zionism. At the same time, the units are interrelated at several complementary—and nonmutually exclusive—levels: *chronological, analogical,* and *theoretical.* The chronological connection is built-in. The first unit describes the encounter between Zionism and Arab Jews in the colonial context of the early 1940s and indicates the point at which the Arab Jews were "discovered" as a reservoir for immigration. The second unit (chapter 3) describes networks of national emissaries and their patterns of operation between 1942 and 1945 and lays out the symbiotic relationship between nationalism, religion, and ethnicity—the three categories that make up the ideological project known as "Zionism." Chapter 4 focuses on the Jews of Iraq in the 1950s prior to, and upon, their arrival in Israel and the manner in which national accounting linked this population with that of the Palestinian refugees. The final chapter deals with the Mizrahim—a new title given to Arab Jews in Israel—over a period of thirty years, from the mid 1970s to the present.

The analogical connection tells the story of the interplay between nationalism, religion, and the ethnicity of Arab Jews on four different analogical screens. The first is the colonial screen, the second the religious, the third the economic-political, and the fourth that of memory. Thus, for example, I analyze the religiosity of the Arab Jews not only as a phenomenon bearing theological meaning but also as a screen on which additional social, political, and cultural questions are displayed. I argue that the religion described in the reports of the Zionist emissaries is a marker of ethnicity that finds concentrated symbolic expression in the religious category. The four screens, which appear in the different chapters, enable alternative multivocal presentations of the Arab Jews, their identity, and their relations with Zionist/Israeli nationalism. The screens, then, are not only historical stages but also four fundamental identity options that are realized or assume high visibility at certain historic moments.

The theoretical connection between the units is manifested through a triangle that describes the components of the Zionist project: nationalism, religion, ethnicity. I argue that in order to get a grip on the Zionist encounter with the Arab Jews, Zionism needs to be conceptualized as an ideological practice that is anchored in these three symbiotically related categories.

These three categories—nationalism, religion, ethnicity—tend to appear simultaneously, and the ties between them cannot be unraveled easily.[6] This connection, as it is shaped within national thought, resembles the form of relationship that Foucault posits between knowledge and power. Knowledge does not lead to power, and power does not lead to knowledge, Foucault says. Knowledge/power appears as one seemingly inseparable unit (Foucault 1980). Paraphrasing Foucault, it can be said that nationalism, religion, and ethnicity are not only related in Zionist thought, they are almost interchangeable, or intertwined. Each of these categories is a necessary but insufficient condition for the whole, and each category requires the other two in order to produce the "Zionist subject." Only when these three categories co-appear do they succeed in manufacturing a coherent Zionist identity.[7] Despite the fact that Zionism ideologically fuses these three categories, it nonetheless continues to treat them as if they were mutually exclusive.[8] The remarkable success of the Zionist project during the twentieth century can be understood only in relation to the hegemonic status that it obtained through mobilization, cooperation, and co-optation—through these categories—rather than as based on coercion or repression (as far as the Jewish subjects of the project are concerned).

In each of the chapters, I choose alternative relationships between these categories and seek to dismantle their ostensible binarism. I point to their symbiotic relationships, as well as the ambivalence in modes of representation. For example, I show that although nationalism does in fact appear simultaneously with ethnicity in national thought and practice, its appearance at once creates and negates ethnicity. This is why every attempt by the Arab Jews to reconstruct their past within the Zionist discourse forces an "ethnic approach" on them, and the denial of the "ethnic approach" by the agents of nationalism paradoxically cleaves the national logic into Mizrahim and Ashkenazim. Furthermore, note that I use the three—nationalism, ethnicity, religion—as categories of practice, not only as conceptual categories. In practice, nationalism is identified as an outcome of dispersed political practices rather than as an a priori, predisposed category.

My intention in this book, then, is to undo the national-religious-ethnic package and expose the mechanisms by which its components acquire a unifying logic. The analysis will be accomplished by a methodological dismantling of each category into diverse voices and multiple, heterogeneous logics. In my analysis, nationalism does not speak in one voice, just as ethnicity and religion are not closed categories, but fractured and multiple. For these and other reasons, I also maintain that it is impossible to understand the construction of the identity and the status of the Arab Jews in Israel without closely tracing the colonial roots of these social processes. The formative stage of the "discovery" of the Arab Jews by the Zionist movement and its attempt to transform them into objects of migration are deeply embedded in a colonial context. Although a number of earlier pioneering works in the past decade have focused attention on the colonial context of the Arab Jews (e.g., Shohat 1989, 1997a, 1997b, 2001), the canonic academic discourse continues to downplay its importance and shies away from the use of postcolonial analysis in regard to Israeli society. The conclusions of this book clearly show the need to place the repressed colonial setting at the center of discussion. Notwithstanding the differences between the colonial experiences of the Jews in Iraq and the Jews in North Africa, I show that the colonial setting is the place from which any discussion of the Arab Jews must begin. As postcolonial theory suggests, the remnants of this colonial logic vis-à-vis the Arab Jews remain embedded in Israeli culture and politics to this day.

In the course of the book, I use the category of Arab Jews (or Mizrahim) to represent the Jews from the Islamic countries as a whole. It should be noted that the use of such generalizing sociological categories is the result of a dialectical game with the categories that hegemonic Zionism itself has identified and manufactured over the years. The Zionist institutions and then the state made use of these and other classifications as essentialist categories that define all the "Arab Jews" as a homogeneous, uniform identity group and blur the differences among them.[9] In retrospect, the shared life-experience of the Arab Jews in education, the army, the development towns, the factories, or on the margins of the lower middle class had the effect of ratifying the common definitions and in practice created a homological sameness between the different groups of origin among Jews from Islamic countries.

My starting point is provisionally to accept the hegemonic definition and counterpose a critical opposition to it. Acceptance of the hegemonic definition is a well-known move in identity politics. The minority group challenges the hegemonic definition of themselves by imputing a different meaning to it. This may result in a strategic posture that Homi Bhabha and Gayatri Spivak would call "strategic essentialism." Like the "new ethnicities" throughout the Western world (Hall 1996a, 1996b), the Arab Jews in Israel accepted the hegemonic image of identity and sameness and tried to imbue it with political meaning that was positive and assertive (see also Regev 1995, 2000; Regev and Seroussi 2004). My use of the discursive category of Arab Jews accepts the generalizing dimension of the hegemonic category in the first stage, but contests its political implications.

A similar phenomenon occurred in North America and Europe when the identity category of "blackness" was applied to blacks from different ethnic groups. It acted as an umbrella concept that gave rise to the assertive identity experience that Paul Gilroy (1993) terms "the Black Atlantic," and with it to the possibility of joint struggle by blacks as blacks. Similarly, the category of "queer" began as a pejorative in reference to gays and lesbians but ultimately acquired an implication of self-empowerment. This occurred even though queer theory does not believe in gender-based preferential identity or in a limited number of gender categories between which one can move (Butler 1991).

The first stage in identity politics is therefore to accept the hegemonic definition and reverse its substantive meaning. Research practice shows that in the second stage of identity politics, researchers begin to dismantle the essentialist definition and conduct separate critical analyses for separate identity groups. In this stage, an attempt is made to articulate a variety of definitions through which it is possible to dismantle the essentialist definition, based on the insight that identity is not a closed category (Butler, Laclau, and Žižek 2000). Recently, for example, "African American" became a term for debate in the United States. During the twentieth century, many black Americans shifted from "colored" to "Negro" to "black," and then to "African American." However, with the demographic shift due to immigration from sub-Saharan Africa and the Caribbean, the use of the term has diverged into additional subcategories, such as "Nigerian American" and "Jamaican American."[10] A similar process occurs in the Israeli context and in this book as well.

The archival materials on which the analysis is based refer primarily to the Jews of Iraq, beginning in 1941, and to some extent to Iranian and Yemenite Jews. Plainly, the focus on Iraqi Jewry is closely bound up with my personal biography. However, in light of the fact that the dominant conception in the hegemonic discourse adds the Jews of Iraq to the identity category of Mizrahim and tends not to distinguish between them and Jews of Moroccan or Yemenite origin, for example (and also in light of the fact that this generalization is often accepted among Jews from Iraq themselves), I consider it legitimate to use the Iraqi example as a tentative case study for the encounter between the Zionist movement and all the Arab Jews.

At the same time, it is clear that this study does not constitute a representative work encompassing all the Arab Jews. The necessity for the different points of view stems precisely from the dialectical character of the use of the category of Mizrahiness. That dialectic is manifested by being, on the one hand, a "true" category as used by various agents, establishments (e.g., the state and its branches, the media, and academe), and critical agents (e.g., protest groups); yet, on the other hand, it is plain that its use is an invention resulting from defining historical circumstances. Deconstructing those circumstances necessitates the adoption of additional points of view. It is more than likely that an analysis based on the Jews of Yemen or of Morocco instead of Iraqi Jewry would cite a different terminus a quo and very possibly arrive at conclusions that differ from mine. Such an approach invites additional alternative Mizrahi points of view. These might demonstrate that Mizrahiness is not the opposite of Ashkenaziness but is a category with broad margins, whose boundaries have to be clarified within its historical and discursive context. These theoretical questions are extensively discussed throughout the book.

Finally, I would note that the complex connections between nationalism, religion, and ethnicity, as they emerge in this book, constitute one analysis, or one show, in a complex pageant that is rich in additional variables. Because of the complexity of the critical project with which this book deals, together with the nature of the historical encounters that are its focus, the gender perspective is not included as one of the modes of looking at Zionist and

Mizrahi history.¹¹ That perspective can turn the nationalism-religion-ethnicity triangle into a quadrangle and give rise to an additional observation point that challenges the Zionist narrative and exposes further relationships within it—among concepts of gender, nationalism, ethnicity, and religion—as well as problematizing each concept separately. Examples of the fascinating questions that I was unable to address in this book would include an analysis of the connection between concepts of gender in Zionism and the method by which Zionism approached and constructed the Jews in the Arab countries; the connection between gender otherness (of women in the Zionist project) and ethnic otherness (of the Arab Jews within the project); the national-ethnic-religious place to which the Zionist project assigned Arab Jewish women (see Melamed 2002); and the way in which these women themselves perceived their ethnicity (see Khazzoom 2002), religiosity, and nationality in relation to Mizrahi men, on the one hand, and the national project, on the other. A study of these and other questions could help dismantle the monolithic character of the national discourse, generate new starting points, and add new precincts of memory and alternatives to the Zionist narrative.

NOTES

1. I am indebted to Meir Wigoder (2001) for the title "History Begins at Home."
2. Ironically, Arendt was otherwise critical of European imperialism (see, e.g., Arendt 1951).
3. I am not suggesting that the concept of "denial" reflects the totality of the aspects (discursive and political) of the Mizrahi identity. In the course of the book, I shall propose different interpretations for modes of identity construction and contest the theoretical use of the term "denial." I shall show that speech about Mizrahiness is not necessarily denied but undergoes a process of depoliticization by the discussion being shifted into other arenas. In other words, I shall show that Mizrahi identity can appear openly and referentially in one layer of discourse, yet at the same time disappear from its other layers. Moreover, because Mizrahi identity is organized as a hybrid category and is amenable to multifaceted articulation, it can also be supervised and manufactured in "acceptable" tracks of Mizrahiness ("Mizrahiness as folklore" is legitimate and acceptable) and in tracks that are not acceptable (such as those that create continuity between Mizrahiness and Arabness). The result will be to show that although "denial" reflects on the experience of Mizrahim in the context of identity politics, the concept of "denial" is overly reductive in the theoretical context. Theoretically, I shall point to a dual process in which construction and denial appear simultaneously. This goes along the lines that Latour (1993) suggests in his analysis of modernity. He points to the manner by which a hybrid reality is being constructed into distinct and mutually exclusive categories. Denial corresponds to what Latour (1993) would call "work of purification." For example, Jewish religious identity is being used in the construction of nationalism, but at the same time, its relevance is rejected in the Jewish national consciousness (i.e., nationalism and religion are seen as separate entities). My use of it at this stage of the discussion arises from the fact that it is a "key" concept in the phenomenology of Mizrahi identity politics, on which I would like to reflect in a critical manner.

4. See esp. Shohat 188 and also her "Reflections by an Arab Jew," http://www.bintjbeil.com/E/occupation/arab_jew.html .

5. See, e.g., Meir-Glitzenstein 2002, who discusses Iraqi immigrants in Israel in the 1950s; Rozin 2002. To be sure, there are also plenty of studies of Arab Jews in their home countries. These studies, however, are seen to belong to Jewish history, and as such they hardly make the necessary link between their historical origin and their position in Israeli society. Mostly, those studies subscribe to methodological Zionism and its theoretical assumptions. For example, a common assumption is the teleology of immigration. They assume that the status of the Arab Jews (they never use the term "Arab Jews," since it is not accepted in the Zionist lexicon) in those countries is ephemeral, a stage prior to an inevitable immigration to Israel.

6. The triangle image is for heuristic purposes. One can extend this framework by using additional categories. A natural candidate is "gender"; see further Hazan 2001.

7. The symbiosis between the categories is never a simple one, but is based on a series of contingencies where each of these categories exerts a veto right over the whole. Theoretically, we can refer to Althusser's concept of interpellation (or hailing), which suggests that ideology "recruits" individuals and "transforms" them into subjects of a particular order. In our case, I would argue, transformation of the individual (or the group) into a "Zionist subject" is based on the interrelationships between the three categories. For example, in order to be included in the "project," the religious needs to assume a national identity, the secular to subscribe to political theology, and the Arab Jew to assume a religious and national identity by which he/she relinquishes Arab identity. Notwithstanding, this relinquishment is never definitive. Zionism asks the Arab Jews to relinquish their Arab identity, but this demand never fully satisfies. According to Althusser, interpellation is never fully or completely achieved, and it therefore generates a crisis and antagonism in the subject (Althusser [1969] 1971, 174).

8. The display of these categories as autonomous is based on the practice of "translation" and "purification" (Latour 1993), as is shown throughout the book. Thus, for example, Zionist thought is based on incessant hybridization of nationalism and religion, but at the same time, it is also based on the purification of these categories, so as to appear as two separate ontological and sociological zones.

9. For a discussion of the categories, see Ben-Dor 1999; Yanow 1999.

10. To be sure, the debate revolves around the question of who can claim to be called "African American"; some American-born blacks argue that the term applies only to the descendents of slaves brought to the United States, not to newcomers "who have not inherited the legacy of bondage, segregation and legal discrimination" (*New York Times*, August 29, 2004, 1, 20).

11. For fascinating analyses of gender, sexuality, and race in colonial context, see Stoler 1995, 1997.

REFERENCES

Althusser, Louis. [1969] 1971. "Ideology and Ideological State Apparatuses." In *Lenin and Philosophy and Other Essays*, 162-183. New York: Monthly Review Press.

Arendt, Hannah. 1951. *The Origins of Totalitarianism*. New York: Meridian Books.

Arendt, Hannah, and Karl Jaspers. 1992. *Hannah Arendt/Karl Jaspers Correspondence, 1926–1969*. Trans. Robert and Rita Kimber. Ed. Lotte Kohler and Hans Saner. New York: Harcourt Brace Jovanovich.

Beck, Ulrich. 1994. "The Reinvention of Politics: Towards a Theory of Reflexive Modernization." In *Reflexive Modernization*, ed. Ulrich Beck, Anthony Giddens, and Scott Lash. Palo Alto, Calif.: Stanford University Press.

Ben-Dor, Zvi. 1999. "The Amazing History of the Mizrahim." In *The Mizrahi Revolution*, ed. Inbal Perlson [in Hebrew]. Jerusalem: Center for Alternative Information.

Butler, Judith. 1991. "Contingent Foundations: Feminism and the Question of Postmodernism." *International Praxis* 2:150–165.

Butler, Judith, Ernesto Laclau, and Slavoj Žižek. 2000. *Contingency, Hegemony and Universality*. New York: Verso.

Cohen, Yinon, and Yitzchak Haberfeld. 1998. "Second Generation Jewish Immigrants in Israel: Have the Ethnic Gaps in Schooling and Earnings Declined?" *Ethnic and Racial Studies* 21: 507–528.

Deshen, Shlomo, and Moshe Shokeid, eds. 1984. *Jews of the Middle East: Anthropological Perspectives on Past and Present* [in Hebrew.] Tel Aviv: Schocken.

Dittgen, Herbert. 1997. "The American Debate about Immigration in the 1990s: A New Nationalism after the End of the Cold War?" *Stanford Humanities Review* 5 (2): 256–286.

Fallaci, Oriana. 1976. *Interview with History*. Boston: Houghton Mifflin.

Fanon, Frantz. 1952/1967. *Black Skin, White Masks*. New York: Grove Press.

Foucault, Michel. 1980. *Power/Knowledge: Selected Interviews and Other Writings ,1972–77*. Ed. Colin Gordon. New York: Pantheon Books.

Gilroy, Paul. 1993. *The Black Atlantic: Modernity and Double Consciousness*. Cambridge, Mass.: Harvard University Press.

Hacohen, Dvora. 1994. From *Fantasy to Reality: Ben-Gurion's Plan for Mass Immigration, 1942–1945* [in Hebrew]. Tel Aviv: Ministry of Defense.

———. 1998. *The Grain and the Millstone: The Settlement in the Negev in the First Decade of the State* [in Hebrew]. Tel Aviv: Am Oved.

Hall, Stuart. 1996a. "Who Needs 'Identity'?" In *Questions of Cultural Identities*, ed. Stuart Hall and Paul Du Gay. London: Sage Publications.

———.1996b. "New Ethnicities." In *Stuart Hall: Critical Dialogs in Cultural Studies*, ed. David Morley and Kuan-Hsing Chen, 441–449. London: Routledge.

Hazan, Haim. 2oom. *Simulated Dreams: Israeli Youth and Virtual Zionism*. New York: Berghahn Books.

Khazzoom, Aziza. 1998. "The Origins of Ethnic Inequality Among Jews in Israel." Ph.D. diss., Department of Sociology, University of California, Berkeley.

———. 2002. "Becoming a Minority, Examining Gender: Jewish Iraqi Women in the 1950s in Israel." In *Mizrahim Be Israel*, ed. Hannan Hever, Yehouda Shenhav, and Pnina Mutzaphi-Haler [in Hebrew]. Tel Aviv. Hakibbutz Hameuchad and the Van Leer Jerusalem Institute.

———. 2003. "The Great Chain of Orientalism: Jewish Identity, Stigma Management, and Ethnic Exclusion in Israel." *American Sociological Review* 68: 481–511.

———. 2005. "Did the Israeli State Engineer Segregation? On the Placement of Jewish Immigrants in Development Towns in the 1950s." *Social Forces* 84 (1): 115–134.

Latour, Bruno. 1987. *Science in Action: How to Follow Scientists and Engineers through Society*. Cambridge, Mass.: Harvard University Press.

———.1993. *We Have Never Been Modern*. Cambridge, Mass.: Harvard University Press.

———. 2005. *Reassembling the Social*. Oxford: Oxford University Press.

Meir, Yosef. 1973. *Beyond the Desert: Underground Activities in Iraq* [in Hebrew].Tel Aviv: Ma'arakhot.

———. 1983. *Zionist Movement and the Jews of Yemen* [in Hebrew]. Tel Aviv: Afikim.

———.1989. *Social and Cultural Development of the Jews of Iraq* [in Hebrew]. Tel Aviv: Naharayim Center for the Diffusion of Iraqi Jewish Culture.
Meir-Glitzenstein, Esther. 1997. "The Riddle of the Mass Immigration from Iraq: Causes, Circumstances and Consequences" [in Hebrew]. *Pe'amim* 71:25–53.
———. 2001. "From Eastern Europe to the Middle East: The Reversal in Zionist Policy vis-à-vis the Jews of Islamic Countries." *Journal of Israeli History* 20 (1): 24–48.
———. 2002. "Our Dowry: Identity and Memory among Iraqi Immigrants in Israel." *Middle Eastern Studies* 38:165–186.
Memmi, Albert. 1975. "What Is an Arab Jew?" In *Jews and Arabs*, ed. Albert Memmi, 19–29. Trans. Eleanor Levieux. Chicago: J. Philip O'Hara.
Morris, Benny. 1987. *The Birth of the Palestinian Refugee Problem, 1947–1949*. Cambridge: Cambridge University Press.
Ofer, Dalia, ed. 1996. *Between Veterans and Immigrants, 1948–1951* [in Hebrew]. Jerusalem: Ben-Zvi Institute.
Offe, Claus. "New Social Movements: Challenging the Boundaries of Institutional Politics." *Social Research* 52:4 (1985): 817–868.
Regev, Motti. 1995. "Present Absentee: Arab Music in Israeli Culture." *Public Culture* 7:433–445.
———. 2000. "To Have a Culture of Your Own: On Israeliness and Its Variants." *Ethnic and Racial Studies* 23:223–247.
Regev, Moth, and Edwin Seroussi. 2004. *Popular Music and National Culture in Israel*. Berkeley: University of California Press.
Rozin, Orit. 2002. "Hygiene and Parenthood of Immigrants from Islamic Countries" [in Hebrew]. *Iyunim Be Tkumat Israel* 12:195–238.
Shafir, Gershon. 1989. *Land, Labor and the Origins of the Israeli-Palestinian Conflict, 1882–1914* (Cambridge: Cambridge University Press).
———. 1996. *Land, Labor and the Origins of the Israeli-Palestinian Conflict, 1882–1914*. (Berkeley: University of California Press).
Shohat, Ella. 1988. "Sephardim in Israel: Zionism from the Standpoint of Its Jewish Victims." *Social Text* 7: 1–36.
———. 1989. *Israeli Cinema: East/West and the Politics of Representation*. Austin: University of Texas Press.
———. 1997a. "Columbus, Palestine and Arab Jews: Toward a Relational Approach to Community Identity." In *Cultural Identity and the Gravity of History: Reflections on the Work of Edward Said*, ed. B. Parry et al., 88–105. New York: Lawrence & Wishart.
———. 1997b. "The Narrative of the Nation and the Discourse of Modernization: The Case of the Mizrahim." *Critique* 10:3–18.
———. 1999. "The Invention of the Mizrahim." *Journal of Palestine Studies* 1:5–20.
———. 2001. *Forbidden Memories* [in Hebrew]. Tel Aviv: Bimat Kedem.
Stoler, Laura Ann. 1995. *Race and the Education of Desire*. Durham, N.C.: Duke University Press.
———. 1997. "Making Empire Respectable: The Politics of Race and Sexual Morality in Twentieth-Century Colonial Cultures." In *Dangerous Liaisons: Gender, Nation, and Postcolonial Perspective*, ed. Ann McClintock, Aamir Mufti, and Ella Shohat, 344–373. Minneapolis: University of Minnesota Press.
Wigoder, Meir. 2001. "History Begins at Home: Photography and Memory in the Writings of Siefgried Kracauer and Roland Barthes." *History and Memory* 13:9–59.
Yanow, Dvora. 1999. "From What *Edah* Are You? Israeli and American Meanings of Race-Ethnicity' in Social Policy Practice." *Israel Affairs* 5 (2): 183–199.

15

A Mizrahi Call for a More Democratic Israel

PNINA MOTZAFI-HALLER

Last night, my son Yoni asked me to help him with his homework. The subject of his studies is *Moshavot Rishonot* (First Agricultural Settlements). When I first heard that this subject would be a distinct part of the class curriculum, to be taught along with Math or Hebrew Lit, I asked the school mistress, a woman of Yemeni origin, if there would also be a topic of studies called *Ayarot Pituah Rishonot* (First Development Towns). This was my way of commenting about a particular kind of historiography that privileges Ashkenazi pioneers over the Mizrahi immigrant settlers of peripheral towns (known as Ayarot Pituah). She said something playful and we never discussed the issue again.

The storyline of *Moshavot Rishonot*, the book Yoni brought home, is built around three imaginary families and traces in thirty-three detailed chapters their struggles to survive as they founded Petach Tikva, Rishon LeZion, and other *First Moshavot*. It is an endearing story that invites the young reader to identify with its two key protagonists: Miraleh, a nine-and-a-half-year-old girl who emigrated with her parents from Hungary, and her best friend Sarahleh, who came from Russia. Into the evolving plot enters a single young Halutz who is the romantic address for both Miraleh and Sarahleh. We are told that he came to Israel from Romania. It was not until chapter 22 that I finally found the only Yemeni person in this Zionist story—the Little Yemeni Boy. He enters the story through Miraleh's eyes, who describes him as "a small boy, darker and thinner than all the kids I have ever known. One could see he ate like a little bird. He wore a long, gray dress called *galabiya*. He had lots of small, black very dense curls and two *peot* on his cheeks. He spoke a strange language, a bit Arabic, a bit Hebrew: something unclear."

Reprinted, by permission, from *Tikkun: A Bimonthly Interfaith Critique of Politics, Culture and Society* 13, no. 2 (1988): 50–52.

Lest we have any doubt, our Miraleh makes it clear this boy is different: *"I must say, any way I looked at him he was different from any child I had ever known."* Miraleh, however, proves much more tolerant than her mother and the other people in the neighborhood who do not buy the Little Yemenite's cheese because they think he is Arab. She believes he is Jewish and is the only one who listens to his story. He tells her he and his family (all twenty of them) live in a cave, that they walked all the way from Yemen to Jerusalem, that he is the only hope for any income for his family, and so forth. She heroically convinces her mother and the other women to buy the little boy's cheese.

The representation of the Yemenites within this single chapter is not complete without the obligatory photographs of a Yemenite bride, the embroidery of Yemenite women's pants, and other similar pictures that document the "folklore" of Yemenite Jews. There is also a section directed to the "interested student" who might want to try a recipe of something called "Yemeni food," as well as instructions on how to perform Yemeni dance steps. The chapter concludes by asking student readers who are children of Moshavot if Yemenite Jews have settled in YOUR *moshava*? If so, how many years ago did THEY come to YOUR *moshava* and what work did THEY perform?

I have presented this textbook and the way it represents the Israeli "Self" and the Yemeni "Other" at some length because I want to illustrate how the exclusion of Mizrahi Jews is carried out in Israel today, fifty years after the establishment of the Zionist state. The Yemeni boy remains nameless. He represents a category of people whose entry into the main narrative is through their exotic food, customs, and dance steps. His poverty, unlike that of Hungarian, Russian, and Romanian Jewish immigrants, is not heroic. He is not included as a subject, as a person who is part of the historical doing of the time. He is forever the "Other" who came to do a particular kind of work in Our *Moshava*.

I could give many more examples of the exclusion of Mizrahim, Yemenites as well as other Jews of Arab Lands, from the historical narrative that defines the Israeli national Self. Recently, I saw a photograph of a man holding a few pages of a book. The caption reads "nine out of four hundred." It is a powerful visual representation of the limited space (nine pages) accorded to Mizrahi history within the four-hundred-page Jewish history textbook used by Israeli schools today. Like the story of the Little Yemenite Boy, this photo reminds us of the intrinsically Euro-centered and Orientalist view of the non-Ashkenazi Jew as the "Other" whose only salvation comes when he is distinguished from the despised Arab due to his *strange* yet acceptable Jewishness.

This practice, whereby a ruling group writes a *national history* from its narrow particular perspective in ways that exclude the role played by other groups in the historical process, is not unique to Israeli Zionist historiography. As an anthropologist, I have analyzed and written about similar processes in Africa and elsewhere. Yet, as a Mizrahi intellectual, I have been deeply affected by the dominant Zionist historiography that distorts, disfigures, and destroys the historical agency of Mizrahim. What my son and other children learn through such stories only reaffirms the message that being a Mizrahi means you are associated with processes in Africa and elsewhere. Yet, as a Mizrahi intellectual, I have been deeply affected by the dominant Zionist historiography that distorts, disfigures, and destroys the historical agency of Mizrahim. What my son and other children learn through such stories only reaffirms the message that being a Mizrahi means you are associated with lack of progress, dark traditionalism, ignorance. The unavoidable outcome is self-contempt and lack of dignity. The only way to become Israeli is to erase any trace of that identity.

Despite the Zionists' best efforts to create a homogeneous Israeli society, fifty years after independence Israeli society is more fragmented than ever. The emergence of a clear, assertive, and unapologetic Mizrahi voice over the last decade is part of such a process of fragmentation. I would like to argue here that such fragmentation is positive, is healing rather than destructive, and that it signals the hope for a more democratic future for Israel in a post-zionist era.

But let me return to mainstream Zionist historiography and the very real damage it has caused, not only to Mizrahim in Israel but to the kind of society it justifies. Zionist historiography distorts, disfigures, and destroys the past of the Mizrahim. While the brave New Historians have begun over the past few years to write a more balanced historiography that looks at the Palestinian perspective in the Zionist saga, no coherent, critical, Mizrahi-centered narrative has been developed yet in Israel.

Over the past few years, I have spent many months examining archival material from the 1950s with an eye for the missing story, the silenced story of the Mizrahi immigrants about their experiences during the first critical years of Israeli statehood. My reading led me to the amazing testimony of Eliyahu Elyashar, a leader of the Sephardim who had been living in Palestine generations before the arrival of the first Zionist settlers. In two voluminous texts, *To Live with Jews* and his recent, posthumous *To Live with Palestinians*, Elyashar depicts in great detail the struggle for power among the various Jewish segments of the population in the pre state era, and their shifting relationships with resident Palestinians, and with the Turkish, and later the British colonialists. Elyashar's historical trajectory brings to light other historical scenarios that the Zionists ruled out. For example, he speaks about attempts to establish coexistence with Arab neighbors, and to fight against the demonization of the Arab by the Eastern European Zionists. But Elyashar's books are not part of the school curriculum, nor have I seen a serious analytical effort to integrate his records into a fuller, more complete historical narrative.

My historical exploration did not convince me, on the one hand, that Sephardim in the pre-state era, or that Mizrahim in the early years of statehood, were all noble, good people, nor, on the other hand, that they were the hapless victims of Ashkenazi oppression. Instead, my work has enabled me to see beyond the distortions and exclusions built into the dominant, official Zionist historiography and to realize that the actual historical outcome—the rise to hegemony of the secular socialist Zionists led by East European Jews—was not inevitable, nor was it the only force that had shaped the emerging society.

One of my exhilarating discoveries was the realization that Mizrahis, a group generally represented as traditionalists who could not grasp the essence of Western democracy, had, in fact, a clear and powerful vision of equality. Such a discovery clearly has rehabilitative value. It allows Mizrahim to see that there is nothing to be ashamed of in their recent past. It restores a sense of dignity and pride. But beyond that, such historical reconstruction presents a genuine critique of the incoherence of Euro-centered Zionism's idea of a democratic state as a state that grants civil rights only to particular sectors of the population and not to others. As the title of the well-known Mizrahi writer Sammi Michael's recent book suggests, such historiography illustrates that the rhetoric of socialist equality was empty and that there have always been in the Jewish state *Equal and More Equal* people.

I have argued that dominant Israeli claims to universalism must be exposed, and that hegemonic Zionist narratives must be understood for what they are—the views of a particular social group of Eastern European, secular Zionists with an increasingly narrowing social base in today's Israel. That is, the group that succeeded in controlling the state is as particularistic, as *ethnic*, as the Mizrahi collective identity they worked so hard to *absorb*—that is, to eliminate. Mizrahiyut is no more exotic than East European Zionism. It is not an unchanged culture common to a population of people whose father was born in Asia-Africa (as the increasingly more convoluted definitions of the Central Bureau of Statistics will have us believe). It is an identity that has become a significant force in Israeli social reality because it was constituted within specific relations of power. Thus, Mizrahiyut is clearly an Israeli social phenomena and it is defined within a social and political reality that defines other, similarly partial identities.

The conclusion of this analysis is inevitable: the argument that the ruling group can represent all groups (what I have called its *claims to universality*, or what popular discourse calls the *melting pot*) must be put aside because it conceals a thinly disguised version of a totalitarian dream. It is more and more apparent in contemporary Israel that the social base of these narrow elites is becoming increasingly more limited. In fact, the heightened social and political struggles in Israel in the 1990s suggest that the claims to knowledge and historical truth by the dominant secular Zionist sectors have been under growing attack. Contemporary, assertive Mizrahi voices (note the plural form) are participating in a process of *breaking the center*, a process that involves other ethnic categories (Soviet Jews, Palestinian citizens of the state) and groups defined along gender and religious lines. And here is my second conclusion:

the only way of reaching a reconciled society in Israel is to accept the multiple claims by the various groups that make up contemporary Israeli society.

The Mizrahi voice enters into the recent proliferation of groups at two critical points: in the religious agenda of Shas, and in the secular, leftist social agenda of Keshet (Hakeshet Hademocratit Hamizrahit). These two explicitly Mizrahi-centered movements are radically different in nature and in their visions of a future Israeli society. A political party that swept ten Knesset seats only to join the Likud coalition, Shas draws on mostly lower-class Mizrahi voters and boasts an impressive grassroots Mizrahi religious alternative educational system that stretches from daycare centers to Yeshivas. Keshet is a fledgling two-year-old movement of intellectuals with a stated claim of staying out of party politics. Most observers place Keshet and Shas on the two extreme ends of the transforming Israeli scene.

Yet, in their very different ways, these two contemporary movements pose the same radical challenge to existing definitions of Israeli-hood and Zionist ideology. In their assertive claims to Mizrahi identity as a viable base for Israeli-hood, in their refusal to accept Mizrahi identity as a deformed, lacking version of an Ashkenazi, Euro-centered model of the Israeli self, these two movements expose the claims to universalism by the ruling elite as essentially particularistic and Orientalist. Such Eurocentric definitions have bred cultural paternalism and inequality among Jews, and a cycle of wars with Palestinians and Arab neighbors. Both Shas and Keshet defy the hegemonic definition of Mizrahiyut as an identity that must be left out, erased, in order to enter the Israeli collective.

Shas' defiance takes the avenue of reclaiming the religious content of Mizrahi life. For Shas, Jewish identity is an ontological identity that justifies their right to live and to act in a Jewish state. Keshet fights for a social agenda of equality that includes not only Mizrahim and their civic rights (Keshet currently is campaigning for the Mizrahi rights to state lands now sold by kibbutzim and for an equal share of Mizrahi cultural creation in state funds, for example), but also the equal rights of women and Palestinians. Keshet argues that Mizrahim, as well as women, Palestinians, and other oppressed groups, have an inalienable right to have access to good schools, to employment, and to participate in the public space of society. In its most fundamental thesis, Keshet defends the right to difference as a universal right, and sees itself as the real (and only) left in contemporary Israel. Its struggle is not to gain power, but to work against the exclusion of other groups from the sharing of power and resources.

The way to a postzionist society must begin not with the cancellation of all differences (as the melting pot ideology has it), but rather with the acknowledgment of distinctions. Existing Ashkenazi-Zionist ideals and institutions have in this sense to be deconstructed, because they are based on unexamined assumptions that have proven destructive and oppressive. Further, the democratic process in Israel can be considerably deepened and expanded if it is made accountable to the demands of those sections of the populations—Mizrahim, women, Palestinians—who traditionally have been excluded from it. To that end, new assertive Mizrahi voices are joining the increasingly assertive voices of feminists and Palestinians in a multifaceted struggle to expand democratic practices.

This leaves us, however, with an apparent, perhaps irresolvable paradox. The Mizrahi agenda advanced by both Shas and Keshet is one of social reform, not of revolution. However, while struggling through legislative reforms to change the present Israeli institutional setting, both movements also assert that these very institutions and settings are rooted in the cultural and political values of the dominant Ashkenazi, male, Euro-centered segments of society. Especially for Keshet, the inherent contradiction is always there: do we accept government grants for an alternative school that advocates Mizrahi-centered curriculum, or do we reject the system that dictates culturally biased tests as the entry ticket for higher education? The simultaneous acceptance of the system in an effort to reform it from within while at the same time rejecting its foundations condemns Keshet (much more than Shas) to ambiguous, peripheral relations with the existing establishment. The outcome has had paralyzing political effects.

Is it possible to resolve this paradox? I think it is not. But the absence of a solution is the very precondition for a really democratic Israel. The articulation of a vision of equality by minority groups, by feminists, and by oppressed segments of the population should inform concrete, daily struggles. That is what makes democratic interaction possible.

Gender and Sexuality:
Women, Gays, and Lesbians

16

Body and Territory

Women in Israeli Cinema

ORLY LUBIN

Jacky is a drug dealer trying to move up in life: trying to progress from dealing minor, "soft" drugs (grass) to "the real thing," hard-core, big-money "heavy stuff" (heroin). A request from a client, a Kibbutz member catering for a volunteer to the Kibbutz, serves as the trigger. The only problem is, where to get the stuff: Would the regular dealers welcome the newcomer into their midst, or would they guard their territory? Thus, the struggle over territory, a constant component in commercial life, becomes the backbone of the narrative, as is often the case when illegal commerce (drugs, sex, weapons) is concerned. In *Jacky*, Rachel Esterkin's 1990 short film (written with Shemi Zarchin), which takes place in a development town at the outskirts of Kibbutz territory, or possibly in a neighborhood on the outskirts of bourgeois Ashkenazi city territory, Jacky tries to carve out a territorial niche within the province of drug commerce.

It is here, on the margins—where the fields of socialist Zionism and Ashkenazi hegemonic Zionism end and the "Other" Israel begins, the Israel of Arab Jews, Jews of North African descent, the Mizrahi Jews—that the space of the ethnic "home," the location of the excluded, is situated. The margins can supply such a space, a space for the creation of Otherness as accepted, a "normative" center, since they, the margins, are located far from the centralized gaze of the monitoring, policing hegemony. The margins are where ethnicity can find a home, can create a home, within which it will not be marked as "ethnic otherness," but will claim for itself the status of the putatively "non-marked" or "nongendered"—a status normally reserved for the white, Ashkenazi male, who supposedly constitutes the all-encompassing "universal," marked neither by ethnicity nor by gender. In the margins, where there is no

Reprinted, by permission of Indiana University Press, from Orly Lubin, "Body and Territory: Women in Israeli Cinema," *Israel Studies* 4, no. 1 (1999): 175–187.

watching eye to constitute morality,[1] where people are not visible to the gaze of hegemony, where they are outside the frame within which morality happens as the by-product of the upper-class gaze, there otherness can construct itself by itself. It is the gaze of the norm, of the normative hegemony, which constitutes and structures the subject and the community as moral, and as ethnically marked; it is away from the normative gaze that Otherness can construct life on its own terms.

Thus, for example, the films of Moshe Mizrahi—*The House on Shlush Street* (1973), *I Love You, Rosa* (1972), *Abu El-Banaat* (1973), or *Love in the Skies* (1986)—create a space for Mizrahi ethnicity that avoids all relations with Ashkenazi life. In them, the protagonists, all Mizrahi, live their individual and communal lives in a separate sphere, unrelated to Ashkenazi hegemony, which either does not appear on screen at all, or is there only as a marker of power relations between the two spheres. The protagonists conduct their lives in their languages (Ladino, Arabic, French, and Hebrew), eat traditional, ethnically marked food, and enjoy cultural manifestations that are marked "folklore" (legends, proverbs, fables) and thus are considered inferior by conventional agents of hegemony.

But most importantly—they do not subordinate their lives and the temporal order of their lives to national history. Rather, they ignore national events, or participate only to support their material needs, but not as ideologically committed subjects. They run their private, familial lives parallel to—and not in accordance with, against, or as critique of—the national hegemonic Ashkenazi historical narrative. Had they been related in any way to that story, whether as critics or as adherents, their lives would become derivative of the Ashkenazi normative narrative. By disconnecting from the narrative altogether, by creating a temporal axis and cultural commitments that are separated from the authorial, "exclusive" historical narrative and national commitments, their lives have the representational appearance of independence and may be termed nonderivative. Hence, "ethnicity" creates itself, for itself: in Mizrahi films, power relations with the Ashkenazi hegemony are clear and visible but do not subordinate the "ethnic other" to their dictate, whether through the hegemony of nationality or through that of culture.[2]

In the very same way, *Jacky* separates itself from hegemonic norms and narratives. Here, too, the narrative carries no national implications; the story concerns an individual who shows no interest in constructing nationality, in national events, or in participating in creating national history or culture, as is the normative conduct of protagonists of products of Hebrew and Israeli canonical culture. The protagonists' aspirations are totally material and private and bear no relevance to the national endeavor. Moreover, Ashkenazi subjects appear only in the guise of purchasers in commercial relations, thus foregrounding the power relations (Ashkenazim with the money, Mizrahim in need of money) which obtain here. This asymmetry also hints at a past romance between Jacky and a Kibbutz member, a failed relationship, of course—and one that is certainly insufficient grounds for the Mizrahi community to structure itself.

Ethnic territory is separated as well. As in the films of Moshe Mizrahi, and in films about the Ma'abarot (the small shanty towns built in the 1950s to house new immigrants), so in Jacky, territory is totally segregated. Despite the formal establishment claim found in government documents and propaganda pamphlets, that the Ma'abarot were built as "rings" in "a chain of settlements" since they were located at the borders to serve the interests of security and territorial expansion (thus portraying the Ma'abarot as part of the pioneering effort and assimilating them to the Halutzic ideological project), the films in question show how the Ma'abarot—and in *Jacky,* the development towns and peripheral neighborhoods that developed from the Ma'abarot—were actually secluded, isolated, and far from adequate for their stated task: the great *effort to assimilate* the newcomers (mostly Mizrahi) into the hegemonic (Ashkenazi) society and ideology.[3] *Jacky* is located entirely in one such closed neighborhood, with people coming from the outside only to purchase drugs, and with Jacky exiting for a short episode to Jaffa to get the heroin, an episode engulfed in fear, distress, escape from the police, and a quick return to the safety of the enclosed territory. In this secluded territory the hegemonic gaze does not underpin normative morality or judgment: the inhabitants structure their lives according to their own needs, and not those of the "other" ethnicity—the Ashkenazi one.

In *Jacky,* however, there is one further complication: Jacky is a woman. *Jacky* is the story of her attempt to create her own space, both as a professional career woman (an independent drug dealer) and as an independent woman not adhering to the dictates of societal norms. At this juncture of gender, ethnicity, and territory, the constitution of the subject comes sharply into focus.

Jacky is a young, single woman who lives in her own space (a small house characteristic of residences in development towns: a single room built of cheap materials, falling apart and almost leaning on other such "houses") in an undefined, unnamed settlement. The place's identification by the viewer is achieved through the visual signs of the social and financial status of its inhabitants, and even more so by their ethnic makeup. The structure and look of the space, the furnishings, the clothes, the occupations portrayed (Jacky's father owns a rundown, arak-serving coffeehouse, while her boyfriend is a drug dealer), as well as the stereotypical modes of behavior (her brother-in-law beating up her sister), all combine to create that which Igal Bursztyn describes as Israeli cinema's attempt at a visual language of realism: in this case, that of territory, of realistic site.[4] Jacky refuses to marry her boyfriend and "settle down," as everybody—the boyfriend, her sister, her neighbor—expect and urge her to do. She wants her freedom; even more so, she has her own terms—the boyfriend should study some profession, stop dealing drugs, and most important, let her go to work. Jacky's demands try to reverse two accepted patterns. The first is a true-to-life sociological fact: in a development town there is not much other than drug-dealing for the boyfriend to do, and as a Mizrahi who grew up in such a place, he did not get the kind of education and opportunities that would actually equip him for anything else. The second reversal concerns the stereotypical portrayal of woman as dependent on her husband for support.

For Jacky, too, dealing drugs is the most accessible and feasible way to make a living. As long as she sticks with soft drugs, it is accepted by her family and neighbors as one of her eccentricities, to be cured when she finally gets married. It is when she tries to move on to hard drugs that the community rejects her. At this point, she transgresses too many borders, not only of gender (acting as a man) but also of territory—both the territory of men and the actual territories allocated to certain dealers. When she tries to get the heroin, they all try to persuade her to hand the client over to her boyfriend or her brother-in-law; when she refuses and moves out of the familial territory into the wilderness of street drug-dealings, she is perceived as a messenger for the men in her family.[5] This, finally, brings about territorial fights, ending with her boyfriend not only leaving her but also being knifed. The short film ends with him being rushed to the hospital and with Jacky, all alone, moving around in an erotic dance in the empty café.

In her insistence on being, and remaining, financially independent—and even more so, in her attempt to become an independent, professional woman who is part of the professional community—Jacky does something very few women, perhaps only one before her, dared do in Israeli cinema: she constitutes her subjectivity via her participation in public life as a working, professional woman. Women in Israeli films have repeatedly been portrayed as housewives, as prostitutes, as related to soldiers (wives of, widows of, mothers of), or as having no occupation or no position in life. When they do work, it is always in a stereotypical female profession (nurse, teacher), or in a profession which has no bearing on the narrative. The center of the public sphere—that of community life and active, professional life—is reserved for the male protagonists. They are the ones to determine not only the narrative and the action on screen, but also the fate of the family and its relation to the community. In this way, the films genderize—or rather, develop in accordance with the genderization of—the Zionist ethos, in which professional life and community life are the most important components of the individual's daily materialization of ideology. Zionism privileges the working body over the sexual body; the public, communal sphere over the private, intimate sphere; the professional individual over the nonprofessional, *luft gesheft* [nonworking] moneymaker. But this opposition is also genderized: the center of the Zionist scene, that of professional, communal, working life, is totally occupied by men, whereas the periphery, that of private life, is all that is left for women.

Historically, Israeli cinema has not tried to change this strict division of labor between the genders. Women in Israeli movies rarely work, develop a career, or promote a nonstereotypically female profession. The very few female protagonists who have tried to create communal, professional life for themselves have failed. Jacky is a case in point. She tries to penetrate the commercial circle dominated by men, to transcend her function as merchandise and become a merchant herself—not the stereotypical female merchant selling sex, but a merchant selling merchandise circulating outside the borders of her own valuable property: her body. The outcome is, of course, that Jacky finds herself all alone, and the cause of disaster. She fails and loses her private, intimate, sexual life, her professional future, and her position and status in the community. Her way of life poses too strong a threat to the accepted separation of the spheres, in which the only valuable item a woman has to negotiate her terms with in the world is her body, her very private sphere. It is when this private sphere of the sexual body, privacy which Peter Brooks calls the most intimate privacy,[6] becomes public that a woman can become a merchant herself, entering market relations as she who sells that which is usually sold by other men: her own body. Trading her body for money or for any other item of market value (food, a job, familial shelter), she becomes an active participant in market relations, rather than an object of trade only. She then gains entrance into this very guarded public sphere of trade and commerce, of communal life and financial independence, of having control over one's own destiny—the public sphere of male domination.

Nevertheless, even as she becomes thus independent, the woman trading her body does not necessarily also become an active "desiring," as well as a desired, subject. Her entrance into the circle of market relations and commerce, while enriching her in terms of finance and public visibility, does not free her from her status of an object of desire. On the contrary—rather than being an object of desire in her private home, she becomes a public object of desire, like the female protagonist on the screen. She becomes a public object of desire when selling her body means prostituting her sex, or submitting its desire to the laws of the market. Jacky avoids such a price, such loss, as she chooses—the only female protagonist in Israeli cinema to do so—not to trade her body, her sex, and not even to settle for control over her sexual body only, but actually to participate in the public sphere trading merchandise which is not her own body.

Her failure then becomes unique. The only other woman in Israeli cinema who tries to constitute herself via her profession, Tikva, the protagonist of the third episode in the film *Tel-Aviv Stories* (Ayelet Menachmi and Nirit Yaron, script with Shemi Zarchin, 1992) fails, since, even when she succeeds, she cannot carry out her own ambitious, liberating plan and gives it up. After managing to create an alternative setup that will enable her long overdue divorce, she changes her mind and opts for the normative, hegemonic mode of conduct, which objectifies her, and in which she becomes the stereotypical woman: one who prefers revenge over freedom. Jacky's failure, on the other hand, is not so much her own, as society's failure—the result of society's inability to create a basis for the independence of Mizrahi women. Thus, *Jacky* is a critique of Israeli society on several scores: gender, ethnicity, class, and social structure. On one hand, the film follows the normative representation of women in Israeli cinema in that it, too, does not have the power to change the social structure within which men occupy the communal, professional center and women are pushed to the periphery. But on the other hand, in its failure to enable its protagonist to carry out her plan, it also offers harsh criticism of the social structure and cultural depictions that are the cause of exactly this crippling positioning of women. It is probably in place to stress the point that it is the only film in Israeli culture to do so: other cinematic texts have had to resort to different modes of subjectivization, not so much through criticism as through subversion. *Jacky*'s uniqueness, though, does not make this film a milestone, since it does not have precursors and other films have not, to date, followed in its footsteps. The attempt to shake the center, the domination of professional and communal life, and locating a woman in this center, remains one of a kind. Which only goes to show that the domination of the center by men is still so strong within the Zionist ethos that it cannot be challenged without having to pay too high a price. Subversion, then, is still the more available mode of representing women as self-constituting subjects in Israeli cinema. Subversion, and not change—not even up-front resistance; subversion is that which is practiced when overall change, or a revolution, is unavailable. Subverting hegemony thus becomes the principle way of exposing oppressive apparatuses, or of actually practicing some alternative kind of control even when under hegemonic oppression.

This type of subversion is present in *Jacky* as well. Even though it is a film dealing with the very exclusion of women from the center of communal, professional action, it is not willing to give up the very special mode of subversion developed in Israeli films to focus on female experience. Hence the ending of *Jacky*, which seems to many spectators superfluous—her erotic dance, which adds nothing to the story nor to her characterization—is, finally, a remnant of the specific kind of subversion found in films such as *Sharona Motek*, in *Tel-Aviv Stories*, and *A Thousand and One Wives* (Michal Bat Adam, 1989). In these films, since the woman cannot gain control over her public, professional life, she transfers the focus of control to the sexual body. She does not sell her sexuality to gain financial control over her life; rather, her control empowers her to practice this sexuality in her own way and with the partners she chooses. She becomes a desiring subject, rather than remaining the peripheral, inactive desired object. In these films, interested in representing female experience and in supplying their protagonists with modes of controlling their destiny in some manner—be it minor and futile but still some manner of control—the focus of subject constitution is transferred to constructing active desire.

Sexuality, marginalized in Zionist culture,[7] becomes an empty cultural space ready to house the marginalized: woman. Whereas the power of Zionist culture renders difficult any effort to position women as the center socially and professionally, through the very act of rendering the sexual body as Other and marginalizing it, Zionism has also provided women artists with an empty space in which to constitute a female subject.

In the case of films, the move to place the sexual body and its control at the center entails not only a thematic focus on the corporeal, but also the return of the gaze. The apparatus of the gaze, dominant in Hollywoodian movies, which reifies the female body and marginalizes women as Other, as passive desired objects, is now used, not in order to objectify woman as the object of male sexual voyeuristic gratification, but as means of female control. The corporeal takes center stage, not as male property and not as a means of commerce, but as actual matter that occupies actual space, and as the focus of desire and activity. Jacky, who is shown in the film to have practiced sexuality, controlled her sexual body, and gratified her desire, dances erotically in the film's final scene but to herself, for herself. There is no gaze other than that of the camera, but the camera serves also as the point of view of the above-mentioned critique of her exclusion to the margins as an Other. Hence, the camera's gaze in itself, since it is also a point of departure for criticism, is not an objectifying apparatus. The only control left for Jacky to practice is over her sexual body, and that she does: she externalizes this control in her slow movement, explicitly sexual but also explicitly her own.[8]

The final scene of the film leaves the spectator with no objectifying agency: s/he is left to decide whether to join the position of critique, offered by the lack of male gaze to watch (over) Jacky's sexual and moral conduct, or the position of the absent gaze. The cinematic apparatus, the camera, offers both positions: that of the hegemonic, patriarchal, Ashkenazi norm, criticizing Jacky and the other characters for lack of normative behavior, and that of critical leverage, suggesting to the viewer a means of subversion even as she is being oppressed. The camera, then, while assuming hegemonic norms when it does not let Jacky succeed, also teaches the female viewer, indeed any other viewer from the margins. It teaches all oppressed viewers how to negotiate these norms and how to create some measure of control—control, for instance over her sexualized body in a situation where it is not yet possible to change woman's positioning altogether. For the viewer, then, hegemonic norms are exposed both as powerful (causing Jacky's failure)—and as an apparatus—that is, a man-made means of oppression—rather than biological givens. Women are so positioned in society and culture as part of a normative, ideological apparatus and not because "that's the way they were born." Subversion, then, becomes a possibility: whereas it is useless to try to change positioning in the case of biological determination, it becomes possible when ideological apparatuses are exposed. Their very exposure makes it possible to undermine them.

The strength enabling such subversion arises here, and in many other cultural products, out of the stereotype, since the representation of woman solely as a sexual being is, of course, highly stereotypical. This strength is the result of appropriating stereotypical characterization as a starting point for self-constitution. Empowerment occurs when the name of the characteristic is internalized—but not its evaluation, and when the empty space thus created is colonized and adopted as subject-location. The space of the stereotype is thus an empty niche available for the marginalized, the oppressed, the excluded, and the repressed to occupy, to be there in her/his place and not in the place of (an)other as only its guardian.[9] The stereotype provides, then, a space for self-construction. When Jacky focuses on her sexual body, she does not strengthen the stereotype, but uses it as a site for herself: her body, not as the stereotypical focus of male gaze or sexual commerce, but as a corporeal, space-occupying, desiring active agent.

Jacky constitutes herself, finally, as a sexual and self-owned subject. The empty space of the stereotype is rendered concrete through the empty café, the public domain of patriarchy, and Jacky's failure (her lack of communal participation) is replaced by the exposure of apparatuses of oppression: the apparatus of economics and commerce, the market value of woman, or gender relations as commercial relations. Finally, territory becomes a major constituent of subject-construction and position-location: territory is that which marks the limits of professional conduct, the borders of community, the location of the ethnic, and the space of gender. The territory of the drug dealer marks the limits of Jacky's ability to act as an independent merchant; the territory of the development town marks the border of the assimilation of Arab Jews into Israeli Ashkenazi society; and the private territory marks the boundaries of female self-constitution. For Jacky, there is no transcending of boundaries, no crossing of borders, no breaking the limits; but within the territory she is able to occupy, the ethnic, gendered, and national subject is finally located as itself. Even though Jacky fails, and does not manage to break out, the space she occupies now becomes home to her own corporeal body and its cultural markers. Ethnic, gendered, and part of nationality on her own terms, Jacky is located on national territory and speaks the national language, but rejects its belief system and ideological norms—politics of identity as location politics. Territory becomes the site of struggle over identity and subjectivity.

The traditional Zionist-Palestinian struggle over national territory is replaced with a gendered, ethnic struggle over naming the territory. Jacky is not party to the national struggle: she is not a soldier, nor is she related to one, and fighting over land and territory to be claimed as "Israeli" is not part of her heritage. Rather, she is in the process of changing the function of each of the territories she occupies: the house, the "home," the settlement. Since all of them are feminized (the house and the home as the female's traditional domain, and the settlement as part of the feminization of the Mizrahi in Israeli culture),[10] claiming them as spaces of action, as the spaces of an active agent, would mean renaming them as "male" spaces. In *Jacky*, this means marking these territories as spaces for her action, she, the woman, acting differently. They are not marked as "male" since they are feminized and since Jacky does not "become" "a man." But they lose their mark as "female," since their femaleness is contaminated by Jacky's masculine name and profession, by her active rather than passive conduct, and by her appropriation of female stereotypes as locations of power. Hence, "house," "home," and "Mizrahi space" are marked, not by the dichotomous opposition of genders, which means genderizing the private and the public spheres, nor by the limitations placed over Mizrahi territorial expansion. "Territory" becomes a site of critique and is marked by the critical stance of the camera's point of view. National struggle over land, commercial struggle over street control, gender struggle over public and private spheres, and ethnic struggle over settlement expansion are replaced by the struggle over the limits of criticism, the limits of resistance, and the limits of change.

Jacky is not trying to gain control over any of those territorial markers. Rather, she is trying to constitute her own subjectivity at the juncture where they intersect. Her control over who she is will be gained as a result of their juxtaposition, which also means their mutual constitution. Thus, none is rendered exclusive nor is granted absolute authority; each territory, each territorial marker becomes only one option for subject-constitution, but never the only one, never the leading one. As a result of this collision between axes of subjectivity, ethnic oppression is exposed through gender oppression and vice versa; and the national repression of the Palestinian "other" is revealed through his absence from the ethnically marked settlement.

Territory is the site, not of struggle over actual land, but of the struggle over identity markers. The Palestinian-Israeli struggle over territory is the struggle of marking territory as national; Jacky's struggle over territory is virtual—she is not fighting for control over certain streets for drug dealing, nor is she looking for control over the "home" and "backyard" territory. Rather, she marks territory, not by controlling it, but by placing her corporeal body in it—in the café at the end, and en route as she looks for the drugs to buy. For her, the placing of her body, her material and sexual flesh-and-blood body, serves as marker, as a virtual marker, which does not end up with placing national flags in its stead nor in guarding the entrance door, but in the residues left behind by her body: scent, footsteps, acts. Thus, she both places her corporeal body in an actual space, and wins that space, not by remaining there, but by marking it, by naming it differently, by undermining the name it has. This she achieves by contaminating, in her dual presence as active (male) and stereotypically sexual (female), as independent (male) and unsuccessful (female), both male and female markers of house, settlement, and nation.

Territory becomes a site. "Site" is where subjectivity can be constituted. As in the films portraying the *Ma'abara,* and in Moshe Mizrahi's films, the enclosed territory—the development town, the *Ma'abara*, the backyard, the home—becomes the site of ethnic constitution. Through the feminization of the Mizrahi in Israeli culture and the location of the ethnic within the feminized domain (the home and the backyard), this site is marked not only as ethnic but also as genderized. It is there that the axes of nationality (Israeli), ethnicity (Arab Jew), and gender (woman) intersect and simultaneously constitute each other—and collide and collapse onto each other. The juncture of identity-axes, located at the backyard of the Mizrahi private home in Zion, is also the site of their mutual exposure as apparatuses of control and oppression. As such, this juncture is also the site of the constitution of alternative subjectivities of the kind that Jacky represents: a woman marked both corporeally and culturally, both as sexual and as independent, both as active and as critical, as resistant and subversive, but also bearing the mark of failure. Thus, Jacky is an aberrant subject, an ethnic Mizrahi who is nevertheless central, someone who in her self-marking also marks that which is usually not marked: the "universal" Ashkenazi. Jacky is both marginalized to the periphery—where she offers a critique of hegemonic morality as a nonhegemonic agent—and positions herself as central in her disregard of that hegemony. Finally, the territorial mark of nationality—which supposedly endowed development towns with the mark of Halutzic participation, and which excludes women from their public sphere to their private, underprivileged sphere—is replaced with the marking of the territory, and the control over it is the mark of weakness. Jacky, in her virtual territorial marking, locates her corporeal body at the center of the narrative: the men's control over territory, both on the streets and in the home (her brother-in-law beating up her sister), turns out to be insufficient and is not strong enough to exclude Jacky. "Territory" is conquered, rather, by her marking it and not by a man asserting his control over it. In naming her body her own, she will mark and name, through her body's presence, the sites she populates as she moves along as sites for her subject-constitution. Jacky realizes that conquering a street or a home will not lend her power; it is through her marking locations with the presence of her actual body that she changes their function and their names.

Jacky presents an option for Israeli woman on screen: to use the position of to-be-looked-at-ness[11] (the apparatus of the objectifying gaze) in order to undermine through it the price paid because of it: the loss of agency. In using her corporeal body as the marker of virtual territory she uses the stereotypical mark of female sexuality as a mode of subversion. The corporeal body is the agent of action, and the to-be-looked-at-ness—the marker of passivity and female stereotype—becomes an inflection of the mode of subversion practiced by women in Israeli cinema. By not adhering to the territorial markings of ethnicity, gender, and nationality, Jacky undermines the power of territory and replaces it by the power of the site, the virtual territory marked by the corporeal body, which creates the alternative gendered, ethnic, and national subject. Jacky, then, is a catalog of the possibilities and options of critical representation of woman's experience in national culture and society as they are manifested and actualized in Israeli cinema.

NOTES

1. Mary Poovey, "The Production of Abstract Space," in *Making Worlds: Gender, Metaphor, Materiality,* ed. Susan Hardy Aiken, Ann Brigham, Sallie A. Marston, and Penny Waterstone (Tucson, Ariz., 1998), 69–89, esp. 72–77.
2. For a reading of Mizrahi films, esp. *The House on Shlush Street* and *I Love You, Rosa,* see Orly Lubin, "Nationality, Ethnicity, and Women," *Cinemateque* 75 (September–October 1994): 16–19.
3. On the formal and cinematic representations of the *Ma'abarot,* see Orly Lubin, "From Periphery to the Center: The Subversion of the *Ma'abarot* Movies," *Zmanim* 39–40 (Winter 1991): 141–149.
4. Igal Bursztyn, "From 'The Little Coins' to 'The Master Version,'" in *Scripts 1,* ed. Rennen Schorr and Orly Lubin (Jerusalem: Jerusalem Film and Television School and Kinneret Publishing House, 1990), 5–24. See especially pages 22–24 on *Coordania,* by Dina Zvi-Riklis, in which Bursztyn describes the efforts made regarding the visual code of the *Ma'abara.*
5. On the impossibility of street independence, see Judith Butler's ingenious reading of the plaintiffs' discourse in the New Bedford gang rape case in her article "Contingent Foundations," in *Feminists Theorize the Political,* ed. Judith Butler and Joan W. Scott (New York and London, 1992), 3–21, esp. 12–13.
6. Peter Brooks, *Body Work: Objects of Desire on Modern Narrative* (Cambridge, Mass., 1993), esp. chap. 2, "Invasions of Privacy: The Body in the Novel," 28–53.
7. See, for example, David Biale, *Eros and the Jews: From Biblical Israel to Contemporary America* (New York, 1992).
8. For a longer discussion of women in Israeli cinema, see Orly Lubin, "Woman as Other in Israeli Cinema," in *The Other in Jewish Thought and History,* ed. Laurence J. Silverstein and Robert L. Cohn (New York and London, 1994), 305–325.
9. Luce Irigaray, *Speculum of the Other Woman,* trans. Gillian C. Gill (Ithaca, N.Y., 1985), 76.
10. On the feminization of the Mizrahi (Sephardi) Jew, and on the stereotyping of Mizrahi Jews, and especially on the relations between Mizrahi and Ashkenazi Jews, see Ella Shohat, *Israeli Cinema: East/West and the Politics of Representation* (Austin, Tex., 1989); and her "Sephardim in Israel: Zionism from the Standpoint of Its Jewish Victims," *Social Text* 19–20 (Fall 1988): 1–35.
11. Laura Mulvey, "Visual Pleasure and Narrative Cinema," *Screen* 16 (Autumn 1975): 6–18; see also, Mulvey, *Visual and Other Pleasures* (Bloomington and Indianapolis, 1989), 14–26; Constance Penley, ed., *Feminism and Film Theory* (London and New York, 1988), 57–68.

17

Introduction to *Beyond Flesh:* *Queer Masculinities and Nationalism in Israeli Cinema*

RAZ YOSEF

Beyond Flesh critically explores the complex and crucial role played by Israeli cinema in the construction of heterosexual masculinity, as well as its attempt to marginalize, sequester, discipline, and normalize queerness in Israeli national masculine identity. These issues are analyzed along the axes of cardinal historical and sociopolitical discourses of the Israeli society that have informed the representation of Israeli manhood: namely, the Zionist project, the military culture, the interethnic tension between Mizrahim (Sephardi/Oriental Jews) and Ashkenazim (Eastern European Jews) in Israel, the Jewish/Israeli-Arab/Palestinian conflict, and the emergence of Israeli lesbian and gay consciousness.

I shall argue that Israeli heterosexual masculinity and its seemingly unified collectivity cannot imagine itself apart from the conception of externalized, sexualized ethnic and racial "others" on whom it was founded and which it produced. Zionist phallic masculinity is constituted through the force of exclusion of the queer, the (homo)eroticized Mizrahi and the Palestinian male "others," a repudiation without which the national subject cannot emerge. The dominant subject is produced not by the refusal to identify with the sexualized "other," but rather through identification, a disavowed identification, with the abject "other." The process of incorporation through disavowal means that the "other" is structurally present within normative masculinity as a space of transgression and negation. In this sense, the "other" *internally* marks the dominant national masculinity, opening an epistemological gap in maleness itself that threatens to undo the national, sexual, and racial authority on which Israeli male heterosexual identity is based.

Reprinted by permission of Rutgers University Press, from Raz Yosef, *Beyond Flesh: Queer Masculinities and Nationalism in Israeli Cinema* (New Brunswick, N.J.: Rutgers University Press. 2004), 1–15. Copyright © 2004 by Raz Yosef.

Zionism was not only a political and ideological project, but also a sexual one, obsessed with Jewish masculinity and especially the Jewish male body. The political project of liberating the Jewish people and creating a nation like all other nations was intertwined with a longing for sexual redemption and normalization of the Jewish male body. In fin-de-siècle antisemitic scientific-medical discourse, the male Jew's body was associated with disease, madness, degeneracy, sexual perversity, and "femininity," as well as with homosexuality. This pathologization of Jewish male sexuality had also entered the writings of Jewish scientists and medical doctors, including Freud.

In this context, we should understand the desire of the Zionist movement to transform the very nature of European Jewish masculinity as it had existed in the Diaspora. Thinkers such as Theodor Herzl and Max Nordau were convinced that the invention of a physically stronger, healthier heterosexual "Jewry of Muscles" would not only overcome the stereotype of the Jewish male as a homosexual, but also would solve the economic, political, and national problems of the Jewish people. Unlike the passive, ugly, femme diasporic Jewish male, the new Zionist man would engage in manual labor, athletics, and war, becoming the colonialist-explorer in touch with the land and with his body. This notion of a new Jewish masculinity became the model for the militarized masculine Sabra—the native-born Israeli in *Eretz Yisrael* (the land of Israel).

Documentary and narrative Zionist cinema, designed to attract potential pioneers from Europe, as well as financial and political support, was an important tool in the creation of Jewish male heterosexual subjectivity. However, in this book the history of the Israeli cinema will not be examined as a documentation of new Hebrew masculinity versus "feminine" diasporic Jewish manhood. This kind of analysis runs the risk of reinforcing and reproducing the dichotomized categories of the imaginary homogenous and coherent national Zionist narrative. Moreover, it does not theorize the place from which the queer Jew can speak *within* the framework of the dominant Zionist discourse. The relationships between the new Jew and the queer Jew are examined not in terms of dichotomies, but rather in terms of ambivalence, displacement, and disidentification. The overriding premise here is that the queer Jew is not the "other" of the new Zionist "self," but rather a structural element of it.

At the same time, the "Zionist body Master Narrative" must be understood in terms of race and ethnicity. In her groundbreaking study on Israeli cinema, Ella Shohat critiqued the Orientalist and Eurocentric foundations of the Zionist movement that remained faithful to the ideological habits of the European colonial mind.[1] Shohat deconstructed the structural mechanisms of the Ashkenazi Zionist ideology that regarded Mizrahim and Palestinians through a prejudicial grid shaped by European culture. Examining the Zionist propaganda films, for example, she argued that the Ashkenazi pioneers embody the humanitarian and liberationist project of Zionism, carrying with them the same banner of a "universal," "civilizing mission" that European powers propagated during their surge into the "underdeveloped world." Shohat's insightful observations explain the relationships between the Zionist body politics and its colonial discourse of the Oriental body. A more complete analysis of the Zionist body Master Narrative, however, must consider the negative effects of Ashkenazi Zionist sexual politics, not only on the construction of Ashkenazi queers, but also on the (homo)sexual constructions of Palestinian and Mizrahi manliness.

Zionism's fantasy of a hypermasculine heterosexual Jewish male was intertwined with discourses on the breeding of children, body hygiene, and racial improvement. This fantasy was structured by Orientalist perspectives about the East, especially that of Eastern bodies, associated with lack of hygiene, plagues, disease, and sexual perversity. By assigning the Eastern population as objects of death and degeneration, Zionism created internal biologized enemies against which the Zionist society must defend itself. In the name of maintaining and securing life and the reproduction of the new Jewish "race," the Zionist society kept the right not only to discriminate and to oppress its enemies, the Palestinians, but also its citizens, the Mizrahim. Through the discourse of the new male Jew's sexuality, which was structurally linked to discourses on hygiene and racial/national survival, the Zionist society reinforced and legitimized its nationalism. Thus, Zionism produced a normalizing society through the discourse of sexuality and a kind of racism inscribed within it.

This book traces representations of masculinities from the first Zionist film pioneers' attempts to produce films in Palestine in the twenties and thirties, through the emergence of a national cinema after the establishment of the state of Israel in 1948. Its major focus is on the feature-film productions of the last five decades. Documentaries of the pre-state period, when feature filmmaking was limited, are also examined, as are those short films and television series that offer gay and lesbian cultural production. This book is not a chronological history of Israeli cinema, but rather an analysis of representations of the male body and sexuality in films that address major discourses on Israeli ideas of manhood: primarily, Zionist masculine ideology, as well as the Israeli military, tensions between Mizrahim and Ashkenazim, conflicts between Israelis and Palestinians, and the new queer culture. My approach to analysis of those texts is largely synchronic—namely, I move forward or backward to follow a comprehensive trajectory of an idea, to draw a trope, or to trace a discursive practice.

More specifically, the methodology of textual analysis used in this volume draws upon and reformulates recent developments in queer theory and postcolonial theory. Queer theory seems to lack any coherent methodology and its analysis draws upon a wide variety of theoretical positions (feminism, psychoanalysis, deconstruction, the work of Michel Foucault, or a mixture thereof) and their associated strategies and techniques. An attempt to summarize queer theory and to identify it as a homogeneous school of thought risks domesticating it and fixing it in ways that queer theory resists fixing itself. As Judith Butler puts it, "normalizing the queer would be after all, its sad finish."[2] As a theoretical model, it still encapsulates active and unresolved disputes among several scholars (such as Leo Bersani, Michael Warner, and David Halperin), and this book will not try to solve them, but rather attempt to add to the field's heterogeneity.[3]

As a working definition for this book, "queer theory" is understood as a form of analysis that systematically challenges any theoretical or political discursive practice of naturalness in sexuality. Historically in Western society, those practices naturalized heterosexuality and enforced heteronormativity. The term "queer" defines itself against the norm rather than against the heterosexual. Queer theory argues that the normative regimes inhabited and embodied by heterosexuals are ideological fictions rather than natural inevitabilities. Thus, in this context, heterosexuality is also queer.

This volume does not attempt to locate "positive" or "negative" images of queers in Israeli cinema, nor does it critique the fetishization, objectification, and stereotypical figuration of gays as a "misrepresentation" of preexisting queer experience. Neither will it critique the absence of queer subjects from cultural representation. Such an approach runs the risk of not only producing an essentialized queer subject and reinforcing a dichotomous codification of sexual differences that are inherent in the compulsory heterosexual Zionist culture, but also assumes that queer people and queerness are marginal or invisible. In fact, in most of the films that are explored, there are no ostensibly gay characters and, on the face of it, the films do not deal with homosexuality. In some of the films, the word "gay" is not even mentioned in any form or context—for example, in Zionist propaganda films. Instead, this book traces complexities of queer desire and identification and tries to explain the positioning of "femininity" within the articulation of male homoeroticism, as well as the construction of male heterosexuality through and against the specter of homoeroticism.

The Israeli dominant cultural articulation seeks to conceal the artificial and historically motivated character of heterosexual masculinity it brings into effect by naturalizing the work of representation. The forming of the normative Israeli national subject requires identification with the Zionist phantasm of sexuality, identification that takes place through a disavowal of the threatening spectacle of "feminine" maleness. As Butler states, any "refusal to identify with a given position [suggests] that on some level an identification has already taken place."[4] Butler poses this as a question: "What is the economic premise operating in the assumption that one identification is purchased at the expense of another? If heterosexual identification takes place not through the refusal to identify as homosexual but through an identification with an abject homosexuality that must, as it were, never show, then can we extrapolate that normative subject-positions more generally depend on and are articulated through a region of abjected identification?"

Zionist male heterosexuality is a function of a disavowed identification with an imaged queerness, upon which Israeli straightness never ceases to depend. Zionist homophobia is not only a fear of queerness, but also a disavowal of this dependence on male queers, of the *structurating necessity* of this negation. That is, queerness is an essential structural element in the construction of Zionism—a structural element that must be disavowed. This abjected identification threatens to destabilize and unveil the self-establishing structural presumptions of the heterosexual male subject. This study exposes how the Israeli heterosexual subject's fear of and desire for queer masculinity undo the fixity of his identity, make him feel a sense of fluidity, estranged from himself, make him feel a painful need for "otherness." *Beyond Flesh* also investigates and historicizes the emergence of Israeli gay cultural products, such as the films of Amos Guttman and Eytan Fox. It analyzes how and in what ways these queer filmmakers in their cultural texts challenge and construct an alternative to the dominant Zionist body Master Narrative, or sometimes reconfirm and reinforce it.

While queer theory has questioned the seemingly "natural" status of epistemological assumptions of sex, it nevertheless has not been fully responsive to questions of race, ethnicity, and nationalism. Postcolonial theory in the last two decades has addressed questions of race, nation-state relations, class, and gender, among others, through analysis of texts of imperial cultures and has exposed structural contradictions in their colonialist ideologies and processes. Like queer theory, the field is strongly influenced by several methodologies (poststructuralism, Marxism, feminism, psychoanalysis, the works of Michel Foucault and Frantz Fanon), and even the term itself has been the subject of controversy ("post-colonial," "postcolonial," "postcoloniality," "anticolonial-critique") by scholars such as Arif Dirlik, Anne McClintock, Robert Stam, Ella Shohat, and Aijaz Ahmad.[5] However, postcolonial theory is a method of analysis that investigates the construction of societies whose subjectivity has been constituted in part by the subordinating power of colonialism, as well as a set of discursive practices involving resistance to colonialism and colonialist ideologies and legacies. Edward Said's genealogical critique of Orientalism as a discursive practice, by which European culture was able to manage—and even to produce—the Orient during the post-Enlightenment period,[6] is crucial for the understanding of how ethnic and racial power relations operate within Israeli society, as Shohat had already eloquently discussed in her book on Israeli cinema.

In Orientalist discourse, the East is produced as aberrant, underdeveloped, and inferior in order to constitute the Occident's "self" as rational, modern, and superior, as well as to justify the West's privileges and aggressions. While Said discusses the differences and oppositions between colonizer and colonized, Homi Bhabha's work examines the complex mix of attraction and repulsion, fear and desire that characterize their relationship.[7] The colonial subject's attitude toward the "other" is not a simple rejection of difference but an acknowledgment and a disavowal of an "otherness" that holds an attraction and poses a threat. Hence, colonial identity is a problem arising in between colonizer and colonized, an ambivalent hybridized condition of fantasy and fear, far different from the clear-cut authority that the colonial domination wants to present. Therefore, ambivalence is a structural element of colonial discourse, undesired by the colonizer.

The colonizer seeks to constitute compliant subjects who mimic his assumptions and values. For example, Israeli cinema in the seventies expressed an anxiety about the emergence of a new Mizrahi macho masculinity and made an effort to domesticate Mizrahi men by disavowing ethnic differences, using practices of mimicry that were enforced through the military and interethnic marriage, compelling Mizrahim to reflect an image of Ashkenazi heteronormativity. Indeed, Bhabha describes mimicry as "one of the most elusive and effective strategies of colonial power and knowledge."[8] However, those practices of mimicry have the potential to constitute hybridized colonial subjects who threaten to disclose the ambivalence of the discourse of colonialism, which the use of stereotype tries to conceal. In his films, the Mizrahi filmmaker and actor Ze'ev Revach exploits strategies of mimicry and passing in order to transgress visible borders of sexuality and ethnicity and to present a version of Mizrahi manhood that deconstructs the heteronormative stereotype imposed on Mizrahi men by exposing masculinity as masquerade and spectacle.

In postcolonial scholarship, with a few notable exceptions,[9] there has been a general critical tendency to minimize the role of sexuality, and particularly homosexuality. This study insists on the importance of understanding the intersectionality of discourses on race and ethnicity and the discourse of (homo)sexuality within the particular national discourse of Israeli cinema. The terms "race" and "ethnicity" in this study refer to historical and ideological discourses rather than to ahistorical or biological categories. In Israeli cinema, the representation of Mizrahi and Palestinian men as savages, primitive and violent, reproduces certain Zionist ideological fictions and psychic fixations about the sexual nature of Oriental masculinity and the "otherness" that it is constructed to embody. Zionist colonial fantasy projected its own fears of and desires for homosexuality onto the male Mizrahi and Palestinian imagined sexuality and body. In the film *Paratroopers* (Judd Ne'eman, 1977), for example, the construction of the Mizrahi man as homophobic—that is, as repressed homosexual—enabled the Ashkenazi male protagonist to allay his own anxieties about homosexuality. In another film, *Hamsin* (Dan Wachsman, 1982), the Israeli man's fear of miscegenation between Arab men and Jewish women displaced his own homoerotic fantasies about interracial sex. The Oriental body was forced to stand in, to mimic, to be a mirror-image upon which the Israeli-Ashkenazi (sexual) ego props itself. However, other films, mainly produced by Mizrahi filmmakers, resisted these kinds of representations of the Oriental male body. They problematized the issue of self-representation and made the Zionist Ashkenazi fiction of identification visible, exposing it as a historically constructed identity dependent upon binaries of East/West, Arab/Jew, Palestinian/Israeli, Mizrahi/Ashkenazi, feminine/masculine, homo/hetero.

This study emphasizes that the categories of "race" and "ethnicity" are not exclusive properties of "truly" raced people, such as Palestinians and Mizrahim, but also constitute the identity of the Ashkenazim themselves. In Israeli cinema, Ashkenazi people have escaped and enjoyed the privilege of not being marked as part of an ethnic group. Instead, they imaged themselves as the norm. Zionist films articulate Ashkenazi pioneers as "whites," a construction that defines itself against the image of the "black" diasporic Jew and the Middle Eastern population. The "white" identity of the Zionist pioneer is founded on a paradoxical notion of being part of a race—the Jewish race—and, at the same time, of being an individual and universal subject who is not part of his racial genealogy. The figure of the Sabra, who is at once Jewish but born from nothingness—from the "elements"—embodies this paradoxical construction of Ashkenazi "whiteness." This book will try to embody the disembodied manifestation of "Ashkenaziness" in Israeli cinema.

My work is indebted to the growing field of masculinity and the representation of the male body in film studies. Starting with mid-eighties articles by Paul Willemen about the films of Anthony Mann, Richard Dyer on the male pin-up, and Steve Neale about the spectacle of masculinity in popular cinema, and continuing with series of books in the early nineties such as Steven Choan and Ina Rae Hark's edited volume *Screening the Male,* Peter Lehman's *Running Scared,* Paul Smith's *Clint Eastwood,* and Dennis Bingham's *Acting Male,* these works contributed to the deconstruction of Western heteronormative masculinity and its institutions of power.[10]

Willemen describes two ways in which the male hero is displayed in Mann's Westerns. First the male body is represented as spectacle, producing an erotic visual pleasure for the (male) viewer. This erotic objectification of masculinity can be threatening for the normative subject; therefore it is always followed by the physical destruction of the male body through beating or mutilation. Those two representations are understood in terms of the sadistic/masochistic doublet. The objectification of the male body is linked to the sadistic gaze and the bodily destruction to masochistic pleasure. Following Willemen, Neale explores the implications of Laura Mulvey's observation about the sadistic nature of the cinematic gaze for issues of masculinity, arguing that the male body in popular imagery is "feminized" and objectified by the apparatus of the cinema and the viewer. However, as Smith eloquently states:

> Neale's contention, that in order for the male body to be thus objectified it has to be "feminised," is open to question, not least because it relies

upon a sweeping generalization (increasingly often doubted in film studies) about the conventions and the apparatus of cinema—namely, upon the argument that they are oriented primarily and perhaps exclusively to the male spectator and his processes of identification. Neale's argument is in a sense self-fulfilling, or at least circular. If it is first assumed that the apparatus is male, geared to a male heterosexual gaze, then any instance of objectification will have to involve the "feminisation" of the object."

Indeed, a generalization of the kind leads to theoretical deadlock that minimizes the complexities of desire and identification in representations of masculinity in cinema.

This book attempts to identify more liberating possibilities of masochism, based on the work of Leo Bersani, Gilles Deleuze, Gaylyn Studlar, and Kaja Silverman, for the production of "new" male sexualities.[12]

In *Running Scared*, Lehman offers a more flexible approach—informed by a variety of critical methods, including close textual analysis, feminism, psychoanalysis, auteurism, and cultural studies—for exploring the representation of the male body in film and culture. His book "confront[s] the silence surrounding the male body, particularly the male genitals."[13] Lehman focuses mainly on the (in)visibility of the male penis—its size, shape, color—unveiling and demystifying the taboo and awe surrounding its representation in popular and scientific discourses. The pivotal attention that Lehman gives to the male penis reinforces his frame of analysis: the construction of heteromasculinity. This is, in part, because identification of heterosexual masculinity demands prioritization of the penis as the only legitimized site of male eroticism.

This volume turns critical attention to another erogenous zone of the male body: the male anus. Even more than the penis, the male anus is surrounded by compulsive sexual fears, fantasies, and fundamental cultural taboos. As Eve Kosofsky Sedgwick and Michael Moon write: "On the conventional road map of the body that our culture handily provides us the anus gets represented as always below and behind, well out of sight under most circumstances, its unquestioned stigmatization a fundamental guarantor of one's individual privacy and one's privately privatized individuality."[14] Following the writings of D. A. Miller, Lee Edelman, and Leo Bersani, I would like to suggest that the anus is a structural element in both the construction of heterosexual and homosexual masculinity in Israeli national cinema.[15] The anus, as a site of penetration, operates for men as a phobic orifice that must be repudiated, if the male subject submits to the laws of castration and heterosexuality. In phallocentric culture, the anus is associated with "feminine" passivity and castration, something that must be disavowed and repressed in order for male phallic identification to succeed. Accordingly, the heterosexual national subjectivity emerges through a disavowed identification with anal penetration. In this sense, anality takes a repudiated constitutive part in heterosexual masculinity.

Gay men have a different relationship to the anus. Anality is an important zone for gay men in their deconstruction of phallic masculinity. In the act of anal sex, homosexuals embrace castration and passivity that is antithetical to fantasies of male phallic mastery and authority. Through anal passivity, the homosexual male subject summits the phallic male body to violation and transgression. In short, phallic masculinity is present in male homosexuality through the process of its repudiation. However, this presence is primarily conceived as a desired space of rejection, negation, and transgression.

An approach that only emphasizes the structural ambivalence of male subjectivity can be seen as part of the tendency of discourse analysis to dehistoricize and delocate masculinities from their temporal, spatial, geographical, and linguistic contexts. The emphasis on the plurality of masculinities suggests that dominant Israeli Ashkenazi masculinity is crisscrossed by its "others": queer, Mizrahi, and Palestinian masculinities.

Drawing on Mikhail Bakhtin's concept of "the dialogic imagination," this book examines the dialogic way in which images of male sexualities in Israeli cinema "work," as they circulate in the contingent and contradictory circumstances of historical, cultural, and artistic contexts. This approach does not aim to have the last word on the "value" of a given text, but rather recognizes the contextual character of relations among authors, texts, and audiences as they encounter each other in the worldly spaces of the social sphere.

For Bakhtin, dialogism—defined by Robert Stam as "the necessary relation of any utterance to other utterances"[16]—is the process of generation of meanings and values, which are never finally fixed, but are constantly subject to coalescent and antagonistic efforts of articulation from one discourse to the next. The production of meanings is simultaneously determined from without (the referential status of the utterance, its context) and from within (the semantic and stylistic interaction between various utterances as they circulate endlessly throughout language itself). Any act of enunciation emerges in response to the relevant context, whether in response to the immediate social situation (what the speech performance is about and to whom it is being addressed) or to the wider socio-historical circumstances (the more inclusive economic, political, and cultural environment). In other words, for an utterance to have significance, it must be related to social existence. As Bakhtin states: *"Only that which has acquired social value can enter the world of ideology, take shape, and establish itself there."*[17]

Representations of masculinities in Israeli cinema is analyzed in relation to multiple contexts: political, historical, and cultural, as well as in relation to questions of the politics of positionality of cinematic authors and audiences. What kind of national, racial, ethnic, gender, sexual group do the filmmakers represent? What do they represent and how, and what remains silenced? To whom are those representations being addressed and how are audiences called to identify with them? The same representation could be read differently by opposed groups. The image is always the site of a struggle between multiple and intersecting meanings which, in turn, reflect wider social conflicts. For example, while representations of male-male desire between Palestinians and Israelis—produced by gay Israeli filmmakers and addressed to the Israeli audience—promote interracial sexual unions and subvert the heterocentric national hegemony, at the same time, they cannot be read outside the history of the Israeli occupation of the West Bank in 1967 that turned Palestinians into cheap labor, commodified bodies for sale, not only for work but also for the sexual-visual pleasure of those gay Israeli directors and their audiences. In this analysis of images of male sexualities, text and context, cinema and politics are deeply and structurally intertwined.

However, contextual analysis does not exhaust the representations' significance. For Bakhtin, every utterance not only echoes its time and context, but also depends on a network of other utterances (past and present) for its significance. This kind of dialogic interaction accounts for the utterance's open-ended possibilities of meanings, its multiple and polysemic layers of semantic depth. Bakhtin argues that since a text can generate new meanings, which did not previously exist, it cannot be seen as a reflection of a prediscursive reality, but as part of a wider, infinite intertextual chain: "No one utterance can be either the first or the last. Each is only a link in a chain, and none can be studied outside this chain."[18] In short, for Bakhtin, there is no direct relation between the utterance and the external world, but only a mediated or interdiscursive one.

In this volume, images of manliness are analyzed in relation to other Israeli cinematic texts (past and present) and occasionally in relation to foreign cinemas that influenced Israeli cinema's representation of masculinities, such as Sergei Eisenstein's films, German Expressionism, Hollywood melodramas, and R. W. Fassbinder's cinema. Israeli films are explored in relation to non-cinematic texts—such as literary texts, journalistic articles, medical-scientific reports, and political speeches—in order to view Israeli cinema's discourse of male sexualities as parallel to or structured by them. They are also a part of a larger discursive structure.

While Israel's unique nation formation has been subject to extensive intellectual inquiry in and outside Israel, only a few comprehensive scholarly works have been written about Israeli cinema. Most of the works outline production histories and plot synopses of Israeli films; for example, Nathan Gross and Ya'acov Gross's *The Hebrew Film: The History of Cinema in Israel*; Meir Schnitzer's *Israeli Cinema: Facts, Plots, Directors, Opinions*; Hillel Tryster's *Israel before Israel: Silent Cinema in the Holy Land*; Amy Kronish's *World Cinema: Israel*.[19] Ella Shohat's book *Israeli Cinema: East/West and the Politics of Representation* was the first critical attempt in Israeli cinema studies to come to terms with the Zionist/Israeli national ideology, specifically with its objectification of the Mizrahi and Palestinian subjects, as well as with the absence or marginality of their experience, along axes of race, ethnicity, class, and gender. Following Shohat's work, Israeli cinema scholarship produced a body of critical literature on the history of Israeli cinema, using various theoretical models. For example, Igal Bursztyn's *Face as Battlefield* analyzes Israeli films through the representation of the cinematic close-up; Nurith Gertz's *Motion Fiction: Israeli Fiction in Film* explores the relationship between Hebrew literature and Israeli cinema; Nitzan S. Ben-Shaul's *Mythical Expressions of Siege in Israeli Films* traces metaphors of the "siege syndrome" in Israeli films; Ariel Schweitzer's *Le Cinema Israeli de la Modernite* investigates the modernist aesthetic and politics in Israeli cinema. The anthology *Fictive Looks: On Israeli Cinema*, edited by Nurith Gertz, Orly Lubin, and Judd Ne'eman, offers an interesting collection of essays on Israeli films from neo-Marxist, feminist, postcolonial, and historiographic perspectives.[20]

In this body of scholarship, there has been little attempt to explore questions of male sexuality. This elision is especially striking since one of the central forming elements of the Zionist ideology is the figure of the male Ashkenazi Sabra. Addressing Israeli cinema in the forties and fifties, Nurith Gertz examines the representation of the "new Jew" in relation to his "others": Holocaust survivors, Arabs, and women. She argues that the Israeli cinematic discourse elides the differences between those "others," who are "identified with each other and create hierarchy that supports the imagined homogeneity of the new [masculine] Hebrew identity."[21] By pointing out the identification between those "others," Gertz runs the risk of erasing the important distinctions between the different experiences of oppression of diasporic "queer" Jews, Arabs, and women, making homophobia, racism, and misogyny synonymous. Furthermore, this analogy obscures those who inhabit both identifications of "otherness," such as Mizrahi gay men who confront both racism and homophobia. Rather than suggesting that race, ethnicity, gender, and sexual orientation are "natural" analogies, this book seeks to explore the historical construction of intersections among different categories of identity at a particular cultural moment.

Israeli cinema scholarship as a whole is ensconced within a conspicuously heterocentric interpretative framework. Israeli film theorists remain silent when it comes to critical issues of homosexuality, queer desire, and queer identification. When scholars do address a queer imaginary, it is usually in reference to "openly" gay directors, who deal with "the subject," assuming that queerness can only express "local" concerns of a "special" sexually oriented group. This perspective, which governs Israeli film theory and culture as a whole, implicitly posits heterosexuality as the norm and refuses to *see* homosexuality as a constitutive part of Israeli cultural discourse. In other cases, discussions of homosexuality occur in a homophobic context, identifying gays as "anomalous" or "outcast" figures, even as "freaks." Referring to the films of the gay filmmaker Amos Guttman, Amy Kronish writes, "[Guttman] had a capacity for portraying homosexuality in a way which does not make the viewer uncomfortable. The film [*Amazing Grace*] includes no scenes of male love-making."[22] Homosexual sex frightens Kronish and makes her feel uncomfortable. Therefore, she must disavow the specter of gay intercourse in Guttman's films, despite copious evidence to the contrary.

Jewish Studies theorists, such as Sander Gilman, Daniel Boyarin, and David Biale, have been more attentive to representations of Jewish male (homo)sexuality in Western culture, using, like Boyarin, the Jewish male femme image as a critical practice.[23] I am indebted in many aspects to their insights on the nineteenth-century European discourse of masculinity and Zionist sexual politics. However, while concerned with questions of (Jewish) race within antisemitic discourse, those scholars have almost completely ignored the racial and racist politics of the Zionist project itself. When some of those scholars do address questions of Orientalism, they argue that racism is an effect of the Zionist sexual discourse and that the history of Zionist racial politics began only with the Euro-Jewish pioneers' arrival in Palestine.

On the contrary, Zionist racial and racist discourse is not a byproduct or an effect of Zionist sexual politics, but actually a constitutive element of it. Moreover, the racial thinking of the Zionist leaders, which informed their ideas of a new (hetero)sexuality, began long before the first pioneers reached the shores of Palestine. In addition, critical discussions of the Zionist heteronormatively referred, sometimes not directly, only to the Ashkenazi male body, thus eliding the specific body experience of Mizrahi (male) Jews and the role they played in the Zionist "white" male fantasies. Indeed, the Zionist discourse is structurally sexed, gendered, and raced, as Mizrahi feminism has already pointed out in its ongoing critical debate with Ashkenazi feminism.[24] The challenge of this study is to explore the historical and theoretical intersections between multiple categories of race, ethnicity, gender, sex, and nationalism and to expose them as ideological constructions produced by Zionist culture. Insistence on intersectionality of multiple categories of difference recognizes their instability and structural ambivalence and refuses to assume the fixity of one over the other.

Beyond Flesh offers not only a theoretical and critical account of the construction of masculinities and queerness in Israeli cinema and culture, in particular, but also suggests a model for the investigation of the role of male sexualities within the constitution of national culture, in general. My aim in this book is to challenge the tendency within dominant critical discourses to treat race, sexuality, and nationalism separately. I hope that my insistence on the historical and theoretical intersectionality of race, ethnicity, gender, and sexual orientation within national culture will open up a space in between those multiple categories in which subjectivity is constituted.

NOTES

1. Ella Shohat, *Israeli Cinema: East/West and the Politics of Representation* (Austin: University of Texas Press, 1987).
2. Judith Butler, "Against Proper Objects," *Difference* 2–3, no. 6 (1994): 21.
3. Leo Bersani, *Homos* (Cambridge, Mass.: Harvard University Press, 1995); Michael Warner, "Introduction," in *Fear of a Queer Planet: Queer Politics and Social Theory*, ed. Michael Warner (Minneapolis: University of Minnesota Press, 1993), vii–xxxi; David M. Halperin, *Saint Foucault: Towards a Gay Hagiography* (New York: Oxford University Press, 1995).
4. Judith Butler, *Bodies That Matter: On the Discursive Limits of "Sex"* (New York: Routledge, 1993), 113.
5. Arif Dirlik, "The Postcolonial Aura: Third World Criticism in the Age of Global Capitalism," in *Dangerous Liaisons: Gender, Nation and Post-colonial Perspectives*, ed. Anne McClintock, Aamir Mufti, and Ella Shohat (Minneapolis: University of Minnesota Press, 1997), 492–501; Anne McClintock, *Imperial Leather: Race, Gender, and Sexuality in the Colonial Contest* (New York: Routledge, 1995); Ella Shohat and Robert Stam, *Unthinking Eurocentrism: Multiculturalism and the Media* (London: Routledge, 1994); Aijaz Ahmad, *In Theory: Classes, Nations, Literatures* (London: Verso, 1992).
6. Edward W. Said, *Orientalism* (New York: Pantheon, 1978).
7. Homi K. Bhabha, *The Location of Culture* (London: Routledge, 1994).
8. Bhabha, "Of Mimicry and Man: The Ambivalence of Colonial Discourse," in *The Location of Culture*, 85.
9. See, for example, Kobena Mercer, *Welcome to the Jungle: New Positions on Black Cultural Studies* (New York: Routledge, 1994); Anne McClintock, *Imperial Leather*; Ann Laura Stoler, *Race and the Education of Desire: Foucault's "History of Sexuality" and the Colonial Order of Things* (Durham, N.C.: Duke University Press, 1977); *Talking Visions: Multicultural Feminism in a Transnational Age*, ed. Ella Shohat (Cambridge, Mass.: MIT Press, 1998).
10. Paul Willemen, "Looking for the Male," *Framework* 16 (1981): 15–17; Richard Dyer, "Don't Look Now: The Male Pin-Up," in *The Sexual Subject: A "Screen" Reader in Sexuality* (London: Routledge, 1992), 265–276; Steve Neale, "Masculinity as Spectacle," in *The Sexual Subject*, 277–290; Steven Choan and Ina Rea Hark, eds., *Screening the Male: Exploring Masculinities in Hollywood Cinema* (London: Routledge, 1993); Peter Lehman, *Running Scared: Masculinity and the Representation of the Male Body* (Philadelphia: Temple University Press, 1993); Paul Smith, *Clint Eastwood: A Cultural Production* (London: UCL Press, 1993); Dennis Bingham, *Acting Male: Masculinities in the Films of James Stewart, Jack Nicholson, and Clint Eastwood* (New Brunswick, N.J.: Rutgers University Press, 1994); Susan Jeffrods, *Hard Bodies: Hollywood Masculinity in the Reagan Era* (New Brunswick, N.J.: Rutgers University Press, 1994). See also Paul Smith, ed., *Boys: Masculinities in Contemporary Culture* (Boulder, Colo.: Westview Press, 1996); Gaylyn Studler, *This Mad Masquerade: Stardom and Masculinity in the Jazz Age* (New York: Columbia University Press, 1996); Steven Cohan, *Masked Men: Masculinity and the Movies of the Fifties* (Bloomington: Indiana University Press, 1997); Judith Halberstam, *Female Masculinity* (Durham, N.C.: Duke University Press, 1998); Peter Lehman, ed., *Masculinity: Bodies, Movies, Culture* (New York: Routledge, 2001).
11. Smith, *Clint Eastwood*, 157.
12. Leo Bersani, *The Freudian Body: Psychoanalysis and Art* (New York: Columbia University Press, 1986); Gilles Deleuze, *Masochism: Coldness and Cruelty* (New York: Zone

Books, 1989); Gaylyn Studlar, *In the Realm of Pleasure: Von Sternberg, Dietrich, and the Masochistic Aesthetic* (New York: Columbia University Press, 1988); Kaja Silverman, *Male Subjectivity at the Margins* (New York: Routledge, 1992).

13. Lehman, *Running Scared*, 28.
14. Eve Kosofsky Sedgwick and Michael Moon, "Divinity: A Dossier, a Performance Piece, a Little Understood Emotion," in *Tendencies*, by Eve Kosofsky Sedgwick (Durham, N.C.: Duke University Press, 1993), 246–247.
15. D. A. Miller, "Anal Rope," in *Inside/Out: Lesbian Theories, Gay Theories*, ed. Diana Fuss (New York: Routledge, 1991), 119–141; Lee Edelman, *Homographesis: Essays in Gay Literary and Cultural Theory* (New York: Routledge, 1994); Leo Bersani, "Is the Rectum a Grave?" in *AIDS: Cultural Analysis, Cultural Activism*, ed. Douglas Crimp (Cambridge, Mass.: MIT Press, 1988), 197–222.
16. Robert Stam, *Subversive Pleasures: Bakhtin, Cultural Criticism and Film* (Baltimore: Johns Hopkins University Press, 1989), 13. See also Michael Gardiner, *The Dialogics of Critique: M. M. Bakhtin and the Theory of Ideology* (London: Routledge, 1992).
17. V. N. Volosinov, *Marxism and the Philosophy of Language*, trans. Ladislav Matejka and I. R. Titunik (Cambridge, Mass.: Harvard University Press, 1973), 22 (his italics).
18. M. M. Bakhtin, *Speech Genres and Other Late Essays*, trans. Vern W. McGee, ed. Caryl Emerson and Michael Holquist (Austin: University of Texas Press, 1986), 136.
19. Nathan Gross and Ya'acov Gross, *The Hebrew Film: The History of Cinema in Israel* [in Hebrew] (Jerusalem: privately published, 1991); Meir Schnitzer, *Israeli Cinema: Facts, Plots, Directors, Opinions* [in Hebrew] (Jerusalem: Kinneret Publishing House, 1994); Hillel Tryster, *Israel before Israel-Silent Cinema in the Holy Land* (Jerusalem: Steven Spielberg Jewish Film Archive, 1995); Amy Kronish, *World Cinema: Israel* (Madison-Teaneck: Fairleigh Dickinson University Press, 1996).
20. Igal Bursztyn, *Face as Battlefield* [in Hebrew] (Tel Aviv: Hakibbutz Hameuchad, 1990); Nurith Gertz, *Motion Fiction: Israeli Fiction in Film* [in Hebrew] (Tel Aviv: Open University of Israel Press, 1993); Nitzan S. Ben-Shaul, *Mythical Expressions of Siege in Israeli Films* (Lewiston: Edwin Mellen Press, 1997); Ariel Scweitzer, *Le Cinema Israeli de la Modemite* (Paris, 1997); *Fictive Looks: On Israeli Cinema* [in Hebrew], ed. Nurith Gertz, Orly Lubin, and Judd Ne'eman (Tel Aviv: Open University of Israel, 1998).
21. Nurith Gertz, "The 'Others' in '40s and '50s Israeli Films: Holocaust Survivors, Arabs, Women" [in Hebrew], in *Fictive Looks*, 381.
22. Kronish, *World Cinema: Israel*, 181.
23. Sander L. Gilman, *Difference and Pathology: Stereotypes of Sexuality, Race and Madness* (Ithaca, NY: Cornell University Press, 1985); Daniel Boyarin, *Unheroic Conduct: The Rise of Heterosexuality and the Invention of the Jewish Man* (Berkeley: University of California Press, 1997); David Biale, *Eros and the Jews: From Biblical Israel to Contemporary America* (New York: Basic Books, 1992).
24. On Mizrahi feminism, see, for example, Ella Shohat, "Mizrahi Feminism: The Politics of Gender, Race, and Multiculturalism," in *News from Within*, April 1996, 17–26; Henriet Dahan-Kalev, "Feminism between Ashkenaziness and Mizrahiness," in *Sex, Gender and Politics*, ed. Dafena Izeracli [in Hebrew] (Tel Aviv: Hakibbutz Hameuchad, 1999), 217–266.

18

The Construction of Lesbianism as Nonissue in Israel

ERELLA SHADMI

The Reign of the Heterosexual Woman

The heterosexual woman is one of the building blocks of Israeli culture and Zionist ideology—the ideology on which the Jewish national movement and the State of Israel were founded. From the writings of Theodor Herzl, Zionism's founding father, through the idolization of motherhood and fertility and unto women's status in law and society in contemporary Israel, the heterosexual woman reigns. Lesbianism is absent.

An explicit expression of the exclusion and invisibility of the lesbian option appears in one of the peak moments of the Israeli movie *Moments*, directed by Michal Bat Adam (a woman)—as the scholar Orly Lubin describes:

> On a wide bed in a Jerusalem hotel two women are pampering themselves, revealing their inner worlds, and maybe maybe touching each other slightly . . .
>
> The scene develops into a love scene, but not before the additional, probably inevitable, element—Julia's boyfriend—joins the two women. . . . What started as the ultimate of connectedness between women, as a moment of directedness towards women's love, as the peak of a dramatic joining which constructs female sexuality and love between women, turns into a cliché—of the pornographic genre.
>
> The man's penetrating gaze . . . turns the women, the object of his observation, into objects for his use. The pornographic event goes on with Dayan (the actor) having intercourse with both women. . . . By this intercourse, which has no (lesbian) alternative, the connecting

Reprinted, by permission, from Erella Shadmi, *Sappho in the Holy Land* (Albany: State University of New York Press), 251–264.

between two women is accomplished through and thanks to the male's sex organ. (Lubin 1995, 349)

This scene—whose lesbian aspect was furiously denied by the woman filmmaker at the Eleventh Feminist Conference—reflects the whole story of female heterosexuality in Israeli culture. It expresses the male-centered heterosexist patriarchy in which men are center-staged, women are confined to their heterosexual roles, and women's passion for women is denied. It expresses, indeed, the way in which heterosocial, not only heterosexual, socioeconomic, political, and ideological systems structure our reality.

The centrality and connectedness among God, masculinity, family, and land, constructed by Zionism throughout its history (Shadmi 1992) and fortified by winds of nationalism, messianism, and fundamentalism blowing in the last decades, have established the supremacy of men in Israeli culture and defined the inferior social position of women, whose existence is justified predominantly by their services to men, the family, and the homeland.

Zionist ideology and Israeli culture view motherhood as supremely important for the nationalistic and religious interests it serves (Berkovitch 1999; Yanay and Rapoport 1997; Yuval-Davis 1987). Women's fertility is perceived as the women's national mission (Ben Gurion as cited by Hazelton 1977, 52) and their wombs—as owned by the homeland (Keinan, cited by Hazelton 1977, 57). Social institutions and norms and ideological discourse make traditional coupling and family form the only legitimate options, the only responsible, sensible, and right behavior (Amir 1997).

The Israeli state, through its legal system and social discourse, has constructed motherhood as the only route for women to become a part of the collective (Berkovitch 1999). Motherhood, therefore, is accorded national meaning and appropriated from women's control. Women's sexuality exists for men only—never for themselves or other women (Hazelton 1977, 109–110). Indeed, sexuality has no part in the image of the ideal woman who almost always is portrayed as a part of a heterosexual family (Lahav 1993).

No wonder that Israeli women define themselves in terms of their familial roles (Friedman 1996), that society sees traditional families and traditional feminine roles as central (Bar Yosef 1991; Friedman 1996; Hartman 1991; Shritt 1982), and that the labor market gives priority to working women who have families (Izraeli 1992).

The nationalization and idolization of womanhood and motherhood take heterosexuality for granted and exclude lesbians (and non-Jewish women as well; Berkovitch 1999) from public discourse. The emphasis on marriage and motherhood depoliticizes both women's consciousness (Gluzman 1997, 158) and women's sexuality, which thus cease being an opposition to the existing order. Zionism's assumption of the normality of heterosexual existence, lived within the parameters of the institutionalized family forms, enables the penetration of social and political control over women and sexual outgroups, lesbian included (cf. Whelehan 1995, 95).

The interweaving of heterosexual/heterosocial, masculine, and national narratives was vividly expressed by Herzl, Zionism's founding father, in his formative novel *Altneuland*. Here Herzl views Zionism as the process by which Jewish masculinity would be restored. For him, Zionism is a masculine idea in which women can hold but an auxiliary position (Gluzman 1997). Zionism signifies the turning of the feminine, seemingly queer Jewish male into masculine (Boyarin 1997, 123). The move described by Herzl, from nonerotic to heterosexual desire, is an allegory of a movement from weakness to national power, and the renewed national power is an allegory of heterosexual desire (Gluzman 1997, 154). Thus, through interweaving heterosexual masculinity with nationalism not only do women become secondary, but lesbians are ignored altogether.

The central and exclusive presence of heterosexual women in the Zionist and Israeli narrative have kept lesbians outside society's boundaries and locked in the closet. The lesbian, whose significant other is not a man and who is not a member of a traditional family—in short, the a-nationalized and a-Zionist Israeli woman—undermines the hegemonic ideology and norms. The Israeli lesbian, deviating from "proper" behavior, shatters the national narrative by her mere existence. As she celebrates woman-to-woman bonds as empowering symbols of female strength (cf. Whelehan 1995, 90) suppressed by Zionism, she embodies an alternative model to Zionist norms. She acts "in accordance with her inner compulsion to be a more complete and freer human being," rejecting "the limitations and oppression laid on her by the most basic role of her society—the female role" (Radicalesbians 1973, cf. Clough 1994, 142–143).

Her refusal to become or remain heterosexual means (following Wittig 1992; cf. Whelehan 1995, 102) a refusal to become Zionist or Sabra (as native-born Israelis are called). As Sabra and Zionist are political rather than essential categories, they receive meaning through their insertion into (among other things) the discourse of heterosexuality. Heterosexuality is a category used to enforce women's role as producer, simultaneously encouraging her ideologically to reproduce the conditions of existence of heterosexual institutions (cf. Whelehan 1995). As she betrays her national mission and refuses to sacrifice herself to the national Moloch, she represents a danger to the nation.

The appearance of the feminist movement in the early 1970s created, for the first time, a space for constructing an alternative lesbian identity, indeed, an alternative female sexuality, whose meaning is not derived from the benefits she renders to national events. How, then, has lesbian identity been shaped and how has it developed since the 1970s? This question stands at the center of this chapter.

Some Methodological Comments

This question refers to the issue of identity. Identity is the meaning of a self to itself or to the other, and this identity is created and re-created and, therefore, changeable through a process of "identification," that is, acts of linking the self to something else—be it a person, a group, or an idea (Glaser 1998).

In particular this chapter explores the role played by social change actors—feminists, gay men, and lesbians themselves—in this "identification" process, that is, in constructing the social meaning of lesbianism. Such an exploration will throw light on the nature of the lesbian, feminist, and gay movements as social change movements. Taking my departure from the literature about the New Social Movements (Eder 1985; Offe 1985; Touraine 1985) and its critique (Laclau 1996; Lentin 1999; Johnston and Klandermas 1995; Tarrow 1996, 1998; Waters 1998), I wish to examine the extent to which these movements are revolutionary or conformists and their role in bringing about social change.[1]

Special attention will be given here to the relation between lesbianism and feminism. As a feminist-lesbian of the first generation of out-of-the-closet political lesbians, aware of my ideological standpoint (so insightfully examined, explained, and justified by Zimmerman 1997), I wish to examine how Israeli lesbians have situated themselves in relation to feminism and against it, and vice versa.

Such an exploration seems to me of special interest since feminism, once the theory, ideology, and politics of so many lesbians like myself, has become nowadays an object of so much anger and contempt for many, especially younger, lesbians. Lesbians' position vis-à-vis feminism may reveal their stand toward womanhood, sexuality, and social change and, consequently, the political meaning of lesbianism in Israel.

My goal here is to encourage a discussion on the meaning and problematics of lesbian alliances with various ideologies and political groups, feminism in particular, so lesbians will be able to define their specific voice and politics in a time when so many social change actors, feminists and gay men included, are either co opted by or choose to ally with mainstream politics (Lentin 1999).

The chapter presents my reflections on the history and development of the organized Jewish lesbian community in Israel since the early 1970s. It is based on my experience as a member of this community since the early 1980s and on numerous informal talks with lesbians, feminists, and others throughout these years. Through these talks I had the opportunity to learn about their experience, and I could discern their perceptions and ideas about lesbianism, feminism, ideologies, and Israeli society.

I choose to focus on the (loosely) organized lesbian community not only because I am more familiar with it, but especially because, first, this is the arena, more than any other location, where feminism and lesbianism meet and discourse; second, its boundaries are definable and, therefore, easier for study and; third, as an organized group, it has been more vocal and plays a significant role in the public arena and social discourse. I deal here only with Jewish lesbians since no information about Palestinian Israeli lesbians is accessible to me.

In Search of an Identity

Being excluded and silenced by hegemonic culture, having no role model or known history, and viewed as immoral, sick, and ugly (Oppenheimer 1991), Israeli political lesbians have made an attempt, against all odds, to both survive and construct a new lesbian identity.

Feminism, making its first steps in Israel in the early 1970s, inspired hopes among lesbians for a change in their status and for creating a supportive space in which to "come out" and organize. The feminist demand for women's control of their bodies, the belief that new ways to express and construct women's identities are opening up, and the struggle for social and political rights for all women, all led lesbians, who had spent precious years in the closet, to join the feminist movement.

They were, however, quickly disappointed: heterosexual feminists, homophobic like the rest of society, viewed lesbians not only as a national danger but also as a stick in the revolution's wheels. Lesbians dared not express their voices and needs as lesbians. They stayed invisible and silenced as before. They could express themselves only as radical feminists. Lesbians became the forerunners of the struggle to revolutionize society, politics, and culture, to liberate women's bodies from men's control, and to replace patriarchy with women's value system, hoping that such changes would transform lesbians' status as well. A critique of sexuality and heterosexuality had to await better times.

Radical feminism gave lesbians an outlet for their outrage and a direction for political struggle, but it also silenced the autonomous lesbian voice and kept the lesbian identity in the closet. Lesbians could "pass" as heterosexual radical feminists, giving up the possibility of putting lesbianism on the social or feminist agenda. In fact, they desexualized lesbianism in the hope of meaningful sisterhood.

Like lesbians elsewhere (Zimmerman 1997, 161), Israeli lesbians of the 1970s separated their feminist theory and politics, namely, radical feminism, from their material practice and experience, that is, lesbianism. Unlike lesbians elsewhere, this separation did not lead Israeli lesbians to articulate issues of sexuality and to establish a theoretical and political position of lesbian feminism. Radical feminist lesbians have hardly attempted to critique heterosexuality—except in private conversations—to politicize sex or sexualize politics. Indeed, lesbianism had been portrayed and experienced by these political lesbians as a challenge to Zionist patriarchy, but this portrayal rarely if ever was voiced outside lesbian circles, and it served as a basis for identity formation more than as a politically transformative means. No wonder "sex wars" never erupted in Israel as they did in the United States.

In the mid-1970s liberal feminism headed by heterosexual mainstream women took control of Israeli feminism (Swirski 1991;Wenzel 1996;Yishai 1997). These women acted in mainstream institutions—political parties, academia, and public institutions—to alter legislation, public policy, and education. Feeling rejected and oppressed—as both lesbians and radical feminists—lesbians took little part in these activities. They neither resisted their oppression by heterosexual feminists nor fought for their rights; instead, they turned in on themselves. They went on with their radical feminist politics by, for example, working for battered women and establishing feminist women's centers and consciousness-raising groups. But much of their resources were directed toward building and safeguarding a lesbian community—a space where they could freely and safely form and express their identity and get support and approval from other lesbians. In particular, they organized self-help groups, parties, and discussion events for lesbians only; they made Kol Ha-Isha, the Jerusalem feminist center, a meeting place for lesbians, and they rendered financial and psychological help to lesbians in trouble.

The community, in fact, a lesbian ghetto, enabled lesbians to survive in an oppressive environment. Within the confines of the lesbian community, they could find an island of support in an ocean of hostility, to construct their lesbian selves, and to shape their radical feminist voices. The community provided many lesbians with an environment in which they could address and explore sexual options and desires.

The closeted community, however, joined the radical feminist stand to leave the issue of lesbianism outside public discourse. As before, Israeli lesbians, oppressed by lesbophobic society and silenced by liberal heterosexual feminists, dared not put lesbianism on the public agenda and remained in the closet. Even the attempt to build culturally alternative spaces in the newly opened women's centers, headed predominantly by lesbians, and in the lesbian community, was mainly based on a women's, not lesbian-specific, value system. In other words, women's, rather than lesbian-specific, interests and perspectives dominated the lesbian struggle and thinking.

Interestingly, together with the attempts to build a community, the term "lesbian feminist" first appeared, particularly in titling the lesbians' organization—the Lesbian Feminist Community. From the start and to this very day, this term has been associated with the context of community, namely, a supportive space and social life, and not with the context of politics and theory, that is, social change and political thinking.

Lesbians began to be visible as lesbians (rather than feminists) in the late 1980s. Changes in society at large facilitated this move: Since the early 1970s Israeli society has become more and more liberal, pluralist, and critical. The doctrine of civil rights has begun to take root in politics and social discourse and oppressed groups, especially among Mizrahi Jews, Israeli Arabs, women, and to a lesser degree, gay men and women who have begun to struggle for social change. Past beliefs and myths have been shaken.[2]

Three political struggles, especially since the late 1980s, have had a profound impact on organized lesbians: First, the women's peace movement (Chazan 1992; Emmett 1996; Heiman and Rapoport 1997), which made clear the connection between different kinds of oppression, such as oppression based on nationality, gender, and sexuality (Shadmi 2000a). Lesbians' presence and growing visibility in this movement enhanced the understanding of this connection.

Second was the growing struggle of Mizrahi and Palestinian feminists to shatter the oppressive domination of Ashkenazi women over the Israeli feminist camp, to alter the feminist agenda, and to make the voices, needs, and interests of diverse women heard. This struggle has opened doors to lesbians as well.

Finally, the Association for Individual Rights, struggling for the rights of gay men, lesbians, and bisexuals, has had growing success (Yonai 1998).

As a result of all these changes and of the empowering experience lesbians had within their community and in feminist struggles for women and peace, lesbians began to appear as lesbians at the end of 1980s and during the 1990s. The organized lesbian community, being both encouraged by and active in the developments in the society at large, gradually came out of the closet. It began to develop its main institutions: committees and general assembly, journal and theater, conferences and self-help groups.

Organized lesbians participate, often in leadership positions, in grassroots feminist activities. They represent lesbian interests in the press and political institutions. They are present in mainstream institutions such as politics, business, the free professions, and academia. A growing number of lesbian couples and families live openly and proudly. For the first time lesbians have become visible as lesbians and their voices have begun to be heard in public.

The organized lesbian community has thus undergone major social and political changes reflecting the fortification of the community but also its higher public visibility and the higher integration of lesbians in society. Higher visibility, however, does not make their existence legitimized and socially accepted: their existence has become socially tolerated only as long as it is lived and experienced within the confines of the community and expressed within socially approved discourses. In other words, lesbians have been ghettoized and forced into mainstream ideological frameworks.

Since the late 1980s the organized lesbian community has abandoned radical feminism and adopted a civil rights doctrine as its politics and ideology. Once again lesbian existence has been subordinated to an ideology that suited the hegemonic center.

In line with the civil rights doctrine, lesbians began to demand a number of rights, economic and cultural as well as political, so as to be treated equally, to enjoy equal satisfaction of basic common rights and needs, and not to be discriminated against on the basis of their sexual preference. They fought for equal opportunities in employment, for legitimizing lesbian families and motherhood, and for respecting lesbian culture and identity.

For the first time lesbians demanded that their distinctiveness be acknowledged and their culture embraced by society. And for the first time, lesbianism became the basis for lesbian politics and a public issue.

The civil rights doctrine reflects the organized lesbians' striving to be included by society and to become an integrated and legitimate part of it. This doctrine worked to reposition certain varieties of lesbianism through rehabilitating lesbianism from bad sex to good sex (cf. Whelehan 1995, 176). By adopting this doctrine, however, sexuality had been deemphasized and lesbians failed to critique the "naturalness" of heterosexuality. Lesbianism has become no more than a specific feature of a marginal community unmixed in many areas of social behavior and demanding its right to construct and preserve its traditions. Lesbian sex was taken out of the context of politics and put in terms of individualistic sexual behavior bared of its political and revolutionary meaning. No wonder that the legal and familial discourses became the main ones through which lesbianism was expressed. Sexuality was not dealt with at all and the ways heterosexuality is constructed as "natural" was not critically analyzed. Only rarely were accepted definitions of sexuality investigated and an attempt to redefine intimate relations made—and often only within the secure but closed frameworks of community discussions or gay and lesbian journals.

This doctrine reflects organized lesbians' withdrawal from revolutionary aspiration and critical thinking and their acceptance of the existing order and its institutions (family, politics, military, religion) and power structure. By adopting this doctrine lesbians abandoned their effort to make an impact on the course of social developments; to resist the pressure to be heterosexual (Oppenheimer 1991); to question heterosexual institutions prevailing in Israel, such as familialism, motherhood, traditional womanhood, and the fertility cult ; and to shatter systems of heterosexuality, andocentrism, and patriarchy. Instead, their struggle has been directed toward enlarging the boundaries of the collective so they can be included. They adopted the prevailing norms and lifestyles and left behind the revolutionary drive, their main feature only twenty years earlier. As such, civil rights lesbians seem to serve the interest of the establishment more than they promote lesbian interests (Jeffreys 1990). Lesbianism has become tolerated (at least to some extent) as an individualistic lifestyle, but the critique of compulsory heterosexuality, namely, the enforcement of heterosexuality through the ideological and political control of women's sexuality (Rich 1980), has been forgotten.

Interestingly, the turn toward civil rights doctrine coincided with both the AIDS epidemic and the gradual though still limited decrease in the centrality and power of the military in Israeli society. As a result many critics turned to the complexities of male homocentrism and masculinity. Lesbians exist at the margins of this discourse, often ignored altogether.

The greater social interest in masculinity, the relatively successful joint struggle of gay men and women for civil rights, and the recognition of the privileges of gay men (as males in an andocentric society) have strengthened alliances of lesbians with gay men. Their joint actions have led to a new militancy in the form of queer politics in the streets and queer theory in the academy. As queer thinking deconstructs normative categories of gender and sexuality and is inclusive of all transgressive sexual minorities, Israeli lesbians, more than ever before, have dealt with issues of sexuality and subjectivity, specifically with questions of pleasure, desire, fantasy, and difference, and challenged the difference and opposition between heterosexuality and homosexuality. Queer lesbians in Israel celebrate, so it seems, their difference, admire transgressive behavior, and are tolerant of various types of "sexual minorities." Their strategies seem subversive, joyous, transformative, and, therefore, attractive to many.

Nevertheless, queer theory avoids the difference between lesbians and gay men up to the point of inclusion of female and male homosexuality in one monolithic category—the category of queer. Queer politics has been appropriated by gay men who subsume and negate lesbian sexuality (cf. Jeffreys 1990). Queer perspective represents a movement of the lesbian community toward a sexual identity that draws its meaning from the gay men's community, which rejects femininity and abandons the female body. In their stead we find enthusiasm for cyborgs, female-to-male transexuality, and Barbie, creatures beyond gender, efficient, clean, and sexless—far away from the female body (Lauretis 1996, 47). As a theory growing in man-controlled academic circles—in Israel as elsewhere—the queer perspective is distanced from socially lived experiences and femininity, that is, from the female body and the lesbian experience.

Once again lesbianism has been subsumed to a discourse that, although constructive in some ways, nevertheless works to obscure lesbianism and take it off the public agenda.

Ignoring Lesbianism—Deradicalizing Lesbianism

Despite the fact that lesbian existence has been increasingly felt in Israel since the early 1970s, lesbianism, that is, same-sex womanhood (rather than homosexuality or feminism), is largely absent from political, feminist, and queer discourses. Lesbianism remains as invisible as before and has thus been constructed as a nonissue.

Viewing lesbians as either radical feminists or queer has denied lesbians political existence through their inclusion either as a female version of male homosexuality, thus erasing their feminine existence, or as a radical version of heterosexual feminists, thus ignoring their sexual existence. In both versions lesbianism becomes marginal and partial: boundaries thus defined leave out major elements of the lesbian experience. Consequently, a handicapped, mutilated identity has been constructed.

The civil rights doctrine made the lesbian community no more than a minority group fighting for its interests and to be included in society. Such a position adopts the assumption that heterosexual women are the norm, a model for emulation, the goal to pursue. The assumptions, beliefs, and rules of heterosexual womanhood are not challenged. Heterosexual women, especially feminists, are not required to understand their bodies; to reflect on their sexual pleasure, passion, and pain; and to look into their sexuality.

The absence of lesbianism is the effect of a political attempt, supported by feminists and gay men, to force lesbianism into conceptual, discursive, and ideological frameworks distanced from lesbian existence: in order to refrain from confronting the lesbian challenge to Zionist ethos, in fact to erase this challenge, lesbian existence has been subsumed to ideologies tolerated by hegemonic groups. Lesbians can act only within the boundaries of such ideological frameworks. By linking lesbianism to these ideas, namely, by the process of constructing its meaning, its revolutionary and threatening potential has been neutralized and the reign of the heterosexual woman preserved.

Feminist scholarship plays an important role in this attempt to avoid lesbianism.[3] Lesbians rarely exist in contemporary academic discourse. Addressing the issue of feminist production of knowledge in the social sciences in Israel, Hannah Herzog avoids the issue of lesbianism altogether (Herzog 1997). Even when she writes about feminist scholars who demand a reflective and critical approach from feminists who create knowledge from a privileged position, she examines only the writings of Palestinian and Mizrahi Jewish women and ignores the writings of lesbians such as Jo Oppenheimer, whose article appears in a collection extensively examined by her.

When Herzog discusses how boundaries between academia and practice are crossed and how social actors' voices become a source of knowledge, she ignores lesbian writings (including lesbians of academe) that appear in two major journals of feminist activists: *Noga* and *CLaF Hazak*.

Orly Benjamin, to take another example, analyzing the impact of self-development on women's attempt to increase partners' domestic participation, does not even raise the possibility of a lesbian couple (Benjamin 1997).

Delila Amir, in another illuminating example, shows how Israeli committees for abortion certification construct the "responsible," "committed," and "clever" reproductive behavior of Israeli women as the one carried out within a legitimate coupling and traditional family form. Amir takes the heterosexual couple and family for granted and, therefore, does not find it necessary to examine the heterosexual discourse of these committees (Amir 1995).

With the ignoring and subsuming of lesbianism, not only is lesbian sexuality kept in the closet but also women's sexuality and the possibility of constructing an alternative womanhood to the Zionist one, one that is not based on women's service to the nation, men, and the family.[4] This avoidance by scholarship and politics in Israel goes hand in hand with the rapid and sharp turn they took from women's and feminist issues to issues of gender and masculinity. The changes toward gender and masculinity reflect not only repackaging of Women's Studies and feminist politics but also the deradicalizing of them (Robinson and Richardson 1996). These changes took place before feminism sank roots in Israeli academe and politics, and they defeat and offset the feminist challenge. Subsuming women's issues to gender issues depoliticizes relations between the sexes and once again excludes the woman-centered feminist perspective and existence—that is, lesbian existence—from feminist discussion and public discourse. Consequently, the revolutionary potential of lesbianism, so threatening to the Zionist ethos and the Israeli culture, has been deradicalized. The subsuming of the political meaning of the lesbian identity to ideologies digestible to hegemonic groups leaves the existing hetero-sexist order in its place, even strengthening it. Feminists and gay men, both scholars and activists, thus become part of the existing regime of knowledge.

Under these circumstances of a lesbophobic society, avoiding the issue of lesbianism, organized lesbians, wishing not only to survive but also to be visible and tolerated by society, have adopted socially approved ideological frameworks and invested much of their energy in building a safe and empowering community. However, by employing these two strategies of survival, organized lesbians have been co-opted by the existing political system. Since the strategy of community building ghettoizes lesbianism, and the strategy of adopting socially approved ideologies depoliticizes it, organized lesbians played a significant role in facilitating the political attempt to strip lesbianism of its political meaning so it becomes part of the existing order rather than a challenge to it. They consented to the tendency to construct lesbianism as a nonissue, to neutralize its revolutionary potential, and, consequently, to uphold the existing order. Organized lesbians in the main adopted the ideologies enforced on them and, willingly or unwillingly, accepted the discursive chains put on them.

The Limits of Social Change

I argued at the opening of this chapter that lesbianism is perceived as a major threat to dominant ideologies in Israel. The history of lesbians since the 1970s, when an opportunity to incorporate lesbianism within hegemonic discourses was opened with the emergence of the feminist movement, indicates that although lesbians receive more than ever before social recognition and legal rights in contemporary Israel, lesbianism has been silenced, ignored, or subsumed by other ideological frameworks.

The reluctance of Israeli society to face lesbianism may be understood. What is striking is the refusal of the organized lesbian community, the feminist camp, and the *gay* struggle—all movements fighting for social change—to deal with this issue. All are found to be guardians of the existing order, at least in terms of women's sexuality and alternative womanhood. In the way they deal with the challenge lesbianism puts to Israeli culture—namely, ignoring, subsuming, and silencing it—they all conform to socially accepted norms, avoiding the option to shatter them.

Drawing on the literature on New Social Movements, two closely related lines may explain this conformist behavior. The first focuses on the movements' socioeconomic composition, and the second on their modus operandi.

According to the first, all three, like New Social Movements elsewhere (Offe 1985) and in Israel (see Sasson-Levy 1995; Shadmi 2000a), are bourgeois, Western, white movements fighting mainly to improve the social positioning of their constituencies.[5] Under the veil of revolutionary rhetoric lies an ambition on the part of middle-class, Ashkenazi women, lesbians, and gay men to get their piece of the national pie. As a result of their ambition to be annexed to the sources of power, they are reluctant to expose the working of oppressive institutions such as heterosexual femininity, so that the existing order in which they wish to be included will not be undermined. Thus, significant currents of Israeli social movements gave up the option of resistance and transformation. The organized lesbian community, the feminist camp, and the gay struggle in Israel are, consequently, no more than an interest group "fighting against the euphemistic treatment of or complete disregard for social problems, thus against its own decline in the status system" (Eder 1985, 888). They fail to become truly transformative social movements that fight "for a radical democratization of social relationship as such (not only social relationships of production)."

However, the symbolic meanings of these three movements in regard to lesbianism cannot be overlooked: They succeeded in altering public discourse regarding homosexuality and lesbianism; they made more citizens, politicians, and public figures aware of oppression on the basis of sexual preference; they succeeded in amending some public policy and legislation; they facilitated the growth of lesbian and homosexual art. And more lesbians are accorded equal opportunities in employment. As such, these movements seem "moral crusaders" "fighting for the recognition of their own culture as the legitimate culture and thus against the prevalent morality" (Eder 1985, 888).

How much these changes have affected the actual lives of lesbians is, however, controversial: these symbolic gains overshadow society's reluctance to deconstruct and reconstruct its hegemonic ideologies on which lesbophobia and lesbians' oppression are based. We may reasonably assume, therefore, that many lesbians still suffer from overt or covert oppression. Since the lesbian agenda is controlled by organized, middle-class, mainly Ashkenazi lesbians, we have little information regarding difficulties encountered by Mizrahi-Jewish, Palestinian, orthodox-Jewish, working-class, handicapped, and elderly lesbians and lesbian experience in rural areas.[6]

Thus, the organized lesbian community's symbolic gains seem to come at the expense of transforming the lives of real lesbians. The organized community succeeded in controlling the public agenda regarding lesbianism, and many other lesbians, whose needs and interests are overlooked, pay the price. The other line of interpretation of the conformist behavior of these three movements lies in an understanding of their mode of functioning. The feminist movement, like other social movements of the 1970s and 1980s, due to the reflexivity of the activists (Touraine 1985), "abandons revolutionary dreams in favour of the idea of structural reform, along with the defense of civil society that does not seek to abandon the autonomous functioning of political and economic systems—in a phrase, self limiting radicalism" (Cohen 1985, 664). In other words, the movement moved through a linear trajectory from revolutionism to moderate radicalism, together with its institutionalization, as a consequence of, among other things, the dominant position of its actors (Lentin 1999). Many social movements organized later and, influenced by different structural conditions, as are the organized lesbian community and the gay struggle, have been institutionally allied, mainstream backed, collaborating with state bodies, and appealing for sociopolitico-legal recognition from their beginning (Lentin 1999). Thus, all three movements either left their revolutionary zeal soon after their start or have never been revolutionary from the beginning.

Thus, the privileged social position of movements' members as well as their moderate radicalism may explain their reluctance to revolutionize society, politics, and discourse. Yet these factors do not sufficiently explain why lesbianism—and not, for example, heterosexuality or feminism—is unspeakable and doomed to be invisible, why the issue of lesbianism becomes an indicator of the limit of social reform in Israel.

I would like to suggest that the explanation lies in a deep subconscious recognition that lesbians escape categories of sex and gender and open the door to females who are not "women." As Wittig correctly said, a lesbian is ungendered, unsexed, neither woman nor man (Wittig 1981). This is because sex/gender is the result of institutional heterosexuality. Within heterosexual systems, "'intelligible' genders are those which in some sense institute and maintain relations of coherence and continuity among sex, gender, sexual practice, and desire " (Butler 1990, 17). Even her anatomy itself is suspect within heterosexist ideology. Thus, "neither anatomy nor desire nor gender can link her securely to the category 'woman,'" and, thus, she "exits the category of 'woman,' though without thereby entering the category 'man'" (Calhoun 1994). As a consequence, lesbianism is neither about enlarging the socially constructed category "woman" nor about recognizing that there might be multiple categories of women. It is about challenging the heterosexual society demand that females be women. For that demand denies the lesbian option, which is to be a not-woman, neither identifiably woman nor man (Calhoun 1994).

Lesbianism, therefore, is the future lived today. And it is a future that is so disturbing that it must be passed over. So it becomes a nonissue.

Epilogue

Since the early 1970s Israeli lesbians have been constantly engaged in a process of identity formation. This process, altering in accordance with changes in cultural and social circumstances, makes the lesbian identity, or, rather, the lesbian "identification," dynamic, permanently in flux, always moving and searching. It therefore encourages lesbian visibility and facilitates lesbian survival.

At the same time, the social mechanisms of ignorance and subsuming, together with the organized lesbian community's refusal to revolutionize society, structure the organized lesbian struggle as guardians of the existing order. Many lesbians might pay the price.

However, two recent developments may alter profoundly the way in which lesbianism is dealt with in Israel: the first is the growing opposition of radical feminists, old and young, to the way the organized lesbian community has developed. This opposition was expressed at the last feminist conference, held in October 1999, when they put compulsory heterosexuality on the feminist agenda and made all women, lesbian and heterosexual alike, face their sexuality and the way it is socially constructed, and the price they pay individually and collectively for this social institution. It also was expressed in the last issue of *CLaF Hazak* (the organized lesbian community's journal, March 2000). The second is the first steps made by Mizrahi-Jewish lesbians to voice their distinctive point of view both in the national feminist conference and in Mizrahi-only conferences. Both work to direct attention to lesbianism (rather than to homosexuality or feminism) and to diversity among lesbians themselves.

These rearticulations of radical lesbian-feminist stands inspire hope that the organized lesbian community is embarking upon a new track in the process of identity formation taking place in the last thirty years. Its constant dynamics might facilitate this search.

NOTES

1. This issue is also dealt with in my work about Women in Black (Shadmi 2000).
2. Numerous studies describe and analyze the recent changes in Israeli society. Among them, Wistrich and Ohana 1995; Ohana and Wistrich 1996; Lissak and Knei-Paz 1996;

Taub 1997; Peled and Shafir 1996; Peres and Yuchtman-Yaar 1998; Peri 1998; Ram 1998; Yona 1998; Kimmerling 1985.
3. For an exception, see Lubin 1995.
4. For an elaborated analysis of the implications of this avoidance in feminist scholarship in Israel, see Shadmi 2000b.
5. No research is known to the author regarding the ethnic and class composition of these three movements. However, based on personal knowledge and talks with activists and scholars, this argument seems plausible. It should be also emphasized that there are Mizrahi people in all three movements, but they either struggle against Ashkenazi domination (see, for example, Shiran 1991 and Dahan-Kalev 1997) or accept unproblematically Ashkenazi domination.
6. In the same vein, it is also debatable whether women's lot, not only public discourse and consciousness, has been altered by the feminist struggle. See, for example, the debate regarding battered women that took place in Israel in the summer of 1999. Police and welfare policies have been altered, ministers and members of parliament voice their outrage with it, and it is unlikely that anyone will publicly endorse it. However, it seems that the number of battered women has not decreased and the severity of the battery has increased.

REFERENCES

Amir, Delila. "Responsible, Committed, and Intelligent: The Construction of Israeli Femininity in the Commission for Stopping Pregnancy." *Theory and Criticism* 7 (1995): 247–254.

Bar Yosef, Rivka. "The Management of the Household in Two Types of Families in Israel." In *Families in Israel*, ed. Lea Shamgar-Handelman and Rivka Bar-Yosef. Jerusalem: Hebrew University Press, 1991.

Benjamin, Orly. "Self-Development in Israel: Does It Affect Women's Attempts to Increase Partners' Domestic Participation?" *Israel Social Science Research* 12, no. 2 (1997): 97–122.

Berkovitch, Nitza, "Eshet Hayal Mi Yimtzaa: Women and Citizenship in Israel." *Israeli Sociology* 1 (1999): 277–317.

Boyarin, Daniel. "The Colonial Masque Ball: Zionism, Gender, Imitation." *Theory and Criticism* 11 (1997): 123–144.

Butler, Judith. *Gender Trouble: Feminism and the Subversion of Identity.* New York and London: Routledge, 1990.

Calhoun, Chesire. "Separating Lesbian Theory from Feminist Theory." *Ethics* 104 (April 1994): 558–581.

Chazan, Naomi. "Israeli Women and Peace Activism." In *Calling the Equality Bluff: Women in Israel*, ed. Barbara Swirski and Marilyn Saffir, 151–163. New York: Pergamon, 1992.

Clough, Patricia Ticineta. *Feminist Thought.* Cambridge, Mass.: Blackwell, 1994.

Cohen, Jean L. "Strategy or Identity: New Theoretical Paradigm and Contemporary Social Movements." *Social Research* 52, no. 4 (1985): 663–716.

Dahan-Kalev, Henriette. "The Oppression of Women by Other Women: Relations and Struggle between Mizrahi and Ashkenazi Women in Israel." *Israel Social Science Research* 12, no. 1 (1997): 31–44.

Eder, Klaus. "The New Social Movements: Moral Crusades, Political Pressure Groups, or Social Movements?" *Social Research* 52, no. 4 (1985): 869–890.

Emmett, Ayala. *Our Sisters' Promised Land: Women, Politics, and Israeli-Palestinian Coexistence.* Ann Arbor: University of Michigan Press, 1996.

Friedman, Ariela. *Annie Oakley Won Twice: Intimacy and Power in Female Identity* [Ba'a Me'ahava]. Tel Aviv: Hakibbutz Hameuchad, 1996.

Glaser, Andreas. "Placed Selves: The Spatial Hermeneutics of Self and Other in the Post Unification Berlin Force." *Social Identities* 4, no. 1 (1998): 7–38.

Gluzman, Michael. "Longing for Heterosexuality: Zionism and Sexuality in Herzl's Altneuland." *Theory and Criticism* 11 (1997): 143–162.

Hartman, H. "The Division of Labor in Israeli Families." In *Families in Israel*, ed. Lea Samgar-Hendelman and Rivka Bar-Yosef, 197–210. Jerusalem: Hebrew University Press, 1991.

Hazelton, Lesley. *Israeli Women: The Reality Behind the Myth.* New York: Simon and Schuster, 1977.

Helman, Sara, and Tamar Rapoport. "'These Are Ashkenazi Women, Alone, Whores of Arafat, Don't Believe in God, and Don't Love Israel': Women in Black and the Challenging of the Social Order." *Theory and Criticism* 10 (1997): 175–192.

Herzog, Hannah. "Ways of Knowing: The Production of Feminist Knowledge in Israeli Social Science Research." *Israel Social Science Research* 12, no. 2 (1997): 1–28.

Izraeli, Dafna. "Culture, Policy, and Women in Dual-Earner Families in Israel." *Dual Earners Families: International Perspectives*, ed. S. Lewis, D. Izraeli, and H. Hootsmans, 19–45. London: Sage, 1992.

Jeffreys, Sheila. *Anticlimax: A Feminist Perspective on the Lesbian Sexual Revolution.* London: Women's Press, 1990.

Johnston, Hank, and Bert Klandermas. *Social Movements and Culture: Social Movements, Protest, and Contention.* Minneapolis: University of Minnesota Press, 1995.

Kimmerling, Baruch. "Between the Primordial and the Civil Definitions of the Collective Identity: The State of Israel or Eretz Israel." In *Comparative Social Dynamics: Essays in Honor of Shmuel Eisenstadt*, ed. Erik Cohen, Moshe Lissak, and Uri Almagor, 262–283. Boulder, Colo.: Westview Press, 1984.

Laclau, Ernesto. *Emancipation(s).* London: Verso, 1996.

Lauretis, Teresa de. "Fem/Les Scramble." *Cross-Purposes: Lesbians, Feminists, and the Limits of Alliance*, ed. Dana Heller, 42–48. Bloomington and Indianapolis: Indiana University Press, 1996.

Lentin, Alana. "Structure, Strategy, Sustainability: What Future for New Social Movement Theory?" *Sociological Research Online* 4, no. 3 (1999).

Lissak, Moshe, and Baruch Knei-Paz, eds. *Israel Towards the Year 2000.* Jerusalem: Magnes, 1996.

Lubin, Orly. "Women in Israeli Cinema." In *A View into the Lives of Women in Jewish Societies: Collected Essays*, ed. Yael Amon, 349–374. Jerusalem: Zalman Shazar Center for Jewish History, 1995.

Offe, Claus. "New Social Movements: Challenging the Boundaries of Institutional Politics." *Social Research* 52, no. 4 (1985): 817–868.

Ohana, David, and Robert Wistrich, eds. *Myth and Memory: Transfigurations of Israeli Consciousness.* Tel Aviv: Van Leer Institute and Hakibbutz Hameuchad, 1996.

Oppenheimer, Jo. "The Pressure to be Heterosexual." In *Calling the Equality Bluff: Women in Israel*, ed. Barbara Swirski and Marilyn P. Saffir, 108–116. New York: Pergamon Press, 1991.

Peled, Yoav, and Gershon Shafer. "The Roots of Peacemaking: The Dynamics of Citizenship in Israel, 1948–1993." *International Journal of Middle East Studies* 28 (1996): 391–413.

Peres, Yohanan, and Ephraim Yuchtman-Yaar. *Between Consent and Dissent: Democracy and Peace in the Israeli Mind.* Jerusalem: Israeli Democracy Institute, 1998.

Peri, Yoram. "From Political Nationalism to Ethno-Nationalism: The Case of Israel." In *The Arab-Israeli Conflict: Two Decades of Change*, ed. Yehuda Lukas and Abdalla M. Battah, 41–53. Boulder: Westview, 1988.

Radicalesbians. "The Woman Identified Woman." In *Radical Feminism*, ed. Ann Loedt, Ellen Levine, and Anita Rapone. New York: Quadrangle Books, 1973

Ram Uri. "Citizens, Consumers, and Believers: The Israeli Public Sphere between Fundamentalism and Capitalism." *Israeli Studies* 3 (1988): 24–44.

Rich, Adrienne. "Compulsory Heterosexuality and Lesbian Existence." *Signs* 5, no. 4 (1980): 631–660.

Robinson, Victoria, and Diane Richardson. "Repacking Women and Feminism: Taking the Heat Off Patriarchy." *Radically Speaking: Feminism Reclaimed*, ed. Diane Bell and Renate Klein, 179–187. North Melbourne, Australia: Spinifey Press, 1996.

Sasson-Levy, Orna. *Radical Rhetoric. Conformist Practices: Theory and Praxis in an Israeli Protest Movement.* Jerusalem: Hebrew University, Faculty of Social Science (Hebrew), 1995.

Shadmi, Erella. "Women Palestinians, Zionism: A Personal Account." *News from Within* (October–November 1992): 13–16.

———. "Between Resistance and Compliance, Feminism and Nationalism: Women in Black in Israel." *Women's' Studies International Forum* 23, no. 1 (2000a): 23–34.

———. "Lesbians' Absence: Silencing the Personal and the Feminine in the Public and Feminist Discourse in Israel." Paper presented at the Annual Conference of the Israeli Association of Women's Studies, Beit Berl College (Hebrew), 2000b.

Shiran, Vicki. "Feminist Identity vs. Oriental Identity." In *Calling the Equality Bluff: Women in Israel*, ed. Barbara Swirski and Marilyn P. Saffir, 303–311. New York: Pergamon Press, 1991.

Shrift, Ruth. "Marriage: An Option or a Trap?" In *The Double Bind: Women in Israel*, ed. Dafna Izraeli, Ariela Friedman, and Ruth Shrift, 64–112. Tel Aviv: Am Oved, 1982.

Swirski, Barbara. "Israeli Feminism: New and Old." In *Calling the Equality Bluff: Women in Israel*, ed. Barbara Swirski and Marilyn P. Saffir, 285-302. New York: Pergamon Press, 1991.

Taub, Gadi. *A Dispirited Rebellion: Essays in Contemporary Israeli Culture.* Tel Aviv: Hakibbutz Hameuchad (Hebrew), 1997.

Tarrow, Sidney. "States and Opportunities: The Political Structuring of Social Movements." In *Comparative Perspectives on Social Movements: Political Opportunities, Mobilizing Structures, and Cultural Framings*, ed. J. D. McCarthy, M. N. Zald, and D. McAdam. Cambridge: Cambridge University Press, 1996.

———. *Poet in Movement: Social Movements and Contentious Politics.* 2nd ed. Cambridge: Cambridge University Press, 1998.

Touraine, Alain. "An Introduction to the Study of New Social Movements." *Social Research* 52, no. 4 (1985): 749–787.

Wenzel, Mirjam. *Women's Movements in Israel.* Jerusalem: Friedrich Ebert Stiftung, 1996.

Waters, Sarah. "New Social Movement Politics in France: The Rise of Civic Forms of Mobilization." *West European Politics* 21, no. 3 (1998): 431–449.

Wistrich, Robert, and David Ohana, eds. *The Shaping of Israeli Identity: Myth Memory and Trauma.* London: Frank Cass, 1995.

Wittig, Monique. "One Is Not Born a Woman." *Feminist Issues.* 1, no. 2 (1981): 47–54.

———. *The Straight Mind: And Other Essays.* Hemel Hempstead: Harvester Wheatsheaf, 1992.

Whelehan, Imelda. *Modern Feminist Thought: From the Second Wave to "Post-Feminism."* New York: New York University Press, 1995.

Yanay, Nitza, and Tamar Rapoport. "Rituals Impurity and Religious Discourse on Women and Nationality." *Women's Studies International Forum* 20, nos. 5–6 (1997): 651–662.

Yishai, Yael. *Between the Flag and the Banner: Women in Israeli Politics*. Albany: State University of New York Press, 1997.

Yona, Yossi. "State of Its Citizens, Nation-State or a Multicultural Democracy." *Alpayim* 16 (1998): 238–263.

Yonai, Yuval. "The Law Regarding Same-Sex Preference—Between History and Sociology." *Law and Government* 4, no. 2 (1998): 531–586.

Yuval-Davis, Nira. "National Reproduction and Demographic Race." *Racial America* 21 (1987): 37–59.

Zimmerman, Bonnie. "'Confession' of a Lesbian Feminist." *Cross-Purposes: Lesbians, Feminists, and the Limits of Alliance*, ed. Dana Heller, 157–168. Bloomington and Indianapolis: Indiana University Press, 1997.

PART IV

American Jews

19

Diaspora

Generation and the Ground of Jewish Identity

DANIEL BOYARIN AND JONATHAN BOYARIN

Critics of Zionism, both Arab and others, along with both Jewish and non-Jewish antisemites, have often sought to portray Jewish culture as essentially racist. This foundational racism is traced to the Hebrew Bible and is described as the transparent meaning of that document. Critics who are otherwise fully committed to constructionist and historicist accounts of meaning and practice abandon this commitment when it comes to the Hebrew Bible—assuming that the Bible is, in fact and in essence, that which it has been read to be and authorizes univocally that which it has been taken to authorize. Frederick Turner writes, "But the distinctions raised in the covenant between religion and idolatry are like some visitation of the khamsin to wilderness peoples as yet unsuspected, dark clouds over Africa, the Americas, the Far East, until finally even the remotest islands and jungle enclaves are struck by fire and sword and by the subtler weapon of conversion-by-ridicule (Deut. 2:34; 7:2; 20:16–18; Josh. 6:17–21)."[1] The historically and materially defined local practices of a culture far away and long ago are made here "naturally" responsible (like the khamsin, the Middle Eastern Santa Ana) for the colonial practices of cultures entirely other to it simply because those later cultures used those practices as their authorization.[2] One effect of this sudden dehistoricization of hermeneutics has been an exoneration of European Christian society that has been, after all, the religious hegemonic system for virtually all of the imperialist, racist, and even genocidal societies of the West, but not, of course, Judaism. There were no Jewish missionaries in the remote islands and jungle enclaves. It is not the Hebrew Bible that impels the "Societies for the Propagation" but rather Pauline rhetoric like, "For as in Adam all men died, so in Christ all men shall be made

Reprinted, by permission of University of Chicago Press, from Daniel Boyarin and Jonathan Boyarin, "Diaspora: Generation and the Ground of Jewish Identity," *Critical Inquiry* 19, no. 4 (Summer 1993): 693–725. This excerpt begins at page 709.

alive" (1 Cor. 15:22). Jews and Jewish culture will have to answer for the evil that we do (especially to the Palestinians), but it is absurd for "the Jews" to be implicated in practices in which they had no part and indeed have had no part even until now: forced conversion, deculturation, genocide.[3] Even the primitive command to wipe out the peoples of Canaan was limited by the Bible itself to those particular people in that particular place, and thus declared no longer applicable by the Rabbis of the Talmud.[4] It is precisely the very literalism of rabbinic/midrashic hermeneutics that prevented a typological "application" of this command to other groups. It should be clearly recognized, then, that the attempt of the integrationist Zionist Gush Emunim movement to refigure the Palestinians as Amalek and to reactivate the genocidal commandment is a radical act of religious revisionism and not in any way a continuation of historical rabbinic Judaism.

Does this mean that rabbinic Judaism qua ideology is innocent of either ethnocentric or supremacist tenets? Certainly not. What it argues is rather that Jewish racism, like the racism of other peoples, is a facultative and dispensable aspect of the cultural system, not one that is necessary for its preservation or essential to its nature. Perhaps the primary function for a critical construction of cultural (or racial or gender or sexual) identity is to construct it in ways that purge it of its elements of domination oppression. Some, however, would argue that this is an impossible project, not because of the nature of Jewishness but because any group identity is oppressive, unless it is oppressed.

In a recent Marxian analysis of both race and racism, Etienne Balibar has argued that "racism" has two dissymmetrical aspects. On the one hand, it constitutes a dominating community with practices, discursive and otherwise, that are "articulated around stigmata of otherness (name, skin colour, religious practices)." It also constitutes, however, "the way in which, as a mirror image, individuals and collectives that are prey to racism (its 'objects') find themselves constrained to see themselves as a community." Balibar further argues that destruction of racism implies the "internal decomposition of the community created by racism," by which he means the dominating community, as is clear from his analogy to the overcoming of sexism that will involve "the break-up of the community of 'males.'"[5] This is, however, for us the crucial point, for the question is, obviously, if overcoming sexism involves the breaking up of the community of males, does it necessarily imply the breaking up of the community of females? And does this, then, not entail a breaking up of community, *tout court*? Putting it another way, are we not simply imposing a more coercive universal? On the other hand, if indeed the very existence of the dominant group is dependent on domination, if identity is always formed in a master-slave relationship, is the price not too high? What we wish to struggle for, theoretically, is a notion of identity in which there are only slaves but no masters, that is, an alternative to the model of self-determination, which is, after all, in itself a Western, imperialist imposition on the rest of the world.

We propose Diaspora as a theoretical and historical model to replace national self-determination.[6] To be sure, this would be an idealized Diaspora generalized from those situations in Jewish history when Jews were both relatively free from persecution and yet constituted by strong identity—those situations, moreover, within which Promethean Jewish creativity was not antithetical, indeed was synergistic with a general cultural activity. Another way of making the same point would be to insist that there are material and social conditions in which cultural identity, difference, will not produce even what Balibar, after P. A. Taguieff, has called "differentialist racism," that is, "a racism whose dominant theme is not biological heredity but the insurmountability of cultural differences, a racism which, at first sight, does not postulate the superiority of certain groups or peoples in relation to others but 'only' the harmfulness of abolishing frontiers, the incompatibility of lifestyles and traditions; in short, it is what P. A. Taguieff has rightly called a *differentialist racism*" ("I," 21).

To our understanding, it would be an appropriate goal to articulate a theory and practice of identity that would simultaneously respect the irreducibility and the positive value of cultural differences, address the harmfulness, not of abolishing frontiers but of dissolution of uniqueness, and encourage the mutual fructification of different lifestyles and traditions. We do not think, moreover, that such possibilities are merely utopian. We would certainly claim that there have been historical situations in which they obtained without perfect success in this radically imperfect world. The solution of Zionism—that is, Jewish state hegemony, except insofar as it represented an emergency and temporary rescue operation—seems to us the subversion of Jewish culture and not its culmination. If represents the substitution of a European, Western cultural-political formation for a traditional Jewish one that has been based on a sharing, at best, of political power with others and that takes on entirely other meanings when combined with political hegemony.

Let us begin with two concrete examples. Jewish resistance to assimilation and annihilation within conditions of Diaspora, to which we will return below, generated such practices as communal charity in the areas of education, feeding, providing for the sick, and the caring for Jewish prisoners, to the virtual exclusion of others. While this meant at least that those others were not subjected to attempts to Judaize them—that is, they were tolerated, and not only by default of lack of Jewish power—it also meant that Jewish resources were not devoted to the welfare of humanity at large but only to one family. Within Israel, where power is concentrated almost exclusively in Jewish hands, this discursive practice has become a monstrosity whereby an egregiously disproportionate measure of the resources of the state is devoted to the welfare of only one segment of the population. A further and somewhat more subtle and symbolic example is the following. That very practice mentioned above, the symbolic expression of contempt for places of worship of others, becomes darkly ominous when it is combined with temporal power and domination—that is, when Jews have power over places of worship belonging to others. It is this factor that has allowed the Israelis to turn the central Mosque of Beersheba into a museum of the Negev and to let the Muslim cemetery of that city to fall into ruins.[7] Insistence on ethnic speciality, when it is extended over a particular piece of land, will inevitably produce a discourse not unlike the Inquisition in many of its effects. The archives of the Israeli General Security Services will one day prove this claim eminently, although already we "know" the truth.

We are not comparing Israeli practice to Nazism, for that would occlude more than it reveals and would obscure the real, imminent danger of its becoming the case in the future; the use of *Lebensraum* rhetoric on the part of mainstream Israeli politicians and the ascent to respectability and a certain degree of power of fascist parties in Israel certainly provide portents of this happening. Our argument is rather for an as yet unrealized but necessary theoretical compatibility between Zionist ideology and the fascism of state ethnicity. Capturing Judaism in a state transforms entirely the meanings of its social practices. Practices that in Diaspora have one meaning—for example, caring for the feeding and housing of Jews and not "others"—have entirely different meanings under political hegemony. E. P. Sanders has gotten this just right:

> More important is the evidence that points to Jewish pride in separatism. Christian scholars habitually discuss the question under the implied heading "What was wrong with Judaism that Christianity corrected?" Exclusivism is considered to be bad, and the finding that Jews were to some degree separatist fills many with righteous pride. We shall all agree that exclusivism is bad when practiced by the dominant group. Things look different if one thinks of minority groups that are trying to maintain their own identity. I have never felt that the strict Amish are iniquitous, and I do not think that, in assessing Jewish separatism in the Diaspora, we are dealing with a moral issue. (The moral issue would be the treatment of Gentiles in Palestine during periods of Jewish ascendancy. How well were the biblical laws to love the resident alien [Lev. 19:33–34] observed?)[8]

The inequities—and worse—in Israeli political, economic, and social practice are not aberrations but inevitable consequences of the inappropriate application of a form of discourse from one historical situation to another.

For those of us who are equally committed to social justice and collective Jewish existence, some other formation must be constituted. We suggest that an Israel that reimports diasporic consciousness—a consciousness of a Jewish collective as one sharing space with others, devoid of exclusivist and dominating power—is the only Israel that could answer Paul's, Lyotard's, and Nancy's call for a species-wide care without eradicating cultural difference.[9] Reversing A. B. Yehoshua's famous pronouncement that only in a condition of political hegemony is moral responsibility mobilized, we would argue that the only moral path would be the renunciation of Jewish hegemony qua Jewish hegemony.[10] This would involve first of all complete separation of religion from state, but even more than that the revocation of the Law of Return and such cultural, discursive practices that code the state as a Jewish state and not a multinational and multicultural one. The dream of a place that is ours founders on the rock of realization that there are Others there just as there are Others in Poland, Morocco, and Ethiopia. Any notion, then, of redemption through land must either be infinitely deferred (as the Neturei Karta understands so well) or become a moral monster. Either Israel must entirely divest itself of the language of race and become truly a state that is equally for all of its citizens and collectives or the Jews must divest themselves of their claim to space. Race and space together form a deadly discourse.

Genealogy and *territorialism* have been the problematic and necessary (if not essential) terms around which Jewish identity has revolved. In Jewish history, however, these terms are more obviously at odds with each other than in synergy. This allows a formulation of Jewish identity not as a proud resting place (hence not as a form of integrism or nativism) but as a perpetual, creative, diasporic tension. In the final section of this chapter, then, we would like to begin to articulate a notion of Jewish identity that recuperates its genealogical moment—family, history, memory, and practice—while it problematizes claims to autochthony and indigenousness as the material base of Jewish identity. "The Tanak and other sources of Judaism reveal certain ideas concerning The Land that reflect, or are parallel to, primitive Semitic, other Near Eastern, and, indeed, widespread conceptions about the significance of their land to a particular people. Israel is represented as the center of the Earth. . . . The religious man desires to live as near to this sacred space as possible and comes to regard it, the place of his abode, his own land, as the centre of the world" (*T*, 1; see also p. 87).

There are two diametrically opposed moments in the Jewish discourse of the land. On the one hand, it is crucial to recognize that the Jewish conception of the Land of Israel is similar to the discourse of the land of many (if not nearly all) "indigenous" peoples of the world. Somehow the Jews have managed to retain a sense of being rooted somewhere in the world through twenty centuries of exile from that someplace (organic metaphors are not out of place in this discourse, for they are used within the tradition itself).

It is profoundly disturbing to hear Jewish attachment to the land decried as regressive in the same discursive situations in which the attachment of native Americans or Australians to their particular rocks, trees, and deserts is celebrated as an organic connection to the Earth that "we" have lost.[11] The uncritical valorization of indigenousness (and particularly the confusion between political indigenousness and mystified autochthony) must come under critique, without wishing, however, to deny the rights of native Americans, Australians, and Palestinians to their lands precisely on the basis of real, unmysterious political claims. If, on the other hand, Jews are to give up hegemony over the land, this does not mean that the profundity of our attachment to the land can be denied. This also must have a political expression in the present, in the provision of the possibility for Jews to live a Jewish life in a Palestine not dominated by one ethnic group or another.

On the other hand, the biblical story is not one of autochthony but one of always already coming from somewhere else. As Davies has so very well understood, the concept of a divine promise to give this land that is the land of others to His People Israel is the sign of a bad conscience for having deprived the others of their land (see *T*, 11–12).[12] Thus at the same time that one vitally important strain of expression within biblical religion promotes a sense of organic, "natural" connectedness between this people and this land—a settlement in the land—in another sense or in a counterstrain, Israelite and Jewish religion is perpetually an unsettlement of the very notion of autochthony.

Traditional Jewish attachment to the land, whether biblical or post-biblical, thus provides a self-critique as well as a critique of identities based on notions of autochthony. Some myths about "the tree over there from which the first man sprung," along with European nationalist myths about Atlantis,[13] have been allowed to harden into a confusion of "indigenous" (the people who belong here, whose land this rightfully is—a political claim, founded on present and recently past political realities) and "autochthonous" (the people who were never anywhere else but here and have a natural right to this land). The Jewish narrative of the land has the power of insisting on the connection without myths of autochthony, while other narratives, including the Zionist one, have repressed memories of coming from somewhere else. The confusion between indigenousness and autochthony is of the same kind as the confusion in Michaels's text between any kind of genealogically based racism belonging to a people and modern scientific racism.

These very conflations are complicitous with a set of mystifications within which nationalist ideologies subsist. Harry Berger argues that "the alienation of social constructions of divinity and cosmos by conquest groups resembles the alienation of socially constructed kinship and status terms from domestic kin groups to corporate descent groups—in anthropological jargon, from the ego-centered kinship system of families to the more patently fictional ancestor-centered system of lineages."[14] Distinguishing between forms of "weak transcendence" and "strong transcendence," Berger argues that "family membership illustrates weak kinship; tribal membership, strong kinship." Strong transcendence is more aggressive because it is more embattled and does more ideological work; that is, according to Berger, it serves to justify land control. "Status that depends on land is generally more precarious and alienable than status inscribed on the body; mobile subsistence economies tend to conceptualize status in terms of the signifying indices of the body—indices of gender, age, and kinship—rather than of more conspicuously artificial constructions, and are closer to the weak end of the weak-to-strong scale" ("L," 121). The place of the first of these alienations can, however, be taken by the alienation of a socially constructed connection to a land by myths of autochthony and the unique belonging of this land to a people, an alienation that can serve the interest of conquerors, as easily as by the transcendental legitimation of kings. Thus if Berger, following Walter Brueggemann, contrasts two covenants, one the Mosaic, which rejects "the imperial gods of a totalitarian and hierarchic social order" ("L," 123), and one, the Davidic, which enthrones precisely those gods as the one God, we could just as well contrast two trajectories, the one toward autochthony and the one against it, in the same way. The first would support the rule of Israelite kings over territory; the second would serve to oppose it.[15] "The dialectical struggle between anti-royalism and royalism persists throughout the course and formative career of the Old Testament as its structuring force. It sets the tent against the house, nomadism against agriculture, the wilderness against Canaan, wandering and exile against settlement, diaspora against the political integrity of a settled state" ("L," 123).

Our argument, then, is that a vision of Jewish history and identity that valorizes the second half of each of these binary systems and sees the first as only a disease constitutes not a continuation of Jewish culture but its final betrayal.

Berger, however, has also implicated "ancestor-centered systems of lineages" as ideological mystifications in the service of the state power of conquest groups while we have held up such an organization as one feasible component of an alternative to statism. Empirically, tribal organization, with its concomitant myths of the eponymous ancestor, is nearly emblematic of nomadic peoples. Berger's own discourse, however, is inconsistent here, for only a page later he will refer to the premonarchic period of Israel ("roughly from 1250 to 1000 B.C.") as a sociological experiment in "the rejection of strong transcendence in favor of a less coercive and somewhat weaker alternative, the tribal system that cuts across both local allegiances and stratificational discontinuities" ("L," 123). Thus Berger first puts tribalism on the side of "strong transcendence" and then on the side of "weak." Against Berger's first claim on this point and in favor of his second, we would argue that talk of the eponymous ancestors, of the patriarchs, is conspicuously less prominent in the "Davidic" texts of the settlement than in the "Mosaic" texts of the wandering. As Berger himself writes, David "tried to displace the loyalties and solidarity of kinship ties from clans and tribes to the national dynasty" ("L," 124). We suggest that descent from a common ancestor is rather an extension of family kinship and not its antithesis and thus on the side of wilderness and not on the side of Canaan. Even the myth of descent from common ancestry belongs rather to the semantic field of status through the body and not to the semantic field of status through land. Diaspora, in historical Judaism, can be interpreted then as the later analogue to nomadism in the earlier set of material conditions and thus as a continuation of the sociological experiment that the Davidic monarchy symbolically overturns.[16] With the rabbinic "invention" of Diaspora, the radical experiment of Moses was advanced. The forms of identification typical of nomads, those marks of status in the body, remained, then, crucial to this formation. Race is here on the side of the radicals; space, on the other hand, belongs to the despots.

One modernist story of Israel, the Israeli Declaration of Independence, begins with an imaginary autochthony—"In the Land of Israel this people came into existence"—and ends with the triumphant return of the people to their natural land, making them "re-autochthonized," "like all of the nations." Israeli state power, deprived of the option of self-legitimation through appeal to a divine king, discovered autochthony as a powerful replacement. An alternative story of Israel, closer, it would seem, to the readings of the Judaism lived for two thousand years, begins with a people forever unconnected with a particular land, a people that calls into question the idea that a people must have a land in order to be a people. "The Land of Israel was not the birthplace of the Jewish people, which did not emerge there (as most peoples have on their own soil). On the contrary it had to enter its own land from without; there is a sense in which Israel was born in exile. Abraham had to leave his own land to go to the Promised Land: the father of Jewry was deterritorialized" (T, 63).[17] In this view, the stories of Israel's conquest of the land, whether under Abraham, Joshua, or even more prominently under David, are always stories that are compromised with a sense of failure of mission even more than they are stories of the accomplishment of mission, and the internal critique within the Tanakh (Hebrew Bible) itself, the dissident voice that is nearly always present, does not let us forget this either. Davies also brings into absolutely clear focus a prophetic discourse of preference for "exile" over rootedness in the land (together with a persistent hope of eschatological restoration), a prophetic discourse that has been totally occluded in modern Zionist ideological representations of the Bible and of Jewish history but was pivotal in the rabbinic ideology (see T, 15–19).

The rabbis produced their cultural formation within conditions of Diaspora, and we would argue that their particular discourse of ethnocentricity is ethically appropriate only when the cultural identity is an embattled (or, at any rate, nonhegemonic) minority. The point is not that the land was devalued by the rabbis but that they renounced it until the final redemption; in an unredeemed world, temporal dominion and ethnic particularity are impossibly compromised. Davies phrases the position just right when he says, "It was its ability to detach its loyalty from 'place,' while nonetheless retaining 'place' in its memory, that enabled Pharisaism to transcend the loss of its Land" (T, 69).[18] Our only addition would be to argue that this displacement of loyalty from place to memory of place was necessary not only to transcend the loss of the land but also to enable the loss of the land. Political possession of the land most threatened the possibility of continued Jewish cultural practice and difference. Given the choice between an ethnocentricity that would not seek domination over others and a seeking of political domination that would necessarily have led either to a dilution of distinctiveness, tribal warfare, or fascism, the rabbis chose ethnocentricity. Zionism is thus a subversion of rabbinic Judaism, and it is no wonder that until World War II Zionism was a secular movement to which very few religious Jews adhered, seeing it as a human arrogation of a work that only God should or could perform.[19] This is, moreover, the basis, even to this day, for the anti-Zionist ideology of such groups as Neturei Karta.

The dialectic between Paul and the rabbis can be recuperated for cultural critique. When Christianity is the hegemonic power in Europe and the United States, the resistance of Jews to being universalized can be a critical force and model for the resistance of all peoples to being Europeanized out of particular bodily existence. When, however, an ethnocentric Judaism becomes a temporal, hegemonic political force, it becomes absolutely, vitally necessary to accept Paul's critical challenge—although not his universalizing, disembodying solution—and to develop an equally passionate concern for all human beings. We, including religious Jews—perhaps especially religious Jews—must take seriously the theological dimension of Paul's challenge. How could the God of all the world have such a disproportionate care and concern for only a small part of His world? And yet, obviously, we cannot even conceive of accepting Paul's solution of dissolving into a universal human essence, even one that would not be Christian but truly humanist and universal, even if such an entity could really exist.[20] Somewhere in this dialectic a synthesis must be found, one that will allow for stubborn hanging-on to ethnic, cultural specificity but in a context of deeply felt and enacted human solidarity. For that synthesis, Diaspora provides a model, and only in conditions of Diaspora can such a resolution be even attempted. Within the conditions of Diaspora, many Jews discovered that their well-being was absolutely dependent on principles of respect for difference, indeed that, as the radical slogan goes, "no one is free until all are free." Absolute devotion to the maintenance of Jewish culture and the historical memory was not inconsistent with devotion to radical causes of human liberation; there were Yiddish-speaking and Judeo-Arabic-speaking groups of Marxists and anarchists, and some even retained a commitment to historical Jewish religious practice.[21] The "chosenness" of the Jews becomes, when seen in this light, not a warrant for racism but precisely an antidote to racism. This is a Judaism that mobilizes the critical forces within the Bible and the Jewish tradition rather than mobilizing the repressive and racist forces that also subsist there and that we are not denying.

Within conditions of Diaspora, tendencies toward nativism were also materially discouraged. Diaspora culture and identity allows (and has historically allowed in the best circumstances, such as in Muslim Spain), for a complex continuation of Jewish cultural creativity and identity at the same time that the same people participate fully in the common cultural life of their surroundings. The same figure, a Nagid, an Ibn Gabirol, or a Maimonides, can be simultaneously the vehicle of the preservation of traditions and of the mixing of cultures. This was the case not only in Muslim Spain, nor even only outside of the land. The rabbis in Diaspora in their own land also produced a phenomenon of renewal of Jewish traditional culture at the same time that they were very well acquainted with and an integral part of the circumambient late antique culture. Diasporic cultural identity teaches us that cultures are not preserved by being protected from "mixing" but probably can only continue to exist as a product of such mixing. Cultures, as well as identities, are constantly being remade. While this is true of all cultures, diasporic Jewish culture lays it bare because of the impossibility of a natural association between this people and a particular land—thus the impossibility of seeing Jewish culture as a self-enclosed, bounded phenomenon. The critical force of this dissociation among people, language, culture, and land has been an enormous threat to cultural nativisms and integrisms, a threat that is one of the sources of anti-Semitism and perhaps one of the reasons that Europe has been much more prey to this evil than the Middle East. In other words, diasporic identity is a disaggregated identity. Jewishness disrupts the very categories of identity because it is not national, not genealogical, not religious, but all of these in dialectical tension with one another. When liberal Arabs and some Jews claim that the Jews of the Middle East are Arab Jews, we concur and think that Zionist ideology occludes something very significant when it seeks to obscure this point. The production of an ideology of a pure Jewish cultural essence that has been debased by Diaspora seems neither historically nor ethically correct. "Diasporized," that is, disaggregated, identity allows the early medieval scholar Rabbi Sa'adya to be an Egyptian Arab who happens to be Jewish and also a Jew who happens to be an Egyptian Arab. Both of these contradictory propositions must be held together. Similarly, we suggest that a diasporized gender identity is possible and positive. Being a woman is some kind of special being, and there are aspects of life and practice that insist on and celebrate that speciality. But this does not imply a fixing or freezing of all practice and performance of gender identity into one set of parameters. Human beings are divided into men and women for certain purposes, but that does not tell the whole story of their bodily identity. Rather than the dualism of gendered bodies and universal souls, or Jewish/Greek bodies and universal souls—the dualism that the Western tradition offers—we can substitute partially Jewish, partially Greek bodies, bodies that are sometimes gendered and sometimes not. It is this idea that we are calling diasporized identity.

Crucial to this construction of Jewish history and identity is the simple fact, often consciously or unconsciously suppressed, that Diaspora is not the forced product of war and destruction—taking place after the downfall of

Judea—but that already in the centuries before this downfall, the majority of Jews lived voluntarily outside of the Land.[22] Moreover, given a choice between domination by a "foreign" power who would allow them to keep the Torah undisturbed and domination by a "Jewish" authority who would interfere with religious life, the Pharisees and their successors the rabbis generally chose the former (see T, 68).[23]

The story we would tell of Jewish history has three stages. In the first stage, we find a people—call it a tribe—not very different in certain respects from peoples in similar material conditions all over the world, a people like most others that regards itself as special among humanity, indeed as the People, and its land as preeminently wonderful among lands, the Land. This is, of course, an oversimplification because this "tribe" never quite dwelled alone and never regarded itself as autochthonous in its land. In the second stage, this form of life increasingly becomes untenable, morally and politically, because the "tribe" is in cultural, social, and political contact with other people. This is, roughly speaking, the Hellenistic period, culminating in the crises of the first century, of which we have read Paul as an integral part. Various solutions to this problem were eventually adopted. Pauline Christianity is one; so perhaps is the retreat to Qumran, while the Pharisaic Rabbis "invented" Diaspora, even in the land, as the solution to this cultural dilemma.

The third stage is diasporic existence. The rabbinic answer to Paul's challenge was to renounce any possibility of domination over others by being perpetually out of power:

> Just as with seeing the return in terms of the restoration of political rights, seeing it in terms of redemption has certain consequences. If the return were an act of divine intervention, it could not be engineered or forced by political or any other human means: to do so would be impious. That coming was best served by waiting in obedience for it: *men of violence would not avail to bring it in.* The rabbinic aloofness to messianic claimants sprang not only from the history of disillusionment with such, but from this underlying, deeply engrained attitude. It can be claimed that under the main rabbinic tradition Judaism condemned itself to powerlessness. But recognition of powerlessness (rather than a frustrating, futile, and tragic resistance) was effective in preserving Judaism in a very hostile Christendom, and therefore had its own brand of "power." (T, 82)

As before, our impulse is only slightly to change the nuance of Davies's marvelously precise reading. The renunciation (not merely "recognition") of temporal power was to our minds precisely the most powerful mode of preservation of difference and, therefore, the most effective kind of resistance. The Neturei Karta, to this day, refuse to visit the Western Wall, the holiest place in Judaism, without PLO "visas" because it was taken by violence.

This response has much to teach us. We want to propose a privileging of Diaspora, a dissociation of ethnicities and political hegemonies as the only social structure that even begins to make possible a maintenance of cultural identity in a world grown thoroughly and inextricably interdependent. Indeed, we would suggest that Diaspora, and not monotheism, may be the most important contribution that Judaism has to make to the world, although we would not deny the positive role that monotheism has played in making Diaspora possible.[24] Assimilating the lesson of Diaspora, namely that peoples and lands are not naturally and organically connected, could help prevent bloodshed such as that occurring in Eastern Europe today.[25] In Eastern Europe at the turn of the century, the Jewish Workers' Bund, a mass socialist organization, had developed a model for national-cultural autonomy not based on territorial ethnic states. That program was effectively marginalized by the Bolsheviks and the Zionists. Diaspora can teach us that it is possible for people to maintain its distinctive culture, its difference, without controlling and, a fortiori without controlling other people or developing a need to dispossess them of their lands. Thus the response of rabbinic Judaism to the challenge of universalism that Paul, among others, raised against what was becoming, at the end of one millennium and the beginning of the next, increasingly an inappropriate doctrine of specialness in an already interdependent world may provide some of the pieces to the puzzle of how humanity can survive as another millennium draws to a close with no messiah on the horizon. The renunciation of difference seems both an impoverishment of human life and an inevitable harbinger of oppression. Yet the renunciation of sovereignty (justified by discourses of autochthony, indigenousness, and territorial self-determination), combined with a fierce tenacity in holding onto cultural identity, might well have something to offer to a world in which these two forces, together, kill thousands daily.

Appendix: Statement of the Neturei Karta

We the Neturei Karta (Guardians of the City—Jerusalem),[26] presently numbering in the tens of thousands, are comprised of the descendants of the pioneer Jews who settled in the Holy Land over a hundred years before the establishment of the Zionist State. Their sole motive was to serve G-d, and they had neither political aspirations nor any desire to exploit the local population in order to attain statehood.

Our mission, in the capacity of Palestinian advisers in this round of the Middle East Peace Conference, is to concern ourselves with the safeguarding of the interests of the Palestinian Jews and the entire Jewish nation. The Jewish people are charged by divine oath not to seek independence and cast off the yoke of exile which G-d decreed, as a result of not abiding by the conditions under which G-d granted them the Holy Land. We repeat constantly in our prayers, "since we sinned, we were therefore exiled from our land." G-d promised to gather in the exiled Jews through His messiah. This is one of the principles of the Jewish faith. The Zionist rebelled against this divine decree of exile by taking the land away from its indigenous inhabitants and established their state. Thus are the Jewish people being exposed to the divine retribution set down in the Talmud. "I will make your flesh prey as the deer and the antelope of the forest" (Song 2:7). Our advice to the negotiating contingent of the Palestinian delegation will remain within the framework of Jewish theology.

Zionist schoolings dictate a doctrine of labelling the indigenous Palestinian population "enemies" in order to sanction their expansionist policies. Judaism teaches that the Jew and non-Jew are to coexist in a cordial and good neighbor relationship. We Palestinian Jews have no desire to expand our places of residence and occupy our neighbors' lands, but only to live alongside non-Jewish Palestinians, just as Jews live throughout the world, in peace and tranquility.

The enmity and animosity toward the non-Jewish population, taught to the Zionist faithful, is already boomeranging. King Solomon, in Parables 27:19, describes reality "as one's image is reflected in water: so one's heart toward his fellow man"—so an enemy's heart is reflected in his adversary's heart. The Intifada is "exhibit A" to this King Solomon gem of wisdom. We hope and pray that this face-to-face meeting with imagined adversaries will undo the false image created and that both Jew and Arab in Palestine can once again live as good neighbors as was the life of yesteryear, under a rule chosen by the indigenous residents of the Holy Land—thus conforming with G-d's plan for the Holy Land.

Inchallah! [27]

NOTES

1. Frederick Turner, *Beyond Geography: The Western Spirit against the Wilderness* (New York, 1980), 45. In his book *Storm from Paradise: The Politics of Jewish Memory* (Minneapolis, 1992), 134 n. 13, Jonathan Boyarin has provided a summary critique of Turner's book. See also on this theme Regina Schwartz, "Monotheism, Violence, and Identity," in *Religion and Literature*, ed. Mark Krupnick (forthcoming).

2. A particularly extreme and explicit version of this naturalizing and dehistoricizing move vis-à-vis biblical hermeneutics is found in Donald Harman Akenson, *God's Peoples: Covenant and Land in South Africa, Israel, and Ulster* (Ithaca, N.Y., 1992), who writes, "For certain societies, in certain eras of their development, the scriptures have acted culturally and socially in the same way the human genetic code operates physiologically. That is, this great code has, in some degree, directly determined what people would believe and what they would think and what they would do" (9).

3. See Marc Shell, "Marranos (Pigs); or, From Coexistence to Toleration," *Critical Inquiry* 17 (Winter 1991): 306–335, for the argument that Jewish reluctance to convert others is built into the system and not merely a result of later material and historical conditions. We think, however, that Shell underestimates the potential for grounding racist thought in other aspects of biblical discourse.

4. See Jonathan Boyarin, "Reading Exodus into History," *New Literary History* 23 (Summer 1992): 523–554.

5. Etienne Balibar, "Is There a 'Neo-Racism'?" in Balibar and Immanuel Wallerstein, *Race, Nation, Class: Ambiguous Identities* (London, 1991), 18; hereafter abbreviated "I."

6. To the extent that this diasporic existence is an actual historical entity, we ourselves are not prey to the charge of "allegorizing" the Jew. It may be fairly suggested, however, that the model is so idealized as to be in itself an allegory.

7. A highly ingenuous, or more likely egregiously disingenuous, claim by Abba Eban is given the lie in every page of Israeli history, particularly the last ones. Beersheba may have been "virtually empty," but that is little consolation to the Bedouin who were and continue to be dispossessed there and in its environs. And the refugees in camps in Gaza, as well as the still-visible ruins of their villages, would certainly dispute the claim that Arab populations had avoided "the land of the Philistines in the coastal plain . . . because of insalubrious conditions" (Abba Eban to W. D. Davies, in Davies, *The Territorial Dimension of Judaism* [1982; Minneapolis, 1992], 76; hereafter abbreviated *T*).

8. E. P. Sanders, "Jewish Association with Gentiles and Galatians 2:11–14," in *The Conversation Continues: Studies in Paul and John in Honor of J. Louis Martyn*, ed. Robert T. Fortna and Beverly R. Gaventa (Nashville, Tenn., 1990), 181.

9. See Jonathan Boyarin, "Palestine and Jewish History," chap. 7 of *Storm from Paradise*.

10. Shell argues, following Spinoza, that temporal power is necessary for toleration ("Marranos [Pigs]," 328 n. 75). We are suggesting the opposite, that only conditions in which power is shared among religions and ethnicities will allow for difference with common caring.

11. An aboriginal Australian recently began her lecture at a conference with greetings from her people to the indigenous people of the United States, of whom there were two representatives in the audience and whom she addressed by name. Much of her lecture consisted of a critique of the rootlessness of Europeans. Daniel Boyarin had a sense of being trapped in a double bind, for if the Jews are the indigenous people of the Land of Israel, as Zionism claims, then the Palestinians are indigenous nowhere, but if the Palestinians are the indigenous people of Palestine, then Jews are indigenous nowhere. He had painfully renounced the possibility of realizing his very strong feeling of connection to the land (this connection having been co-opted by the state) in favor of what he and Jonathan Boyarin take to be the only possible end to violence and movement toward justice. Are we now to be condemned as people who have lost their roots?

12. Davies remarks that this sense of "bad conscience" can be found in texts as late as the first century B.C.E. We think he underestimates this. The classical midrash on Genesis, Bereshith Rabba, a product of the fourth and fifth centuries C.E., begins with the question, "Why does the Torah open with the creation of the world?" It answers, "So that when the Nations will call Israel robbers for their theft of the Land, they will be able to point to the Torah and say: God created the earth and can dispose of it at his will!" (our trans.).

13. See Pierre Vidal-Naquet, "Atlantis and the Nations," trans. Janet Lloyd, *Critical Inquiry* 18 (Winter 1992): 300–326.

14. Harry Berger Jr., "The Lie of the Land: The Text beyond Canaan," *Representations* no. 25 (Winter 1989): 121; hereafter abbreviated "L."

15. For an even more nuanced reading of tensions within the Davidic stories themselves, see Schwartz, "Nations and Nationalism: Adultery in the House of David," *Critical*

Inquiry 19 (Autumn 1992): 142. Schwartz's forthcoming book will deal with many of the themes of identity in the Bible that this essay is treating, albeit with quite different methods and often with quite different results.

16. It is important to emphasize that this analysis is indifferent to the historical question of whether there were nomadic Israelite tribes to begin with or the thesis (made most famous by the work of Norman K. Gottwald, *The Tribes of Yahweh: A Sociology of the Religion of Liberated Israel, 1250–1050 b.c.e.* [Maryknoll, N.Y., 1979]) that ascribes them to a "retribalization" process taking place among "native" Canaanites. For a discussion of this thesis, see "L," 131–132. For our purposes, the representations of the tribes as nomadic and the ideological investments in that representation are indifferent to the "actual" history.

17. Also, "The desert is, therefore, the place of revelation and of the constitution of 'Israel' as a people; there she was elected" (*T*, 39). Davies's book is remarkable for many reasons, one of which is surely the way that while it intends to be a defense and explanation of Zionism as a deeply rooted Jewish movement, it consistently and honestly documents the factors in the tradition that are in tension with such a view.

18. We think that Davies occasionally seems to lose his grip on his own great insight by confusing ethnic identity with political possession (see *T*, 90–91 n. 10). The same mixture appears also when he associates, it seems, deterritorialization and deculturation (93). It is made clear when he writes, "At the same time the age-long engagement of Judaism with The Land in religious terms indicates that ethnicity and religion . . . are finally inseparable in Judaism" (97). We certainly agree that ethnicity and religion are inseparable in Judaism, but we fail to see the necessary connection between ethnicity, religion, and territoriality. Moreover, a people can be on their land without this landedness being expressed in the form of a nation-state, and landedness can be shared in the same place with others who feel equally attached to the same land. This is the solution of the Neturei Karta, who live, after all, in Jerusalem but do not seek political hegemony over it.

19. Davies states that "for religious Jews, we must conclude, The Land is ultimately inseparable from the state of Israel, however much the actualities of history have demanded their distinction" (*T*, 51). Yet clearly many religious Jews have not felt that way at all. Although we do not deny entirely the theological bona fides of religious Zionism as one option for modern Jewish religious thought, the fact that they are the historical "winners" in an ideological struggle should not blind us to the fact that their option was, until only recently, just one option for religious Jews, and a very contested one at that. Even the theological "patron saint" of religious Zionists, the holy Rabbi Loewe (Maharal) of Prague, who, as Davies points out, "understood the nature and role of nations to be ordained by God, part of the natural order," and that "nations were intended to cohere rather than be scattered"; even he held that "reestablishment of a Jewish state should be left to God" (*T*, 33). Rabbi Nahman of Bratslav's desire to touch any part of the land and then immediately return to Poland hardly bespeaks a proto-Zionism either (*T*, 33). Davies nuances his own statement when he remarks, "Zionism cannot be equated with a reaffirmation of the eternal relation of The Land, the people, and the Deity, except with the most cautious reservations, since it is more the expression of nationalism than of Judaism" (*T*, 64). Davies is right, however, in his claim that Petuchowski's statement—that there can be a "full-blooded Judaism which is in no need to hope and to pray for a messianic return to Palestine" (J. J. Petuchowski, "Diaspora Judaism—An Abnormality?" *Judaism* 9 [1960]: 27)—is missing something vital about historical Jewish tradition. The desire, the longing for unity, coherence, and groundedness in the utopian future of

the messianic age is, as Davies eminently demonstrates, virtually inseparable from historical Judaism (*T*, 66). There is surely a "territorial theological tradition." At issue rather is its status in premessianic praxis.

20. Judith Butler asks, "How is it that we might ground a theory or politics in a speech situation or subject position which is 'universal' when the very category of the universal has only begun to be exposed for its own highly ethnocentric biases?" Judith Butler, "Contingent Foundations: Feminism and the Question of 'Postmodernism,'" *Praxis International* 11 (July 1991): 153.
21. Lenin's minister of justice, I. N. Steinberg, was an orthodox Jew.
22. Davies is one scholar who does not suppress this fact but forthrightly faces it. See *T*, 65.
23. Once again, the Neturei Karta, in their deference to Palestinian political claims on the Land of Israel, are, it seems, on solid historical ground.
24. Sidra Ezrahi has recently argued that monotheism and Diaspora are inextricably intertwined (personal communication with Daniel Boyarin).
25. Our point is not to reallegorize the Jew as wanderer but simply to point to certain aspects of the concrete realities of Jewish history as a possible, vital, positive contribution to human political culture in general. The implicitly normative call on other Jews to participate in our image of Jewishness is, we admit, ambivalent and potentially coercive, but how could it be otherwise? Even coercions can be ranked.
26. This statement was made by the Palestinian Jewish (Neturei Karta) members of the Palestinian delegation to the Middle East Peace Conference in Washington, D.C., 1992, and has been translated here from the New York Yiddish weekly *Di yidishe vokhnshrift*, September 4, 1992. We are not including this statement with our essay in order to advance Neturei Karta as an organization, nor are we members of Neturei Karta, some of whose policies we are in sympathy with and others of which we find violently objectionable. We include it because we consider it to be eloquent evidence of the kind of radical political rhetoric available within a highly traditional diasporic Jewish framework and in particular for its insight into what could be called the construction of the demonized Other.
27. The word is the traditional Muslim prayer, "May it be God's [Allah's] will."

20

From Diaspora Jews to New Jews

CARYN AVIV AND DAVID SHNEER

"Homeland?" He turned the word contemptuously back on the odious little firebrand.

"I suppose by this you mean some wilderness on the other side of the globe, on which I have never laid eyes, and which I don't even know how to picture, but which, from the description, even by those who profess themselves its eternal lovers, can promise me *nothing*.

"And yet, if I am to believe the arguments of people like you, it is that place, and not here in the Europe of my birth, and of my father's birth, and of my father's father's birth, that I am to think of as my authentic homeland? . . . I would ask you please not to impose upon me a destiny that I could never experience, but as entirely forced and artificial."

–Jascha, from Rebecca Goldstein, *Mazel* (1995)

A home is relatives and Jews.

–"Shai," interview with Naama Sabar

The metaphor of a people longing to go home is compelling. It also is outdated.

–Larry Tye, *Homelands* (2001)

On the first day of a class David teaches on Zionism and nationalism, a student asked him, "Where's the diaspora? And when writing my papers, should I capitalize it or not? Do you say that Jews in the United States are *in* diaspora or are *the* diaspora?" David explained that much of the class would be asking

Reprinted, by permission, from Caryn Aviv and David Shneer, *New Jews* (New York and London: New York University Press, 2005), 1–25.

those very questions and, when possible, figuring out some answers. He asked her where she learned the word.

"In Hebrew school and from my parents. We're diaspora Jews."

"Well, then do you have an answer to the question 'Where is the diaspora?'"

"Yeah, any place but Israel. . . . Well, at least for Jews."

"So it must be a place, or a lack of a place. But what about before Israel existed? Was there a diaspora?"

"Oh, that's a good point."

"How about Israelis who don't live in Israel? Do they become diaspora Jews?"

"No, it's about where you're born."

"So if you move to Israel, you're still really a diaspora Jew?"

"Well, no, because by moving to Israel and making *aliyah*, you're becoming an Israeli."

In only a few questions, this exchange raises some of the fundamental questions about modern Jewish identity and Jews' understanding of their place in the world. David wanted to respond to her: "If the word 'diaspora' is too amorphous and doesn't really seem to mean anything, why don't you get rid of it?" but decided that would only add to her confusion.

This book is an answer to her questions. We want to uncover the assumptions people make about diaspora. We show how some Jews are rethinking their ideas about Israel and the tensions between exile and home, diaspora and homeland, here and there. Jews are dismantling the very idea of diaspora in the way they live their lives.

Jewish Exile, Diaspora, and Home

Diaspora: 1a: the settling of scattered colonies of Jews outside Palestine after the Babylonian exile. b: the area outside Palestine settled by Jews. c: the Jews living outside Palestine or modern Israel. 2: a dispersion abroad. (Webster's)

"Diaspora" has become a popular term to describe how ethnic groups live in the world today. As air travel becomes cheaper, as Web phones make virtual visual communication over thousands of miles instantaneous, people are finding new ways of creating communities across time and space. The idea of diaspora assumes that global communities have a center, a place that Africans in the African diaspora, Irish in the Irish diaspora, and Mexicans in the Mexican diaspora can identify with and think about, and perhaps yearn to return to.

The word "diaspora" means dispersion. It originated in the Septuagint, one of the original Greek translations of the Bible: Deuteronomy 28:25: "thou shalt be a diaspora in all kingdoms of the earth." The very word summons up images of Jewish seeds scattered about the earth.[1] The term "diaspora" solidified into European consciousness and the English language only in the modern era. The *Oxford English Dictionary* cites its first use in English in 1876. More recently, dozens of collective groups have appropriated the term to explain their geographically scattered communities. Dictionary definitions of the word "diaspora" differ—some refer to actions, others to people, and others to places, depending on how the term is used. However, the word the Greeks translated from the original Hebrew as "dispersion" might, more literally, read, "thou shalt become a *horror* to all the kingdoms of the earth [*ve-hayitah le-za'avah le-chol mamlechot haarets*]." *Za'avah*, the word in question, means anything from atrocity and outrage to horror and terror, but it does not mean dispersion. That which came to symbolize the Jews' scattering among nations had a much more ominous and threatening tone in the original.

Jews' understanding of their "diaspora" has had a more negative connotation than the rather benign-sounding "dispersion," although the historian Erich Gruen and others have shown that the practices Jews developed to create Jewish diaspora communities were frequently different from the words Jews used to describe the experience of exile. In Hebrew and Yiddish, the term *galut (golus)* is a closer equivalent to "diaspora" than *za'avah*. But even in this case, *galut* is an inherently negative term, suggesting spiritual diminishment and exile, rather than just dispersion from a homeland. In Modern Hebrew, the adjective *galuti*, which should simply be translated as "diasporic," in fact is generally translated pejoratively as "ghetto-like, of ghetto nature, exilic, diasporic," suggesting that Jews' relationship to place has changed since the advent of modern Hebrew, Zionism, and the founding of Israel.[2]

Within some Jewish cultures and memories, then, diaspora as *galut* has signified a diminished spiritual and eschatological condition, connected to the negative idea of exile, homelessness, and a yearning for a return to Zion under the guidance of the Messiah. Traditional Jewish texts always figured (and continue to figure) a mythic Zion as the eternal Jewish home, the place to which the Messiah would return Jews. But this was and continues to be a mythic home, a nirvana, a glimpse of the world to come. Many Jews who actually lived in the land we now know as Israel during the two-thousand-year "exile" still conceived of Zion as a mythic place from which they were exiled. Even after the establishment of the state, within and outside Israel, after Jews "forced the hand of history" by doing that which the Messiah had not yet done, there have been religious Jews, namely the ultra-Orthodox groups Reb Arelach and Neturei Karta, that live in Israel but do not recognize Jewish political sovereignty over the land.[3] In the 1970s, the leader of Lubavitch Hasidism, M. M. Schneerson, declared that Jews who lived in the Holy Land were just as much in exile as those who lived in the diaspora.[4]

Historically, Jews' understanding of home and diaspora was made up of everyday practices and relationships to local communities and to mythic homelands, no matter where one lived. The first theoretician of diaspora, the prophet Jeremiah, who witnessed the destruction of the First Temple in 586 B.C.E. and the subsequent Babylonian Exile, suggested one particular survival strategy. Jews needed to craft a concept of diaspora that would allow them to be at home wherever they were, while still maintaining a memory of place that connected them to Zion. Jeremiah was still too fresh from the real experience of expulsion to move beyond a diaspora/homeland dichotomy, but he told Jews to root themselves in their new communities: "Build houses and live in them, plant gardens and eat their fruit.... Multiply there, do not decrease. And seek the welfare of the city to which I have exiled you" (Jeremiah 29:5–7). Although Jews were yearning for their lost homeland when they said the words "If I forget thee, O Jerusalem" (Psalms 137:5), Jeremiah called on Jews to maintain a dynamic tension between movement and rootedness, between being at home and recalling a mythic homeland.

Many Hellenistic Jews in the Second Temple Period (513 B.C.E.–70 C.E.), for example, *chose* to live outside the borders of the Holy Land. While living throughout the Hellenistic empire, they sent money to Jerusalem and conceived of Jerusalem as the *patris*, the homeland, but did not long to return there. In the words of Erich Gruen, "The self-perception of Second Temple Jews projected a tight solidarity between center and diaspora. [But] the images of exile and separation did not haunt them.... The respect and awe paid to the Holy Land stood in full harmony with commitment to local community and allegiance to Gentile governance."[5]

While living in exile following the destruction of the Second Temple—what had been the locus of Jewish political and spiritual power and the symbol of Jewish rootedness in Judea—in 70 C.E., Rabbinic Jews crafted a diaspora that allowed them to be home where they were while maintaining cultural differences from the other people with whom they lived. They had to construct senses of home wherever they were in diaspora, because there was no real homeland anymore. In this way, the historic Jewish diaspora differs from many postmodern diasporas, which have an actual political entity, rather than only a symbolic one, that they may call a homeland. If contemporary diasporas create relationships to both a real and a mythic homeland, Jews in Exile only had the mythic, messianic Zion to imagine.

Over the course of several centuries, Jews added varied practices (like Hellenistic Jews' sending of money to the Temple before the Exile) to their repertoire of cultural strategies for remembering the homeland while firmly "rooting" diasporic Jewish cultures in their local places. Jews recited lamenting psalms about exile on fast days and repeated the line "next year in Jerusalem" every Passover, and some made pilgrimages to the Holy Land. Some Jews continued to send money to help support the Jews who remained behind in Zion after the expulsion. And, culturally, many Jews maintained a mythic connection to the Holy Land, a connection celebrated (and sometimes satirized) in liturgy and literature. In S. Y. Abramovitch's classic Yiddish story, *The Brief Travels of Benjamin the Third*, the little town of Tuneyadevka marvels at the arrival of a date from the Holy Land: "You should have seen the town come running to look at it. A Bible was brought to prove that the very same little fruit grew in the Holy Land. The harder the Tuneyadevkans stared at it, the more clearly they saw before their eyes the River Jordan, the Cave of the Patriarchs, the tomb of Mother Rachel, the Wailing Wall. . . . For a moment . . . the whole of Tuneyadevka was in the Land of Israel."[6]

In addition to remembering the mythic Exile from the Holy Land, Jews also had strategies for rooting themselves in places. For example, Jewish communities established cemeteries—a very concrete act of claiming both place and space for themselves that meant acquiring land and investing it with cultural and metaphysical power. Cemeteries are holy ground (and are also impure ground), and no matter how much one culture can wipe away cultural traces of another by destroying buildings, eliminating languages, or killing people, bodies are rooted *in* the ground, not *on* the ground.[7] Jews also established traditional schools (*b'tei midrash*) and ritual bathhouses (*mikva'ot*)—places off-limits to the cultures and peoples around them. These private spaces within the community served as foundations from which to construct community. They are also places that have historically been associated with gender and sexuality, and with the segregation of space and knowledge. These three spaces—cemeteries, bathhouses, and schools—were cornerstones of how Jews practiced home in multiple ways for several centuries, across geographies and cultures.

Although the majority of contemporary Jews no longer use bathhouses and traditional schools as their way of making home, many still perform acts of marking Jewish space by hanging a mezuzah on a doorpost. Ask most American Jews, and they'll say that hanging a mezuzah is one of the most important symbols that visibly and publicly renders a home as "Jewish." Within a mobile modern American culture, the symbol of the mezuzah roots Jews in homes and creates a sense of community. When a Jew moves, she is supposed to leave the mezuzah on the house, rather like Jews leaving bodies in the ground. From the beginning of the mythic diaspora, Jews have created rituals, built structures, and developed relationships to places that simultaneously create a sense of home in the places they live and assert Jews' difference from those around them by remembering Zion.

Jewish Peoples and Jewish Diasporas

Although Jews' relationship to the mythic Zion has always been one of the markers of Jewish difference from the people around them, Jews have always had many diasporas and homelands—from Sephardic Jews who were expelled from medieval Spain in 1492 and longed for a mythic return, to nineteenth- and twentieth-century German Jews, who, before the Holocaust, viewed Germany as their homeland. German Jews made up the bulk of Jewish immigrants to the United States in the nineteenth century. In the years shortly after their primary migration, in the mid-nineteenth century, these Jews maintained strong relationships with Germany by bringing in German rabbis, traveling across the Atlantic, and even importing German forms of Judaism, such as the Reform movement, to America. Similarly, many Jews who left Germany in the 1930s during Nazi rule still thought of Germany as the homeland from which they had been exiled.

At the same time, many Jews were already starting to see themselves as rooted in the places they lived, rather than in diaspora from their former home. German Jews who remained in Germany after it became a country in 1871 increasingly crafted German national identities for themselves. They served in the German army, spoke German, and read German literature. When Eastern European Jews started immigrating to Germany in the 1880s and 1890s, established German Jews often used these new *Ostjuden,* or Eastern Jews, as foils against which they judged their own rootedness in Germany.[8] In the United States, Hebrew Union College, Reform Judaism's American seminary, founded in 1875 in Cincinnati, began to produce the first generation of American-born Reform rabbis. From that point on, German Jews in the United States became deeply invested in seeing America as home by forming organizations, such as the Hebrew Immigrant Aid Society, to expedite the Americanization process for new immigrants coming from less acculturated parts of Europe. Although many American Jews who traced their roots to Germany retained symbolic connections to Germany and to German language and literature, the communal structures they established firmly rooted them in their new homeland.[9]

It was not just German Jews who began to see the places they lived as home. Many new Eastern European immigrants felt that America was their true Jewish homeland. The Eastern European Jewish immigrant writer Mary Antin suggested as much when she said, "Not 'may we be next year in Jerusalem,' but 'next year—in America!' So there was our promised land."[10] Today, many Jews living in the American Jewish diaspora, in Phoenix, Atlanta, Denver, and elsewhere, long for a metaphorical "return," or at least a routine pilgrimage, to the American Jewish homeland—New York. A friend of ours who lives in Denver, Colorado, returns to New York six times a year to "recharge her Jewish batteries."

Like American German Jews in the nineteenth century, at the turn of the twentieth century, the new American Jewish immigrants were living in a traditionally conceived diaspora, but not one with its origins in Zion. Most American Jews trace their roots back to the large wave of Jewish migration from Eastern Europe to the United States between 1881 and 1924 and have maintained traditional diasporic connections with family, friends, business connections, and others who "stayed home." Many American Jews retained some connections to Eastern Europe until World War II, speaking the Eastern European Jewish vernacular, sending money back "home," and establishing *landsmanshaftn,* community self-help groups organized around immigrants' hometowns.[11]

The application of the term "diaspora" to early-twentieth-century American Jewry becomes more complicated when discussing the ideal of a mythic return. Most American Jews in the first half of the century saw themselves as emigrants from Eastern Europe, immigrants to America, traversing two distinct places and cultures even as those cultures informed each other. Some traveled back and forth; some came to the United States and then returned to Eastern Europe; most stayed permanently in America.[12] They did not see themselves in "diaspora," if by diaspora one presumes a desire to return home. American Jews of Russian and Eastern European descent became very good Americans, embraced the rhetoric of assimilation, and did not generally see tsarist and then Communist Russia as a place of return. They did, however, feel responsible for those "back home" and maintained relationships with their countries of origin. And most American Jews, even most self-professed Zionists, did not think of Israel/Palestine as the yearned-for homeland. Most American Zionists before World War II supported the establishment of Zion as a refuge for persecuted, downtrodden Jews, but not for themselves.

After the Holocaust, and especially after the cold war, American Jews' notion of placement and roots changed again. In the words of the noted Jewish Studies scholar Deborah Dash Moore, "The destruction of European Jewry shattered the familiar contours of the Jewish world and transformed American Jews into the largest, wealthiest, most stable and secure Jewish community in the diaspora."[13] In a post-Holocaust world, many American Jews came to see Eastern Europe no longer as the real place from which to draw roots but as a mythic home, not one that they want to return to but one that they want to bear witness to. It is a land of Jewish ghosts and of lost cultures. If, for example, Hebrew was once the holy tongue that became the modern Jewish vernacular, Yiddish, the former Jewish vernacular, now has a sense of nostalgic sacredness, of a language and culture now lost. The ways in which Eastern Europe has become a mythic part of the Jewish past and not an imagined mythic home in the future is central to understanding how American Jews see themselves at home in America.

More recently, Jews have migrated to the United States from Iran, the former Soviet Union, and even the "promised land" of Israel itself.[14] New York's and Los Angeles's multiple and multiethnic Jewish communities from around the world complicate the notion of diasporic generations and point to the need for mapping the global spaces and communities that Jews inhabit and call home. Researchers have found that many Israelis, avowedly secular residents of the "Jewish" state, develop their first meaningful connections to organized Judaism when living in the United States. Even more interesting is the phenomenon of Israelis who have immigrated to the United States and who later return to Israel as newly minted *American* Jews. They demonstrate their Americanness by participating in the rituals that American Jews have developed around Israel, such as holding a bar or bat mitzvah at the Western Wall in Jerusalem.[15]

Zionism and the End of Exile

Although Jews have always had multiple diasporas and multiple homes, the overarching diaspora in Jewish culture has always been the Exile from Zion. In a world in which the mythic is upstaged by the real Zion, how do Jewish communities reinscribe Zion as the mythic home of Jews, especially as Jews around the world make homes for themselves wherever they are? Why is Zion still so central to the construction of Jewish identity in a global world? How did Jews' ideas of home change once the mythic had become the real, once the ghost of Jewish sovereignty had come "back to life," once Jewish nationalists had established political hegemony over the place that had been a place of memory?

Zionism, the nationalist movement to establish Jewish political independence based on the idea that Jews needed their own territory to be truly safe in the modern world, was predicated on ending the Jews' two-thousand-year exile in other people's homelands. For Jews, Israel evokes particularly resonant, complicated meanings of home. Centuries of migration, history, politics, culture, and religious yearning have layered upon Israel multiple and conflicting meanings of home and homeland. For whom is Israel home, and how so? Has Israel been the "homeland" of Jews since "time immemorial," as some would claim? Is "home" the current state of Israel, with its contested borders, complex struggles for political power, shifting diplomatic alliances, and persistent violence? How should that home be governed, and who should live there as a fully enfranchised citizen? Is Israel a theocratic home where all Jews should live as one nation under God (as interpreted by Orthodox rabbis), or is it a polyglot of cultures and languages, a secular democracy? Is it all of those things? Or none of the above?

The idea of Israel has never been stable. Early debates about Zionism focused on the question of whether Jews should be in search of *a* Jewish homeland or *the* Jewish homeland. The founder of political Zionism, Theodore Herzl, believed that the purpose of a Jewish homeland was to be a place of refuge and thought that any territory governed by Jews would suffice as a Jewish homeland. In the late 1890s and early 1900s, there were plans to establish Jewish homes in such "non-Jewish" places as Uganda and Argentina.[16] But other Zionists emphasized that place and home were not just about territory but also involved memory, myth, and emotion. These Zionists insisted that the Jews' homeland needed to be the historic, mythic Zion, and thus was born the movement to settle Jews in the territory that would eventually become Israel. Once the Zionist movement placed territory in Palestine at the center of Zionism, the next question was, would Jews from around the world move there?

Early Zionists argued that living outside one's historic home was destructive to constituting a stable, modern Jewish identity. Only the establishment of a political place in the Jews' historic homeland would create a fully modern Jew. The reminders and remainders of Exile—language, cultural practices, and religious ideologies—needed to be suppressed or minimized in order to make way for the "new Jews," an identity based on a heroic, explicitly masculine notion of citizenship and belonging.[17]

The founding of a political state was fraught with even more questions about this new Jewish homeland's position in the (Jewish) world. Would it be a European, parliamentary-style democracy in the Middle East that happened to have a lot of Jews? Would the state rely on its nationalist origins and become a Jewish state, possibly compromising some of the ideals of equality, democracy, and universalism? How would the hundreds of thousands of non-Jews who already lived there fit into this vision? In 1950, the Knesset, the Israeli parliament, answered some of these questions when it crafted the "Right of Return," a law that allowed Jews anywhere in the world automatic citizenship in the new country if they moved to Israel. The question of who would fit into this category was and still is one of the most complicated questions for the Israeli government and Israeli society to wrestle with, as demonstrated by recent decisions by the Israeli supreme court to recognize conversions to Judaism facilitated by non-Orthodox rabbis.[18]

The centrality of the idea of return shows that Zionism, first and foremost, envisioned Israel as the future homeland of *all* Jews, an idea summed up in the phrase that describes Israel's primary function—a place for "the ingathering of the exiles." Even the name of the new state, Israel (the historic word connoting the Jewish people—am *yisrael*), suggests a group of people well beyond the country's borders. But the use of the word "right" in the original law also shows that the Israeli government could not insist on this ingathering. It needed to persuade Jews around the world that they should move to Israel voluntarily and take themselves out of their dispersion. Some did. For most Jews who chose not to physically relocate in Israel, the very least they could do was to recognize and celebrate Israel as the center of Jewish culture and as an emerging and viable source of Jewish identity. And, most important, they could support it financially.

Financial support, in fact, was one of the foundations of the relationship between American Jews and early Zionists in Israel.[19] In 1921, according to the historian Melvin Urofsky, the Twelfth Zionist Congress approved a $6 million budget, 75 percent of which was to come from American Jews. From its inception, the (re)building of the Jewish state would depend on diaspora dollars, most notably American diaspora dollars.[20] The anthropologist Jeffrey Shandler coined the term "impresario culture" to describe the entrepreneurial role

American Zionists played in helping to fund the state—primarily as directors and producers—from the safe and relatively removed confines of American Jewish urban enclaves.[21]

The idea that American Jews would participate from a distance, financially and politically, was enshrined in the well-known conversation that took place in 1950 between the first president of Israel, David Ben Gurion, and the then-president of the American Jewish Committee, Jacob Blaustein. Ben Gurion stated unequivocally that "The Jews of the United States . . . have only one political attachment and that is to the United States of America. We should like to see American Jews come and take part in our effort. . . . But the decision as to whether they wish to come . . . rests with the free discretion of each American Jew himself." Blaustein responded, rather curtly: "We must sound a note of caution to Israel and its leaders . . . the matter of good-will between its citizens and those of other countries is a two-way street: that Israel also has a responsibility in this situation—a responsibility in terms of not affecting adversely the sensibilities of Jews who are citizens of other states by what it says or does. In this connection, you are realists and want facts, and I would be less than frank if I did not point out to you that American Jews vigorously repudiate any suggestion or implication that they are in exile. . . . To American Jews, America is home."[22] Israel would be *a* Jewish home, not *the* Jewish home.

Remaking the Diaspora after the Establishment of Israel

After World War II and the establishment of Israeli statehood, the Jews with the most financial and cultural capital were located primarily in North America. Because of this, Zionist discourse sought to reinterpret the hierarchical relationship between "diaspora" and "homeland." Until World War II, "Israel," literally and figuratively, was not on the map of the majority of Jews.[23] Only after the war did Israel and Zionism move to the center of Jewish identity, politics, and overall aspirations for the American Jewish community. After the destruction of the vibrant socialist circles and many religious Jewish communities of Eastern Europe, Zionism became the dominant political ideology.

The discursive and power relationships that shaped global Jewish communities changed dramatically. After the war, the majority of American Jews moved out of the working classes and into the suburbs.[24] They lost their tangible connection to Eastern Europe, where many formerly Jewish towns had been decimated, and in its place began creating the mythic Eastern Europe that haunts American Jews today. As American Jewish identities, practices, and communal affiliations increasingly became options, and as more Jews married non-Jews, Israel became a convenient focal point around which to rally in solidarity.

Jewish communal organizations worldwide have gradually made support for Israel a civic religion around which to build a modern secular Jewish identity. Mainstream American Jewish organizations have used and expanded historical, religious, and cultural tropes in Judaism to cultivate among Jews a sense of connection and belonging to Israel and, through Israel, to one another. These organizations have encouraged "diaspora Jews" to connect to Israel through philanthropy, education, tourism, lobbying, and business ventures. We call these networks of power, finance, and culture that have used Israel to foster diasporic Jewish identities the "diaspora business."

The civic religion of Israel (and the diaspora business that helps build it) evokes resonant meanings and memory. For many Jews, Israel as a physical place remains an emotionally laden, highly effective symbol of Jewish solidarity that often induces powerful feelings of ownership, and belonging. Even in the prestate period, such acts as purchasing wine, oranges, and other food products from Jewish farms in Palestine were championed as acts of Zionism. (These rituals had roots in premodern Jewish rituals about mythic Zion. Recall the town of Tuneyadevka's messianic ecstasy upon the arrival of the date.) The spatial meaning of Zion became something decidedly tangible, a romantic place to which one could send money for trees, daycare centers, and kibbutzim. Many rituals of American Zionism that had been developed in the prestate period became generalized rituals of American Jews. It became traditional for Jewish grandparents to give grandchildren Israeli bonds for a bar mitzvah or for a family to plant trees in Israel.[25] Giving money and claiming land became and still are the responsibility of "good" American Jews.

Through music, art, and other forms of creative expression (or forms of kitsch, depending on one's aesthetic taste), Jews have interpreted and imagined Israel as a physical place of meaning, memory, and community. In countless nostalgic songs from the Israeli folkloric tradition, lyricists have waxed poetic about the shores of the Sea of Galilee, the sand dunes that later became the sprawling metropolis of Tel Aviv, and Jerusalem as a city of gold. American Jews purchase paintings, posters, and knickknacks that symbolize their connection to Israel through images of the Western Wall, the Chagall windows at Hadassah Hospital, the Temple Mount, and the Dead Sea. The body care company Ahava has built its reputation on its romantic connection to the waters and muds of the Dead Sea.[26]

But memory, of course, is always an unpredictable and complex process of construction and myth, particularly in a place as contested as Israel. Yael Zerubavel, in her book *Recovered Roots: Collective Memory and the Making of Israeli National Tradition,* has explored how the Zionist project relied heavily on the selective interpretation of history and traditions to reinvent memories around specific places, such as the fall of Masada and the Temple Mount in Jerusalem. Instead of remembering Masada as a gruesome site of mass suicide, Zionist shapers of memory (including educators, scholars, and military officials) sought to transform Masada into a place that symbolized steadfastness, conviction, and heroism. The physical space of Masada has now become thoroughly touristed and transformed into a national shrine, where American Jewish teenagers now hike the mountain at dawn to see the sun rise over Jordan.[27]

Visions of heroic, powerful Israel became widespread among Jews after the 1967 war, a war laden with emotional rhetoric about an impending second Holocaust. Israel's dramatic victory changed its relationship with global Jewry. For Soviet Jews and other Jews who never left Eastern Europe, Jews who were made invisible by the ghosts haunting global Jewry or were silenced by the cold war, Zionism was a way to assert Jewishness and was a common way of expressing dissent. Jews in the Soviet Union, and throughout the Eastern bloc, celebrated the 1967 victory and began clamoring for the right to emigrate, especially as anti-Zionist politics became an important facet of Communist political rhetoric. A generation of young American Jews, influenced by the messages of the civil rights movement and the images of heroic Israeli soldiers recapturing the Western Wall, decided to immigrate to Israel and integrate as much as possible into Israeli culture.[28] Many American Jews latched onto Zionism as a source of Jewish pride, even as Israel's occupation of the West Bank, the Gaza Strip, and the Sinai Peninsula became a political liability in the world community.

By the 1970s, everything associated with Israel became important to Jewish communal policymakers, but not for the same reasons as in earlier generations. For American Jewish policymakers, Israel was an important way to sustain and bolster the continuity of American Jewish identities and communities. The Hebrew language was established as part of the curricula in colleges and Jewish high schools in the United States (even the Israeli pronunciation of Hebrew pushed out the once common Eastern European pronunciation taught in American Jewish schools, which is why our parents say "*Yisgadal, ve'yiskadash*," while we were both trained to say "*Yitgadal, ve'yitkadash*"); Israel came to rival local Jewish charities as the leading recipient of Jewish donations; and a trip to Israel became an important part of a child's Jewish education. In many ways, Zionism reflected a cornerstone of Jewish culture and identity globally. Zionism showed that diaspora discourse was very successful, some say too successful. Israel became the place that would save global Jewry and also preserve an American Jewish identity, or so the policymakers hoped.

Except among leftist and socialist Jews, there was very little debate about Israeli politics and the Israeli government until the 1980s. Immediately after the 1967 war, third-world nationalist movements, socialist governments, and radical movements in the United States began to criticize Israel and Israeli policies toward the Palestinians in the territories, and, by the 1980s, the Zionist idea was no longer immune to criticism within the Jewish world, especially within Israel itself. The 1982 Israeli invasion of Lebanon, and the 1986 Palestinian uprising known as the Intifada, turned Jewish victims into "Zionist oppressors" in some parts of the world. Jews in Israel began to engage in open debate and to criticize Israeli militarism for the first time. Communal leaders around the world began questioning whether too much attention was paid to Israel and not enough to "the home front." The British chief rabbi, Jonathan Sacks, pointed out, in 1994, that the dispatch of the greater part of Jewish charitable funds to Israel showed how British Jews had too deeply internalized the idea that they were somehow located on the periphery of Jewish life. He argued that British Jews should spend their Jewish pounds "at home," by which he meant Britain.[29] In Western public opinion, Israel was no longer the sweetheart of the world, the refuge for the oppressed, but was now seen by some as an oppressor in its own right and the object of too much Jewish attention.

Jews beyond Zionism

Some secular and religious Jews have gone so far as to question the certainty of the Zionist idea. Is there a place for a Jewish state in a multicultural, transnational world? Is it ethical to have two tiers of Israeli citizenship based on one's ethnic background, a system in which Jews were given more status than Arabs? By the 1990s, the Jewish voices of criticism, especially within Israel but also around the world, became louder. And thus was born the idea of postzionism—an ideology formulated by Israelis who questioned the foundational myths and ideologies of Israel. A whole generation of scholars and intellectuals, known as the "new historians," challenged passionately held beliefs about Israel's founding and about Israel's role in the Jewish world.[30] Did Israel need to be a "Jewish state," or should it become a secular democracy? Did Israel need to deny the messier and unsavory parts of its past in order to make people proud of it as a country? Did Israel still need to demand an ingathering of all global Jews, or could it develop a healthy partnership *with* global Jews? For some, postzionism led to the question of whether a secular Jewish national state was even necessary for Jews to find pride in Jewish culture.[31]

This fear of the disunity of global Jewry has caused some to retrench. The United Jewish Appeal, in its campaigns to increase fund-raising among American Jews, emphasizes Jewish unity and vulnerability to make American Jews feel responsible for their embattled brethren around the world. And, in a grandiose statement of unity, in 1998, members of the Knesset and some leaders of American Jewry signed "A Covenant between the Jewish People of North America and Israel" that reiterated the popular slogan "We are one."

In contrast, as the Jewish Studies scholars Deborah Dash Moore and S. Ilan Troen state, "the intensity and frequency with which such declarations [about unity] are made indicate a growing need to counter a contrary reality."[32] Moore and Troen suggest that the Jewish world is moving toward a reality of greater diversity, toward a multiplicity of identities—"we are many." They are not alone. In the new book *Cultures of the Jews,* David Biale and the many participating authors show that the dynamic tension between unity and diversity has always defined Jews and their cultures from the days of the Bible.[33]

Since the 1980s and 1990s, some Jews have searched for alternatives to Zionism and Israel as the bases of secular Jewish identity and new interest in the diversity of Jewish culture. One place people turned to was the culture that was destroyed in the Holocaust—the Yiddish culture of Eastern Europe. Concerts of traditional folk music from Eastern Europe known as *klezmer* are sold out worldwide, Yiddish Studies courses have spread across college campuses, and publishing houses have begun publishing vast numbers of Yiddish books in English translation. Many of the people who began this search—often progressive, feminist, and queer Jews, but also the *haredim* (ultra-Orthodox) who nostalgically remember pre-Holocaust Eastern European Orthodox culture as the apex of religious Jewish life—felt marginalized by the dominance of Zionism and Israel in American Jewish culture. A second place has been the recovery of Sephardic history—of Jews who derive their roots from medieval Spain—and of Mizrachi cultures of Jews from the Middle East, two centers of Jewish life that historically have been marginalized by the dominance of Ashkenazi elites in the United States and Israel. Witness the rise of the Shas political party and the maintenance of separate North African Jewish communities in Israel, the emergence of IVRI-Nasawi (an association of Sephardic/Mizrachi writers and artists) in the United States, the incorporation of the American Sephardi Federation into New York's Center for Jewish History, the production of Ladino plays and cultural exhibits, and educational projects designed to challenge Ashkenazi hegemony.[34] The seeds of new types of Jewish cultures have begun to flourish, from both the right and the left.

Another direction or place people have turned is to celebrate diaspora. Rootlessness and wandering are valorized, diaspora nationalism is studied, Jews in far-flung lands in as many languages as possible are mapped, as the embrace of diaspora becomes the leftist critique of a positivist Jewish history that ends in the establishment of Israel. The historian Howard Wettstein, in the collection *Exiles and Diasporas,* suggests that "exile" and "diaspora," traditionally treated as synonyms, are in fact distinct concepts within Jewish culture and history. Exile, according to Wettstein, presumes expulsion from a home and a sense of things being "not as they should be. Diaspora, on the other hand, although it suggests absence from some center—political or religious or cultural—does not connote anything so hauntingly negative."[35] Laurence Silberstein, a scholar of Jewish culture, writes that Jewish Studies scholars should embrace the concepts and theories of hybrid and fragmented identities that postcolonial theorists have used to describe South Asian, African, and other historically colonized people.[36] Several popular writers, most of them American, have taken up the task of charting Jewish communities around the globe and have used the traditional idea of Jewish diaspora to capture not Jewish rootlessness but Jewish diversity in the modern world.[37] Finally, the noted scholars Daniel and Jonathan Boyarin argue that the two-thousand-year relationship Jews had with Zion as a mythic and messianic place sublimated the potential for political violence that such nationalistic yearnings for land could have had. "The solution of Zionism—that is, Jewish state hegemony, except insofar as it represented an emergency and temporary rescue operation—seems to us the subversion of Jewish culture and not its culmination. . . . Capturing Judaism in a state transforms entirely the meanings of its social practices."³⁸ As a mythic notion, Zion helped to maintain cultural continuity, community, and collective identity, without fostering a Jewish nationalism expressed in a desire for political power.

The work of the Boyarins has been instrumental in deconstructing static notions of Jewish identity by theorizing an antizionist politics without negating the importance of Jews' connection to a place called Zion. The Boyarins turn to diaspora as a solution. "We propose Diaspora as a theoretical and historical model to replace national self-determination."³⁹ The Boyarins see a future of permanent and celebrated diaspora, not just for Jews but for all people. The Jews' two-thousand-year history of living apart from, and as part of, others' societies is a model for future interaction of various groups. For the Boyarins, such a conception "allows a formulation of Jewish identity not as a proud resting place (hence not as a form of integrism or nativism) but as a perpetual, creative diasporic tension."⁴⁰ This conception of diaspora allows Jews, like many indigenous peoples of the world, to have a connection to a land without having dominion over that land, a memory of place without power over place. Some contemporary European Jewish intellectuals, such as Richard Marienstras, call for a revival of diaspora Judaism through secular Hebrew and Yiddish culture, which he calls a "cultural politics of the Diaspora."⁴¹ And scholars and writers have heeded this call by filling Jewish bookshelves with books about the Jewish diaspora.

We question whether the rise of diaspora as the concept that best articulates this kind of group and individual identity in the modern world has discounted or overshadowed the extent to which people—as individuals and as groups—are creating new forms of home in a more mobile world. Many scholars of other diasporas have shown the problems of presuming that "imagined communities"—groups that identify as a collective without each person knowing every member of the group—have centers and peripheries. And, as James Clifford points out, global people do not live "in diaspora," because global people do not live either "at home" or "in exile." For global people, home is constantly shifting.⁴²

While Clifford and other scholars are interested in movement, mobility, frontiers, borders, and fluidity—ideas central to the body of theory known as transnationalism—we are interested in how people construct something called "home" and root themselves to those homes. The literary scholar Leah Garrett suggests that observers have seen the "Jewish condition" in one of two ways: "Critics often see Jews as having 'legs,' not 'roots.' If they are merely walking over the land, rather than rooted in it, their placement must always, and necessarily, be in relation to the lands that they traverse ('their' lands). The other choice becomes Zionist nationalism, where 'we' are at home on our land." Garrett argues that Yiddish literature offers a third alternative "of understanding how Jews on the cusp of modernism envisioned the world beyond 'Diaspora' and 'Zionism' . . . the third possibility is what we see in the literature of travel: the use of literature to revise the world and to envision the 'here and now' of Eastern Europe as our here and now. Jewish writers, then, were re-envisioning the Jewish map, reconceiving the relationship between here and there, as part of modernization." For these writers, Zion could be right where they were.[43]

The following chapters [of *New Jews*] explore the ways in which Jews today craft identities, not as diasporic, homeless, or exilic subjects but as people rooted in and tied to particular places. These roots shape how new Jews identify themselves and view the world and how new Jews also traverse many places as part of the process of communal identity formation.

Methodologically, we approach these questions as a historian and a sociologist, and this book reflects our interdisciplinary approach. We interweave historical analysis, literary readings, interview data, and ethnographic research in each of these chapters to show the many ways Jews are thinking about the end of diaspora.[44] We interrupt the narrative flow of the text to include stories and notes from our research trips as a way to show how we ourselves are implicated in these processes, since our own lives are evidence of Jewry going global. We are both scholars and activists who have traveled to many places to do research, visit families, and go on holiday, while approaching each of these places as American Jews raised in the suburbs in the 1970s. Caryn has visited Israel numerous times and also lived there to write her dissertation during the Oslo peace process of the 1990s, while David lived in Moscow during the same period.

Politically, we want to question the centrality of Israel in Jewish geography, culture, and memory. And intellectually, we want to move beyond the term "diaspora" as a mode of explaining postmodern collective identity, since such a conceptualization reinforces notions of centers and peripheries and emphasizes motion and rootlessness, often at the expense of home and rootedness.

Rather than refer to Jews as "in Israel" or "in (the) diaspora," we refer to new Jews as "global" and break down the inherent dichotomy that the Israel/diaspora metaphor maintains. In this postzionist, post-Soviet, post-American-melting-pot moment, we show that looking at Jews as global rather than diasporic/Israeli serves several purposes.

First, we wonder why people still break down Jewish identity and Jewish geography into two metacategories—Israel and everyone else commonly referred to as "the diaspora." Such labeling has the homogenizing effect of suggesting that everyone not in Israel has something in common and that all those in Israel share a common experience. In this way, we question the place of privilege of Jews who live in Israel within the Israel/diaspora dichotomy.

Second, we question the very notion of a unified Jewish people who live within these two categories of Israel and diaspora. We argue that a collective unified whole, "the Jewish people," does not describe how Jewish identities and communities operate and instead use the idea of Jewish peoples. The idea of unity is often mobilized to create a semblance of collective solidarity in response to historical persecution or in order to make Jews feel responsible for people with whom they may have very little in common.[45] As Jews, especially in America, feel more secure socially and economically and have power over place and space, they are beginning to examine internal differences. The question of Jewish difference has become all the more pressing with the mass migration of Jews from the former Soviet Union to Israel, Germany, and the United States. These groups of Jews speak different languages from the Jews in their new host countries, maintain different senses of Jewish identity, and often maintain separate communal institutions. By examining how Jews feel rooted in different places, such as Los Angeles, Moscow, and Jerusalem, and how Jews experience places and their Jewishness differently, we emphasize Jewish diversity. What does, in fact, an upper-middle-class professional, secular Jew in Los Angeles have in common with a working-class Israeli Sephardic religious Jew in Bnei Brak except the fact that each one calls herself a Jew?

Third, by deemphasizing "diaspora," which connotes powerlessness, and "homeland," which connotes power, we suggest that power within the Jewish world—cultural, political, economic—flows in many directions and to and from diverse places.

Jews Dismantling Diaspora

We believe that the valorization of diaspora has been useful, not just for Jews but for all groups of people who live in multiple places, for deconstructing notions of permanence and of the assumed confluence of space, place, and culture. But the rise of diaspora—the celebration of displacement, rootlessness, exile, and hybridity—has overshadowed the ways in which many Jews are remaking their sense of home and establishing new kinds of roots, not just to particular pieces of land but also to concepts, ideas, stories, and spaces. To understand Jewish cultural and identity formations in the contemporary world, we believe that, as Barbara Kirschenblatt-Gimblett put it, "we need to theorize how space is being reterritorialized in the contemporary world."[46] Kirschenblatt-Gimblett also suggests that the ability of people, money, and culture to move around the world easily and rapidly "not only divides and disperses people and activities that once occupied a contiguous space—and not only or necessarily by means of violence—but also collapses spaces of dispersal by abbreviating the time it takes to get from here to there.[47] She encourages us to consider the "uncoupling of displacement, dispersion, and diaspora." Zvi Gitelman agrees that "we are moving to a global shtetl; Jewish people have been drawn into closer and more frequent contact with each other by contemporary communications, by increased travel due to technology and affluence, by a sense of mutual responsibility stimulated by the Holocaust as evinced in the campaigns for Soviet, Syrian, and Ethiopian Jewry, by greater access to the former Soviet Union and Eastern Europe, and by the centrality of Israel as a common denominator for world Jewry."[48] Maybe people who have some kind of collective identity, or who make up an imagined community, can be dispersed without the experience of displacement.

But why rely on diaspora at all? The term has become a catch-all phrase to describe complex spatial and identity formations in a fragmented world. Since all imagined communities live in multiple places, one could easily argue that all groups could fit under the rubric "diaspora." If anyone can consider himself or herself a part of a diaspora, then the word loses its meaning. Another problem with the term "diaspora" is that it still presumes that there is a single center of a given community, an idea that the example of contemporary Jewry shows is simply not true. As Kirschenblatt-Gimblett states, "New spaces of dispersal are produced—traversed and compressed by technologies of connection and telepresence. Physical locations can be experienced as accidents of proximity, while common interest, rather than common location, can become the basis of social life in a medium where location is defined not by geographical coordinates but by the topic of conversation."[49] Among those who study Jews, according to Biale, "the categories of Israel and Diaspora no longer occupy the central place in scholarly agendas they once held."[50]

Young Jews understand this. Kol Dor (Voice of a Generation), an international network of twenty- and thirty-something Jewish leaders from twelve countries, including Israel, met for its first conference in May 2004. One of the group's first resolutions stated that participants refuse to use any kind of "Israel-Diaspora" discourse and instead would speak in terms of a "global Jewish discourse."[51] Some young Jews from around the world, then, are abandoning diaspora because it envisions the Jewish world hierarchically with Israel on top, "the diaspora" on bottom. Young American Jews are also questioning the links between Israeli Jews and those in other parts of the world. In the recent National Jewish Population Survey, only 20 percent of Jewish college students felt "very emotionally attached to Israel."[52]

We suggest that a global politics that recognizes the tensions between rootedness and movement and the realness of both should guide our thinking about identities and spaces. In this book, we explore ways Jews are making home in a global, not diasporic, world. We examine how Jews use travel, money, memory, organizations, and power to constitute new identities and to create new relationships to real and mythic homelands, and we show that often the real and the mythic are the same place. We also show how the ability to be rooted, to live in a postdiasporic moment, is a sign of affluence, power, and privilege as Jews have "made it" in many of the societies in which they live.

Chapter 1, about Jews in Moscow, describes the activities of Jews who resist the notion that they somehow do not live at home where they are and should live in Israel or the United States. Moscow's Jews are the ones who spurned the Exodus narrative that Israeli and American Jews created for them during the cold war. By seeing how today's Jews in Moscow struggle to assert their own forms of identity and community, we want to emphasize diversity within global Jewry and to expose the financial, cultural, and social power dynamics that shape Jewish identities and communities. In chapter 2, we use the experiences of American Jews who travel to and live in Eastern Europe and Israel to introduce the idea of the "diaspora business" and to question what it means to be an Israeli or an American Jew. We examine March of the Living and taglit-birthright israel, two teen/young adult Jewish identity travel programs, to show how diaspora discourse is taught, spread, and contested.[53] We ask why Jews in America feel that they need to send their children to Israel in order for them to feel Jewish and how Jews create a new Jewish map by imagining Eastern Europe (where more than 1.5 million Jews still live) to be a graveyard, while Israel is envisioned as the land of triumph. Chapter 3 explores two Jewish museums in Los Angeles and asks what it means to be a Jew in America. We compare the Museum of Tolerance, one of the first Holocaust museums in the United States, with the Skirball Cultural Center to show how different Jewish communities and generations present America as a homeland for Jews. Chapter 4, about lesbian, gay, bisexual, and transgender Jews in Israel and North America, explores the multiple identities of Jews who traverse many global communities. We explore how national cultures and roots to those cultures affect individual and communal identities.

Our final chapter shows that New York is the place around which the global Jewish world pivots. We show how New York is the center of the diaspora business, home of the largest Russian-speaking Jewish community in the world, ahead of Moscow,[54] home to the most important Jewish art museum and one of the most innovative Jewish historical museums in the world, the site of the only queer Jewish synagogue in the world, with two full-time rabbis and several rabbinic interns, and also the home of multiple and multiethnic Jewish communities.

In all of these chapters, we examine the national, symbolic, and intimate processes of homemaking by showing Jews exerting power over space and place, and over one another, across different geopolitical boundaries, and through various media and cultural practices. To call a place home is a statement of power (Zionists know this best). By arguing that a place is home, Jews express a sense of entitlement, control, and familiarity. Home is a place where people practice identity and intimacy. We examine both the ways that Jewish discourses reinscribe diaspora into the language of global Jews and at the same time how global Jews encounter these discourses, sometimes actively resisting, others times passively ignoring the idea of diaspora.

If the Boyarins lament the founding of a political state as that which undermined the traditional, benign relationship of Jews to a mythic Zion, Palestinians lament the founding of a political state as that which made Palestinians into a diaspora. Jews in the United States, Russia, Germany, and elsewhere are, in many ways, privileged, because they can choose where to live and can visit family members and friends in multiple places around the world. Palestinians do not have such a choice. The Right of Return is a privilege that allows Jews to construct new kinds of relationships to their mythic and real homes, and the presence of a diaspora business allows Jews to root themselves in, and route themselves to, many places. If (or, more likely, when) a Palestinian state comes to exist, Palestinians around the world will, we hope, have the opportunity to decide where to live and will have the privilege and choice of asking, "Where is home?" as Jews have. We recognize that this discussion implies power over place, both discursive power and military power, and we also recognize that discourse and guns are not the same thing. Our attempt to unravel the power dynamics that shape Jewish communities and identities in a global world is meant to expose both the diversity and the privilege of global Jewish experience.

That Jews are privileged may feel ironic precisely because many global Jews feel embattled, vulnerable, and under siege. The research for this project took place both before and after September 11, 2001, before and after the decline of the Israeli economy, the start of the second Intifada, the American occupation of Iraq, and the recent rise in criticism of Israeli policies that at times elides into criticism of global Jewry. Ironically, it is the very idea that Israel is the Jewish homeland and, therefore, that all Jews are tied to this political entity that has also blurred the boundaries between criticism of Israeli politics and criticism of Jews writ large. If Jews have trouble drawing a line between global Jewry and the State of Israel, it is no wonder that others do, too.

In this climate, we recognize that some Jews do not feel privileged, some Jews do not feel safe, and some Jews no longer feel rooted. Most Jews we talk to these days feel a heightened sense of precariousness about their identities as Jews in this historical period of uncertainty. Jews in Europe feel threatened by an increase in anti-Semitic acts. Some of the Americans in Israel described in chapter 2 have left Israel and returned to the United States as violence has increased and the opportunities for employment have vanished. Taglit-birthright israel has at times struggled to recruit American Jewish students to take advantage of its free trips to Israel. Parents of teenagers on the March of the Living have been afraid for the children's safety, not in Poland but in Israel:[55] As American rabbis tell their congregants to stop traveling to "anti-Semitic" Europe and go "support the Jewish state" with their tourist dollars, many Israelis are simultaneously leaving Israel for calmer waters in the United States. And, late in 2004, two key figures on the Israeli political scene resurrected the Zionist imperative to move to Israel. Ariel Sharon called on French Jewry to abandon the land of Jewish emancipation and the French Revolution, a place he referred to as the home of the "wildest anti-Semitism," for safer ground in the Holy Land. Not surprisingly, some French Jewish organizations took offense at the notion that they were somehow not at home in France.[56] More disturbingly, the former chief rabbi of Israel, Rabbi Israel Meir Lau, declared that Jews should all leave Europe: "I'm telling you there is no future for European Jewry."[57]

No home is permanent, no group is ever permanently rooted or permanently diasporic, and power over places, communities, and identities can be gained or lost. As Jews feel threatened and as criticism of Israeli policies mounts, many cling to ideas of safety and refuge and reassert the unity of the Jewish people. But perhaps it is precisely in times of turmoil, when home feels unsafe, when others are clamoring for power, that Jews should not see power as a zero-sum game but should recognize their privileged position in the world as a people with internal diversities and multiple homes and should engage the world not out of fear but out of the power of rootedness.

NOTES

1. Stefan Helmreich, "Kinship, Nation, and Paul Gilroy's Concept of Diaspora," *Diaspora* 2, no. 2 (1992): 245. Helmreich bases his definition of "Diaspora" on the *Oxford English Dictionary*. See also Erich Gruen's *Diaspora* (Berkeley: University of California Press, 2001), which examines the origins of the concept after the dispersions of Jews from the Kingdom of Israel first through the Hellenistic and then through the Roman empires.

2. These definitions of the terms *galut* and *galuti* come from R. Alkalay, *The Complete Hebrew-English Dictionary* (Jerusalem: P. Shalom Publications, 1981).

3. The Boyarins cite Neturei Karta as an example of this new form of diaspora because of their rejection of Jewish political hegemony over the land. See Daniel Boyarin and Jonathan Boyarin, "Diaspora: Generation and the Ground of Jewish Identity," *Critical Inquiry* 19, no. 4 (1993): 724–725. For a fuller discussion of Neturei Karta's ideology and its conception of Jewish identity, see Mitchell Judah Heifetz, "Jewish Anti-Zionism: A Case Study in Political Ideology" (Master's thesis, Case Western Reserve University, 1972). For an ethnographic description of the Reb Arelach sect in Mea Shearim, see Sam Heilman, *Defenders of the Faith: Inside Ultra-Orthodox Jewry* (New York: Schocken, 1992).

4. See Immanuel Jakobovits, "Religious Responses to Jewish Statehood," *Tradition* 20 (Fall 1982): 192, as cited in Bernard Wasserstein, *Vanishing Diaspora: The Jews in Europe since 1945* (Cambridge, Mass.: Harvard University Press, 1996), 86. As he grew older, Schneerson mellowed his religious antizionist stance and supported Chabad activities in Israel.

5. Erich Gruen, "Diaspora and Homeland," in *Exiles and Diasporas: Varieties of Jewish Identity*, ed. Howard Wettstein (Berkeley: University of California Press, 2002), 32, 36.

6. S. Y. Abramovitch, *Tales of Mendele the Book Peddler*, ed. Dan Miron and Ken Frieden (New York: Schocken, 1996), 307.

7. See Daniel Elazar, "Community," in *Encyclopedia Judaica*, CD-ROM version, 1997, or David Roskies, *The Jewish Search for a Usable Past* (Bloomington: Indiana University Press, 1999), chap. 7.

8. See Steven Aschheim, *Brothers and Strangers: The East European Jew in German and German Jewish Consciousness, 1800–1923* (Madison: University of Wisconsin Press, 1981); George Mosse, *German Jews beyond Judaism* (New York: Hebrew Union College Press, 1985).

9. For more on the formation of particularly American forms of Jewish religious identities in the nineteenth century, see Jonathan Sarna, *American Judaism: A History* (New Haven: Yale University Press, 2004).

10. Mary Antin, *The Promised Land* (New York: Houghton Mifflin, 1912), 141.

11. See Rebecca Kobrin, "Conflicting Diasporas, Shifting Centers: The Transnational Bialystok Émigré Community in the United States, Argentina, Australia, and Palestine, 1878–1949" (Ph.D. diss., University of Pennsylvania, 2002).

12. See, for example, Irving Howe, *The World of Our Fathers* (New York: Schocken, 1976), 58. Howe cites the statistic that while two-thirds of the total number of immigrants to the United States in the years between 1908 and 1924 remained in the country permanently, 94.8 percent of Jews did so.

13. Deborah Dash Moore, "Jewish Migration in Postwar America: The Case of Miami and Los Angeles," in *A New Jewry? America since the Second World War: Studies in Contemporary Jewry*, ed. Peter Medding (New York/Oxford: Oxford University Press), 102. We would push Moore to ask why the most stable and secure Jewish community in the world is still the diaspora.

14. See R. Stephen Warner and Judith G. Wittner, eds., *Gatherings in Diaspora: Religious Communities and the New Immigration* (Philadelphia: Temple University Press, 1998); Steven J. Gold, "Gender and Social Capital among Israeli Immigrants in Los Angeles," *Diaspora* 4, no. 3 (1995): 267–309.

15. Naama Sabar, *Kibbutzniks in the Diaspora* (Albany: SUNY Press, 2000), 104–106.

16. In the early Zionist movement, there was much debate about whether the new Jewish homeland had to be on the same territory as the original Jewish homeland in Palestine or whether Jews could use any territory to create their home. The most famous nonzionist proposal was the Uganda Proposal made by the British to give Jews territory in Africa for Jewish ingathering. In 1903, the proposal was rejected in favor of a Zion-or-nothing platform. See Geoffrey Wheatcroft, *The Controversy of Zion: Jewish Nationalism, the Jewish State, and the Unresolved Jewish Dilemma* (Reading, Mass./New York: Perseus Books, 1996), 108–110; Jonathan Frankel, *Prophecy and Politics: Socialism, Nationalism, and the Russian Jews, 1862–1917* (Cambridge/New York: Cambridge University Press, 1981), 133–171.

17. Ella Shohat, *Dangerous Liaisons: Gender, Nation, and Postcolonial Perspectives* (Minneapolis: University of Minnesota Press, 1997); Yael Chaver, *What Must Be Forgotten: The Survival of Yiddish Writing in Zionist Palestine* (Syracuse: Syracuse University Press, 2004); Baruch Kimmerling, *The Invention and Decline of Israeliness: State, Society, and the Military* (Berkeley: University of California Press, 2001).

18. The Supreme Court decision was handed down February 20, 2002. See the Israeli Foreign Ministry's Web site, http://www.mfa.gov.il/mfa, for details about the ruling.

19. Tom Segev, *Elvis in Jerusalem: Post-Zionism and the Americanization of Israel* (New York: Metropolitan Books, 2001), chap. 1.

20. Melvin Urofsky, *American Zionism from Herzl to the Holocaust* (Lincoln: University of Nebraska Press, 1995), 312–313.

21. Jeffrey Shandler, "Producing the Future: The Impresario Culture of American Zionism before 1948," in *Divergent Jewish Cultures: Israel and America*, ed. Deborah Dash Moore and S. Ilan Troen (New Haven: Yale University Press, 2001), 53–71.

22. David Ben Gurion and Jacob Blaustein, "An Exchange of Views," *American Jewish Year Book* 53 (1952): 564–568.
23. Wheatcroft, *The Controversy*, 254–273.
24. Karen Brodkin, *How Jews Became White Folks* (New Brunswick: Rutgers University Press, 1998). On the relationship between American Jews and the idea of Diaspora, see Naama Sabar, "Kibbutz L.A.: A Paradoxical Social Network," *Journal of Contemporary Ethnography* 31 (February 2002): 68–94.
25. On the prestate material culture of American Zionism, see Shandler, "Producing the Future," 58–61.
26. To read how Ahava invokes romantic images of Israel, see its Web site, http://www.ahava.com/general/about_us.asp.
27. Yael Zerubavel, *Recovered Roots: Collective Memory and the Making of Israeli National Tradition* (Chicago: University of Chicago Press, 1995).
28. Kevin Avruch, *Critical Essays on Israeli Society, Religion, and Government* (Albany: SUNY Press, 1997).
29. *Jewish Chronicle*, February 10, 1994.
30. See for example the work of the historians Benny Morris, Ilan Pappe, and Tom Segev and of sociologists such as Baruch Kimmerling and Meron Benvenisti.
31. On the idea of postzionism, see Laurence Silberstein, *The Postzionism Debates: Knowledge and Power in Israeli Culture* (New York: Routledge, 1999).
32. Deborah Dash Moore and S. Ilan Troen, "Introduction," *Divergent Jewish Cultures: Israel and America* (New Haven: Yale University Press, 2001), 5.
33. David Biale, ed., *Cultures of the Jews* (New York: Schocken, 2003).
34. On North African Jewish communities in Israel, see Yoram Bilu, "Moroccan Jews, Shaping Israel's Geography," in Moore and Troen, *Divergent Jewish Cultures*, 72–86; on Ivri-Nasawi, see Loolwa Khazoom, "United Jewish Feminist Front," in *Yentl's Revenge*, ed. Danya Ruttenberg (San Francisco: Seal Press, 2000). See the organization's Web site at http://www.ivri-nasawi.org/.
35. Howard Wettstein, ed., *Exiles and Diasporas: Varieties of Jewish Identity* (Berkeley: University of California Press, 2002), 2.
36. Laurence Silberstein, ed., *Mapping Jewish Identities* (New York: NYU Press, 2000).
37. See Larry Tye, *Homelands: Portraits of the New Jewish Diaspora* (New York: Owl Books, 2000); Howard Sachar, *Diaspora: An Inquiry into the Contemporary Jewish World* (New York: HarperCollins, 1985); and James Ross, *Fragile Branches: Travels through the Jewish Diaspora* (New York: Riverhead, 2001).
38. Boyarin and Boyarin, "Diaspora," 712–713.
39. Ibid., 711.
40. Ibid., 714.
41. Richard Marienstras, *Etre un peuple en diaspora* (Paris: F. Maspero, 1975), and his "On the Notion of Diaspora," in *Minority Peoples in the Age of Nation-States*, ed. G. Chaliand (London: South Asia Books, 1990), 119–125.
42. James Clifford, "Diasporas," *Cultural Anthropology* 9, no. 3 (1994): 303.
43. Leah Garrett, *Journeys beyond the Pale: Yiddish Travel Writing in the Modern World* (Madison: University of Wisconsin Press, 2003), 170–171.
44. A few methodological notes: We have given pseudonyms to the informants who appear in the book to protect their privacy. Our statistics in each chapter come from

a variety of sources, as noted. When it comes to debates about Jewish demographics, statistics are particularly politicized. Israeli government officials want immigration statistics to be higher; American Jews want the Jewish population of the United States to increase; and those who think Eastern Europe is dead want to show tiny numbers in Moscow and other major Eastern European cities. It is impossible to extricate oneself from these problems; therefore, we try to provide ranges, to give several sources, or, when we are feeling polemical, to offer a statistic that supports our point while showing that it is one of many possible statistics. For more on the problem with statistics, see Joel Best, *Damned Lies and Statistics: Untangling Numbers from the Media, Politicians, and Activists* (Berkeley: University of California Press, 2001).

45. On how Jewish philanthropies use a language of unity to encourage donation, see Kerri Steinberg, "Contesting Identities in Jewish Philanthropy," in Wettstein, *Exiles and Diaspora*, 253–278.

46. Barbara Kirschenblatt-Gimblett, "Spaces of Dispersal," *Cultural Anthropology* 9, no. 3 (1994): 342. See also her book *Destination Culture: Tourism, Museums, and Heritage* (Berkeley: University of California Press, 1998).

47. Ibid.

48. Zvi Gitelman, "The Decline of the Diaspora Jewish Nation," *Jewish Social Studies* 4, no. 2 (1998): 127.

49. Kirschenblatt-Gimblett, "Spaces of Dispersal," 342.

50. Biale, *Cultures of the Jews*, xxix.

51. Yair Sheleg, "A Pan-Jewish Jewish Approach," *Haaretz*, May 11, 2004.

52. "Jewish College Students" (a special report for the National Jewish Population Survey, 2000–2001), 19.

53. The official name of the program uses lowercase letters for "birthright" and "israel." The word "taglit" means discovery, in this case a double entendre in that students on the program are supposed to discover both Israel and their Jewish selves.

54. See Sam Kliger, "Russian Jews in America: Status, Identity, Integration" (Paper presented at conference "Russian-Speaking Jewry in Global Perspective," Bar Ilan University, June 2004). Kliger estimates the number of Russian Jews in New York at 350,000. In 1999, Mark Kupovetsky, a leading historian of Soviet Jewry, estimated the core Jewish population of Moscow at 320,000, although other sources put the number at closer to 250,000. The only survey to put Moscow's Russian-speaking Jewish population higher than New York's is that by the Federation of Jewish Communities of the Commonwealth of Independent States (FJC), which claims that there are 500,000 Jews in Moscow, despite the 2002 census figures, which showed 120,000. See http://www.fjc.ru/news/newsArticle.asp?AID=108529.

55. As peace prospects improved in 2005 after Yassir Arafat's death, student interest in taglit-birthright israel programs increased.

56. That said, the umbrella organization for French Jewry, Le Conseil Representif des Institutions juives de France (CRIF), condemned only the fighting between France and Israel, not the specific comment by Sharon, and said that it is up to the individual or the family to decide whether or not to move to Israel. For the CRIF press release, see http://www.crif.org (in French).

57. "Ex-Chief Rabbi: European Jewry Has No Future," *J: The Jewish News Weekly of Northern California* 108 (December 10, 2004): 21a.

21

The Charge of Antisemitism

Jews, Israel, and the Risks of Public Critique

JUDITH BUTLER

> Profoundly anti-Israeli views are increasingly finding support in progressive intellectual communities. Serious and thoughtful people are advocating and taking actions that are anti-Semitic in their effect if not their intent.
> –Lawrence Summers, president of Harvard University, September 17, 2002

When the president of Harvard University, Lawrence Summers, remarked that to criticize Israel at this time and to call upon universities to divest from Israel are "actions that are anti-Semitic in their effect, if not their intent,"[1] he introduced a distinction between an effective and intentional antisemitism that is controversial at best. Of course, the countercharge has been that, in making his statement, the president of Harvard has struck a blow against academic freedom, in effect, if not in intent. Although he himself made clear that he meant nothing censorious by his action, and that he is in favor of these ideas being "debated freely and civilly,"[2] his words nevertheless exercise a chilling effect on political discourse, stoking the fear that to criticize Israel during this time is to expose oneself to the charge of antisemitism. He made his claim in relation to several actions that he called "effectively antisemitic," which included European boycotts of Israel, antiglobalization rallies in which criticisms of Israel were voiced, and fund-raising efforts for organizations with "questionable political provenance." Of local concern to him, however, was a divestment petition drafted by MIT and Harvard professors who oppose the current Israeli occupation and the treatment of Palestinians. Engaging with this initiative critically, Summers asked why Israel was being "singled out . . . among all nations" for a divestment campaign, suggesting that the singling-out

Reprinted, by permission of Judith Butler, from *Precarious Life: The Powers of Mourning and Violence* (London and New York: Verso, 2004), 101–127.

was evidence of an antisemitic aim. And though Summers claimed that aspects of Israeli policy "can be and should be vigorously challenged," it was unclear how such challenges could or would take place without being construed in some sense as anti-Israel, and why those foreign policy issues, which include "occupation" and are, therefore, given the dispute over legitimate state boundaries, domestic policies as well, ought not to be vigorously challenged through a divestment campaign. It would seem that calling for divestment is something other than a legitimately "vigorous challenge," but we are not given any criteria by which to adjudicate the difference between those vigorous challenges that should be articulated, and those which carry the "effective" force of antisemitism.

Of course, Summers is right to voice concern about rising antisemitism, and every progressive Jew, along with every progressive person, ought to be vigorously challenging antisemitism wherever it occurs, especially if it occurs in the context of movements mobilized in part or in whole against the Israeli occupation of Palestinian lands. It seems, though, that historically we are now in the position in which Jews cannot be understood always and only as presumptive victims. Sometimes we surely are, but sometimes we surely are not. No political ethics can start with the assumption that Jews monopolize the position of victim.[3] The "victim" is a quickly transposable term, and it can shift from minute to minute from the Jew atrociously killed by suicide bombers on a bus to the Palestinian child atrociously killed by Israeli gunfire. The public sphere needs to be one in which *both* kinds of violence are challenged insistently and in the name of justice.

If we think, though, that to criticize Israeli violence, or to call for specific tactics that will put economic pressure on the Israeli state to change its policies, is to engage in "effective antisemitism," we will fail to voice our opposition out of fear of being named as part of an antisemitic enterprise. No label could be worse for a Jew. The very idea of it puts fear in the heart of any Jew who knows that, ethically and politically, the position with which it would be utterly unbearable to identify is that of the antisemite. It recalls images of the Jewish collaborators with the Nazis. And it is probably fair to say that for most progressive Jews who carry the legacy of the Shoah in their psychic and political formations, the ethical framework within which we operate takes the form of the following question: will we be silent (and be a collaborator with illegitimately violent power), or will we make our voices heard (and be counted among those who did what they could to stop illegitimate violence), even if speaking poses a risk to ourselves. The Jewish effort to criticize Israel during these times emerges, I would argue, precisely from this ethos. And though the critique is often portrayed as insensitive to Jewish suffering, in the past and in the present, its ethic is wrought precisely from that experience of suffering, so that suffering itself might stop, so that something we might reasonably call *the sanctity of life* might be honored equitably and truly. The fact of enormous suffering does not warrant revenge or legitimate violence, but must be mobilized in the service of a politics that seeks to diminish suffering universally, that seeks to recognize the sanctity of life, of all lives.

Summers mobilizes the use of the "antisemitic" charge to quell public criticism, even as he explicitly distances himself from the overt operations of censorship. He writes, for instance, "The only antidote to dangerous ideas is strong alternatives vigorously defended." But with what difficulty does one vigorously defend the idea that the Israeli occupation is brutal and wrong, and that Palestinian self-determination is a necessary good, if the voicing of those views calls down upon itself the horrible charge of antisemitism?

Let us consider his statement in detail, then, in order both to understand what he means and what follows logically from what he has said. In order to understand Summers's claim, we have to be able to conceive of an "effective antisemitism," one that pertains to certain kinds of speech acts, which either follows upon certain utterances or is said to structure those utterances, even if it is not part of the conscious intention of those who make the utterance itself. His view assumes that such utterances will be taken up by others as antisemitic or will be received within a given context as antisemitic. If his claim is true, then there will be one way or, perhaps, a predominant way of receiving them, and that will be to receive them as antisemitic arguments or utterances. So it seems we have to ask what context Summers has in mind when he makes his claim; in what world, in other words, is it the case that any criticism of Israel will be taken to be antisemitic.

Now, it may be that what Summers was effectively saying is that, as a community, largely understood as the public sphere of the United States, or, indeed, of a broader international community which might include parts of Europe and parts of Israel, the only way that a criticism of Israel can be heard is through a certain kind of acoustic frame, such that the criticism, whether it is of West Bank settlements, the closing of Birzeit University, the demolition of homes in Ramallah or Jenin, or the killing of numerous children and civilians, can only be taken up and interpreted as an act of hatred for Jews. If we imagine who is listening, and who is hearing the former kinds of criticisms *as* antisemitic, that is, expressing hatred for Jews or calling for discriminatory action against Jews, then we are asked to conjure a listener who attributes intention to the speaker: "so and so" has made a public statement against the Israeli occupation of Palestinian territories, and this must mean that "so and so" actually hates Jews or is willing to fuel those who do. The criticism is thus not taken for its face value, but given a hidden meaning, one that is at odds with its explicit claim. In this way, the explicit claim does not have to be heard, since what one is hearing is the hidden claim made beneath the explicit one. The criticism against Israel that is levied is nothing more than a cloak for that hatred, or a cover for a call, transmuted in form, for discriminatory action against Jews.

So whereas Summers himself introduces a distinction between intentional and effective antisemitism, it would seem that effective antisemitism can be understood only by conjuring a seamless world of listeners and readers who take certain statements critical of Israel to be tacitly or overtly *intended* as antisemitic expression. The only way to understand *effective* antisemitism would be to presuppose *intentional* antisemitism. The effective antisemitism of any criticism of Israel will turn out to reside in the intention of the speaker as it is retrospectively attributed by the one who receives—listens to or reads—that criticism. The intention of a speech, then, does not belong to the one who speaks, but is attributed to that speaker later by the one who listens. The intention of the speech act is thus determined belatedly by the listener.

Now it may be that Summers has another point of view in mind—namely, that critical statements *will be used* by those who have antisemitic intent, that such statements will be exploited by those who want not only to see the destruction of Israel but the degradation or devaluation of Jewish people in general. In this case, it would seem that the discourse itself, if allowed into the public sphere, will be taken up by those who seek to use it, not only for a criticism of Israel, but as a way of doing harm to Jews, or expressing hatred for them. Indeed, there is always that risk, a risk that negative comments about the Israeli state will be misconstrued as negative comments about Jews. But to claim that the only meaning that such criticism can have is to be taken up as negative comments about Jews is to attribute to that particular interpretation an enormous power to monopolize the field of reception for that criticism. The argument against letting criticisms of Israel into the public sphere would be that it gives fodder to those with antisemitic intentions, and that those who have such intentions will successfully co-opt the criticisms made. Here again, the distinction between effective antisemitism and intended antisemitism folds, insofar as the only way a statement can become effectively antisemitic is if there is, somewhere, an intention to use the statement for antisemitic aims, an intention imagined as enormously effective in realizing its aims. Indeed, even if one did believe that criticisms of Israel are by and large heard as antisemitic (by Jews, by antisemites, by people who could be described as neither), it would then become the responsibility of all of us to change the conditions of reception so that the public might begin to learn a crucial political distinction between a criticism of Israel, on the one hand, and a hatred of Jews, on the other.

A further consideration has to take place here, since Summers himself is making a statement, a strong statement, as president of an institution which assumes its value in part as a symbol of academic prestige in the United States. In his statement, he is saying that he, as a listener, will take any criticism of Israel to be effectively antisemitic. Although in making his remarks he claimed that he was not speaking as president of the university, but as a "member of the community," his speech was a presidential address, and it carried weight in the press precisely because he exercised the symbolic authority of his office. And in this respect, he models the listener or reader we have been asked to conjure. If he is the one who is letting the public know that he will take any criticism of Israel to be antisemitic, that any criticism of Israel will have that effect *on him* and, so, will be "effectively" antisemitic, then he is saying that public discourse itself ought to be constrained in such a way that those critical statements are not uttered. If they are uttered, they will be taken up and interpreted in such a way that they will be considered antisemitic. The ones who make those arguments will be understood as engaging in antisemitic speech, even hate speech. But here it is important to distinguish between antisemitic speech that, say, produces a hostile and threatening environment for Jewish students, racist speech which any university administrator would be obligated to oppose and to regulate, and speech that makes a student politically uncomfortable because it opposes a state or a set of state policies that any student may defend. The latter is a political debate, and if we say that the case of Israel is different because the very identity of the student is bound up with the state of Israel, so that any criticism of Israel is considered an attack on "Israelis" or, indeed, "Jews" in general, then we have "singled out" this form of political allegiance from all the other forms of political allegiance in the world that are open to public disputation and engaged in the most outrageous form of silencing and "effective" censorship.[4]

Indeed, not only, it seems, will Summers regard such criticisms as antisemitic, but he is, by his example, and by the normative status of his utterance, recommending that others regard such utterances that way as well. He is setting a norm for legitimate interpretation. We do not know how he would rule on various cases if they were to reach his desk, but his current utterance gives symbolic authority to the claim that such utterances are impermissible, in the same way that racist utterances are. What is complicated, however, is that his understanding of what constitutes antisemitic rhetoric depends upon a very specific and very questionable reading of the field of reception for such speech. He seems, through his statement, to be describing a sociological condition under which speech acts occur and are interpreted—that is, describing the fact that we are living in a world where, for better or worse, criticisms of Israel are simply heard as antisemitic. He is, however, also speaking as one who is doing that hearing, and so modeling the very hearing that he describes. In this sense, he is producing a prescription: he knows what effect such statements have, and he is telling us about that effect; they will be taken to be antisemitic; he takes them to be antisemitic; and in this way, rhetorically, he recommends that others take them to be so as well.

The point is not only that his distinction between effective and intentional antisemitism cannot hold, but that the way the distinction collapses in his formulation is precisely what produces the condition under which certain public views are taken to be hate speech, in effect if not in intent. One point

Summers did not make is that anything that the Israeli state does in the name of its self-defense is fully legitimate and ought not to be questioned. I do not know whether he approves of all Israeli policies, but let us imagine, for the sake of argument, that he does not. And I do not know whether he has views about, for instance, the destruction of homes and the killing of children in Jenin, which, last year, attracted the attention of the United Nations but was not investigated as a human rights violation when Israel refused to let the UN survey the scene. Let us imagine that he objects to those actions and those killings, and that they are among the "foreign policy" issues that he believes ought to be "vigorously challenged." If that is the case, then he would be compelled, under his formulation, not to voice his disapproval, believing, as he does, that the voicing of that disapproval would be construed, effectively, as antisemitism. And if he thinks it is possible to voice that disapproval, he has not shown us how it might be voiced in such a way that the allegation of antisemitism might be averted.

If one were to decide not to voice a criticism of those killings, for fear that that criticism might be taken as critical of the Jews, say, as a people, or as stoking the fires of antisemitism elsewhere, one would be compelled to choose between exercising the right or, indeed, obligation to wage public criticism against forms of violent injustice, on the one hand, and fomenting antisemitic sentiment through the exercise of that right, on the other. If Summers did object to such policies, would he censor himself and ask that others do the same?

I do not have the answer to this question, but his logic suggests the following: one could conclude, on the basis of a desire to refrain from strengthening antisemitic sentiment and belief, that certain actions of the Israeli state—acts of violence and murder against children and civilians—must not be objected to, must go unremarked and unprotested, and that these acts of violence must be allowed to go on, unimpeded by public protest or outrage, for fear that any protest against them would be tantamount to antisemitism, if not antisemitism itself.

Now, it is surely possible to argue, as I would and do argue, that all forms of antisemitism must be opposed, but it would seem that now we have a serious set of confusions about what forms antisemitism takes. Indeed, the actual problem of antisemitism is elided here by the strategic way that the charge of antisemitism works, which means that when and if the charge ought to be made, it will have been made less robust by its use as a threatened interpellation. Indeed, if the charge of antisemitism is used to defend Israel at all costs, then the power of the charge to work against those who demean and discriminate against Jews, who do violence to synagogues in Europe, and who wave Nazi flags and support antisemitic organizations is radically diluted. Indeed, many critics of Israel now dismiss all claims of antisemitism as "trumped up," after having been exposed to the use of the claim as a means to censor political speech, and this produces an insensitivity and refusal to acknowledge existing political realities that is worrisome at best. One reason, then, to oppose the use of the charge of antisemitism as a threat and as a means to quell political critique is that the charge must be kept alive as a crucial and effective instrument to combat existing and future antisemitism.

Summers, on the other hand, does not tell us why divestment campaigns or other forms of public protest *are* antisemitic, if they are. Rather, it seems that "antisemitism" functions here as a charge, one that does not correspond to a given kind of action or utterance, but one that is unilaterally conferred by those who fear the consequences of overt criticisms of Israel. According to Summers, there are some forms of antisemitism that are characterized retroactively by those who decide upon their status. This means that nothing should be said or done that will be taken to be antisemitic by others. But what if the others who are listening are wrong? If we take one form of antisemitism to be defined retroactively by those who listen to a certain set of speech acts, or witness a certain set of protests against Israel, then what is left of the possibility of legitimate protest against a given state, either by its own population or by those who live outside those borders? If we say that every time "Israel" is uttered, the speaker really means "Jews," then we have foreclosed in advance the possibility that the speaker really means "Israel."

If we distinguish between antisemitism and forms of protest against the Israeli state (or, indeed, right-wing settlers who sometimes act independently of the state), acknowledging that sometimes they do, disturbingly, work together, then we stand a chance of understanding that the Jewish population of the world does not conceive of itself as one with the Israeli state in its present form and practice, and that Jews *in Israel* do not conceive of themselves as one with the Israeli state. In other words, the possibility of a substantive Jewish peace movement depends upon (1) a productive and critical distance from the state of Israel (one that can be coupled with a profound investment in what future course it takes), and (2) a clear distinction between antisemitism, on the one hand, and forms of protest against the Israeli state based on that critical distance, on the other.

I take it that Summers's view, however, relies on the full and seamless identification of the Jewish people with the state of Israel, not only an "identification" that he makes in coupling the two, but also an "identification" that he assumed to be subjectively adopted by Jews themselves. His view seems to imply a further claim as well—namely, that any criticism of Israel is "anti-Israel" in the sense that the criticism is understood to challenge the right of Israel to exist.[5]

I'll turn to the problem of identification in a moment, but let's first consider the latter claim. A criticism of Israel is not the same as a challenge to Israel's existence, and neither is it the same as an antisemitic act, though each could work in tandem with each of the other claims. There are conditions under which it would be possible to say that one leads to the next. A challenge to the right of Israel to exist can only be construed as a challenge to the existence of the Jewish people if one believes that Israel alone is what keeps the Jewish people alive or if one believes that all Jewish people have their sense of perpetuity invested in the state of Israel in its current or traditional forms. Only if we make one of these assumptions, it seems, does the very criticism of Israel function as a challenge to the very survival of the Jews. Of course, one could argue that criticism is essential to any democratic polity, and that those polities that safeguard criticism stand a better chance of surviving than those that do not. Let us imagine, for the sake of argument, that one set of criticisms do challenge the basic presuppositions of the Israeli state, ones that produce differential forms of citizenship, ones that secure the Right to Return for Jews, but not Palestinians, ones that maintain a religious basis for the state itself. For a criticism of Israel to be taken as a challenge to the survival of the Jews or Jewishness itself, we would have to assume not only that "Israel" cannot change in response to legitimate criticisms, but that a more radically democratic Israel would be bad for Jews or for Jewishness. According to this latter belief, criticism itself is not a Jewish value, and this clearly flies in the face not only of long traditions of Talmudic disputation, but also of all the religious and cultural sources for openly objecting to injustice and illegitimate violence that have been part of Jewish life for centuries, prior to the formation of the contemporary state of Israel, and alongside it.

So it seems that the very meaning of what it is to be Jewish or, indeed, what "Jewishness" is has undergone a certain reduction in the formulation that Summers provides. Summers has identified Jews with the state of Israel as if they were seamlessly the same, or he has assumed that, psychologically and sociologically, every Jew as such an identification, and that this identification is essential to Jewish identity, an identification without which that identity cannot exist. Only on the basis of such presumptions, then, does it follow that any criticism of Israel strikes against a primary identification that Jews are assumed to have with the state of Israel. But what are we to make of Jews who *dis*identify with Israel or, at least, with the Israel state (which is not the same as every part of its culture)? Or Jews who identify with Israel (Israeli or not), but do not condone or identify with several of its practices? There is a huge range here: those who are silently ambivalent about how Israel handles itself now, those who are half-articulate about their doubts about the occupation, those who are very strongly opposed to the occupation, but within a Zionist framework, those who would like to see Zionism rethought or, indeed, abandoned, and either do or do not voice their views in public. There are Jews who may have any of the given opinions listed above, but voice them only to their family, or never voice them to their family, or only voice them to their friends, but never in public, or voice them in public, but cannot go home again. Given the extraordinary range of Jewish ambivalence on this topic, ought we not to be suspicious of *any* rhetorical effort to assume an equivalence between Jews and

Israel? The argument that *all* Jews have a heartfelt investment in the state of Israel is simply untrue. Some have a heartfelt investment in corned beef sandwiches or in certain Talmudic tales, memories of their grandmother, the taste of borscht or the echoes of the Yiddish theater. Some care most about Hebrew songs or religious liturgy and rituals. Some have an investment in historical and cultural archives from Eastern Europe or from the Shoah, or in forms of labor activism that are thoroughly secular, though "Jewish" in a substantively social sense. There are sources of American Jewish identification, for instance, in food, in religious ritual, in social service organizations, in diasporic communities, in civil rights and social justice struggles that may exist in relative independence from the question of the status of Israel.

What do we make of Jews, including myself, who are emotionally invested, critical of its current form, and call for a radical restructuring of its economic and juridical basis precisely because they are so invested? Is it always possible to say that such Jews do not know their own best interest, that such Jews turn against other Jews, that such Jews turn against their own Jewishness? But what if one offers criticism of the Israeli state in the name of one's Jewishness, in the name of justice, precisely because, as it were, such criticisms seem "best for the Jews"? Why wouldn't it always be "best for the Jews" to embrace forms of radical democracy that extend what is "best" to everyone, Jewish or not? I signed one such petition, "Open Letter from American Jews," and there were finally 3,700 of us who, identifiably Jewish, opposed the Israeli occupation.[6] This was a limited criticism, since it did not call for the end of Zionism per se, or for the reallocation of arable land, for rethinking the Jewish right of return, or for the fair distribution of water and medicine to Palestinians, and it did not call for the reorganization of the Israeli state on a more radically egalitarian basis. But it was, nevertheless, an overt criticism of Israel. Let us assume that a vast number of those who signed that petition undergo something we might reasonably term *heartache* when taking a stand against Israeli policy in public, and that hands shook as they entered their names on that list. The heartache emerges from the thought that Israel, by subjecting 3.5 million Palestinians to a military occupation, represents the Jews in a way that these petitioners find not only objectionable, but truly terrible to endure, *as Jews*; it is precisely *as Jews*, even in the name of a different Jewish future, that they call for another way, that they assert their disidentification with that policy, they assert another path for Jewish politics, they seek to widen the rift between the state of Israel and the Jewish people to produce an alternative vision. This rift is crucial for opening up and sustaining a critical relation to the state of Israel, its military power, its differential forms of citizenship, its unmonitored practices of torture, its brutality at the borders, and its egregious nationalism.

One could take the psychological view and say that these petitioners suffer from internalized antisemitism, but Summers, to be fair, does not make this statement, even if, *effectively*, the statement seems to follow logically from what he does say. If one calls for universities to divest from the state of Israel, as I, along with many others, have done, that is not the same as condoning the position that Israel should be "driven into the sea," and it is not, as a public speech act, tantamount to driving Israel into the sea. The speech act calls upon Israel to embody certain democratic principles, to end the occupation and, in some instances, to reject the Zionist basis of the current state in favor of a more egalitarian and democratic one. The petition exercises a democratic right to voice criticism, and it seeks to impose economic pressure on Israel by the United States and other countries to implement rights for Palestinians otherwise deprived of basic conditions of self-determination. The criticisms of Israel can take several different forms, and they differ according to whether they are generated within the state or from the outside: some wish for the implementation of human rights; some wish for the end of the occupation; some call for an independent Palestinian state; and some call to reestablish the basis of the Israeli state itself without regard to religion so that a one-state solution would offer citizenship on an equal basis to all inhabitants of that land. According to this last call, Jewishness would no longer be the basis of the state, but would constitute one multivalent cultural and religious reality in that state, protected by the same laws that protect the rights of religious expression and cultural self-determination of all other people who have claims to that land.[7]

It is important to remember that the identification of Jewishness with Israel, implied by the formulation that maintains that to criticize Israel is effectively to engage in antisemitism, elides the reality of a small but dynamic peace movement in Israel itself. What do we make of those who are to the left of Peace Now, who belong to the small but important postzionist movement in Israel, such as the philosophers Adi Ophir and Anat Biletzki, the professor of theater Avraham Oz, the sociologist Uri Ram, or the poet Yitzhak Laor? Are we to say that Jews, nay, Israelis who are critical of Israeli policy or, indeed, call into question the structure and self-legitimating practices of the Israeli state are therefore self-hating Jews, or that they fail to be sensitive to the ways in which these criticisms can fan the flames of antisemitism? Could it be instead that these critics hold out a different path for the state of Israel, and that their politics, in fact, emerge from other sources of political vision, some clearly Jewish, than those that have currently been codified as Zionism? What are we to make of the new organization Brit Tzedek in the United States, numbering close to 20,000 members on last count, which seeks to offer an alternative American Jewish voice to AIPAC,[8] opposing the current military occupation and struggling for a two-state solution?[9] And what about Jewish Voices for Peace, and Jews Against the Occupation, Jews for Peace in the Middle East, the Faculty for Israeli–Palestinian Peace,[10] Tikkun, Jews for Racial and Economic Justice, Women in Black, or, indeed, the critical mission of Neve Shalom–Wahat al-Salam, the only village collectively governed by both Jews and Arabs in the state of Israel, which also houses the School

THE CHARGE OF ANTI-SEMITISM 379

for Peace that offers instruction in conflict resolution that opposes Israeli militaristic strategy.[11] What are we to make of the Israel/Palestine Center for Research and Information in Jerusalem?[12] And what do we make of B'tselem, the Israeli human rights organization that monitors human rights abuses on the West Bank and in Gaza, or Gush Shalom,[13] the Israeli organization against the occupation, or Yesh Gvul, 2003,[14] the Israeli soldiers who refused to serve in the occupied territories? And, finally, what do we make of Ta'ayush (which means "living together" in Arabic)? This last is a coalition that not only seeks peace in the region, but also, through Jewish-Arab collaborative actions, opposes state policies that lead to isolation, poor medical care, house arrest, the destruction of educational institutions, and a lack of water and food for Palestinians living under the occupation. Let me cite from one member's description of that group sent to me in the fall of 2002, a young literary critic named Catherine Rottenberg:

> It is a grassroots movement which emerged after the October 2000 events—the outbreak of the second intifada and the killing of 13 Arab citizens within Israel. The Israeli peace camp, particularly Peace Now, did nothing to bring people to the streets; in fact, there was barely a murmur of protest. It began when some professors at Tel Aviv University and Palestinian citizens of Israel from Kfar Kassem decided that a new and real Arab-Jewish movement was desperately needed. There were a dozen activists at the time. Now there are Ta'ayush branches all across Israel and about a thousand activists.
>
> Many of us were tired of going to protests to stand—once again—with a sign in our hand.... We were thinking more of resistance than of protest. Basically, we use non-violent civil disobedience to convey our message (which is similar to the one endorsed by the American Jewish academics [see "Open Letter..."]—but more radical). In Israel, we are probably best known for our food and solidarity convoys that defy the military siege, often breaking through physical barriers, not only the psychological ones. Jewish and Palestinian citizens of Israel travel in convoys made up of private cars (our last convoy included approximately a hundred cars) to West Bank villages where we establish—in advance—strong ties through months of dialogue. We try to break the walls—physical, psychological, and political—separating the two peoples and expose the brutality of the occupation. We bring humanitarian aid, but we use it more as a political tool to break the siege than as humanitarian relief. It doesn't look good in the international press when Israel prevents humanitarian aid from reaching the villages—although it does it all the time!
>
> We usually manage to get some media attention. We have also helped organize many demonstrations; these are always in coalition with other organizations (like the Women's Coalition for a Just Peace).

> Yesterday (August, 2002), Ta'ayush tried to reach Bethlehem—to break the curfew and to demonstrate with the residents against Israel's draconian policies. The police didn't let us enter the city, of course, and used tear gas and water hoses to disperse us. But we demonstrated anyway, near the checkpoint, calling our Palestinian partners (in Bethlehem) by cell phone so that they could speak to the crowd.
>
> In the past few months, we have also worked within Israel, trying to expose and fight discrimination against the Palestinian population. Last week we organized a work camp at one of the many unrecognized villages in the North and next week a water convoy will go to unrecognized Bedouin villages that still do not have running water.
>
> I have been an activist for many years, but Ta'ayush is something extraordinary. It has been an amazing learning experience—both in terms of democracy, as well as how to negotiate gender, class, sexuality and race in times of crisis. We all have different political agendas, but we have always managed somehow to maintain dialogue and work together. There is no office, no official positions, it is democracy at work and consequently we have hours and hours and hours of meetings. We have created a real community and as far as I can see, it is the only light (small that it is) at the moment.[15]

Such organizations are not only expressing notions of "Jewish" collectivity, but, like Neve Shalom, undercut a nationalist ethos in the interests of developing a new political basis for coexistence. They are, we might say, diasporic elements working with Israel itself to dislodge the pervasive assumption of nationalism. As Yitzhak Laor remarks, "a joint life means relinquishing parts of a national ethos."[16]

It seems crucial not only for the purposes of academic freedom, but surely for that as well, that we consider these issues carefully, since it will not do to equate Jews with Zionists or, indeed, Jewishness with Zionism. There were debates throughout the nineteenth century and the early twentieth, and indeed at the inception of Israel, among Jews whether Zionism was a legitimate political ideology, whether it ought to become the basis of a state, whether the Jews had any right, understood in a modern sense, to lay claim to that land—land inhabited by Palestinians for centuries—and what future lay ahead for a Jewish political project based upon the violent expropriation of the land of Palestinians, dispossession on a massive scale, slaughter, and the sustained suspension of fundamental rights for Palestinians. There were those who sought to make Zionism compatible with peaceful coexistence, and others who made use of it for military aggression, and still do. There were those who thought, and who still think, that Zionism is not a legitimate basis for a democratic state in a situation where it must be assumed that a diverse population practices different religions, and that no group, on the basis of their ethnic or religious views, ought to be excluded from any right accorded to citizens in general. And there are those who maintain that the violent appropriation of Palestinian lands, and the dislocation of 700,000 Palestinians at the time that Israel was founded has produced a violent and dehumanizing basis for this particular state formation, one which repeats its founding gesture in the containment and dehumanization of Palestinians in the occupied territories. Indeed, the new "wall" being built between Israel and the occupied territories threatens to leave 95,000 Palestinians homeless. These are surely questions and issues to be asked about Zionism that should and must be asked in a public domain, and universities are surely one place where we might depend upon a critical reflection on Zionism to take place. But instead of understanding the topic of "Zionism" to be something worthy of critical and open debate, we are being asked, by Summers and by others, to treat any critical approach to Zionism as "effective antisemitism" and, hence, to rule it out as a topic for legitimate disagreement and discussion.

What better time, though, to ask after the history of Zionism, the implications of its implementation, the alternatives that were foreclosed when it took hold in 1948 and before, and what future, if any, it ought to have? A crucial history needs to be uncovered and opened to new debate: what were Hannah Arendt's objections to Zionism, and why did Martin Buber come to disavow its project? What were the movements critical of the Israeli state from its inception from within the community of Jews in Palestine: B'rith Shalom, the Matzpen Movement? In the academy we ask these questions about U.S. traditions of political belief and practice; we consider various forms of socialism critically and openly; and we consider in a wide variety of contexts the problematic nexus of religion and nationalism. What does it mean to paralyze our capacities for critical scrutiny and historical inquiry when this topic becomes the issue, fearing that we will become exposed to the charge of "antisemitism" if we utter our worries, our heartache, our objection, our outrage in a public form? To say, effectively, that anyone who utters their heartache and outrage out loud will be considered (belatedly, and by powerful "listeners") as antisemitic, is to seek to control the kind of speech that circulates in the public sphere, to terrorize with the charge of antisemitism, and to produce a climate of fear through the tactical use of a heinous judgment with which no progressive person would want to identify. If we bury our criticism for fear of being labeled antisemitic, we give power to those who want to curtail the free expression of political beliefs. To live with the charge is, of course, terrible, but it is less terrible when you know that it is untrue, and one can only have this knowledge if there are others who are speaking with you, and who can help to support the sense of what you know.

When Daniel Pipes established "Campus Watch" in the fall of 2002, he produced a blacklist of scholars in Middle Eastern Studies who were, in his view, known to be critical of Israel and thus understood to be antisemitic or to be fomenting antisemitism. An e-mail campaign was begun by Mark Lance, a philosopher at Georgetown University, in which a number of us wrote in to complain about not being listed on the site. The point of the e-mail initiative was to undermine the power of "blacklisting" as a tactic reminiscent of McCarthyism. Most of us wrote in to say that, if believing in Palestinian self-determination was adequate for membership on the list, we wished to be included as well. Although we were subsequently branded as "apologists" for antisemitism, and listed on the Web under this heading, there were no individuals who were part of this campaign who accepted the notion that to criticize Israel or to promote Palestinian self-determination were antisemitic acts. Indeed, when Tamar Lewin from the *New York Times* contacted me after my name was associated with the beginning of this campaign, she said she was doing a story on rising antisemitism on campus, implying that the opposition to the Daniel Pipes Web site was evidence of this rise. I explained to her that I was, like many others who wrote in, a progressive Jew (handling the discourse of identity politics for the moment), and that I rejected the notion that to support Palestinian self-determination was in itself an antisemitic act. I referred her to several Jewish organizations and petitions that held views such as my own and suggested that this was not a story about antisemitism, but about how the charge of antisemitism plays to silence certain political viewpoints. Her story in the *New York Times,* "Web Site Fuels Debates on Campus Antisemitism" (September 27, 2002), skewed the issue significantly since it accepted the assumption that there were "pro-Israel" and "pro-Palestinian" positions that did not have any overlap, and it refused to name as Jewish several of us who opposed the Web site and its neo-McCarthyism. Indeed, the article managed to associate those who opposed Pipes with antisemitism itself, even though we had, in conversation with her, made clear our profound revulsion at antisemitism.

So many important distinctions are elided by the mainstream press when it assumes that there are only two positions on the Middle East, and that they can be adequately described by the terms "pro-Israel" and "pro-Palestinian." Various people are said to hold views that are one or the other, and the assumption is that these are discrete views, internally homogeneous, nonoverlapping. And the terms suggest that if one is "pro-Israel," then anything Israel does is all right, or if one is "pro-Palestinian," then anything Palestinians do is all right. But true views on the political spectrum do not fall easily into such extremes. So many complex formulations of political belief are erased from view. One can, for instance, be in favor of Palestinian self-determination but condemn suicide bombings, and still differ with others who share both views on what form that self-determination ought to take. One can, for instance, be in favor of Israel's right to exist but still ask, What is the most legitimate and democratic form that such an existence ought to take? If one questions the present form, is one therefore anti-Israel? If one holds out for a truly democratic Israel/Palestine, is one therefore anti-Israel? Or is one trying to find a better form for this polity, one that may well involve any number of possibilities: a revised version of Zionism, a postzionist Israel, a self-determining Palestine, or an amalgamation of Israel into a greater Israel/Palestine where all race- and religion-based qualifications on rights and entitlements would be eliminated? If one is against a present-day version of Zionism, and offers reasons, reasons that would eliminate all forms of racial discrimination, including all forms of antisemitism, then surely one is involved in a critique of Israel that does not immediately qualify as antisemitic.

This is not to say that there will not be those who seize upon the fact of critique to further their antisemitic aims. That may well take place, and it surely has taken place. I do not mean to dispute this possibility and this reality. But the fact that there are those who will exploit such a critique is not reason enough to silence the critique. If the possibility of that exploitation serves as a reason to quell political dissent, then one has effectively given the domain of public discourse over to those who accept and perpetrate the view that antisemitism is authorized by criticisms of Israel, including those who seek to perpetuate antisemitism through such criticisms and those who seek to quell such criticisms for fear that they perpetuate antisemitism. To remain silent for fear of a possible antisemitic appropriation is to keep the very equation of Zionism and Jewishness intact, when it is precisely the separation between the two that guarantees the conditions for critical thinking on this issue. To remain silent for fear of an antisemitic appropriation that one deems to be certain is to give up on the possibility of combating antisemitism by other means.

What struck me as ironic here is that Summers himself makes the equation of Zionism with Jewishness and, so it seems, of Zionists with Jews, even though this is the very tactic of antisemitism. At the same time that this was happening, I found myself on a listserv in which a number of individuals opposed to the current policies of the state of Israel and sometimes opposed to Zionism itself started to engage in this very slippage, sometimes opposing what they called "Zionism" and other times opposing what they called "Jewish" interests. Every time the latter equation took place on the listserv, a number of us objected, and as a consequence several people took themselves off the listserv, unable to bear the slippage any longer. The controversial academic in Manchester, England, Mona Baker, who dismissed two Israeli colleagues from the board of her translation studies journal in an effort to boycott Israeli institutions, offered a weak argument in defense of her act, claiming that there was no way to distinguish between individuals and institutions. In dismissing these individuals, she claimed she was treating them as emblematic of the Israeli state, since they were citizens of that country. But citizens are not the same as states: the very possibility of significant dissent depends upon the difference between them. The presumption of a seamless continuity between Israeli citizens and the Israeli state not only made all Israelis equivalent to state interests, but makes it more difficult for academics outside of Israel to ally with dissidents inside who are taking strong and important stands against the occupation. Mona Baker's conflation of citizens with states was quickly followed, in her own discourse, by a collapse of "Israeli" interests with "Jewish" ones. Her response to the widespread criticism of the act in which she dismissed Israeli scholars from her board was to send around e-mails on the "academicsforjustice" listserv complaining about "Jewish" newspapers, labeling as "pressure" the opportunity that some such newspapers offered to discuss the issue in print with those she had dismissed. She refused such conversation. At that moment, it seemed, she was not only in a fight against current Israeli policy or, indeed, the structure and basis of legitimation of the Israeli state, but suddenly, now, with "Jews," identified as a lobby that pressures people, a lobby that pressures her. She not only engaged established antisemitic stereotypes but also collapsed the important distinction between Jewishness and Zionism. In her defense, Baker pointed out that one of the Zionist journals enlisting her to participate was called *The Jewish Press*, but the slide from proper name into generic entity remains nevertheless unfortunate. The same criticism that I offered to Summers's view thus applies to Baker as well: it is one thing to oppose Israel in its current form and practices or, indeed, to have critical questions about Zionism itself, but it is quite another to oppose "Jews" or fear from "Jews" or assume that all "Jews" have the same view, that they are all in favor of Israel, identified with Israel, or represented by Israel. Oddly, and painfully, it has to be said that at this point, on these occasions Mona Baker and Lawrence Summers make use of a similar premise: Jews are the same as Israel. In the one instance, the premise works in the service of an argument against antisemitism; in the second, it works as the effect of antisemitism itself. Indeed, it, seems to me that one aspect of antisemitism or, indeed, of any form of racism is that an entire people is falsely and summarily equated with a given position, view, or disposition. To say that all Jews hold a given view on Israel or are adequately represented by Israel or, conversely, that the acts of Israel, the state, adequately stand for the acts of all Jews, is to conflate Jews with Israel and, therefore, to recirculate an antisemitic reduction of Jewishness. Unfortunately, Summers's argument against antisemitism makes use of this antisemitic premise (which does not mean that he is antisemitic). We see the antisemitism of the premise actively expressed in the remark that Mona Baker makes about the "Jewish" press that is presumptively identified with Israeli state interests (which does not mean that she *is* antisemitic).

In holding out for a distinction between Israel and Jews, I am calling for a space of critique and a condition of dissent for Jews who have criticisms of Israel to articulate, but I am also opposing antisemitic reductions of Jewishness to Israeli interests. The "Jew" is no more defined by Israel than by antisemitic diatribe. The "Jew" exceeds both determinations, and is to be found, substantively, as this diasporic excess, a historically and culturally changing identity that takes no single form and has no single form. Once the distinction between Israel and Jews is made, an intellectual discussion of both Zionism and anti-semitism can begin, since it will be as important to understand critically the legacy of Zionism and to debate its future as it will be to track and oppose antisemitism as it is promulgated throughout the globe. A progressive Jewish stance will pursue both directions, and will refuse to brand as antisemitic the critical impulse or to accept antisemitic discourse as a legitimate substitute for critique.

What is needed is a public space in which such issues might be thoughtfully debated, and for academics to support the commitment to academic freedom and intellectual inquiry that would support a thoughtful consideration of these issues. What we are up against here is not only the question of whether certain kinds of ideas and positions can be permitted in public space, but how public space is itself defined by certain kinds of exclusions, certain emerging patterns of censoriousness and censorship. I have considered the way in which the charge of antisemitism against those who voice opposition to Israeli policy or to its founding ideology seeks to discredit that point of view as hatred or, indeed, hate speech, and to put into question its permissibility as protected speech or, indeed, valued political commentary. If one cannot voice an objection to violence done by the Israeli state without attracting the charge of antisemitism, then the charge works to circumscribe the publicly acceptable domain of speech. It also works to immunize Israeli violence against critique by refusing to countenance the integrity of the claims made against that violence. One is threatened with the label "antisemitic" in the same way that within the United States to oppose the most recent U.S. wars earns one the label of "traitor," or "terrorist sympathizer," or, indeed, "treasonous." These are threats with profound psychological consequence. They seek to control political behavior by imposing unbearable, stigmatized modes of identification which most people will want more than anything to avoid identification with. Fearing the identification, they fail to speak out. But such threats of stigmatization can and must be weathered, and this can only be done with the support of other actors, others who speak with you, and against the threat that seeks to silence political speech. The threat of being called "antisemitic" seeks to control, at the level of the subject, what one is willing to say out loud and, at the level of society in general, to circumscribe what can and cannot be permissibly spoken out loud in the public sphere. More dramatically, these are threats that *decide* the defining limits of the public sphere through setting limits on the speakable. The world of public discourse, in other words, will be that space and time from which those critical perspectives will be excluded. The exclusion of those criticisms will effectively establish the boundaries of the public itself, and the public will come to understand itself as one that does not speak out, critically, in the face of obvious and illegitimate violence—unless, of course, a certain collective courage takes hold.

NOTES

1. David Gelles, "Summers Says Antisemitism Lurks Locally," *Harvard Crimson*, September 19, 2002. The full transcript can be found at http://www.yucommentator.com/v67i4/israelcorner/address.html.
2. Remarks reported in the *Boston Globe*, October 16, 2002.
3. For an extended discussion of how Zionism itself has come to rely upon and perpetuate the notion that Jews, and only Jews, can be victims, see Adi Ophir, "The Identity of the Victims and the Victims of Identity: A Critique of Zionist Ideology for a Post-Zionist Age," in *Mapping Jewish Identities*, ed. Laurence Silberstein (New York: New York University Press, 2000).
4. Robert Fisk writes, "The all-purpose slander of 'antisemitism' is now being used with ever-increasing promiscuity against people who condemn the wickedness of Palestinian suicide bombings every bit as much as they do the cruelty of Israel's repeated killing of children in an effort to shut [those people] up." "How to Shut Up Your Critics with a Single Word," *Independent*, October 21, 2002.
5. Note in the full version of the statement offered as an epigraph to this essay how Summers couples antisemitism and anti-Israeli views: "Where anti-Semitism and views that are profoundly anti-Israel have traditionally been the primary reserve of poorly educated right-wing populists, profoundly anti-Israeli views are increasingly finding support in progressive intellectual communities." In this statement he begins by coupling antisemitism with anti-Israeli views, without precisely saying that they are the same. But by the end of the sentence, antisemitism is absorbed into and carried by the term "anti-Israeli" (rather than *anti-Israel*, as if it were the people who are opposed, rather than the state apparatus) so that we are given to understand not only that anti-Israeli positions but antisemitism itself is finding support among progressive intellectual communities.
6. One can see this letter and its signatories at http://www.peacemideast.org.
7. See Adi Ophir's discussion of Uri Ram's vision of postzionism: "For the post-Zionist, nationality should not determine citizenship, but vice-versa: citizenship should determine the boundaries of the Israeli nation. Judaism would then be regarded as a religion, a community affair, or a matter of a particular ethnicity, one among many." Ophir, "The Identity of the Victims and the Victims of Identity," 186. See also Uri Ram's contribution along with other pieces in *The Post-Zionist Debates: Knowledge and Power in Israeli Culture*, ed. Laurence Silberstein (New York: Routledge, 1999).
8. AIPAC, the America Israel Public Affairs Committee, is the largest Jewish lobby in the United States and is almost always supportive of Israel in its current form and practices.
9. See http://www.brittzedek.org.
10. See http://www.ffipp.org.
11. See http://oasisofpeace.org.
12. See http://www.iperi.org.
13. See http://www.btselem.org and http://www.gush-shalom.org.
14. See http://www.shministim.org for information on Yesh Gvul. See also Ronit Chacham, *Breaking Ranks: Refusing to Serve in the West Bank and Gaul* (New York: Other Press, 2003).
15. See http://taayush.tripod.com. Citation quoted with the permission of the author.
16. Yitzhak Iaor, "Will the Circle Be Unbroken?" *Haaretz*, August 2, 2002.

ABOUT THE CONTRIBUTORS

CARYN AVIV is a lecturer with the Center for Judaic Studies and academic coordinator of the Certificate in Jewish Communal Service in the Graduate School of Social Work at the University of Denver. She writes and teaches in the areas of Israel studies, global Jewish communities and identities, and gender and sexualities. She is coauthor/editor of three books with David Shneer: *New Jews: The End of the Jewish Diaspora*, *American Queer: Now and Then*, and *Queer Jews*. Her current book project uses social movement theories of emotion, space, and gender to map Israeli-Palestinian coexistence work.

ARIELLA AZOULAY teaches visual culture and contemporary philosophy at the Program for Culture and Interpretation, Bar Ilan University. She is the author of *The Civil Contract of Photography*, *Once Upon a Time: Photography Following Walter Benjamin*, *Death's Showcase*, and *Training for ART*. She has also directed the documentary films *At Nightfall*, *I Also Dwell among Your Own People: Conversations with Azmi Bishara*, *The Chain Food*, *The Angel of History*, and *A Sign from Heaven*.

AZMI BISHARA is a well-known Arab writer and intellectual. He is a Palestinian citizen of Israel, professor of philosophy at the Bir Zeit University in the West Bank (1986–1996), and a member (1996–2007) of the Knesset, the Israel parliament, representing the cause of turning Israel into the state of its citizens. He has published seven books in philosophy and political science and two literary works.

DANIEL BOYARIN was raised with his brother Jonathan in a Jewish farm community in New Jersey. He is the Taubman Professor of Rabbinic Culture at the University of California at Berkeley and author of *Unheroic Conduct: The Rise of Heterosexuality and the Invention of the Jewish Man*, *Carnal Israel: Reading Sex in Talmudic Culture*, and *A Radical Jew: Paul and the Politics of Identity*.

JONATHAN BOYARIN is the Kaplan Professor of Modern Jewish Thought at the University of North Carolina–Chapel Hill, and author of several books, including *Thinking in Jewish*, *Storm from Paradise: The Politics of Jewish Memory*, and *Polish Jews in Paris: The Ethnography of Memory*.

JUDITH BUTLER is Maxine Elliot Professor in the Departments of Rhetoric and Comparative Literature at the University of California at Berkeley. Her most recent book, *Giving an Account of Oneself*, was published by Fordham University Press (2005). She is currently working on essays pertaining to Jewish philosophy, focusing on prezionist criticisms of state. She is a board member of Jewish Voice for Peace, USA Executive Committee of Faculty for Israeli-Palestinian Peace, and the Freedom Theatre in Jenin.

HANNAN HEVER is chair of the Department of Hebrew Literature at the Hebrew University in Jerusalem. His recent books include *Producing Modern Hebrew Canon, Nation Building and Minority Discourse, Toward the Longed-for Shore: The Sea in Hebrew Culture and Modern Hebrew Literature*, and *The Narrative and the Nation: Critical Readings in the Canon of Hebrew Fiction*.

ALEXANDRE (SANDY) KEDAR is a senior lecturer at the Law School at Haifa University in Israel. His principal research focus is on legal geography, legal history, and land regimes in settler societies and in Israel. Dr. Kedar does not consider himself a postzionist. He is the author of several published works, the latest of which is "Land Regimes and Social Relations in Israel" (with Oren Yiftachel), forthcoming in *Swiss Human Rights Book*, edited by Hernando de Soto and Francis Cheneval.

BARUCH KIMMERLING was a professor of sociology at the Hebrew University of Jerusalem. He authored numerous books in English and Hebrew, including *The Interrupted System: Israeli Civilians in War and Routine Times, The Invention and Decline of Israeliness: State, Society, and the Military*, and *Palestinians: The Making of a People* (with Joel S. Migdal).

ORLY LUBIN is an associate professor at Tel Aviv University specializing in cultural studies, with a major focus on feminist theories. She has published extensively on literature, cinema, theater and visual culture, analyzed from the perspectives of feminist, postcolonial, and queer theories. She is currently working on a book about the representations of the material, the site of the body in culture, and issues of recognition, acknowledgment, and accountability.

JOEL S. MIGDAL is Robert F. Philip Professor of International Studies at the University of Washington's Henry M. Jackson School of International Studies. The founding chair of the University of Washington's International Studies Program, his books include *Peasants, Politics, and Revolution, Palestinian Society and Politics, Strong Societies and Weak States, State in Society, Through the Lens of Israel, The Palestinian People: A History* (with Baruch Kimmerling), and *Boundaries and Belonging*.

ABOUT THE CONTRIBUTORS

BENNY MORRIS was born in Kibbutz Ein Hahoresh, south of Haifa, in December 1948 and grew up in Jerusalem and New York. He served in the Nahal paratroops and earned his undergraduate degree (1973) at the Hebrew University and his Ph.D. (1977) in Cambridge University. He worked as a journalist at the *Jerusalem Post* (1978–1990). Since 1997 he has taught modern Middle East history at Ben-Gurion University.

PNINA MOTZAFI-HALLER teaches social anthropology at Ben Gurion University, Israel. She is the author of numerous essays and a book on African societies and culture; the editor of a book on gender in the Middle East; and coeditor of two books published in Hebrew on ethnicity and class in Israel. She is completing a book based on her three-year ethnographic research among working-class Mizrahi women in Yeruham. Her current research deals with cleaning labor in Israel. She lives with her two sons, David and Jonathan, in Sde Boker.

ADI OPHIR is the founding editor of *Theoria ve-Bikoret*, an Israeli venue for critical theory and cultural studies. He teaches political philosophy and critical theory at the Cohn Institute for the History and Philosophy of Science and Ideas, Tel Aviv University. His recent publications include *The Order of Evils* and "The Sovereign, The Terrorist, and the Humanitarian," in *Non-Governmental Politics*, edited by Michel Feher.

URI RAM is a member of the Department of Sociology and Anthropology at Ben Gurion University, Israel. His published books include *The Globalization of Israel: McWorld in Tel Aviv, Jihad in Jerusalem, The Time of the "Post": Nationalism and the Politics of Knowledge in Israel, The Changing Agenda of Israeli Sociology: Theory, Ideology and Identity*, and *In/Equality* (coeditor).

ERELLA SHADMI is a lesbian feminist activist and scholar living in Israel. She teaches feminist theory, women's studies, and the sociology of policing. She has published several articles about women's issues in Israel and is currently working on a book about radical feminist critique of Israeli society and women's position. She is also coediting a book on crime and criminal justice in Israel. Professor Shadmi served as a senior police officer at the Israel Police Headquarters and published several critical analyses of the Israeli police.

GERSHON SHAFIR is a professor in the Department of Sociology at University of California at San Diego and director of the Institute for International, Comparative, and Area Studies. He is the author of *Land, Labor, and the Origins of the Israeli-Palestinian Conflict, 1882–1914*; *Being Israeli: The Dynamics of Multiple Citizenship* (with Yoav Peled), which won the 2002 Middle Eastern Studies Association's Albert Hourani Award for best book on the Middle East; and *National*

Insecurity and Human Rights: Democracies Debate Counterterrorism (coedited with Alison Brysk).

ANTON SHAMMAS is a Palestinian writer and translator of Hebrew, Arabic, and English. His novel *Arabesques* was chosen by the *New York Times Book Review* as one of the seven best novels of 1988. He teaches comparative and modern Arabic literature at the University of Michigan.

YEHOUDA SHENHAV is a professor of sociology at Tel-Aviv University. He is the editor of *Theory and Criticism* (Hebrew) and senior editor for *Organization Studies*. His recent books include *The Arab Jews*, *What Is Multiculturalism* (with Yossi Yonah), and *Manufacturing Rationality*. He is currently working on political theology, colonial bureaucracy, and state of exception.

DAVID SHNEER is director of the Center for Judaic Studies and associate professor of history at the University of Denver. His books include *Queer Jews*, *Yiddish and the Creation of Soviet Jewish Culture*, and *New Jews: The End of the Jewish Diaspora*. His newest book project looks at the lives and works of two dozen World War II military photographers to examine what kinds of photographs they took when they encountered evidence of Nazi genocide on the Eastern Front.

ELLA SHOHAT teaches cultural studies and Middle Eastern studies at New York University. Her published books include *Unthinking Eurocentrism* (with Robert Stam), *Flagging Patriotism: Crises of Narcissism and Anti-Americanism* (with Robert Stam), *Taboo Memories, Diasporic Voices*, and *Israeli Cinema: East/West and the Politics of Representation*. She has coedited several volumes, including *Dangerous Liaisons: Gender, Nation and the Postcolonial Perspective*, *Multiculturalism, Postcoloniality and Transnational Media*, and *The Cultural Politics of the Middle East in the Americas*.

LAURENCE J. SILBERSTEIN is Philip and Muriel Berman Professor of Jewish Studies in the Department of Religion Studies, Lehigh University, and director of the Philip and Muriel Berman Center for Jewish Studies. He is the author of *Martin Buber's Social and Religious Thought* and *The Postzionism Debates: Knowledge and Power in Israeli Culture*. His edited and coedited books include *New Perspectives on Israeli History: The Early Years of the State*, *Mapping Jewish Identities*, and *Impossible Images: Art after the Holocaust* (with Shelley Hornstein and Laura Levitt).

OREN YIFTACHEL teaches political geography and urban planning at Ben-Gurion University of the Negev, Beer-Sheva. He is the founding editor of *Hagar: Studies in Culture, Politics, Identities*. His recent articles include "Towards a Theory of Ethnocratic Regimes: Learning from the Judaization of Israel/Palestine" (with

A. Ghanem) in *Rethinking Ethnicity: Majority Groups and Dominant Minorities*, edited by E. Kaufam, and "Walls, Fences and 'Creeping Apartheid' in Israel/Palestine" (with H. Jacobi) in *Writing against the Wall*, edited by M. Sorkin. His book *"Ethnocracy": Land and Identity Politics in Israel/Palestine* was published in 2006 by the University of Pennsylvania Press.

RAZ YOSEF teaches in the Film and Television Department at Tel Aviv University and at Sapir College, Israel. He is the author of *Beyond Flesh: Queer Masculinities and Nationalism in Israeli Cinema*, as well as numerous articles on issues of gender, sexuality, and ethnicity in Israeli visual culture.

INDEX

Aaronsohn, Ran, 49
Abdullah (king of Transjordan), 36, 37, 39, 43
Abraham, 336
Abramovitch, S. Y., 349
Abu El-Banaat (film), 284
ACRI (Association of Civil Rights in Israel), 148, 152–153
After the Eagles Landed: The Yemenites of Israel (Lewis), 248, 249
Ahmad, Aijaz, 298
AIPAC (America Israel Public Affairs Committee), 378, 386n8
Akenson, Donald Harman, 341n2
Alcalay, Amiel, 7
aliyah: and Diaspora, 346; and Mizrahim, 239–241, 242, 253; modernization associated with, 247; in Zionist historiography, 108, 109–110
Alliance Israelite Universelle, 244
Almog, Shmuel, 105, 116n12
Althusser, Louis, 272n7
Altneuland (Herzl), 310
America Israel Public Affairs Committee (AIPAC), 378, 386n8
American Jews, 327–386; attitude toward Zionism, 353, 354, 356; Brit Tzedek, 378; as cautious about criticizing Israel, 20; college students' declining attachment to Israel, 362; "A Covenant between the Jewish People of North America and Israel," 357; differences among, 361; Eastern European Jews, 350–351; emigrate to Israel, 356, 364; financial support for Israel from, 353–354; German Jews, 350; Israel as civic religion for, 354–355; Israeli Jews live in U.S., 351–352, 364; Israelism among, 27n65; on Israel/Palestine as homeland, 351; lobbying on behalf of Israeli politicians, 133; lose their connection to Eastern Europe, 354; new vision of Israel after 1967 war, 356; New York City, 350, 351, 358, 363, 368n54; "Open Letter from American Jews," 377; postzionism among, 5, 7, 18–21; United Jewish Appeal, 357; Zionist influence among, 7, 18
American Sephardi Federation, 358
Amir, Delila, 317–318
Ana'im, Muhammad, 213
anality, 301–302

Antin, Mary, 350
antiquity, 112–113
antisemitism: antizionism equated with, 215n5; Campus Watch blacklist, 381–382; criticizing Israel seen as, 369–386; effective, 369, 370, 371–373, 381; femininity associated with Jews in, 295; increasing in Europe, 364; intentional, 372; Jewish exceptionalism on, 111; on Jewish racism, 329; Jewish threat to nativism as source of, 338; Muslim, 244; protest against Israeli state distinguished from, 375; Zionism as revolt against, 96
antizionism: antisemitism equated with, 215n5; Palestinian critics of Zionism associated with, 92; postzionism contrasted with, 89–90, 95; postzionism equated with, 5; without negating importance of Jews' connection to Zion, 359; on Zionism as human arrogation of God's work, 337
Arabesques (Shammas), 193–216; arabesque as richly articulated vehicle for minority discourse, 195; detective-story organization of, 196; dynastic political genealogy genre parodied by, 200; Hebrew language of, 14, 193–194, 210, 211, 212–215; Hegel's master-slave relationship and, 208–209; Israeli Jews placed in uneasy position by, 212; as minority literature, 13–14, 210–212; "narrator" versus "narrative" sections of, 196–198, 199, 202, 206; negationist stance of, 195; oral tales in, 206–207, 212–213; Oz on, 193; politicization in, 210; as protest, 194; seen as most truly Israeli novel yet, 195; as semiautobiographical, 196; spatial patterning of, 205; textual interrelationships in, 207–208; treatment of time in, 202–205; two Anton Shammases in, 197–198; two-faced nature of Israeli public discourse exposed by, 200, 201; women in, 202–203, 205; Yehoshua as model for Bar-On, 201
Arab Higher Committee, 40
Arab-Israeli conflict. *See* Israeli-Arab conflict
Arab Jews. *See* Mizrahim
Arab Jews (Shenhav), 16
Arab Legion, 31, 32, 36, 37, 38
Arab Liberation Army, 39

Arabs: Ben-Gurion associates Nazis with, 95; collusion against Palestinian statehood, 1947–1949, 36–37; manufactured as common perennial historical enemy, 243. *See also* Israeli-Arab conflict; Israeli Arabs; Palestinian Arabs
Arafat, Yassir, 228
Araydi, Na'im, 213
Archives Law, 34
Aref, Aref al-, 31
Arendt, Hannah, 95, 261–262, 271n2, 381
Argentina, 352
Arieli, Yehoshua, 116n12
Ashkenazim: as charter group in Israel, 127; cultural dissonance between Arab Jews and, 244; defined, 142n4; as ethnic group, 278, 300; feminism among, 305, 314; increasing assimilation between Mizrahim and, 138; intra-Jewish residential segregation, 131–132, 137–138; Israeli scholars as, 14; in *Jacky*, 283, 284, 289, 292; lesbians, 319, 320, 322n5; and Mizrahim in Zionist historiography, 275–280; as percentage of Israeli Jews, 127; "white" identity of, 300; Yemeni Jewish babies adopted by, 248; Zionism seen as European-Ashkenazi-White-Colonial movement, 65; and Zionist hypermasculine heterosexual male, 295–296, 299–300, 305
Ashkenazi Revolution, The (Katznelson), 247
Association for Individual Rights, 314
Association of Civil Rights in Israel (ACRI), 148, 152–153
Auschwitz, 86
Australia, Aboriginal land rights' cases in, 155–156
autochthony, 334–335, 336, 339
Aviv, Caryn, 19
Avneri, Uri, 6, 95
ayarot pituah (development towns), 131, 263, 275, 285, 286, 292
Azoulay, Ariella, 10, 11, 13, 63

Babylonian Exile, 348
Babylon Jewish Museum, 247
Baer, Yitzhak Fritz, 104, 116n10, 116n12
Baghdadi Jews, 240, 244, 250
Baker, Mona, 383–384
Bakhtin, Mikhail, 302, 303
Balibar, Etienne, 330, 331
Ballas, Shimon, 265
Barak, Aharon, 121, 148, 151–152, 154, 155, 156, 157, 158, 159
Bar-Joseph, Uri, 116n7
Bar Kokhba syndrome, 113, 119n35
Bar-Zohar, Michael, 33
Bat Adam, Michal, 288, 308–309
Bechor, Guy, 70
Beck, Ulrich, 265
Bedouins: dwellings, 141–142, 147n74; romanticizing, 246
Beersheba, 332, 342n7
Beit-Tzaffafa (Jerusalem neighborhood), 177
Ben-Eliezer, Uri, 140

Ben-Gurion, David: acceptance of partition by, 35–36; on American Jews, 354; on expulsion of Arabs, 33, 39; on Jewish Agency after establishment of Israel, 62; Nazis and Arabs associated by, 95; on peace agreement in 1948–1949, 42, 43–44; portraits of, 225
Benjamin, Orly, 317
Benjamin, Walter, 262
Ben-Shaul, Nitzan S., 304
Benvenisti, Meron, 6
Ben Zvi, Yitzhak, 225
Berger, Harry, Jr., 334–335
Bergman, Hugo, 104
Bersani, Leo, 297, 301
Bethlehem, 380
Bevin, Ernest, 36
Beyond Flesh (Yosef), 294–307
Bezalel Museum, 167, 181n5
Bhabha, Homi, 65, 265, 266, 269, 298–299
Biale, David, 215n5, 305, 357, 362
Bible, Hebrew, 329, 330, 335
Biletzki, Anat, 378
Billig, Michael, 124
Bingham, Dennis, 300
Birth of Israel, The (Flapan), 35, 55n7
Birth of the Palestinian Refugee Problem, 1947–1949, The (Morris), 35, 39, 93
Bishara, Azmi, 15, 92, 140, 180n1
Blaustein, Jacob, 354
"Bond of Silence" (Shenhav), 263
Bonné, Alfred, 104
Boyarin, Daniel, 17, 19, 305, 342n11, 358–359, 364
Boyarin, Jonathan, 19, 342n11, 358–359, 364
Brief Travels of Benjamin the Third, The (Abramovitch), 349
Brinker, Menachem, 62
Britain and the Arab-Israeli Conflict, 1948–51 (Pappe), 35, 37, 42
B'rith Shalom, 95, 381
Brit Tzedek, 378
Brooks, Peter, 287
Brown v. Board of Education, 155, 163n43
Brueggemann, Walter, 335
b'tei midrash, 349
B'tselem, 177, 379
Buber, Martin, 6, 95, 104, 381
burden of proof in land cases, 154
Bursztyn, Igal, 285, 304
Butler, Judith, 19, 20, 297–298, 344n20
by-pass roads, 146n56

Calhoun, Chesire, 321
Campus Watch, 381–382
Canaanite movement, 6, 214, 216n19
Canaanites (people), 113, 330, 335, 343n16
capitalism: economic liberalization, 52–53, 66–67, 156; ethnic logic of, 124–125; post-Fordist, 9, 66, 67, 71
Carmeli Brigade, 40
Carr, E. H., 103
cemeteries, 349
Center for Jewish History (New York), 358
Chalutz, 88

INDEX

Chinski, Sara, 7
Choan, Steven, 300
cinema, Israeli. *See* Israeli cinema
Cinema Israeli de la Modernite, Le (Schweitzer), 304
civil marriage, 136
civil rights: apartheid system of citizenship for guaranteeing Jews', 96; Association of Civil Rights in Israel, 148, 152–153; cultural impact of Israel on Arabs seen in terms of, 15; in democracies, 133, 139; in Israel, 139; Israeli Arabs denied, 127, 278; Jewish settlements ignore Palestinian, 135; lesbians adopt doctrine of, 313–316, 317; and *Qaadan v. Katzir*, 121, 152
CLaF Hazak (journal), 317, 321
"Clash of Civilizations" thesis, 70
Clifford, James, 359
Cohen, Eli (Kamal Amin Thabat), 259–261, 262
Cohen, Erik, 62
Cohen, Gavriel, 117n24
Cohen, Jean L., 320
Cohen, Nadia, 260
Collusion across the Jordan (Shlaim), 35, 42
community (private) settlements, 131–132, 150–151
contractualism, Western corporativism versus Islamic, 203
conversion, 229, 353
corporativism, Islamic contractualism versus Western, 203
"Covenant between the Jewish People of North America and Israel, A," 357
critical sociology, 8–9; academic authority of, 95; Megged on, 46, 50; on Mizrahim, 65; precursors of, 95; Ram on, 61; Shafir on, 50–51; on victim identity, 88
Cultures of the Jews (Biale), 357

Dakuar, G'amil, 164n64
Dante, 213, 220
David, King, 113, 335–336
David Tower Museum, 167
Davies, W. D., 334, 336–337, 339, 342n12, 343n17, 343n18, 343n19
Davis, Uri, 95
Davis, Yuval, 69
Dayan, Moshe, 43, 169
de-Arabization, 128–129, 137, 261, 262
Declaration of Independence, 222, 336
decolonization: in other settler societies, 156; peace process seen as, 51–54. *See also* postcolonialism
Deleuze, Gilles, 10, 13, 14, 23n23, 26n54, 171, 210–212, 301
democracy: calls for more Israeli, 377, 378; characteristics of, 133; demos required for, 133–134; ethnocracy compared with, 121, 125, 126, 139; illiberal, 143n17; Israel considered democratic, 12, 14, 67–68, 92, 112, 127, 132, 134, 139–141, 152, 198, 200, 201, 226–227, 352, 353, 357; Judaization conflicts with, 128, 129, 130; Mizrahi call for more democratic Israel, 275–280; and orthodox agenda, 134–137

Democratic Mizrahi Rainbow, 164n66
demos, 133–134
Derrida, Jacques, 212, 213
development towns (*ayarot pituah*), 131, 263, 275, 285, 286, 292
dialogism, 302
Diaspora, 329–344; biblical origins of, 346–347, as catch-all phrase, 362; celebrating, 358–359; as creative force with Judaism, 19; cultural politics of, 359; diaspora business, 355, 363, 364; from Diaspora Jews to new Jews, 345–368; dictionary definitions of, 346, 347; of different Jewish peoples, 349–352; dismantling, 361–365; as dissociation of ethnicities and political hegemonies, 340; and exile, 346–349, 358; femininity attributed to, 295; and home, 346–349; as imagined community, 359; Jeremiah on, 348; Jewish cultural creativity in context of common life of surroundings, 337–338; Jewish return means rupture with, 234; as model for synthesis of universal and particular, 337; negative connotations of, 347; Negev land sold to Jews from, 142; nomadism as analogue for, 335–336; as not forced product, 338–339; organizations have statutory powers in Israel, 133; postzionism's meaning for, 90; problems with term, 362; remaking after establishment of Israel, 354–357; as replacement of self-determination model, 331, 359; resistance to assimilation and annihilation during, 331; Zionist rejection of, 18, 19, 95
Dinur (Dinaburg), Ben Zion, 104, 116n10, 116n12
Dirlik, Arif, 298
DirYassin massacre, 93
Don-Yehiya, E., 146n51
dress, Arab Jewish, 244–245
Dubnow, Simon, 105
Dwiri, Ibrahim and Hilda, 159
Dyer, Richard, 300

Eastern European Jews: destruction of, 354; immigration to United States by, 350–351. *See also* Ashkenazim
East Jerusalem: Arab population in 1967, 58; as factor against separation, 53; Israeli Jews residing in, 133; Israeli occupation of, 166, 167, 173; Rockefeller Museum, 167–168
Eban, Abba, 42, 342n7
Edelman, Lee, 301
Eder, Klaus, 319
Egypt: Ghosh on Jews of, 251; Israel rejects 1948 peace proposal of, 43–44
Eichmann, Adolf, 85, 95, 261
Eisenstadt, S. N., 62, 118n27
El-Aqsa Mosque, 167
Elbogen, Ismar, 104
Eliraz, Yisrael, 213
Elkosh (Deir el-Qasi), 223–224
Elon, Amos, 6
El-Tal, Abdallah, 169

Elyashar, Eliyahu, 277
Encyclopedia Hebraica, 110
Equal and More Equal (Michael), 278
Eretz Israel (Land of Israel): antiquity attributed to Jewish roots in, 112–113; boundary-drawing after 1967 war, 112; *Encyclopedia Hebraica* article on, 110; in invention of Jewish nation, 242; as not birthplace of Jewish people, 336; as renounced until final redemption, 336–337; two opposed moments in Jewish discourse of, 333–334; in Zionist historiography, 105, 107–108, 117n18
Esterkin, Rachel, 283
Ethiopian Jews, 127, 362
ethnicity: Ashkenazim as ethnic, 278, 300; denial of ethnic problem in Israel, 262–264, 271n3; as ideological category of Zionism, 267–268; intersection of discourses of sexuality and, 299–300; in Israel citizenship, 64, 68, 357; in *Jacky*, 283, 284, 285, 291, 292; melting pot ideology, 97, 224, 278, 279, 360; purification in Jerusalem, 177–178. *See also* ethnocracy; ethnonationalism; racism
ethnocentricity, 336, 337
ethnocracy, 121–147; characteristics of, 125–126; defined, 125; democracy compared with, 121, 125, 126, 139, 143n16; examples of, 139, 143n16; and globalization, 124–125; and intra-Jewish residential segregation, 131–132; Israel as, 12, 67–68, 92, 112, 127, 132, 137–139; Judaization of Israel/Palestine, 126–130; and orthodox agenda, 134–137; selective openness in, 126; theorizing, 122–125
ethnonationalism, 123–124; in backlash against postzionism, 71; boundary-drawing after 1967 war, 112; of community settlements, 148; global dominance of, 124; as Israeli citizenship regime, 64; in neozionism, 69, 70; in Zionist historiography, 105
Ettinger, Shmuel, 116n12
European Union (EU), 126
Evron, Boas, 6
exceptionalism, 110–111
exile: Diaspora and, 346–349, 358; Zionism and the end of, 352–354. *See also* "ingathering of the exiles" (*Kibbutz Galuiot*)
Exiles and Diasporas (Wettstein), 358

Face as Battlefield (Bursztyn), 304
"Facing the Forests" (Yehoshua), 208, 209
Faculty for Israeli–Palestinian Peace, 378
Fallaci, Oriana, 264
Fanon, Frantz, 298
Farouk, King, 43
feminism: doubts about accomplishments of, 322n6; heterosexual women take control of, 313; of *Jacky*, 17, 286–287; lesbian, 313, 321; lesbians' relationship to, 311, 312; Mizrahim join in multifaceted struggle, 280; Mizrahi versus Ashkenazi, 305, 314; political marginalization of lesbians supported by, 317, 319; radical, 312, 313, 314, 317, 321; as reformist, 320; as space for constructing alternative lesbian identity, 310, 318
fertility cult, 308, 309, 315
Fictive Looks: On Israeli Cinema (Gertz, Lubin, and Ne'eman), 304
Fifth Aliyah, 109
films. *See* Israeli cinema
Finkelstein, Norman, 59n5
Finland, 128, 141
First Aliyah, 109, 110
First Temple, destruction of the, 348
Fisk, Robert, 386n4
Flapan, Simha, 35, 36, 37, 55n7, 95, 116n7
Fordist capitalism, 66, 67
'48 generation, 3, 34
Foucault, Michel, 10, 13, 25n46, 63, 64, 165–166, 170–171, 265, 268, 296, 298
Fourth Aliyah, 109
Fox, Eytan, 298
Franciscan Museum, 167
Frankenstein, Karl, 247
French Jews, 364–365, 368n56
Freud, Sigmund, 295
Friedlander, Saul, 86
"From Sea to Sea," 223
From Time Immemorial: The Origins of the Arab-Jewish Conflict over Palestine (Peters), 57, 59n5
frontier culture, 122, 129

Galilee, Mitzpim established to Judaize, 150
galut, 347
Garrett, Leah, 359–360
Gat, Moshe, 250
gay men: alliances with lesbians, 316; political marginalization of lesbians supported by, 317, 319; "queer" beginning as pejorative but acquiring implication of self-empowerment, 269; queer masculinities and nationalism in Israeli cinema, 294–307; as reformist, 320; transformative potential of, 14; Zionism as marginalizing and excluding, 17–18
Gaza Strip: Arab population in 1967, 58; in Egyptian peace proposal of 1948, 43; Israel offers to take in 1949, 44; as separated from West Bank, 53; state-subsidized colonization drive in, 53. *See also* occupied West Bank and Gaza
gaze, the, 284, 289, 292, 300, 301, 308
gender, 281–325; diasporized gender identity, 338; in Israeli films, 286–288; Jewish community spaces associated with, 349; subsumption of women's issues under gender issues, 318; Zionism's masculine discourse, 17–18, 294–298, 304, 305, 310, 353. *See also* sexuality; women
German Jews, 350
Gertz, Nurith, 304
Ghanem, Asad, 140
Ghosh, Amitav, 250–251
Giladi, Naeim, 254n9

Gilbar, Gad, 59n5
Gilman, Sander, 18, 305
Gilroy, Paul, 269
Gitelman, Zvi, 361–362
Glaser, Andreas, 311
globalization: and ethnonationalism, 124–125; and Israeli land regime, 156; and post-Marxist postzionism, 66, 67; postzionism shaped by, 3, 9
Gold of the Jews, The (Zertal), 93
Goldstein, Rebecca, 345
Gorny, Yosef, 49
Gottwald, Norman K., 343n16
Graetz, Heinrich, 105
Gramsci, Antonio, 54, 126, 140
Greek Orthodox patriarchy, museum of, 167
Green Line: Arabs left in Israel as "Green Liners," 222; in Jerusalem, 169, 173–174, 175, 176, 182n18
Gross, Nathan, 303
Gross, Ya'acov, 303
Gross, Yosef, 255n17
Gruen, Erich, 347, 348
Guattari, Félix, 14, 23n23, 26n54, 210–212
guest workers, 96
Gush Emunim, 85, 86, 135, 330
Gush Shalom, 379
Guttman, Amos, 298, 305
Guttnick, David, 145n40

hagirah, 108
Haifa, exodus of Arabs from, 39–41
Halacha, 135
Hall, Stuart, 7
Halperin, David, 297
Hammer, Z., 135
Hamsin (film), 299
Harel, Yisrael, 67
Hark, Ina Rae, 300
Harkabi, Yehoshafat, 43, 113
Haskala, 67
Hassollelim, Kibbutz, 159
Hausner, Gideon, 261, 262
Hebrew Bible, 329, 330, 335
Hebrew Film, The: The History of Cinema in Israel (Gross and Gross), 303
Hebrew Immigrant Aid Society, 350
Hebrew language: in American Jewish education, 356; exile of Palestinian refugees done in, 220; Hebrew culture emerging around, 229; of Jewish immigrants from Arab world, 224; as Jewish not Israeli language, 219; as "language of grace," 213, 214, 220; as new synthetic language, 213; *Qaadan v. Katzir* on, 152; revival of, 129, 219; in Shammas's *Arabesques*, 14, 193–194, 210, 211, 212–215
Hebrew Union College, 350
Hebrew University, 104–105, 116n11, 247
Hegel, Georg Wilhelm Friedrich, 208–209, 214, 247
Hellenistic Jews, 348
Helmreich, Stefan, 365n1
Herzl, Theodor, 219, 222, 225, 295, 308, 310, 352
Herzog, Hannah, 317

heterotopias, 166, 170–172
Hever, Hannan, 10, 13–14, 23n25, 26n52, 26n54
Hiram, Ephraim, 261
historiography: critique of Zionist, 106–113; Israeli-Jewish, 102–120; making a Zionist, 104–106; Mizrahim and Zionist, 234, 243, 245, 275–280; nationalist, 103; in sociopolitical hegemony, 114–115. *See also* new historiography
History of the Jewish Community in Eretz Israel, 111, 117n24
Histradut, 48, 66–67
Hobsbawm, Eric, 106–107
Holocaust, the (Shoah): American Jews' attitude toward Palestine affected by, 351; in construction of Jewish identity, 84–85; and criticism of Israel, 370; Eichmann trial, 85, 95; exceptionalism attributed to, 111, 118n26; institutions and products in commemoration of, 82–83; loss of the land associated with, 85, 86; in Zionist historiography, 110
Holocaust Memorial Museum (Washington), 82
Holy Land: Jews maintain mythic connection to, 348. *See also* Palestine
Homelands (Tye), 345
homosexuality: Israeli cinema scholarship as silent on, 304–305; queer synagogue in New York, 363; seen as one monolithic category, 316, 317. *See also* gay men; lesbians
Horowitz, Dan, 49
House on Shlush Street, The (film), 284
human rights, 98, 249, 374, 378, 379
Huntington, Samuel, 70
Husayni, Haj Amin al-, 36
Hushi, Abba, 223
Husseini, Faisal, 182n23

Ibn Gabirol, 338
Ichud movement, 95
ideology: critique of Zionist, 94–99; "end of ideology" thesis, 62; Labor Zionism as, 48–49; postideological perspective on postzionism, 62–63, 70
I Love You, Rosa (film), 284
immigrant-settler society: building an, 102–103; and ethnocracy, 122–123; "pure settlement" colonies, 50, 51, 122–123, 126; selective openness in, 126
In an Antique Land (Ghosh), 250–251
Independence Day, 219, 222–223
indigenousness, 333–334, 342n11
"ingathering of the exiles" (*Kibbutz Galuiot*): in dominant Israeli sociology, 9; and intra-Israeli segregation, 138; and Israel as homeland for all Jews, 353; and Israeli exceptionalism, 111; and Mizrahim, 16, 233–234, 236, 239, 245, 247; modernization associated with, 248; in "myth" of Zionism, 2; narrative of unique Jewish suffering for legitimating, 242; and Palestinian "others," 11; versus partnership with global Jews, 357

In Praise of Normalcy (Yehoshua), 62
Institute for Jewish Studies (Hebrew University), 104
intifada: Israeli security apparatus seen as unable to subdue, 52; limited self-rule results from, 138; the other seen as victim in, 95–96; postzionism affected by second, 69; turns Jewish victims into "Zionist oppressors," 356
Iranian Jews, 351
Iraqi Jews, 237, 239, 240, 241, 244, 247, 250, 254n4, 262
Irgun Zvai Leumi (IZL), 41, 93–94
Islamic Museum, 167
Israel: American Jews as cautious about criticizing, 20; American Jews immigrate to, 356, 364; American Jews' support for, 353–354; apartheid aspects of, 92, 96, 98, 228; broadening middle class in, 138; characterizations of regime of, 139–140; citizenship regimes of, 64, 68, 377; as civic religion for secular Jews, 354–355; clear boundaries lacking for, 132, 133, 136, 140; collectivist social regime of traditional, 66; as common denominator for world Jewry, 362; continual conflict and responses to criticism of, 20; criticizing seen as antisemitic, 369–386; criticizing versus challenging right to exist, 375–376; Declaration of Independence, 222, 336; as democratic, 12, 14, 67–68, 92, 112, 127, 132, 134, 139–141, 152, 198, 200, 201, 226–227, 352, 353, 357; demos lacking in, 133–134; Diaspora conditions compared with state power in, 331–332; elections of 1996, 134, 138; as ethnocracy, 12, 68, 92, 127, 132–134, 137–139; fascist tendencies in, 19, 332; fortress mentality in, 194; fragmented society of, 277; identification of Jewish people with, 375, 376–380, 384–385; immigration statutes of, 128; as invented nation, 242; investment and aid after Six-Day War, 227; Israeli Jews in U.S., 351–352, 364; as Jewish state, 12, 14, 15, 19, 90, 127–128, 134, 135, 141, 152, 158, 198, 200, 201, 222, 226–227, 228, 333, 352, 353, 357; Judaization of Israel/Palestine, 126–142; land and labor in Israeli-Palestinian conflict, 46–55; land policy of, 130, 149, 156; *Lebensraum* rhetoric in, 332; lesbianism constructed as nonissue in, 308–325; making visible power relations in, 10, 25n42; militarism begins to be criticized, 356–357; minority discourse in, 191–325; Mizrahi call for more democratic, 275–280; modernization as mechanism of policy making in, 246; name's meaning, 353; as national refuge, 2, 8–9; "proper," 133, 140, 145n43; racist tendencies in, 19; religious character of state, 136; remaking Diaspora after establishment of, 354–357; sense of having been duped in, 93–94; as settling ethnocracy, 137, 160n6; as theocracy, 134–137, 352; victim position as asset to, 87–88; world Jewry in politics of, 133, 139, 145n40; Zionism's teleological model of history of, 16. *See also* Eretz Israel (Land of Israel); Israeli-Arab conflict; Israeli Arabs; Israeli cinema; Jerusalem; occupied West Bank and Gaza; political parties

Israel before Israel: Silent Cinema in the Holy Land (Tryster), 303
Israeli-Arab conflict: ethnonationalism encouraged by, 70; "old" history and attitudes toward, 33; as total conflict, 103; Yom Kippur War of 1973, 11; in Zionist historiography, 108, 109. *See also* Lebanon invasion of 1982; Six-Day War (1967); War of Independence
Israeli Arabs, 217–229; binational state for, 228, 229; changing nomenclature for, 27n61; discriminatory policies against, 130; equal citizenship structurally denied to, 141; equal participation demanded by, 228–229; exclusion from Israeli society, 111–112, 127; expropriation of land of, 130, 150; ghettoization of, 130; as having little to celebrate in 1998, 226–229; identification with Palestinian people, 15, 27n61; integration desired by, 54; in Israel citizenship categories, 96; in Israeli social stratification, 127; and Israeli welfare state, 68; Israelization of, 228; and Jewishness of Israeli state, 15; Keshet on rights for, 279; and law of return, 26n59, 128, 235, 364, 376; long history of discrimination against, 198; as marginalized and disempowered, 11, 12, 14–15, 226, 228; middle class and intelligentsia of, 227; orthodox groups on, 135–136, 137; as percentage of Israel's population, 126; population in 1967, 58; in postcolonial postzionism, 65; postzionism accepts separation between Israeli Jews and, 91; prefer to retain their collective identity, 158, 164n64; prevented from buying land, 130; public land allocation to, 160n14; in *Qaadan v. Katzir*, 12, 148–164; Rabin supported by, 227–228; religious divisions among, 127; response to changes after 1967, 227–228; right to vote given to, 226–227; separate neighborhoods for, 138; Shammas's personal testimony of an "Israeli Arab," 219–225
Israeli cinema: queer masculinities and nationalism in, 294–307; scholarship on, 303–304; women in, 286–288. *See also Jacky* (film)
Israeli Cinema: East/West and the Politics of Representation (Shohat), 303–304
Israeli Cinema: Facts, Plots, Directors, Opinions (Schnitzer), 303
Israeli settlers: as citizens, 12; criticism of and anti-Semitism, 375; in electoral politics, 134; expansion of settlements, 228; Gush Emunim supports, 135; intra-Jewish residential segregation, 131–132; penetrate into Arab areas, 130; postzionism influenced by, 3; rationales

for settlement, 131; as self-styled persecuted victims, 199
Israelism, 27n65
Israeli Society: Critical Perspectives (Ram), 9
Israel Land Administration (ILA), 148, 151, 158, 161n22
Israel Lands (Mekarkei Israel), 150, 160n10, 161n22
Israel Museum, 167
Israel/Palestine Center for Research and Information, 379
IVRI-Nasawi, 358

Jabareen, Tawfik, 163n51
Jacky (film), 283–293; constitution of the subject in, 285–290; as critique of majority Israeli society, 17, 288; ending of, 288, 289; realism in, 285; setting of, 283, 285; as subversive, 288, 289, 292; territory in, 285, 290–293
Jaffa, exodus of Arabs from, 40, 41
Jameson, Fredric, 209
Jenin, demolition of homes in, 371, 374
Jeremiah, 348
Jerusalem, 165–187; American Jews' symbolic connection to, 355; annexations since Six-Day War, 182n20; checkpoints in, 176–177; competing interests attempt to shape, 176, 182n19; ethnic purification in, 177–178; exodus of Arabs from, 40, 41; functions as single urban unit, 176; Green Line drawn in, 169, 173–174, 175, 176, 182n18; Hellenistic Jews and, 348; heterogeneity of, 173–180; as heterotopia, 166, 170–172; Israeli unification policy for, 165, 173, 174, 177, 180, 180n2; Jewification of, 13, 177–178, 181n16; Kol Ha-Isha feminist center, 313; loopholes in borderlines of, 178; museums in, 167–168; Muslim conquest of, 167; no-man's-lands in, 169, 181n9; partition of, 180n2; population ratio of Jews to Palestinians in, 174; refugee camps on outskirts of, 177; three-thousandth-anniversary celebration, 166. *See also* East Jerusalem
Jerusalem School (historiography), 105, 114, 116n12
Jewish Agency: Ben-Gurion on, 62, and democratization of Israel, 134; in establishment of Katzir, 148; in Israeli land system, 130; Jewish agriculture subsidized by, 224; Negev lands sold to, 142; in *Qaadan v. Katzir*, 151–152, 154, 155, 163n41, 164n61; in three-party leases, 151
Jewish Community in Crisis, A: The Exodus from Iraq, 1948–1951 (Gat), 250
Jewish Museum (New York City), 244
Jewish National Fund (JNF), 48–49, 130, 134, 148, 151, 157, 160n10
Jewish Publication Society of America, 116n13
Jewish Voices for Peace, 378
Jewish Workers' Bund, 340
Jews: beyond Zionism, 357–361; "chosenness" of, 337; from Diaspora Jews to new Jews, 345–368; dual representation as majority and minority, 194, 198, 199, 208–209, 212; genealogy and territoriality in Jewish identity, 333; as "guarantors for one another," 136; history steeped in suffering, 194; identifying with Israel, 375, 376–380, 384–385; ideology of pure Jewish cultural essence, 338; as invented nation, 242; Israel as Jewish state, 12, 14, 15, 19, 90, 127–128, 134, 135, 141, 152, 158, 198, 200, 201, 222, 226–227, 228, 333, 352, 353, 357; as "making it" in societies in which they live, 362; New Jew, 233, 234, 236, 295, 304, 353; Palestinians as Israeli Jews', 201–202; as percentage of Israel's population, 126; as percentage of Jerusalem's population, 174; population residing in occupied territories, 133; racism associated with, 329–330; separatism among, 332; three stages of history of, 339; unity attributed to, 361; victim position assumed by, 84–85, 100n6, 242, 243, 370. *See also* American Jews; antisemitism; Ashkenazim; Diaspora; Holocaust, the (Shoah); Mizrahim; Sephardim
Jews for Peace in the Middle East, 378
Jews for Racial and Economic Justice, 378
JNF (Jewish National Fund), 48–49, 130, 134, 148, 151, 157, 160n10
Jordan: Abdullah, 36, 37, 39, 43; annexation of West Bank, 43; in Arab-Israeli war of 1948, 36, 37, 38; in division of Jerusalem, 169, 173
Joshua, 336
Judaism: conversion, 229, 353; as ethnic and/or religious, 135; national character attributed to, 105; rabbinic, 330, 336–337; Reform, 350; in Zionist historiography, 103. *See also* Jews; Orthodox Judaism
Jutte, Robert, 105, 116n9

Kahane, Meir, 201
Kamen, Charles, 55n9
Kanyuk, Yoram, 213
Katzir: establishment of, 148, 150, 164n60. See also *Qaadan v. Katzir*
Katznelson, Kalman, 247
Kaufmann, Yehezkel, 104
Kedar, Alexandre (Sandy), 10, 11, 12
Kedourie, Elie, 103
Keshet (Hakeshet Hademocratit Hamizrahit), 279, 280
Khatib, Muhammad Nimr al-, 32
Khdhuri, Haham Sasson, 239, 250
Kibbutz Galuiot. See "ingathering of the exiles" (*Kibbutz Galuiot*)
kibbutzim: build without planning permission, 142; construction, 1949–52, 131; decline of, 227; as exclusivist, 49; land allocated to, 150; as model for Jewish frontier settlement, 129; *Qaadan v. Katzir* and, 157
kidnapping Yemeni Jewish babies, 248–249, 256n23, 256n24
Kidron, Peretz, 33

Kimmerling, Baruch: on exclusion of Palestinians from Israeli historiography, 8, 11, 25n45; and Foucault, 25n46; on Israeli control system, 126; Megged's criticism of, 21n15, 119n38; postzionist critique of, 10, 62; and Shafir, 24n33, 46
kinship, family versus tribal, 334–335
Kirschenblatt-Gimblett, Barbara, 361, 362
Kiryati Brigade, 32
Klausner, Joseph, 104
Klein, Samuel (Shmuel), 106
Kliger, Sam, 368n54
Knesset, 127, 128, 133, 135
Kolatt, Israel, 116n12, 117n15, 117n24
Kol Dor, 362
Kol Ha-Isha, 313
Kosher food, 136
Koushinski, Rouja, 256n23
Kronish, Amy, 303, 305
Kupovetsky, Mark, 368n54

labor: Arab Jews as cheap, 250; in ethnocracy, 124; Histradut, 48, 66–67; Israeli system of, 97; Palestinian Arabs as cheap, 54, 112, 127, 199, 209, 303
Labor Party: criticism of postzionism from left wing of, 68; decline after 1967, 227; economic strategy of, 66; sectoral parties overshadow Likud and, 138
Labor Zionism: economic institutions dismantled, 52–53; as ideology, 48–49; separatist legacy of, 53–54
Lance, Mark, 382
land: Bedouins prevented from using, 141–142, 147n74; Israeli land policy, 130, 149, 156; Israeli state expands its holdings, 130, 150; in Qaadan v. Katzir, 148–164; and race, 333; redemption through, 333; seen as belonging to Jewish people, 129, 130, 135; unidirectional character of transfers, 130. See also Eretz Israel (Land of Israel); nationalization of land
Landau, Sigalit, 166
Land Day, 227
Landers, Yisrael, 4, 21n13
landmanshaftn, 351
Lanzmann, Claude, 82
Laor, Yitzhak, 7, 378, 380
Latour, Bruno, 265, 271n3, 272n8
Lau, Israel Meir, 365
law (right) of return, 26n59, 128, 204–205, 234, 235, 333, 353, 364, 376
Lebanon: supreme court outlaws using abducted Lebanese as "trading cards," 152. See also Lebanon invasion of 1982
Lebanon invasion of 1982: deception about reasons and planning for, 94; postzionism shaped by, 3; Sabra and Shatila massacre, 93; turns Jewish victims into "Zionist oppressors," 356; victims of, 95
Lebensraum, 332
Lehman, Peter, 300, 301
Lesbian Feminist Community, 313
lesbian feminists, 313, 321
lesbians, 308–325; in academic discourse, 317–318; alliances with gay men, 316; civil rights lesbians, 313–316; deradicalizing, 318; feminism as space for constructing alternative lesbian identity, 310, 318; and heterosexual woman as building block of Israeli culture, 308–310; ignoring and subsuming, 316–318; limits of social change regarding, 318–321; organized, 314–315, 318, 319, 320, 321; "queer" beginning as pejorative but acquiring implication of self-empowerment, 269; and queer theory, 316; relationship to feminism of, 311, 312; in search of an identity, 312–316; seen as female version of male homosexuality, 316, 317; symbolic gains for, 319–320; transformative potential of, 14, 18, 320–321; Zionism as marginalizing and excluding, 17, 18, 310
Levy, Shabtai, 40
Levy, Yitzhak, 116n7
Lewin, Tamar, 382
Lewis, Bernard, 115
Lewis, Herbert S., 248, 249
liberalism: illiberal democracies, 143n17; liberal citizenship regime, 64, 68; liberal Zionism, 67–68, 90–91; neoliberalism, 66, 68, 71, 124, 138; postzionist preference for, 69; *Qaadan v. Katzir* and, 149, 151, 152, 156, 157, 163n53; racist discourse of Israeli, 201
liberalization, economic, 52–53, 66–67, 156
Lieberman, Avigdor, 142
Liebman, Charles, 62
Likud: economic liberalization under, 66; postzionism opposed by, 69–70; sectoral parties overshadow Labor and, 138; Shas joins coalition, 279
Linz, J., 145n39
Lissak, Moshe, 49, 117n24
Livnat, Limor, 1, 2
Livneh, Neri, 68, 69
Loewe (Mahara'l) of Prague, Rabbi, 343n19
Lorch, Netanel, 32
Los Angeles, 351, 361, 363
Love in the Skies (film), 284
Lubin, Orly, 17, 304, 308–309
Lydda, 31–33, 39, 43
Lyotard, Jean-François, 63, 81, 332

Ma'abarot, 285, 291
Mabo v. Queensland, 156
Madmoni, Shoshana, 256n23
Mahler, Raphael, 104
Maimonides, 338
"making the desert bloom" trope, 248
Makleff, Mordechai, 40
mamlachtiyut ideology, 66
Mann, Anthony, 300
Mapam Party, 35, 225
March of the Living, 363, 364
Marienstras, Richard, 359
market forces, Israeli economy gives greater role to, 52–53, 66–67, 156
Marxism: Jewish Marxists, 337; post-Marxist approach to postzionism, 65–67, 71

Masada myth, 113, 355–356
master-slave relationship, 208–209, 330
Matzpen, 6, 95, 381
Mazel (Goldstein), 345
McCarthy, Justin, 59n5
McClintock, Anne, 298
Megged, Aharon, 4, 21n15, 46, 50, 119n38
Meir, Golda, 36, 57, 264
Meir, Yosef, 266
Mekarkei Israel (Israel Lands), 150, 160n10, 161n22
melting pot ideology, 97, 224, 278, 279, 360
Memmi, Albert, 264
Menachmi, Ayelet, 287
Meshulam, Uzi, 256n24
messianism, 85–86, 96
mezuzah, 349
Michael, Sammy (Sammi), 240, 278
Migdal, Joel, 8, 21n15, 119n38
mikva'ot, 349
Miller, D. A., 301
Milstein, Uri, 116n7
mimicry, 299
minority literature, 13–14, 210–212
Miron, Dan, 64
Mitzpim (Lookouts), 150, 155, 157
Miyoshi, Masao, 180n3
Mizrahi, Moshe, 284, 285, 291
Mizrahim, 231–280; ambivalence of, 242; and Arab nationalism, 237, 239, 241; call for more democratic Israel by, 275–280; as category with broad margins, 270; class-based approach to, 266, 267; a critical Mizrahi studies, 251–254; cultural affinity with Arab Muslims, 245, 264; defined, 142n4; denial of ethnic problem in Israel, 262–264, 271n3; development towns and inner-city ghettos of, 263, 275; dischronicity of, 246–248; dislocation of, 235–238; dismemberment of culture of, 242–246; displacement of, 238–242; dissonant methodologies in studying, 248–251; essentialist approach to, 266–267, 269–270; as "exotic," 244, 246, 249, 250, 252; feminism of, 305, 314; feminization of, 290, 292; in films, 284, 299–300; in frontier urban neighborhoods, 131; history begins at home, 257–274; increasing assimilation between Ashkenazim and, 138; intra-Jewish residential segregation, 131–132, 137–138; in Israeli social hierarchy, 127, 137; and Israeli welfare state, 68; in *Jacky*, 17, 283, 284–285, 288; lack of progress associated with, 277; lesbians, 321; macho masculinity emerges in, 299; as main group of later immigrants to Israel, 127; as marginalized and disempowered, 12, 15–17, 251–252; modernization imposed on, 246–248; and Palestinian Arabs, 234–235, 239, 241–242, 253, 254n8, 280; as percentage of Israeli Jews, 127; as percentage of Israeli population, 264; postcolonial postzionism on, 65; postzionism influenced by emerging identity of, 3; recovery of history of, 358; as reinventing their cultural identity, 235; religionization of, 265; scholarship marginalizes, 11; in Six-Day War, 260; socioeconomic gap with Ashkenazim, 127, 252, 264; terminological variety for, 236–237; in textbooks, 276; traditionalism associated with, 67, 277, 278; transformative potential of, 14; as two categories spliced together, 264; Zionist discourse and study of, 233–256; versus Zionist hypermasculine heterosexual male, 294, 295, 296, 299, 305
modernization: hegemonic paradigms rely on theories of, 252; ingathering associated with, 234; Mizrahim and, 246–248; romanticizing and modernizing narratives, 249
Moments (film), 308–309
monotheism, 340
Moon, Michael, 301
Moore, Deborah Dash, 351, 357
Morris, Benny, 7–8, 23n31, 24n32, 47, 48, 91, 93, 115n7, 266
Moscow, Jews of, 363, 368n54
Moses, 335, 336
Moshavat Rishonot (textbook), 275
motherhood, 308, 309, 315
Motion Fiction: Israeli Fiction in Film (Gertz), 304
motion pictures. *See* Israeli cinema
Motzafi-Haller, Pnina, 15, 16–17, 65
Muhareb, Mahmoud, 263
Mulvey, Laura, 300
Museum of Tolerance (Los Angeles), 363
Myers, David N., 105, 116n12
Mythical Expressions of Siege in Israeli Films (Ben-Shaul), 304

NAFTA, 126
Nagid, 338
Nahman of Bratslav, Rabbi, 343n19
Nancy, Jean-Luc, 332
Naqash, Samir, 265
nationalism: decline of, 71; historiography and, 106–107; hyphenated identities and, 65; as ideological category of Zionism, 267–268; of left wing of Labor Party, 68; nationalist historiography, 103; political Zionism in creation of new, 103; postmodernist critique of, 63; and queer masculinities in Israeli cinema, 294–307; transnationalism, 359–360. *See also* ethnonationalism
nationalization of land: channels of, 150; in Israeli land policy, 149; in Judaizing Israel/Palestine, 130; privatization and, 156–157; *Qaadan v. Katzir* and, 151, 154, 158
National Religious Party, 135
national self-determination. *See* self-determination
"National Unity" slogan, 97, 98
nativism, 337, 338
Neale, Steve, 300–301
Ne'eman, Judd, 299, 304

Negev: Bedouins prevented from using land in, 141–142; Beersheba, 332, 342n7; in Egyptian peace proposal of 1948, 43
Neiman v. Central Elections Committee, 141, 147n72
neocolonialism, 54
neoliberalism, 66, 68, 71, 124, 138
neozionism, 67, 69, 70, 71
Netanyahu, Benjamin, 86, 133, 145n40
Neturei Karta, 333, 337, 339, 340–341, 344n23, 344n26, 347
Neve Shalom—Wahat al-Salam, 378–379, 380
new historiography, 7–8, 31–45; academic authority of, 95; Megged on, 46, 50, 119n38; and Mizrahim, 277; Morris as coiner of term, 91, 115n7; precursors of, 95; Ram on, 61; Shafir on, 47, 50–51; on victims, 87, 88; Zionist foundational myths challenged by, 357
New Jew, 233, 234, 236, 295, 304, 353
New Social Movements, 319
New York City, 350, 351, 358, 363, 368n54
Nimni, Ephraim, 22n20
1949: The First Israelis (Segev), 2
Noga (journal), 317
Nordau, Max, 295
normalcy, 246

occupied West Bank and Gaza: boundary-drawing after 1967 war, 112; community (private) settlements in, 131–132; criticism of occupation seen as antisemitic, 369, 371, 377; demand for Palestinian state in, 227, 228; displacement of absolute loss in, 85–86; in elections of 1996, 134; Gush Emunim supports settlement in, 135; Israeli Jews residing in, 133; Israeli soldiers who refuse to serve in, 379; Israeli undermined by desire to hold, 198; military rule in, 226; mutual dependence between majority and minority created in, 199; occupation becomes political liability, 356; occupied territories called simply "territories," 117n19; Palestinian Arab population of, 126; Palestinian Arabs as commodified bodies for sale in, 303; postzionism shaped by, 3; Ta'ayush activities in, 379–380. *See also* Israeli settlers
Oovda (television program), 256n23
"Open Letter from American Jews," 377
Operation Dani, 31–33, 38
Operation Yoav, 43
Ophir, Adi, 10–11, 26n52, 63, 378, 386n7
Oppenheimer, Jo, 317
Orientalism: of Arendt, 262; dominates Israeli society, 17; in Israeli ethnic and power relations, 298–299; on Mizrahim, 249, 253, 259, 262, 265, 276, 279; and Zionist hypermasculine heterosexual male, 296, 305
Origins of the Palestinian Refugee Problem, The (Morris), 7
Orren, Elhannan, 32–33
Orthodox Judaism: growing political influence of, 134–137; as percentage of Israeli Jews, 127; separate neighborhoods for, 138; in theocratic conception of Jewish state, 352. *See also* ultra-orthodox
Oslo agreement: as de-escalating over a century of conflict, 51; occupied territories still Israeli controlled after, 126; Palestinian resistance leads to, 138. *See also* peace process
Ostjuden, 233, 254, 350
Our Man in Damascus (Ben-Hanan), 260
Oz, Amos, 193, 194

Palestine: American Jews' attitude toward return to, 351; Arab population at end of colonial period, 118n29; during British colonial period, 111; imaging as empty, 234, 248; Judaization of Israel/Palestine, 126–130; Klein on Jewish right to settle in, 106; "making the desert bloom" trope in Jewish claim to, 248. *See also* Gaza Strip; Israel; Palestinian Arabs; West Bank
Palestine Liberation Organization (PLO), 51, 53
Palestinian Arabs: Arab collusion against statehood for, 1947–1949, 36–37; in boundary-drawing after 1967 war, 112; calling for Palestinian self-determination seen as antisemitic, 371, 378, 382; as cheap labor for Israel, 54, 112, 127, 199, 209, 303; as commodified bodies for sale, 303; countermythology of, 113; de-Arabization, 128–129, 137, 261, 262; demolition of villages of, 129; diaspora of, 364; dislocation at time of Israel's establishment, 381; exclusion from Israeli history, 8; feminism among, 314; film representations of, 299; historiographical debate over origins of, 56–60; in Israel citizenship categories, 96; as Israeli Jews' Jews, 201–202; in Jerusalem, 166, 173, 174, 178, 182n22; Jordanian annexation of West Bank, 43; Keshet on rights for, 279; land and labor in Israeli-Palestinian conflict, 46–55; media stereotypes of, 59; Mizrahim and, 234–235, 239, 241–242, 253, 254n8, 280; Neturei Karta and, 340–341; 1948 war as *al Naqba* for, 8, 51, 59n1; number governed by Israel in after 1967 war, 58; origins of refugee problem, 38–42, 44; population in occupied territories, 126; in postcolonial postzionism, 65; postzionism influenced by emerging nationalism of, 3, 4; pre-state Sephardim seek coexistence with, 277; in "pure settler society" model, 123; refigured as Amalek, 330; refugee land confiscated, 130, 150; represented as non-Jewish obstacle to Jewish/Israeli national trajectory, 243; scholarship marginalizes, 11; seen as willingly leaving their homes in 1948, 2, 7–8, 38–39, 94; in *Tekumah* television series, 1; as unprepared for 1948 war, 37–38; Zionism in shaping of, 58; Zionism's resurgence in response to violence of, 70; Zionist colonization seem from point of view of, 113, 119n39; in

Zionist historiography, 108; versus Zionist hypermasculine heterosexual male, 294, 295, 296, 299. See also *intifada;* Israeli Arabs
Palestinian Authority, 228
Palestinians: The Making of a People (Kimmerling and Migdal), 8, 119n38
Pappe, Ilan, 5, 7, 25n44, 35, 37, 42, 47, 48, 69, 91, 116n7
Paratroopers (film), 299
parties, political. *See* political parties
Passover, 348
Pat (Jerusalem neighborhood), 177
Paul, St., 329–330, 332, 337, 339
Peace Now, 378, 379
peace process: deception about, 94; Judaizing accelerated by, 146n56. *See also* Oslo agreement
Peled, Yoav, 64, 68, 91, 140, 144n30
Perah (newspaper), 244
Peres, Shimon, 51, 134
periodization, historiographical, 108–110
personal memoirs, 114
Peters, Joan, 57, 59n5
Petuchowski, J. J., 343n19
phallocentrism, 301, 302
Pharisees, 336, 339
Philistines, 113
Pinkas sherut (Rabin), 33
Pipes, Daniel, 381–382
PLO (Palestine Liberation Organization), 51, 53
pluralism, 71, 112
pogroms, 243
political parties: Keshet, 279, 280; Mapam Party, 35, 225; National Religious Party, 135; Shas, 135, 279, 280, 358. *See also* Labor Party; Likud
political Zionism, 102–103
population exchange, 239, 241
Porath, Yehoshua, 113, 116n7
postcolonialism: applying to Diaspora, 358; Arab Jews and postcolonial studies, 265, 268–269; as not temporal term, 23n25; postcolonial perspective on postzionism, 64–65, 68, 71; postcolonial theory in film criticism, 296, 298–300; postzionism as connected to, 9, 10; Yosef's use of, 18
post-Fordist capitalism, 9, 66, 67, 71
postmodernism: diaspora as mode of explaining collective identity of, 360; postmodern historiography, 91; postmodernist perspective on postzionism, 63–64, 70–71; postzionism associated with, 9, 10, 25n43, 91, 92, 98; as set of historical conditions versus cultural position, 89
postzionism: among American Jews, 5, 7, 18–21; antizionism equated with, 5; common denunciations of, 93; as consequence of Zionist success, 98; as critical enterprise, 6, 9–13; decline in early 2000s, 69–70; as displacement of contradictions in Zionism, 99; early use of term, 22n16; emergence of, 357; as epoch versus cultural critique, 89–90; future prospects for, 69–71; historical forces in shaping of, 3–4; ideological controversies surrounding, 67–69; impact on Israeli culture, 70; as label, 90–94; as minoritarian discourse, 6, 23n23; and Mizrahim, 235; as multicultural, 68, 69; positive and negative, 63; postcolonial approach to, 64–65, 71; postideological approach to, 62–63, 70; post-Marxist approach to, 65–67, 71; postmodernism associated with, 91, 92, 98; postmodernist approach to, 63–64, 70–71; precursors of, 6; as regulative discourse, 5–6; as reproducing Zionism's main fault, 91; shifting meaning of, 5; *Tekumah* series associated with, 1; theoretical approaches to, 61–67, 70–71; Zionist critique of, 4–5
privatization, 52, 66–67, 124, 164n55, 164n66, 226
procedural obstacles to affirmation of nonsettler land rights, 153–154
progress: discourse of, 246, 247–248; history seen as catastrophic not progressive, 262; Mizrahim associated with lack of, 277. *See also* modernization
"pure settlement" colonies, 50, 51, 122–123, 126

Qaadan v. Katzir, 148–164; difficulty in deciding, 121, 148; as drawing line between past and future, 155, 158; equality jurisprudence as major innovation of, 12, 152–153, 161n24; as first step, 157–158; as forward-looking precedent, 149, 158; interference with discriminatory land allocation, 149–151, 158; interference with discriminatory mechanisms, 153–155; as isolating case from collective context, 155–157; legal escape devices maintained in, 157, 158; limited interpretation of Jewish-Zionist state tenet in, 151–152, 158; as not ordering respondents to permit Qaadans to live in Katzir, 12, 148, 158, 164n61; potential to lead in various dimensions, 158–159
queer theory, 18, 269, 296–297, 298, 316
Qumran, 339

Rabin, Yitzhak: agreements with PLO, 51; Arab electoral support for, 227–228; assassination of, 94, 135, 228; on legitimacy of Palestinian national aspirations, 24n34; in Operation Dani, 31–32, 33
Rabinowitz, Dan, 7, 26n49, 27n61
racism: "chosenness" of Jews and, 337; criticism of Israel compared with, 373; differentialist, 331; of European Christian society, 329–330; of Israeli liberals' discourse, 201; Jewish culture associated with, 329–330; law of return seen as racist, 204; against Mizrahim, 241, 247; scientific, 334; two aspects of, 330–331; in Zionism, 19, 96, 98, 305

radical feminism, 312, 313, 314, 317, 321
Ram, Uri, 9, 90, 91, 140, 378, 386n7
Ramle, 32, 33, 39, 43
Raz-Kratotzkin, Amnon, 7, 91, 92, 95
Reb Arelach, 347
Recovered Roots: Collective Memory and the Making of Israeli National Tradition (Zerubavel), 355
Reform Judaism, 350
religious right: Gush Emunim, 85, 86, 135, 330; postzionism influenced by rise of, 3; in West Bank settlements, 132. *See also* ultra-orthodox
"resident suitability" tests, 132
Revach, Ze'ev, 299
right (law) of return, 26n59, 128, 204–205, 234, 235, 333, 353, 364, 376
rights: human, 98, 249, 374, 378, 379. *See also* civil rights
Rockefeller Museum, 167–168
romanticizing ethnography, 249
Rosenne, Shabtai, 44
Rosenzweig, Uri, 256n23
Rottenberg, Catherine, 379–380
Rouhana, Nadim, 140
Ruppin, Arthur, 104
Russian-speaking immigrants: as percentage of Israeli Jews, 127; separate neighborhoods for, 138; status in Israeli society, 127; in United States, 361, 363, 368n54

Sa'adya, Rabbi, 338
Saban, Ilan, 153
Sabar, Naama, 345
Sabbath, 136
Sabra, 18, 236, 295, 304, 310
Sabra and Shatila massacre, 93
Sacks, Jonathan, 357
Said, Edward W., 65, 204, 262, 265, 298
Sallah Shabbati (film), 235–236
Sanders, E. P., 332
Schapira, Hermann, 116n11
Schindler's List (film), 82
Schneerson, M. M., 347
Schnitzer, Meir, 303
Scholem, Gershom Gerhard, 104, 105
School for Peace, 378–379
Schueftan, Dan, 42
Schwartz, Regina, 342n15
Schweid, Eliezer, 63, 67
Schweitzer, Ariel, 304
Second Aliyah, 109
Second Temple, destruction of the, 348
Sedgwick, Eve Kosofsky, 301
Segev, Tom, 2–3, 7, 91, 93
segregation, intra-Jewish residential, 131–132, 137–138
selective openness, 126
self-determination: calling for Palestinian seen as antisemitic, 371, 378, 382; Diaspora as replacement for model of, 331, 359; in ethnonationalism, 123–124; Judaizing Israel/Palestine for, 135, 139, 141; Zionism based on, 96

"separate but equal" doctrine, 155, 163n43
separation of religion from state, 333
Sephardim: cultural dissonance between Ashkenazim and, 244; Elyashar on pre-state population, 277; expulsion from Spain of, 349; Katznelson on, 247; recovery of history of, 358; strict meaning of, 237; in terminological crisis of Mizrahim, 236
September 11, 2001, attacks, 69, 70
settlers, Israeli. *See* Israeli settlers
settlers' courts, 153, 162n34
settler society. *See* immigrant-settler society
Seventh Million, The (Segev), 93
sexuality, 281–325; Jewish community spaces associated with, 349; Zionism marginalizes, 286, 289. *See also* gender; homosexuality
Shabak, 159
Shadmi, Erella, 18
Shafir, Gershon, 8, 64, 68, 93, 144n30, 266
Shalev, Michael, 3–4, 93
Shalev, Mordechai, 208, 209
Shammas, Anton: debate with Yehoshua, 201; on Hebrew and Arabic, 216n16; as Israeli Christian Arab, 194–195; on Israeli culture's effects on Palestinians, 14–15, 26n59; in Israeli mass media, 194, 212; personal testimony of an "Israeli Arab," 219–225; refuses to label himself a Palestinian, 201; rejects polarized images of himself, 195. *See also Arabesques* (Shammas)
Shamosh, Amnon, 260–261
Shandler, Jeffrey, 353–354
Shapira, Anita, 46–47, 119n39
Shapiro, Yonattan, 140
Sharett, Moshe, 42, 43, 44
Sharon, Ariel, 1, 364–365
Shas, 135, 279, 280, 358
Shell, Marc, 341n3, 342n10
Shenhav, Yehouda, 15, 16, 23n25, 64–65
Shlaim, Avi, 35–37, 42, 43–44, 47, 48, 95, 116n7
Shmueli, Avshalom, 258
Shneer, David, 19
Shoah. *See* Holocaust, the (Shoah)
Shoah (film), 82
Shohat, Ella, 15, 16, 18, 23n28, 265, 266, 295, 298, 303–304
Silberstein, Laurence, 63, 92, 358
Silverman, Kaja, 301
Silwan, 166
Simon, Ernst, 104
Six-Day War (1967): Arab Jews participate in, 260; East Jerusalem occupied by Israel, 166, 167; Holocaust preoccupation and, 85; investment and aid to Israel after, 227; new vision of Israel after, 356; unifying effect attributed to, 3; West Bank and Gaza Strip conquered in, 198; Zionists embrace victim position after, 95
Skirball Cultural Center (Los Angeles), 363
Smith, Paul, 300–301
sociology, critical. *See* critical sociology
Solomon, 341
Soviet Jews, 356, 361, 362

Soysal, Y. N., 123
Spielberg, Steven, 82
Spivak, Gayatri, 269
Stam, Robert, 298, 302
Stepan, A., 145n39
Stern Group, 93
Stockwell, Hugh, 40
strategic essentialism, 269
Studlar, Gaylyn, 301
suicide bombings, 370, 382
Summers, Lawrence, 20, 369–378, 381, 383, 384, 386n5
Swirsky, Shlomo, 140
Syria: Eli Cohen spy case, 259; Israel rejects 1949 peace proposal of, 43, 44

Ta'ayush, 379–380
Taeubler, Eugen, 104
taglit-birthright Israel, 363, 364, 368n55
Taguieff, P. A., 331
Talmon, Jacob, 116n12
Tekumah (television series), 1–2, 22n21, 240
Tel-Aviv Stories (film), 287–288
teleological explanations, 110
Temple Mount, 167, 181n15
terra nullius doctrine, 156
theocracy, 134–137, 352
Theory and Criticism (journal), 11
Third Aliyah, 109
Thousand and One Wives, A (film), 288
three-party leases, 151
Tikkun, 378
Tilly, Charles, 110
Tokhnit Dalet, 41
Toldat Milhemet Ha'kornemiut, 32
To Live with Jews (Elyashar), 277
To Live with Palestinians (Elyashar), 277
torture, 152, 377
Transjordan. *See* Jordan
transnationalism, 359–360
Tree Day, 224
tribalism, 334–335, 339, 343n16
Troen, S. Ilan, 357
Tryster, Hillel, 303
Tsahor, Zeev, 49
Turki, Fawaz, 58, 60n6
Turkish Jews, 244
Turner, Frederick, 329
Tye, Larry, 345

Uganda, 352, 366n16
Ulmart, Ehud, 181n16
ultra-orthodox: on return to Zion, 347; separate neighborhoods for, 138; in Yiddish revival, 358
United Jewish Appeal, 357
United States. *See* American Jews
universalism: Israeli elite's claims to, 278, 279, 283, 292, 296; Jewish state as compromising, 353; Pauline, 337
Urbach, E. E., 104
Urofsky, Melvin, 353

victims, 81–101; being a victim of identity, 86–88; identity of the victim, 84–86; Jewish fascination with victim position, 84–85, 100n6, 242, 243, 370; other than Jews, 94; position of the victim, 81–84; Zionists assume position of, 95–96
Victoria (film), 240

Wachsman, Dan, 299
Warner, Michael, 297
War of Independence: "David and Goliath" myth about, 37–38, 94; exceptionalism attributed to, 111; expulsion and flight of Palestinians during, 129; Flapan on "myths" of, 35; Israel's lack of emphasis on achieving peace, 42–43; Jerusalem divided after, 169; massacres of Arabs in, 42; new historiography on, 31–45
Weber, Max, 265
welfare state, 66, 68
West Bank: apartheid system in, 228; Arab population in 1967, 58; Jordanian annexation of, 43; as separated from Gaza Strip, 53; state-subsidized colonization drive in, 53. *See also* occupied West Bank and Gaza
Wettstein, Howard, 358
Wik v. Queensland, 156
Willemen, Paul, 300
Wittig, Monique, 320
women: as depicted in Israeli culture, 17; diasporized gender identity, 338; heterosexual woman as building block of Israeli culture, 308–310; house and home as traditional domain of, 290; inferior social position of, 309; in Israeli films, 286–288; Israeli welfare state and, 68; in *Jacky*, 283–293; Keshet on rights for, 279; motherhood, 308, 309, 315; sexuality of, 309, 321; in Shammas's *Arabesques*, 202–203, 205; as Shin-Bet informers, 221; transformative potential of, 14; Zionism as marginalizing and excluding, 17. *See also* feminism; lesbians
Women in Black, 378
women's peace movement, 314
World Cinema: Israel (Kronish), 303

Yadin, Yigael, 38
Yad va-Shem, 82
Yaron, Avner, 257–258, 259
Yaron, Nirit, 287
Yehiya, Eliezer Don, 62
Yehoshua, A. B., 62, 201, 208, 209, 332–333
Yemeni Jews, 240, 246, 248–249, 266, 275–276
Yerdor case, 128
Yesh Gvul, 379
Yiddish, 351, 358, 359, 360
Yiftachel, Oren, 10, 11–12, 68, 149, 160n6
Yiftah Brigade, 31–32
Yom Kippur War (1973), 3
Yosef, Raz, 17–18

Za'im, Husni, 44
Zarchin, Shemi, 283, 287
Zertal, Idith, 7, 93

Zerubavel, Yael, 355
Zion: movement to settle Jews in, 352–353; as mythic Jewish home, 347, 349, 352, 358–359, 364; spatial meaning becomes tangible after establishment of Israel, 355. *See also* Palestine
Zion (periodical), 105
Zionism: academicians in service of, 11; American Jews influenced by, 7, 18; American Jews' support for, 353, 354, 356; as charismatic movement become routinized, 62; Christian European context of, 243; as colonialism, 8, 46–50; contingency of definitions of, 10; critique of historiography of, 106–113; critique of ideology of, 94–99; Diaspora rejected by, 18, 19; as dominant discourse in Israel, 10; earlier critics of, 95; and the end of exile, 352–354; as epoch versus discursive regime, 89–90; fascism compared with, 332; forests as symbols for, 208; Hebrew as language of, 211, 213; heterosexual woman in ideology of, 308, 309–310; identification of Jews with, 380–381, 383; ideological categories of, 267–268, 272n8; ideologization of, 48; as ingrained in population, 69; Jewish Workers' Bund marginalized by, 340; Jews move beyond, 357–361; liberal, 67–68, 90–91; as majoritarian discourse, 5–6; making a Zionist historiography, 104–106; masculine discourse of, 17–18, 294–298, 304, 305, 310, 353; methodological, 265, 272n5; Mizrahim and Zionist historiography, 234, 243, 245, 275–280; as nationalist discourse, 6; neozionism, 67, 69, 70, 71; Neturei Karta criticism of, 341; normality attributed to, 6; Palestinian identity shaped by, 58; Palestinian violence in resurgence of, 70; postzionism criticized by, 4–5; as "pure colonial settler" movement, 127; racist and fascist tendencies in, 19, 96, 98, 305; as reductive and exclusionary, 16; seen as European-Ashkenazi-White-Colonial movement, 65; Segev on "myths" of, 2–3; sense of having been duped by, 93–94; as settler movement, 127, 144n23, 152; sexuality marginalized in, 286, 289; as subversion of Jewish culture, 331, 337, 343n19, 347; teleological model of Israeli history of, 16; victim position as asset to, 87–88; victim position assumed by, 95–96; Zionist discourse and the study of Arab Jews, 233–256. *See also* antizionism; postzionism
Zionist Federation, 130
Zuckermann, Moshe, 91
Zurayk, Constantine, 59n1
Zureik, Elia, 140